To GMG 3 Harry Thom
My shipmate and fi
Bay, Republic of Vi
aboard PCF 46 and 52.
Their mission was to deny infiltration
of arms and contraband to the VietCong
enemy. The record stands that did
not happen due to the diligence,
and combat competence of these
PCF crews.

Our Navy and Nation owe a
deep debt of gratitude to these
courageous sailors.

With deep respect and
admiration,

Roy F Hoffmann
RADM USN (ret)
CTF-115 Vietnam 1968-69

THIS IS LATCH

THIS IS LATCH

The Rear Admiral Roy F. Hoffmann Story

by WEYMOUTH D. SYMMES

PICTORIAL HISTORIES PUBLISHING COMPANY, INC.
Missoula, Montana

Copyright © 2007 by Weymouth D. Symmes

All rights reserved.

Library of Congress Control Number 2007937992

ISBN 978-1-57510-137-8

First Printing October 2007

PRINTED BY
Jostens Printing and Publishing
Visalia, California

TYPOGRAPHY, BOOK & COVER DESIGN
Arrow Graphics, Missoula, Montana

PUBLISHED BY
Pictorial Histories Publishing Company, Inc.
713 South Third Street West, Missoula MT 59801
phone (406) 549-8488, fax (406) 728-9280
phpc@montana.com
website: pictorialhistoriespublishing.com

CONTENTS

Foreword by John O'Neill vii
Preface ix

PART ONE. EARLY LIFE TO KOREA
CHAPTER 1. The Early Years 3
CHAPTER 2. World War II and the Demobilization 19

PART TWO. KOREA TO VIETNAM
CHAPTER 3. Sinking of the USS *Pirate* 41
CHAPTER 4. Back to Korea and the USS *Harry E. Hubbard* 58
CHAPTER 5. The "Peacetime" Navy 79
CHAPTER 6. In Command 104

PART THREE. VIETNAM TO RETIREMENT
CHAPTER 7. Commander Task Force 115 157
CHAPTER 8. Commands and Retirement 327

PART FOUR. CIVILIAN AND SWIFT BOAT VETERANS AND POWS FOR TRUTH
CHAPTER 9. Civilian 397
CHAPTER 10. Swift Boat Veterans and POWs for Truth 414
EPILOGUE. Admiral Roy F. Hoffmann Foundation 495

Appendix 501
Glossary 504
Sources 507
Index 515

FOREWORD

I FIRST HEARD OF Admiral Roy Hoffmann while I was in Swift Boat Training School in Coronado, California—then a sleepy semi-isolated peninsula. Admiral Hoffmann was then the Task Force 115 commander, which included all Swift boats in Vietnam. He was a loyal subordinate of Admiral Elmo Zumwalt, Commander of Naval Forces in Vietnam and a Navy legend as well.

Admiral Hoffmann's courage was legendary; the stories about him were numerous. Unlike almost all of the young officers and enlisted men who served under him, he had seen the deadly face of war before, most notably in Korea where he nearly died in the frigid waters off the Sea of Japan, after the sinking of his ship. He was truly an "old salt," not only baptized and nearly drowned in the sea, but also shaped and molded by years of naval service. He was not a self-promoter, just a leader who commanded immediate respect from the force of his personality and the distinction of his service. He shared the abysmal conditions and the bullets with his men.

In 2004, I along with several hundred other Swift boat sailors received word that "Latch," Admiral Hoffmann's Vietnam call sign, was once again, after the passage of 35 years, summoning us to service for our Nation. John Kerry, whom we all knew to be profoundly unfit to serve as Commander-in-Chief, was lurching towards the presidency of the United States. Amazingly, he was doing so using the political theater of "reporting for duty," claiming his short and controversial time in Vietnam qualified him for the Nation's highest office, while continuing to vilify those with whom he had served. Admiral Hoffmann went to his attic, pulled out ancient records, and began one by one to locate and contact those he had known so long before. His wonderful wife Mary Linn acted as his secretary and introduced her mid-20th century sailor-husband to the marvel of e-mail. When Latch called, almost all of us who were able came on that last great voyage of 2004. He truly was like Tennyson's *Ulysses*, summoning one last effort from an aged crew—"one equal temper of heroic minds made weak by time and fate but strong in will . . ." And so men like Bob Elder came from his bank in Delaware, Wey Symmes from retirement in Montana, Dick Pees from Ohio, Larry Thurlow from the plains of Kansas, Joe Ponder bearing his wounds from Vietnam with dignity. And then these men were joined by former Prisoners of War, men like Medal of Honor recipient Col. Bud Day, Paul Galanti, Jim Warner and Ken Cordier. People who could never have been hired at any price came for Duty, Honor, and Country, at the summons of a 79-year-old man that many had not seen or heard from in 35 years.

Neither lesser duty, nor a lesser man than the Admiral, could have caused these men to endure the grief and abuse of 2004. Each of us knew that we would be vilified and that there would be no personal reward other than fulfilling our duty to our nation, our friends, and those in the uniform of our nation's armed forces.

Admiral Hoffmann and his wife Mary Linn were repeatedly threatened and insulted during the 2004 election. The abusers never understood the mettle of these patriotic Americans. They never understood the call of Duty, Honor, and Country. And because of that miscalculation history profoundly changed.

—John E. O'Neill

John E. O'Neill comes from a Navy family. His father was a distinguished Naval aviator in World War II and retired from active duty as an admiral. Mr. O'Neill is a 1967 honors graduate of the U.S. Naval Academy. He was Officer in Charge of a Swift boat in Vietnam (PCF 94). He came to national attention defending Vietnam veterans against John Kerry's false atrocity charges on the *Dick Cavett Show* in 1971. Mr. O'Neill went on to receive has J.D. from the University of Texas in 1973, graduating first in his class. He clerked for Justice William H. Rehnquist on the U. S. Supreme Court from 1974–1975.

Mr. O'Neill is the co-author of the bestselling *Unfit for Command*. His wife was the late Anne O'Neill and he has two grown children. He is in private law practice in Houston, Texas, specializing in large-scale commercial litigation. He is now married to Diane O'Neill.

PREFACE

My introduction to the world of Admiral Roy F. Hoffmann came in a typically late evening (his eastern standard time) phone call. It was March 9, 2004, and with a gruff voice, without preliminaries, he introduced himself as "Roy Hoffmann" and asked if I was Weymouth Symmes and had I served on Swift boats during any part of the time John Kerry was in Vietnam. I replied I was and I had. He asked if I had read *Tour of Duty* by Douglas Brinkley, the then new biography of John Kerry. Again I replied in the affirmative. He asked what I thought of the book. I replied that I was shocked at the portrayal of John Kerry as indicated by the book. I had not realized Kerry left Vietnam after only three months in combat, using as his exit gambit three questionable Purple Hearts. I was further shocked by his postwar radical antiwar activities. Finally, I felt Kerry's general characterization of the Swifties I had served with was grossly inaccurate and unfair.

Meanwhile, I was puzzled. Who was calling? I knew from *Tour of Duty* that then-Captain Roy Hoffmann had been the commander of the task force under which I had served in Vietnam, and that same individual had then gone on to retire as a rear admiral in the U.S. Navy. I knew who that Roy Hoffmann was, but who was this? It may surprise the reader to know that admirals did not routinely call me. In fact, an admiral had never before called me since I left the Navy in 1970.

He then asked me if I knew who was calling and I said no. He replied: "This is Latch," which had been his call sign in Vietnam. It turned out that he was calling all of the former Swift personnel he could locate to explore the idea of opposing what was certain to become the candidacy of John Kerry for President and thus Commander in Chief of the United States armed forces.

Along with over 350 other Swifties and POWs I joined the Admiral's effort to inform the American public about John Kerry. During the course of my involvement I eventually came to understand and appreciate the great service career military personnel provide to America, service well represented by men such as Admiral Hoffmann. As I came to know him better I also came to appreciate that his rich and varied service would make a story well worth telling.

That story begins with the Admiral's father in the trenches of France in World War I; and growing up during the Great Depression and enlistment during World War II. We continue the chronicle in the mine-filled waters off Wonsan in Korea and the loss of the USS *Pirate* with Roy Hoffmann aboard. We will share the Admiral's journey to command, first of ships and then of Task Force 115, pursuing the enemy on the coastal and inland waterways of Vietnam. Our story will conclude with additional commands; the achievement of flag rank; and finally with forming and leading a group that may have been the deciding influence in the 2004 election.

As with any strong figure bearing great responsibilities, a career like the Admiral's was not without controversy. Not everyone appreciated his leadership style, his aggressiveness, his attention to detail, and his demands for excellence. Not everyone liked his methods, but I found nearly universal respect. Almost everyone said if they had to go to war they hoped it would be with Roy Hoffmann.

It is apparent to me that the United States armed forces have two primary purposes: To prepare for war and to fight a war. The effectiveness of the former in many ways determines the success of the latter. Those who believe, as I do, that Admiral Hoffmann's demands for excellence prepared his commands for the ultimate test of war in exemplary fashion will find much to admire in this book. Those who think the military should be an exact reflection of the greater American society; or who, in John Kerry's term, think we should prepare for and fight a more "sensitive" war will find less to admire.

This book is also the story of Mary Linn Hoffmann, the Admiral's wife and partner for over 55 years. Mary Linn is a strong, independent woman, who during much of the Admiral's service anchored their family through raising five daughters, 25 family moves and the demands of the Navy. The service of the career military spouse is difficult and vital. Those who feel, as I do, that strong, independent women who choose to focus on and put their families first are worthy of our great respect, will find much to admire in Mary Linn Hoffmann. Those who subscribe to the more modern feminist notion of "fulfillment" will perhaps find less to admire.

It was a great privilege to tell the story of these fine people. America seems increasingly mired in a celebrity culture of movie and television stars whose status is based on fantasy, not real accomplishment; media creations of no accomplishment; preening politicians; and often thuggish and drug-addled rock/rap stars and athletes. The pleasure of writing about two people of consequence and accomplishment was an anecdote to today's world for this author.

This book could not have been written without the Hoffmanns' help, support and encouragement. The Admiral provided all documents from his career that I needed and was always willing to clarify any point, or to straighten out this civilian when I strayed too far from Navy dogma. Similarly, both of the Hoffmanns were generous with their time, patiently sitting through hours of taped interviews. Quotes from the Admiral and Mary Linn in the following chapters come from those interviews. Their help in steering me to people with whom they had served was also indispensable.

Thanks are also due to the many I interviewed in connection with the book. They were almost all willing and indeed eager to talk about the Admiral and their service. Their names may be found under "Sources" and I here extend my appreciation.

Thanks to the staff at Pictorial Histories for their support, and in particular to Stan Cohen for making it possible. Thanks also to Kitty and Bill at Arrow Graphics for their fine work, on this, my second book.

Thanks to my wife, Terry, for the love, support and understanding that it takes to create and market a book. To her I dedicate *This Is Latch*.

And finally, a note about the Navy system of officer rank, which can be confusing since the Navy doesn't use the designations followed by the Army, Air Force and Marines.[1] Obviously Admiral Hoffmann's rank changed as he moved up through the Navy system, and he retired as a rear admiral. Changing references to his rank as he received promotions can be confusing for the reader. In this book, then, "the Admiral," when capitalized always refers to Roy F. Hoffmann.

---

1. For example, the Admiral retired in grade 0–8, the equivalent of a Major General. The glossary contains Navy rank designations with equivalents in the other service branches.

PART ONE

EARLY LIFE TO KOREA

Any man who may be asked in this century what he did to make his life worthwhile . . . can respond with a great deal of pride and satisfaction: "I served in the United States Navy."

—President John F. Kennedy
1963, Annapolis, Maryland

1

THE EARLY YEARS

THE ADMIRAL'S FATHER, Roy Walter Hoffmann,[1] was born on October 5, 1894, in Victoria, Missouri, the son of Frederick Herman and Hannah Mary Hoffmann. He grew to manhood in Missouri. Before his 20th birthday World War I broke out in Europe, starting almost by accident in August of 1914,[2] with the "Allied" powers (Great Britain, France, Russia, Belgium, Italy and Japan) ultimately fighting the "Central" powers of Germany, Austria-Hungary, Turkey and Bulgaria. By the time America entered the brutal conflict in 1917 the major combatants (England, France, Russia and Germany) had fought each other nearly to exhaustion. Thirty million people died in the war, ten million on the battlefield and 20 million of hunger and other war-related causes. Six million more were carried off the battlefield, crippled for life.

By early summer of 1918 Roy Walter had enlisted in the fabled Rainbow Division of the U.S. Army after having been passed over by the Navy due to his small stature. Activated in August of 1917, the Rainbow Division was composed of National Guard divisions drawn from 26 states and the District of Columbia. Roy Walter Hoffmann had joined a remarkable American effort.

In January of 1917 there were 200,000 soldiers in the U.S. Army. By the end of the war there were over 4,000,000 in the U.S. armed forces, two

---

1. Roy Walter Hoffmann was born Walter Roy Hoffmann and later reversed the order of his first and middle names.

2. It was a mundane start for such a terrible war. On June 28, 1914, a Serbian nationalist assassinated Austrian Crown Prince Franz Ferdinand at Sarajevo. Austria, with Germany's blessing, then declared war on Serbia. Russia mobilized, Germany declared war on Russia and then on France, Britain entered the war in support of Belgium and France, and so it went.

million of whom went to Europe to fight under the American Expeditionary Force (AEF). Over 1.3 million of them got into action.

They were commanded by "Black Jack" Pershing, who got his nickname in Cuba while with a regiment of Negro cavalry, whose capabilities he respected and promoted. Pershing, according to Robert Leckie in *The Wars of America*, ". . . was almost inhumanely controlled, this Iron Commander of the thin, set lips, flinty gray mustache, impeccable uniform and cold, colorless voice." In 1915 he had lost his wife and three small daughters in a fire and his reported reaction when told was only to grow grayer. He commanded respect from his troops but never had their devotion. His insistence that the American Expeditionary Force be an American army, not an adjunct to British and French forces, instilled pride in U.S. troops and respect on the battlefield, secured in the battle of Belleau Wood.

Roy Walter Hoffmann took his recruit training at Fort Dodge, Iowa. Roy was visited in camp by Zettamae Pruneau Hoffmann, his wife, and Hannah Hoffmann, his mother, providing him a break from the ten hours of drilling per day the doughboys were going through to prepare for war. In those days he drilled in the same uniform he would wear on leave and eventually wear to march off to war. Upon completion of recruit training, Roy shipped out for the killing fields of France, joining Co. C. of the 850th Infantry.

As Roy Walter Hoffmann was moving up in the trenches the Germans began a massive final offensive in 1918, driving the Allies back to the Marne. The Allies, bolstered by the American Expeditionary Force, went on the counteroffensive. From September 26 to November 11, 1.2 million U.S. troops were involved in the Battle of Meuse-Argonne, sweeping the Germans before them. On November 9 Kaiser Wilhelm II of Germany abdicated. Two days later the war ended on the 11th hour of the 11th day of the 11th month of 1918. The doughboys could come

Admiral Hoffmann's father, Roy Walter Hoffmann, to the left. HOFFMANN PHOTO

How they came home from the trenches: A beat up troop transport, Newport News, Virginia, 1918. HOFFMANN PHOTO

home, after leaving 130,174 dead and missing on the battlefield, and suffering over 200,000 wounded.

Roy's letter to "My dear wife," written from "Somewhere in France" after the Armistice was signed, was circumspect as it was read by an Army censor, but his relief at coming home was apparent. By the end of 1918 he was back in Newport News, Virginia, arriving on a rusty and dilapidated troop transport.

Roy Walter Hoffmann and Zettamae Pruneau Hoffmann settled into Crystal City, Missouri, after the war. Crystal City is so named because of the glass works there for which it is known. Crystal City was a small, one industry town on the bluffs of the Mississippi River and in the foothills of the Ozarks. Thirty miles from St. Louis, it was dominated by the Pittsburgh Plate Glass Company (PPG), which had come to town in 1895. The silica sand rock on the east side of Plattin Creek proved excellent for glass making. Crystal City Works Nine became the largest plate glass plant in the world. In 1925 around 3,500 people lived in Crystal City.

The union of Roy and Zettamae lasted over 50 years and produced four children. Roy was the easy going one, with a pleasant personality, and the ability to get along well with people.

Zettamae was born on January 4, 1899, in Kokomo, Indiana. Her father was first generation French and a skilled glass worker. The family transferred from Kokomo to Crystal City, where Zettamae's father worked as a glass cutter for PPG. Zettamae was a strong-willed woman and ran the family. Roy Walter supplied the heavy spanking when the Hoffmann siblings needed discipline, but it was usually on instructions from Zettamae.

Roy and Zettamae had two boys and two girls. One daughter died early of strep throat, an infection that came on quickly and raged unhindered in those days before antibiotics. Juanita was born five years before her brother Roy, who was born November 18, 1925, followed by brother Paul Ivan, born in 1927. Juanita was married after high school to a linotype operator from Billings, Montana. Paul, who is as easy going as his father, enlisted in the U.S. Army in 1946. After his service he worked for PPG in Crystal City. Both siblings are still living, Paul on his farm in Crystal City and Juanita in Covington, Tennessee.

Mary Linn Thompson, who in 1950 would marry Roy F. Hoffmann, was born December 4, 1927. Her father was Robert Linn Thompson, who was born in Missouri on January 23, 1894. He had served in the Army during World War I at Fort Monroe in Virginia.

At the end of World War I he married Christine Marchand, whose father had been born in the Alsace-Lorraine section of France. He had immigrated to Massachusetts with his family at age 16.

Robert Thompson completed the 8th grade only, but he was a hard worker, excellent with his hands. He was an exceptional machinist, practical engineer, and had an aptitude for mechanics. He would spend his entire work career with the St. Joseph Lead Company, starting as a mechanic and driver for the company president. He maintained the company's automobile fleet, but as his skills became apparent he was eventually moved into corporate headquarters where he worked in a small mechanical laboratory. He designed a specialized micrometer that measured the circumference of the cables used to hoist ore and men out of the mines, recognizing that as the huge cables aged they stretched and became smaller and less reliable.

Robert was a good man and parent; Christine was a good parent as well, albeit more social than Robert. She chose to focus on her family and never worked outside the home.

There were three children born of the union of Robert and Christine. Elizabeth was the oldest, born in 1920, followed by Mary Linn in 1927 and Robert Lee in 1929. Elizabeth had a scholarship to a Catholic School as a youth and so was not often around when Mary Linn was growing up.

Elizabeth eventually married a naval aviator who flew both Catalina and Coronado seaplanes in the Atlantic and Pacific during World War II; he went on to work for McDonald Douglas as an aeronautical engineer. Robert Lee served during the Korean War in the Army. After the war he went on to a distinguished career as a design and production engineer.

ON SEPTEMBER 3, 1929, the Tuesday after Labor Day, the Dow-Jones average stock market price reached its all time high. Some stocks, traditionally valued at ten times earnings, were by 1929 trading at 50 times earnings. The Great Crash, which climaxed on Tuesday, October 29, 1929, less than two months after the all-time high, came with shocking suddenness. According to Frederick Lewis Allen in *The Big Change 1900–1950*, "It was a collapse of terrifying proportions and duration." The stock market crash didn't cause the Depression, but was the most dramatic symptom of underlying sick conditions in the United States, and indeed the world.

On October 24, 1929, 12.8 million shares changed hands. By the end of that day 11 prominent men on Wall Street had committed suicide. On October 29 frantic selling continued, totaling 16.4 million shares. In October alone stock values listed on the New York Stock Exchange declined from $87 billion to $55 billion (a 37 per cent decline). And it kept going in an almost uninterrupted two-year decline in the volume of American business. As sales ebbed business income declined. Businesses responded by laying off workers and cutting the salaries and wages of those that remained. As unemployment increased and purchasing power decreased the pool of those who could turn it around spiraled down, leading to further loss of income and further cuts. The country marched toward disaster.

There was no single cause of the Great Depression; rather it was an unhappy confluence of factors assailing the world at once. The U.S. was overproducing capital and goods. There were too many factories, housing was overbuilt, and machines made production more effective with fewer workers required. Credit was too plentiful and cheap, business ethics were lacking as greed overrode the fundamental economic health of the nation. At a time when 50 per cent of Americans lived in rural areas, agriculture was vastly overproducing for the available markets for their produce. International trade was out of balance and the situation was exacerbated by restrictive tariffs in the U.S. The miasma left from World War I had created political and economic unrest in Europe, causing uncertainty and fear.

Finally, the Depression became self-generating, as each bank collapse, each bankruptcy, each friend out of work, each seemingly inept and weak government response drove an ever-deepening spiral. It shattered the American Dream, which held that if you worked hard and lived by the rules you could improve your situation and that of your children. Suddenly, through no fault of their own, Americans' financial world collapsed, marking that generation for all their lives. And in a further blow to that great generation, the Depression planted the seeds for the rise of Adolf Hitler in Germany. The Depression would only end as America geared up for World War II.

St. Louis was the westernmost city in the major leagues in those Depression years, and they hosted not only the Cardinals but also the St. Louis Browns, a hard team to follow, as they were consistent losers. St. Louis was also the major league city closest to the 1930s Dust Bowl that extended from Texas and Oklahoma north into the Dakotas. A short distance away Roy F. Hoffmann and Mary Linn Thompson grew up in this Depression environment.

Before the Depression, Roy's father, Roy Walter, owned a grocery store. In those days people phoned in orders and groceries were boxed and delivered to customer's homes in a Model T delivery truck. Much of the business was done on credit and Roy Walter carried many IOUs as a result. Many of those IOUs became uncollectible with the onset of the Depression, as the customers simply couldn't repay the debts.

Roy Walter Hoffmann ended up losing his business due to an unfortunate fire, from which he could not recover. The fire and uncollectible IOUs left him in debt for much of the Depression, and into World War II. The Depression times were tough, particularly after losing the store.

In fairly typical fashion for that generation, Roy Walter picked himself up after losing the store and went to work. He worked most of his life for A & P grocers as a meat department manager and butcher. Times were tough and Roy Walter had to manage meat departments and the butcher shops within two stores. The stores were over 30 miles apart and to be able to have transportation between the two, Roy W. sold Chevrolets on the side. The job provided a demonstrator model, the chief advantage of the position.

Roy F. had this to say about the Depression, "Frugality was an absolute necessity, for jobs were scarce and pay for fathers fortunate enough to have a job was minimal. Frills such as candy, ice cream and soda pop were almost exclusively reserved for major celebrations such as Independence Day, Christmas and the family picnic for Grandma's birthday."

For those families lucky enough to have work, life had some semblance of normalcy. They heated their homes mostly by coal, delivered to their homes by truck and a sooty driver, who dumped the dusty coal through a cellar window. Their refrigerator was actually an icebox, and they had their blocks delivered by an iceman who brought them in multiples of 25 pounds, up to 100.

Women were respected and treated with courtesy. Men opened doors for them, gave them their seats on busses and street cars, stood up when they entered a room and always removed hats in their presence. Women were respected not because they were like men, but mercifully were not like men at all. They were the strong, yet gentle, better side of all our natures. For this, they held a special place in society.

When people went to the dentist in those days they sat in the chair for an hour or two of agony, as slow drills ground away, the pain untouched by Procaine, which was mixed at the chair and not very effective. There were no antibiotics, almost no health insurance, and if you were sick you stayed home, usually attended by a physician who made house calls. Parents who could afford to sent their children away for part of the summer, partly because of fear of polio.

They listened to an Atwater Kent, Philco, Silvertone or Majestic radio

Before the Crash: Roy W. Hoffmann in his grocery store (to right), circa 1929. Uncle Leo Pruneau to the left. Hoffmann Photo

set, which aired variety shows starring Jack Benny, Rudy Vallee, Fred Allen, George Burns and Gracie Allen, Bing Crosby, Edgar Bergen and Charlie McCarthy; to the "Grand Old Opry;" and to serials like "Amos 'n' Andy," and "The Lone Ranger." They went to see Mae West in the motion-picture theaters, and read *Tender Is the Night* by F. Scott Fitzgerald, *Goodbye, Mr. Chips* by James Hilton, *Gone with the Wind* by Margaret Mitchell and *The Thin Man* by Dashiell Hammett.[3]

With the proliferation of sports teams and entertainment for today's public it is very difficult to understand the special place baseball had in the hearts of Americans in those days. Then there was only baseball. Tickets were 50 cents and hotdogs five cents. Despite that, attendance kept dropping during the Depression and the Cincinnati Reds, Boston Braves and the Philadelphia Phillies nearly went out of business.

The 1934 St. Louis Cardinals fielded the Gashouse Gang of Frankie Frisch, shortstop Leo Durocher, The Dean Brothers (Dizzy and Daffy), Pepper Martin and Wild Bill Hallahan. Jay Hanna "Dizzy" Dean won 30 games that year and his brother, Paul "Daffy" Dean won 19 as a rookie. Left fielder Joe "Ducky" Medwick (so called because he ran like one) hit .319, and third baseman Pepper Martin passed out exploding cigars, put sneezing powder into the hotels' ventilation systems and then dropped water balloons out the windows. He was called the Wild Hoss of the Osage and played all out baseball without a jockstrap. The Cards met Detroit in the World Series. Dizzy got hit on the head by a thrown ball while running the bases and was carried off the field. The next day he said: "They took an X-ray of my head and found nothing." Dizzy shut out Detroit in the deciding game of the series. He was a second grade dropout ("I didn't do so well in the first grade, either," he said). Dean later went into sports casting and this author as a youth remembers him saying of a runner: "He slud into base." English teachers across the land were appalled.

Babe Ruth's career was coming to an end. After his estranged wife was killed in a house fire the night of January 11, 1929, the Babe married his mistress, Claire Hodgson. To her may be attributed the last few years of the Babe's great career, as she set down and enforced rules for him: No hard liquor during the season, no hot dogs or sodas before a game, in bed (with her only) by 10:00. She traveled on the Yankee train to make sure he toed the line. In 1933 the Babe hit "only" 34 home runs, drove in 103 runs and had to endure the humiliation of a

---

3. Description of the 1930s from William Manchester, *The Glory and the Dream* (New York: Bantam Books, 1974), *passim*

35 per cent pay cut. In 1934 the Yankees released the 39-year-old Ruth, and the next year he hit his 714th and final home run. His body had given out and he could barely hobble around the bases. He spent his final days waiting for the call to manage, which never came.

DESPITE THE DEPRESSION, it is clear Roy F. Hoffmann had a happy childhood. His parents kept the kids in line but weren't overbearing disciplinarians. He attended public grammar school with what might today be termed a "diverse" student body: A mixture of students of European nationalities, some of foreign birth with little or no ability to speak English. Those that couldn't speak English had family members translate for them until they could learn to speak English, which they quickly mastered. Roy counted himself one of the lucky ones in that his father had a job. Many of his friends' fathers were on the pick and shovel working for the WPA.

There were virtually no organized sports or playgrounds. There was little class structure since everyone was in essentially the same boat economically. The parents tried to cushion the worst of the Depression from their children, and those children made do with what they had. They played street hockey with elm branch sticks and tin cans for pucks. In softball and hardball both teams used the same gloves, transferring them as the teams transitioned from offense to defense. Normally there were only enough gloves for the infielders; outfielders were expected to catch fly balls with their bare hands. Anyone who had his own glove was "up in the high cotton." The balls were used until the ragged and dirty hide covers fell off. They skied in the winter with barrel staves.

Roy was an average student, relatively small compared to his peers, and not especially athletically talented, although he was aggressive and participated in most sports except basketball. He tried to play football but was restricted by his size. He stuck with it because his coach was interested in developing leadership skills and manhood—Roy practiced against the first team and learned how to persevere and grow. He got in at game time when the game was hopelessly lost or the team was so far ahead they couldn't lose.

He was very active in Boy Scouts, an organization producing leaders from then to now. His leadership skills manifested themselves early as a patrol leader, where he organized and led a team which collected many tons of scrap metal and waste paper in the nationwide program to rearm the U.S. military in the pre-war and early years of World War II.

Roy had his share of fights as a youth; despite his size he never backed down. After age 12, when he started delivering and selling newspapers, he never again had to ask for money. Working in knickers and carrying the papers in a bag, he delivered each paper on foot. The Sunday paper was special, as he made a penny profit on each one.

He stocked shelves in the grocery store and worked as a soda jerk in a dairy, which had a fountain as most did in those days. There was no air conditioning in the insufferable Missouri summers and it was a real treat for families to go to the fountain for sundaes.

His best friends were brothers Jim and Jerry Pfeiffer, Sylvester "Syl" Pagano and Bill Coolidge. James Pfeiffer became a sergeant in the 15th Army Air Force and was assigned to a B-17 bomber as a navigator/radioman. He was engaged in the massive offensive-bombing operations in Central Europe during World War II.

Gerald Pfeiffer was a glider trooper in the 101st Airborne Division. He was severely wounded by German artillery on September 22, 1944, during the early stages of the allied offensive assault in the European lowlands. After extensive surgeries, hospitalization and rehab he was medically discharged in 1945. He retired as a Missouri state employment executive. His wounds from World War II on occasion still bother him.

Bill's dad was the chief engineer for the PPG. Roy was Bill's best man when he married. Bill and Roy joined the Navy together after the start of World War II. Syl's mother died when he was a child. As was done in those days, his father went to Sicily, where he married and brought back a widow. She brought her three boys, none of whom could speak English. So it came to pass that Syl started the second grade with three new stepbrothers. He translated for them until they learned the language. All of the boys graduated from high school fluent in English.

Mary Linn was also lucky to have a father who worked two jobs during the Depression. The St. Joseph Lead Company did as well as it could for its employees, laying none off but cutting back on hours for those who remained. The company, with little or no demand for its products, cut back its operations to one week per month. During the summer months the company provided garden spots for employees so they might raise food for their families, and in the winter gave permission to cut wood on company lands for heating and cooking fuel. During the Depression the company borrowed ten million dollars and stockpiled thousands of tons of lead concentrate so each employee might have some money for his family needs. By the end of 1936 operations were increasing and with Hitler on the move in Europe the company returned to a five-day workweek.

Mary Linn remembers her childhood fondly. She came from a conservative, religious family, which never went into debt. Her parents were not politically oriented, although they had a high regard for Franklin Delano Roosevelt. On occasion, they cancelled out each other's ballot.

Mary Linn was an athlete, a catcher on a fast pitch softball team sponsored by the local shirt factory. At other times she played tennis with her dad. Her best friend was Pat Mabery (Terry). They are still in touch and Pat still lives in Missouri, retiring there after she and her husband spent their careers in education.

Mary Linn's fondest wish was to get away from Bonne Terre.

FEW MEN WOULD come to dominate their times as Franklin Delano Roosevelt did. In the election of 1932 Americans had turned to him as a man who seemed to understand their distress, and even more importantly was willing to do something about it. He was reelected in 1936. Roosevelt had promised to balance the budget in 1932, but instead the country was running an annual deficit of six to seven billion dollars. Seven million Americans were still out of work. Most newspapers were anti-Roosevelt; Hearst called the New Deal the Raw Deal. But unemployment in 1936 was half what it had been in 1932, industrial production was climbing, the banks had been saved, and business profits were rising. The Republicans had nominated Alf Landon for president. Landon gave bad speeches and campaigned poorly. He famously said: "Wherever I have gone in the country, I have found Americans." Roosevelt finally put Landon out of his misery on November 3, 1936, winning the greatest victory in American politics to that date. Landon won only two states (Maine and Vermont) and the electoral vote was 523 to eight.

BY 1923 GERMANY had descended into the chaotic legacy left by the Treaty of Versailles after World War I: The economy was in ruins, inflation raged, and the German currency was not worth the paper it was printed on. In this chaos Fascism thrived.

By June of 1932 the National Socialist Workers Party (of which the word Nazi is a contraction) had become the largest party in the Reichstag, holding 230 seats out of 608. Adolf Hitler, who in January of 1933 became the chancellor of Germany, led the Nazis.

In March of 1936 Hitler reoccupied the Rhineland that had been demilitarized under the provisions of the Versailles Treaty and the Locarno Agreement. The French and British filed a meek protest, further emboldening Hitler. Then, on March 13, 1938, the Germans annexed Austria in the Anschluss, proclaiming the unfortunate region a province of the German Reich. In the fall, on September 30, 1938, Hitler and English Prime Minister Neville Chamberlain signed the Munich Pact, a vague friendship agreement between the two countries. The British and French allowed Hitler to annex the Sudetenland, an area of Czechoslovakia with a largely German-speaking population. Chamberlain returned home with the agreement and proclaimed to the cheering crowd below the window of No. 10 Downing Street: "I believe it is peace for our time." Ever the realist, Winston Churchill understood it better: "Britain and France had to choose between war and dishonor. They chose dishonor. They will have war." Hitler triumphantly entered the Sudetenland on October 3, 1938.

Unfortunately for the world and for Germany, it's clear that Hitler had misread the will of the British and the American people. He had ample reason to so read the attitudes of the two exemplars of democracy. Hitler disdained America: "There's nobody more stupid than the Americans . . . I'll never believe the American soldier can fight like a hero." At many American colleges, militant pacifism ruled. At Columbia and Berkeley only eight per cent were willing to fight for America under any circumstances. In 1935 over 150,000 students demonstrated in a nationwide Student Strike for Peace. "Subsequently a half-million undergraduates signed a pledge that if Congress declared war they would refuse to serve . . . Their concept of what they called 'the system' was not far removed from 'the establishment' their children would later learn to loath."[4] As to the British, there was good reason as well to question their will before Churchill. British youths of the Oxford Union passed a resolution which read in part: " . . . this House will in no circumstances fight for its King and Country."[5]

On March 14, 1939, Hitler invaded the rest of Czechoslovakia after having taken the Sudetenland in October of the preceding year. By the end of the month Britain and France had guaranteed to protect the Polish and the Rumanians against foreign aggression; by so doing they made World War II inevitable.

On September 28, 1939, Germany and Russia partitioned Poland, which had been caught in a pincer movement when Russia invaded from

---

4. These '30s protestors were a tired predecessor to college antiwar students of the '60s and '70s. "They were opposed to compulsory ROTC, violations of academic freedom and student rights; they wanted reform of college administrations. Radicals were members of the Student League for Industrial Democracy (SLID), a forerunner of the Students for a Democratic Society." Manchester, *The Glory and the Dream*, pp. 126–127.

5. Robert Leckie, *The Wars of America* (Edison, NJ: Castle Books, 1998), p. 683.

the east on September 17, two weeks after Germany entered Poland from the west. Two days after the German invasion Great Britain and France formally declared war on Germany.

Next, on November 30, 1939, the Soviets invaded Finland and were met with a ferocious defense. On March 13, 1940, the armistice between the USSR and Finland was signed. The Finns had suffered terribly, losing 25,000 dead and 45,000 wounded. The Soviets also suffered in a harbinger of the massive casualties they were to suffer in the war, with 48,000 dead and 158,000 wounded.

On March 18, 1939, Benito Mussolini and Hitler announced Italy's formal alliance with Germany against England and France. Mussolini called this the "Axis" on which Europe will revolve; Germany, Italy and Japan would eventually be called the Axis powers. Mussolini, the son of a blacksmith, was called *Il Duce* (the leader). He came to power in October 1922 with his march on Rome, so cowing the king that Mussolini was made prime minister. He organized Italian World War I veterans into the rabidly nationalistic "blackshirts" which he used to intimidate his opponents. Inept and venal, he proved an uncertain and cumbersome ally for Hitler.

On April 9, 1940, two German divisions under the command of General Kaupitsch invaded Denmark; Copenhagen fell within 12 hours. The Norway landings also began, and on April 10, 1940, the Norwegian government and royal family left Oslo and Vidkun Quisling was installed to lead a puppet government. After the war Quisling was tried for high treason by his fellow countrymen and executed by firing squad. For his treachery his name would come to symbolize the word traitor.

On May 8 Chamberlain resigned and another of the giants of the 20th Century, Winston Churchill, officially took his office two days later. It now seems that Churchill was inevitable, that " . . . indomitable, jut-jawed and glowering . . . living embodiment of John Bull . . ."[6] Repudiated before by the British, they turned to him in their dire hour of need.

On May 10, 1940, the Germans began their attack in the west. By the end of the day it was clear the Belgian and Dutch armies weren't going to hold out long enough for British and French help to do any good. At 1100 hours on May 15 the Dutch army capitulated. Less than two weeks later King Leopold surrendered the Belgian army. In those dark days Prime Minister Churchill had little to offer other than ". . . blood, toil, tears and sweat."

---

6. Leckie, *The Wars of America*, p. 698.

From May 26 to June 4 the "Miracle of Dunkirk" evacuation occurred. When it was done, the Royal Navy, assisted by hundreds of small fishing and merchant ships sailing from the shadows of the White Cliffs of Dover, evacuated 338,226 men, including 112,000 French soldiers. On June 4 Churchill declared:

> We shall go on to the end. We shall fight in France, we shall fight in the seas and oceans . . . we shall defend our Island, whatever the cost may be. We shall fight on the beaches, we shall fight on the landing grounds, we shall fight in the fields and the streets, we shall fight in the hills; we shall never surrender . . . our empire beyond the seas . . . would carry on the struggle, until, in God's good time, the New World, with all its power and might, steps forth to the rescue and liberation of the Old.[7]

OLD EUROPE TOPPLED as on June 5, 1940 Germany invaded France. France had been lulled into a false sense of security by the Maginot Line that stretched from Switzerland to Longway just below the Ardennes Forest in Belgium. The guns were set in place and pointed where the Germans were supposed to appear. The French Army matched its inadequacy:

> The French Army was rotten. It had never recovered from the shock of the last war, and since 1936 it had been shabbily armed and its will to fight weakened by the indifference and pacifism of the leftist Popular Front. The French nation was also sick. France had been bled white in the last war and was further depleted by a declining birth rate.[8]

PARIS FELL TO THE Germans on June 14, 1940. France surrendered and a pro-German government, welcomed by many of the French, was installed in the city of Vichy. In London, a Free French government headed by General Charles de Gaulle vowed to fight on.

In the United States, Roosevelt eased a reluctant American public into preparation for war. On July 20, 1940 Congress authorized $4 billion for the construction of a two-ocean navy. On September 3 Roosevelt gave 50 American destroyers to England in exchange for the right to construct bases in British possessions in the Western Hemisphere, inspiring the Lend-Lease program which became law when signed by Roosevelt on March 11, 1941. Essentially it meant that Britain could continue to order American materials without necessarily having the cash to pay for them. It narrowly passed

---

7. Leckie, *The Wars of America*.
8. Ibid., p. 702.

Congress as isolationist sentiment remained strong. On September 16 the Selective Training and Service Act required men from 21 to 35 years of age to register for military training.

On November 5, 1940, Franklin D. Roosevelt won reelection for an unprecedented third term, defeating Republican Wendell Willkie. Roosevelt carried 38 states with 449 electoral votes and won 55 per cent of votes cast. Willkie carried only ten states with 82 electoral votes. In one of his baser pandering moments, Roosevelt said only five days before the election, in Boston: "And while I'm talking to you mothers and fathers I give you one more assurance. I have said this before, but I say it again: Your boys are not going to be sent into any foreign wars." It was of course clear to Roosevelt by then that war was inevitable.

Operation Barbarossa, the German attack on the Soviet Union, began at 0300 on June 22, 1941. It was the most fateful decision of Hitler's career, an astounding mistake and one of the worst blunders by a war leader in recorded history. With Barbarossa Hitler opened up a vast second front against a country with a poor road system, disabling the fabled blitz that sputtered to a halt as the immobilizing Russian winter set in.

In the 1920s Japan reinvented itself in a way that led to war in the 1930s. It developed a state religion, Shinto, which was an ancient religion of nature worship coupled with a belief in a divine emperor. Shintoism was perverted into an endorsement of a modern, totalitarian state. Around this foundation was built a militarized version of the old code of the samurai, a class of noble warriors, the Bushido. The Japanese came to believe that the greatest good was fighting and dying for the emperor. If you were to die in his service, you would be transported to the Yakakuni Shrine, a Japanese warrior paradise reminiscent of the virgins awaiting today's Muslim terrorists. Tragically, it became the justification for murder, torture and cruelty on a scale unprecedented in Japanese history.[9]

In September of 1931 Japan sent its army to occupy south and central Manchuria. In the face of weak Chinese resistance the Japanese had largely completed the conquest by early 1932. By 1934 Japan was spending nearly half its budget (937 million yen out of 2,112 million yen) on the army and navy.

---

9. Paul Johnson, *Modern Times: The World from the Twenties to the Nineties* (New York: HarperPerennial, 1991), p. 181

In December of 1937 Japanese forces advancing from Shanghai reached and captured the Chinese capital, Nanking. In the four weeks after the Japanese entered the city they engorged themselves in one of the worst massacres in human history, hunting men, women and children to their deaths. Some 20,000 male Chinese of military age were marched out of the city and bayoneted and machine-gunned to death. The killings continued until February 6, 1938; by the time it was over the Japanese Army had killed between 200,000 and 300,000 Chinese.

In June and July 1938 the Japanese advance was halted near Chengchow by massive flooding caused by the Chinese breaching the dams along the Yellow River. An estimated one million Chinese peasants died in the flood.

On July 16, 1940, the brilliant General Tojo became Minister of War in Japan. Just over a year later, after Roosevelt was informed Japanese forces had invaded French Indochina, he froze Japan's assets in the U.S. This stopped trade between the countries, essentially cutting off Japanese oil supplies.

AND SO, THE COURSES of the lives of Roy F. Hoffmann and Mary Linn Thompson, and millions of their fellow citizens were set. It would be war after all. They followed the news, mostly in the newspapers and on radio, as that's the way they got it in those days. They watched and waited, well aware of the Nazi threat. And then the Japanese attacked Pearl Harbor.

2

WORLD WAR II AND THE DEMOBILIZATION

On July 2, 1941, Lou Gehrig, legendary first baseman of the New York Yankees, died of Amyotrophic Lateral Sclerosis (ALS), the disease which would forevermore bear his name. On the 17th of that same month Yankee center fielder Joe DiMaggio's 56-game hitting streak ended in a game with the Cleveland Indians. The extraordinary streak had begun on May 15 and it is likely it will never be broken.

Baseball was a diversion from the raging wars in Europe and Asia as that same month of July brought an embargo ordered by President Roosevelt on shipments of scrap iron and gasoline to Japan. Roosevelt was reacting to the assault by Japanese forces into the French colony of Indochina. That action, coupled with his order freezing Japanese assets in the U.S., assured the war that was to come on December 7, 1941.

The Japanese decision to attack Pearl Harbor was a colossal blunder on the scale of Hitler's decision to attack Russia the preceding year.[1] The attack, coming without a formal declaration of war, united an America saddled with a deep isolationist and antiwar sentiment.

There was ample warning the Japanese would attack, but most military strategists thought the attack would come in the Philippines, America's major base in the Pacific. The commanders at Pearl Harbor thought they were secure from attack because of the strength of the garrison there, and distance from an

---

1. Admiral Nagumo, the Japanese Navy Chief of Staff, and Admiral Yamamoto, their most able Navy commander, knew the Japanese could not hope to win an all-out war with America and Britain. Admiral Nagumo said: "If I am told to fight regardless of the consequences I shall run wild considerably for six months or a year. But I have utterly no confidence in the second or third years." America out produced the Japanese 20 to 1 in steel, 100 to 1 in oil, 10 to 1 in coal, 5 to 1 in aircraft production, 2 to 1 in shipping and 5 to 1 in overall labor force. Paul Johnson, *A History of the American People* (New York: HarperCollins, 1997), p. 777.

attacking force. Sabotage was thought to be the greater threat, and so the battleships were berthed tightly together in the harbor and planes were parked neatly together in rows in the middle of Hickam Field.

The Japanese fleet under Admiral Nagumo sailed from the Kurile Islands on November 26, 1941, for Pearl Harbor, struggling through mountainous waves that broke over the ships, sweeping men overboard. The fleet received the message "Climb Mount Niitake" on December 2, which meant, "Proceed to the attack."

There were eight battleships moored along Battleship Row in Pearl Harbor, some side by side. Five cruisers and 26 destroyers were berthed in the harbor as well. By a stroke of luck three carriers and seven other cruisers were out to sea when the attack occurred.

At 7:02 A.M. a radar operator on Oahu reported a large force of incoming aircraft which was the first wave of 40 torpedo bombers, 51 Val dive bombers and about 50 twin-engined Betty bombers escorted by 50 Zero fighters on the way to attack Pearl Harbor. His superior officer told him to ignore the blips thinking they were probably U.S. planes coming from the mainland.

The "Japs" or "Nips" ("Nip" was short for "Dai Nippon," the Japanese word for their homeland), as they were called then, had launched their planes from carriers located approximately 230 miles north of the island of Oahu. The first wave achieved complete surprise, and it was followed by a second wave of 170 planes. By 1000 hours it was over. All but 47 of the 359 land-based Army, Navy and Marine planes on Oahu were damaged or destroyed. All eight battleships in the harbor were damaged and five smoking metal hulks sunk into the mud. The *Arizona* was lost with many of her crew trapped aboard. There were an additional three cruisers and three destroyers sunk. In all 19 ships were sunk or damaged. The massive oil storage tanks were left intact as Nagumo declined to send in a third attack. Three thousand Americans died at the hands of the Japanese.

That weekend Roosevelt was in his study, wearing an old pullover sweater, going through his stamp collection. He was stunned by the attack. The next day he addressed a joint session of Congress, asking for a declaration of war against Japan. The Senate responded with a unanimous vote in favor and the House followed with a 388–1 vote for war.[2]

Three days later Germany and Italy declared war on the United States. On December 17 Admiral Chester Nimitz replaced Admiral Husband E.

---

2. The sole vote against was by pacifist Representative Jeanette Rankin of Montana, who has become something of a darling of the antiwar movement. Her meaningless vote squandered a legacy as the first woman elected to the House. As in 1917, when she voted in the House against World War I, her vote against World War II caused the voters of Montana to send her packing after another single term in office.

Devastation at Pearl Harbor following the Japanese attack. The USS Oklahoma (BB 37) is capsized and the USS Arizona (BB 39) has gone down.
OFFICIAL U.S. NAVY PHOTO, STAN COHEN COLLECTION

Bracketed by plumes of smoke are the sunken USS West Virginia and the USS Tennessee. The West Virginia was hit by two armor-piercing bombs and by seven to nine torpedoes, literally blowing open the port side of the ship.
OFFICIAL U.S. NAVY PHOTO, STAN COHEN COLLECTION

The shock next day. Los Angeles Times, *December 8, 1941.* Courtesy Stan Cohen

Kimmel as Pacific Fleet commander, who, along with Lieutenant General Walter C. Short, was made a scapegoat for the Pearl Harbor attack. The United States had entered the greatest, most costly and deadly war in world history. Before it was done 38 million lives would be lost worldwide; American casualties killed and wounded would be over one million.

WHEN THE NEWS came that Pearl Harbor had been attacked Roy Hoffmann was working at his job as a soda jerk. The radio, which was always on in the fountain, was airing standard programming when the announcement came that the Japs had attacked Pearl Harbor. There was a stunned silence in which a dropped pin would have echoed in the room. For ten to 15 minutes after the announcement the customers sat engrossed by the news.

Mary Linn was a freshman in high school when she heard the news. It was a few days after her birthday and she had just been to Mass with her mother, sister and brother. They got the news at their home and all of the males (of military age) said they would be going into the service. There were no lamentations, no griping, just acceptance of their duty to their country.

Soon there were men lined up for blocks in front of recruiting offices to enlist. Since both parents had to consent to enlistment at age 17, some lied about their age to get in.

AFTER THE ATTACK on Pearl Harbor the Japanese offensive continued with the invasion of Luzon in the Philippines on December 10, 1941. Later that month Wake Island fell after 400 U.S. Marines made a heroic 15-day stand defending the Island. Next Manila fell on January 2, 1942, forcing U.S. and Philippine forces under MacArthur to withdraw to the Bataan peninsula. On March 17 General MacArthur was ordered to leave Bataan by President Roosevelt, as it was apparent the Allied forces would fall. Bataan fell on April 9 resulting in the surrender of 75,000 American and Philippine troops. The next day the brutal Bataan Death March began at dawn. American and Philippine prisoners marched 100 miles in six days on one meal of rice and with Japanese bayonets and gun butts brutalizing them along the way. In less than a week 5,200 Americans and many more Filipinos dropped dead along the trail, from executions, thirst and starvation.

For four months the Japanese conducted a one-sided war without serious setback. Then, on April 18, carrier-launched bombers under the command of Lieutenant Colonel James H. (Jimmy) Doolittle conducted an air raid on Tokyo, providing a major boost for American morale and a blow to the Japanese, who thought their islands impregnable. Flying North American Aviation's twin engine B-25s, Doolittle's Raiders got off the deck of the *Hornet* with no way to land back on the carrier after the mission. Task Force 16, under the command of Vice Admiral William F. Halsey, escorted the *Hornet* within 600 nautical miles of Japan. At that point the TF began to encounter Japanese picket boats, one of which managed to send a radio message before being sunk. Thinking the mission compromised, Halsey and Doolittle decided to launch the 16 planes, each with a crew of five (pilot, co-pilot, navigator, gunner and bombardier), at once. It was a huge gamble as the planes had a 2,000-mile trip before they could hopefully land behind Nationalist lines in China after hitting Japan. Doolittle led off down the 467 feet of available runway on the carrier. Thirteen of the Raiders hit Tokyo.[3] Eventually 11 crews, including Doolittle's, had to bail out, while three crash-landed. The Japanese captured eight of the crewmen; three were executed and one died in captivity. Doolittle later received the Medal of Honor for the mission.

The Battle of the Coral Sea was fought May 4 through 8, 1942, between the American and Japanese navies. The overall strategy of Admiral Isoroku Yammamoto was to capture the Midway Atoll and force a battle with the Americans in which he could destroy the carriers missed at Pearl Harbor. Coral Sea was the first naval battle fought in which neither fleet came in sight of the other. Despite the sinking of the U.S. carrier *Lexington*, which was struck by two torpedoes and at least two bombs, the Battle of Coral Sea was a heavy blow to the Japanese. They lost seven warships to the depths of the ocean, as well as 77 of their 108 operational aircraft.

The Battle of the Coral Sea was followed by the Battle of Midway, June 4–6, 1942. Despite overwhelming superiority in surface warships and submarines, the Japanese squandered their advantage by dividing their Combined Fleet into no fewer than ten separate formations, which were so separated they couldn't provide the others support. Planes from the carriers *Enterprise*, *Hornet* and *Yorktown* caught Nagumo's carriers with recovered planes on their decks. Three squadrons of *Devastator* torpedo bombers led the first attack, which they gallantly made despite losing 35 of 41 planes. Their attack drew the Japanese Zeros to the wave tops at the precise moment *Dauntless* dive-bomber squadrons reached the scene, striking the Jap carriers again and again. Despite American losses of two ships and over 300 men, the Japanese losses were far worse, damaging or destroying assets the Japanese could ill afford to lose.

On August 7, 1942, the U.S. Marines landed on Guadalcanal in the Solomon Islands and so began the brutal island hopping battles that defined the Pacific War. In the naval battle of Guadalcanal, November 12–15, the U.S. fleet under Admiral William "Bull" Halsey sank 28 Japanese warships and transports,

---

3. The remaining three hit Nagoya, Osaka and Kobe.

rendering them unable to reinforce their troops on Guadalcanal. U.S. Marines finally took control of Guadalcanal after four months of savage combat.

It was tough going in Europe for U.S. forces as well, as the Americans were defeated by the Afrika Korps of Field Marshal Erwin Rommel at the Kasserine Pass in Tunisia, February 14–25, 1943. The Americans regrouped under George S. Patton and stopped the Nazi drive, linking up with British forces under Field Marshal Montgomery. Eventually Montgomery would link up in Tunis and force the surrender of all German and Italian forces in North Africa.

ON APRIL 1, 1943, President Roosevelt, in a move to stem inflation, froze wages, salaries and prices. At the same time meats, fats and cheeses were rationed, joining earlier rationing of shoes, gasoline and coffee. For Roy Walter Hoffmann the rationing of beef would prove to be a blessing in disguise. He had acquired a farm outside Crystal City where he was able to raise and slaughter beef for sale. He always made sure he had extra beef on hand in his butcher shop for the families that had servicemen home on leave during the war. The remainder provided extra income, eventually enabling him to settle the debts he had left from the store fire.

In May of 1943 17-year-old Roy F. Hoffmann graduated from Crystal City High School. At the end of the preceding month he had enlisted in the Navy Reserve. He would have joined earlier except his parents wouldn't sign a waver for him to enlist—they insisted he finish high school first. He joined with a

The costs of war: Memorial services on Midway Island, June 1942.
ASSOCIATED PRESS PHOTO FROM THE U.S. NAVY, STAN COHEN COLLECTION

U.S. Navy gun crews in action against Japanese-held Wake Island, October 5–6, 1943.
Associated Press Photo from the U.S. Navy, Stan Cohen collection

sense of patriotic duty, or as he put it: "Joining the Navy was not a decision; it was almost automatic. Where I came from if you weren't 4-F you were expected to go."

He had picked the Navy for two reasons. First, he had seen submarines built on the Great Lakes floated down the Mississippi on their way to New Orleans. "When I saw that I thought 'there's a ticket out of the Ozarks.'" Second, it was about the time the USS *Missouri* was commissioned, with an all-Missouri crew.

While still in high school he had taken a battery of military aptitude tests, which determined six of the students (out of 70) were considered to have officer potential. Of the six young Roy received a commission, another eventually received a battlefield commission, and the remaining four were called into the battle in Europe. Roy had hoped to qualify for Naval Aviation Training, with the Army Air Corps as his second choice.[4]

---

4. The U.S. Air Force was not created as a separate branch of the U.S. Military until after World War II. During the war air operations were limited to the Army and Navy.

Roy F. Hoffmann at enlistment, 1943. HOFFMANN PHOTO

At home American women went to work to support the war effort. They became known collectively as "Rosie the Riveter" from a *Saturday Evening Post* cover by Norman Rockwell. "Rosie" was in coveralls with goggles pushed up on her forehead, brawny yet feminine and appealing at the same time. During the war more than six million women took up what formerly had been "men's work," breaking down what had been previous high barriers to employment.

One of those working women was Zettamae Hoffmann, who went to work as an inspector at a huge munitions plant at Wentzville, Missouri. The plant manufactured small arms ammunition and Zettamae worked there throughout the war.

MEANWHILE, MARY LINN Thompson was in high school, following the news of the war on radio and in newspapers. There were no "body counts" released in those days, and the news was censored to insure there were no leaks of Allied war plans. Every Monday the students got a pop quiz on news of the war.

She had a teacher, Mr. Barrow, who got her involved in sports. He was a strict disciplinarian, tolerating no foolishness in the classroom or on the field. Severe nuns in their black habits at her school reinforced discipline. They handed out corporal punishment liberally. Mary Linn worked hard for Mr. Barrow, not wanting to disappoint him. Naturally competitive, she played the catcher position for the softball team. According to Mary Linn, Navy Waves were the toughest opponents she played in adult leagues. Also, she was forced to wear a chest protector one season as the league enforced the rule that women catchers must wear one.

ROY F. HOFFMANN had joined with zeal to get into the action ("Fly over Tokyo" in his words). So with eager anticipation he reported to the Federal Building in St. Louis, where he and the other recruits were put in cattle cars and taken to Lambert Field, which was a Naval Air Station (NAS) during the war. The next day the recruits lined up in front of the drill sergeants (Navy chief petty officers [CPOs] and Marines). "Where are we going, chief?" asked young Roy. "What do you mean where are you going," was the reply, "you're going *here*." How embarrassing. He had joined to fight Japs and he was stuck 45 miles from home.

His friend in recruit training was Arthur Green, who was Jewish. On one break from training Roy took Arthur to the family farm, where he got to watch the pigs being slopped. Arthur's only comment was: "It's no damn wonder we don't eat pork."

After two to three months Roy was shipped to Portage Des Sioux near St. Charles at the confluence of the Missouri and Mississippi. He wasn't making much progress getting away from home, and going on liberty in uniform without any ribbons wasn't much fun either. His next stop was Missouri Valley College in Marshall, Missouri, where he majored in chemistry and physics, two subjects he had done well with in high school.

He was enrolled under the Navy's V-12 College Training Program, initiated in 1943 to meet the need of the Navy for commissioned officers to man the ships, fly the planes and command troops in World War II. When the draft age was lowered to 18 in November 1942, the Navy saw it would face a shortage of college-educated officers. Also, hundreds of colleges and universities in the U.S. were facing financial collapse when classrooms emptied as men enlisted. The V-12 participants consisted of students already enrolled in Marine and Navy reserve programs; enlisted men recommended by their commanding officers; and high school seniors who passed nationwide qualifying examinations. Eventually 125,000 college-age participants were enrolled at 131 colleges and universities in the three years of the program from 1943 to 1946. All of the men were on active duty, in uniform and subject to very strict military discipline. They worked hard, studied all year, carried over 20 credit hours and engaged in a minimum of nine and one-half hours of physical training each week. The heavy workload and responsibilities under the program paid off, as it eventually produced 38 admirals (including Rear Admiral Roy F. Hoffmann and Vice Admiral Rex Rectanus) and 20 Marine generals.

Blacks enrolled in the V-12 program starting late March 1943. They were a ground-breaking group. One of the black graduates, Vice Admiral Samuel L. Gravely, Jr., became the first black to command a Navy warship and the first black to advance to the rank of Admiral.[5] Other notable V-12 veterans were Johnny Carson, Robert F. Kennedy, Jack Lemmon and Senator Daniel Patrick Moynihan (D-NY).

ON JULY 10, 1943, the invasion of Sicily commenced under the command of General Dwight D. Eisenhower. By August 17 the island was captured, giving the allies control of Mediterranean shipping. By then Mussolini was done and

---

5. Admiral Gravely said, "The V-12 program was a turning point in my life. It gave me an opportunity to compete on an equal footing with people I had never competed with before. It gave me an opportunity to prove to myself that I could succeed if I tried." V-12 Navy College Training Program Internet Web site, by Carolyn Alison.

the new Prime Minister, Pietro Badoglio, started the process for the eventual end of Italian military resistance. The invasion of Salerno followed, met by fierce German resistance.

January of 1944 brought the invasion to the coastal town of Anzio near Rome, followed the next month by a massive bombing campaign against German aircraft production centers. Bombing raids continued against Berlin.

June 6, 1944, saw the largest invasion force in history hit the beaches of Normandy. Now famous as D-Day, Operation Overlord was a huge risk due to the vagaries of weather and the entrenched Germans on the coast. Eisenhower's courageous decision sent the allies ashore at beaches given names like Omaha, Utah and Juno. After four days of fierce fighting the allies established their beachhead and a million Allied troops were soon ashore. It would take nearly another year of pounding before the Germans ultimately surrendered.

On August 25 Paris was taken and the German occupation ended. The Allies fought across the continent, pushing the Germans to their homeland. On December 16, 1944, the Germans counterattacked in the desperate Battle of the Bulge. The Allied troops were pushed back in Belgium's Ardennes Forest (creating the "bulge" at the center). After two weeks of brutal fighting in deep snow the Germans were stopped—the end was near for them as they rapidly collapsed.[6]

On October 20, 1944, General Douglas MacArthur waded ashore at Leyte Island in the Philippines, fulfilling his promise to return. Three days later the Japanese suffered a major naval defeat in the Battle of Leyte Gulf. Their fleet decimated, the Japanese began to resort to *kamikaze* ("Divine Wind") suicide attacks on American ships. These suicide missions, in which Japanese pilots dived at ships desperately firing at them, were devastating when the bomb-laden planes struck. The attacks caused 400 American ships to go down with the loss of nearly 10,000 sailors.

In Europe American bombers hammered Berlin, and the brutal firebombing of Dresden commenced, eventually incinerating 100,000 Germans. In February in a former Tsarist place at Yalta, Churchill, Stalin and a weak and ill Roosevelt met to discuss the final assault on Germany, creation of a peace organization (eventually the United Nations), and the groundwork

---

6. An indicator of the American élan as fighting men was General Anthony McAuliffe's reported response when presented with a German demand he surrender when his 101st Airborne Division was surrounded in Bastogne: "Nuts."

for the post-war division of Europe. That division laid the groundwork for the "Cold War" between the Communists and the democracies that would drag on for 40 years after the conclusion of World War II. On March 7 the American First Army crossed the Rhine at Remagen; by the end of that month all German forces were pushed back into Germany.

In the Pacific, on March 16, the month long battle for the rocky, eight square mile volcanic island of Iwo Jima ended with an Allied victory. The fighting was almost unbelievably difficult, with the Marines suffering some 25,000 casualties. The next month U.S. troops invaded Okinawa. This, the bloodiest battle of the Pacific lasted until June 21, and when it was done the Americans had suffered some 80,000 casualties (12,500 dead) and the Japanese lost some 160,000 men on the island.

On April 12, 1945, President Roosevelt suffered a massive cerebral hemorrhage and died at his retreat in Warm Springs, Georgia. With him was his long time mistress, Lucy Rutherford. His death brought to the presidency Harry Truman, whom Roosevelt had kept uninformed of many of the secrets of the war, including the Manhattan Project, which had developed the atom bomb. On July 16, 1945, the first atomic bomb was successfully detonated at Alamogordo, New Mexico.

On April 30, 1945, with a backdrop of Russian shells falling on Berlin, Hitler married his mistress Eva Braun deep within his fortress bunker. After poisoning Eva, Hitler ended his miserable life with a pistol shot. A week later the Germans surrendered to General Eisenhower at Rheims in France and to the Soviets at Berlin. President Truman proclaimed Victory in Europe (V-E) Day, May 8, 1945.

MEANWHILE, A FRUSTRATED Roy Hoffmann had spent much of the war in Marshall, Missouri. When the time came to go to flight school he couldn't pass the eye examination, and so he was ordered to enroll in the Navy Reserve Officers Training (NROTC) program at Notre Dame. The selection process to Notre Dame was "very selective" as the Admiral now puts it. They were all lined up and everybody with a last name starting with the letters "A" through "G" went to Rice and the remainder went to Notre Dame.

Roy Hoffmann majored in chemistry at Notre Dame. Additionally, he took the Naval Science curriculum that emphasized engineering. He played in the school band as a percussionist. The news of V-E Day was the cause of a great celebration, the Admiral remembered. "Everyone was having a hell of a time. Somehow or other I ended up in Chicago and I don't remember a whole lot about that."

PRESIDENT TRUMAN MADE the decision to use the atomic bomb to end the war in the Pacific. The first bomb was dropped on Hiroshima by the U.S. B-29 Superfortress *Enola Gay*, August 6, 1945. This first destructive blast was followed by a second bomb dropped on the city of Nagasaki. The will of the Japanese to fight effectively ended with these two bombs.[7] Victory in Japan (V-J Day) was proclaimed on August 15, 1945. On September 2, 1945 General MacArthur accepted the unconditional surrender of Japan aboard the USS *Missouri* (BB 63) in Tokyo Bay.[8]

IN SEPTEMBER OF 1945 Mary Linn Thompson entered Flat River Junior College in Flat River, Missouri, and lived at home while at school. She had hoped to go to the University of Missouri, but former GIs were mustering out of the service in record numbers, taking advantage of the GI Bill and overwhelming the colleges. At Flat River she took Rhetoric, European History, Botany, English Composition, French and Spanish. It was not an easy course load; as she had done in high school she excelled in her studies.

Eventually it came time for her younger brother to enter college and Mary Linn had to drop out because the family couldn't afford two children in college. She speaks of the event without rancor. In those days it was assumed the man would have to be the breadwinner for the family and so his education was simply more important.

---

7. In the worst kind of historical revisionism, Truman has been harshly criticized for his decision to drop the atomic bombs. In reality the Japanese were prepared to fiercely defend their homeland; Allied casualties would have been enormous in an invasion of Japan; and the war-weary Allies had already suffered terribly in the war. Allied experiences from Guadalcanal to Okinawa led to the belief that the Japanese would fight to the death. There were still six million battle-hardened troops defending the Japanese homeland. Our military had estimated there would be between 500,000 and a million casualties in an invasion of Japan. Even if the casualties were half their estimate the losses would have been unacceptable. "Each successive island that the Americans invaded was defended fanatically, at immense cost on both sides. The Japanese military code, centuries old and steeped in the samurai tradition, showed no tolerance for surrender." Kenneth C. Davis, *Don't Know Much About History* (New York: Avon Books, 1990), p. 317.

8. The *Missouri* entered combat early in 1945 and was the flagship of Admiral Halsey's Third Fleet. Truman selected the *Missouri* for the surrender ceremony because it was named for his home state and had been christened by his daughter Margaret. As often happens, politics prevailed over right. The honor should have gone to the USS *Enterprise*, which had fought throughout the war in the Pacific. Naval Historical Foundation, *The Navy* (New York: Barnes and Noble Books, 2000).

In 1947 Mary Linn started as a medical records librarian at the St. Joseph Lead Company's hospital. While working there she impressed the doctors and staff and was encouraged to go on to medical school, but she concluded it would be difficult competitively for a woman in practice in those days. Patients simply had more confidence in male physicians.

Roy Hoffmann was still enrolled at Notre Dame when the war ended. In June of 1946 he graduated from NROTC Unit 1, even though he hadn't completed his requirements for a Bachelor of Science degree in chemistry at Notre Dame, and was commissioned as an ensign in the U.S. Navy Reserve. In a great honor for the new Navy officers, Admiral Chester Nimitz, Commander in Chief of the U.S. Pacific Fleet from December 17, 1941 to the end of the war, presided over the ceremony.

Orders to the USS *Quick* (DD 490) followed. The Federal Shipbuilding and Dry Dock Company at Kearny, New Jersey, built the *Quick* in 1941. She was commissioned on July 3, 1942, Lieutenant Commander R. B. Nickerson commanding. She was assigned to escort duty in the shipping lanes of the Caribbean and the Gulf of Mexico, lanes that in preceding months had suffered the greatest losses to German U-boat activities in the western Atlantic. She was then ordered to Safi, Morocco, where she took up station for the Southern Attack Group of operation "Torch," the invasion of North Africa. After returning to the U.S. she again returned to North Africa, then sailed for Sicily and participated in operation "Husky." She later returned to escort work in the North Atlantic and on Mediterranean runs until the end of the war in Europe.

The war in the Pacific still raged on, and on June 13, 1945, she entered the Charleston Naval Shipyard where she was converted to a high-speed destroyer-minesweeper, emerging as DMS-32. The *Quick* was fast, 33–34 knots, and very rough riding. Originally she had four 5-inch gun mounts; the fourth was taken off to accommodate the mine sweeping gear on the fantail. When Roy Hoffmann reported aboard the *Quick* she was home-ported at the Embarcadero at the foot of Market Street in San Francisco. He had traveled by train to San Francisco with a folded dollar bill, which new officers carried to give to the first person that "signs" (salutes) them. He had gone all the way to San Francisco without a salute; the first came from the sentry at the pier. When he reported aboard it was his first time on a Navy ship.

He reported to a ship manned by a mostly inexperienced wardroom and crew. There were three experienced officers on board (the CO, XO and one lieutenant j.g.) and several senior chief petty officers, but the balance of the crew was inexperienced. In those days an ensign was to be seen and not heard at the wardroom table. The CO was Lieutenant Commander Foote, a Naval Academy graduate, and a good officer who ran a disciplined ship.[9]

After two months the ship deployed for the Western Pacific (West Pac). Roy Hoffmann was assigned to damage control and minesweeping. The transit to Hawaii could only be described as tough. The narrow beamed, rough riding ship was battered by heavy seas, and suffered through 15- to 20-degree rolls. The new ensign must have wondered if he was destined for a Navy career. He spent the whole transit "on the rail," puking over the side, seasick. He was so sick he sometimes thought it would be better to go over the side. His only consolation was there were plenty of other sailors lined up with him. He did manage to scale the main mast to a crow's nest high above the main deck, holding on for dear life.

Heavy seas were dangerous for the destroyer men. On those early classes of destroyers there was no fore-aft interior passageway, so to transit the length of the ship it was necessary to go out on the main deck. There was a cable that stretched fore and aft which sailors clutched for dear life while transiting the main deck, which could be awash with heavy seas. Perhaps inevitably, a sailor was swept overboard in the heavy seas and never recovered. The storms were so substantial the ship required topside repairs at Pearl Harbor. Pearl Harbor still showed the aftermath of the attack by the Japanese. There were oil slicks on the water and the superstructures of sunken ships were still visible.

From Pearl the ship sailed to Yokosuka, Japan. There the military clubs and quarters were staffed with Japanese employees. They were a disciplined lot, so it was difficult to tell what they were thinking. They were mostly concentrating on survival, as the post war years were difficult for them. The Americans were generous in sharing their leftover food with the hungry Japanese.

The Japanese inland sea had been heavily mined by Allied B-29s during World War II. The architect of the mining was General Curtis LeMay, a strong

---

9. Navy captains were more remote figures in those days, often intimidating. Given the Admiral's later reputation for ship handling he relates a revealing story about captains at that time. The Admiral was given a chance to land the ship and he promptly hit the pier, causing no damage to the ship, but some to the pier. The captain looked at the then young ensign and said imperiously in a deep voice: "Well." Roy Hoffmann looked at him and the captain said "Back out and do it again." I asked the Admiral in the interview: "How'd you do the second time?" "I did it," was his response. The captain's comment: "That's better."

proponent of mine warfare. The *Quick* engaged in sweeping operations to clear the inland sea and Tokyo Bay of mines. The *Quick* also did some fleet support, practiced gunnery and towed Japanese barges full of stockpiled ammunition and sunk them. Meanwhile, young Ensign Hoffmann gained valuable experience and an appreciation of the importance of the Navy mission.

He was there during MacArthur's tenure as an all-powerful potentate in Japan. The Japanese had the highest respect for MacArthur. Thousands of Japanese would gather to see MacArthur come out of his headquarters in Tokyo and get into his big Packard staff car.[10] When MacArthur eventually left Japan hundreds of thousands of Japanese lined the streets to see him off.

By 1947 the Admiral had decided that he wanted to make a career of the Navy. He liked the responsibility, the possibility of doing something significant with his life and the camaraderie with his fellow officers. It was, then, a shock when he got a set of orders to proceed to San Diego for de-activation. He had been caught in the massive drawdown of U.S. military forces in the wake of the end of World War II. Reserve officers were the first to go.

Ensign Hoffmann went to the Executive Officer of the *Quick* (one didn't go directly to the remote Commanding Officer). He expressed to the XO that he hoped his performance would justify his staying on active duty. The XO said he could recommend him and took the request to the captain, who agreed. The CO sent a message saying that Ensign Hoffmann was performing above the standards expected of a newly commissioned junior officer and that it would be in the best interests of the Navy that he be retained on an active duty status. In other words, Ensign Hoffmann was a strong candidate for a U.S. Navy career.

The message was sent to the Bureau of Naval Personnel (BUPERS) and the one word message came quickly back: "CARBASORD" (carry out basic orders). He was to become a civilian again, against his will. Soon a very depressed Roy Hoffmann was loaded up aboard the USS *Princeton* and headed for home and discharged. In June of 1947 he was transferred to the Inactive Reserve. It appeared his Navy career had ended.

THE 1947 WORLD to which the Admiral returned was settling into post-war prosperity. Many had expected a post-war depression but the opposite happened, despite a raging inflation.

A new Ford sedan cost $1,236 and a Chevrolet convertible cost $1,750

---

10. The story goes that sometimes it was a double and not MacArthur who got into the car.

in those days. Jackie Robinson signed with the Brooklyn Dodgers on April 10. The St. Louis Cardinals threatened to strike if he played. To National League President Ford Frick's great credit he told them: "If you do this you are through, and I don't care if it wrecks the league for 10 years. You cannot do this, because it is America."[11] Robinson hit .297 that year, led the league in stolen bases and won the Rookie of the year award. His courage and dignity brought the color barrier crashing down in baseball.

The top box office stars were Bing Crosby, Betty Grable, Gary Cooper, Humphrey Bogart, Bob Hope, Clark Gable and Alan Ladd. On radio people tuned in to Jack Benny, Bob Hope, Red Skelton, "Fibber McGee and Molly," "Superman," "The Shadow," and "Amos 'n' Andy." The Best Picture was awarded to the great film *The Best Years of Our Lives*, presented in a ceremony hosted in Hollywood by Jack Benny. Ronald Reagan, president of the Screen Actors Guild, narrated clips taken from Oscar winning movies.

FACED NOW WITH finding a civilian position, Roy decided to complete his education, enrolling at the University of Nebraska. The University of Missouri was too close to home, and besides he had decided to become a veterinarian. He applied to the School of Veterinary Science at Nebraska and was accepted. He loaded his car and trailer and off he went to school in September of 1947.

When he got to the Agriculture school at Lincoln, Nebraska he checked in with the registrar. "What's your major?" she asked. "Veterinary Science," Roy replied. The woman gave him a puzzled look and said, "We don't offer Veterinary Science."

Roy said, "Sure you do," and pulled out his letter of acceptance.

She looked at the letter and said it was a mistake—the main campus should never have issued the letter of acceptance for a program they didn't offer. Roy asked for an audience with the dean, which was granted. The dean graciously called other veterinary schools and they were all booked up for several years. Roy said, "to hell with it," took out a coin and flipped it. If it came up heads he would major in chemistry and if it came up tails he would choose physics. It came up chemistry. He received his BS in chemistry from the University of Nebraska in July of 1948.

In October of 1948 he went to work for the St. Joseph Lead Company in Bonne Terre, Missouri, as an analytical chemist.

The St. Joseph Lead Company was one of the great lead and zinc mining

---

11. Rita Lang Kleinfelder, *When We Were Young* (New York: Prentice Hall, 1993), p. 21.

companies of the world. Lead had been mined in southeastern Missouri since the time of the earliest French and Spanish explorations. The early process of blasting, moving, breaking, crushing, jigging and smelting ore was arduous, but by 1866 250 tons of pig lead were sold by the company. Under the leadership of Charles Parsons (whose education was in the field of dentistry) the company began to grow and prosper. The company smelter was moved to Herculaneum, Missouri; a railroad to move the ore followed. The company progressed and expanded during World War I and the twenties, even investing in mines in Argentina. The Depression years had been tough, but the company rebounded during World War II. On February 1, 1947, B. Franklin Murphy replaced Louis Sicka as General Manager.[12]

Roy Hoffmann's job consisted of taking core samples and analyzing them for their percentage of lead, zinc and trace metals. In December of 1948 he met Mary Linn Thompson. One of her friends, Joe Pratte, had called and wanted to know if he could bring a friend to her home. She thought he meant a girlfriend and said yes. As it turned out he brought Roy Hoffmann, with whom he worked. Her first impression was that he wasn't very big, but was handsome and well dressed. Roy seemed courteous, nice. Joe asked if they would double date for an all-class reunion. They made the date, but Mary Linn "wasn't too taken, initially." And there it ended for the time being.

Meanwhile, Roy and other company men would come to the bowling alley and watch the girls, including Mary Linn, bowl. Between games they would talk. He soon asked her to go to a hockey game in St. Louis. She knew nothing about hockey but was into sports and gladly accepted. Roy turned out to be, in her words, "a good date." He was patient and explained the game to her. He planned their dates meticulously. He took her to see "Oklahoma" in St. Louis. They went to see the Cardinals play in St. Louis. Mary Linn's favorite player was Enos "Country" Slaughter. Slaughter had gone from first to home to win the 1946 World Series for St. Louis. The outfielder had missed the 1943, 1944 and 1945 seasons due to military service during World War II. In 1946 the 30-year-old Slaughter batted .300 and drove in 130 runs to lead the team. By 1954 his skills had declined and the Cards dealt him to the hated Yankees where he finished out his career as a pinch hitter.

For music in 1949 they would have listened to new artists Fats Domino, Tennessee Ernie Ford, Burl Ives and Dean Martin. And at the movies they would have seen Bob Hope, Bing Crosby, Abbott & Costello, John Wayne,

---

12. Internet "History of St. Joe Lead Company," Special Edition, Fall 1970.

Gary Cooper, Betty Grable, Humphrey Bogart and Clark Gable.

Eventually Roy proposed in Washington State Park in the Ozarks; Mary Linn initially turned him down. She was saving money for her last two years of college. His comment was: "Well, if you're going back to school you're going back married."

According to Mary Linn, "It looked like he wasn't going away."

And of course, married they were, on January 1, 1950. As the Admiral tells it they picked that date so he could remember their anniversary, but Mary Linn said she had already taken her paid vacation for the preceding year and so they waited until the new year to get married. They both wanted to get out of Bonne Terre and checked out chemist positions in Houston during their honeymoon, which was mostly spent in New Orleans.

They returned to Bonne Terre, settled in to their young married life. Their world was about to dramatically change as the North Koreans invaded South Korea that summer of 1950.

PART TWO

KOREA TO VIETNAM

Mediocrity defines what's normal and therefore what's human; excellence is an attack on all the others. It's the nightmare side of democracy. . . .

—David Denby
Great Books

The Korean Peninsula
MILES
0 20 40 60 80 100
USSR
MANCHURIA
MANCHURIA
Yalu River
NORTH KOREA
Wonsan
Heartbreak Ridge
Pyongyang
Bloody Ridge
The Punchbowl
Panmunjon
Sea of Japan
Seoul
Inchon
Kimpo Airfield
Yellow Sea
SOUTH KOREA
Pusan
Chenju Island

3

SINKING OF THE USS *PIRATE*

IN JUNE OF 1949 the last United States forces in Korea were withdrawn. They had been occupying the southern portion of the Korean peninsula since the end of World War II. Only a small military mission remained. The withdrawal of American troops was an invitation to aggression, and it occurred when 90,000 Soviet- and Chinese-backed North Korean troops poured over the 38th parallel border on June 25, 1950. Kim Il Sung's armed forces were equipped with Soviet tanks, artillery and combat aircraft. The Korean War came as a shock, as Communist forces invaded the southern Republic of Korea, bringing to a harsh and desolate land a war no one wanted.

The North Koreans encountered only token resistance from South Korean forces, and within three days they had captured the South Korean capital of Seoul, 40 miles from the border. President Truman sought and received approval from the U.S. Congress for military intervention to help the South Koreans repel the naked aggression from the North. A U.N. Security Council cease-fire resolution followed on June 27, followed by a later resolution to commit forces to support the South Koreans.

Truman also wanted to prevent the Chinese from invading Taiwan, where Chiang Kai-shek was fighting against the mainland Communists. He ordered the *Valley Forge* (CV 45), the heavy cruiser *Rochester* (CA 124) and eight destroyers to sortie from Subic Bay in the Philippines. That show of force probably prevented a Communist invasion of Taiwan and gave pause to Stalin's expansionist strategy in the area.

On June 30, 1950, General Douglas MacArthur visited the collapsing South Korean lines and called for U.S. troops. Truman responded with an American Navy blockade of the Korean coast; the next day U.S. ground forces landed in Korea. On July 8, 1950, MacArthur was named

Commander of United Nations forces in Korea. He would command a largely American and South Korean Army, although ultimately soldiers from 16 nations—including forces from Australia, Great Britain, Turkey and the Philippines— would fight in that harsh land.

The United States was ill prepared for war. The available U.S. troops came from Japan, where they had been on occupation duty since the end of World War II. They were out of shape and lacked modern arms. U.S. military strength was at its lowest state of readiness since Pearl Harbor. Air power saved the allies in the early going as they were pushed to a defensive perimeter at Pusan, where they were finally able to stop the North Korean offensive.

On August 4, 1950, Truman authorized a call-up of 62,000 U.S. Army reserves. As the country lurched toward a war footing, those who had served the country so well in World War II would be called on once again.

Roy Hoffmann had stayed in the Navy reserves after the termination of his service in 1947. He had applied for the Army reserves as they were reorganizing in Missouri and would have a unit closer to him. The Navy reserves were on the other side of St. Louis, a long commute in those days before interstate highways.

When the Korean War broke out he knew that as an experienced reserve line officer with a mine warfare designator he would be recalled. He decided he would rather be in the Navy per his training and inclinations. Unsure of the status of his Army application, he nevertheless volunteered for the one-year enlistment the Navy was then offering. The Admiral knew the one-year enlistment was a nebulous thing, particularly during a war.

He and Mary Linn had discussed his volunteering. They both agreed it was best for him to volunteer rather than wait to be called back. Mary Linn was then experiencing a difficult pregnancy, her first, which had caused her to become a patient in the hospital where she worked. After the decision had been made, Roy returned from a reserve meeting and visited her in the hospital. He brought with him a portable typewriter and a book on naval correspondence and together they composed and she typed a letter volunteering him for active duty. When asked about how difficult it must have been to be pregnant, hospitalized and about to lose her husband to the Navy Mary Linn replied: "It's a war, again, and you can't put your own interests before those of the country."[1]

---

1. The Hoffmann's first child, Harriet Ann Hoffmann, was born February 12, 1951, in Bonne Terre, Missouri.

There matters stood until August 15, 1950, at which time orders arrived from the Commandant, Ninth Naval District. They arrived at the Admiral's parents' home, 30 miles away. The Admiral picked the orders up on a Friday on his lunch hour. He was ordered to quit his job immediately and proceed to the U.S. Court House, Kansas City, on Saturday for a physical. If found physically qualified he was to report to the Commandant, Twelfth Naval District, San Francisco, California on Monday.[2] There he was to take the first available government transportation to Yokosuka, Japan, where he would report to the USS *Pirate* (AM-275) for the reactivation of that ship.

Mary Linn worked on Saturdays, but she drove him to Lambert Field before work, where he got on a plane for Kansas City. She picked him up on his return that afternoon. In the meantime, he had been promoted to lieutenant j.g. as a reservist, and so a half-stripe had to be added to his lower uniform sleeves. Mary Linn shopped for a new uniform that reflected his recent promotion. Unfortunately the tailor in St. Louis put the small stripe underneath the large one, the reverse of the proper order. A local tailor corrected the error over the weekend.

On Sunday the young lieutenant j.g. said goodbye to his family and on Monday Mary Linn took him to the airport for his TWA flight to California.[3] He proceeded to Honolulu via Navy air, arriving at 0700 hours August 26, 1950. On August 29 he left Honolulu, again via Navy air, and reported aboard the *Pirate* September 2. To his surprise the *Pirate* commission pennant was flying; she had already been activated. The drydock was flooded and she was floating, ready for sea trials.

The *Pirate* had been in Drydock No. 6 in Yokosuka from August 14 to August 28, 1950, where Lieutenant Cornelius E. McMullen had assumed command. Captain McMullen was a capable officer who had stayed in the Navy after World War II. He spent his career mostly on destroyers and retired as a captain. He was a classic disciplinarian, efficient, aloof; his capabilities would soon serve him in good stead.

The *Pirate* was of the *Admirable* class of mine sweepers. She had seen service

---

2. One is not surprised to learn the Navy had so abruptly ordered such a sea change in the young couple's lives. Roy had to quit his job; report all the way across the state to Kansas City, when he could have taken his physical 60 miles away; and he had to say goodbye to his pregnant wife, his parents, and fly across the country in just over a weekend.

3. The young call-up went to war absent any current training. "My refresher training in California was the time it took to grab a cab from the San Francisco airport to NAS Alameda and board a USN Mars aircraft for island hopping to Japan."

during World War II, just missing the Allied final drive on Okinawa in 1945. The ship then reported to the Service Force Pacific Fleet in December 1947 for deployment in Japanese waters in a caretaker status, where she remained, out of service in reserve for the next several years. In July of 1950 the *Pirate* was back on duty as part of Mine Division 32, under the command of Lieutenant Commander Bruce Hyatt.

The ship was mostly manned by recalled Navy veterans who had experience during World War II. When Roy Hoffmann arrived on board "the captain welcomed me aboard and immediately asked: 'Are you a qualified underway Officer of the Deck (OOD)?'" His response was yes he was, but he hadn't been to sea for over two years. "Good!" Captain McMullen responded. "We're underway at first light tomorrow for extended operations. We now have three qualified OOD's. You have the second watch."[4]

The ship got underway at 1300 on September 3, 1950. Their route took them from Yokosuka to Sasebo, Japan. *Pirate* was the guide with the Commander of Mine Division 32 embarked aboard. They steamed with the *Incredible* on station 1,000 yards astern. The ships conducted emergency drills, gunnery and training exercises.[5]

Lieutenant j.g. Hoffmann was assigned as gunnery and minesweeping officer. The armament wouldn't take much of his time, as it consisted of one slow-fire 3-inch 50 on the bow and two twin 40s. His fire control station was on top of the open bridge, where he had a 360-degree view. His secondary duty was as supply and commissary officer; he was amazed at the lack of inventory control. At the first general quarters he discovered there weren't enough life jackets for the crew, unacceptable going into a war zone. He informed the CO who sent a message to the flagship, the heavy cruiser *Rochester* (CA 124), requesting more life

---

4. "Recollections of Mine Warfare Experience in the Early Months of the Korean War–1950." RADM Roy F. Hoffmann, USN (ret.) October 31, 2000.

5. There were seven ships that were to play a major role in the events about to unfold: The *Pirate* (AM 275), *Pledge* (AM 277), *Incredible* (AM 249), *Osprey* (AMS 28), *Redhead* (AMS 34), *Kite* (AMS 22) and *Endicott* (DMS 35). Navy ship designations are arcane but descriptive of the purpose of the vessel. Thus, an AM is a steel hulled fleet minesweeper and the workhorse of the mine fleet; an AMS is a wooden hulled auxiliary mine sweeper, ideally suited for sweeping influence type mines, and in a supporting role during major sweeping operations as a Danning and mine destruction vessel; and a DMS is a versatile destroyer minesweeper, usually used for open water clearance, where deep draft and lessened maneuverability were acceptable. They were also an excellent fire support ship.

jackets. The *Rochester* ordered them aside and with a painter (a rope attached to the bow of the ship) off the starboard bow towed the *Pirate* as though it were a whaleboat. Men on the *Rochester* tossed down sufficient life jackets for the *Pirate* crew. In light of what was to come the life jackets would be sorely needed.

From September 8 to 1800 hours on September 9 the *Pirate* steamed to Pusan 1,000 yards behind the guide *Osprey*. As they entered the war zone the ships darkened from sunset to dawn. They moored at Pier 1 and at 1800 hours got underway for patrol duties. From September 9–19 Mine Division 32 conducted daily routine moored and influence minesweeping of the entrance channel, and conducted sonar patrol and identification of in-bound traffic when not engaged in minesweeping.

Moored minesweeping required good team training and supervision by experienced petty officers. The *Pirate* was fortunate to have men aboard with World War II experience, as sweeping is arduous and hazardous, particularly in moderate to heavy seas. One snap of a cable could mean the loss of a limb or death for an inattentive sailor. A typical day of sweeping saw the ship underway before dawn with the gear streaming aft by first light. Fourteen to 16 hours of grinding work followed as the ship swept all day, and the men retrieved the gear after sunset. The evening was spent repairing and preparing the moored gear for the next day. There were only two proficient signalmen aboard, and they supplemented the navigation team for continuous precision positioning during sweep ops. In this day of satellite positioning it is difficult to understand how arduous yet critical these navigators were during sweep ops. They ended the day exhausted from their tense labors.

Meanwhile, it was apparent the perimeter defense ashore at Pusan had stabilized and the allies were not going to be driven into the sea. The men of the *Pirate* watched as carrier attack aircraft bombed and strafed enemy positions. Although the *Pirate* was in range of the North Korean long range artillery the small ship seemed not to be a priority for the enemy. Pusan at that time was a relatively small port crammed with ships of all descriptions. It was the principal staging port for the forthcoming assault on Inchon.

On September 19, 1950, the *Incredible* relieved the *Pirate* and she steamed to Sasebo, Japan, to undergo main engine repairs, maintenance and replenishment in preparation for the planned amphibious assault on Wonsan.

Meanwhile, in mid September, Vice Admiral Arthur Struble, Commander of the Seventh Fleet, led 230 ships toward North Korea and into the Yellow

Sea. The armada approached the narrow channel leading to Inchon in the early morning of September 15. In the preceding days ships and carrier aircraft bombarded enemy defensive positions ashore at Inchon. At 0633 hours on September 15, 1950, 1,950 fleet amphibious landing craft disembarked the 5th Marine Regiment of the 1st Marine Division on Wolmi Do in Inchon Harbor, beginning the Inchon invasion. The goal was to relieve South Korean and U.N. forces hemmed in at Pusan, and to recapture Seoul. It was a brilliant stroke conceived by General MacArthur.

After several days of hard fighting by the Marines, South Korean troops and elements of the Army's 7th Infantry Division, allied forces captured the port at Inchon and nearby Kimpo airfield. On September 21st U.S. Army units that had broken out of the Pusan perimeter linked up with Inchon forces. A week later the 1st Marine Division captured Seoul after bloody, street-by-street fighting. The Inchon assault was brutal on the enemy, inflicting 20,000 casualties and began the disintegration of the North Korean Army.

By September 29 U.N. forces reached the 38th parallel, and South Korean President Syngman Rhee announced he intended to cross the parallel and reunite Korea under his rule. He was fully backed by MacArthur, who loudly announced his support. Meanwhile, nearly one million Chinese troops were massing in Manchuria. The stage was set for MacArthur's eventual dismissal by Truman.

IN THE MEANTIME, General MacArthur was planning another amphibious assault at Wonsan on the Sea of Japan. He intended strategically to destroy the North Korean Army completely and intended to occupy northeast Korea. The Navy would land the X Corps and the 1st Marines at Wonsan, where they would advance overland to the Yalu River, thence into the People's Republic of China. South Korean troops, in advance of his strategy, got to Wonsan on October 10, 1950, five days before the planned invasion. Later the Navy would discover the Communists had placed somewhere between 2,000 to 4,000 Soviet-made magnetic and contact mines in the approaches to the harbor. As the Navy approached the harbor they didn't know what they were facing, only that a path had to be cleared through the minefield before the 1st Marine Division could begin moving ashore.

THE KOREAN PENINSULA was almost ideally suited for defensive mine warfare. Many of the coastal waterways were shallow—ideal for defensive mining; the waters were often muddy and perfect for concealment; and ocean currents in the Sea of Japan and Yellow Sea disbursed floating mines launched from junks and sampans inland. In 15 days the deadly mines would traverse the entire length of the peninsula.[6]

Sea mines were originally known as "torpedoes."[7] They evolved into four basic types. The Contact Mine was anchored to the floor of the ocean so that the mine bobbed ten to 20 feet beneath the surface. On the mines were several triggering "horns" (the minesweep sailors called them "horned monsters"). If a passing ship were to make contact with one of horns the chemical vials within triggered the firing circuit on the mine and it exploded.

These mines were swept by cutting the cables holding them to the anchor. The minesweeper would stream sweep cables from the stern of the ship with "depressors" and "otters" to hold the gear at the right angle and depth. Floats or "pigs" kept the cable from running too deep. Serrated cables and "cutters" cut the cable so the mine would bob to the surface. Cutters worked like a hedge trimmer; as the mine is drawn into the cutter a charge slams the cutter together, theoretically slicing the cable.

Magnetic Mines were detonated by the shifting lines of the force of the earth's magnetic field as a ship's hull passed nearby. Magnetic sweep gear (two cables with a short "leg" and a long "leg") with copper electrodes at the end was streamed from the stern of the minesweep. Pigs kept the cables buoyant. The long leg drifted some 1,200 feet astern. A generator on the ship transmitted a powerful current creating a strong magnetic field theoretically detonating mines within reach of the current.

Acoustic mines were detonated by "hearing" engines or propeller noise of a passing ship. When the internal diaphragm vibrated it closed the switch and the mine exploded. These mines were destroyed by dragging equipment called a "hummer" or a "bumblebee" through the water, replicating the sound of a ship's propeller.

---

6. There is an indispensable guide to the intricacies of mine warfare as it relates to the Korean War, and this author has drawn heavily on the following cited article, as well as Admiral Hoffmann's experience. It is an arcane subject but a very dangerous endeavor when you are in the midst of a mine field of the proportions of Wonsan. Much of what follows is drawn from: Malcolm W. Cagle and Frank A. Manson, "Wonsan: The Battle of the Mines." *U.S. Naval Institute Proceedings*, Vol. LXXXIII No. 6, June, 1957, pp. 598–611; Hoffmann, "Recollections of Mine Warfare Experience in the Early Months of the Korean War—1950," passim; and R. F. Hoffmann interviews, July, 2005.

7. And so, Admiral Farragut's famous order at Mobile Bay, "Damn the torpedoes, Four Bells [Full Speed Ahead]!" referred to the crude mines used by Confederate forces during the Civil War. Cagle, "The Battle of the Mines," p. 599.

A more unsweepable mine and thus more dangerous was the Pressure Mine, which exploded with the negative pressure of a passing ship. They must be swept by duplicating the change in water pressure, which was achieved by towing a hull (called a "guinea pig") through the minefield.

Finally, the toughest of all was the modern mine, or Combination mine, which used two or more of the above types. And, defensive mine layers may build into mines "counters" which will only allow the mines to explode after five to ten or more ships have passed by them.

The mines at Wonsan came from Soviet stockpiles sent to Korea by rail during the period from July 10–20, 1950. They were turn of the century vintage Magnetic and Contact (Type MKB) mines. They were assembled and laid under the supervision of the Soviets, who departed on October 4, 1950. Some 3,000 mines were laid off Wonsan, using 32 small boats, beginning somewhere between July 10 and August 1, 1950. The primitive technology brought the planned allied invasion to a halt. "The hard fact . . . remained that the landing force [the largest assembled since World War II] . . . suffered a three week delay in schedule because of enemy mines . . . A small maritime nation with little technical experience . . . and a minimum of equipment can at small cost deny the use of its landing areas to a large and modern naval force."[8] The great Pacific minesweeping force of World War II, which had consisted of some 525–550 ships, had been dismantled, and only ten minesweepers were available to clear Wonsan.

On September 26, 1950, the USS *Brush* (DD 745) was severely damaged when a mine blew off her bow on Korea's northeast coast. Two South Korean vessels struck mines: YMS 509 on September 28 and YMS 504 on October 1, 1950. That same day a mine escaped the sweeping gear of the USS *Magpie* and struck her starboard bow. Of the 33-man crew only 12 survived.

On October 2, 1950, Vice Admiral Arthur D. Struble, riding anchor at Inchon aboard his flagship *Rochester*, ordered Joint Task Force 7 reformed for the Wonsan amphibious assault. He further ordered that all Seventh Fleet minesweepers get underway for Wonsan as soon as possible.

Admiral Struble was an experienced mine warfare officer, serving at the end of World War II as Commander Mine Force Pacific. He felt the Wonsan sea

---

8. Lieutenant Colonel Harry W. Edwards, "A Naval Lesson of the Korean Conflict," *U.S. Naval Institute Proceedings* (Vol. LXXX No. 12), December, 1954, p. 1,338.

approaches would be mined and that his task force would come under fire from entrenched enemy artillery at the Wonsan approaches. As Commander Harry W. McElwain, Intelligence Officer for Task Force 90 put it: "When they said 'go' on the Wonsan operation, mines were our biggest headache."

Pirate got underway from Sasebo at 0400 October 6, 1950. The ship joined the small flotilla under Captain Richard T. Spofford at 0900 on October 7. Spofford knew little about Wonsan's harbor other than its geography and bathymetry.[9] Earlier discovery of minefields at Inchon and Chinnampo made it almost certain there were mines present. He also lacked intelligence about enemy status on the various islands in the harbor. It was likely they were garrisoned by North Korean troops with artillery to use against the minesweeping operation. He had neither information on how many mines were in the harbor, nor what types they were. It was a minesweeping nightmare. After the sinking of the *Pirate* and *Pledge* they discovered the Wonsan minefield covered 400 square miles, and numbered more than 3,000 mines of the Contact and Magnetic type. To confront this dangerous threat were six minesweepers initially.

With an October 15 landing date looming Captain Spofford decided to risk a direct sweep approach, sending the *Pledge* and the *Incredible* on an exploratory run straight from the 100 fathom curve to the landing beaches by the shortest and most direct route. The minesweepers got underway shortly after sunrise on October 10, 1950. The Officer in Tactical Command (OTC), Lieutenant Commander Bruce Hyatt, was riding the *Pledge* since his flagship *Pirate* was conducting minesweeping on behalf of gunfire support ships south of Wonsan.[10]

The *Pledge* began sweeping from the west edge of the 100-fathom curve in a direct line to the landing beaches. Astern of the *Pledge* were the *Incredible*, *Osprey* and *Mockingbird*, each ship streaming its gear. Two more minesweepers followed the formation: The *Chatterer* dropping orange-colored Dan buoys to mark the edge of the swept channel and the *Partridge* riding shotgun to destroy by gunfire any mines brought to the surface by the other minesweepers. Ahead was a hovering helicopter from the USS *Worchester* spotting mines beneath the water.

By late afternoon these courageous sailors had swept a 3,000-yard wide channel from the 100-fathom to the 30-fathom curve, a distance of about 12

---

9. Measurement of the depth of large bodies of water.
10. *Pirate* had commenced sweeping October 7 through 9 with negative results.

miles. They had cut and destroyed 21 contact mines without casualty. About the same time B. D. Pennington, the *Worchester* helicopter pilot, reported seeing five distinct lines of mines inside the 30-fathom curve directly ahead in the assault path to the beach. This verified reports from the minesweepers sonar operators, whose sonar echoes had verified the presence of dozens of mines. "Every officer and man was weary and somewhat taken aback by the discovery."[11] At dusk the minesweepers filed out of the channel and anchored in swept water near the 30-fathom curve. *Pirate* had experienced port engine problems and remained outside the 100-fathom curve until 1830 hours, at which time she proceeded to anchorage in company with the USS *Kermit Roosevelt*.

In light of the heavy minefield Captain Spofford decided to shift the sweeping effort to the Russian navigation channel. His force was augmented that night by the arrival of the *Pirate, Redhead* and *Kite*.

The next day, October 11, as the U.S. Navy continued sweeping, the 1st Republic of Korea (ROK) Corps captured Wonsan. Later that day the *Pirate* entered unswept waters as the guide in an Oboe type sweep. The *Pirate* was in a port echelon formation with the *Pledge* and *Incredible*, followed by the Danning vessels *Redhead* on station on the *Pirate's* starboard float and the *Kite* on the *Incredible's* port float.

The *Pirate* swept five contact mines and collectively at least 18 mines were cut. As dusk descended the formation turned to return to swept waters, and started to retrieve their gear. On the *Pirate* they retrieved their port sweep wire with extreme caution as the tension meter was showing a steady and unusually heavy strain, indicating there was probably something snagged on the wire. Suddenly the boatswain's mate in charge shouted: "Avast heaving! Avast Heaving! Mine! Mine! Mine fouled on the cable!"

"Believe me," the Admiral years later recalled, "this horned monster bobbing 20 feet off your stern got your undivided attention."[12] They eased the wire off several fathoms, holding it there to avoid a possible bottom detonation as Captain McMullen advised the OTC of the danger and the *Pirate* headed for the open sea. Topside lights from the fleet ships anchored offshore suddenly lit up as the *Pirate* towed its dangerous cargo to the open sea. Once past the 100-fathom curve the crew cut the cable to jettison the mine. The men of the *Pirate's* sweep crew then spent most of the remainder of the

---

11. Cagle and Manson, "Wonsan: The Battle of the Mines" p. 606.
12. Hoffmann, "Recollections of Mine Warfare Experience in the Early Months of the Korean War."

night breaking out new serrated cable and re-rigging the port sweep gear. A tired but confident crew had the ship ready for sweeping operations at daybreak. As one expert put it, "The nerve strain of this duty would be hard to bear were it not for the amount of physical exertion required in handling heavy tackle; keeping busy tended to check-rein the adrenal system."[13]

Captain Spofford held a midnight conference and decided to make an all-out effort to clear the Soviet channel the next day. It was a fateful decision as before the next day was done two of the lead vessels were blasted apart by mines and sunk within minutes of each other. The surviving ships pulled the survivors out of the frigid waters of the harbor under the fire of enemy shore batteries.[14]

ON THE MORNING of October 12 Captain Spofford decided to try and clear the minefield with an air strike by Task Force 77. It was a spectacular show that failed to clear the mines, as they had an anti-mining device that prevented detonation by a close explosion. The slow and dangerous job would have to be done by the minesweepers.

In late morning, after the counter-mining air strike, the minesweepers proceeded on a westerly course at six knots toward the harbor. There were three islands ahead, Yo-do on the left, Ung-do on the right and Sin-do almost dead ahead. Lieutenant Commander Bruce Hyatt was aboard his flagship *Pirate*, leading the formation. *Pledge* and *Incredible* followed astern. *Redhead* was laying Dan buoys astern the *Pirate*, and *Kite* was on shotgun duty astern the *Incredible*. Laying off ready to give gunfire support with their 5-inch guns were the *Diachenko*, the *Doyle* (DMS 34) and the *Endicott* (DMS 35).

At 1045 hours the formation changed course to 258, speed eight knots, and at 1112 hours the formation entered unswept waters. The ready boxes on the *Pirate* were undogged and the 3-inch gun manned, ready for enemy shore fire. Condition Able was set and the ship reported ready in three minutes.[15] Roy Hoffmann was at his battle station on top of the pilothouse,

---

13. Edwards, "Naval Lessons of the Korean Conflict," p. 1,337.
14. The danger of mine sweeping is indicated by the casualties: " . . . the mine force which comprised only two per cent of the naval personnel in the Far East suffered twenty per cent of the total casualties." Ibid., p. 1338.
15. Able was a special minesweeping condition bringing all personnel not necessary for the operation of the ship to topside. The crew was dispersed to minimize casualties in the event the ship struck a mine. The three-minute *true* ready condition report would become a fixation in the Admiral's later career; undoubtably his experiences in Wonsan hard wired the importance of it in his mind.

right above the open bridge; he could see and hear everything that happened there. It was a bright sunny day with minimal wind. Although he could hear the radio it seemed unusually quiet, with only the subdued chatter of the navigation team and an occasional rudder command intruding on the quiet. The captain had the conn and the Commodore and XO were close at hand.

Pirate's sweeping gear severed two mine cables and the mines popped to the surface aft. By 1154 hours four more were cut. The mines were 50 yards apart, at an estimated depth of 15 feet, and lay on a north-south line between Yo-do and Ung-do. Within three minutes *Pledge*, maneuvering astern through mines already cut by the *Pirate*, swept three more mines with her port gear. *Incredible*, still in formation, cut four more. The small ships were in extreme danger, in a thick minefield with mines popping to the surface all around them. Still, the sailors carried on calmly and professionally.

Then, the spotter helicopter from the carrier spotted three more mine lines ahead about the same time a sonar report came from below decks that there were mines 100 yards dead ahead. Both Hyatt and McMullan considered a turn at this critical juncture dangerous and so continued on course. This was standard operating procedure in mine warfare as turns were dangerous, exposing the beam of the ships to the minefield.

Captain McMullen got a sonar report on a mine dead ahead as he threaded his ship through the treacherous minefield. Suddenly the bow lookout threw off his headset, wheeled around and hauled aft,[16] shouting up at the bridge: "Mine! Mine! Starboard bow—dead ahead!" The captain calmly ordered hard left rudder, anxiously waited about ten seconds, then ordered hard right rudder, hoping to clear the mines. The turns were slow at six knots and with sweep gear astern. Suddenly there was a huge explosion as the mine made contact with the ship, blowing a gaping hole just aft of amidships, obliterating the engine room. The explosion broke the main deck into two parts.[17]

Roy Hoffmann was hurled into the air, spiraling, spinning, and seeing black and white, black and white as he turned toward and away from the sun. Although he doesn't remember it, he landed on top of the Executive Officer on the open bridge, bleeding profusely from a head wound.

---

16. Or hauled ass as the Admiral puts it.

17. The green horned monster would have been made of steel and weighed 984 pounds. It would have had five horns protruding, and had a hydrostatic arming switch. It would have been charged with 506 pounds of TNT with a tetryl booster.

The USS Pirate *strikes a mine at 12:01 PM, October 12, 1950. In the smoke and water plume are parts of the ship and deck equipment.*
Official U.S. Navy Photo, Hoffmann collection

At 1201 hours a huge plume of black smoke rose above the stricken ship, pieces of ship and deck equipment caught up in it. Then, at 1202, the ship listed sharply to port; at 1203 back to a severe starboard list; at 1204 the ship capsized and went into a boiling sea of muddy, oily water as splashes from enemy shore batteries began to hit around the area. By 1205 hours the *Pirate* was gone.

The next thing Roy Hoffmann remembered was the XO bending over him and picking him up, saying, "Hoffmann! Hoffmann! Abandon ship!" The ships standard compass stand, the binnacle, had rolled over on his arm and he found it difficult to get up. The ship had already heeled back to starboard and was going down. He went to the open bridge bulwark and climbed down a ladder to the O-1 deck and slipped into the frigid water.[18]

He was concerned about the mast coming down on him as the ship capsized, so he began to swim away from the *Pirate*. Meanwhile, he couldn't figure out why he wasn't getting any buoyancy from his life jacket. Then he remembered as the damage control officer he didn't have on a kapok,

---
18. The water was a cold 56 degrees; hypothermia was a real danger if you were in it long, particularly when wounded, as many of the men were.

Lifeboats pick up survivors from approximately 12:30 until 3:00 P.M.
OFFICIAL U.S. NAVY PHOTO, HOFFMANN COLLECTION

the standard flotation battle gear, which is too bulky to get around the ship under damage conditions. Instead, he had on an inflatable; he pulled the lanyard, which started the CO_2 cartridge to inflate the jacket.

It was hard to see at surface level, but he saw an island close by, and began swimming toward it. He was within shouting distance of a CPO who was also swimming to the island. Suddenly, splashes began to appear around them. He yelled at the CPO: "Is somebody shooting at us?" "They sure as the hell are!" was the reply. They began to swim as fast as they could back to where the ship had gone down.

By then a rescue operation was underway. A PBM was dropping smoke near survivors and other ships in the area were dropping life rafts into the water. Some men had been blown off the *Pirate*, and the *Pledge* had launched her whaleboat to help with the wounded in the water (the *Pirate* had gone down so quickly there was no opportunity to launch rafts or her whaleboat). At that point enemy shore batteries began to zero in on the *Pledge* and the men in the water. The *Pledge* returned fire. Then the *Incredible* lost her load, experiencing complete engine failure, and went dead in the water (DIW). The *Redhead* came alongside her as a tug would and towed her out of the area. It was chaotic, bloody, and dangerous; the men on the ships reacted magnificently.

The *Endicott* began to engage the enemy with 5-inch gunfire support and launched her rescue boats as well. At this critical juncture a mine struck the *Pledge* amidships.

Lieutenant Richard O. Young commanded the *Pledge*, which immediately hove to when the mine hit the *Pirate*. As she was launching her motor whaleboat, shore batteries on Sin-do opened fire on the sinking *Pirate* and her crew in the water. The *Pledge* responded with her 3-inch gun and the shore fire began to shift to her. Meanwhile, she was in waters where 13 floating mines were bobbing on the surface and countless others lurked beneath the surface.

Captain Young's first thought was to rescue survivors from the *Pirate* and to continue the sweep. Events overtook him as he came under fire and realized he couldn't pass through the *Pirate's* floating sweep gear without enmeshing his own ship. He ordered all battle stations manned to counter shore batteries from Sin-do and small arms fire coming from Yo-do. He cut his minesweeping gear as he radioed for air support.

He soon expended the ship's ready 3-inch ammunition; enemy shore batteries had bracketed the *Pledge*, and Young realized his situation was becoming untenable. He decided to make a turn into waters that had already been swept and ordered "Left-full rudder; starboard engine ahead two-thirds." The ship had turned approximately 30 degrees when, at 1220 hours, she struck a mine. The explosion occurred amidships on the starboard side near the forward engine room, causing great damage throughout the ship. Decks and bulkheads ruptured from the keel to the open bridge and water poured into the gaping hole on the starboard side. The blast knocked Captain Young out for about 30 seconds. When he regained his senses he saw saving the ship was hopeless and gave the order to abandon ship. All on the open bridge had been seriously injured (Captain Young suffered a broken leg). He hobbled to CIC and found one man dead, one seriously injured and a third conscious; all were pinned down by wreckage.

He tried to remove the men from CIC but his broken leg rendered him unable to help. He made his way to the boat deck for help as the bow of the ship was awash with water. Fortunately a UDT team arrived and began rescue operations of the remaining men in CIC and two more from the pilothouse. They then abandoned ship right before it went down. They were unable to recover the dead sailor in CIC and he went down with the ship.[19]

---

19. Six were missing from the ship and 41 injured, one of whom later died of the injuries. *Pirate* suffered similar casualties: Six killed and 43 wounded.

Then U.S. Navy carrier attack aircraft roared in and silenced the shore batteries. It appeared the men in the water might survive after all. Roy Hoffmann spoke for all the men that day, speaking of the arrival of the attack aircraft: "What a beautiful sight! My everlasting gratitude to the tail-hookers!"

MARY LINN HOFFMANN was working, less than a month away from her 23rd birthday, married less than a year and five months pregnant when the *Pirate* went down. She had been out with one of the nurses on staff and the wife of one of Roy's friends that day. She came home and one of the neighbors and her mother's brother were standing by the back door. She thought their greeting was odd, restrained as she breezed in the door. "What's the matter with them," she remembers wondering. As she entered the house she found her mother crying.

Mary Linn's first thought was that her brother-in-law, Ted, who flew for the reserves on weekends, had been hurt. Her mother then informed her there was bad news and she should sit down. The radio had just announced the *Pirate* and *Pledge* had gone down in Wonsan harbor.[20]

For those who know her it is no surprise that Mary Linn reacted with calm and control. She called the telegraph office—there was no telegram for her from the Navy. She next called the Red Cross for information and they reacted somewhat indignantly, saying, "Ma'am, that news will not be released until the next of kin are notified." Imagine her surprise that she didn't qualify for information.

Fortuitously, Mary Linn had recently gotten a letter from Captain McMullen's wife, who lived in Fall River, Massachusetts, so she had her address and phone number. She called, and Mrs. McMullen said she had heard the same news by radio. She later called with information on the number of casualties but still had no specific information.

She then had to call her husband's parents. They took the news hard, but she calmed them down and they later joined her to wait for further developments. A telegram later arrived for his parents, well after the fact.

Mary Linn had faith her husband was alive. She knew if he got in the water he could swim well and was resourceful. Still, it was a most anxious time.

---

20. Similar press releases shocked other families. Reports reached the media of the minesweeper USS *Magpie* sinking with 21 missing; and two destroyers were damaged after striking mines off the east coast of Korea. The USS *Brush* suffered 11 dead, three missing and ten injured; the USS *Mansfield* had 26 injured.

MEANWHILE, ROY HOFFMANN finally made it to a life raft, still bleeding from his head wound; his fellow sailors helped him into the raft. Most of those in the raft with him were wounded as well, most commonly with fractured legs and head wounds. Their raft was towed to the *Endicott*, where he had to be helped aboard due to weakness from loss of blood and hypothermia. They were then transferred to the hospital ship *Repose*. He was there about a day and was then transferred to an old World War I British hospital ship, the *Maine*, a red flag Royal Navy ship manned by Corsican merchant marines.

He was on the *Maine* for less than a week, recovering from his wound. In addition to the many wounded sailors aboard from Wonsan, there were many wounded Marines and Army men from the Inchon invasion. Next to the Admiral was an Army lieutenant with severe burns. From the *Maine* he was transferred to the Kobe Army hospital in Japan. There he was finally able to communicate with Mary Linn, thanks to a ham radio operator in Kobe, who put him in phone communication with her. She had received notice that she would get the call within 24 hours. He sounded tired, but was very matter of fact and reassured her he was not seriously wounded.

Within a week he was pronounced fit for duty and informed he would be transferred back to the United States. All he owned were the clothes he had on when the ship went down, and his wallet. He borrowed a uniform from a soldier and flew back to San Francisco on Flying Tiger Airlines.

THE *PIRATE* AND *PLEDGE* had sunk in very shallow water (the mast of the *Pirate* was still visible above the water). There were a number of mines still floating around the wreckages and they had to be cleared before the UDT teams could retrieve any bodies left aboard; destroy the encryption devices; and destroy what was left of the ships.

The crew of the *Pirate* received the Presidential Unit Citation and many Purple Hearts (including one for the Admiral) for their wounds. Lieutenant McMullen and Lieutenant Commander Bruce Hyatt both received Silver Stars for their actions the day of October 12, 1950.[21]

---

21. In 1952 Captain McMullen received an anonymous package containing the *Pirate*'s 48 star American flag. Within was a note explaining that as CO he might like the flag. On May 28, 1985, Cornelius McMullen donated the flag to the Naval Historical Center, where it is now part of the Korean War exhibit.

4

BACK TO KOREA AND THE USS *HARRY E. HUBBARD*

November of 1950 saw a difficult turn in the war for Allied forces. Early that month General MacArthur reported there were Communist Chinese troops in action with North Korean troops. Their involvement forced the overextended U.S. Army, Marine and South Korean units to retreat south, the forerunner of a massive Chinese counteroffensive that began on November 4. A million "volunteer" troops of the Communist Chinese People's Liberation Army emerged from the snow-covered mountains of North Korea and streamed across the Yalu River, which separated Korea from Manchuria. Not surprisingly, MacArthur announced this was a major threat to his command, and demanded reinforcements. He also announced a plan to bomb the Yalu River bridges, which was overruled by Washington.

He began the political campaign that was to prove his undoing, wherein he favored an all-out war with China that would reunite Korea and topple the Communist government in China. Strategically he was in trouble as well, as the Chinese drove through his forces, which he had split.

By December 5, U.N. troops abandoned Pyongyang and eventually were pushed out of the north. The X Corps[1] had to fight their way back to the coast in bitter cold and howling winds. The Chinese continued their offensive, promising to drive the Americans into the sea. Most of the ground troops fought their way to the coast where Navy ships put a wall of fire between the infantry and the enemy.

On December 16 President Truman declared a national emergency and called for an army buildup of 3–5 million men. By Christmas Eve day the Navy's Amphibious TF 90 had completed withdrawing 105,000 troops, 91,000 civil-

---

1. Units included the 1st Marine Division, the 3rd and 7th Infantry Divisions of the Army, and three South Korean divisions of the I and II Corps.

ian refugees, 350,000 tons of cargo and 17,500 military vehicles. At the end of the year General MacArthur publicly announced the U.S. should attack China with tactical atomic weapons, and advocated the use of half a million Nationalist Chinese (Taiwanese) troops to overthrow the Communist government in China. At the start of 1951 it appeared the world was hovering on the brink of World War III, particularly since Chinese troops broke through the defensive perimeter around Seoul on January 1 and took Inchon and the Kimpo airfield. There seemed no way to stop them.

Lieutenant j.g. Roy Hoffmann arrived at Travis A.F.B. in the United States just before Thanksgiving, 1950. While still in Japan he had been given an Army uniform to wear and he had gotten a pair of single silver lieutenant j.g. bars from a Marine for his collars. He was wearing a p-cutter for a hat without an emblem. To say he was out of uniform understates the situation. No sooner had he gotten on an Air Force transit bus than an Air Force M.P. detained him for not having travel orders and impersonating an officer.

There wasn't much young Lieutenant j.g. Hoffmann could say except, "If you're going to arrest me at least turn me over to the Navy." The 12th Naval District Headquarters were right on Market Street in San Francisco. Fortunately the M.P. agreed and marched him up to the Officer of the Deck at Navy Headquarters, who didn't believe the Hoffmann story either.

"You can't come to the United States without orders!" the OOD said.

"Oh yes I can," he replied. He was marched up to the Chief of Staff who said, "Well, your story is so ridiculous there has to be some truth to it."

Lieutenant j.g. Hoffmann asked the chief of staff to send a message to Naval Forces Japan and ask them to verify his situation, which they did within three or four days. Meanwhile he called the Bureau of Naval Personnel (BUPERS) and got a detailer who told him, "You'll be very pleased to know we are ordering you to the command of a minesweeper."

He responded that he was very honored, but he didn't know if he was ready for a minesweeper command. He had, after all, only returned to active duty a short time ago. He thought he might do the Navy more good if he got more experience. He requested a destroyer, and the detailer said that with his record that wouldn't be a problem, *if that were what he really wanted.*[2]

---

2. [author emphasis] Clearly this was an important point in the Admiral's career, and he took the responsible position. He was 25 years old and did lack the experience required to command a ship. However, in retrospect, he was probably as well qualified as other officers who received a command, and it may have been an accelerator to his career to take the position.

Meanwhile, he was due 30 days of "survivors leave," and he left for Missouri, arriving there Thanksgiving Day with his mix and match uniform and all he owned in a shoebox.

IN THE UNITED STATES the public followed the war news anxiously on radio, in the newspapers, and on the relatively new medium of television. In January 1950 the famous Boston Brink's robbery occurred when after 7:00 P.M. seven men broke into the Express Company and got away with $1.2 million in cash and $1.5 million in money orders. The FBI would spend $129 million over the next six years trying to catch the robbers. Eventually one of the gang members (Specs O'Keefe) confessed and the case was solved. The Federal government got a nominal return on its expenditure: $50,000 of the take was recovered.

That same month Alger Hiss was convicted of perjury and sentenced to five years in prison. Hiss was a former advisor to President Roosevelt and the president of the Carnegie Endowment for International Peace. Despite his denials Hiss was a member of the Communist Party and had passed secret papers to the Soviets while working for the State Department. The Hiss case brought national attention to a young war veteran from California, Representative Richard Nixon. He would hold that stage well beyond his resignation from the presidency in disgrace in 1972.

In July the U.S. population passed 150 million (it has doubled at this writing). In October Communist China invaded Tibet and in May of the following year Peking forced Tibet to formally accept Communist control. Their heavy-handed control wrecked havoc on the country as their temples, libraries and monasteries were destroyed. By 1975 the Chinese had killed an estimated one million Tibetans.[3]

On November 1 two Puerto Rican terrorists tried to shoot their way into the Blair House, where the Trumans had been temporarily residing during the renovation of the White House. After shooting and killing an Army private at the front gate, one of the gunmen was shot down and the other eventually received a death sentence, later reduced to life by Truman. Truman had watched the unfolding event from the balcony, causing the Secret Service apoplexy.

The Timex watch ("It takes a licking and keeps on ticking") came out

---

3. This sorry event in world history is commemorated by thousands of "Free Tibet" bumper stickers in the United States today. Bumper sticker diplomacy notwithstanding Tibet remains under the thumb of our new most favored trading partner, China. Offering proof that even evil has a redeeming side, China in 1950 did outlaw polygamy and the sale of women.

that year, as did Sugar Pops and the Paper-Mate ballpoint pen, which neither leaked nor smudged. The first copy machine to use xerography came out, which would later be known by the trade name Xerox. Charles Schulz' cartoon strip, *Li'l Folks*, was picked up by United Features Syndicate and renamed *Peanuts*; Mort Walker introduced the comic strip *Beetle Bailey*; and Louis L'Amour wrote his first book, *Westward the Tide*.

People listened to "Mona Lisa" by Nat King Cole, "Music! Music! Music!" by Teresa Brewer, "Bibbidi-Bobbidi-Boo" [this one didn't win any prizes for lyrics] by Perry Como and "Frosty the Snowman" by Gene Autry; and went to the movies to see *The Asphalt Jungle* with Sterling Hayden, *Cyrano de Bergerac* with Jose Ferrer, *Sunset Boulevard* with Gloria Swanson and William Holden, and the Disney classic, *Cinderella*.

Popular television shows that year were "The George Burns and Gracie Allen Show," "The Jack Benny Show,"[4] "What's My Line,"[5] and "You Bet Your Life," with Groucho Marx as emcee.[6]

When Mary Linn first saw her husband in Missouri he was still recovering from his wounds. His eyes were still blackened and he had a scar on his temple. They both knew his wounds could have been much worse, and were also aware he was probably heading for the open bridge head first when landing on the XO broke his fall.

He didn't have much to say about the sinking, although it was on his mind, at least subconsciously, as one would expect. One night on this first leave he awakened Mary Linn with his arms and legs thrashing about, uttering words she had not heard in her Catholic school days. It was apparent he was having a nightmare about swimming toward the island after the mine struck the *Pirate*, coming under fire and swimming back to the site of the sinking.[7]

---

4. This television show would run until 1965 and featured the now-famous cast of Jack Benny, Eddie "Rochester" Anderson, Don Wilson, Dennis Day and Mary Livingston.

5. Featuring John Daly as moderator and panelists Arlene Francis, Dorothy Kilgallen and Bennett Cerf.

6. Rita Lang Kleinfelder, *When We Were Young* (New York: Prentice Hall, 1993), pp. 61–81, passim.

7. Almost everyone has some sort of reaction to combat trauma. The factors that make it worse in some are unknown, but certainly the intensity and duration of the trauma count for a lot; and recovery has much to do with the support system in place to deal with it. Korean veterans, as Vietnam veterans, had to find their own support in the face of an indifferent public and a military culture not trained to recognize it. For a good review of the universality of the experience read *Achilles in Vietnam* by Jonathan Shay (1994). He draws parallels between the combat trauma exhibited by Achilles in *The Iliad* and Vietnam veterans he had treated for PTSD.

The survivor's leave flew by and the Hoffmanns parted again; he had to meet his new ship on Christmas Day. And so he left, a month and a half before the due date of the birth of his first child.

Roy Hoffmann reported aboard the USS *Harry E. Hubbard* (DD 748) on Christmas Day, 1950. She was swinging at the hook and he took a water taxi out to get aboard.

The *Hubbard* was named in honor of Commander Harry E. Hubbard who had been killed in the Solomon Islands campaign of World War II while commanding the USS *Meridith*. The ship was commissioned in 1944 at the New York Navy Yard, with Commander Hubbard's daughter Jean in attendance. During World War II she arrived off Okinawa on May 8, 1945, as part of Destroyer Flotilla 5, to serve as a picket destroyer guarding against waves of Japanese aerial raids and suicide runs of kamikaze planes. For nearly two months the *Hubbard* fought off the savage Japanese raids, shooting down four suicide planes in the process.

When the picket ships USS *Evans* (DD 552) and USS *Hadley* (DD 774) were badly damaged defending against some 50 kamikaze planes on May 11, 1945, the *Hubbard* was first on the scene, rendering fire-fighting, damage control and medical aid. On May 25 she shot down two suicide planes as she escorted the USS *Barry* (APD 29) from picket station into Kerama Rhetto. One of the kamikazes was blown out of the air a scant 50 yards from the ship.

The *Hubbard* was decommissioned at San Diego in 1947; she was recommissioned in October of 1950 following the invasion of South Korea, Commander Burris D. Wood, Jr., commanding. A native of New Orleans, Commander Wood was a pleasant career Navy officer, who had graduated from the U.S. Naval Academy at Annapolis in 1931. After a varied career, the *Hubbard* was that coveted first command for Burris Wood. He was easy-going, not a disciplinarian and was loved by his crew. He was a religious man but did not wear it on his sleeve. He ran a good ship and his greatest ability may have been to delegate to more competent officers things in which he didn't excel.[8] The Executive Officer was Lieutenant Commander Harry A. Burns.

On January 29, 1951, the *Hubbard* deployed for the Western Pacific in company with the USS *Brown* (DD 546), the USS *O'Brien* (DD 725), and the USS *Bradford* (DD 545). Roy Hoffmann was assigned the Gunnery

---

8. Captain Wood attended *Hubbard* reunions for many years; he passed away within the last few years.

USS Hubbard *(DD 748) steaming close aboard, Korean waters.* Official U.S. Navy

Officer position. He was fortunate to inherit a highly trained gunnery and fire control crew, most of whom were World War II veterans. The First Class Petty Officer in charge of the Fire Control console spent all of World War II in the Pacific on destroyers. Once he left the United States he didn't return until the end of the war. He was an experienced engineer and had been a design engineer for the food processing industry when recalled for the Korean War.

The ship made a three and one-half week stop at Pearl Harbor for minor voyage repairs, and for liberty in the great port for the sailors. For Lieutenant j.g. Hoffmann, it was a most fortuitous stop, as he was able to call Mary Linn, who had just delivered their first child, Harriet Ann Hoffmann, born February 12, 1951, in Bonne Terre, Missouri.

Roy Hoffmann's roommate on the *Hubbard* was Harry Train, who would later go on to retire as an admiral (four star). They went on the beach to celebrate the birth of Roy Hoffmann's first born while they were in Hawaii; the result was Harry Train had to help a very inebriated Roy Hoffmann back to the ship.[9]

---

9. Admiral Harry Train, USN (ret.) interview, October 10, 2006.

MARY LINN HAD delivered Harriet in the same hospital where she had worked for several years. Everyone knew her circumstance (that her husband was headed for the Korean War), and friends surrounded her.

Hoffmann had first called Mary Linn's mother and been informed that she was in the hospital, where he was able to reach her. She didn't have much privacy for the call, as there were other patients there, and her co-workers as well, who were friends in the small, 92-bed hospital. He called in the evening and somehow got a bouquet of flowers to her.

The birth was normal and Mary Linn spent about ten days in the hospital. Harriet, who would eventually show signs of disability, appeared normal at birth. Mary Linn took her home where they lived with her parents. She stayed home to raise her daughter and didn't return to work.

ONCE UNDERWAY from Hawaii the *Hubbard* steamed west, stopping for four hours at Midway to refuel. There the sailors encountered the famous "gooney birds," the Laysan albatross. These birds are so ungainly that at take off they run like an out of control bus and land as a plane would that had totally lost power, yet were beautiful when in flight. Midway was where they bred by the thousands. Held in reverence by the mariners of old, it was this bird the Ancient Mariner had heartlessly shot.[10] On March 7 the ship arrived in Sasebo, remaining there only long enough to take on fuel, ammunition and urgent supplies. She then sailed to join fast carrier TF 77 in offensive operations along the east coast of Korea.

For the next 22 days the *Hubbard* acted as one of the screen destroyers for the carriers *Princeton* (CV 45), *Philippine Sea* (CV 47), and *Valley Forge* (CV 45), whose planes were making almost around the clock strikes against the enemy. Her duties were as varied as could only be carried out by a destroyer: radar and radio countermeasure watches, mine destruction, plane guard duties and gunnery exercises.

On March 31 the *Hubbard* returned to Sasebo for R & R, but by April 8 she was back on station in Song-jin, well above the 38th parallel, conducting shore bombardment against the Communists. On May 13 the *Hubbard* started screening duties again with TF 77. She struck an underwater obstruction and had to return to Sasebo for dry-docking and inspection of

---

10. In the *Rime of the Ancient Mariner* by Samuel Taylor Coleridge, the albatross was a bird of good omen. The poem deals with the supernatural punishment and penance of a seaman who must periodically repeat the experience.

her screws, rejoining TF 77 on June 2, 1951. Ten days later another horrific explosion hit the fleet.

As MARCH DREW to a close the U.S. armed forces neared the three million mark, nearly double the strength they had been at the start of the Korean War. The numbers and training began to tell as on March 14 U.S. forces recaptured Seoul. By then Truman had had it with MacArthur. He relieved him of all commands on April 11, and replaced him with Lieutenant General Matthew Ridgway. The breaking point for Truman came when MacArthur openly defied Truman's plan to negotiate a Korean peace. MacArthur returned home a national hero. On April 19 General MacArthur addressed a joint session of Congress, where he defended his Korean positions and declared his military career to be at an end. He paraphrased an old Army ballad when he said, "I now close my military career and just fade away, an old soldier who tried to do his duty as God gave him the light to see that duty." There was a huge outcry against Truman and there were calls for his impeachment, but the sad truth is MacArthur's sometime megalomania had done him in.[11] It was a sad end to a career spent in service to his country.

TASK FORCE 77 WAS under the command of Rear Admiral G. R. Henderson. With three carriers and a battleship it was a huge task force, the largest assembled since World War II. This required an equally large screen around the carrier group. Hence, there were three destroyer divisions in Screen Group 77.2, which was under the command of Captain R. S. Smith. Within the Screen Group four destroyers comprised Destroyer Division 132: The *O'Brien* (DD 725), *Brown* (DD 546), *Walke* (DD 723), and *Hubbard* (DD 748).[12]

On June 12, 1951, the *Walke* and *Hubbard* were steaming with the carriers *Bon Homme Richard* (CV 31), *Princeton* (CV 37); the battleship *New Jersey* (BB 62), and the *Des Moines*-class heavy cruiser *Helena* (CA 75). The destroyer *Bole* (DD 755) reported engine trouble and moved to the south of

---

11. Harry Truman, in his inimitable fashion, had this to say about the firing: "I fired him because he wouldn't respect the authority of the President. That's the answer to that. I didn't fire him because he was a dumb son of a bitch, although he was, but that's not against the law for generals. If it was, half to three-quarters of them would be in jail." Kenneth C. Davis, *Don't Know Much About History* (New York: Avon Books, 1990).

12. The primary sources for the events of June 12 were the Log Books of the *Hubbard* and *Walke*; the Action Report dated June 17, 1951, by Commander Destroyer Squadron 7; the Action Report by Commander Carrier Division Five (Commander Task Force 77), dated June 26, 1951; and the experiences of Roy Hoffmann.

the formation. At the start of June 12 the *Hubbard* was steaming on boilers #2 and #3, steering course 090 at 15 knots. At 0300 she changed course to 275 to get into position to act as plane guard for the *Bon Homme Richard* as she conducted air operations from 0352 to 0410, and again from 0538 to 0559 hours. At 0605 a battle-damaged F4U from the *Bon Homme Richard* made an emergency landing on the *Princeton*.

The weather conditions at 0734 hours, June 12 were a light wind of six knots and an easy sea with three-foot swells; the sky was overcast at 1,500 feet with visibility of 15 miles; and the temperature was 57 degrees. The *Walke* was in screen station #4 in the formation and the *Hubbard* was immediately aft. Suddenly a tremendous explosion hit the *Walke* on the port side. Captain Thompson assumed the *Walke* conn as the ship slowed to 5 knots and went to general quarters. By 0742 hours the bridge received word that the explosion had taken place on the port quarter about frame 170. The explosion hit two aft berthing compartments, causing high casualties and massive flooding.

At 0744 the *Hubbard* went to general quarters and moved ahead at flank speed to render assistance to the stricken *Walke*. As Roy Hoffmann assumed his battle station at the main battery director (a high point on the ship) he could see the gaping hole in the *Walke*, big enough to drive a Greyhound bus through.[13] As *Hubbard* came alongside the first priority was to save the *Walke*. The *Hubbard* began transferring damage control personnel to the *Walke*, and between the two crews they did a magnificent job of saving the ship. They assisted in controlling the flooding of the damaged living compartments, in medical aid to the many casualties, and in providing cover against a submarine attack.

There was confusion as to the cause of the explosion. The *Hubbard* had a positive sonar contact, indicating an enemy submarine in the area, but a floating mine was also a possible source of the explosion. Meanwhile, the task force prudently left the area in a move to protect the carriers and battleship from what was a potential submarine attack. The *Hubbard* and *O'Brien* stayed behind to assist.

At 0753 hours all hands topside on the *Walke* shifted to starboard to reduce the list. By 0758 the Hubbard was alongside and at 0808 had the highline rigged, as flooding was confined to two compartments aboard the Walke.

---

13. There was a hole in the hull about 18 feet wide and extending from below the turn of the bilge to four feet above the water line. Compartments C-203L and C-204L were wide open to the sea and free flooding. Water was about five feet deep in C-205L when pumping commenced.

At 0759 hours the *Bradford*, in Station #2, reported a mine passing 25 yards to starboard; she left the formation to destroy it. The mine was approximately three feet in diameter, with no visible horns and painted a dark grey. When the *Bradford* destroyed the mine the resulting explosion appeared to the *O'Brien* exactly like the explosion that had struck the *Walke*.

On the *Walke* the damage control crews removed the exploders from the depth charges on the port side throwers and port stern racks. They then jettisoned 24 Mark 9 depth charges and three Mark 14 depth charges.

At 0812 the *Walke* changed to course 335 at 3 knots as Dr. Donahue (lieutenant j.g.) and medical supplies were transferred from the *Hubbard*. At 0831 a helicopter delivered two hospital corpsmen to help with the wounded. By 0845 all of the wounded were out of compartment C-203L, although the dead were still inaccessible. At 0850 the *Helena* closed to send over two doctors, two more corpsmen, and medical supplies, which arrived by boat at 0902.

Due to a severe port list, ballasting commenced as they pumped fuel from the port fuel oil tanks. The Chief Engineer continued pumping oil over the side until the ship had achieved a 5-degree starboard list to relieve pressure on the damaged port doors below decks.

At 1000 seven men were transferred to the *Helena*. At the same time 11 dead were ordered transferred to the *Hubbard* for further delivery to the *New Jersey*. An additional 15 men were missing and presumed dead.

At 1002 the *O'Brien* reported two more mines, as it was underway to rendezvous with the *Bradford*. At 1040 the *Walke* reported a sonar contact at 270, 1200 yards, which the *Hubbard* then confirmed with her gear. She made an urgent depth charge attack, and at 1149 the *O'Brien* and *Bradford* completed five additional depth charge attacks. Subsequent to these attacks they reported hearing a series of underwater explosions, and some light oil and debris were sighted on the surface after the attacks. At 1240 the *Hubbard* reported regaining sonar contact and she made another depth charge attack.[14]

At 1445 hours the *Hubbard* proceeded to the *Walke* to transfer casualties. At 1538 she commenced receiving remains of the 11 dead sailors, loading her boats with bodies of the dead. It was a gruesome task as the bodies

---

14. It is Admiral Hoffmann's opinion that the *Walke* was hit by a floating mine, not a torpedo fired from an enemy submarine. Although floating sea mines are against the Geneva Convention, it's clear there were floating mines in the area that day. Given that fact, plus the similarity of the explosion reported with the destroyed mine, one has to agree that a mine caused the explosion on the *Walke*. However, that doesn't discount the fact there may have been an enemy submarine on the scene that day.

were bloody, some of the bodies were unidentifiable and in some cases they had only body parts to identify. At 1942 hours the *Hubbard* rejoined the formation with 11 bodies from the *Walke* and at 2220 commenced transfer of the remains to the *New Jersey*. By midnight the exhausted crew of the *Hubbard* had returned to Screen Station #6.[15]

At 1740 hours 33 more wounded were listed, in addition to those previously reported. Their injuries included lacerations, lymphatic membrane perforations (from the blast), concussions, fractures, burns, abrasions and contusions. The final toll on the *Walke* was: 13 dead, 13 missing and presumed dead (mostly casualties in the flooded living compartments) and 42 wounded.[16]

AT ABOUT THIS TIME, at home, Mary Linn began to suspect something was not quite right with their daughter Harriet. She could not hold her head up well, she was not eating well and appeared listless—she lacked the sparkle in her eyes that Mary Linn thought she should have. She made sounds but Mary Linn didn't think she was progressing as she should.

Mary Linn mentioned her concerns to the doctor who had delivered Harriet and he pronounced: "Oh, you first time mothers, you read books and if the child isn't doing exactly what the book says you get upset."

Mary Linn wanted to take Harriet to St. Louis to see a specialist, but she knew they would ask for Harriet's records from her doctor. He was a very close friend and she didn't want to hurt his feelings, "So I just thought I'd wait until Roy gets home and we'll go to California and find a specialist out there." She did not express her concerns to her husband. "It was not the time," she said.

ON JUNE 27, 1951, the *Hubbard* returned to Sasebo, Japan. Ten days later the ship returned to Songjin where Captain Wood assumed command of Task

---

15. Again, this was a defining moment in the Admiral's career, reinforcing his insistence on Damage Control when *he* was in command. He would always put one of his best officers (if not the best) in Engineering on Damage Control. "Damage control is difficult to enforce; when it comes to Damage Control discipline is the number one word. Watertight doors have to be closed and dogged properly; when you shut a valve you want to make sure it is properly shut. All battle lanterns have to be operating properly—you're in deep trouble if power fails and battle lanterns aren't ready—you can't see a damn thing," he said. "We're not talking about chicken shit," he insists, but there is always an element of that in Navy discipline.

16. Over 1,177,000 Navy personnel served during the Korean War. Four hundred fifty-eight sailors were killed in action, 1,576 were wounded and 4,043 died from either injury or disease.

Element 95.22, the northernmost bombardment group off eastern Korea. In addition to naval bombardment the *Hubbard* had on board a group of Republic of Korea (ROK) marines. The crew of the *Hubbard* assisted in putting the ROK marines ashore, made many landings in enemy territory, and obtained valuable intelligence by taking enemy prisoners for interrogation.

On July 23 the *Hubbard* proceeded southward to Wonsan so Commander Wood could assume tactical command of Task Element 95.21 of the Wonsan bombardment group. It was pressure time on the crew and their gunnery officer, Roy Hoffmann, as they conducted interdiction firing on an around the clock basis. The enemy was continuously attempting to move supplies through the area and using large caliber guns located in the hills surrounding the bay to drive U.N. forces from the Wonsan harbor. Because of major transportation facilities connecting the enemy front lines with Russian and Chinese supply areas, the Wonsan port was a vital link to enemy forces. The bombardment made it more difficult for the enemy to supply their troops.

The enemy responded with fire from shore and the *Hubbard* experienced repeated near misses. After just over a month of shore bombardment the *Hubbard* was relieved and she returned to Yokosuka, and then on August 20 she rejoined TF 77 for one last operational line period before returning to the United States. On August 25, 1950 the *Hubbard*, USS *Rodgers* (DDR 876) and the USS *Helena* (CA 75) went on a special mission to act as a radar picket and life guard ship in conjunction with a 30 plane raid on Rachin, a transportation center just eight miles south of the Russian border, and 36 miles from the approaches to the large Russian naval base at Vladivostok.

ON SEPTEMBER 22, 1951, Division 31 relieved the *Hubbard's* division and she set sail for San Diego via Yokosuka, Midway and Pearl Harbor. On the cruise the ship had traveled 69,860 miles, used 930,000 barrels of fuel oil (at a cost of $1.86 million in 1951 dollars), and fired 8,342 rounds of 5-inch ammunition (57,000 rounds total or 190 tons of main battery ammunition) against the enemy. It was an average of one shell every eight minutes, 24 hours a day for the entire period they were on the line.

THE *HUBBARD* RETURNED to San Diego and Roy Hoffmann flew back to Missouri to bring his family to Long Beach, California, where the ship had gone into the yard. The Hoffmanns had driven across the country with most of their possessions in their car; what didn't fit they had shipped by Railway Express. They rented a second-floor apartment on Ocean Boulevard that faced the ocean. It had been difficult to find a place that would accept an eight-month-old child. Some of the newspaper rental ads said: "No Navy, no kids."[17] Fortunately they found a rare landlord who welcomed them with the comment: "I've never had an eight-month-old burn a hole in the upholstery with a cigarette." The rent was $125 per month.

In January of 1952 the Hoffmanns moved from Long Beach to 627 Westbourne Street in La Jolla, north of San Diego. The exclusive community would lead one to believe, as the Admiral put it, that they were "high in the cotton." In truth, their apartment was above a garage. Mary Linn became part of a close group of Navy wives. In particular, they were close to a couple from the *Hubbard* with a young daughter, Lieutenant j.g. John C. and Mary Snodgrass of Houston, Texas.

Looming was another deployment to the Korean War zone. The Admiral was home long enough to help conceive another child. Mary Linn had taken Harriet to a pediatrician who recommended she take her to a specialist, which she determined to do after the *Hubbard* deployed again.

In March the family moved again, from La Jolla to 712 Tourmaline in Pacific Beach. On June 1st Roy Hoffmann received his promotion to lieutenant and the ship departed for another WESTPAC cruise.

CHRISTINE LINN HOFFMANN, the second daughter born to the couple, arrived August 30, 1952. Mary Linn hired a practical nurse to stay with Harriet while she had Christine. She had a lot of friends there to help after the birth, and not all of them were Navy families.

In the meantime, she had taken Harriet to a specialist in San Diego, which the Hoffmanns had to pay for since in those days the Navy didn't pay for private care.

It is too kind to say the doctor had a lousy bedside manner. He confirmed her concerns about Harriet. She was autistic, unable to speak or hear, and she couldn't bite or chew. Her food had to be pureed for her to survive, but she knew her parents and was an affectionate child. Mary Linn said, "It is something you learn to live with."

It was easier for the Hoffmanns to accept that nothing could be done than it was for the doctors. The San Diego specialist told Mary Linn: "You must tell your husband right away."

"He doesn't know," she replied.

---

17. It was not unusual to find such an attitude toward the military. This author remembers seeing lawn signs in the late 1960s in San Diego saying: "No dogs or Navy allowed."

"Where is he?" he asked.

"He's on a ship in Korean waters."

"He must know right away," the doctor repeated.

"He has more crucial things on his mind right now," she replied.

"If you don't tell him, I will."

"You'll have a heck of a time finding out who he is and where he is," she replied. He arrogantly insisted that Harriet go into a residential home and Mary Linn said no, "I'll take care of her."[18]

It is true that Mary Linn had to deal with much of this on her own, but it would be a mistake to make simple characterizations of her motivations. She was not some Pollyannaish figure "standing by her man," nor was she a martyr soldiering on in the face of great adversity. The truth, in this author's opinion, is more complex. The Navy was, in fact, a great adventure for a woman who had spent 23 years in the somewhat stifling environment of a small town. Long separations and frequent moves were just part of the deal. She was a strong, resourceful woman and the challenges were intriguing. By her own admission she was never homesick a day in her life, and she took to the gypsy lifestyle. The *Hubbard* was her first taste of Navy life and it made a positive impression on her. It was a lifestyle she chose, not one inflicted on her.

MEANWHILE, THE Korean War was festering along. In January of 1952 peace talks, which had begun in July of 1951 between the U.N. and China, had stalled. The war slogged on, fought primarily in North Korea's cold, rugged mountain terrain. These battles, for Heartbreak Ridge, Bloody Ridge, and the Punchbowl ended in bloody stalemate reminiscent of the trench warfare of World War I.

In July of 1952 the Republican National Convention nominated national hero General Dwight D. Eisenhower for president, with Senator Richard M. Nixon of California as his running mate. The Democrats nominated Governor Adlai E. Stevenson of Illinois for president, with Senator John J. Sparkman of Alabama his running mate.

In October Eisenhower vowed to go to Korea if elected and seek an early and honorable conclusion to the war. On November 4, 1952, he was overwhelmingly elected president, winning 39 states (to nine for Stevenson), 442 electoral votes

---

18. The Hoffmanns had Harriet in their home until 1973, when she went into a training center in Fairfax, Virginia. Today they pick her up for frequent visits to their home in Richmond, Virginia, where she stays for a week at a time.

(to 89 for Stevenson), and almost 34 million votes to Stevenson's 27.3 million. The Republicans also gained a one vote majority in the Senate, and gained 22 seats in the House for a 221 to 211 majority. Eisenhower's immense popularity and an unpopular war had done the Democrats in.

On November 29, 1952, Eisenhower, as president-elect, fulfilled his campaign promise and flew to Korea. On a three-day trip he inspected U.N. forces and visited front-line positions. His visit was kept secret until he returned from the war zone.

IN JULY OF 1952 the *Hubbard* rejoined the 7th Fleet for another tour of duty in Korean waters. As the ship commenced its bombardment exercises Gunnery Officer Roy Hoffmann met and became acquainted with the Commodore of the Destroyer Division, Captain John D. Bulkeley. Captain Bulkeley was already a Navy legend, brilliant, eccentric, controversial, and one of the most fascinating men to ever wear a U.S. Navy uniform.[19]

John D. Bulkeley was the subject of John Ford's moving 1945 film, *They Were Expendable*, one of the greatest films to come out of World War II. Bulkeley (renamed "Brickley" for the film) was played by Robert Montgomery, in one of his best performances.[20] John Wayne played Lieutenant j.g. "Rusty" Ryan, the hotheaded XO, who with Lieutenant Brickley struggled to get the Navy to accept PT boats as a valuable instrument of war. It is the story of Lieutenant John Bulkeley, commander of Motor Torpedo Boat Squadron No. 3, and the fall of Bataan and Corregidor to the Japanese early in the war.

As is often the case, the truth is more interesting than fiction. Bulkeley was born August 19, 1911, in New York, New York, and was raised in New Jersey. He was unable to gain an appointment to the Naval Academy from his home state, so he wrangled an appointment from Texas.[21] As money for

---

19. Unless otherwise noted, much of the information on Admiral Bulkeley's life is from his son's eulogy to his father in Captain Peter W. Bulkeley, "Vice Admiral John D. Bulkeley, USN," The Board of Inspection and Survey (INSURV).

20. Robert Montgomery was a real-life Naval officer, and Director John Ford had seen action himself in the South Pacific as a documentary filmmaker for the Navy. Then Captain Ford had lost 13 men in his unit; his experiences probably enhanced the accuracy of the film and its somewhat somber tone.

21. The salt spray of navy life was in his veins. His ancestor, Richard Bulkeley, fought on HMS *Victory* with Lord Nelson at the Battle of Trafalgar in 1804; John Bulkeley of HMS *Wager* served under Captain Bligh during his service with Anson's Squadron; and Charles Bulkeley raised the Union Jack for the first time on an American warship, the *Alfred*, which was commanded by John Paul Jones. Ibid., p. 1

the military grew tight during the Depression, only half of the 1933 Academy class received a commission on graduation. John Bulkeley was one of those who didn't, so he joined the Army Air Corps, then a year later joined the Navy as a commissioned officer on the cruiser USS *Indianapolis*.

In the mid 1930s he went into the Japanese ambassador's stateroom, removed his briefcase, and delivered it to U.S. Naval Intelligence. He compounded his affront in 1939 when he lectured the Japanese in Tokyo about what fools they were for being led down the path to disaster by the Emperor. There was no greater affront he could have made to the Japanese and he was arrested for his seditious remarks. It took the U.S. State Department to get him out of jail.

He was next assigned as Chief Engineer of the coal-burning gunboat, the USS *Sacramento* (PG 19), known as the "Galloping Ghost of the China Coast." He met Alice Wood, a young, attractive English girl, at a dinner party aboard the HMS *Diana*, whom he married and divorced more than once, as she periodically grew frustrated with him during their marriage. During their courtship they witnessed the invasion of Swatow and Shanghai by Japanese troops.

John Bulkeley loved opera and he loved animals. He was always compassionate with animals, caring for any that sought his help. He was hard on the outside, but in the early days of World War II he wept over the decision to leave our army at Bataan behind to face an enemy of overwhelming strength.

At the dawn of World War II, Bulkeley was in command of Motor Torpedo Boat Squadron Three, a Philippine-based tactical command of six motor torpedo boats. He proved to be a daring, resourceful and courageous leader who wanted to fight to the last man against Japanese forces attacking the Philippine Islands. He extracted General of the Army Douglas MacArthur, his family and his immediate staff from Corregidor after they were ordered to leave. Their escape was made in a 77-foot motor torpedo boat through enemy lines and over 600 miles of hostile ocean. When he delivered MacArthur to Mindanao, MacArthur told him, "You have taken me out of the jaws of death. I shall never forget it." George Cox, skipper of PT 41 said in 1943 of Bulkeley, "I would follow this man to Hell if asked." For the extraction of MacArthur and other actions around the Philippines Bulkeley was awarded the Congressional Medal of Honor.

In 1944 General Eisenhower sent for Bulkeley to bring in a contingent of PT boats to support the upcoming D-Day invasion and to provide protection against German E-boats. His PT boats were based in England and British King George VI came aboard Bulkeley's PT 504 for an inspection. The King talked to the crew, telling them he had taken part in the momentous Battle of Jutland as a midshipman in 1916. During the visit he had a cup of coffee after which the boat's cook would brook no complaints about his coffee from his boat mates—if it was good enough for the King of England it damn well should be good enough for them.[22]

Bulkeley again showed his great courage during the D-Day invasion, leading his PT boats and minesweepers in clearing the lanes to Utah Beach, keeping German E-boats from attacking the landing ships, and picking up wounded sailors from three sinking ships: the steel-hulled minesweeper USS *Tide*, the destroyer escort USS *Rich* and the destroyer USS *Corry*. The *Tide* (AM 125) had been operating off Utah Beach on D-Day plus one (June 7), when she struck a German magnetic influence mine. Observers on other ships said the explosion caused the *Tide* to come perhaps five feet out of the water. Motor Machinist's Mate Bill Branstrator went up like a rocket and landed with grievous injuries. As the *Tide* started to sink, PT 504, commanded by John Bulkeley, came alongside to take off survivors. Branstrator was laying wounded on the deck and asked for a cigarette. Bulkeley took the one from his mouth that he was smoking and put it in Branstrator's mouth.[23]

Bulkeley took command of his first ship, the destroyer USS *Endicott* (DD 495), engendering in him a love of destroyers and destroyer men. One month after D-Day his ship came to the aid of two British gun ships under attack by two German corvettes. Charging into the scene with only one operational gun he engaged both enemy vessels at point blank range, sinking both of them. "What else could I do?" he later said. "You engage, you fight, you win. That is the reputation of our Navy, then and in the future." His standards were high, as one of the enemy captains of the corvettes learned. As he came up the sea ladder he wouldn't salute the colors on the *Endicott*, and Bulkeley had him tossed into the sea. He came up a second time with the same result. On the third time up he had learned his lesson, saluted the flag and was allowed on board and taken prisoner.

Highly decorated by the end of the war, Bulkeley commented, "Medals and awards don't mean anything. It's what's inside you, how you feel about yourself, that counts."[24]

---

22. Naval Historical Foundation, *The Navy* (New York: Barnes & Noble Books, 2000), pp. 122–123.

23. Branstrator was eventually evacuated to England for medical care. He would lose a leg and endure more than 50 operations as a result of the wounds received June 7, 1944. Ibid., pp. 124–125.

24. Bulkeley, INSERV, p. 3.

AND SO LIEUTENANT Hoffmann encountered then Captain Bulkeley as his Division Commander. He admired Captain Bulkeley and considered himself fortunate to have spent quite a bit of time with him. He felt that Bulkeley's endorsement of his request to transfer from the reserves to the regular Navy was one of the reasons he made it. Only 12 black shoes and 13 aviators made it into the regular Navy in the first round.

Captain Bulkeley would brook no mispronunciation of his name. "It's JOHN D. BULKELEY," he would say. "IT'S ENGLISH—GOT IT? —NOT IRISH!"

To say that Captain Bulkeley had a temper is understating it. As Roy Hoffmann puts it, "It wasn't very nice to have John Bulkeley on your ass, I can tell you that." Think of Captain Wood, who had to give up one of his living accommodations to Captain Bulkeley, since there were no separate quarters for the Commodore on the *Hubbard*. The Commodore took over Wood's sea cabin and he retained his cabin on the main deck. Unfortunately for Captain Wood, he had a problem with heavy seas and seasickness, so he had rigged a gimbal (a device consisting of two rings mounted at right angles to each other so that an object—the bunk in this case—theoretically will remain stationary on a horizontal plane between them regardless of the ship's motion) to secure his bunk from the roll of the ship. Bulkeley couldn't believe a destroyer man would have a gimbal on his bunk. "Bulkeley damn near had a stroke," Roy Hoffmann said. "What the hell's happening to this Navy?" Bulkeley yelled.

The *Hubbard* did a great deal of firing.[25] The east coast of North Korea is mountainous and the North Koreans had to build the railroad beds right along the coast. The routes were interlaced with tunnels, where the North Korean trains would hide during the day, then at night they would come out and make runs between the tunnels. Commodore Bulkeley's reaction was, "We'll get those bastards." So the destroyer would get close in, shut down the blowers, turn out the lights and set the guns on the mouth of the tunnels. The minute the train exited the tunnel the ship would fire, catching the train in the open. One time Lieutenant Hoffmann caught hell from Commodore Bulkeley when he blew up the engine and left the rest of the

---

25. According to Captain John Culver, USNR (ret.), the whole ship would "shake, rattle and roll" with all the gunfire. The ship shot all night so sleep was virtually impossible. They would say, "It's Roy Hoffmann and his damn guns." Captain. John Culver, USNR (ret.) interview, September 17, 2006.

train in the tunnel. "Goddamnit," Bulkeley yelled, "the cargo's in the cars not the engine!"

Despite his outbursts, Bulkeley was approachable, and not an intimidating figure. He loved to tell sea stories, not all of which were necessarily believable. He drove a souped up Chevrolet that had a PT boat for a hood ornament. He had designed an electrical switch activator for his fuel-fill access, way ahead of his time. He also hooked up a two-way radio in his wife's car so they could stay in touch, a harbinger of the ubiquitous cell phone.

As with all aggressive and ambitious Navy men Bulkeley's fondest wish was to make admiral. He was passed over twice for advancement to admiral, but it finally came when former PT boat sailor John F. Kennedy was elected president. Rear Admiral Bulkeley ended up in the backyard of the old Kennedy nemesis, Fidel Castro, as the Commandant of the Guantanamo Naval Base. There he met the bluster and threats of Communist Fidel with his typical resolve. When Castro threatened to cut off the base water supply Bulkeley ordered the installation of desalinization equipment to make the base self-sufficient and then cut the water supply pipe himself. He so offended Fidel that he ended up with a price on his head of 50,000 pesos, dead or alive, for this " . . . guerilla of the worst species." The Marines that guarded the base loved the admiral and he loved them in return.

He ended his career as President of the Board of Inspection and Survey (INSERV), conducting his inspections by the book in strict accordance with standards, but his love for the sailors always came through. After 55 years of commissioned service he retired to private life in 1988, and died on April 6, 1996.

While operating on the east coast of Korea the *Hubbard* came alongside a British aircraft carrier to receive fuel. After the lines were over they proceeded to pump fuel to the *Hubbard* as the two ships steamed together at about 10 knots. Suddenly the captain of the aircraft carrier yelled over on a bullhorn, "I've got two battle damaged planes coming in and I've got to recover them—can you stay with me?" Captain Wood responded they could, and the *Hubbard* steamed up to about 25 knots, staying about 60 feet from the British carrier with all the hoses out during the recovery of the aircraft. Roy Hoffmann was on the bridge at the time, receiving more valuable training in seamanship.[26]

---

26. Captain John Culver, USNR (ret.) interview, September 17, 2006.

THE *HUBBARD* CONTINUED its fine record of gunfire support, driving the ship's mascot, Rowdy, crazy. Rowdy was a bulldog with an attitude, whose General Quarters station was in a box under a radar set in CIC. He hated the naval gunfire and that may explain why he had a habit of biting the crew, although Harry Train, Roy Hoffmann's roommate on the *Hubbard*, provided an alternative explanation. According to Admiral Train the dog was trained by the enlisted men to bite officers, which they accomplished by harassing the dog by waving khakis in front of his nose. His reaction was to bite at the sight of khaki (which couldn't have made the CPOs happy).

Once Rowdy bit Lieutenant Hoffmann on the hand as he was climbing up a Jacobs ladder. When his hand reached the top rung Rowdy latched on and in typical bulldog fashion wouldn't let go. He also shredded the sleeve on his foul weather jacket by latching on to his arm.[27]

---

27. Admiral Harry Train interview, October 10, 2006.

Lieutenant Albert W. Coset, Rowdy, and Lieutenant j.g. Roy F. Hoffmann, USS Hubbard (DD 748). HOFFMANN COLLECTION

ONE OF THE SHIPS the *Hubbard* operated with was the USS *Barton* (DD 722). The Barton had arrived in Yokosuka on June 18, 1952; she then joined TF 77 as a member of a hunter-killer group for operations along the east coast of Korea. On August 10, 1952, while silencing enemy batteries on the island of Hodo Pando, the *Barton* was hit on her number one stack by a 105 mm shell from an enemy shore battery; two men were wounded.

Then, after repairs at Yokosuka she rejoined TF 77. While operating with the *Hubbard* on September 16, 1952, she struck a floating mine that blew out the forward fire room. She was the last ship in the line, and the *Hubbard* was the closest ship to her. The Task Force commander ordered the *Hubbard* alongside to see if they could render assistance, but things were under control due to effective damage control by her crew. There were five men missing and seven wounded on the crippled ship.

BY DECEMBER OF 1952 the *Hubbard* completed her tour of duty and returned to San Diego. As the ship went into the yard at Long Beach the Hoffmann family moved there in January, into a pleasant apartment on East 4th Street. There they stayed until the ship was ready to deploy again, in June 1953.

5

THE "PEACETIME" NAVY

On July 27, 1953, an armistice was signed at Panmunjon, ending the direct fighting in the Korean War. The war had staggered to a conclusion that left the status quo as it existed before the North Koreans invaded in 1950. North Korea would exist as a brutal Communist dictatorship and South Korea would see its economy boom under the twin engines of capitalism and democracy. They still face off in hostility today as North Korea suffers under an unstable dictatorship isolated from much of the world.

In 1952 Dwight D. Eisenhower had campaigned that he would end what had become an increasingly unpopular war. His tough stance (he had hinted he might use nuclear weapons) and Stalin's death brought it to a close.[1] It was another extraordinary feat of American and Allied arms, a brutal stalemate won by the capabilities and courage of the American military. The cost was high for America: More than 54,000 dead either on the battlefield or by accidents and injury; 7,955 were missing in action; and over 100,000 were wounded. More than 2 million Koreans were killed in the fighting.

At home, Americans realized they could no longer stay isolated from the rest of the world, recognizing the threat the Soviets, Chinese and other ruthless dictators represented. America began a massive buildup of conventional nuclear forces; the Cold War replaced the shooting war in Korea.

In June of that year Julius and Ethel Rosenberg were executed at Sing Sing Prison in New York. They had passed secrets about the atom bomb to the Russians, for which they lost their lives. That month a U.S. Air Force C 124 Globemaster crashed near Tokyo after reporting "one engine out . . . returning to field." One hundred twenty-nine people were killed in the crash.

---

1. As is often the case, the U.S. had to mostly go it alone. South Korea and the U.S. provided 95 per cent of U.N. troops.

Americans were reading *The Bridges at Toko-ri* by James Michener, *The Light in the Forest* by Conrad Richter, and *Battle Cry* by Leon Uris. On the radio they listened to "How Much Is That Doggie in the Window," by Patti Page; "Don't Let the Stars Get in Your Eyes," by Perry Como; and "Your Cheatin' Heart," by Hank Williams. In the movie theaters they watched *Shane* with Alan Ladd and Jack Palance; *Stalag 17* with William Holden; *From Here to Eternity* with Burt Lancaster and Deborah Kerr; *It Came From Outer Space* with Richard Carlson; and *The Naked Spur* with James Stewart and Janet Leigh. The top box office stars were Gary Cooper, John Wayne, Alan Ladd, Bing Crosby, Marilyn Monroe, James Stewart and Susan Hayward.

When the television was on in the evening they watched "The Danny Thomas Show;" "General Electric Theater," with host and star Ronald Reagan; and "The Life of Riley," with William Bendix.

Roy Hoffmann received orders to the Naval Ordnance Center as a Naval Weapons Ordnance and Ballistics Instructor in weapons using liquid propulsion. The Navy felt that with his education and experience that would be a good fit for him. At the last minute his orders were changed and he was ordered to the Naval Reserve Officers Training Center (NROTC) program at Illinois Tech as a Naval Ordnance and Ballistics Instructor. He was somewhat disappointed but as it turned out it was a fortuitous change in orders. Liquid weapon propellants lost out to solid propellants and he thus would have spent two years in a program that was on the way out. His thought at the time was that NROTC would be a neutral in terms of a career move. It was an advantage to go in as a junior officer; if you went in as a Lieutenant Commander or Commander it was probably a death knell for further advancement, even though they assign good people to the school. For a captain it was referred to as a "pasture job."

His interim assignment before reporting to Illinois Tech was to Northwestern University for what they called "charm school," designed to teach the techniques of teaching.

In June of 1953 the Hoffmanns packed up and left Long Beach for Chicago, Illinois, where they rented a home at 12509 South Ada Street. It was the first shore assignment in their young marriage and the first opportunity for a good family experience. Despite the shore duty, it was a busy time. The Admiral had lessons to prepare and papers to grade. In addition, he was taking a German course that was the final core requirement for his degree from Nebraska. As the

Admiral relates, he was not an exceptional student ("I helped maintain the averages," he says). Illinois Tech was an exceptional educational facility with students who in some cases were intellectually superior to him.

It was a challenge to stay up with them, and he maintained his humor, particularly when the student knew a quicker way to a mathematical solution. "Come up to the blackboard and show us," he'd say, instead of blustering through it. He gained their respect for his practical experience and his willingness to learn with them.

Illinois Tech was on the Southside in one of the worst neighborhoods in Chicago. The campus was located on 3300 South Federal Street, a kind of oasis in the tough neighborhood. He had a fairly long commute to work through Chicago. It was bumper to bumper with trucks on your tail through the roughest part of the city. "Everybody on the staff had some kind of accident in my two years there, including yours truly." Fortunately his accident was a fender bender, and they had been briefed by the local police that if you got in an accident get away and report to the nearest police station.

Mary Linn was busy raising the kids, and their family continued to grow with the birth of daughter Cecile on October 23, 1953. There was little time for socializing and they saw little of Chicago. Harriet's disabilities were such that it was not always possible to get a sitter, so most of their friends in the predominantly civilian neighborhood were accommodating and came to the Hoffmann home to socialize. In the evenings the parents would gather on the front porch to talk, checking periodically on the kids.

Since they were both still in their twenties, they were asked to chaperone at Fraternity dances and at the houses. One of the Fraternities had what they called a "shipwreck" party, where young girls showed up who should not have been invited. After one of the girls disappeared upstairs Mary Linn and another faculty couple went up and got her.

Comiskey Park, the stadium of the Chicago White Sox, was only a block away from where Roy Hoffmann was teaching. He had always been a Ted Williams fan and so when the Boston Red Sox came to town Lieutenant Hoffmann went to the games. He could get seats behind the visiting team's dugout, where he could watch friends and former Naval aviators Ted Williams and Nellie Fox talk.

NELLIE FOX WAS the 5-foot, 10-inch, 160-pound second baseman for the Chicago White Sox. He and Jackie Robinson were considered the premier second basemen during the 1950s. Fox led the American League in hits four times and was the most difficult player for pitchers to strike out year after year. He played in the big leagues for 19 years and only struck out 216 times in over 9,900 times at bat.

Ted Williams broke into the major leagues in the spring of 1939 with the Boston Red Sox. He was tall, thin, high-strung, cocky (he called his manger Joe Cronin "Sport"), independent, and *really good*. As a rookie he batted .327, hit 31 home runs and drove in 145 runs. It is not an exaggeration to say that it was the greatest rookie batting performance in baseball history.[2]

He liked to call himself "the Kid" and "Teddy Ballgame." He had an eccentric mother who was a Salvation Army street worker, half French and half Mexican. Wherever she was you knew it because she was so loud. As Williams later related, "I was embarrassed about my home, embarrassed that I never had quite as good clothes as some of the kids, embarrassed that my mother was out in the middle of the damn street all the time. Until the day she died she did that and it always embarrassed me."[3] When Williams was playing in the Pacific Coast League for the San Diego Padres (at $150 per month), his mother would work the stands at the home games " . . . loudly declaring herself the mother of the star and demanding funds for her cause."[4] It is probably not surprising that later in life Ted Williams would say, "All I want out of life is that when I walk down the street folks will say, 'There goes the greatest hitter that ever lived.'"[5] He probably succeeded.

In 1941 he had a .39955 average going into the final two games of the season, which rounded to .400. The night before the game Boston manager Joe Cronin offered to keep Williams on the bench so as not to jeopardize the storied .400 mark. His pride wouldn't let him sit it out. "If I couldn't hit .400 all the way," he later said, "I didn't deserve it." He played the two games (a season ending doubleheader), getting 6 hits in 8 at bats, and ended up at .406 for the season.[6]

Bob Feller signed up for the military the day after Pearl Harbor, Joe DiMaggio eventually volunteered, but Ted Williams sought a delay so he could put away enough money to provide for his mother, who was divorced

---

2. Geoffrey C. Ward and Ken Burns, *Baseball An Illustrated History* (New York: Alfred A. Knopf, 1994, p. 257.
3. Ibid., p. 257.
4. Ibid., p. 257.
5. Ibid., p.271.
6. Lawrence Ritter and Donald Honig, *The Image of Their Greatness* (New York: Crown Trade Paperbacks, 1992), p. 173.

and a little loony. As usual, he went his own way, angering Boston fans until he became a Navy flier. In all some 340 major leaguers entered the military in World War II as did some 3,000 minor leaguers. Lieutenant Warren Spahn participated in the Battle of the Bulge and Bob Feller served as the chief of a gun crew aboard the battleship *Atlanta*. Feller kept in shape by jogging around the decks of the ship between air attacks.

Ted Williams made his only World Series appearance in 1946 when the heavily favored Red Sox faced the St. Louis Cardinals. The Cards devised a new defense called the "Williams shift," which took advantage of the hitter's pull hitting and inflexibility. The Cards stacked the infield to the right side and Williams refused to adjust, despite Ty Cobb's offer to help him hit to the huge open hole on the left of the infield. Boston ended up losing the seventh game of the series, 4–3, and Williams hit just .200 with no home runs and no RBIs. When it was over he boarded the train for home and later related, "I just broke down and started crying, and I looked up and there was a whole crowd of people watching me through the window."[7]

In 1952 Ted Williams was 33 years old, married, a father and presumably exempt from service in the Korean War. But he had remained in the Marine reserves after World War II and the Marines desperately needed pilots. He was bitter at being recalled and at missing more baseball seasons (he would miss five in all between World War II and Korea). He survived 39 combat missions over Korea, including one fiery crash landing, and when he returned recurrent viruses and severe loss of hearing in one ear plagued him. On his return in August 1953 he hit .407 in the remaining 37 games in which he got to play. He retired in 1960 as perhaps the greatest hitter the game of baseball has seen. After his final at bat he refused to come out of the dugout and acknowledge the crowd.

FROM 1947 TO 1954 the Navy didn't have an augmentation program for line officers to transfer from the reserves to the regular Navy. Therefore Roy Hoffmann was always on somewhat tenuous ground for a Navy career, as the reserves would be the first to go in a drawdown of the military. In the initial year of the transfer program from reserve (USNR) to regular Navy (USN) there were 25 line officers selected—13 aviators and 12 "black shoes" (surface Navy). Roy Hoffmann was one of those 12 black shoes, a boost to his career and assurance that he would have a position in the Navy as long as he performed.

---

7. Ward and Burns, *Baseball*, p. 288.

As his tour at Illinois Tech came close to the end Lieutenant Hoffmann filled out his preference card for destroyer duty. Flag rank was far from his mind; he wanted to command a ship.

IN 1955 THE WORLD of music consisted of sedate early hits "Sincerely" by the McGuire Sisters, "The Ballad of Davy Crockett," by Bill Hayes, "Cherry Pink and Apple Blossom White" by Perez Prado, "Dance With Me Henry" by Georgia Gibbs, "The Yellow Rose of Texas" by Mitch Miller and "Love is a Many-Splendored Thing" by the Four Aces. In July of that year "Rock Around the Clock" by Bill Haley & His Comets shot to Number One on the charts, followed in September by a Pat Boone cover of a Fats Domino tune, "Ain't That a Shame." New artists that year were Chuck Berry and Little Richard; just around the corner was Elvis Presley and the explosion of Rock and Roll, which would forever change what teenagers, listened to; and how they dressed, acted and thought. It was a revolution not only in music but also in the behavior of a generation of America's youth.

Their parents were introduced to James Bond by reading Ian Fleming's *Live and Let Die* and *Moonraker*; they also read *The Quiet American* by Graham Greene, *Andersonville* by MacKinlay Kantor, the then shocking *Lolita* by Vladimir Nabokov, and *79 Park Avenue* by Harold Robbins. There were gritty movies that year: *Blackboard Jungle* with Glen Ford and Sidney Poitier; *East of Eden* and *Rebel Without a Cause* with James Dean,[8] *The Man from Laramie* with James Stewart; *Marty* with Ernest Borgnine and *The Night of the Hunter* with Robert Mitchum and Shelly Winters.

New television shows that year were "The Adventures of Robin Hood" with Richard Greene; "Cheyenne" with Clint Walker; "Gunsmoke" (which was to run for 20 years) with James Arness, Milburn Stone and Amanda Blake; "The Honeymooners" with Jackie Gleason, Art Carney, Audrey Meadows and Joyce Randolph; "The Life and Legend of Wyatt Earp" with Hugh O'Brien; and "The Phil Silvers Show" with Phil Silvers and Paul Ford.

In 1955 First Secretary Nikita Khrushchev emerged as the Soviet Union's power figure. With the ascension of the belligerent Communist, Cold War tensions were destined to increase, culminating with the face off with President Kennedy in the Cuban Missile Crisis of 1962. Nuclear war was considered to be a real threat and everyone lived under its shadow. In June, 53 U.S. cities ran "Operation Alert," a three day mock Hydrogen bomb

---

8. Dean died in a fiery crash while driving his silver Porsche, September 30, 1955.

drill, after which evaluations showed 8.5 million Americans would have died. In July of that year President Eisenhower, who had seen the face of war firsthand, offered the Soviets a disarmament plan that suggested the four nuclear powers (Britain, the U.S., France and the USSR) exchange complete military blueprints and allow periodic aerial inspections to deter surprise attacks. The Soviets failed to respond and squandered the opportunity. The Cold War continued with its threat of massive mutual destruction.

Racial problems in the United States continued to fester just barely beneath the surface, as an entire race was treated under the great American democracy as second-class citizens. The Federal Government made tentative steps to redress the grievances of the black community, but the real problem was based in denial of American ideals by a substantial portion of the balance of the population. Led by individuals that year (Rosa Parks and Martin Luther King, Jr. in particular), the black community began to demand the rights guaranteed them under the United States Constitution.

WHEN ROY HOFFMANN first received his orders to Destroyer Flotilla TWO (DESFLOT TWO) his first reaction was: "Aide and Flag *Secretary*. What the hell is that?" So he called the Bureau of Naval Personnel (BUPERS) to find out what a Flag Secretary did. He was told that this was a sea-going assignment for a demanding admiral who was interested in someone for the position who had been at sea and knew something about ships. He had turned down several candidates before he had gotten to Lieutenant Hoffmann, who was acceptable to him. BUPERS wasn't about to change the orders. As it turned out, it was a good career assignment. DESFLOT TWO was in charge of strategy and tactics relating to the escort of convoys, and the Flag Secretary reviewed all correspondence coming in or going out. The Flag Secretary decided if it needed some kind of action, after which he would handle it himself or assign it to someone for action, and keep a record that it had been done. The Flag Secretary also stood flag watches as the Officer in Tactical Command (OTC), another career enhancing opportunity.

The new orders brought another move, so in September of 1955 the Hoffmanns left Chicago for 74 Shore Drive, a rental, in Middletown, R.I. There they resided while their first owned home was constructed at 290 Middle Road. They felt financially it made sense to build and own a home. Their personal finances had stabilized, it was a good financial move to own, and the home could be readily rented because of the large Navy presence there. The home had three bedrooms, one bath, two fireplaces, a nice family room and a two-car garage underneath. It was a good home for a family with three small children and one on the way. (Hilarie Jean Hoffmann was born October 11, 1955, in Newport, R.I.)

Despite the fact that the Admiral was at sea about 50 per cent of the time, they were not extended tours, and he had more family time. When he was in port he stood one and three watches.

Mary Linn joined an organization for parents of retarded children (she was secretary of the organization). In those days there was neither a school nor classes for retarded children, so the organization started their own. They got a building in a park and rec area that they used for half of the day. They hired a teacher and other parents volunteered as aides. Mary Linn would speak to Navy wives' luncheons to recruit volunteers to help out in the school. They got names of people needing assistance from one of the cooperating school districts; the other district wouldn't help as they said it was too "personal." As busy as she was, she still had time to go bowling and play softball. "I never had a chance to be bored."[9]

Rear Admiral Walter Price was the Commander of DESFLOT TWO. He was succeeded by Rear Admiral Robert Taylor Scott Keith, described by the Admiral as "the epitome of what an admiral should look and act like." Rear Admiral Harold E. "Dutch" Deutermann, a sailor's sailor, succeeded Admiral Keith. Deutermann was different from his predecessors, easier going than Admiral Keith, who could be somewhat aloof.

DESFLOT TWO commanded one transatlantic convoy on a major NATO exercise that involved both the *Nautilus* and *Seawolf*, prototypes for the nuclear submarine force. It was an important test of their ability to protect transatlantic convoys from the latest nuclear submarine capabilities. In those days they were still using the ungainly looking "bloopy bags" for convoy duty. The dirigibles operated out of Brunswick, Maine. Facing heavy winds the blimps could actually lose ground and fall behind the convoy. The submariners soon learned that by going barely over the horizon and putting up their periscope they could spot the bloopy bags, giving away the position of the convoy. DESFLOT TWO countered by positioning the blimp away from the convoy to lure the submarine away.

---

9. Mary Linn won the batting championship in the Rhode Island Women's Hard Pitch Softball League, batting .433 for the year as a catcher. She could also throw a bullet to second base.

Destroyer Flotilla TWO (DESFLOT TWO) personnel, Rear Admiral Walter Price at center, front row. Three staff officers from this photo ultimately made admiral, including Lieutenant Roy F. Hoffmann, seated to the far left, front row.
OFFICIAL U.S. NAVY PHOTO, HOFFMANN COLLECTION

CVE 112, flagship of DESFLOT TWO, with Dealy Class DE 1006 *alongside on fleet exercises.* OFFICIAL U.S. NAVY PHOTO, HOFFMANN COLLECTION

DESFLOT TWO Operations, circa 1954, the "bloopy bags."
OFFICIAL U.S. NAVY PHOTO, HOFFMANN COLLECTION

At sea Lieutenant Hoffmann had valuable experience as OTC, standing many watches. DESFLOT TWO had tactical responsibility to maneuver escorting screen ships in the convoy and to reposition them when submarine contact was made. His watches were normally stood in the Flag plot, which was usually shared with the Combat Information Center (CIC) of the flag ship.

Admiral Price was a light sleeper, and his cabin was right below the Flag plot, so he could hear people walking, chairs moving and conversations above him. One night Lieutenant Hoffmann was standing a steaming watch in CIC when the awakened Admiral Price called up and said, "If you're trying to irritate me you're doing a damn good job." Lieutenant Hoffmann and the others spent the rest of the watch in their socks and in silence.

Lieutenant Hoffmann was the flag OTC one night when the convoy was approaching Newport with the ships still in a dispersed circular formation. Suddenly in the center of the formation, close by, Lieutenant Hoffmann picked up an unidentified radar contact on the screen that he hadn't seen before. "Oh shit!" he thought. "How did *this* happen?" He called up Admiral Price and said, "We have an unidentified contact bearing and range (such and such)."

Admiral Price responded, "*What!* How in the hell could you possibly have missed *that?* Call your relief."

A very dejected Lieutenant Hoffmann sent the boatswain's mate of the watch to get his relief. The relief called up and said, "What in the hell's going on? I'm not due to relieve you yet."

Lieutenant Hoffmann responded, "Don't question me, just get up here."

When his relief arrived Lieutenant Hoffmann explained the situation and the relief took over the watch. Roy Hoffmann went down to his bunk thinking, "My career is over."

He was upset but finally managed to get to sleep. The next thing he knew the boatswain's mate of the watch was shaking his bunk, saying, "Lieutenant Hoffmann, you have the watch."

"What do you mean I've got the watch?" he asked. "I just got down here a couple of hours ago." So he called the flag bridge and said, "What the hell is going on?"

The flag watch officer said, "Don't give me any gas, just get your butt up here."

When he arrived on the bridge he asked the OOD what was going on. He was told, "The old man's so mad he's gone through the entire watch."

Lieutenant Hoffmann picked up the phone, called the admiral and said, "This is Lieutenant Hoffmann reporting. I have the watch, sir."

The admiral says, "Who?"

"Hoffmann."

The admiral responded, "I thought I told you you were relieved."

"You did, sir," Lieutenant Hoffmann replied.

Then the admiral started laughing. "You mean I've gone through the whole watch?"

That was the end of the incident. It turned out a submarine had surfaced in the middle of the task force in preparation for entering port; future admiral Hoffmann's career was back on track.

At the end of 1957 the Admiral received new orders to the USS *Lloyd Thomas* (DDE 764) as Executive Officer (XO). Two months later he was advanced to lieutenant commander and a career that had been stuck on lieutenant for a long time began to take off again. He was a member of the "hump group," that unusually large group of officers that had been commissioned shortly before or immediately after World War II, a group for which promotions were slow.[10]

---

10. The draw down of forces after World War II resulted in many decommissioned ships, severely reducing the number of officer billets available in relation to the number of officers.

The Honor Guard of the USS Lloyd Thomas *(DE 764), 1956.*
OFFICIAL U.S. NAVY PHOTO, HOFFMANN COLLECTION

Before he left for his new assignment on the *Lloyd Thomas*, Admiral Dutch Deutermann took him aside and said, "Roy, I've got one piece of advice for you as you depart for your new ship. No matter how much paperwork you've got piled up on your desk, get up off your butt and get around the ship at least twice a day. If you have to deep six that paper—do it."

Admiral Hoffmann emphasized the advice in an interview with this author. "You can't be a good XO without knowing the ship and the crew," he said. "Get down to engineering, get down to the fire room and talk to the watch there, get to the sonar room and the fire control center (the main battery plot). Talk to the seamen and find out what's going on in their lives. Find out what motivations they do and don't have. Talk to the chief petty officers—have lunch with the chiefs. You can't be their buddy, but the crew will respect you, even if they don't want you around, because you are showing an appreciation for their job and in the readiness of the ship."

A SEVERE RECESSION in the United States, the worst since World War II, ushered in 1958. Almost seven per cent of the workforce was unemployed, with the bedrock of the economy, manufacturing, the hardest hit.

Internationally, Khrushchev ousted Bulganin in the USSR and assumed leadership of both the Communist Party and the state, which had been separated since the death of Stalin in 1953. Vice President Richard Nixon's motorcade was attacked during a goodwill tour of Latin America; the incident became one of Nixon's "crises" about which he would later write. In August Communist China bombarded the Nationalist garrison on Quemoy, a small island off the mainland. In response the Eisenhower administration moved the Seventh Fleet into the Formosa Straits.

In November the Democrats solidified their hold on national life by taking control of the House (282 seats out of 435) and the Senate (62 out of 96 seats). They would not relinquish that control until 1994.

Rock and Roll continued to co-exist with more sedate forms of music, but as the "Baby Boom" generation increased its buying power Rock and Roll won out. "Nel Blu Dipinto di Blu (Volare)" by Domenico Modugno, "Sugartime" by the McGuire Sisters, and "Catch a Falling Star" by Perry Como were being overwhelmed by "It's Only Make Believe" by Conway Twitty, "Poor Little Fool" by Ricky Nelson, "Hard Headed Woman" and "Don't" by Elvis Presley, "Great Balls of Fire" by Jerry Lee Lewis, "Sweet Little Sixteen" by Chuck Berry and "Rock-in' Robin" by Bobby Day. Presley made the big news that year after being drafted, by actually going in the Army and receiving no special treatment while doing so. He had his head shaved, went to Germany, and returned having lost much of the momentum generated by his earlier explosion onto the music scene. Meanwhile, Jerry Lee Lewis married his 13-year-old cousin, a harbinger of what many Rock and Roll stars would bring to the culture of the United States.

New television shows that year were, "Peter Gunn" with Craig Stevens, "The Rifleman" with Chuck Connors and Johnny Crawford, "77 Sunset Strip" with Efrem Zimbalist, Jr. and Roger Smith, and "Wanted: Dead or Alive" with Steve McQueen.

THE USS *LLOYD THOMAS* (DD 764), a *Gearing* class destroyer, was commissioned in 1947, J.I. Cone commanding. She was named for Lieutenant j.g. Lloyd Thomas, a naval aviator who lost his life fighting in the Battle of Midway during World War II. He was awarded the Navy Cross while serving as a pilot in

Torpedo Squadron 6 based off the USS *Enterprise*. In 1949, after conversion to a hunter-killer destroyer at the San Francisco Navy Yard, *Lloyd Thomas* joined the Atlantic Fleet, home ported at Newport, R.I.[11]

Lieutenant Commander Hoffmann felt good about the orders to the *Lloyd Thomas*, as it was a stepping-stone to command. Another advantage was that with a homeport of Newport the Hoffmanns could stay in their home. Shortly after their arrival their last daughter, Emilie Frances Hoffmann was born, on February 3, 1958.

Captain of the ship was Commander Clarence "Breezy" Brooks.[12] He commanded a ship that materially was not in very good shape. There were problems in engineering and the ventilation system was deficient. It was also a ship to which things just seemed to happen. The ship had run aground while mooring in Narragansett Bay, just before Roy Hoffmann came aboard.[13] Some time after Lieutenant Commander Hoffmann reported aboard he got a call from the Officer of the Deck (OOD). "We've had a light oil spill," the OOD said.

The spill had occurred while they were pumping out the bilges into a floating container called a sludge ring. Executive Officer (XO) Hoffmann only lived two miles from the destroyer berth, and when he got within sight of the harbor he saw that the slick extended from the berth to the ocean. "You said you had a *light* spill?" he asked the OOD. The *Lloyd Thomas* was outboard of a destroyer tender, which was covered with the black oil on the port side. Despite advance warning of a severe nor'easter, the crew had not moved the sludge ring to a secure leeward position.

In those days they threw out carbonized sand on the oil slick, which absorbed the oil, causing it to sink with the sand. Unfortunately it didn't remove the oil; it only got the problem out of sight. It worked fine except every time a ship got underway in the harbor its screws stirred up the mess at the bottom, bringing it to the surface again.

The *Lloyd Thomas* also had a post office robbery on board the ship, which had to have been one of the more unusual crimes committed aboard a U.S. Navy ship—the classic "inside job." A Laundryman from the ship committed suicide; it seemed like it was always something.

The *Lloyd Thomas* was a DDE, an antisubmarine warfare ship. At the time the Soviet Navy was the largest threat to the U.S. Navy, and as a result

---

11. The ship was decommissioned in 1973 when she was transferred to Taiwan and renamed the *Dang Yang*. She was eventually sunk as an artificial reef.
12. His nickname came from his track star days in college.
13. Narragansett Bay is a deep inlet of the Atlantic southwest of Newport.

the ship spent a great deal of time "boring holes" in the Atlantic Ocean. Much of 1958 was spent in the Caribbean with Operation Springboard in the spring, and in refresher training in September and October. In 1959 the ship participated in hunter-killer training off Norfolk; made a summer cruise to Quebec to open up the St. Lawrence Seaway; and participated in NATO operations in the Atlantic.

The *Lloyd Thomas* was a great learning experience for Roy Hoffmann. Ship handling was not one of Breezy Brooks' skills, and he increasingly turned to his XO to handle the ship. Newport is not an easy port to get into, particularly in the winter, when you have fog, strong currents and heavy wind to contend with. The destroyers normally made up to mooring buoys in Narragansett Bay, usually in nests.[14]

Landing the ship meant controlling 3,000 tons of momentum coming into a pier or mooring buoy. One must always be aware of the three elements of ship handling: Wind, current (seas), and visibility. A destroyer is a twin-screwed ship with a tremendous amount of power relative to her size. With rudders sitting behind each screw the power serves as an advantage in ship handling. The ship is landed using the engines in opposition in concert with the rudder. For example, the OOD will give a command of "Full left rudder, starboard engine ahead two thirds, port engine back one third." The helmsman then repeats the language back exactly.

The helmsman controls the rudder directly but the engine command is telegraphed to the engine room, where they will respond, but after a delay. Landing involves working with the chief engineer and the other engineers to accommodate for the delay. To preserve the engineering plant you don't want to go from an ahead bell to an astern bell without coming through stop first. That gives the engineers time to control the steam pressure. Of course, in an emergency that isn't possible—if an emergency back full order is given then the engineers must ignore the stop.

On the bridge, mooring requires discipline, teamwork and a helmsman you can count on. If you are on the wing of the bridge when it's raining and windy you need a strong voice to give commands and the helmsman

---

14. The Admiral did not share much of his Navy life with his family. Once Breezy Brooks cornered Mary Linn at a party and said, "I bet you wonder why I let Roy get underway and bring the ship in so much. It's because I want him to have the experience." Mary Linn later asked her husband, "Do you do a lot of the ship handling?" "Well, yes I do," he replied. "Is it because Breezy wants you to have the experience?" "No," her husband replied, "it's because he can't do it."

needs one back to you. You also have to be in good communication with the forecastle in case you want them to let go the hook (anchor) in heavy winds or currents. Seldom if ever do you have the same landing—currents, wind and visibility will be different every day. The Admiral has come into Newport where the fog was so heavy you literally couldn't see anything in front of you and were reliant on the men on the pier shouting directions to you. Eventually you got a reputation in the fleet as either a good or bad ship handler. It is safe to say Roy Hoffmann was legendary among his peers in the Navy for his ship handling ability.

Roy Hoffmann personally and professionally got along well with his commanding officer, but there was a problem between the division commander, Commodore Clark, and Breezy. Clark and Brooks had had a run-in before. Clark had given Breezy either a poor or mediocre fitness report that Clark felt should have prevented Brooks from ever having a destroyer command. Unfortunately, the *Lloyd Thomas* was the flagship when Clark arrived as division commander. So Breezy Brooks ended up as Commodore Clark's flagship CO—the last man Clark wanted to see in that position.

The situation was like oil and water; they didn't get along at all. It was more the Commodore than Breezy. The *Lloyd Thomas's* XO found himself caught in the middle between the two of them. Commodore Clark was an excellent mariner and tactician but he had a short fuse and minimal tolerance for personal deficiency. The Commodore would tell XO Hoffmann to do something and Roy Hoffmann would say, "I'll tell the Captain." He would then go to Breezy who would say, "Is he giving you orders again?"

"Yes, sir," was the response.

"Well, don't worry about it," Breezy, who understood the situation, would say.

Commander Bob Byer relieved Breezy Brooks. Byer was a highly experienced destroyer man and an authority on antisubmarine warfare (ASW). As it turned out Commander Byer had some health issues that affected his stamina, which again provided an opportunity for his Executive Officer to become a more proficient ASW officer.

Tracking submarines required stamina, particularly if you were on a submarine contact. Sometimes the tracking can go on for days, through often-rough weather in the Atlantic. Roy Hoffmann had the stamina to stay in CIC with the conn, or supervising young officers with the conn. You had to keep the contact out of the baffles; if he got on your stern you lost him. A primary submarine tactic was to maneuver the tracking ship into heavy seas, which would cause the ship to pitch violently, lifting the bow out of the water, causing the loss of sonar contact.

ASW operations were hard on the crew.[15] Hard rudder turns caused the ship to roll violently in rough weather. In the wardroom and mess decks they would rig a "fiddle board," which was a wood board that sits about three inches above the table. The fiddle board had holes cut in it to hold plates and glasses in place in foul weather. Without it the food would go flying across the room. Sometimes the only food you could eat was a sandwich. As the Admiral puts it, "You haven't lived until you've been aboard a destroyer in rough weather trying to eat."

They had stanchions set up in the wardroom to hold on in rough weather. In the mess decks they had benches instead of chairs. If the sailor on one end started sliding "the poor bastard on the other end would get shoved off."

Sleeping was just as difficult. They had straps to fasten themselves in during rough seas; otherwise you could go flying out of your bunk. As the XO, Roy Hoffmann had his own cabin. The CO had two cabins, an in-port cabin and a sea cabin. The sea cabin was on the bridge level just aft of the bridge. The XO's living quarters were the same size as the other staterooms, except it wasn't shared with another officer. It contained a small locker, writing desk, a loose chair and a safe. The XO had control of the alcohol and drugs in the safe, plus any miscellaneous cash.

Accommodations aboard a destroyer were austere. It was before general air conditioning. What air conditioning existed was reserved exclusively for the electronic equipment. The wardroom was where the officers went for camaraderie, for rest and for meals. Stewards served the meals (Stewards Mate was a regular Navy rating), and there was a certain decorum observed in the wardroom—it wasn't necessarily a place to lounge around.

The stewards were a mix of blacks or Philippinos. Some of the stewards hated the duty and some liked it (not unlike the rest of the enlisted in the other divisions). Probably some were assigned against their will. The head of the wardroom mess was usually a CPO or first class petty officer. It was his responsibility to purchase supplies for the officers' meals. The CO ate in the wardroom and always had a personal steward. One officer was usually appointed president of the mess and he worked with the stewards.

Even in the late 1950s there was racial strife aboard the ship. It wasn't on the surface, but it was there. If you wanted to really know what was going

---

15. That, along with the harsh Newport winters caused a low ship-over (retention) rate.

on in the ship the steward was a good sounding board. If you could develop a personal relationship with the steward, often he would open up and tell you what was really going on with race relations.

Roy Hoffmann once asked a black steward, "Why do so many blacks live in Boston?" It was 50 miles away from Newport, through heavy traffic. "I don't understand it," he said. Newport was ostensibly open minded about racial issues (a supposed example of "tolerance"). Sailors (black and white) mixed in the bars and the Admiral had never observed any problems.

The steward replied, "No, there isn't a problem in the bars, but let me give you an example. In [he named a popular restaurant], if I go in there I'm the last one to get waited on. Even if the place is empty when I get there, when someone white comes in that's the one they will wait on first. It's almost that way anywhere in the town." There were two standards for service—one for white and one for black.

Blacks would come up from the south with their families to serve on the ship and couldn't find affordable living accommodations. In the winter there were cases of children with frozen fingers and toes from the cold as the parents were forced to spend the night in their car, inadequately clothed, without proper jackets. Sometimes the children would end up in the Navy hospital.

It wasn't necessarily widespread, but, according to Hoffmann, "when they tell you all the racism is in the south, that's a bunch of baloney."

AT THE START OF 1959, after a two-year guerilla campaign in Cuba, Fidel Castro's revolutionaries overthrew the dictatorship of Fulgencio Batista. Castro was a classic Communist dictator, and his brutal tactics solidified his hold on the impoverished nation. Somewhat astoundingly he has been the darling of American liberals, who have been his apologists since 1959.[16] He started his reign of terror executing by firing squad 621 "war criminals." International outrage stopped him initially, but he was back at it by the end of the year.

In 1959 both Alaska and Hawaii were admitted to the Union as the 49th and 50th states. Alaska is a huge state, comprising nearly 20 per cent of the landmass of the contiguous 48 states combined.

The Soviet nuclear threat loomed ever large, and in response the United States began construction of a Ballistic Missile Early Warning System that

---

16. Even former presidents aren't immune; Jimmy Carter has visited the island and has been one of the chief apologists.

would eventually cost $1 billion. In July Vice President Richard Nixon had his first face-to-face meeting with Nikita Khrushchev in Moscow. They engaged in a daylong political debate in front of an exhibit of U.S. household appliances. Nixon reasonably asked, "Would it not be better to compete in the relative merits of washing machines than in the strength of rockets?" Nixon was generally credited with winning the debate. At the invitation of President Eisenhower Premier Khrushchev visited the U.S. later in the year. Nothing substantive happened, other than Khrushchev voicing his disappointment because the Secret Service wouldn't let him visit Disneyland.

On July 8, 1959, the first U.S. servicemen were killed in Vietnam at Bien Hoa, South Vietnam, by the Vietminh (the forerunner of the Viet Cong).[17] The Cold War would end up being fought in surrogate countries with America backing the right of self determination and the Soviets and Chinese backing usually vicious Communist regimes.

Popular music that year included "Smoke Gets in Your Eyes" by the Platters, "Mack the Knife" and "Dream Lover" by Bobby Darin, "Heartaches by the Number" by Guy Mitchell, and "Donna" by Ritchie Valens. By the time "Donna" was released Valens had died along with Buddy Holly and J. P. Richardson (the "Big Bopper") in a fiery plane crash outside Mason City, Iowa, while flying to a concert.

People read *Advise and Consent* by Allen Drury, *Goldfinger* by Ian Fleming, *My Wicked, Wicked Ways* by Errol Flynn[18] and *The Status Seekers* by Vance Packard. At the movies they saw *Anatomy of a Murder* with James Stewart and Lee Remick; *Ben-Hur* with Charlton Heston; *Journey to the Center of the Earth* with James Mason and Pat Boone; *Rio Bravo* with John Wayne, Dean Martin and Ricky Nelson; and *Some Like It Hot* with Jack Lemmon, Tony Curtis, Marilyn Monroe and George Raft.

New television shows that year were "Bat Masterson" with Gene Barry; "Bonanza" with Lorne Greene, Michael Landon, Dan Blocker and Pernell Roberts;[19] "The Many Loves of Dobie Gillis" with Dwayne Hickman and Bob Denver; "Rawhide" with Eric Fleming and Clint Eastwood; "The Twilight Zone" with Rod Serling as host; and "The Untouchables" with Robert Stack.

---

17. The soldiers were Major Dale Buis and Master Sergeant Chester Ovnard. By year-end there were some 760 U.S. Military personnel in Vietnam.

18. Flynn's wicked ways led to his death by heart attack in 1959, probably speeded along by heavy drinking. One of the handsome men of Hollywood, by the time of his death he was bloated and dissipated. His many extramarital affairs led to the expression "In Like Flynn."

19. "Bonanza" would have an incredible run on television, from September 1959 to 1973.

IN JUNE OF 1959 Lieutenant Commander Roy Hoffmann received a new set of orders and left the *Lloyd Thomas*. The orders entailed a move for the family from Portsmouth, R.I. to Falls Church, Virginia. In August he reported to the Chief of Naval Personnel, Bureau of Naval Personnel (BUPERS) in Washington, D.C., as a Destroyer Placement Officer for the Atlantic Fleet. BUPERS is a powerful bureaucracy, which heavily influences the careers of every officer in the Navy.

The Hoffmanns rented their home in Portsmouth to another Navy family and rented from a Navy family in Falls Church. Each family had a two-year tour of duty so it worked out well. The home in Falls Church was in a mixed Navy and civilian area. Mary Linn remained busy with Harriet and raising the other children. At this point the girls adjusted well to the moves and even looked forward to them.[20] The girls were registered in a Catholic school and the family settled in. It turned out to be a very demanding job, so it was not family enhancing. Eight-hour days and five-day workweeks really didn't exist for detailers and placement officers in BUPERS, if you wanted to do the job right. As always, Mary Linn, if called on, could handle most of the household duties, except, she says, "The only thing I won't fool with is electricity."

BUPERS was located at the Navy Annex on the Pentagon side of the Potomac River, on a hill overlooking the Pentagon. The Annex was located next to Arlington National Cemetery, on Columbia Pike Avenue. At the time BUPERS shared the building with the Marines, who now have sole occupancy of the building, BUPERS having moved to Millington, Tennessee. The Chief of Naval Personnel at the time was Vice Admiral William Smedberg II and the assistant chief was Rear Admiral B.J. Semmes, two of the Navy's finest.

BUPERS was Lieutenant Commander Hoffmann's first introduction to the inside of the Navy bureaucracy, and after checking around he found it was a very good career assignment.[21] The Navy wanted for the position an executive officer who had just completed a successful tour, one who had a significant amount of sea duty on destroyers, and one who understood the administration and organization of a destroyer.

---

20. Once one of her daughters announced to Mary Linn, "There's a moving van at a house down the street. When are *we* going to get to move?" Eventually their attitudes changed as they got to high school age and didn't want to leave their friends.

21. Shore assignments can be career enhancing, neutral or negative. This was definitely a career enhancing assignment, made possible by a good record as the XO of the *Lloyd Thomas*.

The job turned out to be not only demanding but one that carried tremendous responsibility. Not only were you handling the careers of young Navy officers you were also responsible for getting the right people into the right ship at the right time.

There were two stages involved in the assignment of officers: The detailers and the placement officers. Detailers were assigned to desks by rank, from ensign through commander. The senior detailer is a captain and is also the captain detailer. The staff in the CNO's office handled flag officers.

Both detailers and placement officers spent hours reviewing performance records of junior and senior officers. The detailer would be notified when officers came up for reassignment, and he would then go through the record to try and place the individual in a good position. He would then send a recommendation along with the officer's folder to the placement officer.[22]

All commissioned officers filled out preference cards for their desired assignments. They tried at BUPERS to give them good advice. If, for example, a young lieutenant j.g. puts in for shore duty, because he wants to be with his wife, the detailer is probably going to pick up the phone and say, "Hey look Jones (or Smith), we understand where you're coming from, but if you're serious about a career in the Navy, you're going to make a big mistake by requesting shore duty." Navy careers are made at sea.

Similarly, it was best to leave wide latitude to the Navy for assignment. If you put in for a department head on destroyer you would be well advised not to ask for a specific homeport. If you were willing to go anywhere the detailer would look at the card and say, "This is my kind of man (or woman in today's Navy)—he's willing to go anywhere."

The detailer's job was to try and get the individual into the best job he could to enhance his career. His objective was to take care of the individual, and he could best do that by getting the officer a good seagoing assignment (a fleet billet). He would try and get the best people into destroyers, because there were not enough destroyer billets to go around and he couldn't get them all in.[23] The next tier of duty would be a cruiser, battleship or carrier, not as desirable because a young officer would have more responsibility on a destroyer.

There was an informal network in which the detailers worked, and that may be best described as an officer's "fleet reputation." If a detailer thought

---

22. The description that follows relates to the surface Navy, as that is what the Admiral's section handled. There were comparable sections that handled the submariners and tactical air billets for the aviators.

23. Most destroyers had 18 to 20 officer billets available.

he remembered something about an officer he could go to another department in BUPERS where track was kept of the famous and the infamous. Your fleet reputation could be either good or bad. The detailer would call down and ask, "Do you have a 'flag' on this officer?"

The response would normally be, "You know we can't discuss this."

"I know that," the detailer might respond, "all I want to know is: Do you have a flag on him?" If the detailer wanted to get a fitness report on one of the famous or infamous it had to ultimately be approved by the Chief of Naval Personnel. Records were tightly controlled.

When the jacket did come up it might disclose, as an example, that the officer was charged and court martialed for homosexuality, but beat the rap. Technically he couldn't be denied the assignment, but his fleet reputation was damaged by the charge. The same was true of poor ship handlers and known alcoholics, to cite other examples. Neither would necessarily show on the official record but would be part of the officer's fleet reputation.

The detailer would then send the recommendation for assignment to the placement desk for decision. Organizationally, there was a commander who had the title of Destroyer Placement Officer. Across the hall was his counterpart, the Submarine Placement Officer. If there was a dispute between the detailer and the placement officer the file went up to the senior detailer in charge, a Navy captain. He would then make the decision except in the case of command decisions, which had to go through a board.

The placement officer's interest was to enhance war readiness by getting the best officer he can onto a ship, without ruining an officer's career. The placement officer's job is to do the best he can for the command. He regularly communicated with the COs and XOs of fleet ships. The fleet then was larger than today's fleet, and Placement Officer Hoffmann had around 125 destroyers to work. The homeports they mainly had to work with were Newport, Norfolk, Charleston, Mayport, Key West, New London and Philadelphia.

At least twice a year the placement officers tried to get out to the home ports and visit with the COs. Often the detailer would go with him to talk to the individuals while the placement officer talked to the command. While visiting with the COs the placement officer could suggest to the captain that he "fleet-up" one of the men in his command, meaning advance an officer already on the ship. As an example, the CIC officer might become the operations officer on the ship.

Typically, the CO will ask, "How long can I keep him?"

The response might be, "Well, you can have him for at least a year."

"I don't want an ops officers for just a year."

"Maybe we can work out a deal to leave him 18 months but you can't have him any longer. The detailer won't put up with any longer because he wants to move him to a higher position." And so the negotiations went.

Sometimes the CO might have a complaint. "You sent this damn Drama major as the engineering officer. I've given him a chance but he just doesn't have it. He still can't tell a compressor from a turbine."

It was during this period of the Admiral's career that he acquired the nickname "Nails," as in hard as. The MSO (small craft) placement officer first started calling him that, for his hard and demanding performance evaluations. The BUPERS personnel spent a lot of time reading fitness reports. There are some funny and apocryphal evaluations that always circulate, such as "Ensign Jones is profiting from his past mistakes; unfortunately he has succeeded in emulating all known mistakes of former junior officers and is adept at innovating new ones to his historical repertoire of blunders. He is available for reassignment." Or: "His men would follow him anywhere, but only out of curiosity." Or: "Since my last report he has reached rock bottom and has started to dig." Or: "Sets low personal standards and consistently fails to achieve them"; Or: "The only ship I would recommend this officer for is citizenship"; Or: "Works well when under constant supervision and when cornered like a rat in a trap."

There were other funny stories. Once a newly commissioned Navy officer, the son of a prominent politician whose name would be instantly recognizable, asked for an assignment to a minesweeper. Placement Officer Hoffmann took the request and handed it to the minesweeper desk and they assigned the officer to a minesweeper. The next thing they knew there was a congressional inquiry. It turned out his wife (they were newly married) had written to their congressman complaining that she couldn't understand how her husband could be assigned to such a menial task. She thought he should have gotten a much more responsible assignment.[24]

A detailer got the inquiry and as a joke put a memo in the file saying, "We should acknowledge we made a big mistake. We should have assigned him to a stud farm in Nebraska and ordered his wife to the command of a destroyer. She is a real tiger." It was funny, that is, until the memo ended up

---

24. Something like the commanding officer of an aircraft carrier was the joke at BUPERS.

on some congressman's desk. The Chief of Naval Personnel called in the detailers and placement officers and was about half way through chewing them out when he broke out laughing, got up out of his chair and walked out. The congressman was probably as amused as they were at BUPERS.

Other duties at BUPERS included the "Tombstone Watch," representing the CNO at the many funerals that go on at Arlington; and the "Wallflower" assignments at places like the White House and other official functions. "They normally took the tall, handsome and sharp looking guys that wouldn't stumble on the carpet and could make small talk with the guests," the Admiral now says. "I never made that."

When John F. Kennedy was inaugurated he wanted the PT 109 crew at the inauguration. BUPERS put out a notice to find them and about three times the number that had actually been on PT 109 responded. They all got to go.

Congressional complaints were a common headache. "Why hasn't Johnny made CNO yet?" the joke went. "He's been in the Navy four years already."

On another occasion a Navy multi-engine plane crashed into the Sierra Madre Mountains in Spain and disappeared. Eventually two crewmen walked out, but all the rest were lost. The Department of Defense had issued a strong directive to BUPERS that no information would be given out pending notification of the next of kin.

Roy Hoffmann happened to have the duty after the tragedy. He got a call from a southern farmer who said he got a notice from the Defense Department that his son, a boatswain's mate, was killed in the crash in Spain.

Knowing he was breaking the rules, but in sympathy with him, Roy responded, "Yes, sir, I regret to inform you that the message you have is accurate. It was a tragedy and I have no way of expressing my sympathy for what happened."

The farmer replied, "These are all decisions the Lord makes that we don't have much control over. But, I'm just calling to see how the rest of the men made out." He had accepted the fact he had lost his son, but was very much concerned for the rest of the crew.

Another plane went down with the entire Navy band aboard; two survived that crash as well. Air controllers in Buenos Aires had directed the plane right into Sugarloaf Mountain in a dense fog. The pilots were following the air controllers' instructions when they plowed into the mountain. The impact broke off the tail and it spiraled into the harbor. It was in the tail section where two sonarmen survived.

As his time at BUPERS came close to an end, Roy Hoffmann requested a destroyer command as his next assignment. One of the advantages of being in BUPERS is, with approval, you could write your own orders. It turned out the *Dealey* class (DE) USS *Cromwell* was available. As a relatively new class of ship it was an attractive command.

Then Lieutenant Commander Harry Train had been a shipmate of Roy Hoffmann on the *Hubbard*, and was now on the submarine side of BUPERS. The Navy was first going to send the Admiral down to ASW School in Florida before he reported to the *Cromwell*. "I don't know why the hell they've got me ordered down to ASW School, I've already taken the course and I just came from a DDE."

Harry Train asked him if he wanted to go to a submarine course instead. The Admiral responded that he didn't think he would be very welcome in the submarine school since he was going back to destroyers. But he said, "I think that would be a pretty good move. I'd learn more about submarines there than I ever would at ASW School."

Harry Train responded, "Do you really want to go?"

"Well, yes, but I don't think I can get in."

Train responded, "Sure you can—if you want to go, I'll write it." Which he did. Roy Hoffmann became one of the few destroyer men to go through the two-week PCO and PXO submarine school at New London.[25]

---

25. Admiral Harry Train interview, October 10, 2006.

6

IN COMMAND

USS Cromwell (DE 1014)

The USS *Cromwell* (DE 1014) was named after Captain John Philip Cromwell, who commanded Submarine Divisions 43 and 44 during World War II. Cromwell was aboard the *Sculpin* (SS 191) with his pennant when on November 19, 1943 the *Sculpin* received severe damage from enemy depth charges off Truk. According to the ship's history, "Captain Cromwell elected to remain on board rather than risk capture and endanger the security of the submarine tactics and strategy, scheduled fleet movements, and the important plans for the invasion of the Gilbert Islands, which he might have been forced to reveal under torture or drugs." For his bravery Captain Cromwell was posthumously awarded the Medal of Honor.

The *Cromwell* was built by Bath Iron Works in Bath, Maine and commissioned in 1954 with Lieutenant Commander E. J. Cummings, Jr. commanding. She was a *Dealey* class destroyer escort, 315 feet long, 37 feet at the beam, and had a top speed of approximately 25 knots. She had one engine room, two boilers, one screw and twin balanced rudders beneath the water line.

Lieutenant Commander Roy Hoffmann was familiar with the *Cromwell* from his days at DESFLOT TWO. He had taken orders to the then captain of the *Cromwell*, instructing him to get underway to assist the *Andrea Doria*, which was in distress and sinking. He also knew and liked the other commanding officers in the escort squadron.

The orders to the *Cromwell* pleased both Roy and Mary Linn Hoffmann, and there was a lot of excitement with his first command. Mary Linn related her husband's reaction: "He was extremely pleased with the new orders, although he

USS Cromwell *(DE 1014) and* USS Hammerberg *(DE 1021) steaming side by side, Panama Canal, September 1961.* OFFICIAL U.S. NAVY PHOTO, HOFFMANN COLLECTION

is not one to show it. It was a happy time for all of us." The new command meant they could move back into their home, a familiar place with great neighbors. Harriet seemed glad to be back and her parents were pleased that she recognized the home as one she had been in before. The other girls got involved with Girl Scouts, got into music and played musical instruments in bands.

Roy Hoffmann was fortunate to have for his first command an outstanding wardroom and crew. Layton Dale Smith was the XO, a capable officer with a marvelous sense of humor. He and his wife Rose became lifelong friends of the Hoffmanns. Already aboard when Roy Hoffmann arrived were Bill Dudley, Joe Roxe, Greg Nolan and J. Kent Hewitt, all of whom were interviewed for this book.[1] The arrival of Roy Hoffmann, ac-

---

1. Much of the material for this section of Chapter 6 was taken from interviews with the Admiral and Mary Linn Hoffmann; and interviews with Captain Louis Colbus, USN, Ret., June 16, 2006; Bill Dudley, November 20, 2005; J. Kent Hewitt, September 13, 2005; and Joe Roxe, September 13, 2006. All specific quotations and references come from those interviews.

The responsibility of command: Waiting to come alongside for an underway replenishment, Cromwell, *1960.* GREG NOLAN PHOTO

cording to these men, was a breath of fresh air for the officers and men of the *Cromwell.*

Hoffmann's predecessor on the ship was a controversial figure lacking people skills, unsure of himself and exceedingly tough on everyone on the ship. "In a very short time morale of the ship went from very sluggish and undesirable [under the former CO] to a ship's crew that was ready to do anything for our commanding officer."[2]

One example of Roy Hoffmann's predecessor as CO will suffice. Often the destroyers would nest together and as the CO would depart they would sound

---

2. J. Kent Hewitt interview, September 13, 2005. Hewitt is a Cornell graduate who spent his three years of active duty in the Navy aboard the *Cromwell.* He started in the gunnery department of the ship and eventually became the gunnery officer. After the Navy he went to medical school and became an M.D. specializing in gastroenterology.

two bells on the quarterdeck and announce, "*Cromwell*, departing." Once, when the former CO departed, a cheer went up from everyone before the mast. The captain turned around and stormed up to the then XO, a nice guy named E. P. Fontaine (who went on to become an admiral). The CO put the XO in hack over the incident, which meant he was restricted to the ship, a particularly onerous punishment as he was married and lived in Newport. The preceding is an example cited by Joe Roxe of the tension and difficulty that existed on the ship before the arrival of Roy Hoffmann. In part the good feelings that existed toward the new skipper came from ill feeling toward the previous CO, but he would still have to perform to maintain the respect of the officers and men.[3]

The new CO had barely reported aboard when the ship deployed for Operation Unitos II on August 7, 1961. The U.S. had for the preceding four years sent a task group consisting of four destroyer escorts, a submarine, and a patrol squadron of three or four P2V aircraft to South American waters to conduct combined air/surface antisubmarine warfare (ASW) operations with their Latin American counterparts. Often the American ships operated with Latin American ships that would have been scrapped long ago by more modern navies.[4]

Unitos II, which lasted three months, was an extended cruise with minimal logistic support, often conducted under severe weather conditions. The long and arduous exercises at sea (it was 1,900 miles from Newport, Rhode Island, to Trinidad, transiting each coast) were accompanied by equally demanding social events ashore. It was a test of the new captain and a tremendous learning experience. Before it was over there were two incidents that put in jeopardy his future career advancement.

The genesis of the combined operations was the experience of the Allies during World War II, when German submarines had operated in South American waters, disrupting and sinking Allied shipping. The threat from the long range and effective Soviet submarine fleet was even greater than

---

3. Joe Roxe interview, September 13, 2006. Roxe is a Princeton graduate, who was assigned to the *Cromwell* after completing OCS in April of 1959. His initial commitment was for three years, but he was extended due to the Berlin Crisis. After completion of his Navy service he received an MBA from Harvard Business School. His early career was spent in the oil business in Mobile, and he currently owns his own investment holding company in New York.

4. There was a huge discrepancy among the various navies, from very capable, to an almost laughable "McHale's Navy" mentality. The U.S. was allied with the Latin American nations through the Rio Pact; the Inter-American Defense System assisted them by providing ships, aircraft and submarines by sale or loan. At the time of Unitos II, Chili had the most professional Navy.

that presented by Admiral Donitz in World War II. The vulnerability of the Panama Canal during war from sabotage or attack, and the necessity to move the vast natural resources of the continent would vastly increase ship traffic on the west and east coasts of South America, exposing that shipping to enemy attack.[5] Thus it was strategically important to have South American allies with enhanced antisubmarine capabilities.

Operation Unitos II was under the command of Rear Admiral Louis A. Bryan, Commander of the Atlantic Fleet's Destroyer Flotilla Two. The task force flagship was the USS *Norfolk* (DL 1). She was accompanied by the destroyer escorts *Courtney*, *Cromwell* and *Hammerberg*; the submarine *Clamagore*, and P2V Neptune aircraft from Patrol Squadron II. On the trip down the west coast the American Navy ships conducted ASW operations with units of the navies of Venezuela, Colombia, Ecuador, Peru and Chili. After a transit through the Magellan Straits to the Atlantic Ocean, the American Navy conducted ASW exercises along the east coast with navy units from Argentina, Uruguay and Brazil.

The *Cromwell* was ideally suited for ASW warfare. The ship had a large hurricane bow, an advantage in rough weather. In heavy seas the ship didn't plunge into the sea; rather it was designed to ride over the waves. Good ASW ships have a shallow counter.[6] The *Cromwell* had a normal hull configuration from the bow to about two-thirds aft, where instead of a straight keel all the way back it curved sharply up, with a shallower draft at the after third of the ship. The hull configuration was an advantage in that the ship could make turns with a submarine, which planed under water as an aircraft would. With the shallow counter the *Cromwell* could make a complete circle in about 240 yards. The disadvantage of the shallow counter came in heavy seas as they kicked the stern around like a yo-yo, causing the Second Division sailors to occasionally get thrown out of their bunks. In contrast, a destroyer (DD) was faster but couldn't turn as fast, nor could it ride the heavy seas as well. A favorite tactic of a submarine was to head into heavy seas where a destroyer would have to slow down to maintain sonar contact, taking away her advantage of speed.

Reminiscent of the *Harry E. Hubbard*, there was a mascot aboard the *Cromwell*. On the latter ship it was a stuffed seagull the crew had named "Poncho." Captain Hoffmann's first encounter with Poncho was when, "I opened the door [to the head] and there sits the damn bird."

---

5. The important strategic asset of the Panama Canal was turned over to Panamanian control, due to an initiative by President Jimmy Carter.

6. That part of a ship's stern from the water line to the extreme outward swell.

USS Cromwell, *"The Starboard Engine," Panama Canal, 1961.* GREG NOLAN PHOTO

The first port was a logistics stop at Trinidad, which had an almost idyllic bay with crystal clear water. Located nearby was a former United Fruit plantation crawling with snakes, where the fruit trees were then growing wild. At the officers' club they had a beautiful Macaw that had been there at least since World War II. In the intervening years the bird had picked up an affinity for beer, which would lead him to perch on the table and put his beak into your beer glass. He spoke a few words, perhaps slurred after an evening of drinking with the boys.

Next port of call was Puerto Cabello, Venezuela, land of orchids, beautiful beaches and petroleum. The socialistic country required that a pilot guide the ship in for docking, a good thing as it turned out. As they were going in the XO/navigator positioned the ship on the chart provided by the port caption. With some alarm the XO told the pilot he was taking them out of the channel. "No, no," the pilot responded, "chart no good, channel not where it says." By then the XO was having a fit, but the ship finally got tied up, after which the XO went up to Captain Hoffmann and said, "I want to show you where we are." According to the chart they were moored on land, high and dry. Most of the charts they were using had been originally drafted by Sir Francis Drake and never properly updated.

Next stop was Cartegena, Colombia, a beautiful place where there were fortifications left over from the days of the conquistadors in this most Spanish of all Latin American cities. They spoke the same Castilian as in central and northern Spain, and the women were beautiful and popular with the bachelors aboard the U.S. Navy ships. Unfortunately for the men, Spanish custom called for a chaperone to accompany the young women on dates.

On August 29, 1961, the small task group arrived at Colon, at the beginning of the Panama Canal transit zone. Panama was an independent republic, except for the strip of land surrounding the Canal, which was then leased to the U.S. and under U.S. jurisdiction. *Cromwell* went through the Canal abreast her sister ship *Hammerberg*. Once in the locks, ships do not transit the Canal under their own power. Engines called "mules" pulled them along. The mules of that era were the Westinghouse electric engines originally built for the Canal during Teddy Roosevelt's time.

After the transit of the Canal the task group turned south on the west coast of South America, crossing the equator on September 2, 1961. There the pollywogs, lowly sailors who had never crossed the equator, were hazed by shellbacks, worthy sailors who had crossed before. The traditional Navy ceremony ended with the former pollywogs kissing the belly of King Neptune, the Imperial Ruler of the Raging Main (the fattest CPO they could find), whose belly was smeared with engine room black grease.

The submarine *Clamagore* moored alongside the *Cromwell* when they reached Ecuador on September 5. Submariners of that day had somewhat primitive living conditions, with limited water and very basic meals. *Cromwell* was always generous in sharing showers and meals with the submariners, and the crews often went on liberty together. There was a friendly competition with the submariners, who enjoyed telling the ship's crew how many times they had "sunk" them with torpedoes.

As the task force got to the north coast of Peru they encountered the Humboldt currents, full of vast schools of fish, so thick they would brightly illuminate the sonar. At about this time the *Norfolk* suffered a major engineering casualty, going dead in the water. Half her size, *Cromwell* towed the *Norfolk* back toward Panama until a sea going tug took over the towing duties.

From there they went to Callao, the seaport for Lima, Peru. The major fishing port processed the produce of their fleets, then dumped the cleaned entrails directly into the water, where it produced a smell of sulfur dioxide so strong it would knock you over. The foul air even tarnished the gold braid on officers' uniforms, turning it black.

The final port of call before the Straits of Magellan was the excellent liberty port of Valparaiso, Chili, which the Chileans call "Chico" and the sailors call "Valpo." It is a cosmopolitan city, European in makeup (with descendents from Spain, Germany and the United Kingdom), and a semi-tropical resort. From there the task force entered the Inland Straits (discovered by Sir Francis Drake), and then entered the storied Straits of Magellan.

The Inland Straits meander through a 360-mile, tortuous, narrow course. They are totally uninhabited and the scenery is breathtaking. The water in the Straits is very deep, but there were no navigational aids, so the lead ship had a pilot aboard for guidance through the many islands. *Cromwell* transited the Straits as the last ship in the column. At one point she nearly ran aground as a crossing current pushed the following ships away from the pilot ship; fortunately the ship's navigator caught the change in the depth of the water.

Ferdinand Magellan discovered the Magellan Straits during his first voyage around the world. The Magellan Straits form the waterway link between the South Atlantic and South Pacific Oceans, and vary between two and 20 miles in width. Bracketed by snow-covered mountains, the Straits separate the islands of Tierra del Fuego from the mainland of South America. There may be found penguins by the thousands and a strange bird known as a Steamboat Duck. The Steamboat Duck does not fly; rather it propels itself through the water while flapping its wings, water and foam flying as this strange creature navigates the Straits.

THE *CROMWELL* HAD A FUN and relaxed wardroom on the cruise. Kent Hewitt was an accomplished musician who played the piano and accordion. Encouraged by Captain Hoffmann, he organized the wardroom sing-alongs, actually getting the group to sing songs others might recognize. Roy Hoffmann loved to sing. He would call down and say, "Hewitt, get up here with your squeeze box; we are going to do some singing." Often accompanied by Bill Dudley on the guitar they would sing over dessert and coffee.

According to Bill Dudley, they sang ballads and folk songs. Hoffmann's favorite was "Oh Shenandoah," which he could sing in an acceptable tenor. He often had nicknames for his officers, and Bill's was "Gringo," because he

ABOVE: *The Shellbacks, waiting to initiate the Pollywogs into the Domain of the Golden Dragon, Cromwell, 1961.*
GREG NOLAN PHOTO

RIGHT: *Even Chief Gunners Mate Buitenhuis "Got no respect," Pollywog initiation, Cromwell, 1961.*
GREG NOLAN PHOTO

USS Cromwell *entering the Straits of Magellan, 1961.* Greg Nolan Photo

and the supply officer, Steve Stevens, had gone ashore in Callao and come back with cheap trinkets from a street vendor. Soon everyone in the wardroom was calling him Gringo.

Serving on a destroyer escort was good duty. The ship was small enough that you knew everyone, and the sailors had a sense of ownership and pride in the ship's performance. They also watched out for each other. There were many young sailors on the ship for whom this was their first formative adult experience. In some of the ports the "women of the night" were a great attraction for the young men. A combination of too much to drink and the attractions of the women left these young sailors in jeopardy of missing ship's movement, a most serious offense in the Navy. Joe Roxe remembers going

A classic Navy pose, signalman aboard the Cromwell, *1961.* Greg Nolan Photo

through the skivvy houses with a CPO and picking up *Cromwell* sailors to make sure they didn't get left behind.[7]

In addition, officers worked directly with their enlisted sailors and relied on them; the sailors in turn had direct knowledge of the competency of the officers. Roxe gives a great example of this in "high lining," which occurs when the destroyer pulls alongside another ship to take on

---

7. Joe Roxe interview, September 13, 2006. Joe enjoyed the duty so much he considered making the Navy a career, but decided against it for three reasons. First, Roxe wasn't a "ring knocker." A ring knocker is a Naval Academy graduate that knocks his Academy ring on the table to remind everyone he has an Academy education and thus supposedly holds an advantage over the non-ring knocker. Second, he wasn't married and loved being at sea, but he could see how hard it would be to maintain a family life in the Navy. Finally, the Navy didn't pay very well in relation to private industry.

A wild ride over heavy seas, 1960. GREG NOLAN PHOTO

fresh food, supplies, fuel, new movies, etc. The same might occur as they pulled alongside a carrier for the exchange of personnel. The maneuver is started by the deck crew firing over a rope with a monkey fist at the end to the other ship, after which larger lines are transferred across and the replenishment begins.

In high lining personnel a gantline holds the boatswain's chair as it moves between the ships. On the *Cromwell* the deck force maintained the tension as the ships moved along at 15 knots, rolling together and then apart, with the blue seas roiling up between the ships. The line goes slack as the ships roll together and snaps up when they roll apart. When Roxe was high lined across he always could tell how his men felt about him at that particular moment. If they weren't particularly happy with him the tension would slack and he'd get a good dunking in the water.

Kent Hewitt attributed his survival during his first year on the ship to a boatswain's mate (a career 25-year man) who took him under his wing, educated him and provided the link to the real-world Navy. Hewitt states, "It was an extraordinary act of generosity to take a greenhorn ensign under his wing and provide me with support, guidance, encouragement, and admonishment when I needed it."

One day Joe Roxe was on bridge watch as the OOD when he wasn't as sharp as he should have been (he had been on sonar all night). Captain Hoffmann, observing his lackadaisical demeanor, came up and ". . . gave me a kick in the ass. It was one of the nicest things that anyone has done for me, because I was feeling sorry for myself, tired and out of sorts." But he was engaged in a military operation, requiring his undivided attention. "It was his [Hoffmann's] friendly way of saying 'get your act together.'"

Captain Hoffmann could be tough on his officers as well. One early morning about 0300 Bill Dudley was awakened from a sound sleep by the OOD, who had come down from the bridge. The OOD said that Hoffmann had ordered him to call his relief, Dudley in this case. Hoffmann had awakened and arrived on the bridge, where he discovered contacts closing on the ship, which the OOD had failed to track and report. He simply had not been paying attention. It was a lesson on what happened if you screwed up as an OOD.

THE FIRST STOP ON THE CRUISE up the east coast was to Argentina. A map does not do justice to the size of the South American country. Over a million square miles, Argentina is equivalent in size to the portion of the U.S. lying east of the Mississippi River. The northern portion, which borders Brazil, Paraguay and Bolivia, is subtropical, while the south contains the bleak Patagonia steppes and the rainy Tierra del Fuego. It was sparsely populated in those days, with a population of only 21 million; more than 3.5 million lived in Buenos Aires, the third largest city in the southern hemisphere.

It was the land of Generalissimo Juan Domingo Peron and his wife Maria Eva Duarte de Peron. Peron was overthrown in 1955; the current president was Arturo Frondizi, elected to a single six-year term in 1958.

The task group went up the muddy Rio de la Plata, arriving in Buenos Aires on October 19, 1961. Navigation up the river was somewhat hazardous, as the river wasn't frequently dredged, so they did the smart thing and got closely astern of a big tanker and followed it up. During the transit the *Courtney* damaged a screw, putting her out of commission until a replacement could be flown in from the U.S.

Spanish settlers founded Buenos Aires in 1536, after which they were plagued by frequent attacks from the Querandi Indians. That same year the Indians attacked the town, forcing the Spaniards out. The area was resettled in 1580, this time for good. It became the seat of government and housed the Presidential

Palace and Congress Hall. Buenos Aires was known as the Paris of the South for its nightlife and fabulous food, with a primarily Italian culinary influence.

There was some tension beneath the surface with the American Navy, due to the close relationship between the U.S. and Great Britain, and the latter's claim on the Falkland Islands. The Falkland Islands, known to the Argentineans as the Malvinas, had been in ownership dispute for two centuries. Most of the inhabitants were descended from British settlers who arrived in the 1820s, but the Argentineans considered the islands part of their territory. War between the countries finally broke out on Friday, April 2, 1982. Without any warning or declaration of war, a large Argentinean amphibious force invaded and occupied the British crown colony. The invasion caught the British by surprise, and they had no significant military presence in the area with which to respond to the attack. Prime Minister Margaret Thatcher, as tough as her U.S. counterpart, President Ronald Reagan, was determined to recover the islands.

Thatcher sent an expeditionary force 8,000 miles with that goal in mind. The expeditionary force had a naval escort and light air cover from two British carriers equipped with Harriers. With behind the scenes help from the Reagan administration, the Brits succeeded in recovering the islands. The British submarine *Conqueror* sank the Argentine heavy cruiser *Belgrano*, after which the Argentine Navy retired from the scene. The Argentine Air Force put up a better fight, sinking four British warships and transports. On June 14 the Argentine garrison surrendered. Between the *Belgrano* and the land fighting the Argentineans lost over 1,000 men; British losses were closer to 300. The British victory led to the end of military rule in Argentina and the restoration of democracy in that country.[8]

The task group reached Rio de Janeiro, Brazil, on November 3. Brazil was another huge country, somewhat larger in size than the continental U.S. Brazil is the location of the world's largest river, the Amazon. It was a place of grinding poverty and filth, where many of the citizens lived without running water or sanitation systems. It was a glaring example of class divisions; the socialistic country had miserably failed the people of Brazil.

Brazil had an aircraft carrier with planes aboard without propellers. When Roxe asked his Brazilian counterpart, "Where are the propellers?" the counterpart responded, "Well the Navy controls the carrier but the Air Force controls the planes, and they won't allow the Navy to fly them off the carrier."

---

8. Paul Johnson, *Modern Times The World from the Twenties to the Nineties* (New York: HarperPerennial, 1991).

On Roy Hoffmann's commands he made it his practice to drill the crew at general quarters after clearing the outer sea buoy. He felt it was a chance to shake off the lethargy of the port, get the ship battened down and to check out damage control.[9] The crew had three minutes to get the damage control condition set; they knew if they didn't do it right they would go back to general quarters until they did get it right.

Hoffmann put together a team of reliable chiefs and their job was to go below decks, checking the fittings to insure they were properly set. Usually within ten minutes Hoffmann had a report on the bridge whether the crew had got it right, after which they would secure from general quarters. If the condition was improperly set the ship went back to general quarters until they got it right. If everything was satisfactory he would grant holiday routine for the rest of the day to let the off watch crew "sleep it off."

During general quarters Hoffmann would also concurrently conduct engineering drills, simulating engine casualties. During one of these drills the *Cromwell* experienced a real engine casualty, which was followed by another on their return to the United States. The resulting board of investigation threatened to put a roadblock in front of Roy Hoffmann's advancing career.

To understand the engine casualty it is first necessary to descend to the hot lower decks of a ship with the "Snipes" (engineers) of the Engineering Department.[10] In a typical steam propulsion plant there are boilers, condensers, evaporators, main engines, reduction gears, and propeller shafts leading to propellers, which drive the ship. A boiler is a box-like casing containing hundreds of water-filled steel tubes, which are arranged so heat from the fireboxes passes over them. Heated Navy Standard Fuel Oil (NSFO) is sprayed through nozzles into the fireboxes under high pressure, where it burns intensely, turning the water into steam. The steam then flows through pipes to the turbines. Fresh water for the boilers is made from salt water by evaporators and condensers. Steaming at full speed required the activation of most of the nozzles.

---

9. Because of his experiences in Wonsan Harbor in 1950, Hoffmann was a self-described "bastard" on damage control.

10. Descriptions of ship's power plants from Vincent J. Clayton, "Welcome to Engineering," *Vietnam Magazine*, February 2006, pp. 28–33; and United States Naval Institute, *The Bluejackets' Manual* (Annapolis, Maryland: United States Naval Institute, 1978), pp. 210–211. *Cromwell* was equipped with two Foster-Wheeler boilers and one De Laval geared turbine, which generated 20,000 shp.

Lieutenant Commander Roy F. Hoffmann, commanding officer USS Cromwell, *on the open bridge, 1961.* GREG NOLAN PHOTO

A turbine consists of a revolving rotor with several rows of blades mounted in a steam-tight casing with several rows of stationary blades. The rotor and casing blades are set in alternate rows so that as the steam passes through the turbine each row deflects the steam to the next row. The Cromwell had both high pressure (HP) and low pressure (LP) turbines. After the steam passes through both turbines it is cooled, condensed into water and returned to the boilers. Steam is applied to the main turbine by opening the ahead throttle valve, using a large wheel. Opening the valve allows pressurized steam into the main turbine, where it causes the turbine to turn. The amount of steam let into the turbine chamber regulates the ship's speed. If the ship had to back down, the throttle man had to close the main turbine steam valve and then open the astern turbine steam valve.

Turbines can't be reversed; to reverse the shaft a backing turbine is installed, or, as on the *Cromwell*, an astern element is fitted inside the LP turbine in a separate casing. Because backing stages have fewer rows of blades than the main turbine, and are at lower steam pressure, they produce less power. Thus, a ship never has the power available for backing down as she has for forward movement.

Turbines operate most efficiently at several thousand rpm, but propellers aren't very effective above 400 rpm, so reduction gear is required. With reduction gear, two turbines frequently drive one shaft. The shaft carries power to the propellers. The shaft runs from the reduction gear through long watertight spaces, called shaft alleys, in the very bottom of the ship. They enter the water through stern glands and stern bearings and may be supported outside the hull by struts.

Destroyers had two propellers, as did most submarines. Ships are classed as four-screw (aircraft carriers and cruisers), two-screw and one-screw. Burning NSFO produced a thick residue on the pipes and firesides, and they had to be cleaned and inspected every 500 hours of steaming time.

THE CASUALTY TO *Cromwell's* HP turbine occurred on the transit from Rio de Janeiro to San Juan. The ship went dead in the water (DIW) and Captain Hoffmann waited on the bridge for a report from the chief engineer on the problem. The chief engineer reported they thought they had heard a rub in the HP turbine. To test the turbine they went ahead one third, then ahead two thirds, standard, then ahead full. Everything seemed all right with the turbine so they got underway again.

Two hours later under routine steaming there was another engineering casualty and the ship again went DIW. This time they found the HP turbine rotor had shifted internally, resulting in a rub on the fixed blades—it was a major casualty. The ship had been designed for mass production and there was little redundancy in the engineering plant. However, in the event something happened to the HP turbine they had aboard "crossover piping" which could be used to bypass the HP turbine in an emergency. While the enginemen and firemen installed the piping the ship was DIW for six to eight hours, fortunately in calm seas.

The commodore sent the *Hammerberg* back to stand by the *Cromwell* during the installation of the piping. The two ships were then ordered to Puerto Rico for repairs, the *Cromwell* limping along at about 12 knots on the remaining turbine that they constantly monitored for overheating. The repair facility at San Juan determined they couldn't repair the turbine there, as it would have to be lifted out and rebuilt at a major shipyard.

So the two ships began the long transit back to their home port in Newport, Rhode Island, at a slow 12 to 15 knots, after the long sea deployment on Unitos II. Meanwhile, the cause of the casualty was a mystery, and Captain Hoffmann would certainly have to explain how his ship had become disabled. One would presume the long voyage back gave him plenty of time to think about the consequences if his command had caused the problem.

They finally reached Narragansett Bay where they were to offload their ammunition at a small depot on Prudence Island. As they went in to offload they encountered a strong ebb current, and to get alongside the pier they had to go at standard speed (about 15 knots), and then back down full. The XO got the ship in neatly but at the expense of yet another engineering casualty. Since the HP turbine was off the line and not available to relieve the highly elevated temperatures from the back turbine, the compressed steam blew a gasket on the LP turbine. This repair would have to be added to the major repair coming up at the Boston Navy Shipyard.

The Navy called a Board of Investigation to determine what had been done to disable the main engine on the ship. The Admiral relates now that he was "somewhat" concerned, but one suspects it went beyond that. If his command were found at fault a letter of reprimand would likely go into his file, or at the very least his "fleet reputation" would be affected. Being called before the "green table" was always difficult. As the Admiral puts it, "You have absolute authority and responsibility [as captain of a ship]. You get the glory and you get the blame." It was exactly why he wanted to be in command.

Fortunately the Navy assigned a highly capable and objective captain engineer officer to head the Board of Investigation. He questioned why the safety devices that were installed on the LP turbine to detect a problem before it became a casualty didn't work. Turbines are designed to "float" within a small tolerance, so they don't laterally shift so far the rotor blades would rub on fixed blades. There was a thrust indicator with a dial that was supposed to detect any movement before it got outside the tolerances. The investigation determined that as the *Cromwell* went through the engineering casualty drill out of Rio de Janeiro, a first class petty officer inspecting the gauge in engineering logged the thrust indicator as malfunctioning when it fact it was indicating there were serious problems with the rotor shaft thrust bearing. Had the proper reading been made and reported more serious damage to the HP turbine could have been avoided.

That left the casing leak in the LP turbine, which meant that turbine had to be repaired as well, resulting in more time and expense in the yard. The first casualty could be explained, but what about the second breakdown? Again, the head of the Board interviewed yard personnel, who remembered an incident on the *Cromwell* from before Roy Hoffmann had reported aboard. And that story related to a near human tragedy within the confines of the main condenser.

It turned out that a man striking for shipyard foreman had never been in the main condenser on a *Dealy* class destroyer like the *Cromwell*, and as part of his duties it fell to him to get inside and check it out. The entry was through an inspection plate on the lower side of the turbine's casing, which was barely large enough for a small man to get through. Once in there was only one way out, the way you had come in. After squeezing through the opening you are in a space where you can't turn around; it's a dark, smelly, slimy, hot, and claustrophobic place.

Once the shipyard foreman striker was in he couldn't get out; he became claustrophobic and panicked. The then chief engineer on the *Cromwell* sent one of his smaller sailors to squeeze into the space with soap and water. Once in he took the striker's clothes off and soaped him down to try and get him out. By then the striker was in full panic and helpless. Outside the turbine the chief engineer called the shipyard duty officer and said, "We've got a real problem down here."

After the seaman exited the confined space a shipyard doctor entered the turbine. The doctor checked out the striker and said, "We have got to get this man out of here or he's going to die. He's in a state of shock and he's not going to last much longer." Shipyard personnel eventually cut a larger hole in the LP turbine casing to get him out.

By cutting the hole they saved the man's life. They then re-welded the casing to close the hole. But when they re-welded the casing it created abnormal structural stress and was not properly stress relieved. So when the *Cromwell* backed down landing at Prudence Island, what should have been a 600 degrees Fahrenheit inside the plant got up to well over 1,200 degrees, thus warping the turbine. In the initial repair the shipyard did not properly stress-relieve the casing, which would have required a prolonged and expensive process in the yard.

And so Captain Hoffmann came out the Board of Investigation without a letter of reprimand for either incident. In the first instance it was human error unknown to the senior CPO chief engineer or the captain; and in the second instance it was a mechanical problem beyond the captain's control.

The Admiral now says in retrospect he shouldn't have used a full backing bell to offload the ammo, but of course they weren't aware of the problem with the LP turbine. While there had been no continuity on the *Cromwell* to remember the shipyard incident, fortunately there was continuity at the Boston shipyard.[11]

THE SHIP WAS IN THE Boston shipyard approximately two months while the HP and LP turbines were repaired. Less than four months later the *Cromwell* would be back in the navy yard for serious repairs. The path back to the yard started with a major escort of convoy exercise in the spring of 1962, which was scheduled to take place off the coast of Bermuda. The *Cromwell* arrived on scene just in time for a tremendous and prolonged nor'easter storm.

The storm started out mildly enough and the ships of the task force were able to remain in formation. However, by the start of exercise the seas were heaving. As the full-blown nor'easter arrived the task force commander cancelled the exercise and ordered the TF to set sail for Newport. As the TF plowed through the vicious storm the seas got rougher, and rougher, and rougher, until the ships were contending with hurricane force winds of over 80 miles per hour, and mountainous waves sometimes over 40 feet and higher crashed over them. There was no way to maintain the formation so the task force commander ordered the ships to steam independently and find their way back as best they could. As Bill Dudley put it:

> The ship rolled like an SOB in the troughs and . . . later the commodore basically said it was every man for himself. Men were sick all over the ship and hung on for dear life. I was one of the few who didn't get sick so I spent a lot of time on the bridge. Hoffmann was cool, collected and kept his wits about him, even when the ship was pitching deeply, like an elevator with a broken cable, and taking green water over the bow like you wouldn't believe.

Soon there were SOS emergency signals coming in from ships in distress that could not handle the heavy seas and winds. The closest SOS call to the *Cromwell* was from a Yugoslav freighter that had lost her cargo hatches, was losing freeboard

---

11. There were two ways Roy Hoffmann could have reacted to the Board of Investigation. The event could have made him cautious, tentative and less aggressive. Or, he could put the incident behind him, maintain confidence in his leadership skills and abilities, and make virtually no change in his approach to command. In this author's opinion it is to the Admiral's credit that he chose the latter course. One sees no difference in his approach to subsequent commands after the Board of Investigation than there had been before.

and in real danger of sinking. For the *Cromwell* it was now a matter of saving lives aboard the freighter, but Captain Hoffmann also had to be concerned for the safety of his own ship. The *Cromwell* had taken one wave completely over the ship. Hoffmann was in the captain's seat in the pilothouse when the monster wave approached and he yelled to the OOD on the open bridge to "Hit the deck!" Then the ship's whistle started blowing and Hoffmann yelled to the boatswain's mate of the watch, "Get off the damn whistle." The boatswain replied, "I'm not on the whistle, captain." The wave had bent the housing for the cable of the whistle and the fire room had to cut steam to the whistle to get it to stop.

In the meantime the air search radar antenna was ripped clear off the mast by the fierce winds. As the *Cromwell* tried to maintain headway in the mountainous seas, they attempted to locate the freighter by her position reports, which proved inaccurate. As they continued the ordeal of searching for the freighter in the violent storm Captain Hoffmann's thought was, "What the hell can we do to save them?" *Cromwell's* motor whaleboat had been smashed in the storm. His plan was to put life rafts in tandem on a single line and circle the stricken freighter if they could only find her.

The *Cromwell* eventually located the freighter. Escorted by the *Cromwell*, the freighter, with little freeboard left, managed to get to and seek refuge in Delaware Bay. Meanwhile, during the rescue mission and vicious storm the *Cromwell* had taken a terrible beating. The forward gun mount housing was pounded in and the 3" 50 automatic guns were so out of alignment they were slanted toward each other. Despite the hurricane bow the breakwater was smashed in, and the ship had lost every exterior vertical ladder. The air search radar was gone but they had managed to save the surface radar by allowing it to trail in the wind.[12]

And so, it was back to the Boston shipyard again, the second trip for the new captain in less than a year of command. When he arrived he received another piece of bad news. When the ship got in dry dock, the yard foreman told him, "I hate to tell you this captain, but you've been aground."

It was bad enough to run your ship aground, but to not report it was worse. But in this case, Hoffmann *knew* he had not run his ship aground.

"What do you mean, I've been aground?" he growled.

"Your hull is all bashed in."

"How the hell is that possible?" Hoffmann responded. "My sonar has been working all the time—that's how I've been navigating."

---

12. The Cromwell was not the only ship taking heavy damage. An aircraft carrier had her flight deck bent in the storm.

And the response was, "Well, I've got to report this to the CO of the shipyard."

"Well, I understand, but I'm going down to dry dock right now. I can't believe that."

And with that he inspected his ship and found that sure enough, the keel hull plates that should have been convex, were now concave. The pounding the hull had taken from the heavy seas had buckled the plates inward. He then inspected the huge sonar dome just aft of the stem and found it to be in perfect shape. The condition of the sonar dome was the convincing evidence that the hull had been damaged by the severe pounding of the storm, as the ship could not have run aground without damaging the sonar dome, which projected beneath the keel of the ship.

ONCE OUT OF THE YARD, the officers and men of the *Cromwell* looked forward to fleet operations after extensive yard work. Unfortunately, the *Cromwell* was selected to be the ship open to the general public in Whitestone, New York, over the Fourth of July, 1962. The orders pleased no one, as the ship's crew had to give up their holiday and "turn to" to make the ship shine for the visits of civilians aboard the Navy destroyer. To add insult to injury, hardly anyone showed up to view the ship. It was a ticked off crew that got underway after the "event."

As they left the harbor they had to steam under the Whitestone Bridge. Just as they were passing under the bridge, Captain Hoffmann called down on the squawk box to the Engineering Officer, Ernie Rokowski. Hoffmann ordered, "Blow the tubes!" Rokowski opened up all the steam vents to blow the soot off the tubes, sending " . . . up a cloud of smoke that would have made the Mount St. Helens explosion look like a picnic by comparison."[13] It left motorists on the Bridge choking in a dense fog of black smoke and left the sailors on the *Cromwell* smiling, their morale restored.

ROY HOFFMANN WASN'T THE ONLY officer in those days of a different Navy who was willing to make a statement. The America's Cup races were held south of Newport, Rhode Island from September 15 to 25, 1962.[14] The Navy task group that included the *Cromwell* was returning from Halifax

---

13. Kent Hewitt interview, September 13, 2005.
14. The American defender *Weatherly* defeated the British challenger Gretel, four wins to one that year. The America's Cup was first run in 1851 at the Isle of Wight in England. America's Cup Official Web site, www.americascup.com.

during the America's Cup races. They had been sent to Halifax to gather information on Soviet cannery ships, which cleaned, filleted, processed and froze the Soviet catch for delivery to market. Their dual purpose was to gather intelligence on American Navy ship movements, and the American Navy kept track of their movements.

As the task group returned to Newport they encountered scores of pleasure craft observing the races. The task group had been at sea awhile and the commodore didn't want to wait to get in. He put the DE's in column formation with the *Cromwell* at the head, and hoisted the signal flags "Follow the Guide." The formation went right through the armada of pleasure craft, scattering them as the Navy ships stayed on course. "Of course," Hoffmann relates, "the commodore got his ass chewed out by the destroyer force commander afterward. The commodore just laughed."

On October 3, 1962, the *Cromwell* participated in ceremonies celebrating the 60th anniversary of the commissioning of the first destroyer, the *Bainbridge* (DD 1). The original 600-ton coal burner's name was being bestowed on the world's first nuclear powered destroyer, the guided missile destroyer USS *Bainbridge*. *Cromwell* transited the Fore River in zero visibility to "escort" the *Bainbridge* into the Atlantic Fleet.

Captain John Culver USNR, Ret., remembers going out with a pilot boat to where the *Cromwell* was anchored in Boston Harbor. "It was so foggy you couldn't see your hand in front of your face," he said in an interview. "The dense fog didn't stop Captain Hoffmann and the *Cromwell*. He maneuvered that little ship right into the shipyard. He didn't even flinch when he saw the fog. He steamed that thing right in—unbelievable! Most guys would drop the hook and wait for the fog to go away."[15]

During the week long observance the *Cromwell* and *Sellers* were open to the public. In December Roy Hoffmann was advanced to full commander.

---

15. John Culver interview, September 17, 2006. Ship handling has become a lost art in the current U.S. Navy. A recent article in the U.S. Naval Institute Proceedings (August 2006, pp. 55–58) by Captain Stuart Landersman, USN, Ret., illuminates the differences between the Navy of Hoffmann's era and today's Navy. Landersman relates, "In practice today, almost every port departure, entry and pier landing is done by a civilian ship pilot using tugs. Navy ships use 'valet parking' in their own homeports as well as in distant ports of the world." p. 56. It would seem that aggression, ship handling and seamanship have been replaced by a different ethic of less competence and taking fewer risks in today's Navy.

MEANWHILE, A CRISIS was building which would bring the United States and the Soviet Union to the brink of nuclear war in October of 1962.[16] The crisis came as the result of a monumental miscalculation by Soviet leader Nikita Khrushchev, who had decided after the Bay of Pigs fiasco the preceding April of 1961 that President John F. Kennedy was a weak and vacillating man. Khrushchev saw the botched Bay of Pigs invasion as an opportunity to begin arming Fidel Castro's Cuban dictatorship with nuclear-armed ballistic missiles, only 90 miles from Florida. American spy planes discovered the Soviet missile sites and a tense 13 day standoff between the nuclear powers ensued.

Kennedy reacted by ordering a concentration of naval and other forces into the Atlantic and Caribbean. The Navy established Task Forces 135 and 136 in response to Kennedy's orders. The task forces consisted of the *Enterprise* and *Independence* carrier task groups, six *Polaris* submarines (home based in Holy Loch, Scotland), nearly 30 destroyer and guided missile frigates and an amphibious landing force. Kennedy demanded that the Soviets dismantle the missile sites and remove them from Cuba. To back it up he ordered a naval blockade off Cuba. Meanwhile, the U.S. readied a full-scale invasion of the island.

The tensions were high, and nuclear holocaust was the consequence of a misstep. "A real war will begin, in which millions of Americans and Russians will die," U.S. Attorney General Robert F. Kennedy told Anatoly Dobrynin in a secret memo dated October 27, 1962. It is not an exaggeration to say the stakes were that high.

IN EARLY OCTOBER the *Cromwell* was in Newport, after which she was ordered to go into the yard for a major overhaul, to include enclosing the open bridge. To save money, which was always tight for repairs, *Cromwell* men went ahead and cut off the windshield and some of the stanchion supports on the bridge. They got underway for Earle, New Jersey, to offload ammunition prior to going into the yard. It was a pleasant transit downwind on a chilly but bright day. As they approached the pier they got a flash voice radio message to return to Newport, orders they suspected were related to the impending Cuban crisis.

---

16. Time line and background for the Cuban Missile Crisis were taken from several sources, but most helpful to this author was, David L. Larson, ed., *The "Cuban Crisis" of 1962* (Boston: Houghton Mifflin Company, 1963), *passim*. A good movie has been done on the Crisis, *Thirteen Days* (2000), which deals with the tension through the eyes of political advisor Kenny O'Donnell (Kevin Costner).

When they got into Newport the destroyer pier was a hive of activity. The minute the lines were over they started loading supplies for an extended deployment. Word got out the ship was back, catching many of the families off guard. No liberty was granted. Hoffmann called Mary Linn and said, "We're loading supplies and going south." He needed some things from home so he asked Mary Linn to bring them to the dock. She now relates, "At that time you could drive down on the pier and it was like ants taking supplies aboard."[17]

When the supplies were aboard the crew cast off and *Cromwell*, accompanied by her sister ship *Hammerberg*, set sail for the northern Florida coast. They drilled non-stop on the way down, and brought up live ammunition for the guns. They drilled on small boat boarding parties for search and seizure, they practiced small arms fire, and they drilled, as they never had before.

When *Cromwell* and *Hammerberg* arrived at the designated rendezvous position, they formed an ASW screen with two U.S. Army troop transports, fully loaded with a ready Army assault force. The task group steamed up and down the southeast Florida coastline, boring holes inside the 100-fathom curve. They hugged the coast because of the Soviet submarine threat.

After about a week of steaming the task group was ordered into the Naval station at Mayport, Florida, on the St. Johns River, which was primarily a carrier and destroyer base. The port call was to replenish, give the troops a chance to get off the ship and relieve the crews from the pressure of the events. After two days they got underway again. Shortly thereafter the press correspondents were ordered off the troop ships. *Cromwell* went alongside the Army flagship to high line the correspondents off and transfer them to a pilot boat off Mayport.[18]

They then set a course to a designated beachhead, just east of Havana. There were B-52s droning overhead, as the ship's crew anxiously awaited the signal to

---

17. On October 22, 1962, President Kennedy addressed the nation over radio and TV, briefing Americans on the Cuban Crisis, and the discovery there were medium and intermediate range ballistic missiles and other offensive weapons in Cuba. He informed the country that he had ordered a naval quarantine to prevent further transportation of Soviet offensive weapons to the island. As did millions of other Americans, Mary Linn stored food and water and anxiously followed the news on radio and in the newspapers (the Hoffmann family did not own a television).

18. Years later one of those correspondents gave a talk at a Navy reunion that the Admiral also attended. The correspondent talked about how a destroyer had "damn near killed him" during the Cuban Missile Crisis. He said that he had gone over by high line, the "damn thing jerked around and I thought I was going to drown." The Admiral was the next speaker and he got up and said, "That damn fool that almost killed you was me."

commence the assault phase. It was a stressful time, as the two-ship screen was insufficient for effective ASW operations, and the ships had poor air defense capabilities (two twin 3" 50s weren't exactly overwhelming). Everyone on the ship assumed the assault troops were going in. They could pick up mainland radio stations and followed the events in the unfolding crisis.

ON OCTOBER 23 THE Defense Department released photographs of the Soviet missile sites in Cuba. All Soviet and Warsaw Pact forces were put on an alert basis and Castro ordered the full mobilization of all Cuban military forces. The U.S. went one stage below actual warfare and evacuated all military dependents at Guantanamo and reinforced the garrison there. The U.S. Navy intercepted the Soviet oil tanker *Bucharest*, and then after visual inspection allowed it to proceed. Twelve other Soviet ships headed for Cuba at reduced speed.

On October 25 Ambassador Adlai Stevenson displayed photographs of the missile sites under construction before the U.N. Security Council, and challenged the Soviets to deny the existence of the offensive weapons. The Soviets denied they had offensive weapons outside the USSR. On that day Premier Khrushchev sent a letter to Kennedy with a set of proposals to resolve the crisis. The next day a party of sailors from the destroyers *John R. Pierce* (DD 753) and the *Joseph P. Kennedy, Jr.* (DD 850) stopped and searched the Lebanese-flagged merchantman *Maruda*, which carried Soviet goods destined for Cuba. She was allowed to proceed since she held no military cargo. Other Soviet vessels began to reverse course before they reached the American quarantine line.

On October 26 and 27, 1962, Khrushchev sent letters to Kennedy proposing to withdraw Soviet offensive weapons from Cuba if the U.S. promised not to invade the island, and if the U.S. would remove its own missiles deployed in Turkey, a NATO ally. Kennedy responded favorably to the more positive October 26 letter, and on Sunday, October 28, Radio Moscow announced that their missiles would be crated and returned to Moscow. Although the tension would remain high through the following month as the sites were dismantled, the immediate threat of an exchange of nuclear missiles had been averted.

AS THE CRISIS WOUND DOWN the *Cromwell* was ordered back to Key West for fuel and replenishment, where Captain Hoffmann granted limited liberty to the crew. Jack Bethany was by then the XO of the ship, and, after informing the quarterdeck where they'd be, he and Hoffmann went to the officer's club for a couple of beers. It wasn't long before a messenger came in from the ship and said, "Captain, you have orders to report to the commandant of the Naval base and prepare to get underway as soon as possible."

So, with at least a couple of beers under their belts the captain and XO returned to the ship and had the Shore Patrol notify the sailors on liberty to return to the ship.[19] It was a pitch dark and tricky navigation to get out of the harbor but the XO was a former chief quartermaster and a good one. After determining they had a full navigation team they got underway. As it turned out, they were underway because an enemy periscope had been spotted off the coast of Havana.

The following morning at about 0400, while in transit, Hoffmann got a call from Kent Hewitt, the OOD on the bridge. Hewitt said, "Captain, I hate to get you up, but as we were riding the crest of a wave I looked out the port side and I thought I saw a boat out there with a lot of people on board." The CO responded, "Put the rudder over and I'll be right there." On the *Cromwell* the sea cabin and in-port cabin were combined, so Hoffmann was only half a deck below the bridge level and about three steps away.

They spotted the boat, which was about the size of a motor whaleboat, and it was tossing in the heavy seas. The heading of the boat was such that the *Cromwell* couldn't get alongside without excessive rolls in the heavy troughs. The ship's crew tossed out a painter to pull the boat alongside, but the people on the boat secured it to their stern, which would have swamped it. Fortunately there were Spanish-speaking sailors aboard the *Cromwell* and they ordered the people of the boat to cast off the line and the *Cromwell* would come around and make another approach.

The people in the boat were refugees from Cuba, desperate to escape the Castro dictatorship. There were about 25 people on the boat, including women and children. The boat had an outboard gasoline engine and refugees smoking cigarettes were trying to add gasoline to the engine without a funnel. Gasoline and water the boat was taking on mixed to form a combustible brew sloshing around in the boat.

The *Cromwell* came around again, ordered the refugees to put out their cigarettes, and managed this time to get a painter down to the boat's bow and pulled them alongside. They got the refugees aboard, which was fairly easy with the exception of a *very* pregnant woman whom the sailors bodily lifted onto the ship. After the refugees were all aboard the Cromwell sailors sank the boat so it wouldn't be a navigational hazard.

---

19. About a third of the crew was on liberty. They got all but a few back.

Commander Roy F. Hoffmann, commanding officer, USS Cromwell *(DE 1014), June 25, 1963.*
OFFICIAL U.S. NAVY PHOTO, HOFFMANN COLLECTION

They fed the refugees, and then confined them to a guarded space for security purposes until they could transfer them off the ship. Had the *Cromwell* not picked them up it is a virtual certainty they would have died. They were using an automobile compass to navigate to Florida. *Cromwell* sailors checked it with the ship's standard compass and found it was off by 40 degrees. The refugees were headed straight out to the Atlantic Ocean.

Officially, the U.S. Navy had the obligation to save lives at sea, but not to disembark them into the continental U.S. They transferred the refugees across the pier at Key West to a Coast Guard cutter, and then resumed their station on the Windward Passage patrol to monitor all ships going into and coming out of Cuba. That lasted about a month, after which they returned to Boston and started the delayed shipyard repair.

Within six months Roy Hoffmann received orders to the Naval War College and his days as captain of the *Cromwell* came to an end. It was an eventful and successful first command, and it is best to allow his subordinate officers to speak about their service under Roy Hoffmann.

Kent Hewitt remembered the enormous human friendliness that Roy and Mary Linn Hoffmann represented. "They extended their hearts to other people." Mary Linn has for years corresponded with many at Christmas with hand-written letters detailing the activities of the Hoffmann family during the preceding year. Hewitt said, "She is unbelievable in her dedication to keeping connected to people." Bill Dudley said Roy Hoffmann "... was the best leader of men I met during my active duty in the Navy. He was fair, fun and tough." Joe Roxe said Roy Hoffmann had enormous energy, vitality and enthusiasm. He was a

The Admiral's favorite print, which always hung in a prominent place in either his sea cabin or office. TERRY SYMMES' PHOTO FROM HIS PRINT

good, technically competent skipper. He didn't go to pieces when "stuff got nasty." He was someone you'd want as a leader.

AND SO IN THE TIME-HONORED Navy tradition a Change of Command Ceremony was held on July 19, 1963. The new commanding officer met the officers and crew, then was briefed on the condition of the ship and made the required inspections. The actual transfer of responsibility took place in a formal public ceremony. The uniform normally was full dress, in keeping with the dignity of the occasion. Assembled were the officers, CPOs, and enlisted men, in formation for the ceremony.

At 1400 the commanding officers arrived. After the invocation Commander Roy Hoffmann made his farewell remarks, expressed his appreciation to his officers and men, and read his orders. Then, the prospective commanding officer, Lieutenant Commander Alvin D. Branch, stood, read his orders from the Navy Department to take command, saluted the outgoing CO and said, "Sir, I relieve you." The new CO then turned to the officer conducting the transfer and reported, "Sir, I assume command of the ship." The commission pennant of the relieved commanding officer was then hauled down and the new commission pennant was hoisted. Captain Branch then made a short speech and the ceremony was complete.[20]

Roy Hoffmann was relieved of command and went on to the Naval War College.[21]

THE NAVAL WAR COLLEGE

The Naval War College is located at Newport, Rhode Island. Established on October 6, 1884, it was initially housed in the old building of the Newport Asylum for the Poor.[22] One of the first four instructors was Captain (later Rear Admiral) Alfred Mahan, who became famous for the scope of his strategic thinking and his influence on naval leaders worldwide.[23] Eventually the War College became a laboratory for the development of war plans. Nearly all U.S. Navy operations of the 20th century were originally designed and gamed at the College.

The faculty consists of talented naval officers, officers from other service branches and civilian scholars. In the 1960s two separate programs for U.S. officers were established, one for mid-grade officers emphasizing the operational and tactical elements of command; and one for senior officers emphasizing larger policy and strategic issues. The curriculum included International Relations, Military Management, Economics and Comparative Cultures.

Roy Hoffmann had expected to get shore duty since he had just come from three consecutive tours at sea. The Navy tried to get officers into the College as a junior captain or a senior commander. They wanted officers who were at the peak of their careers and had sufficient time left in the Navy to benefit from the experience. Normally officers were not selected unless they had the potential for a senior command. Attendance was almost required to get your ticket punched. For the Hoffmann family the new orders meant they could move back into their home and arrange for Harriet to go into the Exeter, Rhode Island School for the Mentally Retarded.

---

20. Details of a change of command ceremony from the Naval Historical Foundation, *The Navy* (New York: Barnes & Noble Books, 2000).

21. The fleet workhorse *Cromwell* was stricken from the Naval Register July 5, 1972. She was scheduled to be transferred to New Zealand, but instead was sold for scrap on June 15, 1973.

22. That original building now houses the Naval War College Museum. Background on the Naval War College from the official Web site www.usnwc.edu.

23. Mahan's book *The Influence of Seapower Upon History, 1660–1783* (1890) helped to gain international recognition for the War College.

The teaching at the War College was mostly done in seminars, which were a mixture of Navy personnel, officers from the Army, Air Force, Marines, and State Department personnel. At the time Roy Hoffmann didn't appreciate the experience as he now does. "What a goddamn waste of time," he thought. "I should be at sea."

In one of his classes a crusty old Marine colonel had a dry subject to teach. Soon many in the class fell asleep. The colonel took out a pistol and fired two blanks in the air. He growled, "Look you bastards, if you're not going to listen I'm not going to waste my time up here." It certainly got the attention of the class but it also got the attention of an angry president of the War College, who didn't appreciate the incident.

NINETEEN SIXTY-THREE was the year the United States entered a miasma from which in some respects it has not emerged. One may consider it starting with the November 2, 1963, coup d'etat in South Vietnam, which deposed Ngo Dinh Diem and his brother, Ngo Dinh Nhu, husband of the notorious Madame Nhu, the "Dragon Lady."[24] Diem and Nhu were shot to death in the back of an M-114 armed personnel carrier after Ambassador Henry Cabot Lodge had suggested they accept safe conduct out of the country offered by the rebel generals. Lodge had been aware of the impending coup and did nothing to stop it.

The coup led to a series of unstable governments, which seemed woefully unprepared to defend South Vietnam against the ruthless and repressive Communist regime of North Vietnam, which had as its goal the reunification of Vietnam under the brutal Communist dictatorship. By the end of the month President John F. Kennedy was dead, assassinated on November 22, 1963, by Lee Harvey Oswald in Dallas, Texas. The event seemed to be the impetus for all that was to follow in the next 12 years: The presidency of the dissembling Lyndon B. Johnson; the Tonkin Gulf Resolution; the often violent civil rights movement; the gradual escalation of troop levels and commitment to South Vietnam; the antiwar movement; the breakdown of traditions and morality in America; the election of Richard M. Nixon as president; the "peace" in 1973 in Vietnam, Watergate and the fall of South Vietnam in 1975.

---

24. The standard work on our involvement is Stanley Karnow's *Vietnam A History* (1983). Another excellent source is Lewis Sorley's *A Better War* (1999), which covers the years from 1968 to 1972.

AFTER A YEAR AS A student Roy Hoffmann got orders to the staff of the War College, which would normally be another two-year commitment. He was disappointed with the orders and felt his place was at sea with another command. He immediately started lobbying to get the staff position reduced to a year.

In his new position he was responsible for the civilian staff, including the recruitment of instructors.[25] The President of the War College was a crusty old three star. "He was a little difficult," Hoffmann now relates. He had definite ideas about who would be acceptable to teach at the College. He often said, "Damnit Hoffmann, I want someone who can speak English—English!" Hoffmann's standard response: "Yes sir."

Once Commander Hoffmann brought in an academic from the University of Arkansas as a prospective teacher. The academic came in with a phony Ozark accent and interviewed with the President of the War College—it didn't go well. At the end of the interview Hoffmann asked the president what he thought and his response was, "He left his toothpick in my ashtray." He didn't make the faculty.

On another occasion Hoffmann zeroed in on a professor at Notre Dame, who was Polish. His credentials were good and he was ostensibly a renowned naval historian. Hoffmann called the professor of Military Science at Notre Dame (a Marine colonel) and asked him if he knew the Polish professor.

The colonel replied he didn't know him personally, but he had a good reputation.

"Have you heard him lecture?" Hoffmann asked.

"Yes," the colonel replied, "he gives an interesting lecture."

Remembering the president's admonition, Hoffmann asked. "How about his English?"

"Well," the colonel replied, "he has an accent, but no problem I know of."

"I'm depending on you," Hoffmann told the colonel. "I don't want to spend the money to bring him down here and find it's money down the drain."

Bring him down they did. He turned out to be a short, dumpy man who went bounding up to Commander Hoffmann gave his name and said with a *very* thick accent, "Call me Bill."

---

25. His official title was Director of Civilian Staff. He was also nominally in charge of the library, but there were women at the library "who had been there for 50 years," and they ran the place. He stayed out of their way. While at the Navy War College he received his Master's Degree in International Relations at George Washington University. The program was voluntary and was undertaken in addition to his other duties at the War College.

Hoffmann responded, "Professor, you're the first one up to begin the lectures for the new academic year. We selected you for your knowledge of international fleets and it would be appropriate if you give us a lecture on the strategy of the Soviet fleet."

"That would be fine," he said. After he had prepared the talk he asked Hoffmann to take a look at it. He did look at it and now relates, "It wasn't bad—it was terrible."

Mindful of diplomacy and academic freedom he made a copy of the speech and highlighted those areas where it might be improved.

When the professor got it back and reviewed it he said, "Can you be more specific?"

"Well, for example," Hoffmann said, "you talk about Soviet aircraft carriers. To the best of my knowledge, and I'm fairly positive of this, the Soviets don't have any aircraft carriers."

"A mere technicality," the professor responded. And so it came time for him to deliver his lecture, and it was as bad as Hoffmann had feared. Soon the audience was not only sleeping, some of them were snoring.

"Oh crap," he thought, "I hope the president isn't listening to this." The president was known for sneaking into the back of the auditorium and listening to the lectures. Hoffmann finally got up enough nerve to turn around and see if the president was back there, and sure enough, there he was, his eyes boring holes right through him.

The professor didn't improve much during the year and the president chewed out Hoffmann's boss. Hoffmann summarized the incident: "I could have killed that Marine at Notre Dame."

Each Christmas the CPOs at the Quonset Point Naval Station collected money to provide gifts for the residents of the institution where Harriet lived. In Roy Hoffmann's last year at the War College the Quonset Point Naval Station was going through a Navy directed downsizing, and the continuity was lost to raise the funds. He was asked to step in and organize the fund drive for the Holidays, a challenge he accepted. John Joseph O'Connor, then a Navy commander and the Destroyer Force Chaplain at Newport, helped him with the drive.

O'Connor had been ordained as a Catholic priest in 1945, and he later earned his Ph.D. from Georgetown University. He joined the U.S. Navy in 1952 as a military chaplain, ministering to soldiers in both the Korean and Vietnam Wars. He eventually became the U.S. Navy's Chief of Chaplains, and retired from the Navy with the rank of rear admiral in 1979.

He then went on to serve as auxiliary bishop of New York to Terence

Cardinal Cooke from 1979 to 1983. In 1984 Father O'Connor was appointed archbishop of New York by Pope John Paul II, and was elevated to cardinal the following year. He was an ardent traditionalist and an outspoken defender of Roman Catholic teaching on sexual and moral ethics. His views, particularly his staunch opposition to abortion, often caused controversy. In 1990 his statement that Roman Catholics who were in favor of abortion should be excommunicated caused a fire storm. He died May 3, 2000 in New York.[26]

Sailors in the force contributed the money, and Father O'Connor and Roy Hoffmann went to the exchange to load up shopping baskets for the gifts. Many of the residents of the institution were adults, and as such had adult habits, such as chewing tobacco while working on the farms. One of the shopping baskets was full of chewing tobacco. The clerk looked incredulously at Roy Hoffmann when he came through with the basket of chewing tobacco. Father O'Connor was standing behind him in line, shook his head, and said, "Oh, my friend likes to chew tobacco." The disgusted clerk looked at Roy Hoffmann as though he were out of his mind.

USS *Charles F. Adams* (DDG 2)

On January 26, 1966, at the Charleston, South Carolina Naval Base, Commander Roy F. Hoffmann relieved Commander Robert R. Monroe and took command of the USS *Charles F. Adams* (DDG 2).[27] Monroe had been the fourth captain of the *Adams*, having relieved Commander Emmett H. Tidd in July of 1964.[28] The Executive Officer was Lieutenant Commander Charles A. Reed, a highly capable and experienced destroyer man and Naval Academy graduate. It was a plum assignment to get the ship bearing the class name. Mary Linn Hoffmann relates that her husband was absolutely delighted with the orders and one can understand why.

The *Adams* was the first U.S. Navy ship designed and built as a guided

---

26. O'Connor, John Joseph Cardinal (2006). In the *Encyclopedia Britannica*. Retrieved November 10, 2006, from Encyclopedia Britannica Online: http://www.britannica.com/eb/article-9400553

27. Much of the information for this chapter was developed from interviews with Roy and Mary Linn Hoffmann; and interviews with Judge Robert Andretta on June 14 and August 17, 2006; Matt D'Amico on April 8, 2006; and Pat Sheedy on August 21, 2006.

28. Monroe was an operations analyst specialist. The *Adams* had just completed a Med. Cruise, had good officers and men, and was in excellent material condition. Commander Hoffmann got a good ship when he took over.

Mary Linn Hoffmann (right) presents a check from the Charles F. Adams *crew to Catherine Brancel, a patient of the Crippled Children's Society. With Mary Linn is Mrs. Young, wife of John Young, a Third Class Radarman aboard the* Adams.
Official U.S. Navy Photo, Hoffmann collection

missile destroyer. She was designed with an advanced hull design, and state of the art detection equipment, weaponry and propulsion. She had aboard TARTAR surface to air missiles; ASROC anti-submarine rocket-assisted torpedoes and depth charges; five-inch 54 rapid-fire dual-purpose guns; and a 1200 psi steam plant. Her complement was 18 officers and 319 men.

She displaced 3,370 tons (drawing 22 feet of water), was 437 feet in length and 47 feet across the beam. She had two shaft geared steam turbines (developing 70,000 shp) for 31 knots. The *Adams*'s call sign was "Steam-Cutter." She was nicknamed by her sailors "Charlie Deuce" when they were pleased with their duty and "Sucky Chucky" when they were not. Captain Hoffmann always insisted she be called the *Charles F. Adams* in his presence, never just the *Adams*.

The ship was named after Charles Francis Adams, grandson of John Quincy Adams, and Secretary of the Navy from 1929–1933. He was known for his efforts to promote U.S. Navy sea power in the world's oceans.

She was built at Bath Iron Works in Bath, Maine, and was commissioned at the Boston Naval Shipyard in 1960. She commenced operations as part of Destroyer Squadron Six, an all missile ship squadron organized into two destroyer divisions. The *Adams* was in Destroyer Division 62 (DESDIV 62), which consisted of three DDGs. DESDIV 61 usually had the commodore on board a DLG.

When Roy Hoffmann took command, Robert A. Andretta was already aboard.[29] Bob Andretta was a junior ensign in G Division, assigned as missile officer. He had arrived on the *Adams* in late fall 1965 when the ship was under the command of Captain Monroe. Andretta was pleased with the arrival of Hoffmann, as he thought Monroe was too stuffy for a destroyer command. He relates that almost immediately factions developed on the ship, which either viewed the new captain positively or negatively. But from Andretta's standpoint, "I thought he was pretty good; in fact, I thought he was terrific."

For the first year he did not see Captain Hoffmann as a disciplinarian at

---

29. Bob Andretta served two tours on destroyers, and then went to Vietnam as an advisor to the South Vietnamese Junk Force (see Chapter 7). He is a Naval Academy graduate, class of 1965. He was retired under disability from the Navy in July of 1972, as a result of wounds he received in Vietnam. By the time he retired he was an antiwar, liberal McGovernite. One suspects he is still an unreconstructed liberal today, but was, as with most of the interviews conducted by this author, an absolute pleasure to interview. He recently retired as a Federal Court Judge with the Housing and Urban Development department in Washington, D.C.

all. Andretta relates he thought Hoffmann was fair and well humored and they came to have a warm relationship. Hoffmann called the senior ensign "Bull Ensign," and when Andretta achieved that status Hoffmann began calling him "Bull." When Andretta would come on the bridge the captain would say, "How you doing, *Bull?*" He found he could joke around with the captain *as long as he did his job.* Andretta felt a real affection for the new captain and felt it was reciprocated.

On February 15, 1966, the *Adams* departed for a Mediterranean cruise. The ship had ports of call at Barcelona, Spain; Bari and Brindisi, Italy; and Casablanca, Morocco. As they transited to Casablanca they were warned that most of the African nations claimed a 12-mile territorial waters limit, while the U.S. recognized a three-mile limit. The *Adams* was also made aware there were hostile craft on the sea, equipped with missiles and prepared to enforce the 12-mile limit. Captain Hoffmann decided the quickest route to Casablanca was to cut into that limit by four or five miles. Soon there were three hostile gunboats racing toward the *Adams*. In international flags (and in international waters) the gunboats signaled, "Stop your ship."

In the missile silo on the *Adams* were 40 armed missiles and two test missiles painted blue and gold. The test missiles normally went out when the ship entered port. They weren't real but they looked impressive.

Bob Andretta informed Captain Hoffmann there were missile gunboats coming at the ship and he replied, "Yeah, so what are we supposed to do about it?"

Andretta replied, "How about if I put the test missiles on the launcher and make them look as though they are ready to fire?" And that's what they did. The gunboats, spotting the loaded launcher, turned back to the coast.

Next liberty port was Gibraltar, where their British hosts made them feel welcome. By then the Beatles had captivated the Western world with their music and it could be heard all over the ship.[30] Next up was Alexandroupolis-Kavalla, Greece; and Istanbul, Turkey, the easternmost port of the cruise. Istanbul was the business, commercial and cultural center of Turkey, and a city of then over two million people. The sailors were briefed on Turkish customs before going ashore. They were warned that anyone who insults or curses a Turk in public may be imprisoned for up to three years; Turkish girls should not be spoken to without an introduction; and to stare at or take pictures of Turkish girls without

---

30. "Help," "Yesterday," and "We Can Work It Out," were what the crew was listening to by the Beatles. Other popular songs in early 1966 were "The Ballad of the Green Berets" by SSGT Barry Sadler, "(You're My) Soul and Inspiration" by the Righteous Brothers, "Good Lovin'" by the Young Rascals and "Monday, Monday" by the Mama's & Papa's.

The USS Charles F. Adams *(DDG 2).* Official U.S. Navy Photo, Hoffmann collection

permission was offensive. Turks have great respect for the law—just to curse the law is subject to punishment of up to six years in prison.[31]

Istanbul has been continuously inhabited for over 2,000 years, and the ancient and the modern coexist in the city. The city was once the capital of the Eastern, or Byzantine Empire, which was primarily Greek in ethnic background and culture. The Greeks founded a settlement there known as Byzantium in 685 BC, which later came under the domination of Persia and Macedonia. In 196 AD the city was taken after a three-year siege by Emperor Septinius Severus and thereafter became part of the Roman Empire. In 423 the city fell to Constantine who renamed it Constantinople. In 1205 Latin Crusaders besieged the city. They eventually captured and sacked the city, desecrating its holy places. Constantinople fell to the Turks, under Mohammed the Conqueror, in 1453, after which it was made the chief city of the Ottoman Empire. Turks under Ataturk gained independence in 1923 and in 1924 the city was renamed Istanbul.

---

31. The entire adult population of the United States would be in prison under those circumstances.

Next up was Naples Italy, nestled under the shadows of towering Vesuvius and the ruins of Pompeii; and Palma, Mallorca, a favorite with the sailors for its sunny white beaches, rugged mountain beauty and beautiful bikini-clad Scandinavian girls.

The ship participated in many Navy exercises during the cruise. On a crisp early Mediterranean morning in March of 1966, while cruising on station during NATO War Exercise Fairgame IV, a French *Estendard* jet went down within visual range of the *Adams*. French aviator LT Bernard Birot bailed out of the burning craft and he was rescued and aboard the ship within 15 minutes.

On July 10, 1966, the *Adams* returned from the Med. Cruise. The youth of America, including the young sailors on the *Adams*, were listening to "Hungry" by Paul Revere & the Raiders; "Wild Thing" by the Troggs (the seminal punk hit); "Summer in the City" by the Lovin' Spoonful, the electrified jug band with lead vocalist John Sebastian; and "See You In September" by the Happenings.

Despite the fact Jimmy Hoffa would eventually become a joke after his mysterious disappearance, eliciting more "sightings" than the departed Elvis, in 1966 he was no joke. After a conviction for taking $250,000 in union funds, and despite his status of being out on bail pending appeal, he was reelected to a five-year term as Teamsters President by acclamation. Dr. Martin Luther King, Jr. was engaged in his campaign to make Chicago an "open city" by ending job and housing discrimination with a 40,000-person rally. Also in Chicago, Robert Speck, an itinerant worker, bound and killed, one by one, eight student nurses in their dormitory room.

And in Vietnam, U.S. B-52s from Guam bombed the demilitarized zone separating North and South Vietnam. Defense Secretary Robert McNamara defended the bombing raids with the reasonable explanation that North Vietnam was using the DMZ to enter South Vietnam. In the United States, thousands were entering the military, either voluntarily or by the draft, to supply soldiers for the Vietnam War.

IN LATE SUMMER the *Adams* was ordered into dry dock at the Charleston Naval Yard. As usual funds were tight for the overhaul and ship's company as well as yard personnel worked on the ship. Summer in Charleston was hot and humid and by all accounts it was a miserable yard period. Sailors worked in 120-degree heat in the engine room and topside in the humidity, chipping paint. It is safe to say the miserable working conditions did not endear the captain to the crew.

Lieutenant j.g. Matt D'Amico arrived on the *Adams* just as she came out of the Charleston Navy Yard and headed for refresher training at Guantanamo (called "Gitmo" by the sailors).[32] He was supposed to have been the ASW officer, but when he reported aboard he instead became the First Lieutenant, responsible for, among other things, the appearance and seamanship of the ship. The officer that D'Amico replaced had already left the ship, and as it turned out he had big shoes to fill. "Hoffmann loved him [the former officer]."

D'Amico had a raw crew; his LPO was a first class boatswain's mate, whose view of how the Navy should run didn't necessarily coincide with Captain Hoffmann's. D'Amico remembers Captain Hoffmann walking around with his big cigar, barking at the officers. "Hoffmann rode my butt the whole time in Gitmo," D'Amico said. "It was one of the best things that ever happened to me in my life [in terms of experience]. Hoffmann's standards were exceptionally high, but if he believed in you he would back you one hundred per cent plus. With him, it was all or nothing."

Pat Sheedy was another officer who arrived about this time.[33] He joined the *Adams* as an ensign after a month in gunnery school. When he met Captain Hoffmann he was informed that the ship didn't need a gunner, but they needed a communications officer. Sheedy was made the assistant communications officer and sent off to Newport for Comm. School. He relates that everyone had a different perspective of Captain Hoffmann, largely depending on his level of responsibility. He was harder on department heads than junior officers; harder on junior officers than on chiefs; harder on chiefs than second class and above. Lower rate enlisted men didn't suffer his wrath, as it should have been.

Hoffmann could be moody. "Something could go wrong and he could bite your head off," Sheedy relates. "He would yell at you, but he always was under control, and five minutes later it would be forgotten. Hoffmann never bore grudges. He was always evaluating his officers, but if he thought you were thinking right, he would stand behind you and let you make mistakes. But God save you if he thought you were sloughing off or were hiding something. That's when you could stand by for heavy rolls."

In February 1967 the *Adams* sailed for Fort Lauderdale, where they took

---

32. The *Adams* was D'Amico's second ship. He was a classmate of Bob Andretta at the Naval Academy, class of 1965.

33. Commander Pat Sheedy, USN Ret., is a Charleston native, and a graduate of the Naval Academy, class of 1966.

AFL/CIO official George Harrison and Captain Roy Hoffmann (left), Adams, February 25, 1967. Official U.S. Navy Photo, Hoffmann collection

the AFL/CIO Union Executive Council out for a cruise. Sheedy relates that Captain Hoffmann had a very social side and he excelled in events like that, where guests received first class treatment.

Since the *Adams* had to take the union executives out for a day, Captain Hoffmann felt it was only fair that dependents got to go as well. For this particular event Mary Linn and two of the girls drove down to Florida. Chris, Cecile, Mary Linn, and a fiancée of one of the junior officers on the ship made the trip. Unfortunately, the seas were rough on the Dependents' Day cruise. George Meany, head of the union, didn't go because he was prone to seasickness. The seas were so rough Chris got sick all over Mary Linn. Pat Sheedy brought his parents, his brother and an uncle who was a Catholic priest aboard for the cruise. The priest and Captain Hoffmann got along famously.

From there they went on to Gitmo for refresher training. Again, by all accounts, Hoffmann was on everyone. He wanted a 90 per cent score on everything they did. He was as usual insistent on damage control excellence, and he kept the crew at their battle stations for long periods in the Caribbean heat.

And so, at least initially, according to Matt D'Amico, "Morale at Gitmo—it sucked. But like any team, once they started tasting success it became contagious, and the morale improved with that. Hoffmann had the ability to elevate their talents. A lot of it he did by fear, but once you got to know him his bark was much worse than his bite."

D'Amico gives examples of the captain's methods. The ship had a fake sailor they used for man overboard drills, Oscar the Dummy. "You never knew when Hoffmann was going to be around," D'Amico relates. "He was a terrible sleeper. You could be up on the bridge at 0300 and all of a sudden you'd hear from the fantail, 'Man Overboard!' Hoffmann had grabbed Oscar and thrown him overboard; he wanted to know how fast the crew would react."

On the damage control drills they would set Condition Zebra and the captain would send out teams to check that doors and hatches were dogged down and tight by slipping papers between the door and the jam. Captain Hoffmann would then count up deficiencies. It wasn't enough to set Condition Zebra in three minutes—Hoffmann also wanted to know if it was effective. As D'Amico relates, "In the end we were better for it." Other ships would invite *Adams*'s sailors over to run damage control exercises, her crew was that good. Needless to say, it became a point of pride to be an *Adams* sailor. "The ship was very smart, sharp, and always did things right."[34] By all accounts, the *Adams* was an outstanding ship.

WHILE ON THE GITMO exercises they entered an area where there were no charts. The *Adams* slowed to two knots and Hoffmann put Andretta in a small boat ahead of the ship to take soundings ("Like Mark Twain," according to Andretta). The XO, Lieutenant Commander Charles Reed, was a *very* serious and sober individual who worried about the safety of the ship. As Andretta was ahead of the destroyer in the little boat he thought of ASW operations, in which the lead destroyer is called "brother" and the following destroyer is called "sister," and then they switch off. When they change positions the lead destroyer says "I am brother, you are sister." So, Andretta, who could be something of a smart ass, announced from his small boat, "I am brother, you are sister." When he got back on board the XO was angry about the flippancy, but Hoffmann thought it uproariously funny and bellowed, "Give the Bull some slack."

---

34. Matt D'Amico interview, April 8, 2006.

Adams launches an anti-submarine rocket (ASROC), February 25, 1967.
Official U.S Navy Photo, Hoffmann collection

On underway replenishments (UNREPS) the standard procedure was that the UNREP ship would steam along at 12 knots and the other ship would come up at 15 knots and ease alongside. Not with Captain Hoffmann. His philosophy was that you approach at full speed. As soon the bow passed the stern of the oiler (or carrier), then you would back down full. With him there was no in between.

As Pat Sheedy pointed out in an interview, the above was an example of the difference between the old Navy and the new Navy. In the old Navy, which Roy Hoffmann represented, you wanted to do things with flair. Officially doing the UNREP as Hoffmann did it allowed more control of the ship and decreased the time of the evolution—you wanted it to go as fast as possible—but it was also pretty showy. Sheedy points out, "We'd have guys on the oiler waving goodbye to us as we approached and then their jaws would drop when we got alongside."

Sheedy indicated that in the post Vietnam Navy that was never done—a captain could be court-martialed for the maneuver. In the old Navy you were considered a Top Gun if you were aggressive. Now in the new Navy everyone is afraid of scratching the paint. As Sheedy put it, "Roy Hoffmann represents a part of the Navy that's gone. There's no incentive anymore."

Captain Hoffmann was cognizant of and solicitous of the blue jackets (enlisted men). On many ships the OOD sampled the food served enlisted men on the mess decks. Half the time they didn't do it. Not on Hoffmann's ship. On the *Adams* the officers ate meals once daily on the mess decks. Captain Hoffmann was known to frequently go down on the mess decks and eat there himself to ensure quality.

However, the captain was tough at Captain's Mast. He was relatively easy on rates E 1 through 5, but very tough on chiefs and first class petty officers. He put a lot of responsibility on them. He understood how the Navy worked. He knew ensigns lacked the experience to make the ship run well; the same was true of seamen. It was the first class and chief petty officers, senior officers and captain that could make it an outstanding ship.[35] His favorite punishment for non-rated men was extra duty properly cleaning out the bilges.

IN THE LATE SPRING OF 1967 the *Adams* was assigned to a major air defense exercise in the Caribbean which included midshipmen's training in the Atlantic, after which they were scheduled to go to New Orleans. As it turned out the flagship couldn't pass under the electrical cables spanning the San Jacinto River into Houston, so the *Adams* and the *Courtney* got sent instead to participate in the San Jacinto Day observance. The *Adams* was sent to Houston, which the crew felt was a poor substitute for New Orleans.

At that time the Astrodome had just been built and Captain Hoffmann sent an official Navy message to Judge Roy Hofheinz, owner of the Astros, informing him that the *Adams* was coming into Houston with a group of midshipmen and his crew that loved baseball; would the owner be interested in having the Astrodome host the sailors? The owner agreed, and over the Fourth of July weekend the entire crew of both ships (in shifts), got to go to the Astrodome for at least two games. On Sunday the wardroom of the *Adams* watched the game from the skybox.

---

35. Bob Andretta thought the captain's use of formal court martial for the crew was excessive. Andretta got named as defense attorney a couple of times (this was before he was an attorney). Andretta studied hard; he didn't want to screw up the defense because he didn't know what he was doing. As it turned out he won three of the cases in a row, angering Captain Hoffmann because the cases hadn't gone as he felt they should. As a consequence Hoffmann moved Andretta to trial counsel because he had been successful in defense. That made *him* angry because he was now the antagonist of the sailors. Bob Andretta interview, June 14, 2006.

On August 18, 1967 the *Adams* deployed for another Med. Cruise. By then the ship had a new XO, Lieutenant Commander William D. Watkins. Watkins had joined the Navy in October of 1941. He achieved the rate of chief petty officer in 1956, and was commissioned as a mustang ensign in 1957. Matt D'Amico remembers Watkins as a competent and very nice guy who frustrated Captain Hoffmann. Hoffmann felt he was too nice and that he had to do the discipline part of the XO's job.

But overall, the cruise went well. Captain Hoffmann had a good ship and was always happiest at sea. He believed that sailors should be allowed to wear neatly trimmed beards, even though they were discouraged by the Navy at that time.[36] He let the men of the *Adams* grow beards, which, along with the excellence of the *Adams*, made them stand out in the fleet. As D'Amico puts it, "He didn't give a shit if the admiral saw his men with beards. He was no politician—if he had been he could have been CNO. I marvel at the fact that he actually made flag rank, because he stepped on a lot of toes. He couldn't exist today."

The first stop on the cruise was Valencia, Spain, followed by Valletta, Malta, located 150 miles due south of Sicily in the Mediterranean Sea. The city had withstood three years of constant bombing by the Axis Powers during World War II. From there they went to Barcelona, Spain, where Mary Linn flew to meet her husband, on her first trip to Europe. Next was Brindisi, Italy, where a local chef volunteered to prepare and serve a meal on board ship. Next they went to LaCiotat, France, a small shipbuilding and fishing port on the southern coast of France.

LaCiotat had been taken over by the Nazis in World War II and they had extensively mined the harbor. After the war the U.S. sent an underwater demolition team to clear the minefield. During the clearing of the mines the American lieutenant in charge was killed in the line of duty. Apparently he had time before he died to father a few children in the community. The town erected a statue to him for his successful efforts to open up the port to commerce and shipbuilding.

Around October Matt D'Amico, who was the junior officer of the deck, was on the wing of the pilot house enjoying the sunshine on a beautiful day.

---

36. This was before Admiral Zumwalt was Chief of Naval Operations.

Captain Hoffmann called from the bridge, "D'Amico, come in here. The course is such and such, I have the deck and the conn, and you're taking it over now."

D'Amico wasn't a qualified OOD, but Hoffmann gave him the deck and the conn and he took the ship through a series of formations and drills after which he completed an underway replenishment. The next day the captain called him into his office and said "I'm qualifying you as fleet OOD."

And therein lies one of Hoffmann's strengths: He never looked at where you stood on the seniority list or what your rank was, all he cared about were your capabilities. "I always considered him to be a kind of General Patton type of character," D'Amico relates. "He had a lot of bluster but was a soldier's or sailor's type of officer. Too many leaders can't get their people to elevate their talents, but he could.

"I wasn't his biggest fan," he went on. "It was tough working for him. If you didn't measure up his philosophy was: 'How do I get rid of this officer without hurting him too badly.'

"You always knew when he was satisfied—he'd sit up in the captain's chair with a big old cigar in his mouth, he'd light up the cigar and start telling stories, but until he was satisfied with the performance he'd be chewing on us."

THE SHIP SPENT Christmas and New Year's in Cannes, France, amid the glitter and glamour of the fast-moving city. While in that port one of the radarmen (a third class) deserted. He ended up going to the Russian Embassy in Paris where he said he had information on an American warship. The Russians were not even interested in talking to him. He was never seen again on the *Adams*. They took inventory on the ship and determined there were no classified materials missing. They resumed the cruise and at the Iberian Peninsula the facts came out about the desertion and a report had to be made about it.

At the time it was considered a black mark against you as a captain if one of your crew deserted, even if it had nothing to do with you. Captain Hoffmann had informed the TF commander and the American Embassy of the situation, but he understandably wanted to keep the incident "in house," and didn't want it broadcast throughout the fleet.

He called in the Ops. Officer, the XO and Pat Sheedy to a meeting in the wardroom. The captain wanted to know how the message could be sent to the CNO, Secretary of the Navy and the State Department without it going out on a fleet broadcast. Sheedy advised that it could be sent at the highest

"Who said sailors can't march?" Adams *drill team, Ft. Lauderdale, Florida.* Official U.S. Navy Photo, Hoffmann collection

classification with special limited distribution caveats. And so he worked that night to put it in off-line crypto and get it sent out.

Two days later the message went out on fleet broadcast anyway and they received it on the *Adams*. The Ops Officer decided not to tell the captain, but once they got back to Charleston another captain told him it had gone out.

Bob Andretta relates that when they hit a port Captain Hoffmann was understanding of some of the shenanigans that went on ashore. At Gibraltar, for example, one of local hotels had a huge hammer and sickle Soviet banner (this at the height of the Cold War) flying over the Gibraltar cliffs. One-night junior officers from the *Adams* hauled down the flag and brought it back to the ship.

The next day the ship received a message from the Royal Navy captain of the port alerting the captain of the theft and stating that if it were returned it would be gratefully received with no questions asked. Hoffmann questioned his junior officers, who denied all. "Hoffmann knew goddamned well they were lying," Andretta relates, " but he just reported back to shore that he had looked into it thoroughly and it wasn't done by his men."

As the ship was leaving port Hoffmann discovered the flag on the navigation table. "Oh, shit," he thought. He sent it back to the Royal Navy with a letter of apology from the captain.

From January 15–18, 1968, the ship was in Marin, Spain, home of the

Spanish Naval Academy. One significant change in the Mediterranean was the increasing presence of Soviet warships, mostly cruisers, destroyers and frigates. The Soviets shadowed the American task groups wherever they went. When the U.S. ships entered a liberty port the Russians would lurk off the coast and wait for the U.S. ships to depart. The Russians were a constant presence and were known for harassing the U.S. Sixth Fleet. It became a point of pride to the Americans to strive for superior seamanship. The *Adams* cruise book states, "Ask any *Charles F. Adams* sailor who would be the first to back off [in a confrontation with the Soviets]."

The Soviets were particularly aggressive during UNREPS or carrier operations. On one incident during the Med. Cruise a Soviet ship had been aggressively crowding a carrier in the task force. During the operation the flag watch officer notified Captain Hoffmann on the *Adams* that the Soviet ship was making it a problem for the carrier to turn and maneuver, and requested that the *Adams* move the Soviet ship off. Hoffmann radioed back, "All you have to do is give me the order and we'll be there. Just tell the captain to hold his course and speed because I'm coming down close off your starboard beam and I'll be doing 27 knots. I'm going to make a wide turn under your stern and come right up between you and the Soviet destroyer on your port quarter. Just make sure the captain knows what's going on, because he won't be able to see me. All he'll be able to see is my mast and radar. It will look like we're going to be on your flight deck."

"Roger that," the carrier responded by radio.

Hoffmann put the Soviet ship and the *Adams* on a collision course and ended up between the carrier and the Soviet destroyer. The Soviet ship was forced to back down hard during the maneuver and popped the safeties on her steam plant.

Captain Hoffmann sent a message to the squadron commander, telling him about the maneuver. The squadron commander radioed back, "What the hell were you doing that for?"

Hoffmann sent a quick message back, "I was carrying out a specific order of the task force commander. Will advise you later."

The lessons Matt D'Amico took from incidents like the above were, "You don't take stupid risks, you take calculated risks. You train and train and then train some more so when the test came you were prepared."

THE *ADAMS* RETURNED from the Mediterranean cruise on January 29, 1968. Once into Charleston, Captain Hoffmann let a large contingency of the crew off for leave, as it had been a long cruise. He almost immediately got orders to take the *Adams* to Puerto Rico for a major missile exercise. One of the ships that had originally been ordered down could not respond and so the *Adams* was to replace her. Captain Hoffmann had to recall people from leave, which didn't make the crew very happy.

While they were in the Caribbean Hoffmann received a new set of orders to "Proceed and Report Immediately" to the Commander Surface Surveillance Force, Vietnam. He had four days to report to San Diego. "What the hell is this?" he thought.

It struck Pat Sheedy at the time that Hoffmann was somewhat surprised by the orders and confused as to what his position would be. He was concerned that he was going as the commander of Task Force 115, not merely being ordered to the task force. He soon learned that he was in fact the commander.

Hoffmann anchored the *Adams* at St. Thomas, where he went ashore via motor whaleboat, found a phone at a hotel and called BUPERS. "Where do you think I am?" he asked.

"Charleston," they responded.

"No, I'm not," he replied. "Do you ever look at movement reports? I'm down in the Caribbean."

"Can't you get off the ship?" they asked.

"We're in a major exercise, I'm anchored off St. Thomas and I can't leave the ship until I've been relieved. I'm also scheduled for an INSERV (Inspection and Survey)." This was a major inspection, particularly since the ship was equipped with nuclear tipped weapons. If the ship didn't pass the inspection it was labeled "unfit for warfare," and was out of service until the defects were corrected.

He advised BUPERS to leave him aboard through the inspection, as it would be difficult for a new CO to go through it. BUPERS did modify the reporting date slightly, allowing him more time. Hoffmann wanted to talk to some of the people at the Little Creek Amphibious Base, since he was reporting to the Commander of the Amphibious Force, Pacific. The orders to the Amphibious Fleet didn't thrill him. "What in the hell did I do to deserve this?" he thought. He had volunteered for duty in Vietnam, but had anticipated a destroyer assignment.

In his brief time at Little Creek he did have a chance to talk to a couple of former officers in charge of Swift boats, which would be under his command. One thing they told him was that the Rules of Engagement were so restrictive for the Swift boats in Vietnam they couldn't do much. By the time they got permission to return fire the enemy was gone. As a result, Roy Hoffmann made sure he had a thorough understanding of the Rules of Engagement as part of his preparation for his new command.

AND SO HIS TIME ABOARD the *Adams* ended. By all accounts it was a successful command of a fine ship. As in his previous command, he was very hands on, he wanted everything exact, and there was never any doubt who was in charge. He knew what needed to be done. He may not have been the best liked of captains, but he was the most respected. As Pat Sheedy put it, "If you had to go to war you wanted him to be on the bridge."

BOB ANDRETTA, MATT D'AMICO and Pat Sheedy all ended up volunteering for duty in Vietnam. D'Amico was particularly ready for a change from the *Adams*. There were other reasons he volunteered, but one was to get away from the unrelenting pressure Captain Hoffmann put on the officers. So it was a relief when his orders to Swift boats came through. He was ordered to San Diego to Swift boat training at Coronado.

In his fourth week of training there, "I was sitting in the BOQ in San Diego with Bill Zondorak and Gary Blinn eating lunch when I heard this voice say, 'D'Amico, what are you doing?'

"I look up, and there he is [Hoffmann], in his service dress khakis and he's got a fourth stripe [he was now a full captain]. And I said, Captain Hoffmann, what are you doing here?"

Hoffmann replied, "I'm your new boss."

D'Amico sat back and thought, "Oh my God."

PART THREE

VIETNAM TO RETIREMENT

Never before have our young men been sent into war under such conditions as prevailed in Vietnam and, I regret to say, in their own country. They fought in an unfavorable jungle environment where more often than not they were unable to distinguish friend from foe. They fought under the most severe restraints ever imposed on the members of any armed force. They fought an enemy whose homeland was a land sanctuary . . . and they did all this while many of their own countrymen were making accusations in writings, speeches, and demonstrations that what they were doing was immoral. And in spite of this, they carried out their duty with dedication and true professionalism—equal to, if not surpassing, the performance of American fighting men at any time, in any war.
—Admiral Thomas H. Moorer in a speech given at Pittston, Pennsylvania, March 17, 1973

The essence of war is violence. Moderation in war is imbecility. Hit first! Hit hard! And hit anywhere!
—Admiral Sir John Fisher, 1905

7

COMMANDER TASK FORCE 115

Leaving the Hoffmann Family

Captain Roy F. Hoffmann's new assignment became one of the more dangerous in Vietnam. He would repeatedly put himself In Harm's Way during his year there. What exactly did he leave behind to serve his country?

He had a wife, Mary Linn, to whom he had been married for 18 years. He had five daughters, the oldest of whom, Harriet (age 17), was severely disabled. His other four daughters, Christine Linn (age 15), Cecile (age 14), Hilarie Jean (age 12) and Emilie Frances (age 10), loved and respected their Dad, who reciprocated their love. They were all in their teens or nearly there.

It was a close family; in many respects Harriet made them a stronger family.[1] Harriet is autistic; she doesn't hear or speak, and she can't eat solid food, yet one is struck by how normal the girls felt their life was living with her. Her family nickname is "Boo." Cecile says, "Harriet really colored our lives. We used to go every Sunday when she was in state school in Rhode Island, pick her up and go somewhere. We would spend the afternoon with her, and of course with each other. We had so much fun.

"Harriet was just another member of the family," Cecile says, "We enjoy her. She knows how to wheedle coffee out of people. She thinks all fans should be running—she'll turn them all on high. She has her ways. We all get a kick out of it." "My Dad," Chris says, "is so sweet with Harriet."

When Harriet was home, Emilie says, "If somebody made fun of Boo

---

1. Description of the Hoffmann family developed from interviews with the Admiral and Mary Linn; Chris Hoffmann Carnahan (July 13, 2006); Cecile Hoffmann Gorham (January 10, 2007); Hilarie Hoffmann Hanson (January 11, 2007); and Emilie Hoffmann Crow (October 2, 2006). All quotes are from those interviews.

they took on the whole family." As the next oldest, Chris often defended her older sister. Mary Linn says, "Chris once beat the heck out of a school kid on the bus for making fun of Harriet. At mass one time Harriet was on the pew quietly digging around in my purse. A woman in front of us kept watching Harriet and Chris said, 'You turn around.'"

All of the girls mention what a commitment Mary Linn made to keep Harriet at home. Chris says, "I just can't believe how my mother handled it. I never heard her complain." It was an incredible commitment. Every Sunday the family would go to church (excepting Roy Hoffmann). When he was gone Mary Linn would drive the girls to catechism, then drive back home, because she had Harriet, then she would drive back, take the girls home, and drive back for mass. As Hilarie says, "Just this big, complicated effort, to go to church." One time Mary Linn got a migraine while driving to church. The first thing it affected was her vision, so she had to pull over to the side of the road. It would have been easier to just go home and go to bed, but she didn't; she never took the easy way. When it came time for Chris to go to college she said she would go to Old Dominion, located in nearby Norfolk, so she could help her mom with Harriet. Mary Linn said, "Uh, uh, Harriet is not your job. You get out of here."

The family took frequent moves in stride. Emilie says, "We didn't know any better. We thought it was normal." Hilarie says, "Moving for us was not an issue, it was just the way it was." As a parent now, Hilarie sees that in a way it was easier—there was no decision to make—it was just the way it was. But, "as we got older, each of us had a problem with a particular move, particularly in high school." They had a strong sense of belonging. Cecile says, "I always felt very comfortable—like I belonged."

The girls grew up without television. "We never had a power lawn mower either," Cecile says with a laugh. "We had a push lawn mower. I thought, 'oh my God, we have to be seen in public pushing this lawn mower that doesn't even have an engine on it.'"

As youths, Chris, Hilarie and Cecile were all on the same softball team. "We really had a fun time," Cecile says. "Chris was one of those players you really had to watch out for because she could hit a home run at any time." The girls had grown up watching their mother play softball, and their mother was the team coach.

Their Dad's promotions weren't really celebrated in the family. When they moved to Charleston he started taking Emilie and Hilarie to the ship on Saturdays. "That was a real treat for us," Hilarie says. "He would take two of the girls and we would be there for several hours. It was sharing something he did with us."

His daughters called their dad "D-Boy" which stood for "Daddy-Boy." Chris says with a laugh, "He may be 'altitude-challenged' but he's bigger than life to me." Cecile says her favorite time, as a youth, was bath time. Her dad would "drop us all in the tub at once and get it over with." He taught the girls to sing in three-part harmony in the car on trips. Chris says of her dad, "To me he's a marshmallow. He's a sweet man, he's very tender, but he doesn't like to show it."

He didn't talk about the military, but Cecile echoed all of the girls when she said, "I really admired and looked up to him. Maybe it was because he wore that uniform and always looked so sharp in it. We'd go down to the docks and he'd be up there on the bridge and it was always very impressive." Hilarie says, "We knew his life was the Navy. That's where he excelled and what he was proud of."

Cecile says, "My Dad isn't afraid to tackle anything, even if he doesn't know anything about it. One time we needed a new sidewalk so he took out a sledgehammer, broke up the old one and then they poured a new sidewalk. For me he's been a great example of if you want to get something done do it yourself."

The girls also love and respect their mother. Chris describes her mother as a rock. During the most challenging years of raising the girls "my Dad was gone. She had the toughest job a woman could have—including corporate. She was consistent, she never backed down from her decisions, and as a result we knew our boundaries. We knew there would be consequences if we crossed them and as a result we've been successful in our own lives."

Hilarie says, "She's so strong. She gave all of us a feeling that we could do anything." Cecile says that because of her mother, "I've never once thought 'I can't do this because I'm a girl.'"

Emilie says, "Mom was very strict, but I'm sure she had to be with five of us. I don't ever remember her saying, 'wait until your father comes home.' We'd just as soon get it from Dad." Hilarie describes it as "the look." "Once you got 'the look,' that was it."

The girls all describe Mary Linn as very intelligent, very competitive, very athletic. Hilarie says, "We never, ever, saw or heard our parents fight. We knew it happened. We called it 'the icicles.' You knew they weren't happy but we never heard them fight. It was a very respectful, disciplined environment."

THE GIRLS WERE YOUNG when their dad departed for Vietnam; they were aware of the long deployment but not as much about the danger. Their parents told them that Cam Ranh Bay, where he would be headquartered, was one of the safest places in Vietnam (true enough). The girls were in or near their teenage years and so were in many respects wrapped up in their lives. Without a television they weren't exposed to the daily negative media images of Vietnam much of the rest of America saw. And of course by then the media had misrepresented the Tet Offensive earlier in the year (January 30 to February 24) as a massive setback for America and her ally South Vietnam, when in fact the Offensive had essentially destroyed the Viet Cong in South Vietnam. Most of their battles in the future would have to be fought jointly with enemy soldiers from the North Vietnamese Army.

There exists a photo of the girls taken with their father the day Mary Linn took him to the airport to leave for Vietnam.[2] It was a somber occasion, but the picture indicates that Cecile was the most upset, with downcast eyes. She was a freshman in high school, and the daughter most like her dad. "I was very upset," Cecile says. "I knew my mother was very upset—that was felt throughout the house. I was kind of scared. When I realized he was going away to war it really bothered me."

All of the girls remember Mary Linn being upset with her husband's departure. "For Mom it was a separation for a year and a much more dangerous assignment," Chris now says. "It's one of the very few times in my life I saw my mom cry."[3]

THERE WAS SOME URGENCY for Captain Hoffmann to get to his command. The previous commander had suffered a heart attack, and the Navy required that Hoffmann report without leave or other delays. He was attempting to reach Missouri for his parents' 50th wedding anniversary when he arrived in Atlanta, April 4, 1968, the day Dr. Martin Luther King was felled at age 39 by a sniper's bullet in Memphis. The airport in Memphis, where Hoffmann

---

2. The photo has been on Mary Linn's dresser since 1968. Unfortunately, with the passage of time it was not of sufficient quality to be reproduced for this book.

3. It was most difficult for the Admiral as well. Years later he wrote in response to a question posed by a grandchild: "What was the hardest part of war for you?" "Family separation" he responded, " is the most enduring hardship of war. Missing family holidays and celebrations can be demoralizing; but more important is the realization that you may not be the father you should be."

was to go from Atlanta, was locked down, and the area was bristling with soldiers walking around with guns. Hoffmann's orders barely allowed him enough time to get to Missouri, report to San Diego and then Vietnam. Fortunately he was in uniform and had his orders. He approached the officer in charge in Atlanta and told him, "If I can't fly to Memphis I'm going to miss my mother and father's golden anniversary, which I have promised them I'd make. My schedule is tight with my orders and I've got to get out of here." They let him fly into Memphis, where he got on a Greyhound bus to St. Louis. He made it to the golden anniversary.

MEANWHILE, MARY LINN had issues of her own to deal with. She had been "surprised and concerned" by the orders to Vietnam, which came out of the blue. She had to get a power of attorney to act on his behalf while he was gone, and the lease was up on the home they were renting. She wanted to find another rental in the same school district so the girls would not have to change schools.

She spotted a house for sale owned by a Navy officer she knew. She went up, rang the doorbell and asked, "Would you be interested in renting your house for the year Roy is in Vietnam?" Without hesitation he said yes. His name was Captain Tom Nutt and he was a lifesaver for Mary Linn.

OPERATION MARKET TIME[4]

Roy Hoffmann reported to the Amphibious Base at Coronado, and then flew on to Pearl Harbor, where he had a meeting with Admiral John S. McCain, Jr.[5] Admiral McCain was Commander in Chief, Pacific Command (CINCPAC). As such, he had command of all U.S. forces in the Pacific,

---

4. Much of the documentation for Market Time and SEALORDS operations came from interviews with the Admiral, his official documents from his time as CTF 115, Division Command Histories and some 25 interviews conducted with men who were participants in the events. There are two sources that are excellent on the river wars: Thomas J. Cutler's, *Brown Water Black Beret* and R. L. Shreadley's *From the Rivers to the Sea*. Douglas Brinkley's hagiography of John Kerry, *Tour of Duty*, has much that is accurate, and portions that are not accurate at all. The challenge in using the book for research is to distinguish between the two.

5. Admiral McCain was the father of Arizona Senator John McCain. The distinguished naval history of the McCain family is told in John McCain's 1999 book, *Faith of My Fathers*.

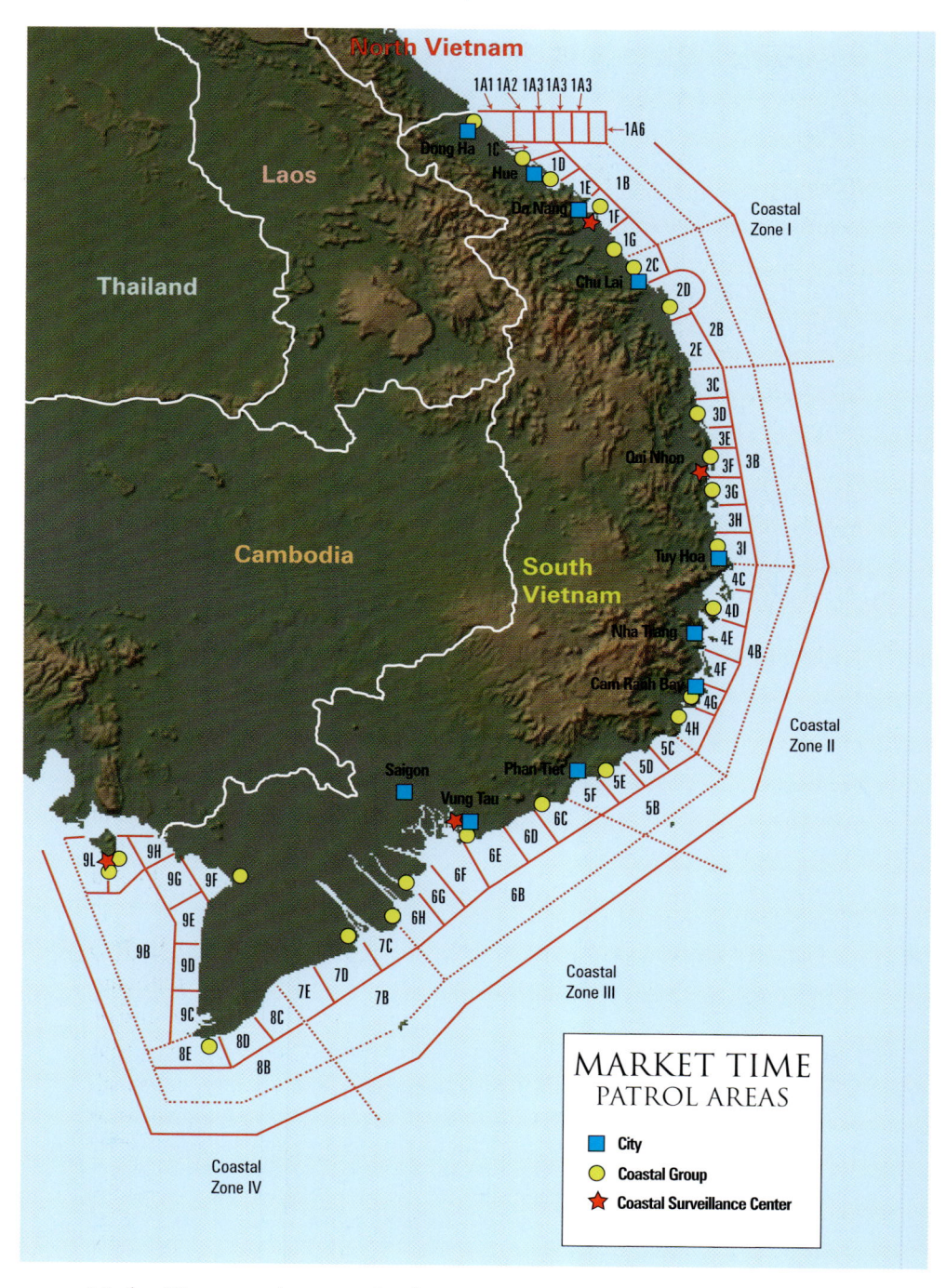

Market Time coastal zones in South Vietnam. MAP BY ARROW GRAPHICS

Briefings were part of the duties; here Captain Hoffmann briefs actor and U.S. Air Force General Jimmy Stewart and his wife, Gloria, on one of their trips to Vietnam.
HOFFMANN PHOTO

the largest military command in the world. It is a geographically immense area, encompassing 85 million square miles, and extends from the Aleutian Islands to the South Pole, and from the west coast of North and South America to the Indian Ocean. It is second only to the office of Chief of Naval Operations in prestige.

Captain Hoffmann asked Admiral McCain if he could meet with his JAG officer; Admiral McCain understandably wanted to know why. Hoffmann told him he had studied the Rules of Engagement prior to going over and he wasn't convinced that they needed the strict application he had heard about in Little Creek and Coronado, where he learned there was entirely too much central control. The Officers in Charge would have to radio headquarters in Cam Ranh Bay to get permission to shoot. By the time that authority came back the enemy was gone. McCain responded, "You know, I agree with you. Go ahead and talk to the JAG." As it turned out the JAG officer also agreed the Rules need not be that restrictive.

On the way to Cam Ranh, Roy Hoffmann drafted his first order, which

The Operation Market Time harbor at Cam Ranh Bay.
Official U.S. Navy photo, Hoffmann collection

Command headquarters, Task Force 115, Cam Ranh Bay, RVN.
Official U.S. Navy photo, Hoffmann collection

indicated that the on-scene commander (after the proper sequence of sirens, lights, warning shots across the bow, etc.) would make the decision on whether to commence firing on a suspected enemy. In the order he wrote that not only did they have the authority, he expected them to use it.

His attitude was, "*We were there to win the war.* I had no intention of just sitting there and letting the clock tick." The task force was in for a change. Douglas Brinkley in *Tour of Duty* had it right when he wrote, "Captain Roy 'Latch' Hoffman [sic], the new commander, was a proud Korean War veteran, a fierce believer in the serious use of force, and not the least bit inclined to sit in the headquarters at Cam Ranh Bay and watch passively. . . . He was short, a bantam rooster who preferred the field to sitting behind a desk, especially if things were hot."

Brinkley then goes on to assert: "Interviews with various Swift boat veterans turned up descriptions of Hoffman [sic] as 'hotheaded,' 'blood-thirsty,' and 'egomaniacal.'"[6] Those are not descriptions that emerged from the extensive interviews this author conducted with Swift boat personnel for the writing of this book.

Rear Admiral Kenneth L. Veth was the Commander of Naval Forces Vietnam (COMNAVFORV) when Captain Hoffmann arrived in country. Admiral Veth was the in country tactical combat commander of Task Forces 115 (Market Time), 116 (Game Warden) and 117 (River Assault Force).

The workhorses of Task Force 116, then under the command of Captain A. W. Price, were the legendary PBRs, 31-foot-long fiberglass boats, which had compiled an impressive record preventing movement of enemy personnel and supplies along and across the major rivers of the Mekong Delta and Rung Sat Special Zone. The task force was comprised of support ships, PBRs, helicopters, minesweepers and, later, SEALs. One of their most important responsibilities was to defend and keep open the Long Tau River. The dark green PBRs were suited for inshore shallow water operations, with their 220 horsepower diesel engines driving water-jet pumps supplied by Jacuzzi Brothers. They were fast, lethal, with twin 50 caliber machine guns forward, and could turn on a dime.

Task Force 117, then under the command of Captain Schermerhorn (later replaced by Robert S. Salzer), conducted operations on the rivers of the Mekong Delta and Rung Sat Special Zone. The Navy element of the Mobile Riverine Force, operating with the 2nd Brigade of the U.S. Army's

---

6. Douglas Brinkley, *Tour of Duty* (New York: William Morrow, 2004), p. 105.

Captain Hoffmann with Rear Admiral Veth, the predecessor to Vice Admiral Elmo Zumwalt. OFFICIAL U.S. NAVY PHOTO, HOFFMANN COLLECTION

9th Infantry Division, was River Assault Flotilla One, comprised of heavily armed and armored boats designed for troop transport, escort and fire support in a riverine environment.

Task Force 115, Captain Hoffmann's command, had succeeded admirably in its mission prior to his arrival. That mission was to secure the coastal regions and major river mouths to prevent the infiltration and movement of enemy forces and materiel by coastal waters. The operation began in March of 1965, and would become the longest single operation in the Vietnam War.

The Market Time Forces formed a barrier of boats, ships and aircraft along the extensive 1,400-mile coastline of South Vietnam. Eventually the Task Force included 84 PCFs (Patrol Craft Fast—the Swift boats), coastal junks, 31 Coast Guard Cutters (WPBs), 5 high-endurance cutters (WHECs), 12 U.S. Navy Destroyer Radar Picket Ships (DERs), ocean and coastal minesweepers (MSOs and MSCs), and P2V *Neptune* and P3 *Orion* patrol aircraft based at the Naval Air Facility at Cam Ranh Bay. Under six Coastal Surveillance Centers (at Da Nang, Qui Nhon, Nha Trang, Cam Ranh Bay, Vung Tau and An Thoi), Coastal Squadron One (COSRON ONE) oversaw six Coastal Divisions (COS DIVs) covering the entire coastal area of South Vietnam. There was also a Harbor Defense element of the Coastal

Part Three: Vietnam to Retirement   167

P3 Orion, *the Navy's version of the Lockheed* Electra, *flies a Market Time patrol off the coast of South Vietnam. The P3, along with U.S. Navy and Coast Guard surface craft, patrolled the entire coast of South Vietnam to keep supplies from the Viet Cong and North Vietnamese fighting in South Vietnam.*
OFFICIAL U.S. NAVY PHOTO, HOFFMANN COLLECTION

U.S. Navy 172-foot non-magnetic ocean minesweeper USS Esteem *(MSO 438) steams off the coast of South Vietnam. Market Time coastal surveillance patrols played an important role in stopping enemy infiltration of men and supplies into South Vietnam by sea.* OFFICIAL U.S. NAVY PHOTO, HOFFMANN COLLECTION

The Coast Guard cutter Winona *stands by while the boarding crew completes the search of a junk. Poles above the junk's decks were used by the Vietnamese fishermen for drying their catch; the stakes flying colorful flags were used as fish net markers.*
OFFICIAL U.S. COAST GUARD PHOTO (BY DALES E. CROSS), A.L. LONSDALE COLLECTION

Surveillance Force under Captain Hoffmann's command, Operation Stable Door, located at Vung Tau, Cam Ranh Bay, Qui Nhon and Nha Trang. The Inshore Undersea Warfare Group One (IUWG ONE) employed Landing Craft Personnel, Large (LCPLs), Harbor Picket Boats and "Boston Whaler" skimmers to patrol the harbors, guarding against infiltration and sappers. There were over 3,500 men and more than 180 patrol boats, ships and aircraft under Hoffmann's command or direction.

The U.S. Coast Guard (USCG), fully integrated with the U.S. Navy, played a major role in Operation Market Time. Over 8,000 men served on Coast Guard units during the Vietnam War, and eight were killed in action. USCG vessels operated along the entire coast of South Vietnam. They interdicted enemy supply vessels; provided naval gunfire support (NGFS); supported the U.S. Navy Swift boats; performed joint amphibious combat operations with U.S. Navy SEAL teams and U.S. Army Special Forces mobile strike teams; performed humanitarian medical and civil action aid to South Vietnam villages; and helped to train the South Vietnamese Navy.

The Market Time Forces performed the often-tedious task of boarding and searching the more than 60,000 junks and sampans plying the waters off the coast of South Vietnam. They boarded and searched more than 500,000 junks and sampans a year, checking I.D. cards and searching for contraband. The Market Time Forces blocked nine major infiltration attempts, including the destruction or capture of six heavily laden North Vietnamese trawlers, each carrying many tons of ammunition. Market Time Forces destroyed or forced back into North Vietnam all but two of the 50 steel-hulled trawlers that tried to run the blockade.

General William C. Westmoreland, the U.S. Commander in Vietnam, commented: "Market Time Forces are a major element of my overall strategy, without which we could not succeed. Market Time Forces have successfully blocked intrusion by sea, forcing the enemy to use the long, tortuous Ho Chi Minh Trail, thus affecting significantly his ability to properly sustain his forces in the South." Before Operation Market Time the Viet Cong received an estimated 70 per cent of their supplies by maritime infiltration; by the end of 1966 that number had been reduced to a trickle of less than ten per cent.

The Swift boats were the first specialized patrol craft used by the U.S. Navy in Vietnam. The initial order of 20 boats in the spring of 1965 was expanded to 54 boats, and then 84 before the first boat arrived. The Swifts were ideally suited for their inshore operations, and the river operations that followed.

In many ways the story of Hoffmann's tour as CTF 115 hinges on the small aluminum Swift and the Navy LSTs, Seawolves, SEALs, Coast Guard cutters and the U.S. Army and Marine, and Vietnamese troops that either supported or were supported by the boats.

Swift boats in Vietnam generally carried a crew of six Americans and a Vietnamese interpreter or trainee. The base crew normally consisted of an Officer in Charge (O in C), usually a lieutenant j.g. or a lieutenant (and later ensigns), a radarman, a boatswain's mate, a gunner's mate and an engineman.

A Swift boat was 50 feet long with a width of 13 feet 6.5 inches and was made of all welded aluminum alloy, less than one-quarter inch thick. The full load displacement was 22 tons, and the draft at full load was 3 feet 10 inches. The height of the boat to the top of the gun tub was 11 feet 6 inches and 16 feet 9 inches to the top of the radar mast. The boats could carry 828 gallons of purified diesel in three tanks. The boats could theoretically attain 24 knots at 2000 rpm, but at that speed the engines burned 75 gallons of

PCF 44 comes alongside a Vietnamese junk while on patrol as part of Operation Market Time. OFFICIAL U.S. NAVY PHOTO, HOFFMANN PHOTO

fuel per hour, limiting the time they could be out without refueling to 10.7 hours, and the total miles they could travel to 250. At 1,600 rpms the boats could still make 17.6 knots, and increased their endurance to 28.5 hours and 400 miles. On open seas, sea height and wind further limited range.

The boats were powered by twin 12V Detroit Diesels, each rated at 480 horsepower, with 1.5:1 reduction gears and N70 type injectors. The diesels drove two shaft driven propellers beneath the waterline; two rudders and opposing engines steered the boat. The engines were housed in a compartment aft on the stern. They were accessed through two large hatches that could be lifted up on hinges to stand at right angles on the deck. In the cramped engine room was a small metal platform between the diesels, where the engineman could work on the bilge pumps, cooling equipment and the diesels.

The fantail on the boats carried on deck a mortar box of finned projectiles of various types: 42 rounds of high explosive (HE), an antipersonnel mortar with point detonating fuses; 15 rounds of white phosphorous (called Willie Pete by the crews), an incendiary mortar that burned with a white-hot intensity when it exploded; and 20 rounds of illumination flares, for marking and for the many night ambushes the boats conducted.

Forward of the mortar box on the deck was a stanchion that held a .50 caliber Browning machine gun with a type M-2 heavy barrel, with an 81mm Mark 2 mortar beneath it. The weapons swiveled and elevated as a unit so the after gunner could swing the gun to either side of the boat when using the .50. The mortar was trigger fired.

There was a cabin forward of the engine hatches. Inside on the port side were a small table, and a gun locker that contained one Ithaca 12-gauge shotgun, two M-79 grenade launchers, three .38 caliber pistols, and foul weather and flak gear. On the starboard side of the cabin was a counter containing a sink, a small refrigerator (that almost never worked), and the radios. The ammunition magazine was beneath the deck in the main cabin, accessed by a metal drop-plate. At the forward part of the cabin was a small doorway that led to a cramped berthing compartment where two bunks were opposite a narrow passageway. Originally this space held commodes, but they were removed as they caused severe leakage in the event of a mine detonating beneath the boat.

On the port side of the cabin, forward, was a two-step ladder that led into the pilothouse, where the helmsman conned the boat from a chair on a raised platform. To his left was a small navigation table where the O in C usually sat while the boat was underway. Behind and above the helmsman, on top of the pilothouse, was the gun turret, where the gunner's mate manned the twin .50 caliber machine guns, an awesome display of firepower crucial for survival in the rivers of Vietnam. The twin .50s were set on a moveable ring so the gunner could swing the guns around to either side of the boat. When the guns were firing, the noise was deafening in the pilothouse as hot, spent shell casings cascaded down. On the mast above the gun tub was a Decca Type D202 radar.

There was a peak tank on the bow, a small compartment large enough for a man to stand with an M-16 in the early days of Market Time. Later, particularly after SEALORDS, the men stood in the peak tank and fired an M-60 machine gun.

CAPTAIN HOFFMANN HAD two tasks initially: First he had to assess the resources he had under his command; second he felt he needed to personally emphasize to the men under his command he expected them to exercise aggressively the new authority granted them in his first Operation Order. He soon realized, in regard to the former, that his task force could do much more with the resources at hand, particularly to deny the inland waterways to the enemy.

As to the second task, he says with irony and with a laugh, "I got in my high powered, twin engine Beech Craft (1937 vintage) and I flew up the coast line." He checked out all the patrol areas, particularly the no-fishing and secret zones. His first stop was Chu Lai, where he assembled the officers and asked them: "Have you received my Directive sub delegating my authority to the senior on scene officer? Let's see your hands." All the hands went up.

"Do you understand it? If you don't raise your hands." When no hands were raised, he went on, "Henceforth, I expect you to carry out my orders, and I'll tell you in advance that you're going to lose the authority if you don't use it." He went on to Da Nang and delivered the same message. The passive culture of coastal patrol began to change.

CAPTAIN HOFFMANN ARRIVED at his new command May 11, 1968. The Paris Peace Talks were just getting underway between the American and North Vietnamese negotiators (the Peace Talks would prove to be more farce than negotiation). Negotiators agreed that, for the time being, participation would be limited to the U.S. and North Vietnam, excluding both Saigon and the National Liberation Front (the Viet Cong). The talks soon moved to secret sessions.

Later in May, in the United States, Senator Eugene McCarthy defeated Senator Robert Kennedy in the Oregon Democratic presidential primary, setting up a showdown in the California primary on June 4. Their candidacies were indicators of the growth of the antiwar movement in the Democratic Party. Robert Kennedy would not survive his visit to Los Angeles.

ALTHOUGH CAPTAIN HOFFMANN'S new aggressive stance would not resonate with Admiral Veth in Saigon, he had guidance from a General Order from General Westmoreland, Commander of U.S. forces in Vietnam, issued May 6, 1968. The message couldn't be more clear:

> Commencing immediately, our objective will be to make a major breakthrough toward military victory in South Vietnam. The fighting will be characterized by aggressive, unremitting, twenty-four hour application of pressure on all enemy elements throughout South Vietnam. U.S. Commanders will take the lead in forging a totally coordinated military offensive.... This must become increasingly their [the South Vietnamese] war. Vietnamese elements must be encouraged, or challenged, to be in the van of the attack. The purpose of fighting in the summer of 1968 will be to hound the enemy, destroy his forces, and rid the land of his influence.

Although there was a culture of coastal patrol in Task Force 115, it's clear now that many of the Swift officers and crews were frustrated at their inability to pursue the enemy to his sanctuaries beyond the estuaries at the entries to the rivers. Most of the crews had volunteered for Swifts when the duty was primarily coastal patrol, but they had come to Vietnam to fight the enemy.

Within the limited confines of their orders they probed the enemy, sometimes pushing beyond the edge of what they knew was allowed. When Captain Hoffmann arrived many of the officers and crews took advantage of the loosened strictures. One such man was Lieutenant F. L. "Skip" Gunther, O in C of PCF 21.[7] His personal call sign was "Mustang Sally," and he was known as the Chu Lai Tiger of TF 115, 1967–1968 era.

Gunther and his crew arrived in Da Nang from Swift school in Coronado in October of 1967. They took over the 21 boat in January 1968, patrolling the Da Nang area, the largest in Market Time, extending south from the DMZ. There was a U.S. Marine amtrack company at the Cua Viet River, which was the border between North and South Vietnam. The river was difficult to transit, particularly during the monsoon season. Gunther frequently exceeded the letter of his operational constraints.

At one point, when on patrol with Hal Gehman's boat (Gunther in area 1 Alpha and Gehman in 1 Bravo), Gunther suggested they patrol together and close in on the coast.[8] It was a moonless night and they thought they might catch an enemy junk on the move along the coast. Gunther cut his engines and dropped the hook while Gehman kept up the patrol, moving south. Gunther had a starlight scope and watched the beach.[9] Soon people began to show up on the beach and it bustled with activity. In the meantime he lost track of the Fathometer reading, which dropped from 20 feet to below six. He felt the boat start to bump along the bottom and the surf was carrying him to the beach. They started the engines to pull away from what had turned into a perilous situation. As they pulled up the anchor they realized the line had been cut—someone from the beach swam out and cut the anchor line.

---

7. Francis L. Gunther was a 1965 graduate of the Naval Academy. He served in Operation Market Time from October of 1967 to October of 1968. All quotes from him are from an interview conducted May 13, 2006.

8. Harold W. Gehman, Jr. would go on from his Swift boat duty to have a long and distinguished naval career, which included command of Atlantic forces; he eventually retired as a full admiral (four star).

9. A Starlight scope was a night vision device that took advantage of the available light for enhanced vision. The images it conveyed were cast in an eerie green hue.

PCF 94 takes a pounding while underway on a Market Time patrol.
Official U.S. Navy photo, Hoffmann collection

They called themselves the Ben Hai Raiders because the Ben Hai River was just north of the DMZ. The entry to the Ben Hai was four to five miles wide. They would run the river, going in two to three miles, transiting the north side where there were enemy caves with large artillery installations. The Swift crew would make a firing run at the cliffs, hosing down the area. They rarely entered the area because it was off limits. On about their third time in they started getting return fire from the cliffs. Once in late February or early March of 1968 a huge round went off in the water about two boat lengths away, raising the boat out of the water. That one turned out to be friendly artillery fire.

The patrols in the north could last for 26 to 28 hours, including transit time. Crews often took a severe pounding during the monsoon season. Once the 21 boat had following seas which pushed them farther and farther away from their base. When they got turned around they were 100 miles away from base and had to turn into the now heavy seas to get back, the waves slamming against the bow and breaking over the boat. The crashing of the waves became so severe the front windshield shattered. As the seas poured through the opening a large sea snake (they could be lethally poisonous) came with them. The crew shot the snake, putting holes in the boat that had to be patched. The only bay they could put into for shelter was VC controlled, so they continued to fight the heavy seas.

It was, Gunther said, his most anxious time. He thought they might broach in the heavy seas and keel over. Despite their life jackets, survival would be uncertain in the heavy seas, and certain capture or death waited on land. It took the boat almost another day to get back—by then they had a helicopter out looking for the boat.

Gunther was patrolling off Hue when the 1968 Tet Offensive started. He and his crew could hear the sounds of the battle coming from the city. For the next two weeks they were constantly on patrol, both providing either gunfire support to embattled Army and Marine units on shore, or patrolling Da Nang harbor.

In May of 1968 they transferred to Chu Lai. The base at Chu Lai received periodic incoming small arms and mortar fire. At first they ducked at the incoming rounds, but eventually they learned to ignore it so that it wouldn't disturb their poker games. Coastal Group 16, comprised of the junk force and SVN indigenous forces, was located there as well, just north of II Corps. The Coastal Group was overrun three times. Gunther and his crew on one of those occasions went in right before the base was overrun and rescued four American advisors. The Swifts also patrolled the Cape Batangan area, playing psychological operations tapes with the almost certainty of receiving enemy fire.

CAPTAIN HOFFMANN'S NEW aggressiveness affected the task force from top to bottom. U.S. Coast Guard Commander Adrian Lonsdale, on April 4, 1968, took over as Commander Gulf of Thailand Surveillance Group (CTG 115.4), and as senior naval advisor to Commander Dang Cao Thang, the Vietnamese Fourth Coastal Zone Commander, at An Thoi on Phu Quoc island.[10] An Thoi was the site of the southernmost Coastal Division (COS DIV 11), and was responsible for the most heavily enemy controlled area in South Vietnam, the Ca Mau peninsula and the U Minh forest. Commander Dang

---

10. Adrian Lonsdale was third generation Coast Guard. He enlisted in the Coast Guard at age 17 in 1945. He graduated from the Coast Guard Academy in 1950, and after a distinguished career retired as a captain. All quotations from Lonsdale are from an interview conducted September 25, 2006.

Cao Thang had been vice chief of naval operations in the South Vietnamese Navy, but his career had been derailed by participation in a failed coup attempt. He had graduated from the Vietnamese Naval Academy in Hanoi and the Naval War College in the United States. He was assigned to Phu Quoc to keep him sufficiently remote from the seat of power in Saigon. He had been fighting the war for 22 years.

If you were part of Captain Hoffmann's command structure you could always expect phone calls. Cam Ranh Bay, 1968. OFFICIAL U.S. NAVY PHOTO, HOFFMANN COLLECTION

Lonsdale reported to three different captains: CTF 115, Commander Coast Guard Squadron One and the senior naval advisor—a difficult situation. He quickly felt the change after Captain Hoffmann arrived in May. He has great admiration for Hoffmann, but says he was a tough man to work for, always on the phone, always wanting to know what was going on. "You had to be on your toes," Lonsdale says, "but he didn't get involved in your business." Captain Hoffmann would make suggestions as to areas to check out, but he never interfered with the operations.

Helicopter support was most difficult to obtain. There was a Navy helicopter unit in Ha Tien; otherwise air support was from Army helicopters. Lonsdale could only request the helos—he couldn't command them. All you could do was hope they would show up. Sometimes they were available for medevacs, but it was more common for the Swifts to bring wounded and dead out to a Coast Guard cutter or Navy LST, which had doctors aboard, as well as decks for the helos.

The day after Lonsdale reported, Lieutenant j.g. Larry Thurlow arrived at An Thoi, where he would spend his entire year tour of duty.[11] Thurlow is an imposing man in person, big, yet soft spoken with a slow Kansas drawl. He was born in 1942 in Garden City, Kansas. His dad was a schoolteacher and coach. Thurlow graduated from high school in 1960 and received his degree from Fort Hays State in Hays, Kansas in 1965, after which he lost his educational deferment. He got his induction notice and was to report for his Army physical when a Navy recruiter said, "Hey, I think I've got a better deal for you." Once you are inducted into the Army they own you, but the Navy recruiter pulled a few strings to allow him to join that branch. The Army allowed the change as long as they were sure the Navy had him, so he didn't dodge the service altogether.

Thurlow entered OCS in Newport in November 1965 and was commissioned as an ensign in April of 1966. He got orders to the amphibious assault ship USS *Princeton* (LPH 5), which was home ported in Long Beach, California, although it was then deployed to Vietnam.[12] He was to meet the ship in Subic Bay in the Philippines, but arrived there just in time to miss ship's movement. The Navy flew him to Dong Ha in a C-130, where upon landing his first sight was of a cart with a tarp covering four American bod-

---

11. Larry Thurlow lives today in Bogue, Kansas, with his wife, Patty. All quotations by Larry Thurlow are taken from an interview on January 10, 2007.

12. The *Princeton* was an old CVS that had been converted to an amphibious assault ship. Her sister ship was the *Yorktown*.

The base at An Thoi. OFFICIAL U.S. COAST GUARD PHOTO, A.L LONSDALE COLLECTION

ies with only the boots showing. He could hear the bombs exploding and smoke swirled in the air. "Welcome to Vietnam," he thought. Marine helos were transferring wounded and killed to the *Princeton*, which was off the coast. Thurlow and 67 other sailors were transferred by helos to the ship as space became available.

He eventually volunteered for Swifts after watching the choppers coming in with Marines either on stretchers or in body bags. He thought to himself, "There are some people putting a hell of a lot more effort into this war than I am." He felt he had to do more, but his options were limited. He wasn't a pilot, or a SEAL or UDT, but he thought Swift duty would present an opportunity for him to contribute to the war effort.

His mother hated the idea that he was going to war. Her only brother had been killed in World War II and is buried in Holland. Thurlow's dad had been drafted into the Army at age 27 in World War II.

Thurlow entered the Swift school at Coronado in February of 1968, heading one of four crews. He brought his crew with him from Coronado to Vietnam. He started Market Time patrols, where he soon learned the coastal patrols were pounding punishment with the heavy seas, particularly during the months of June, July and August with the advent of the Southwest Monsoons. It didn't take him long to figure that the rivers were deep and much calmer. "Some of us started going up the rivers," he says. One of Thurlow's favorites to probe was the Cua Lon, where you had to plow through a shallow alluvial deposit, "leaving a mud wake," to get into the river. The river mouth was a mile wide. They usually went up at night with his boat only. He couldn't tell anyone where he was going because the river was off limits. "The other guys were going up as well," he says, "but they weren't telling anyone either."

NINETEEN SIXTY-EIGHT represented the absolute nadir of the Vietnam War era. The Paris Peace Talks sputtered fitfully along, driven in the United States by a misinterpretation of the 1968 Tet Offensive, the increasingly nihilistic and anarchic antiwar movement and a media drumbeat to get out. On the other side was a North Vietnamese government committed to a much longer view of history. Meanwhile, the U.S. bombed, orchestrating, in George Will's words, "carefully calibrated violence . . . sending signals to an uncomprehending enemy."

THE TWO MAIN CONTENDERS for the Democratic nomination (aside from Vice President Hubert Humphrey) were Robert Kennedy (brother of the slain president), and Eugene McCarthy. They fought over the antiwar votes, all for the privilege of taking on Richard Nixon in the November election. On June 4, Robert Kennedy learned he had won the Democratic presidential primaries in both California and South Dakota. His support from blacks, Hispanic, and labor voters carried the day in California.

That night he addressed his supporters at the Ambassador Hotel in Los Angeles. After he left the meeting he walked through a kitchen passageway where Jordanian immigrant and Arab nationalist, Sirhan Bishara Sirhan waited with a gun. Sirhan Sirhan pumped off all eight rounds in the snub-nosed Iver-Johnson revolver he held. Five people were slightly wounded, but the sixth, Robert Kennedy was mortally wounded after a bullet entered his brain. He died after midnight, leaving behind a wife, Ethel, pregnant with their 11th child.

On June 8 James Earl Ray, the assassin of Dr. Martin Luther King, was apprehended in London. He had left his prints in his Memphis rooming house and the FBI identified him from those. He had a long criminal record, murky motivation, and unexplained cash, the source of which was never explained. He ultimately pleaded guilty and was sentenced to 99 years in prison.

On June 14, Dr. Benjamin Spock, who had dispensed advice to mothers of Baby Boomers for years, the Reverend William Sloane Coffin of Yale, and two others were convicted in Boston Federal District for counseling and aiding draft evasion. Between January 1 and June 15 of 1968, there were 221 major antiwar demonstrations, involving nearly 39,000 students on 101 campuses nationwide. Anarchy was the order of the day, as buildings were dynamited, college presidents and deans were intimidated, buildings were defaced and police verbally and physically assaulted.

June 16, 1968: The Sinking of PCF 19

On June 16, 1968, PCF 19 was sunk five miles south of the Ben Hai River mouth near the DMZ in Quang Tri Province. A missile struck the boat and it went down one-half mile from shore.[13] The 19 boat was on routine patrol the morning of the 16th when a rocket hit it at 0300 hours. There is confusion and controversy as to whether a North Vietnamese helicopter attacked the PCF, but in any event a large explosion engulfed the boat and it sank in less than four minutes.

O in C Lieutenant j.g. John Davis was blinded in the attack and badly wounded. Gunner's Mate Seaman John R. Anderegg, who was also badly wounded, managed to pull Davis and QM2 Frank Bowman off the boat before it went down. Bowman was mortally wounded and died in Anderegg's arms. Bowman slipped beneath the water as Anderegg could not keep both of his crew members with him. Anderegg managed to keep himself and Davis afloat until the USCG WPB *Point Dune* could reach the area and pick them up.

Four Americans (BM2 Anthony G. Chandler of Warner Robbins, Georgia; EN2 Edward C. Cruz of Inarajan, Guam; GMG2 Billy S. Armstrong of West

---

13. James Steffes has written an extensively documented book about the tragedy, *Swift Boat Down*. In the book Steffes argues that the missile was the result of hostile enemy fire from a North Vietnamese helicopter. Admiral Hoffmann, who was on the Court of Inquiry, believes it was a Sidewinder missile from an unidentified U.S. tactical aircraft. As a result of the incident (and others the previous day that were clearly friendly fire) new orders as to command responsibility were issued. If the friendly aircraft were over the sea, tactical command rested with the Navy; anything over land, tactical command was with the senior ground commander.

Helena, Arkansas; and Frank Bowman of Walterboro, South Carolina) and a Vietnamese Navy petty officer went to their watery graves that morning. PCF 12 came under rocket fire as they sailed to help pick up survivors. The minesweeper USS *Acme* was later assigned to recover the bodies; they found three of the Americans and the Vietnamese, but Bowman's body was not recovered.

John Davis eventually regained partial eyesight, but remained haunted during his life by the night of June 16, as was John Anderegg who could not forgive himself for letting Frank Bowman slip away from his grip. John Robert Anderegg died on October 8, 1983, and the last survivor of the sinking, John Davis, died on January 21, 2006.[14]

At the end of June 1968 the U.S. death toll for the year in Vietnam reached 9,557, more than had died in all of 1967. Desecrating the U.S. flag was made a federal crime in the United States. In Vietnam, the COS DIV 11 forces were engaged in Operation Swift Kick in Area 9 Foxtrot. PCFs 5, 10 and 38 came under intense hostile fire on June 26; on July 5 PCFs 3, 5 and 93 destroyed fortified structures as part of the operation. On that day, Radarman Thomas Belodeau was serving on PCF 27. He would later be a participant in the firefight of January 29, 1969, as a member of Tedd Peck's crew, but on this day he won a Bronze Star with Combat V for chasing a VC suspect down and pulling him from the water for interrogation, while enemy fire exploded all around him.[15]

In the meantime, General Creighton Abrams, one of the finest military officers the United States has produced, replaced General Westmoreland as COMUSMACV. He came to Vietnam recognizing the political reality in the United States, that the willingness to fight the Vietnam War was waning. The emphasis of his fine leadership would be to punish and pursue the enemy wherever they were, and to turn over responsibility to the Vietnamese for the war as soon as they could be made ready. All of this was aimed at providing our allies the best possible chance of surviving the inevitable U.S. departure.

On July 7, 1968, he issued Operational Guidance that said in part, "We must concentrate every last element of available combat power on the enemy when he is located." Captain Hoffmann's 1968 Third Quarter report recognized

---

14. John Davis and Skip Gunther were stationed together at Chu Lai. The sinking of the 19 boat occurred on Gunther's birthday. He immediately wrote his family and told them that something had happened with a Swift boat but that he was okay.

15. Brinkley, *Tour of Duty*, p. 264.

Westmoreland's and Abrams' change in guidance, and reflected his growing frustration with the strictures from COMNAVFORV (Admiral Veth) on his operational assets, which weren't being used to their maximum:

> The tenor of these statements [by Westmoreland and Abrams] was that of "increased aggressiveness." Analyzing the strictly defensive role of Market Time as it had been operating for the past several years showed that there was much room for improvement under these new guidelines. Enemy transshipment activity in Market Time area of operation . . . remains a problem. The enemy still controls the majority of the coastline, particularly in the Delta area.

At the end of July Admiral Veth issued his own Operational Guidance, a remarkably passive document, particularly in light of the messages from Westmoreland and Abrams:

> I desire you consider increasing activities in areas where tactically indicated and logistically feasible. The frustration of seeing an evading enemy must be met with renewed vigor and dogged determination to give him no rest. Imagination, cunning, resourcefulness, innovation and daring will be the order of the day for all hands. This will be a Flank speed campaign.

It was no wonder Veth was becoming increasingly marginalized in the command structure of the war, and that COMUSMACV was becoming increasingly frustrated with the Navy.

THE REPUBLICAN NATIONAL Convention closed in Miami on August 8, 1968, with the nomination of Richard M. Nixon for president. He had made a remarkable political comeback after losing to John F. Kennedy in the 1960 election. The Republicans adopted a plank of their platform emphasizing the need for an honorable, negotiated peace and "progressive de-Americanization of the war." In his acceptance speech, Richard Nixon pledged to "bring an honorable end to the war in Vietnam."

ROBERT BRANT WAS another of the outstanding officers who served on Swifts during Roy Hoffmann's tour of duty in Vietnam.[16] Originally from Marquette, Michigan, he committed to the Navy while still a junior in

---

16. Quotations taken from an interview conducted with Robert Brant July 2, 2006. After a 22-year career in the U.S. Navy Brant retired as a Navy commander on September 1, 1989. He and his wife, Barb, currently live in Chantilly, Virginia.

college in Michigan. He initially wanted to be an aviator and actually went to Pensacola for flight training after receiving his commission. After he got there he realized he wasn't enjoying the training. He told them, "I don't think I want to fly." He got a lot of flak about dropping out, but eventually he was assigned to his first ship, the destroyer USS *Douglas Fox*.

The CO of the ship was Commander Horn, and he was in the habit of giving his officers nicknames. Brant is large (larger then as in portly), somewhat cherubic with a florid face and hale manner. Horn decided he should be called "Friar Tuck," and he is known as Friar Tuck or Tuck today. Captain Horn, "a crusty old guy," assigned Lieutenant j.g. Robert Drake to teach Friar Tuck the finer points of Navy life. Drake took Brant out for a big drunk, and they arrived back at the ship at 2:00 A.M. Tuck Brant was not in good shape the next day. ("I could hear my hair grow.")

Eventually Brant volunteered for Swift boat duty. He wanted the duty so much he drove to see his detailer to get the orders. By the time he got back to the ship Captain Horn had the orders in hand, and he asked him, "Tuck, what the hell are you doing? I've got orders here for you to go to Swift training." Horn informed Brant that he thought he had made a bad decision, but wished him the best of luck when Brant said he wanted the duty.

Brant next visited his parents in Michigan. "You're going *where?*" his upset mother said. His father didn't say much. "The day I left home there was Mom all snot and tears because her little boy was leaving." It was upsetting to Brant to see his mother so distraught.

His dad said, "I'll walk you out to the car." He shook Brant's hand and said, "Good luck to you." His dad then gave him a hug and then handed him a box. "When you get down the road apiece stop and open the box."

Tuck Brant drove along the shores of Lake Superior for about 20 miles, and then pulled over and opened the box. Within was a Ka-bar Fighting Knife with Lieutenant j.g. Robert Brant and his serial number engraved on the blade. "It was Dad's way of saying 'it's okay.' That was very important to me." Brant wore the blade for his entire time in Vietnam.

Brant arrived in Coronado in early April of 1968, where he joined a crew of five. After training they all flew over together, arriving first at Cam Ranh Bay. He and the other officers checked in with Commander Charley Plumly, Captain Hoffmann's new chief of staff. Plumly informed them that Hoffmann was in Saigon, but that one of the officers would stay in Cam Ranh, one would be going to Da Nang, and that the rest of them should stay in the barracks because Captain Hoffmann wanted to see them at his Sunday morning briefing.

On Sunday morning they met with Hoffmann. Brant was there with five other Swift officers. Hoffmann said, "in his inimitable way": "There are five of you sitting in those chairs and one of you is probably a chicken shit. You know who you are. Let me know who you are—tell me right now and I'll have you in the States in two days because I don't want you here." Brant thought to himself, "Whoa." After the briefing was over, one of the other officers in attendance, asked, "Did he really say that?" Brant said, "He sure did."

After the briefing Brant then caught a C-47 that took him to Saigon, from where he made the short trip to Cat Lo, arriving there in June of 1968. The DIV COM there was an Academy graduate, a Navy lieutenant with the call sign "Smokey Bear." He slept during the day to get over the hangovers he incurred during the night. He was, Brant says, "a complete asshole." Brant went on a couple of indoctrination patrols and then inherited D.C. Current's boat (PCF 36) and crew when Current was hit and medevaced out.

They did not receive hostile fire until August 8, 1968. That day Brant told his crew, "Let's just drive along the coast and see what we can find." They were in full battle gear, although they did not have on their "flak panties," a piece of flak gear worn below the flak jacket that was supposed to gird their loins and protect their crotch area. Whoever wore the flak panties usually was a subject of derision with their fellow crew members and so most chose not to wear them ("What do *you* have to protect?" was usually the question asked).

Friar Tuck was driving the boat at about the time they reached the mouth of the Bo De River (about which much will be said later). Tuck says, "It happened so quick. I saw these little plops in the water. I heard Fred Prysock (Gunner's mate 2nd class) say on the sound-powered phones, 'They're shooting at us!'" Out the starboard door Brant could see the flashes from the machine gun on shore.

"You just react," he says. "The simplest thing would have been to turn left and head out to sea." All he can remember is thinking "You sons of bitches." As his crew opened fire he spun the wheel right, jammed the throttles forward and drove right at the flashing lights until they weren't flashing anymore. Then, as they swung around out to sea they got two more bursts from shore. "That's when our engineman and loader on the after .50 got hit." He took a slug in his right bicep, right chest cavity and leg. They rendezvoused with an LST, where he was medevaced. He eventually recovered, but never came back.

IN THE NORTH, the enemy had been forced by the effectiveness of Market Time patrols to attempt transshipment of materiel and personnel via the shallow head-

Captain Hoffmann briefing on the effectiveness of Task Force 115 components. August 13, 1968. OFFICIAL U.S. NAVY PHOTO, HOFFMANN COLLECTION

waters of Qui Nhon harbor. A patrol caught a group of enemy sappers and an intense firefight resulted in which three IUWG U.S. Navy men were killed, and one wounded. They managed to kill six of the Viet Cong in the attack. SEAL teams on the Qui Nhon peninsula made significant enemy contact and captured Top Secret enemy documents, including a plan for an attack on Qui Nhon.

ON AUGUST 14, 1968, Lieutenant Commander George M. Elliott relieved Lieutenant David C. Brown as the commander of Coastal Division 11 at An Thoi.[17] Lieutenant Brown had been a roommate of POW Paul Galanti at the U.S. Naval Academy.

As COM COS DIV 11, Elliott worked closely with Roy Hoffmann. Elliott says of his former boss:

---

17. Quotations from George Elliott from various 2006 e-mails and interviews. George Elliott is a 1959 graduate of the U.S. Naval Academy. He spent 26 years in the surface Navy, retiring as a captain in September of 1985. His commands included the USS *Nipmuc* (ATF 157), COS DIV 11 (1968–69), and the USS *Samuel Gompers* (AD 37), 1982–85. He was married to the late Trenny Elliott, who passed away in 2007.

A briefing by Vice Admiral Zumwalt (far right), as Commander Adrian Lonsdale (USCG) and Lieutenant Commander George Elliot (USN) look on.
OFFICIAL U.S. COAST GUARD PHOTO, A.L. LONSDALE COLLECTION

> His reputation was well known to me before we met. We all knew his credo was take the fight to the enemy. He was quick to praise when praise was due and quick to take "corrective action" when he concluded it was necessary. There were never any surprises—everyone in the organization knew that if you were correct in your actions he would go to the mat for you.

ON AUGUST 22 AND 23 enemy forces launched a rocket attack on Saigon. The attack killed 18 and wounded 59. These attacks were followed by rocket and mortar attacks on cities, provincial capitals and military installations. The U.S. airfield at Da Nang was particularly hard hit, as were Hue, Quang Tri and the U.S. Special Forces camp at Duclap, 130 miles northwest of Saigon near the Cambodian border. A ground attack followed the shelling at Duclap involving between 1,200 and 1,500 NVA troops; they lost a reported 643 troops during the three days of fighting that occurred there. It was evident the enemy was still able to move materiel and men with relative impunity across the Cambodian border.

On August 22 three PCFs conducted the first official raid into one of the rivers of the Ca Mau, the Song Ong Doc. The boats provided NGFS for a coordinated ground sweep. The three boats were the 72, 93 and 38; the 38 boat's skipper was Lieutenant j.g. Terrance W. Costello.[18]

Almost everyone who has been around Terry Costello mentions his presence, his intelligence, his calm, and his low key but commanding influence. Larry Thurlow says of him, "He was rock solid, dependable." He's a large and handsome man, and in the now famous picture of the An Thoi O in Cs taken at Saigon on January 22, 1969, he draws your attention standing at the right of the group.

Costello, originally from Eldorado Springs, Missouri, entered the Navy in January of 1966. He was a product of the NROTC program, and got his degree and was commissioned at the University of Missouri. His career started as a damage control officer on a DE operating out of Pearl Harbor (the USS *John R. Perry*). He went to Vietnam from the *Perry*.

His father had been in the Navy both before and during World War II. Terry Costello learned years later his mother was not a supporter of the Vietnam War, but she never said anything to him about it. Costello had one brother in the Army in Vietnam, and another brother (Jimmy) in the Army who was scheduled to go, although he ended up getting sent to Europe. Costello's mother believed in premonitions, and thought Terry would make it out of Vietnam, but she thought if Jimmy went he wouldn't come back.

Costello went through Coronado with six other officers. When he reported to An Thoi in June of 1968 he was assigned the 38 boat, the only boat he ever had during his tour of duty in Vietnam. His crew included Gunner's mate Lucovich, Radarmen Gregory Cybulski and Taylor, Boatswain's Mate Davis and Engineman Richard Hughes.

On the Song Ong Doc operation, George Elliott was riding the 38 boat. They went down from An Thoi the night before. They refueled off a destroyer (using a garden hose), and then decided to get closer in as the seas were pounding them against the ship. They tried to anchor off the mouth of the river but the

---

18. All quotations from an interview conducted with Terry Costello on October 11, 2005. After he left Vietnam he was the weapons officer on the SS *Sample* out of Hawaii, then he was CO of a minesweeper (the USS *Enhance*) out of Long Beach. He received a Master's Degree in International Relations at Oklahoma and a Master's from the War College in National Security Decision Making. He was the CO of the *Stark* and served in Saudi Arabia through Desert Storm. He retired in 1992 as a Navy captain. He now owns a 180-acre cattle ranch in Missouri, about 20 miles from where he was raised. Of his cattle business he says, "I found a good way to lose my money. It's better than gambling in Las Vegas."

swells were so bad the anchors wouldn't hold. They bounced around all night and some of the men got sick and threw up over the side. Costello says they were quite happy to enter the river because of the interior calm waters.

On the way in they stopped and talked to U.S. Army advisors, then moved farther up the river, where they received small arms fire. It was one of the first "official" (as opposed to unofficial) river operations.

On August 29 the Democratic Party convention in Chicago gave the presidential nomination to Vice President Hubert Humphrey, who was in the difficult position of having to defend President Johnson's largely failed Vietnam strategy. Outside the convention hall the streets degenerated into a street battle between some 10,000 antiwar protestors and the embattled Chicago police. On August 28 police had to drive back the nearly 3,000 demonstrators attempting to storm the Conrad Hilton Hotel, headquarters for the Democratic convention.

Tom Hayden, a radical organizer who later married Jane Fonda, urged the antiwar crowds to greater confrontation. The demonstrators waved Viet Cong flags and threw rocks and bottles at police. They yelled "Hell no we won't go" and "Ho-Ho-Ho Chi Minh." The near anarchy, watched by some 50 to 80 million people on television, shocked America.[19]

The chief of staff that Captain Roy Hoffmann inherited at Cam Ranh "was not the type of person I wanted. Although he was an excellent administrator, I needed an experienced fighter. That's how I found Charley Plumly."

Hoffmann called Saigon and said that while his current chief of staff was competent, he wanted "somebody aggressive; someone who is willing to get out of Saigon and get into the action." They sent him Plumly. His job interview was short. Plumly says Hoffmann "only asked me one question: 'Have you ever had command of a ship?'"

Charley Plumly was born and raised in Portland Maine.[20] He graduated

---

19. On August 25, 1968, John Kerry began his Swift boat training at Coronado. Douglas Brinkley in *Tour of Duty* indicates, "John Kerry would be training in San Diego for what he thought would be the purely coast patrolling of Operation Market Time . . . ." Brinkley, *Tour of Duty*, p. 104.

20. All quotations from Charley Plumly are taken from an interview conducted July 3, 2006. Plumly had a distinguished Navy career, which included commanding officer of the ships USS *John Willis* (DE 1027), USS *W. S. Sims*, and the USS *Shenandoah* (AD 26). He retired from naval service as a captain on April 1, 1980. He is married to the former Sibyl Ann Middleton and they have two married children.

Award ceremony, Vice Admiral Zumwalt (left), Commander Charley Plumly, Chief of Staff of TF 115. Official U.S. Navy photo, Hoffmann collection

from the U.S. Naval Academy in 1955. He told his wife Sibyl, regarding his volunteering for Vietnam duty, "I've got to get into this." His wife was supportive even though she didn't like the idea (he also had two young children). He arrived in country in June of 1968 and was initially assigned to NAVFORV headquarters. When he was told TF 115 needed someone he jumped at the opportunity.

He arrived in Cam Ranh in the summer of 1968. Both Hoffmann and Plumly quickly agreed that one of them needed to be in Cam Ranh at all times, and the other would be in the field. For Plumly, that meant getting used to flying in the twin engine Beach Craft, which they called the bug-smasher. They had a pilot available to them, but they had to be careful how much they loaded on board or the plane couldn't get off the ground. "You'd be flying around," Plumly says, "and one or the other engine would start sputtering." Whenever Hoffmann was gone from Cam Ranh he insisted Plumly be in charge of the TF, even though there were other commanders senior to him.

Roy Hoffmann lived in a trailer at Cam Ranh and had a steward to serve him meals. "Hoffmann was strictly a meat and potatoes man," Plumly says. "There was nothing fancy about this guy."

Hoffmann was definitely in charge. Both Plumly and Hoffmann were strong willed and the two men had their arguments. "You had to produce for Hoffmann," Plumly says, "or he didn't want you around. If he starts telling you, 'Listen my friend,' I can tell you you're not his friend." The tempo of operations was intense and decisions had to be made quickly and sometimes without as much information as one would want.

A thin wall separated their offices and when Hoffmann wanted Plumly he would "kick the goddamn wall." Plumly would come in and say, "You rang?" Plumly says that Captain Hoffmann had a great feeling for the enlisted men—he always wanted to make sure they were taken care of.

Plumly now says "I'd do anything for Roy if he called me today."

LIEUTENANT J.G. WILLIAM SHUMADINE started training in Coronado in April of 1968.[21] He flew into Saigon initially, and then flew to Cam Ranh for a two-day indoctrination, after which he took a flight to An Thoi, arriving in June. There he would spend his entire tour of duty, augmenting an already outstanding group of O in Cs.

---

21. William Shumadine retired from the Navy as a commander. He lives today with his wife in Suffolk, Virginia. All quotations are from an interview conducted January 25, 2007.

He was assigned PCF 5 (he had it his entire tour) and a seasoned crew on arrival. He also became, because of his previous top-secret clearance, the registered publications officer. The clearance requirement had the effect of tying him to the division, and they never found a replacement for him (Pat Sheedy was the assistant registered publications officer). Shumadine became a valuable commodity in An Thoi, because of his experience in the rivers and his ability to navigate most of the rivers and canals there. He was given a great deal of responsibility as a lieutenant j.g. He felt, "I can't believe they're letting me do all this—something they wouldn't let me do on a ship."

While in An Thoi, Shumadine kept a logbook that unfortunately has been lost. The book indicated how many times he had been under enemy fire, and he remembers it indicated he was in over 100 separate firefights during his tour there. His experience would prove to be typical for many of the Swifties in the enemy-held stronghold of the Ca Mau and U Minh forest.

He quickly began to patrol areas 8 and 9, coming into An Thoi briefly to replenish food, ammunition and fuel. There it was a brief turnaround and back to patrol, but he did have a little time to enjoy the company of the other officers. Larry Thurlow and Terry Costello became his best friends in An Thoi. Thurlow and Costello, he says, "Had a Kansas-Missouri thing going. You would think the Civil War had restarted with those guys. They were always ribbing each other."

The ribbing could sometimes be unmerciful. Robert W. Hildreth, another of the outstanding officers, "once found a charted shoal" and ran his PCF aground in an area where he was exposed to the enemy. "Bob Hildreth ran aground," Shumadine says, "and thought his life was over because he ran aground on a charted rocky shoal." Although there were no repercussions from the Navy, Hildreth's "worst punishment was having to put up with all his buddies calling him 'Rocky.'" He is known as Rocky Hildreth today.

Radarman David Hemenway served on both Shumadine's and Mike Bernique's crew. Hemenway describes Shumadine as "solid, quiet, and capable. He was laid back, quiet, reserved." Hemenway makes an interesting distinction, rating the officers on their operational ability and their ability to relate to their crew. According to him, Shumadine was outstanding in both regards.[22]

---

22. The other combination for a capable officer was one who was good operationally, but whose relations with enlisted men were less than ideal. Less competent officers were poor operationally but liked by their men, or, the worst type, deficient both operationally and in enlisted relations. Everyone who has ever served in the Navy has encountered all four combinations.

On September 1, 1968, PCF 5 came under fire for the first time. They were patrolling area 9 Foxtrot (in the Three Sisters area) with PCF 3, when they spotted, "a guy in the area who wasn't supposed to be there—it was a no fishing zone. It was a known area where the VC were operating." The PCFs moved in to board and search the sampan and move him out of the restricted area. As they moved in splashes kicked up around the boat. One of Shumadine's crew shouted, "We're taking fire!" The boats turned into the coast, returning fire.

Shumadine vividly recalled it, because that's where he developed his sense of survival and what a firefight was about. "I recall hunkering down," he says. He couldn't see where the fire was coming from; he just knew it was coming from the beach. The boats made several firing runs until the enemy fire was suppressed.

When it was over, and Shumadine was doing his post-engagement assessment, he thought:

> Why was I hunkering down like that? What would protect me? If I'm going to get hit, I'm going to get hit wherever I am. From that point on I would walk the deck while we were taking fire. If it's going to get me it's going to get me anywhere. I wasn't going to go inside the pilothouse or main cabin to hide from the bullets. I'm going to get it when I get it. I took a stoic, fatalistic approach. I can't change that. Why try and hide behind a thin piece of aluminum? I think it made me more effective.[23]

ON SEPTEMBER 4, 1968, Tuck Brant, still operating out of Cat Lo, lost one of his crew members to enemy fire. He was patrolling what they called the "box," their designated area off An Xugen Province on the east side of the Ca Mau peninsula. Brant had been aggressively patrolling the box. The rules allowed him to do H & I (Harassment and Interdiction) fire against the enemy, so every time he went out he shot up his mortar box. He'd go back to the base at Cat Lo and the munitions officer would say, "You son of a bitch, we have to haul all those mortars down to the boat and reload. What are you doing?"

Brant's reply, "They told me to do H & I and I don't want those bastards [VC] sleeping at night."

On September 4 they were cruising close to the coast, "getting bored, just looking into the forest." They came to an estuary (at the mouth of the major river Cua Lon) and "we just stuck our nose in the mouth and then we went up about another four miles. That's when I got into trouble up there."

---

23. He did normally try and stay close to the pilothouse most of the time to listen to the radio and be close to the boatswain's mate piloting the boat.

Brant was sitting on the left side of the raised area where the helmsman's chair was located. They were moving along the river at top speed when Brant sighted a sampan on the left bank. It was painted blue, stacked full of boxes and looked brand new. He didn't spot it until they were abeam of it and they quickly went past. As they roared by all hell broke loose—machine guns opened up on the lone PCF.[24]

They went past the kill zone, and then the boatswain almost turned the boat on its side doing a u-turn in the river. They shot their way through the kill zone. While going out, their radarman, Gerald Pochel of Otis, Oregon, whom the crew had nicknamed "Pooch," took a slug in the side. The slug went in one side and didn't exit.

In the firefight the oil line on one of the diesels was shot through and severed. Tuck thought, "I'll run the engine until it burns up—I don't care, we've got to get out and get Pooch out."

When they cleared the river they gave Pochel artificial resuscitation, "I don't know how long—maybe an hour." He was alive most of the time, but never regained consciousness. They radioed an LST, which turned south for a rendezvous with the Swift boat. The Swift pulled alongside the LST, which dropped a Jacob's ladder to the boat. A corpsman came down, hit Pochel with a shot and said, "He's not there—he's gone."

Brant reported the incident as occurring in the mouth of the river, and so avoided negative repercussions for being up the river. The incident did, however, excite the DIV COM, Smokey Bear, and he flew down on a helo. "Oh crap," Brant thought, "he's never done *that* before."

Smokey Bear got Brant on the fantail of the LST and asked, "What the hell's going on? You know the rules. Brant, I know you were in that fucking river; I'm going to court martial you. Were you in that river?" Brant replied, "No, I was at the mouth."

Meanwhile, as this colloquy was going on, Tuck says, "Pooch is in a body bag on the LST." Smokey Bear next questioned each of the crew members as to whether the boat had been in the river. In the face of an intimidating interrogation the crew stood up for their boat officer and Smokey Bear eventually returned to Cat Lo. The captain of the LST then suggested the crew take a couple of days off on the ship, which they did.

Two patrols later, they had to go out again. Tuck now says, "I have to

---

24. Brant now thinks the sampan was a decoy—the Americans were supposed to stop and check it out and he foiled their ambush by roaring past—"I was brilliant," he says.

be honest, it's pretty scary when you lose somebody. It's upsetting, you're queasy, you're not sleeping and it plays on your mind."

They all got back on the boat and headed for their designated patrol area. Tuck now describes it as everyone being contained within themselves; it's quiet, nobody's talking, an ominous atmosphere. "You could just sense it." Everyone was depressed except the Vietnamese liaison, "who was down in the cabin eating and sleeping, because that's what they did."

Finally, Brant couldn't take it anymore, so he said, "Okay Boats, put the throttles to neutral and just lay to. Everybody on the fantail." The crew gathered there, mostly looking at each other, or down, anywhere but at their O in C. Brant said to them:

> Okay, if you got anything you want to get off your chests, this is your chance. But I'm going to tell you what I think. The other day we were up a river, we were in a firefight, we got some of the sons of bitches, but they got Pooch, and we can't change that. No one's talking today, and we're all out here in our own worlds. And you know what's going to happen guys? One, we don't like the fact that Pooch is dead; two, we're scared; and three, we're going to turn into guys that never go near the coast again. We're going to turn into chicken shits. That will kill us. We've got to shake this. We can't do it by thinking about it, talking about it, so here's what I propose, and we'll vote on it. We're putting our helmets on and we're going up another river right now. If anyone disagrees, you tell me right now.

The crew nodded their heads, put their helmets and flak jackets on and went about a mile and a half up a river north of the Bo De. The run was uneventful and they shortly returned to Cat Lo. When they got in, Smokey Bear was on the pier.

When Brant got off the boat, Smokey Bear, who didn't like Brant and probably wanted him out of his division, said, "Brant, I've got a message here from Sepia.[25] They have every reason to believe that your boat sent an unauthorized transmission."

Despite Brant's denial, Smokey Bear restricted Brant and crew to the base anytime they were in Cat Lo. After Smokey had left Brant's bos'n came up and said, "That was me that sent the transmission."

"I know it was you," Brant replied. His bos'n would pick up the mike every morning and say, "Good morning, Vietnam." One day he had announced over the mike, "Fifty-eight days left."

---

25. Sepia monitored all radio transmissions for the area.

The boatswain said, "Mr. Brant, I'll go up and tell the DIV COM I did it, and then the crew won't be restricted."

Brant replied, "Like hell you will. We'll stay on this boat for the rest of our time in Vietnam if we have to." After staying on the boat for four days, Brant heard they were asking for volunteers to go to An Thoi. He went to his crew and asked what they thought about going to An Thoi. They all replied in the affirmative except one, who was a short-timer. The crew found a sailor from another crew that wanted to go to An Thoi. Tuck asked them one question, "Is he a good guy?" The next day, Steve Luke, sea bag in hand, showed up, thus sealing his fate.

They shoved off for An Thoi on PCF 36 with two other boats. As they were leaving Brant got three signal flags from a WPB: Alpha, Mike, Foxtrot (AMF). The day the three boats left with Brant's boat in the lead, he ran up the three flags, signaling a last message for Smokey Bear: "Adios Mother Fucker."

ON SEPTEMBER 8, 1968, the Swifties lost another, as BM2 John P. McDermott of Pittsburgh, Kansas, was killed aboard PCF 98. The boat was tied up alongside an LST anchored offshore An Xugen Province when a jammed 81mm mortar "round . . . detonated during disarming procedures at the precise moment that McDermott looked down the barrel."[26] The blast blew half of McDermott's head away.

ON SEPTEMBER 18, 1968, Skip "Mustang Sally" Gunther and crew made their last patrol. As one would expect, they didn't just lay off the coast, but actively searched junks along the coastline in the areas 1 Gulf/2 Charlie. As they were searching the junks, water began splashing around the boat as enemy fire commenced from shore. The crew went to general quarters, and threw off the lines to the junk they were searching. They identified the three positions of the ambush and responded first with mortar fire. When they realized they were still receiving heavy automatic weapons fire from the beach, Gunther decided to charge into the fire. They put their beam to the shoreline and all three .50 caliber machine guns on the Swift raked the beach, their tracers stitching a pattern in the trees 100 feet from shore. Gunther says "we just sat there and slugged it out" until they suppressed fire, after which they moved to within M-79 range. The enemy retreated inland.

As Gunther and his crew left country, Captain Hoffmann sent out a message to encourage the men in his northern commands to follow Lieutenant

---

26. Brinkley, *Tour of Duty*, p. 164.

PCF 21, flying its "Last Patrol" flag, rounds a small spit of land at high speed heading south as it nears the base at Chu Lai Harbor. "No man's land" is to starboard. O in C Lieutenant F.L. "Skip" "Mustang Sally" Gunther (known as the "Chu Lai Tiger") is at the after controls. QM2 R. H. Ray (who served on PT boats in World War II) is at the pilothouse door, GMG3 Roger Buie is in the gun tub, QM2 Golburg and EN2 Don Foreman are on the stern. OFFICIAL U.S. NAVY PHOTO, HOFFMANN COLLECTION

Gunther's example. His message said in part that the 21 boat had "been consistently the Top Gun in the Task Force. They have pursued an aggressive, thorough role in surveillance enforcement of restricted zones, and have executed quick decisive action against the enemy." Hoffmann cited their record since May: 41 KIAs (body count); 55 KIAs (probable); numerous junks, sampans, bunkers and structures damaged or destroyed; and 74 detainees taken in. It was exactly what he wanted from his command: Take the war to the enemy in order to win it. Shortly thereafter, Admiral Veth ordered Captain Hoffmann to Saigon.

THEN NAVY CAPTAIN Earl Frank "Rex" Rectanus was the Assistant Chief of Staff for Intelligence to the Commander, U.S. Naval Forces, Vietnam.

He had reported to Vietnam in late May of 1968 and ended up serving under both Admirals Veth and Zumwalt.[27]

"Admiral Veth was ineffective," Rectanus says, "but it wasn't his fault. Admiral Veth was a competent officer who got almost no support from the Navy. He wasn't innovative but he had limited room in which to work." There was an attitude in the Navy that, "this is the Army's war, it's a dirty war; there is no point in losing good sailors in this war. The PBR people were carrying the brunt of the load; Task Forces 115 and 117 were doing a good but inherently limited job."

One cannot overstate the low priority the in country Navy had within the corridors of power in Washington D.C. Leslie J. Cullen wrote:

> There was a larger attitude within the Navy that the in country war in South Vietnam paled in significance to the 'real' war—the air war against North Vietnam. For that reason, South Vietnam gained a reputation at best as a detour from a successful career track, or at worst a 'dumping ground' for inferior officers. In the wider Navy, preoccupied as it was with the Soviet threat—and with Operation Rolling Thunder—the brown water war in Vietnam placed a distant third on anyone's list of priorities.[28]

And then there was the Army problem. General Creighton Abrams held Veth in disdain. Abrams later told Admiral Zumwalt he was getting no help from the Navy in fighting the war. Part of it was the unassertiveness of Veth, part of it was institutional bias—the Army always looked at waterways as a barrier, while the Navy looked at water as an entrée. Rectanus says, "There was tremendous internal opposition to the Navy in South Vietnam. The Army had no time for the Navy. General Abrams wouldn't even see Veth." Part of that reason was that Veth was a two-star, while all the Corps commanders were three-star generals.

Into this political mix came Roy Hoffmann to Saigon. He went with

---

27. Rex Rectanus had a distinguished naval career, both before and after Vietnam. He was advanced to rear admiral on July 22, 1971 and assumed duty as the Director, Naval Intelligence Division, Office of CNO, with the additional duty of Commander Naval Intelligence Command. In February 1973 he became Director of Naval Intelligence and Commander of the Naval Intelligence Command. In September 1974 he was advanced to the rank of vice admiral and retired at that rank on March 1, 1976. All quotations from Admiral Rectanus are from an interview conducted January 26, 2007.

28. Leslie J. Cullen, "Tet and the Genesis of Operation SEALORDS." From the above one may understand why Roy Hoffmann reacted to his orders to Vietnam with less than his full enthusiasm.

both Generals Westmoreland's and Abrams' directives to be more aggressive in his pocket. Veth opened the conference by asking Hoffmann, "Are you aware of the fact that you've been sued by the Vietnamese fishing industry?" "Yes, sir, I am," Hoffmann replied.

"And are you aware that I've also been sued?"

"No sir, I was not aware of that."

With the increased enforcement of no fishing zones and secret zones and the increased aggressiveness against traffic in those areas, there were more vessels sunk than had previously been the case. "Under what authority are you taking these actions?" Veth asked. At this point Captain Hoffmann thought, "My days in Vietnam are going to be pretty short."

He answered, "I thought I was complying with your directives, sir."

It was far short of a dressing down, but it can never be good for a Navy captain to have a two-star admiral imply he wasn't pleased with the way he was conducting his duties. Veth finally dismissed him. As he turned to go, Hoffmann screwed up enough courage, turned around and said, "Admiral, I'm somewhat confused. The commanding general is ordering us to carry the fight to the enemy. I'm not quite sure why I was invited down here and exactly what your orders are at this point. Shall I cease and desist or shall I obey the General's orders?"

Veth looked at him and said, "I'm not God."

Hoffmann said "aye, aye, sir," and the conference was over. Within less than two weeks there was a new commander of Naval Forces in Vietnam. A dramatic change in the Navy's in country role was about to occur.

Operation SEALORDS

On September 28, 1968, the U.S. command in Saigon disclosed that the enemy had substantially increased its use of Cambodia as a staging area and sanctuary. On September 30, Vice Admiral Elmo R. Zumwalt, Jr., the Navy's youngest vice admiral, relieved Rear Admiral Kenneth L. Veth in ceremonies in Saigon. The Navy's contribution to the war effort was about to change dramatically.[29]

---

29. Much of the SEALORDS section of this chapter focuses on Coastal Division 11. This is not to disparage the other forces under the command of Roy Hoffmann, but only reflects the reality of the dramatically altered mission in IV Corps. In fact, Captain Hoffmann's entire command reacted magnificently and with bravery to the altered circumstances.

Part Three: Vietnam to Retirement 199

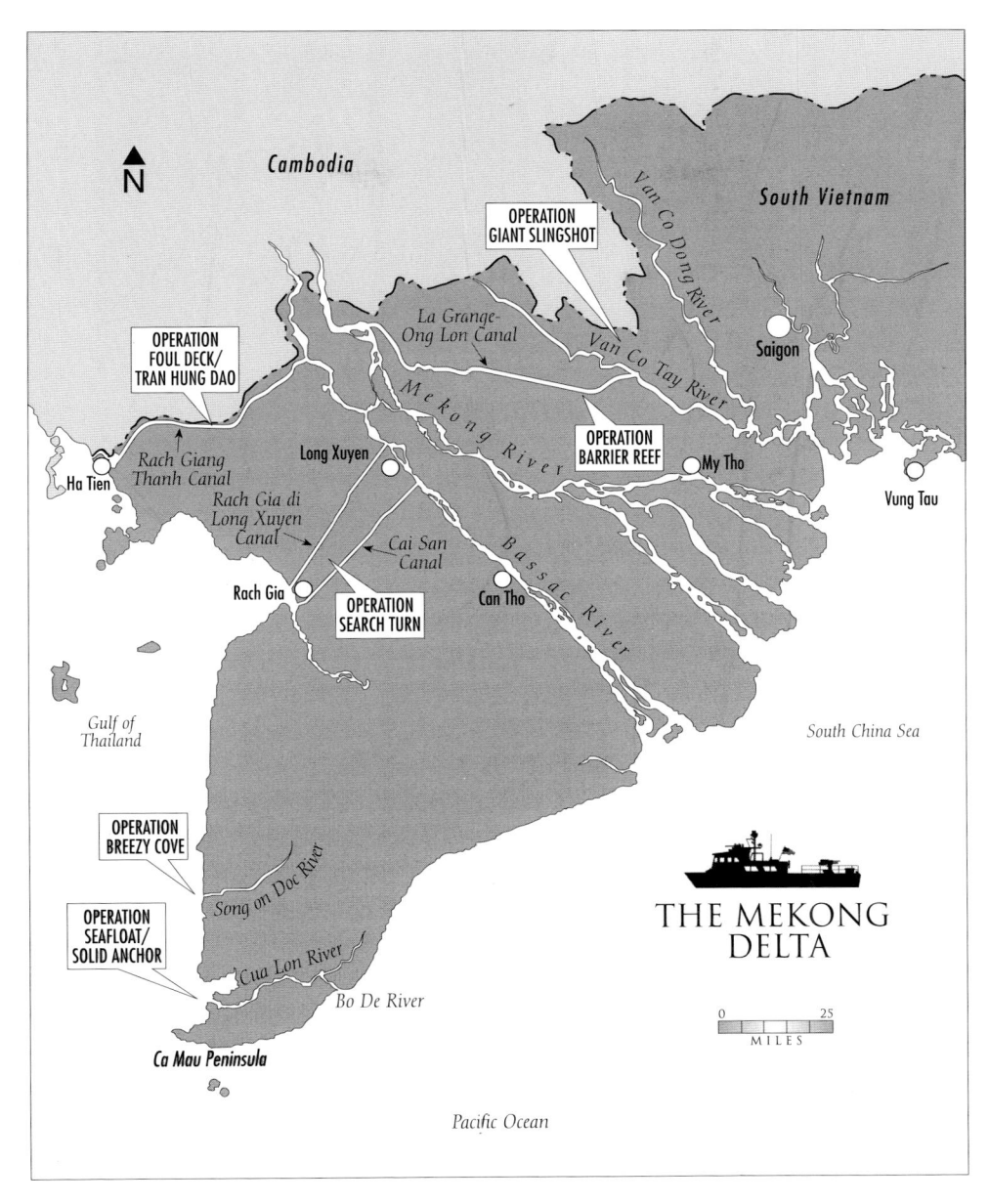

South Vietnam's inland waterways. MAP BY ARROW GRAPHICS

The 1968 Tet Offensive had clearly shown that the Navy's blockade effort had not been able to stop the enemy from infiltrating personnel and materiel into the South. The materiel came down the Ho Chi Minh trail on the backs of coolies, 40 pounds per man. Navy and MACV intelligence also indicated Chinese ships were coming into the port of Sihanoukville and unloading massive amounts of supplies, which were then finding their way over the porous Cambodian border into Vietnam.

Vice Admiral Zumwalt, COMNAVFORV.
ADMIRAL REX RECTANUS PHOTO

As Leslie Cullen pointed out, "The enemy adapted to American patrolling methods and altered schedules of movement and location accordingly. Chased from the Mekong and Bassac Rivers, infiltrators reverted to the lesser rivers and canals that laced the entire southern third of South Vietnam. Many of these waterways ran close to the Cambodian frontier, across which men and logistics moved with relative ease."[30]

Meanwhile, Veth had clung to the old strategy. Veth said, "There was some agitation to go up a lot of the canals with our riverine boats . . . but for the most part we avoided that, again, because the chance of being ambushed by the enemy was so great and there wasn't much to be accomplished."[31]

Admiral Thomas H. Moorer, CNO of the Navy from August 1, 1967 to June 30, 1970, personally picked Zumwalt to relieve Veth.[32] Zumwalt arrived packing three-stars, an upgrade in the Navy's in country status and an indication the Navy had become serious about a change in mission. The Secretary of

---

30. Cullen, "Tet and the Genesis of Operation SEALORDS."
31. *Ibid.*
32. Admiral Zumwalt relates in *My Father My Son* that assigning him to Vietnam was Moorer's way of removing a thorn out of his side—Moorer was an aviator and wanted the aviation community in charge of the Navy. Zumwalt's sponsor was Secretary of the Navy Paul Nitze. Zumwalt thought Moorer's thinking was, "Promote the son of a bitch and nobody will ever hear from him again." p. 41.

An intense Vice Admiral Zumwalt consults with his Market Time Commander, Roy Hoffmann, Cam Ranh Bay. HOFFMANN COLLECTION

Defense wanted the Navy to do its job, and the Navy responded by sending over one of its brightest stars in Zumwalt. Admiral Rectanus now says, "It was a real risk for Zumwalt because no one in the Navy wanted that job." No Navy man had left Vietnam and obtained another job that led anywhere.

Rectanus believes when Zumwalt was sent to Vietnam he knew the handwriting was on the wall. "We were going to leave, sooner than anyone wanted to go." Zumwalt wanted to give the Vietnamese at least a fighting chance to prevent the communists in North Vietnam from overrunning South Vietnam. Rectanus believes that had Zumwalt arrived two years earlier, with the resources he had in 1968–69, the entire course of the war would have been different.

Zumwalt began his tour with an extensive seven-day tour of his new command. He visited his task force commanders; his first visit was to Captain Roy Hoffmann. Hoffmann told him, "Admiral, we've got resources we are not using." He told the new commander he thought his Swift boats were almost ideal for inland waterway operations. He told Zumwalt he had outstanding officers and men on the boats. "I know," Hoffmann said, "we can operate in the rivers because some of our men are already doing it.

"One of my major concerns," Hoffmann told him, "is we have absolutely no coordination with the U.S. Army." He said communications with the other two task forces weren't much better, and he didn't understand why the three task forces couldn't be combined into a more effective organization. The first time Hoffmann had ever seen Captain Art Price, his counterpart in TF 116, was at Zumwalt's change of command ceremony. "We've actually had firefights off the Rung Sat Secret Zone with PBRs." Zumwalt got the same message from the other two task force commanders.

Zumwalt decided immediately that the 38,000 officers and men under his command could be put to greater use. He thought the waterways were the key to securing III and IV Corps. His assistant chief of staff for intelligence, Captain Rectanus, briefed him that Cambodia had become a major enemy supply area. He further briefed the admiral that enemy soldiers and materiel were coming in country across the Cambodian border and traveling along the vast network of rivers and canals deep in the Delta and Ca Mau area. The enemy was in virtual control of the U Minh forest along the western coast and in the Ca Mau peninsula. In many of the areas there had not been a friendly force there for 20 years.

Zumwalt concluded the Navy men were frustrated because the sailors were no longer taking the fight to the enemy. He clearly felt it was time for a change.

He called the three task force commanders into Saigon almost immediately, to tell them he had talked to a very supportive General Abrams in general terms about a change in the Navy's mission, particularly in IV Corps. He asked his three task force commanders to sit down and write an operational plan for better utilization of forces, and he wanted them to call it SEALORDS (the acronym for the awkwardly titled Southeast Asia Lake, Ocean, River and Delta Strategy). The name was for public consumption; the Navy headquarters called it the Strategic Interdiction Campaign.

The plan the task force commanders came up with called for more coordination with the Army's 9th Division; PBRs would become more aggressive, particularly in the Parrot's Beak area, and along the Cambodian border (the result was Operation Giant Slingshot); the Swifts out of Cat Lo would take over the lower Mekong Delta east of the confluence of the Co Chien and Ham Luong rivers; and in the Ca Mau of IV Corps Swifts were to become a river raider operation.

Zumwalt, in Hoffmann's words, "had a brilliant mind. He was a speed reader and could go through a report before I even got through the introduction." Zumwalt took the concept for SEALORDS as presented by the three task force commanders, retained it, and made a masterful presentation to Abrams the same day. Zumwalt's only missteps were mispronouncing some of the Vietnam place names, because he was so new in country. Zumwalt said Abrams, "had a reputation for being a tough man who ate people alive . . . he was also the finest commander under whom I have ever served, and a man who cared deeply for his troops."[33]

As Leslie J. Cullen wrote, "Because SEALORDS—with its post-Tet emphasis on interdiction, denial of sanctuary, and pacification—unified the American naval effort, it is unquestionably one of the better strategies to emerge from the American military experience in Vietnam. By July 1969 a NAVFORV study indicated that the barrier operations . . . generated 900 firefights resulting in more than 1,600 enemy killed." Of equal or greater importance were the more than 160 tons of weapons captured and the disruption of the enemy logistical supply line. That led to, according to Admiral Rectanus, "The revitalization and economic miracle in the Delta starting in late 1968, due in large measure to the operations of PBRs and Swifts . . . and the close support provided by the Seawolves of TF 116."

"It was he [Zumwalt]," Rectanus says, "with the fertile, intellectual mind, the great imagination and the courage to do the job, which no one in the higher echelons of the Navy wanted him to do, who deserves the credit for [one of] the most significant operations of the Vietnam War."

SEALORDS was officially set in motion with the issuance of Operation Plan 111-69 on November 5, 1968. A month before it was officially sanctioned, the Swifties started their assault on the enemy.

DURING THE PERIOD of October 2-4, 1968, Terry Costello and Lieutenant Mike Brown were operating off a USCG cutter in area 9 Charlie, taking turns going out on patrol. Their two crews used one boat, Costello's PCF 38. It wasn't a big operation and the Swifts were operating independently.

On October 4, Mike Brown, whom Costello describes as "rather adventuresome," decided to take the 38 boat into No Man's Land, a place no Swift had been before. With just the one boat, he and his crew went through Square Bay, up the Cua Lon River and out the Bo De, a distance of over 60 nautical miles. As they roared through they fired on targets of opportunity, destroying sampans and structures along the way. While they were exiting the Bo De they came under hostile fire; both O in C Brown and QM2 David

---

33. Zumwalt, *My Father My Son*, p. 42. Abrams understood the reality of Vietnam well. President Johnson, in his typically earthy language, had told him, "General, I want every Vietnamese who carries a peter to be in uniform and to be in this war effort, and I want us to get out as fast as we can."

Clayton were wounded as they fought their way out. "Mike Brown did a hell of a job just getting out of there," Larry Thurlow says.[34]

The battle damaged 38 boat returned to the cutter. "I was always sort of semi-irked at him," Costello says, "because he got my boat shot up. The radar and the fuse panel on the port side where the O in C sat were hit, and never worked right again. The crew constantly rewired the fuse box, but always after that if they wanted to use the searchlight they had to turn the siren fuse on."

Mike Brown made his run ten days before Mike Bernique's famous run up the Rach Giang Thanh. The Swifts were still officially on coastal patrol and little was said about what became known as Brown's Run. Captain Hoffmann, when he became aware of Brown's Run, sent him a message commending the action: "The transiting of the enemy controlled Cua Lon/Bo De . . . by PCF 38 was an outstanding demonstration of seamanship, gunnery and personal courage under extremely hazardous conditions. It was a daylight surface strike into a Communist redoubt that [had] defied intrusion for over two years. It was an action that will . . . shake the morale and confidence of the Viet Cong. Well done."

Meanwhile, Lieutenant j.g. Robert G. Elder, just arriving in the area from Swift training, was aboard a Thai gunboat with Lieutenant j.g. James Harwood when they got the message that Mike Brown had made his run, the boat had been shot up and Brown had been wounded. "Oh my God, I didn't sign up for this," was Elder's first reaction. "These boats are supposed to be out on the open water. Who's this Mike Brown?"[35]

PCFs 9 and 43 arrived in An Thoi on October 10, 1968, after a complete overhaul in the Philippines. On April 12 of the next year the 43 boat would be destroyed in the Rach Duong Keo in the fierce firefight on that day.

On October 11 Bob Elder was assigned the 43 boat, which he says was in beautiful, like-new condition. Bob Elder is tall, handsome, urbane and articulate with a mellifluous speaking voice. Born in 1940, it seems he always had the Navy in his blood. He could remember as a youth the parades given for World War II veterans. In 1960 he was in the Philadelphia Naval Yard during Navy days when they launched the USS *Barney*. He got on the bridge of a ship that day and vowed he would some day stand on a bridge just like it and drive a destroyer.

---

34. Lieutenant Brown was eventually awarded the Silver Star for the operation, and his crew received Navy Commendation Medals.

35. All quotations are from an interview conducted with Bob Elder October 12, 2006. Elder is a banker living today in Pennsylvania with his wife, Mimi.

PCF 43 provides cover for beached Swifts. OFFICIAL U.S. NAVY PHOTO, HOFFMANN COLLECTION

While he was in graduate school at the University of Pittsburgh during the 1963-64 academic season he was recruited to work for Exxon; he went to work for the firm in August of 1964. He never got the Navy out of his blood and, as the Vietnam War heated up, he joined the Navy Reserve in 1965 in order to go to OCS. He started four months of OCS training on January 15, 1966. His "wish list" was to go on destroyer duty. Coinciding with the graduation from OCS he married in May of 1966.

He received orders to the World War II destroyer USS *Soley* (DD 707), home ported in Charleston, South Carolina. He spent three years on the reserve ship *Soley* as the weapons officer. While on the destroyer he heard about Swifts.

In May of 1968 he was in Charleston when his detailer called and said, "Bob, you've got about a month before you muster out of the Navy. I know you are getting out, but we could give you a Swift boat in Vietnam. All it would require you do is sign up for an additional 14 months."

Elder had a wife and 14-month-old baby at home, plus his parents were visiting for the weekend. He was going home and join them for dinner. He was almost out of the Navy and his old job was waiting for him at Exxon. "Without blinking an eye," he says, "I told my detailer to sign me up. To me it was the chance of a lifetime and couldn't believe that anyone wouldn't see that."

He went home that night, sat his wife and parents down, and told them the story. "Instantly, everyone is in tears. I'm looking around like am I the man from the moon or something? Did I say something wrong? I'm a Naval officer, there's a war going on and they've offered me a command at sea in wartime."

After his family settled down and accepted his decision he reported to boat school in Coronado in July of 1968. His best friends at Coronado were officers Virgil Erwin, Doug Armstrong and Jim Harwood. Before leaving Swift training they were told to go into the Swift library and read and memorize the Rules of Engagement (in Appendix Delta). They were told to do so because when they got to Cam Ranh Bay they would be brought in front of someone named Captain Hoffmann, and he was going to want you to quote verbatim from the Rules. "And gentlemen," they were told at Coronado, "Hoffmann is a tough guy, a Jimmy Cagney tough guy."

Elder went to the library thinking, "I can't memorize my name, I can't memorize Mary Had a Little Lamb, I just can't do it." He tried desperately for a week to come up with situations in his mind that would help him remember.

The officers flew over to Vietnam together after training, and sure enough, they were called before Captain Hoffmann, who "was everything they ever told me he was. There's this grizzly guy chomping on a cigar."

"Come in," Hoffmann said gruffly. They went in and didn't sit down. He grilled them on everything imaginable, and then he got to the Rules of Engagement. As it turned out, Hoffmann didn't want rote memory, he wanted to know if they could *think*. He would come up with different scenarios and ask them how they would apply the rules. To his relief, it was exactly how Elder had prepared for the meeting.

After the meeting the four officers split up, Harwood and Elder going to An Thoi and Erwin and Armstrong to Cat Lo. After the flight to Saigon Elder and Harwood ended up at the Grand Hotel in Vung Tau. They had missed their reporting date in An Thoi because no one knew how to get them to the remote area. Elder, thinking he would be court martialed, finally got orders with Harwood to go aboard a 68-foot Coast Guard cutter, which was to take them half way, after which a Thai gunboat would take them the rest of the way.

As they got underway at the height of the monsoon in pouring rain and heavy seas Elder and Harwood were instantly sick. They finally met the

A USCG 82 footer and a Thai gunboat on patrol, An Thoi.
Official U.S. Coast Guard Photo, Lonsdale collection

gunboat at the tip of Vietnam in the middle of the night. The seas were heaving as the boats slammed and crashed together. Elder and Harwood were supposed to jump across to the gunboat with their heavy baggage. They managed to get across without being crushed. The Thais treated them like royalty, delivering them to An Thoi where they reported to George Elliott.

Elder was assigned to George Bates (O in C of the 50 boat) for a week or so of patrols to learn the ropes. Bates took him to Ha Tien for his first patrol, and they went to the NILOs (Naval Intelligence Liaison Officers) office for a briefing. They walked up the hill to get to the post, which was surrounded by barbed wire and claymore mines. Someone yelled, "Don't anybody set those things off."

After the shakedown patrol Elder received the 43 boat and patrolled initially with Terry Costello. Elder describes Costello as strong, silent, possessed with confidence and knowledge, a man with command presence and quiet confidence.[36] Elder's crew consisted of Leading Petty Officer QM2 Rex J. Young; RD2 Jim Thomas; EN2 Danny Lee Anderson; BMSN Howard Hensley, whom Elder describes as the "absolutely fearless" after gunner who had a sixth grade education; and GMG3 Larry Wayne Gilbertson, who "was everything you would think about a dairy farmer from Wisconsin." Elder describes Gilbertson as "a Larry Thurlow kind of guy, solid, reliable, understated, totally fearless." He had inherited a fine crew.

October 14, 1968:
Bernique's Run up the Rach Giang Thanh

Mike Bernique is a large, imposing, intelligent, forceful and articulate man.[37] He was born on December 26, 1943 in Fall River, Massachusetts, and grew up in Germany, France and Washington, D.C. He was educated in France and speaks French nearly as well as he speaks English. His father was wounded in North Africa during World War II, after which he was visited in the hospital by William "Wild Bill" Donovan. His father joined the Office of Strategic Services (OSS), the forerunner to the postwar CIA, and was attached to Chiang Kai-shek. He parachuted into Indo China where he became the American liaison with Ho Chi Minh. He fought with Ho against the Japanese in the last year of World War II.

Mike Bernique's father told him if he ever went in the Army he would "break both your arms and legs. If you don't go in the Navy, you're even more stupid than I think."

Bernique graduated from Notre Dame at the age of 21, after which his Dad came up to him, gave him a hug and said, "Hey, 21, college grad, which is great, I'm really proud of you. You got a job?"

"Nah," Mike responded.

"Any interviews?"

"Nah."

"Do you know what you want to do?"

---

36. Bob Elder ran into Terry Costello at a Swift Boat Veterans for Truth meeting in Washington, D.C. in 2004, 35 years after they had served together in Vietnam. Elder told him, "Terry, in all of my time in the Navy, I never had more of a role model or man I admired more than you." The modest Costello's only reaction was to look mildly surprised.

37. All quotations are taken from an interview conducted with Mike Bernique on June 14, 2006.

"Nah."

"Want to take some time to think about it?"

"Yeah," Mike said.

"Where are you going to do your thinking?" his dad asked.

"At home."

"No, no, you're a college grad, you're on your own, son." Then his dad turned around and walked away. And that was the end of the conversation.

"So," Bernique says in a droll voice, "I joined the Navy."

He went to OCS, "and I loved it." One day a detailer came down to interview him and see what he wanted to do. Bernique says he didn't know it was a trick question, and said, "Well, I don't know. I might stay in the Navy. I kind of like it." The next thing he knew he got all his choices.

He was assigned as a CIC officer on the USS *McCoy* (DE 1038) out of Newport, Rhode Island. Captain Lou Colbus (whom the reader encountered in Chapter 6) was the skipper of the *McCoy*. Colbus was Jewish (he describes himself as "Lou the Jew" and in those days was known as "Big Lou from the BOQ"). He was totally bald and a "fantastic guy" according to Bernique. Colbus credited much of what he knew about seamanship from his association with Roy Hoffmann and Bernique says Colbus taught him everything he knew about seamanship.

Bernique was aboard the *McCoy* when he heard of Swift boats and thought they "sounded like the closest to command at sea I could get." He volunteered, got his orders to Coronado, went through school and arrived in An Thoi in the summer of 1968.

He was assigned to PCF 3 with three of his crew members from Coronado (two others had washed out). David Hemenway, one of the three enlisted men, says they were going to split up the crew when they got to An Thoi because they were short two men. Hemenway now says, "Mr. Bernique had a way of really being forceful sometimes," and the crew stayed together. With the addition of the two new men the crew consisted of GMG2 Robert Hornberger, BM2 Edward Kesselring, RD3 Jimmy Sanford, EN3 Wade Knutson and RDSN David Robert Hemenway.[38] Bernique says

---

38. All quotations from David Hemenway are from an interview conducted March 19, 2007; and from Robert Hornberger in an interview conducted February 10, 2007. Additional interviews for the Rach Giang Thanh run were conducted with Edward Kesselring and Jimmy Sanford during the 2007 Swift Boat Sailors Association reunion in San Diego. David Hemenway, recipient of two Purple Hearts during his service aboard Swifts, came from a Navy family. His dad was in the U.S. Navy during World War II,

today "I loved my crew." The crew was called "Bernique and his hired killers," and David Hemenway says, "when the shit hit the fan there was not a better officer than Bernique around, and I rode with a lot of them." Robert Hornberger echoes him, "Bernique had a lot of guts, and he was a good officer, not afraid of anything."

When Mike Bernique arrived the boats were not to close the beach inside 1,000 yards (one klick). There was an officer's club at An Thoi where there was little to do except read, write and "think a little." Bernique was thinking they could be doing a lot more than they were to take the fight to the enemy.

One day in October the 3 boat was "bobbing around like a cork in the Gulf of Thailand." Bernique was bored. None of the watercraft they stopped had any weapons. "I'm looking at a chart, I'm seeing French canals that were dug and waterways that were magnificent and I'm thinking to myself what self respecting smuggler of weapons is going to go out in the South China Sea when he can go through the canals?" And that was the genesis of Bernique's run of October 14, 1968. In retrospect, knowing now what was going on in Saigon in regard to the planning for SEALORDS, and in light of the aggressive stance of Captain Hoffmann, the Brown and Bernique runs seem low risk to the officers' careers. However, no one in the field knew what was afoot in terms of the changed mission, and they undertook the runs in contravention of standing orders.

The Giang Thanh runs north out of Ha Tien, paralleling the border with Cambodia, to the junction with the Vinh Te canal, where it turns east, then northeast to the city of Chau Doc on the west bank of the Bassac River. It was narrow and winding and totally controlled by the enemy, who crossed it with impunity. Intelligence indicated the Viet Cong had set up tax stations on the Rach Giang Thanh, which had been declared off limits to U.S. patrol boats because of its proximity to Cambodia.

---

serving as a sonarman on a destroyer. He also had an uncle in the Navy during the war and one who served between World War II and Korea. He enlisted in July of 1967, went through boot camp in Great Lakes and then was sent to sub school. He spent about three months on a World War II diesel submarine, and then requested duty in Vietnam. He was ordered to PBR School with Jack Shamley (see below), but the class was too large by nearly a dozen men, so he and Shamley were transferred to Swift school in Coronado in May of 1968. Robert Hornberger also came from a Navy background. His dad was in the Battle of Midway during World War II. Hornberger enlisted in June of 1960 (he eventually put nine years in the Navy) and was assigned to the fleet. His second ship was the USS *John R. Pierce* (DD 753), which participated in the Cuban Missile Crisis, the American ship that stopped the Russian freighter from entering Cuban waters. He volunteered for Swift duty.

The base at Ha Tien. On top of the hill were the Republic of Vietnam forces, captain and family quarters; TF 116 personnel; American advisory team (Army and Navy); and Vietnamese intelligence agents and ARVNs. Weymouth Symmes photo

The crew pulled into Ha Tien; Bernique, armed with his charts, went to the Army base at the top of the hill and asked, "Is this chart right? Is this the way to go?" A couple of the Vietnamese there said, "No go! No go! Numbah ten!"

Bernique: "Numbah ten? Beau coup VC?"

Vietnamese: "Oh, beau coup VC, beau coup VC!" It was what Bernique wanted to hear. He discussed the raid with an enthusiastic Army major at the base (who went along for the ride), and then went back to his crew and told them there was a VC tax collection point up the river and they were going in. David Hemenway remembers thinking, "Oh, really."

As Bernique's DIV COM George Elliott says, "Mike knew the rules but made the run anyway." The Swifties got the boat underway and roared up the narrow waterway. A short time later they rounded a bend where, as Hemenway says, "If you had to stage a VC tax point it was exactly what it would look like. Two sampans were pulled over, and there are guys collecting money." The shocked

VC froze as the Swift swept into view. Robert Hornberger, the twin .50s gunner, says "we charged the river bank, shooting at them as they were running while they shot back at us." Hemenway, who had an M-16 on the bow, states, "I saw that first splash in the water and I knew that this was the real thing. We made one pass by them, we made another pass by them coming back the other way." There were six to eight VC armed with AK 47s; three dropped, unable to reach the tree line, while the others scattered in panic, leaving weapons, ammunition, supplies and documents behind.

The 3 boat beached to retrieve the contraband, and Bernique, Jimmy Sanford and Hemenway ("I was a lot younger then" he says) jumped off the boat. They checked the bodies for documents and began gathering weapons when the VC, who had regrouped in the trees, opened fire. Bernique says, "I'm between the boat and the incoming fire, the boat can't shoot, so the three of us charged their position and they broke and ran."

Afterward, Bernique had "a very interesting choice. I could have kept my mouth shut, but I didn't do that." As they exited the canal he broadcast in the open what he had done. When they got back to the APL that afternoon word was already there they wanted him in Saigon. George Elliott told him the report had gone to Saigon and they wanted him there *now*. Elliott was really nervous and told Bernique "I don't know what's going to happen. You really violated the rules."[39] Meanwhile, Bernique is thinking, "What are they going to do, send me to Vietnam?"

When Bernique arrived in Saigon, he became quickly aware there were two camps. He was first interviewed "by a little guy [the chief of staff], who just lit into me." He basically implied that Bernique deserved a court martial by violating orders. The chief of staff's comment was, "Let me tell you, a hundred VC aren't worth one dead American." Bernique replied, "Look, I'll never trade an American life, but I'll take those odds anytime." Another officer told Bernique that Prince Sihanouk of Cambodia had accused him of killing innocent Cambodian civilians, to which Bernique replied, "You tell Sihanouk he's a lying son-of-a-bitch." Meanwhile, he's thinking, "Wow, I've kicked over a hornet's nest."

George Elliott relates, "I knew that Captain Hoffmann was arguing for Mike with some MACV staffers who wanted Bernique's hide nailed to the wall." One who listened sympathetically was Admiral Zumwalt. Zumwalt listened to the young j.g.'s colorful description of the battle, and carefully

---

39. This would not be the last time George Elliott's aggressive officers would attract attention in Saigon.

Award ceremony (left to right), Vice Admiral Zumwalt, Lieutenant Mike Brown, Lieutenant j.g. Mike Bernique. OFFICIAL U.S. NAVY PHOTO, HOFFMANN COLLECTION

went through the whole operation with him. Bernique was excused from the room, and when he was called back in, Zumwalt asked him what he wanted in terms of operational help. "I want some Marines, some troops on board," he said. Zumwalt, whom Bernique describes as "brilliant," asked him, "Can you get up there [into the Rach Giang Thanh] again?"

Bernique: "Basically I said, you bet your sweet bippy!"

As long as the American Navy was in Vietnam the Rach Giang Thanh would be known as "Bernique's Creek."[40]

THE RUNS OF MIKE BROWN and Mike Bernique seemed to open the floodgates into the rivers and canals of the COS DIV 11 operational area. Three days after Bernique's run, three Swifts crept up the Song Ong Doc in An Xuyen Province, 155 miles southwest of Saigon. The action started as the USCG cutter *Point Cypress* began diversionary fire to the south. At about 0730 PCFs 38 and 93, skippered by Terry Costello and Mike Brown, respectively, turned southward down a narrow north-south canal which lead to the Dam Dong Cung, which would become known as "VC Lake." PCF 11 remained at the northern canal entrance to provide support for the return transit by the other two Swifts.

With U.S. Army *Cobra* helicopters providing cover fire, the two Swifts entered VC Lake at top speed, firing on the suspected VC headquarters there and numerous other structures nearby. The two Swifts remained in the shallow VC Lake for more than an hour, during which time Costello says he could see brown water coming out of his overboard discharge, "and you always get a little nervous then." They exited northward through the canal, firing heavy barrages at enemy structures and watercraft along both banks. They were ambushed on the way out, during which transit both O in Cs and one crewman were wounded. By 1020 hours the operation was complete. They destroyed numerous structures and sampans/junks and set off a huge secondary explosion.

This time, in contrast to Bernique's experience, the officers and men were cited not only by Captain Hoffmann for the "well planned and executed raid . . . a tribute to all involved," but by Admiral Zumwalt, who wrote "I am delighted and excited by the actions of your forces . . . . This initiative and daring displayed by the Swifts supported by Coast Guard and Thai units

---

40. Rather than the court martial he half expected, Bernique was awarded the Silver Star for the action; Sanford and Hemenway received the Bronze Star; and Kesselring, Hornberger and Knutson received the Navy Commendation Medal.

makes us all aware of the caliber of Navy men we have doing the job for us in Vietnam. Your crews are writing a new and significant chapter in the Navy's effort. Well done."

This raid into VC Lake is considered by some to be the first SEALORDS operation. The crews began to hammer the enemy daily. On October 22, 1968, four Swifts thrust their bows into an area in which there had been no allied forces in more than two years. Intelligence had indicated a suspected enemy supply and training complex and so, about 1215 hours, Navy PCFs 11, 50, 93 and 94 entered the western entrance of the Cua Lon River in An Xuyen Province, 168 miles southwest of Saigon. The Swifts pressed eastward into the interior, accompanied by U.S. Army *Cobra* helicopters. The USCG cutter *Wachusett* stood by the western entrance to provide cover fire, while two other Swifts opened up diversionary fire at the east end of the river. PCF 93 led the way as the boats swept into the river at top speed, spraying enemy fortifications and watercraft with intense fire. During the height of the attack the trigger on the mortar of the 93 boat broke off and the gunner grabbed a screwdriver, jammed it into the broken trigger housing and kept firing. The boats went 18.5 miles up the river, receiving fire at the ten-mile mark.

The next day Bernique's crew, accompanied by the 94 boat, caught another VC tax collecting team during a probe of Bernique's Creek, killing all four of the VC. The enemy sanctuaries were no longer off limits to American forces. On October 26, commencing at 0715 hours, PCFs 9 and 93, skippered by Bob Crosby and Rich Baker, respectively, made the first transit of the long and dangerous Ha Tien/Rach Gia canal, and returned. It was a 90-mile round trip and took ten hours to complete. They returned with valuable information of water depth and navigability of the canal in anticipation of future Swift patrols. The next day PCF 50, skippered by George Bates, attempted a probe of the Bay Hap River, but had to turn back when a mine detonated off the boat's port quarter just prior to entering the river.

On October 30, 1968, Swifties engaged in a five-hour battle with enemy forces in the Cua Lon and Bo De Rivers. It was a joint operation with boats from COS DIV 11 in An Thoi and COS DIV 13 in Cat Lo. At 0730 hours PCFs 28, 32, and 103 roared into the river complex from the east and PCFs 3, 36, and 94 entered from the west. The USS *Washoe County* (LST 1165) provided NGFS from the east coast and the USCG *Wachusett* provided west coast fire. The two groups of Swifts raced toward their rendezvous point with Vietnamese AF A-1 *Skyraiders* providing cover overhead.

Fourteen minutes after the boats made the eastern entrance they came under heavy enemy automatic weapon and recoilless rifle fire from both banks of the river. All three boats were hit but they were able to suppress the enemy fire. One of the Swifties was seriously wounded in the battle. The seven Swifts rendezvoused in mid-river, where the wounded crewman was transferred to PCF 94. Accompanied by PCF 50, the 94 boat returned to the west (through the Cua Lon) to take the wounded crewman to the medical facility on board the *Wachusett*.

The remaining five boats then made the return transit to the east (through the Song Bo De). As they approached the eastern river entrance they again came under heavy enemy fire, wounding four more Swift crewmen. During the course of the five hours in the river, the boats destroyed numerous watercraft and enemy fortifications.

Captain Hoffmann again commended the crews for the "courageous and highly successful raid through 'Brown's Run' in the lower Ca Mau peninsula." Zumwalt's message commended the men for "the sudden, coordinated assault . . . on what had been an enemy sanctuary on the Ca Mau Peninsula . . . was a striking example of naval ingenuity and daring. You demonstrated in resounding terms the . . . capabilities of Swift, potent Naval fighting units on restricted inland waterways. You have set a bold new precedent, which the enemy will not soon forget. Keep shooting."

WITH THE ADVENT of SEALORDS in COS DIV 11, the mission broadened to conducting day and night operations in the rivers and adjoining canals of the U Minh forest and the Ca Mau. The U.S. forces interdicted water traffic to prevent infiltration of enemy arms, munitions, food and medical supplies; destroyed enemy watercraft, structures, bunkers, munitions and supplies; gathered intelligence information; and were on call to provide NGFS for U.S. Army and RVN Regional Force/Popular Force outposts.

The boats were operating in the most difficult environment imaginable. Within the Ca Mau were great networks of waterways slithering through dense mangrove swamps. One entered the area with a sense of foreboding as the sluggish brown water carried one deeper and deeper into the remote area. In addition to the monsoons, the crews dealt with huge cockroaches, poisonous water snakes, huge leeches half a foot long, swarming hordes of mosquitoes harboring malaria, all accompanied by 100 degree temperatures and stifling humidity. In the early 1960s the VC had driven the Vietnamese Navy from the Ca Mau and destroyed the region's capital, Nam Can. The

Terrorism is not a recent invention by Muslim fanatics. South Vietnamese schoolteachers such as the women in this photo, were a prime target for the Viet Cong.
Official U.S. Coast Guard photo, A.L. Lonsdale collection

few South Vietnamese people left in the area were wood-cutters and dirt-poor fishermen, most forced into supporting the VC by building bunkers, providing food, transportation and manpower for the enemy.

Around the point of the Ca Mau, on the west side, was the U Minh forest, bordered on the west by the Gulf of Thailand and on the south and east by the Song Ong Doc River. It was an almost impenetrable jungle—in 1952, 500 French paratroopers dropped into the area and were never heard from again.

Overworked and exhausted Swift crews, whose rare days off were spent repairing and maintaining their boats, accomplished the assault on the area. They operated in concert with American Army and U.S. Marine Corps advisors and their Vietnamese and mercenary troops; sparse Army and Navy helicopter support; a few SEALs; and blue-water ships off the coast.

On October 31, 1968, in a televised address to the nation, President Johnson announced a complete halt in U.S. bombing of North Vietnam and the expansion of the Paris Peace Talks to include the National Liberation

218 This Is Latch

The Swifts reach the troop drop off point. Official U.S. Navy photo, Hoffmann collection

South Vietnamese troops with their American advisors move to the bow to disembark.
Official U.S. Navy photo, Hoffmann collection

Going after the enemy; troops disembarking from the bow.
OFFICIAL U.S. NAVY PHOTO, HOFFMANN COLLECTION

Front and the South Vietnamese government. It played well in America, but in Saigon, where the reality of the bombing halt was better understood, President Thieu declared the U.S. had acted unilaterally in the decision. And of course, Nixon and Humphrey were knotted in a tight presidential election, and the utterly callous timing by Johnson could have only been designed to help his vice president, Humphrey, win the election. The last minute surge for Humphrey was nearly enough to put him over the top.

Every political decision made during wartime has consequences for the conduct of the war, often to the detriment of the troops. Captain Roy Hoffmann, in one of his Quarterly Evaluation Reports to COMNAVFORV, pointed out the consequences of the bombing halt north of the DMZ:

> As a result of the bombing halt and suspension of naval activity north of the DMZ, all four of the infiltration type trawlers are now being used as . . . logistical supply ships moving large amounts of cargo south along the coast of North Vietnam. The heaviest activity has been observed off Hon La Island, where large merchant ships have been photographed off-loading cargo to smaller trawlers. In the port of Dong Hoi, photographs have revealed sampans, which can easily transit to the Ben Hai River, alongside infiltration type trawlers that are in the process of offloading.

This enemy materiel, now flowing with impunity, would be used to kill American and South Vietnamese soldiers.

Captain Roy Hoffmann began spending increasing amounts of time in An Thoi as the boats assaulted the enemy-held rivers there. He felt he needed to share the dangers with his men and to understand the operational environment. He spent much of his time on Mike Bernique's boat. Bernique had the highest regard for Roy Hoffmann. He says Latch "was a marvelous field commander ... a mini-George Patton. He was my kind of guy, very courageous, very tough minded, very fair minded, and took care of the enlisted men."

On one visit in November he asked his officers what he could do for them, and the emphatic answer from the O in Cs was *send us M-60s*. Within two days five or six of the light machine guns arrived in An Thoi. By late December they arrived in large numbers. They were referred to as Latch's Christmas presents.

The M-60 was used on the bow by a gunner standing in the small forward compartment called a peak tank (usually this was the radarman's position). The gunners on the boats also added a larger magazine for the after .50 machine gun mount, a large aluminum box that held 400 rounds of ammunition. They hung old flak jackets around the after lifelines and some twin .50s gunners used removable ceramic armor draped around the gun tub. They would need all of it.

BM3 Richard Simon, from Ellsworth, Wisconsin, and Dave Hemenway became friends because they were from the same state. Simon was the first casualty Hemenway would experience after arrival in An Thoi.

The patrol was routine enough. PCFs 36 (Tuck Brant's boat), 43 (Bob Elder's boat) and 50 (skippered by George Bates) raided VC positions in the Song Ong Doc. It was an all day patrol on a beautiful day in the Song Ong Doc, and for most of it nothing happened. George Elliott was riding the 43 boat, which was in the lead. Each boat was given targets to hit, and they beached the boats on the bank for stability and took the targets under mortar fire. They then turned around to leave, and this time the 43 boat was the last boat.

Bob Elder was standing at the port door as a shot rang out from the left side, and right before his eyes Simon, the after gunner on the 50 boat in front of him, "drops dead, just like that." Hemenway says, "we had one shot fired against us all day; it caught him right in the neck." The VC sniper was in a spider hole, and for some reason he got up and started running. He didn't get far as the Swift gunners cut him to pieces. The boats reconnoitered about

200–300 yards downstream and then left the river to take Simon out to the LST for medical help. He was already gone.

IN THE UNITED STATES, on November 5, 1968, Richard M. Nixon was elected president with Spiro Agnew as vice president. The election was a nail-biter, with the lead changing several times. Shortly after midnight Humphrey was leading by 33,000 votes, but by dawn it appeared he couldn't win in the electoral college. Nixon ended up winning 32 states and 301 electoral votes. Humphrey carried 13 states and received 191 electoral votes. George Wallace, spoiler from the South, received 46 electoral votes.

THE BOATS IN THE northern divisions also were responding to the new aggressiveness called for in SEALORDS. Clandestine operation "Dewey Rifle," which ran from November 5-27, saw the PCFs supporting Naval Advisory Detachment/CSC personnel in Da Nang in Ninh Thuan and Binh Thuan provinces.

On November 6 two Swifts blasted enemy positions along the shore 64 miles southeast of Chu Lai. During the course of the action PCF 70 was hit with a 75mm recoilless rifle round, which wounded three sailors, killed EN2 David Merrill of South Bend, Indiana, and hurled passenger Marine Lance Corporal Frederick R. Turner of Columbus, Ohio, into the water. The blast caused extensive damage and a loss of power on the boat. Frederick Turner was not recovered.

The Swifts radioed for help and the USCG cutter *Owasco* arrived on the scene and turned her guns on the enemy. Soon three other Swifts arrived on scene, and PCF 75 towed the damaged boat back to the base at Chu Lai after transferring Merrill and the wounded to the *Owasco*. Pumps provided by the cutter kept the 70 boat afloat.

ON THAT SAME DAY in the United States, students at San Francisco State College began a student strike demanding a third world studies department and an open admissions policy. After daily confrontations between police and students the college closed November 19, and reopened on December 2. New president Hayakawa ordered the school closed early for Christmas vacation. The strike lasted five months.

November 14, 1968, was "National Turn in Your Draft Card Day" in the U.S., which featured draft card burning on many campuses, and rallies against the draft in several cities.

On November 8, 1968, PCF 89 from COS DIV 15 was operating in the South China Sea off Binh Dinh province, when an 81mm mortar accidentally exploded during a combat sea patrol. Lieutenant j.g. Richard C. Wallace of Norfolk, Virginia; BM3 Peter P. Blasko, Jr., of Southern Pines, North Carolina; and BM3 Stephen T. Volz of Lakewood, California, all lost their lives in the explosion.

In the south the Swifts continued their assaults into the Ca Mau. On November 11, Swifts from An Thoi and Cat Lo raided positions in the Cua Lon and Bo De. The Swifts, commencing at 1040 hours, were in the rivers until 1640 hours. They entered the Bo De after an LST provided NGFS at the mouth of the river. As the boats swept up the river they encountered small arms and automatic weapons fire. The boats returned fire, killing two VC and destroying watercraft, structures and bunkers. The USCG cutter *Ingham* provided cover fire as the boats exited the Cua Lon.

Two days later PCFs 31, 50 and 72 raided the Cai Lon River, coming under heavy enemy fire 20 miles upriver. That same day PCFs 3 and 36 raided enemy positions in the Cua Lon, destroying sampans and structures. PCF 36 received a recoilless rifle hit while exiting the river, wounding one of the crewmen. PCF 36 returned fire, destroying the enemy emplacement and causing a huge fireball in a secondary explosion.

November 16, 1968: An International Incident

On November 16 the Swifties ran into another hornet's nest with the enemy, after which the Navy officers had to endure a naval inquiry in Saigon.[41] The planned two-day raid was part of Operation Foul Deck, and involved three Swifts and two Seawolves (UH-1B helicopter gun ships) entering Bernique's Creek pushing up from the south, and PBRs backed by assault craft pushing south from to Bassac River. George Elliott's orders were to take three boats to Ha Tien, run the length of the river, paralleling the Cambodian border, and exit on the Bassac. The next day the boats were to transit the U Minh forest and come out at Rach Gia. The route would take

---

41. Sources for this incident were: Mike Bernique interview, November 16, 2006; Tuck Brant interview, July 2, 2006; Roy Hoffmann interview November 1, 2005; Cutler, *Brown Water Black Beret*, pp. 293–294; Associated Press, "Cambodia Threat to Fight U.S.;" Shreadley, *From the Rivers to the Sea*, pp. 157–158; and Forbes and Williams, *Riverine Force*, p. 126.

The "International Incident," November 16, 1968, showing the burning junk on the Cambodian side of the river. ROBERT "FRIAR TUCK" BRANT PHOTO

Providing vital air support to SEALORDS forces, Mekong Delta, 1969.
OFFICIAL U.S. NAVY PHOTO, HOFFMANN COLLECTION

them through marshes, swamps, dense forests and a rugged area known as the Seven Mountains. It was a transit fraught with peril.

George Elliott made the run on Mike Bernique's 3 boat, which led the way, followed by PCF 38 (Terry Costello) and PCF 36 (Tuck Brant). They started at Ha Tien, and roared up the river about six to seven miles. Because the river follows a tortuous, twisting route the Swifts were not always in sight of each other. At approximately 0840 hours, the 3 boat radioed the others, "We've encountered a VC tax station in the river on the left bank and we're taking the enemy under fire." Costello's boat followed, raking the bank and as he cleared the area he reported a large junk on the bank. Brant's boat, approximately 1,000 yards behind the 38 boat, cleared the bend and saw "the little guys" climbing out from behind the boat, and coming out from the bushes. The VC, who must have thought all the Swifts had passed, were caught by surprise.

The enemy opened up on the lone Swift and the 36 boat crew, with BM2 Steve Luke in the peak tank, GMG3 Prysock on the twin .50s and BM2 Pruett on the after .50, returned fire, chewing up the attacking VC and killing five. The boats encountered an additional tax station, which they took under fire. They continued their transit to the rendezvous with the PBRs, and exited into the Bassac River. Brant says of the uneventful balance of the run, "you would think we were on a cruise." They spent the night on a PBR support barracks ship in the Bassac, where they had a hot meal, saw a movie and bunked for the night. "It was like high cotton," Brant says.

At about 0200 in the morning Elliott awakened Brant. "I've got to go to Saigon," Elliott said. "You get the boats underway in the morning." The next thing Brant heard was a helo on the deck of the barracks ship and Elliott was gone. All they knew in the morning was DIV COM was gone and nobody knew why. The boats got underway in the morning, transiting down the Rach Soi canal to the town of Rach Soi, then onto Rach Gia.

When they got to the Vietnamese Navy base at Rach Gia they were waved over to the pier. The American advisor there told them he had gotten word from An Thoi that the Swifts were to stay the night at Rach Gia. Brant was puzzled; they were only 50 miles from An Thoi. He asked why and was told the only thing they knew was that a helo was coming to take the three O in Cs to Saigon.

The next morning the helo arrived with three other O in Cs to take over their boats for the transit to An Thoi. Then Brant, Bernique and Costello boarded a helo for Tan Son Nhut. When they arrived there a station wagon was waiting to take them to NAVFORV headquarters. Brant says, "we're still in our greens, I've got grenades in my pocket, a pistol strapped on and I smell."

Meanwhile, Roy Hoffmann had been called to Saigon about what was becoming an international incident. Cambodia claimed the three boats under Hoffmann's command had killed not VC but members of a Cambodian military group known as the Khmer Kampuchea Kron (KKK) and ten Cambodian women in a large sampan. In a telegram sent to UN Secretary-General U Thant, the Cambodians threatened to abandon their policy of "neutrality" if America didn't end "its massacre of the civil border population of Cambodia."

The Navy had to report to an international investigation team over the incident, since Cambodia and the U.S. didn't have direct diplomatic relations. Zumwalt ordered Hoffmann to make an on-scene investigation and file a report. George Elliott and the three officers were on the carpet.

Soon after the three skippers arrived they were taken up to a small second floor auditorium with seats on risers. There were three tables at the lowest level with green table cloths (*the veritable green table*). George Elliott was sitting at table number one, and the O in Cs were told to sit at the table in the order they went up the river. Bernique sat with Elliott at table number one; Costello was at table number two; and Brant went to table number three. To Brant, "It seemed like every Navy commander and captain in Saigon was there."

Next they heard "attention on deck!" and Admiral Zumwalt entered, and ascended the steps to the highest row of seats. Captain Roy Hoffmann was in the audience.

Another captain stood up and said, "I am conducting this inquiry."

Brant thinks, "That's not a good word."

The captain then turns to the technician and says, "Start the tape recorders."

Tuck Brant says that at that point, "Popping up in the peanut gallery is old Latch [Roy Hoffmann], and he says, 'Just a minute, just a damn minute.'"

Brant says every eyebrow in the room went up. What is this guy doing?

Hoffmann went on to say, "I just want to say one thing before you do anything. These men were there on my orders, and they were doing their job. These men are not going to take any crap in those rivers. I take full responsibility for their actions. I want the record to reflect that."

Brant says now, "You could see all those guys in their pressed khakis thinking, 'Well, this guy just ended *his* career.' But for me, those were the nicest words I ever heard."[42]

---

42. Tuck Brant now says, "I'd do anything for that man. He was willing to put his career on the line for us."

The O in Cs then gave their testimony, after which Zumwalt said, "This inquiry is over." As they departed Zumwalt came up to them and said, "I'm sorry you had to go through this. We'll get you a flight back to An Thoi."

As they walked out Zumwalt said to Bernique, "Listen, if you cross that border again, drag the bodies back across the line." Bernique said, "Aye, aye, sir."

Hoffmann quickly gathered as much of the conflicting information as he could, drafted a report and took it to Zumwalt early the next morning.

Zumwalt was still awake, propped up by pillows in bed, working on a stack of messages. "What do you have, Roy?" he asked.

His task force commander replied, "The boats were justified in firing, in my opinion. They were under fire."

Hoffmann's report concluded that civilians killed, if any, must have been hiding in the immediate vicinity of the firefight. Hoffmann gave Zumwalt the message he had drafted to go to the Secretary of State under Zumwalt's signature. Zumwalt flipped through the four-page document "faster than I could read the first paragraph," Hoffmann says. Then Zumwalt signed the report.

Hoffmann said, "Admiral, you should read that report before you sign it."

"Don't you have confidence in what you wrote?" Zumwalt asked.

"Yes, sir, I do, I just want to make sure you know what you're signing."

"I do," Zumwalt said, and that was the end of the meeting.

No evidence ever emerged that the men killed that day were anything other than VC. A newsman was aboard Terry Costello's boat, and they flew him to Saigon and developed the film he had taken that day—it clearly showed the boats were taking fire. No bodies of slain women were ever produced. Both Zumwalt and Abrams concluded that the patrol of the border was so vital it was worth the international repercussions that might follow. Evidently Nixon agreed, because the Navy's patrols of the area intensified from that point on.[43]

CAPTAIN ROY HOFFMANN received a Bronze Star Citation with Combat "V" for the period October 1 to November 16, 1968. He was cited for his work in planning and executing SEALORDS, his "brilliant display of tactical acumen," inspiring leadership, and for courageously leading the forces under his command into numerous engagements against the enemy.

---

43. The day after this incident, November 17, 1968, Lieutenant j.g. John Kerry reported for duty to COSRON 1, COS DIV 14, at Cam Ranh Bay, where he would spend a month in training at the relatively secure and quiet area.

Vice Admiral Zumwalt decorates his Task Force 115 Commander, Captain Roy Hoffmann. OFFICIAL U.S. NAVY PHOTO, HOFFMANN COLLECTION

THE FRIENDLY SOUTH VIETNAMESE village of Cai Nuoc, on the Bay Hap River, was surrounded by VC and under siege for much of October and November. The Viet Cong nightly mortared the remote outpost for the 30 days preceding November 20 and probed the weakening village for attack. Seven out of the last ten days the village had been hit by enemy recoilless rife, mortar and ground attacks. Cut off from the world, they were running low on supplies and ammunition, and in danger of being overrun. Their situation was desperate.

Ready for battle on the stern of a Swift. PCF 43 crewmen manning the after .50 caliber (back), M-60 (on the deck), and M-79 grenade launcher (foreground).
OFFICIAL U.S. NAVY PHOTO, HOFFMANN COLLECTION

The Americans made an attempt to resupply the outpost from the air, but the helos couldn't get close enough to drop, due to heavy enemy fire. It fell to three Swift boats, PCFs 5, 43 and 82 (skippered by Bill Shumadine, Bob Elder and Lieutenant j.g. Thomas Herritage II, respectively) to make the seven-mile run to relieve the village. To get there the boats had to traverse the hostile Bay Hap River through largely enemy held territory. Communist gunners lurked in bunkers every 25 yards on both banks along the river entrance. NVA and VC flags fluttered defiantly from crude poles all the way in. The enemy had military buildings and grinders for marching in the area, an indication of how secure they felt there.

Bill Shumadine had been in the Bay Hap once before, in October, on a midnight run. "When you went down the Bay Hap," he says, "you felt like you were in North Vietnam." He had gone in slowly before, on George Bates' 50 boat, mapping the transit at five knots, marking points on the chart. Suddenly a mine went off under the boat, lifting it out of the water, resulting in a pissed off George Bates, "who never forgave me for messing his boat up."

The explosion caused engine problems, which left them DIW in the pitch-dark river. Shumadine says, "I'm visualizing all these World War II movies I'd seen where there are mines all around me and anyway I turn I'm going to hit a mine." He decided they needed to go out the same way they came in so they pivoted the boat in position and crept out. When they cleared the area and opened the throttles, "that's when I knew the boat *really* had some bad damage." It turned out the skags were bent over, the screws were gnarled and the bottom was dished in.

On November 20, gunfire from the USCG cutter *Bibb*, and U.S. and Australian Air Force and Army air strikes preceded the run to Cai Nuoc by the boats. The boats still had to battle their way through a hail of gunfire to reach Cai Nuoc. The Communist gunners, lurking in bunkers, opened up with heavy machine guns, automatic weapons and grenade launchers in an effort to repel the intruding Swifts. Bill Shumadine would later receive a Purple Heart for wounds he got on the way in.

They fought their way to the town and received an enthusiastic and relieved welcome. It was the first time Swifts had ever visited, and Shumadine says the villagers put the sailors up on their shoulders and carried them around Cai Nuoc. "It was unbelievable," he says, "they thought we had saved the day."

The American Special Forces advisors asked how long the boats could stay in the village. Not long, it turned out. A Birddog aircraft was spotting for the boats, and he radioed them, "You guys need to get out of there, the VC are setting up all over the river, and you're not going to make it out. Get out now!"

The Swifties unloaded all the supplies and ammunition they had been able to carry, plus cleaned the boats out, leaving themselves just enough ammunition to shoot their way back out. They left the village a large supply of ammo, fired up the boats and headed out.

They again encountered heavy fire on the way, giving more than they got, and causing heavy damage to the entrenched enemy.[44] As they closed on the river mouth Shumadine's 5 boat helmsman lost attention momentarily as

---

44. The official assessment, usually exaggerated, was still impressive. The three boats were credited with 11 VC killed, 227 military structures and 34 heavy bunkers damaged or destroyed, and over a hundred watercraft damaged or destroyed. The boats also reported a large secondary explosion near an enemy gun emplacement. Most of the attacking VC faded into the underbrush, no longer willing to face the marauding guns of the Swifts.

the guns were firing and ran the boat aground. Shumadine radioed the other boats as they were passing and said, "Hey, stop, we've gone aground."

Tom Herritage radioed back, giving his fellow O in C a hard time, "No way, we're almost out, we're not coming back. I'll get shot if I come back there."

Shumadine didn't see the humor. "This isn't funny," he said. "I'm serious, we can't get off."

The boats came back and threw a line over to pull the 5 boat off the sand bar. Shumadine had worn one of the oversized sound-powered phone helmets during the engagement. The old helmets never seemed to have a chinstrap, and were, like much of their equipment, left over from World War II. As he leaned over to catch the line from the 82 boat his helmet fell into the water and sank out of sight. The boats were still under fire, so the helmet couldn't be retrieved. "My whole life was ruined," Shumadine now laughs, "I was going to be held accountable for this helmet I had lost."

They hooked the line on the bow stanchion and slowly worked the boat around to get it underway again. After this it became standard operating procedure to have a line ready on the stern to expedite pulling a boat that had gone aground. As the enemy would do, the Swifties were learning and adjusting to the new realities in the river.

After the run all the boats were damaged; bullet holes riddled the sides and windows had been shot out of the cabins. When Shumadine went back to Cai Nuoc on a later run the American advisor told him, "That was a key day when you guys showed up. The villagers could see that we were going to stay here and fight with them. People started coming back—they wanted to make a life of it here."

IT WAS A DIFFICULT YEAR for Mary Linn, home in the United States waiting for her husband to return. Her anxiety rarely showed, but once the girls did get to her. They were complaining to her one morning about her not getting up to fix them breakfast "like the other mothers did." It really upset Mary Linn, and Hilarie says, "It was the only time I can remember her showing that something we had said hurt her."

Her husband didn't write much about the war, but occasionally he slipped. One time he told her he was on one of the small Skimmer boats on rough seas, and when the transit was over he said it was like being beat up. Mary Linn wrote him back and said, "What in the heck are you doing? Why were you on the boats?" After that he didn't provide much detail. He did write back and say, "I don't ask my men to do anything I wouldn't do myself."

"I knew he was in harm's way," Mary Linn says, "but I didn't feel he was reckless; he's not that type."

She did get to meet her husband in Hawaii for his R & R, over Thanksgiving, 1968. She made arrangements for Thanksgiving for the girls with friends, and got a sitter for Harriet. Mary Linn had not done much flying, and getting there was an ordeal. The flight was delayed in Atlanta and as a result she missed her flight out of Los Angeles. Mary Linn took one of the women under her wing. The woman was taking an infant to see the child's father, who was coming from Vietnam to see the child for the first time. "I wanted to make sure she got aboard," Mary Linn says.

Good friends John and Mary Ellen Adams met Mary Linn at the airport in Honolulu and she stayed overnight at their home.[45] She went to Fort DeRussy the next morning to meet her husband. The men arrived late as their plane had developed engine trouble. The greeting women were lined up facing each other with a corridor down the center. "No one was talking," Mary Linn says, "you could see they were tense as the men got off the bus and walked down the corridor. There was not a sound as someone next to you or across from you wrapped her arms around some one. It was extremely touching."

Unfortunately, after all of the men were off the bus, there were two women left: A young girl and Mary Linn. She finally was told that her husband was being debriefed and she eventually found him outside a building.

They had cottage-style housing during their brief stay at Fort DeRussy. Roy Hoffmann didn't talk about the war. They talked about the family, went to the beach, sometimes ate on the base. Mary Linn loves pineapple and she ate a lot of it. "It was like a vacation," she says. "It was not stressful. We lived for the day." The five days were over in a flash, and she took him to the airport. "When Roy went on deployments there were never any tears then, or when we parted in Hawaii."

November 24, 1968: The Bo De "Massacre"

On November 24, 1968, five Swift boats entered the Bo De River and ran into one of the most intense enemy ambushes set for the boats during the entire SEALORDS period. The mission as originally conceived was to enter the Bo De

---

45. John Adams retired as a U.S. Navy admiral.

PCF 93 forming up to commence the Bo De River mission. OTC Lieutenant Robert "Friar Tuck" Brant and his crew are on this boat. The USS Washoe County (LST 1165) *is standing by as the mother ship for the mission.*
Tom "Tommy Trees" Forrest and Joe Ponder photo

and transit to a suspected VC general's plantation near the adjoining Dam Doi River, mortar the area and exit through the Cua Lon. The boats were to receive NGFS from a ship off shore before they went in, and were supposed to be supported by two Seawolves from the Vung Tau area. Nothing went as planned.[46]

It started when Tuck Brant, out on patrol, got a radio message to return to An Thoi. When he got there George Elliott was waiting on the pier and said, "Tuck, we've got a mission and I want you to take it. What condition is your boat in?"

"Kind of tired," Brant replied. "I've got a couple of bad injectors."

Elliott assigned Brant the 93 boat and all the equipment. The plan was to go around the Ca Mau at first light and transit the coast to the Bo De. The USS *Washoe County* (LST 1165) was to get in close and shell the mouth of the Bo De with 3-inch gunfire, and two Seawolves from

---

46. The account of this action was taken from interviews conducted with Friar Tuck Brant, July 2, 2006; Terry Costello, October 11, 2005; Bob Elder, October 12, 2006; Jack Shamley, March 13, 2007; Joe Ponder; COS DIV 11 Command History; "All Boats Abort Mission—Shoot Your Way Out!" *The Overseas Weekly—Pacific Edition*; Spec. 5 Randy Woods, "VC Gunners Pounce on Cruising Swift Boats," *Stars and Stripes*; Douglas Brinkley, *Tour of Duty*; and a tape recording made that day by an ABC news correspondent.

Vung Tau were to fly gun support on each bank as the Swifts transited the river.

The LST was off the coast, but the tides were such that they couldn't get in close enough to deliver their 3-inch gunfire, and the rounds fell short. Then, as the boats were steaming to the Bo De they got word the two Seawolves had been diverted elsewhere.[47]

The diesels of five Swift boats could probably have been heard in Saigon as they idled off the coast as the men digested the new information. Tuck Brant always had his PRC 25 (pronounced "prick 25" by the crews) at his feet by the port door. He heard chatter on the radio and they weren't speaking English. There was only one frequency and there were no friendlies in the area. Brant thought, "Those little bastards are in there and they've got captured pricks. They know we're coming."

Brant, who was Officer in Tactical Command (OTC), got on the radio and informed An Thoi they were proceeding up the coast, there had been no NGFS provided, and there were no helos. He recommended they not go in, "because there's no surprise here."

He received a radio message back, "Your orders stand, continue the mission."

"I request you repeat that for the record," Brant said, which they did.

"Aye, aye, sir," he said.[48]

It was late afternoon on a miserable day where a downpour almost obscured the shore as the boats formed up for the run into the river. Jack Shamley says, "Nervousness built the longer we were off the coast. It was dark, nasty weather, the wind was blowing, it was raining, and the seas were rough. We sat off the coast for what seemed like hours. Everyone was getting *real* edgy."

Tuck Brant had their battle flag unfurled—it said "Ho Chi Minh Kiss My Ass" (the banner is pictured in Chapter 10). The boats lined up with Tuck Brant's 93 boat in the lead; Terry Costello's 38 boat was next. He had on his boat ABC reporter Frank Mariano (who made the remarkable recording of the day), and a photographer.[49]

---

47. The Seawolves did arrive at the end of the run out the river and pounded the enemy positions.

48. The reasons for the order to proceed are obscure today. George Elliott says, "This was a fiasco that common sense should have prevented. The boats sat off the river mouth . . . with constant radio chatter . . . it was not Bob Brant's call. It should have been called off. . . ."

49. After the dramatic events of the Bo De run, Costello later received a letter from Mariano with a copy of the tape. "Thanks for the joy ride," the letter said, "and next time I'd like to leave the tape recorder home. Just give me an M-60 and 200 grenades if you plan to get into some shit like that again."

Next was Lawrence Stoneberg's 31 boat, whose crew included GMG3 Joe Ponder manning the twin .50s, QM3 Robert McGowan driving the boat, BM2 Daniel Armstrong on the after .50, GMSN Jack Shamley manning an M-60 on the stern and Spec. 5 Randy Woods, a *Stars and Stripes* correspondent.[50]

Rich Baker skippered the 82 boat and Bob Elder's friend Jim Harwood brought up the rear on the 72 boat. As was typical at the alluvial plains of the Mekong rivers, the boats cut a channel through the silt at the river mouth to get in. (Most of the COS DIV 11 boats had shiny props or nubs for blades from plowing through the silt.)

They got in the river and as soon as the 31 boat cleared the river mouth the enemy cut loose. "There was nothing but machine guns, .51 calibers, B-40 rockets zooming everywhere."

The tape recording tells it best. The correspondent's words are clear, albeit often drowned out by the chatter of twin .50s in the pilothouse. He spent most of his time crouched between the radar and the starboard bulkhead, although at one time during the ensuing firefight Costello looked over and Mariano was shooting out the right door. On the tape in the background is often unintelligible radio traffic. The tape is a fascinating first hand account of a pitched battle between the Swift crews and the attacking enemy. To distinguish the correspondent's voice from the rest, his comments follow in italics.

It looks like very thick jungle in here. I'm not close enough to see exactly, but I can't see any daylight through the jungle at all. There is somebody firing their guns—I can't tell if it's outgoing or incoming. The gunners are… firing on the starboard side, I see tracers hitting the trees. There seems to be a bunker there.

---

50. Larry Stoneberg was then 24 years old and from Chicago. He received a degree in political science from the University of Wisconsin and was commissioned the day he graduated. He had been in Vietnam since July. Jack Shamley is a native of Wolf Point, Montana. He had a cousin who had enlisted in the Navy and told him about Swift boats; Shamley joined the Navy to get the duty. In somewhat typical fashion, he was sent to corpsman school instead, which he didn't like. The Navy next sent him to PBR training, but the class was too large, so 12 to 14 of the men were sent to Coronado for Swift training. Shamley ended up extending three times in An Thoi and served there almost two and a half years (August of 1968 to October 1970). He would go home on leave and find he didn't have any friends there. "After about two weeks I couldn't wait to get back. Vietnam was where my friends were." After the Navy Shamley joined the Lewis and Clark County (Helena, Montana) Sheriffs Department in October 1977. He has three children (Jeff, Jessica and Tommie Jon); his wife Mary died on October 19, 2004. This author and Jack Shamley were friends while serving together in An Thoi and remain so today, living 120 miles apart, the former in Missoula, Montana, and the latter in Helena.

It's a funny thing; once we got inside the mouth of this river . . . the boat seemed to have slowed up some. Maybe it's just my imagination, it seems like we were going a lot faster out in the South China Sea. It's a very uncomfortable feeling here being between two banks and in enemy territory. I see a very well fortified enemy bunker on the starboard side. It looks like, ah, I count one, two, three, four, five bunkers are right here on the starboard side as we're passing. WE'RE RECEIVING FIRE NOW! WE ARE RECEIVING FIRE! ALL THE GUNS HAVE OPENED UP! ALL THE GUNS HAVE OPENED UP! [At this point and periodically through the tape are the sounds of the twin .50s reverberating through the pilothouse, accompanied by the static of radio traffic.] I DON'T KNOW WHAT'S GOING ON . . . BUT EVERYBODY IS FIRING AT THE SAME TIME! THEY'RE FIRING THE MORTARS NOW; THEY'RE FIRING THE MORTARS! THERE SEEMS TO BE FIRE ALL AROUND!

Spec. 5 Randy Woods described the action on the 31 boat:

> Tracers ripped apart the wheelhouse, a few feet away. The pilothouse exploded in a hail of flying glass, tracer flashes, shrapnel, hot shell casings and a pungent haze of gun smoke.... Then the man wrestling the big machine gun behind me screamed [this was Joe Ponder]—his kneecap was ripped open by a .50 caliber slug. The bullet had smashed through the aluminum turret and streaked to within six inches of my head to get to his leg. I turned to see the turret gunner sit down with a thump . . . he was holding his right leg.
>
> "I'm hit," he said.

Woods goes on say "His cry was echoed by the pilot [Robert "Mac" McGowan], who was struck in the head by a piece of flying shrapnel from a bullet through the windshield. Another crewman took his place at the wheel, but couldn't see where the boat was going through the shattered windshield."

Larry Stoneberg's life was saved because he was sitting in the doorway on the port side and the bullets passed over his head. He picked up the radio and said, "Abby November 38, this is 31, my gunners been hit, my gunners been hit, over!" Costello can be heard asking who and one of his crew members said, "Joe's been hit."

Jack Shamley, on the stern, says, "All I can remember for the most part is when the manure hit the ventilator." He remembers the pilothouse taking a hit, and Stoneberg yelling at Shamley to get up to the pilothouse. Shamley was often called on to render aid to the wounded because of his corpsman training. He went through the cabin to get to the pilothouse; when he got there "McGowan is driving and he's got blood all over his face. I turned

SEALORDS mission on the Bo De River, November 24, 1968. PCFs come under heavy enemy fire after the trap is sprung. Pictured is PCF 31; Joe Ponder and Robert "Mac" McGowan have already received their wounds on this boat. Lieutenant j.g. Larry Stoneberg is the skipper of the 31 boat. Tom "Tommy Trees" Forrest and Joe Ponder photo

around and there was Joe holding on to the gun tub and his leg was just hanging by some skin. The first thing I did was give him a shot of morphine. His good leg and arms were basically holding him up. And then for the rest of the time I basically held on to his leg so it wouldn't fall off."

Shamley took Ponder's pulse, "I remember telling him to try and take some deep breaths and relax as much as he can." Shamley was worried about shock, but Ponder "held himself pretty well considering the circumstances."

One of the gunners has been hit; one of the gunners has been hit very badly! It looks like this is going to be a pretty bad day. One of the gunners has been hit . . . one of the gunners is bleeding badly!

"Thirty eight, 38, this is 31, did you get my message, over?"

Costello responded, "This is 38, negative, over."

"My gunner's been shot, my forward gun tub is out of commission, over."

The gunners have opened up again! Number 31 is out of commission; boat 31 is out of commission! The gunner seems to have been killed!

Next an urgent message came from O in C Jim Harwood's 72 boat; "My skipper's foot has just been blown off. We've got to get him the hell out on a medevac right away." Stoneberg came on the radio again and said, "We have another two wounded aboard; we need immediate medevac."

On Rich Baker's 82 boat, a round went through and took out the forward windshield. Baker said, "I felt the concussion as did the crew and we were all blown down by the blast . . . it must have been a B-40 rocket. Thank God no one on my boat got hit." RD3 Gene Hart was one of the crew members aboard the 82 boat that day.[51]

Another round penetrated the hull of the 82 boat and lodged in the ammo magazine in the floor of the main cabin, but did not detonate. Had it detonated it probably would have destroyed the boat. The crew picked up the round and threw it overboard.

As they cleared the kill zone, OTC Tuck Brant got on the radio, and "my actual words to the group (although not good radio words) were: Abby November, Abby November, abort mission! Abort mission! Turn around and shoot your fucking way out!"[52]

As the order came to abort mission, the 38 boat's starboard engine took a hit through one of the cooling hoses and lost power. Chain-smoking Radarman Gregory Cybulski from Belmont, Ohio, the helmsman, said, "When the engine got hit and the oil pressure dropped to zip point nuthin' you better believe I was scared as hell." Above the pilothouse a bullet smashed into the gun tub and glanced off the flak pants of Gunner's mate Paul Lukasiewicz from Worcester, Massachusetts.

Meanwhile, Costello was thinking, "Oh, no, I've got to go back through this and I'm on one engine." Brant's boat pulled alongside the stricken 38 boat and, using braided figure eights made of line, secured the lines to the cleats on each boat. Side by side, with the three engines wide open, Brant on the left bank and Costello on the right, they exited the river.

WE'RE GOING TO ABORT THE MISSION! WE'RE GOING TO ABORT THE MISSION! WE'RE GOING TO HEAD OUT! THE FIFTY CALIBERS HAVE OPENED UP ON THE PORT SIDE NOW . . . AS WE ARE . . . FOLLOWING THE LEADER HERE.

HIT THE STARBOARD SIDE [the rattle of the .50s,] THE STARBOARD SIDE!

---

51. Gene Hart has been a vital member of the Swift Boat Sailors Association, the present day fraternal organization of the Swifties.

52. Tuck Brant told this author, "That's what I said and that's the way I want it remembered." Terry Costello says, "One of the nicest things I ever heard in my life was Friar Tuck saying, 'abort the mission.'"

Everyone's keeping their heads down [rattling .50s]. Everybody's going to get out of here. They're firing the mortars point blank at each bank! The fifties are firing like crazy! 'Keep firing!' the skipper says. Get that port side, port side! [.50s fire]. Our boat's been hit! A crew has been hit amidships; a crew has been hit amidships! Everybody is to fire their way out, everybody. The boat in front of us seems to be hit, it's smoking!

Our boat, number 38, has been . . . hit! Our aft gun just let go! There seems to be a great deal of fire . . . from every bank! No matter where we go there seems to be firing! [.50s firing] We're still taking it! [.50s] There's fire all over the place. [.50s] Our engines have picked up some speed there are rounds coming over this boat! I can hear them! The .50s are firing like crazy now!

There seems to be a medevac, they're calling for a medevac right now. It seems like the LST is firing plenty of rounds right now. We're out of the mouth of the river. The inside of the cabin here is literally filled . . . with spent ammunition, spent cartridges.

[With evident relief] *Well, we're well out of the area now; I don't suppose we are in range of any small weapons fire. It's raining like hell now just to make this day a little bit eerie, just a little more ominous. That was a hellacious 15 minutes, just a hellacious 15 minutes.*

Bob Elder was on patrol on the Rach Giang Thanh while the Bo De operation was going on down south. He was well aware his friend Jim Harwood was on the operation. He had all his radios on and monitored the faint transmissions from the Bo De. Then, "I heard the horror of horrors. Jim got in a firefight and before I get out of my river I hear that Jim may have lost his leg." It was the first of two times in Vietnam Bob Elder would feel an overwhelming sense of guilt for not being there.

Meanwhile the boats tied up at the LST and gave up their wounded for medevac and then made their slow way back to An Thoi. The 82 boat took water the whole way, and by the time they got to An Thoi the boat had about eight inches of freeboard. The 31 boat was without a windshield and with every wave sea water came pouring through the open space.

When they tied up, George Elliott told Brant to report to the area commandant, who wanted a debriefing. Elliott was a little concerned about what the tired, understandably upset and outspoken Brant would say. When they got to the Quonset hut on the beach Brant and Elliott sat in front of the commandant's desk. "Tell me what happened," he said.

PCFs 31 and 72 run at top speed back to the Washoe County *with wounded men Joe Ponder, Robert "Mac" McGowan and Lieutenant James Harwood (aboard the 72 boat). McGowan was wounded in the head, arm and hand; both Ponder and Harwood were severely injured in the ambush.*
Tom "Tommy Trees" Forrest and Joe Ponder photo

Pilothouse damage to the 31 boat. Tom "Tommy Trees" Forrest and Joe Ponder photo

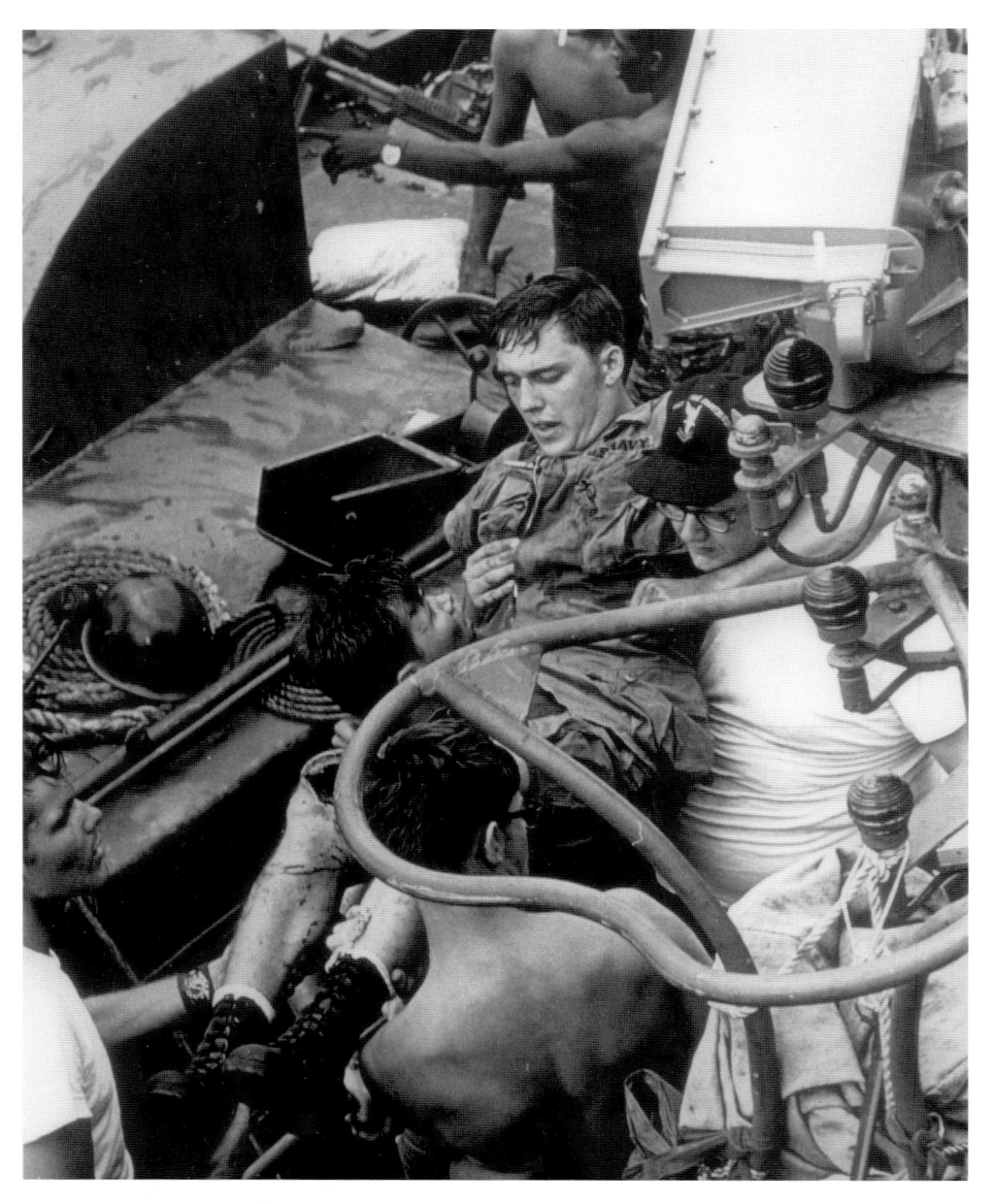

Crewman Jack Shamley (wearing eyeglasses and no shirt) renders assistance to the stricken Joe Ponder. Ponder has been hit in the right knee by an enemy .51 caliber machine gun round. He will be carried to the stern of the 31 boat, placed into a rescue basket, and hoisted aboard the Washoe County *for medical attention and evacuation.* Tom "Tommy Trees" Forrest and Joe Ponder photo

Part Three: Vietnam to Retirement   241

Lieutenant James Harwood is lifted aboard the Washoe County.
Tom "Tommy Trees" Forrest and Joe Ponder photo

U.S. Army medical evacuation helicopter used to transport Harwood, Ponder and McGowan to the U.S. Army's 29th Medical Evacuation Hospital at Binh Thuy for emergency surgery. Tom "Tommy Trees" Forrest and Joe Ponder photo

Tuck Brant said, "I only want to tell you one thing. I can follow orders and I'll go anywhere you send me, but next time we go I want you and your chair sitting on the bow of my boat." The debriefing ended shortly thereafter.

The day after the firefight, Admiral Zumwalt visited Joe Ponder's bedside in the U.S. Army's 29th Medical Evacuation Hospital located at Binh Thuy in the Mekong Delta. For the visit Ponder was cleaned up by Army medics, who washed his hair, gave him a "bird bath" and shave. Ponder wanted to be left alone; even though he had been told that an admiral would come to visit that day, he couldn't believe he would come to visit "only" an E-4.

Soon he heard the sound of a couple of choppers landing nearby, and then he heard "attention on deck!" Admiral Zumwalt, dressed in the standard camouflage uniform, came in and said, "Carry on." He was escorted to Ponder's bedside and he shook Ponder's hand and told him how proud he was of the young sailor and presented him with the Purple Heart Medal. Zumwalt then pulled up a chair and talked to Ponder for about 30 minutes about Ponder's family and asked if there was anything he could do for him.

As Zumwalt got up to leave he leaned over and gave Ponder a hug. "God bless you son," the admiral said, "I wish you the very best."

Joe Ponder says, "I learned weeks later that when Admiral Zumwalt returned to his headquarters in Saigon he wrote a personal letter to my wife telling her of his visit with me the day before."[53]

Douglas Brinkley called the run the "Bo De Massacre," and claimed 17 were wounded in the run. A "massacre" is defined as killing a large number of helpless or unresisting humans under circumstances of atrocity or cruelty. It may be the way Mr. Brinkley views war, but in this context he is engaging in hyperbole. As Tuck Brant says, the notion of a massacre "needs to be dispelled as only three individuals were wounded. We were facing an estimated two companies of VC (about 300 men)." The day was actually a great feat of American arms and leadership, which prevented greater casualties.

As a result of this action Captain Hoffmann began to call the officers and men in his command the "Market Time Raiders," a name that stuck. On November 30, 1968, Admiral Zumwalt flew to An Thoi to

---

53. Joe Ponder has remained active in veteran's affairs since his medical discharge from the Navy. He is on the boards of the Swift Boat Sailors Association and the Admiral Roy F. Hoffmann Foundation. He lives today with his wife, Rebecca, in Keystone Heights, Florida.

present awards, primarily to those involved in the Bo De run.[54] After this, according to Admiral Rex Rectanus, "It seemed to me that Admiral Zumwalt was continually flying to the Delta after firefights to award decorations and to impress on the troops that not only they and their Task Force commander, but Zumwalt himself understood the magnitude of the losses being taken by those brave men . . . and the numbers bear testimony to this fact."

Rectanus goes on to say, "Zumwalt was a people person. At least three times a week he would get in a helo and go down to the Delta, primarily to show the troops he cared about them, he was worried about them."

Zumwalt noted in *My Father My Son* that, "Our river patrol casualties reached an unacceptably high rate of six per cent a month. That meant that anyone serving a year's combat tour . . . had a 70–75 per cent chance of being killed or wounded." One of the ways Zumwalt felt they could reduce those risks was by reducing or removing as much jungle cover as possible. Hence he made the decision to use the toxic herbicide Agent Orange to defoliate the banks of the rivers. Almost every Swiftie serving in the Delta was exposed to the herbicide.[55] Admiral Zumwalt's son, Elmo III, who served on Swift boats, contracted cancer after Vietnam, and died from the disease. His father believed to his dying day that his son's cancer was caused by exposure to Agent Orange.

THE BOATS IN THE NORTHERN divisions responded to SEALORDS with an increased aggressiveness as well. From December 1, 1968, to February 28, 1969, the Swifts stepped up enforcement along the shoreline in area 1 Gulf, the area from Da Nang to Chu Lai. In December the boats made sporadic sweeps through the area and killed 56 enemy evaders. The boats

---

54. Lieutenant Robert Brant (PCF 93) was initially put in for a Silver Star, but for reasons that are unclear he eventually was awarded a Bronze Star. Also awarded the Bronze Star were O in Cs Lieutenant j.g. Terrence Costello (PCF 38), Lieutenant j.g. Richard Baker (PCF 82), Lieutenant j.g. Lawrence Stoneberg (PCF 31), and Lieutenant j.g. James Harwood. Enlisted men EN3 Richard Trussoni (PCF 72) and GMG3 Fred Prysock (PCF 93) also received a Bronze Star. Lieutenant j.g. Harwood (PCF 72), QM2 Robert McGowan (PCF 31) and GMG3 Joseph Ponder (PCF 31) were awarded Purple Hearts. Twenty-three enlisted crew members received the Navy Commendation Medal.

55. Zumwalt, Jr. and Zumwalt III, *My Father My Son*, p. 47. The casualty rates when so extrapolated overstated the casualties. Most of the Swift officers and crews did not spend a full 12 months in the rivers, although some did. Terry Costello, Bill Shumadine, Larry Thurlow, and this author's crew, under O in C Bill Franke, for example, spent one year in the rivers, and the casualty rate held true.

made a concerted effort to clear out all illegal fishing boats, traps and nets. Starting February 24, 1969, one Swift continually patrolled the VC controlled area.[56]

ON DECEMBER 5, 1968, the USCG *Point Cypress* came under hostile fire while conducting a SEALORDS mission in the Rach Giang. One Coastguardsman was killed in the action and two were wounded. On that same day the men of SEALORDS received what was to be the first of two Presidential Unit Citations for Extraordinary Heroism. The award covered the period October 18 to December 5, 1968, and said in part:

> Tasked with routing a myriad of enemy forces from their previous sanctuaries, personnel . . . ventured courageously into little known canals and backwater areas, fighting valiantly through countless intense enemy rocket and automatic weapons attacks. The courage, professionalism and dedication displayed by the officers and men . . . reflected credit upon them and were in keeping with the highest traditions of the United States Naval Service.

ON DECEMBER 6, 1968, John Kerry reported to An Thoi aboard PCF 44. His crew included Leading Petty Officer RD2 James R. Wasser of Kankakee, Illinois; BM3 Drew Whitlow, who would later make a career of the Navy and retire after 26 years; GM Stephen M. Gardner, described by most who knew him as "fearless," and who would be Kerry's longest serving enlisted man (December 6, 1968, to January 21, 1969); EN3 William M. Zaladonis, a good friend of Wasser; and BM Stephen Hatch, a 21-year-old from Altoona, Pennsylvania.

According to Douglas Brinkley, when Kerry got his orders to An Thoi, he clearly didn't want to go. Brinkley says, " . . . by then he [Kerry] had grown more comfortable in Cam Ranh, where his mail arrived regularly and he had time to read and write. The stories he had begun to hear about life in Cat Lo and An Thoi were not appetizing, and going into the danger zone was no longer appealing . . . ." After hearing he was going, "Kerry just stood there for a moment. Then he asked: 'Do I have any choice?' He was informed he had to go."[57]

Kerry was accompanied to An Thoi by 25-year-old Edward "Tedd" Peck from Syracuse, New York. Peck found Kerry standoffish and condescend-

---

56. December 2, 1968, is the date of the "Skimmer Incident," or John Kerry's first "Purple Heart" at Cam Ranh Bay.

57. Brinkley, *Tour of Duty*, p. 150.

ing. "I didn't like anything about him, nothing," Peck said.[58] Peck took PCF 57 down; his core crew consisted of Ken Golden, QM2 Michael Medeiros, QM1 Del Sandusky and EN2 Eugene Thorson. Peck would soon suffer terrible injuries while serving in the rivers of An Thoi.

ON DECEMBER 6, Friar Tuck Brant's PCF 36, accompanied by Lieutenant Ralph P. Dobson's 88 boat, endured another firefight and another loss of a crew member. The enemy lay in wait for the two Swifts as they entered Bernique's Creek for a routine patrol. The VC had settled in heavily fortified bunkers for hours, waiting for the inevitable pounding diesels of the Swifts.

Ralph Dobson was a Naval Academy graduate, a man Tuck Brant describes as "very quiet, very mellow."[59] BM2 Steve Luke was settled into the peak tank of Brant's 36 boat with an M-60 on the deck. Luke had volunteered to go with the 36 boat crew to An Thoi, and cheated death less than two weeks earlier on the Bo De run of November 24, when a VC bullet glanced off his helmet.

---

58. *Ibid*, p. 153.
59. Enlisted men that day were QM2 Kurt Thiele, Jr., EN2 David E. Fultz, GMG3 David L. Richardson, BM2 Steve Luke, SN Billy A. Williams, BM2 Barry E. Wright, BM2 Richard G. Prevett, SN Terry L. Stucker, GMG3 Fred S. Prysock and GMGSN Vern E. Ratcliff.

View of a narrow and muddy canal from the gunner's position on a helicopter. PCF 88 is below. HOFFMANN PHOTO

Recoilless rifle strike on Tuck Brant's boat, PCF 36, December 6, 1969.
Robert "Friar Tuck" Brant photo

The two Swifts were to relieve by noon two other Swifts that had been on patrol in Bernique's Creek for the preceding week. Normally the boats met at Ha Tien or at the river when the patrolling boats emerged. Although Dobson was senior to Brant, he thought Brant should be in charge of the patrol since he had been in the river several times before. The four Swifts tied up at what Brant refers to laughingly as the "international pier," a crude wooden docking area for the boats, instead of meeting in the river.

Dobson and Brant had arrived early for the patrol (about 0900). The two other O in Cs said they had to make one more run up the river because their patrol wasn't over until noon. Brant turned to Dobson and said, "They've been here a week, they shouldn't have to make another run. We're here, why don't we take it now?"

Dobson agreed, and Brant said, "Okay, Ralph, saddle up and I'll take you up the river and you can get the lay of the land." They started up the river and got up seven to eight miles as the other two boats transited to An Thoi. The two Swifts in the river passed a boat full of rice with a couple of people on it. Brant kept on going because it was an orientation run for Dobson. Dobson slowed his boat down to check out the sampan, which turned out to be bait.

Suddenly the boats were in the middle of an intense firefight as the heavily armed enemy force cut loose. Steve Luke opened up with his M-60 on the bow of the 36 boat, getting off about 150 rounds before he was hit with a bullet above his right eye. He would live a short while, but the bullet had taken off the top quarter of his head. The 36 boat also took a 57 mm recoilless rifle hit on the starboard side, which nearly disintegrated the Vietnamese liaison on board; he was blown off the boat. Brant took a shot in the neck and Prysock had the tip of his thumb shot off and two others suffered lesser wounds. The 88 boat had six casualties as well, two requiring medevac.

The boats shot their way through the kill zone, and then went about another mile upriver, where they beached the boats on the mud. They set up a defensive perimeter around the boats and got on the radio to call for medevacs. There was barely enough space for the helos to land, but they did come in and take away Steve Luke and two from Dobson's crew. Although wounded, Tuck Brant stayed with his boat and crew.

The medevac helos brought in members of SEAL Platoon Alfa to replace the wounded and dead on the boats. "They were good warm bodies," Tuck Brant says.

The boats still had to go through the kill zone to get out. As the two Seawolves came back to fly fire support, the boats rearmed, backed the boats off the mud, turned around and headed out. Brant says, "They [the enemy] were still in there. Why they didn't leave, I don't know." With a helicopter gunship on either bank firing their machine guns and rockets through the kill zone, the boats pounded the enemy bunkers as they fought their way through again. Later intelligence indicated the VC left the site carrying about 15 dead and several walking wounded. The Swifties had exacted a terrible price on the enemy for the casualties they took.

Friar Tuck Brant received his second Bronze Star with Combat "V" for the engagement. In addition to the Purple Hearts awarded, Admiral Zumwalt sent a message lauding the men "For outstanding performance of duty." He recognized the "courage and devotion to duty" of the crews of the PCFs, SEAL Platoon Alfa and the Seawolves. The message went on: "The example set here can leave little doubt but what ultimate success in this struggle will be directly attributable to these fine men in Navy blue [actually, camouflage green]. I share your sadness, but I am more than proud of your continuing efforts. Please convey to all participating my sincere admiration for a well-fought operation."

Tuck Brant, after numerous firefights and casualties on his boats, was made maintenance officer at An Thoi. Friar Tuck would go on to run a casino in the officer's lounge on the APL—Bill Shumadine was one of his dealers. It was a good time, a break from the war. The officers sat around the lounge and wrote letters home. "That's how we got away from the boats," Shumadine says. "You were always underway otherwise. You went on board the APL to get away from the noise, pounding diesels, to have some quiet time to write your letters home."

Tuck Brant finished his tour in An Thoi and left country on July 4, 1969, arriving back in the U.S. the same day.

As the Americans shifted tactics, so too did the VC adjust, now increasingly supplemented by main force North Vietnamese Army (NVA). Where once the Swifts had taken advantage of surprise, often-entering areas the enemy had held for 20 years, the VC/NVA forces now began to set more elaborate and deadly ambushes. Their tactic was to inflict maximum damage on the boats; they set up ambushes at hairpin curves where the boats were forced to slow to negotiate the turn (sometimes reducing to 500 rpms). Rocket attacks became more numerous and accurate. The VC began mining the rivers and constructing barricades under cover of darkness. Operating out of slit trenches and heavy bunkers, the enemy had the advantage of protection and surprise over the vulnerable Swifts.

The increasing number of NVA regulars also exacted a toll. Better equipped, more disciplined, better fighters by far than the sometimes part-time VC, they were a different enemy to fight. As Mike Bernique puts it, the primary tactic of the Swifts was to employ concentrated, accurate fire against the enemy, get them to duck their heads, and then send in troops. The first time he tried that with NVA regulars, "they forgot to do something—they didn't duck their heads. I thought, 'oh shit, this is different.'"

On December 7, 1966, John Kerry arrived in An Thoi and reported a pall over the base from the death of Steve Luke the preceding day. Four Swifts were in the Bay Hap that day to resupply Cai Nuoc; they encountered light

NVA graveyard, Ca Mau peninsula, 1969. Weymouth Symmes photo

sniper fire on the run. PCF 80 in the north took a fleeing sampan under fire in the restricted zone off Cape Batangan and killed five Viet Cong. On December 10, PCFs 13 and 75 conducted direct fire on VC targets on Cape Batangan, killing nine and wounding 15 VC.

The COMCOSRON One Commodore, Commander Charles F. "Chuck" Horne, flew down to An Thoi to attend the memorial service for Steve Luke. Horne had relieved the previous commander, Alan J. Hodge, in Cam Ranh on October 4, 1968. During the visit he decided to make his first run up Bernique's Creek.

The next day Bob Elder got word in Ha Tien that Commodore Horne was there and the boats were to take him up the Giang Thanh and out the Vinh Te canal in the middle of the night. Elder's crew was on liberty in Ha Tien when he got the word. Tuck Brant's old boat, PCF 36, would accompany the 43 boat, and Bill Shumadine in his 5 boat was to lay off the coast as a backup.

Horne reported aboard the boat, understandably nervous about his first run through the notorious area. "Bob, where would you like me to stand?" he asked. "What weapon would you like me to hold on to? What should I do?"

Elder now says, "I could understand his concern. He's coming on a Swift where there's not much room."

Horne told Elder to recall his crew from the beach. They were all in town drinking and four of the crew came aboard immediately. Elder asked them, "Where's Hensley?"

"He'll be along," his crew assured him. The 43 boat was tied up to the crude wooden pier (the "International Pier") that had a narrow gangplank connecting it with land. Elder and Horne looked out and Horne said to Elder, "Uh, Bob, who is that on the beach there?"

Elder looked up and saw it was Hensley, crawling on his hands and knees on the pier and up the gangplank, dead drunk. Elder replied, "That's my gunner. Don't worry, by the time we get to the river, he'll be fine." The alarmed Horne helped them get the gunner aboard and somehow the crew got him sobered up for the run.

They got underway in pitch dark and during the transit were hit from the port side while in the middle of a horseshoe turn. Gunner's mate Larry Gilbertson opened up with his twin .50s on the narrow strip of land. The rattling of the .50s was huge as the guns fired, and the cascading spent shell casings sounded initially to Elder like glass shattering in the pilothouse. He thought to himself, "This is it, it's the end." Then he heard a frantic call from the 36 boat, "You're taking us under fire!" The 36 boat was directly opposite the 43 in the turn.

"Cease fire! Cease fire!" Elder yelled. They got through the horseshoe turn and transited all the way to the Vinh Te, which is maybe 30 feet wide—the Swifts could barely turn around in it. They were at full speed and close up because of the firefight. The wake from the leading boat (the 43 was ten to 15 yards behind) was hitting the banks and cascading back at full force. Helmsman QM2 Rex Young was desperately trying to keep the boat steady. Suddenly the powerful wake pushed the fantail of the 43 boat into the beach and they instantly lost their starboard screw. They were ten to 15 miles up the river and Elder's boat was disabled with one engine that could maybe make 500 rpms. They would have to go back through the area of the firefight. "It is going to be a long dangerous transit on the way out," Elder thought.

He put in a call to Shumadine's boat and asked him to come in, meet and assist them. The reader will not be surprised to learn that Shumadine radioed back, "Of course, I'm there." Shumadine had to transit the river alone to get to them, through where the boats had already taken fire. He reached them about three quarters of the way up and together they all exited the river. The enemy didn't fire on them a second time.

From December 10 to 23, PCF 38, under Lieutenant j.g. Terry Costello, provided support for the Navy SEAL Operation Bold Dragon in the Ca Mau peninsula. The 38 boat inserted SEAL units, provided NGFS, conducted night ambushes, removed barricades and conducted intelligence gathering probes during the operation. The boat often made lone transits up VC infested rivers and canals.

The 38 boat and the SEALs operated off the USS *Weiss*, an old converted DE. They transited the Cua Lon, the Bay Hap, and up and down narrow canals. "It was actually kind of suicidal looking back on it," Costello says. "My boat was all the SEALs had."

It was all enemy held territory, although the Swift boat skipper felt better having the SEALs aboard. "I'm not sure how they felt," he says. The Cua Lon was full of fishing stakes, and nets that would foul the screws of the Swifts. They were also logical places for ambushes. Navy UDT teams accompanied the PCF and blew the fish stakes.

The last night of the operation the SEALs wanted to go back in the Cua Lon and leave a sign for future allied incursions; the sign would say in essence: "We were here first and cleared the area for you."

The SEALs were not on the best of terms with the CO of the ship, because the SEALs trashed out the ship (not on purpose, but that was the effect). The senior SEAL was a first class petty officer and he told Costello about wanting to put the sign up. Costello said, "I can't tell the CO because he won't let us do it." So they told a skeptical CO they had to go in and gather intelligence one last time. The CO, who was a commander, told Lieutenant j.g. Costello if they were in there screwing around they were going to be in trouble. Costello said, "Yes, sir."

They went to Fish Island at the mouth of the Cua Lon in the dark and put the sign up.

On December 13, 1968, in response to intelligence indicating a possible forthcoming enemy offensive, 18 PCFs were reassigned to patrol the lower Go Cong, Ham Luong and Co Chien Rivers, allowing intensified PBR operations in the upper reaches of the Delta river tributary complex.[60]

---

60. On this date John Kerry was moved to COS DIV 13 from An Thoi. One of the mysteries surrounding the enigmatic Kerry is why he was moved out of An Thoi so soon after his arrival there.

252 This Is Latch

The operations area north of the Co Chien. Canal at the top is the Rach Bang Cung, which was just west of the infamous "B-40 rocket alley" area. This picture was taken on September 10, 1968, during the wet and rainy season. David Marion photo

View from the gun tub by a twin .50s gunner, 1969. Hoffmann photo

At this point U.S. forces in the country were close to their peak of 550,000 men. Meanwhile, the U.S. death toll in Vietnam passed 30,000. Four of those KIAs were from Naval Inshore Undersea Warfare Group One, Western Pacific Detachment. On December 14, 1968 a monument was dedicated to them at Vung Ro Bay.[61]

On December 17, PCF 51, skippered by Lieutenant j.g. Robert Emory, and PCF 86, skippered by D.C. Current, transited the Bang Cung River (known as Rocket Alley) on a psychological operations mission into the Thanh Phu Secret Zone. On the run EN2 J. R. Hartkemeyer, of Hamilton, Ohio, went below to put on one of the anti-Communist tapes while Robert Emory was standing at the port side door. "Suddenly," Emory says, "a rocket propelled grenade was fired from forward of the boat at the pilothouse. The grenade actually made contact with the boat just behind my legs." The rocket exploded on contact and Emory's body was riddled with shrapnel. The rocket struck just aft of the port side door of the pilothouse and exploded into the main cabin, where Hartkemeyer was standing playing the psychological operations tape. Emory managed to grab the mike and shout, "We are under fire! Under fire!"

As the 86 boat came to their aid, BM3 Steve Bredenko went to check on Hartkemeyer. The shaken Bredenko emerged from the cabin and said, "I can't help him. His head is gone."[62]

A later body count revealed the Swifties in returning fire had killed nine of the VC.

On December 18 Swifties again assaulted the Dong Cung, raiding enemy positions. PCFs 66 and 71 encountered enemy fire during the operation, resulting in damage to both boats and one sailor wounded.

The crews received a message from Captain Hoffmann commending them for their "impressive results under such an explosive situation and in the face of enemy fire. Such consistently superior performance has become the hallmark of PCFs engaged in SEALORDS operations. . . . Please convey my admiration and esteem to every man for a job well done."

In his Quarterly Report to COMNAVFORV Hoffmann cited the three-month results of 185 enemies KIA (body count) and an additional 145 probable KIA. There was also a marked increase in the destruction of junks, sampans, structures and the number of secondary explosions. About this

---

61. The four were: Lieutenant j.g. William T. Morris, RD2 Anthony B. Brown, RM2 Thomas J. Meenan, and ET2 Norman L. McKenney. Captain Roy Hoffmann spoke at the dedication.

62. Brinkley, *Tour of Duty*, pp. 207–208.

Entering the Rach Cai Bai from the Co Chien on an An Nhon raid, February 25, 1969.
David Marion photo

time it was estimated the NVA had somewhere around 140,000 to 160,000 troops in either South Vietnam or nearby in Laos and Cambodia. The fighting strength of the local VC was put at about 40,000. Unlike the American forces, almost all of the enemy troops were fighting men.[63]

Meanwhile, the Swifties lived day to day. Bob Elder received a Christmas present from his wife in November, "and I opened it immediately because I didn't think I was going to be alive at Christmas." On Christmas Day Friar Tuck Brant played Santa Claus for the Vietnamese guards and their families at the POW camp on Phu Quoc Island. In his Santa suit he handed out gifts to puzzled Vietnamese children while saying, "Ho Ho Ho here's for you little boy."

In Captain Hoffmann's year-end report to Admiral Zumwalt, he noted that COS DIV 11 had nine PCFs not operational due to battle damage; COS DIV 13 had two boats not operational and COS DIV 12 had one not operational due to battle damage. There were 70 Swifts then available for operational purposes. Hoffmann singled out the USCG WPBs, noting they

---

63. December 24, 1968, marks the date of John Kerry's "Christmas in Cambodia" story. The story has been largely discredited. In fact, at the time, Kerry's crew was operating in the wide Co Chien River up to its junction with the My Tho. He would not have been allowed into Cambodia from this northern route.

Three RF 246 troops with Co Van Dai Uy (U.S. Army Captain) David Marion, February 1969. DAVID MARION PHOTO

"continued to be reliable and indefatigable in the performance of their missions." They had moved in to keep the inshore surveillance effort intact, and had been underway approximately 80 per cent of the time. Without their efforts the Swifts would not have been able to shift inland.

In response to SEALORDS the enemy built 12 barricades across the Cua Lon and heavily bunkered and fortified the Bo De entrance, temporarily denying the Swift Raiders access to the river complex.

Hoffmann noted that, "The spirit of the entire task force has been and continues to be extremely high. The officers and men of the PCFs involved in the highly hazardous SEALORDS incursions have consistently and aggressively demonstrated unsurpassed courage and determination to seek out the enemy and to defeat him at every opportunity."

An Thoi Swifts logged over 5,000 hours underway each month from October through December. In November they expended over 1,000 mortar rounds and shot 31,700, 57,850 and 36,585 rounds of .50 caliber ammunition in the months of October, November and December, respectively. Since the inception of SEALORDS, COS DIV 11 forces engaged in 110 separate firefights, and were responsible for 121 enemy KIA, and hundreds of structures, sampans, junks and bunkers destroyed.

Hoffmann further noted that, "experienced O in Cs have consistently demonstrated the ability to exercise on scene command authority with sound judgment and to accomplish their missions with a minimum of outside direction from senior commanders." Hoffmann attributed "all combat successes to date to the time proven concept of on scene command with the associated flexibility and I desire to continue this policy wherever possible.

"Each element," he concluded, "has played its part in holding the antiinfiltration line while the PCFs made the highly successful forays . . . deep into the strongholds of the enemy wherever there was sufficient water to float the boat."

BY THE START OF THE New Year the Navy moved a task force of PBRs and armored assault craft into the 56-mile-long canal across the Plain of Reeds, establishing the final link of the 250-mile naval blockade extending from Ha Tien in IV Corps to Tay Ninh City in III Corps. SEALORDS was slowly strangling the enemy.

On January 4, 1969, PCFs 21, 50, 71 and 93 conducted a probe up the Song Ong Doc and then down the Song Bay Hap. They received recoilless rifle, automatic weapons and B-40 rocket fire three times during the run. The battle damage assessment of PCF 21 shows how much punishment the little boats could take. The boat had a four-foot by one-and-one-half-foot hole on the starboard side amidships; 26 one-half-inch holes, nine one-inch holes and two five-inch holes on the port side; plus an additional three two-inch holes in the bottom of the boat. The main cabin overhead was covered with shrapnel holes, the cabin windows were blown, the handrail was covered with shrapnel slashes, there was a five-inch hole in the starboard door, and the gunwale had three shrapnel holes. The boat carried the crew through the firefight.

The next day BM3 Gerald R. Horrell of North Hollywood, California, was killed aboard PCF 71 while operating in the Song Ong Doc. In the Bo De, six Swifts executed a SEALORDS raid; PCF 6 was hit by recoilless and small arms fire; O in C Frank Gilbert was wounded in the engagement.

IN EARLY JANUARY Terry Costello met his wife in Pearl Harbor for his R & R. "It was," he says, "kind of a blurry five days." After it was over he flew back to Saigon, where he was supposed to catch a Market Time flight to An Thoi. He was loaded on a bus full of Army soldiers, and the bus driver inexplicably dropped him off in downtown Saigon, and left him there. Costello spent the night in Saigon, "expecting to be killed. I have no idea why the bus driver did that to me." The next morning the bus driver picked him up again and took him to Tan Son Nhut.

The day after he returned to An Thoi, he and Larry Thurlow were sent out to search at night for a Vietnamese junk force sailor who had been blown off a junk and left behind by Vietnamese sailors. The Vietnamese had gotten in a firefight, the sailor was blown overboard and left there, something American sailors would never do. The Vietnamese was found two days later, floating in the water, dead.

On January 15, eight boats, together with EOD/UDT units, supported by two WPBs and the LST *Terrill County*, conducted operations in the Song Bo De. The Americans expected casualties in the operation. Captain Hoffmann came down from Cam Ranh to be with his men and to go in with the boats on the operation. Since the boats were expecting casualties Hoffmann "borrowed" Dr. Lou Letson from the medical facility at Cam Ranh to accompany him to the LST.[64]

The boats dropped EOD teams ashore to destroy enemy bunkers along the river. It was a successful operation, and the only fire they took was from a lone gunman who shot at the boats and ended up getting return fire from eight Swift boats. "He must have been suicidal," Costello says. At the end of the operation the river transit was more secure for the boats, until the enemy could rebuild their fortifications.

ON JANUARY 20, 1969, on a gray, ugly day, Richard Milhous Nixon was sworn in as the 37th President of the United States. Despite extensive security precautions, and in what historian Stephen Ambrose called "a national disgrace," some 300 to 400 antiwar protestors hurled sticks, stones, rocks, beer cans, bottles and obscenities at Nixon's limousine, the first disruption of an inaugural ceremony in 180 years. The protestors chanted, "Four more years of death," and "Ho, Ho, Ho Chi Minh, the NLF is going to win." The demonstrators burned small American flags the Boy Scouts had distributed, and spat at police.

Nixon's inaugural address should resonate today: "To go forward at all is to go forward together. This means black and white together, as one nation,

---

64. Dr. Lou Letson was the physician who treated John Kerry's first "wound" at the medical facility at Cam Ranh. Letson removed a sliver of metal from Kerry's arm with tweezers. Base Commander Grant "Skip" Hibbard denied a Purple Heart request by Kerry, although Kerry managed to have it issued later in his tour of duty.

A member of a U.S. Navy underwater demolition team prepares to blow up, using gelignite (C-4), an enemy bunker. These canal and riverbank bunkers provided the Viet Cong effective attack points. The bunkers were virtually impregnable to almost every attack except heavy artillery. OFFICIAL U.S. NAVY PHOTO, HOFFMANN COLLECTION

not two . . . to lower our voices would be a simple thing. In these difficult years, America has suffered from a fever of words: From inflated rhetoric that fans discontents into hatreds; from bombastic rhetoric that postures instead of persuades."

ON JANUARY 22, 1969, EN2 Larry D. Villarreal, a native of California, was serving aboard the 82-foot USCG cutter *Point Banks*, home ported out of Cat Lo. During a routine Market Time patrol in the South China Sea the *Point*

Another now-famous photo: Task Force 115 personnel aboard an LST. Task Force Commander Hoffmann may be seen kneeling to the immediate right of Vietnamese forces, center, front row. John Kerry, senator from Massachusetts and failed 2004 presidential candidate, is immediately behind Captain Hoffmann, standing with hands on hips. OFFICIAL U.S. NAVY PHOTO, HOFFMANN COLLECTION

Banks received a message at 0100 hours stating that nine South Vietnamese soldiers were trapped on a beach by two platoons of Viet Cong.

The *Point Banks* reached the scene and the CO asked for volunteers to man a 14-foot small boat and go onto the beach to rescue the out-gunned and out-manned Vietnamese personnel. Villarreal and GM2 Goff volunteered for the mission and launched the boat.

The two men closed the beach, exposing themselves to enemy small arms and automatic weapons fire. As they searched for the Vietnamese soldiers the *Point Banks* provided NGFS. They had been instructed to look for a light the VN soldiers would use to signal their position, but they spotted three lights in different locations. Villarreal and Goff battled heavy surf, which nearly capsized the boat as they closed the beach. At that point VC gunners unleashed a barrage of fire.

Four of the Vietnamese soldiers came running out of the jungle toward the beach, heading directly into the enemy's line of fire. Goff returned fire with his M-60, providing cover for the four Vietnamese, who reached the boat. They took the four soldiers out to the *Point Banks*, and then headed back to get the remaining five in a boat half filled with water. Under enemy fire the men steered their boat toward the beach, only to have the engine fail. Villarreal calmly got it started again and continued toward the beach. Goff and Villarreal provided cover fire for the remaining five Vietnamese soldiers and ferried them back to the cutter. They had saved the nine Vietnamese soldiers from almost certain death or capture, at great risk to themselves. Villarreal was later awarded the Silver Star Medal by the U.S. Navy, thus becoming the third USCG enlisted man to be so decorated in Vietnam.

January 22, 1969: The O in Cs are called to Saigon

Captain Roy Hoffmann had urged Admiral Zumwalt to bring into Saigon the O in Cs of the two COS DIVs taking the brunt of the SEALORDS mission, 11 and 13. Zumwalt quickly agreed and Hoffmann arranged the conference, which had the dual purpose of giving these men recognition for the sacrifices they and their crews were making, and to emphasize the importance of what they were doing and accomplishing.[65]

On January 22, 1969, the O in Cs came in separate groups, one from Cat Lo and one from An Thoi. George Elliott told the An Thoi men that Zumwalt had summoned them to Saigon to explain the mission. They were all given leave from the boats; one of the exceptions was Friar Tuck Brant, who took the only patrol in Area 9 that day. They were not given any instructions as to dress code, and so in what was becoming a hallmark for the Swifties anyway, they all had on different uniforms. Some wore ball caps; some accommodation covers and some had fore and aft caps. No one seemed to care once they arrived in Saigon.

The naval officers left the APL at 0615. They were met at the An Thoi pier by several jeeps and a half-ton pickup and shuttled to the airport. Zumwalt sent a *Caribou* to pick them up. They flew to Saigon and were loaded on a bus and driven through the streets of Saigon to Zumwalt's compound.

---

65. Wade Sanders, O in C of PCF 98, is quoted in *Tour of Duty* as saying "Our divisions were on the brink of mutiny . . . there was just a lot of seething discontent when we arrived in Saigon." Brinkley, *Tour of Duty*, p. 254. This author has found little evidence in the numerous interviews conducted for this book that Sanders' statement is even remotely true.

Shumadine remembers he didn't like riding the bus: "It had bars on the windows and that got my attention." He had been reading about VC terrorists in Saigon and the bus ride made him uncomfortable. "We felt cocky and sure on our own boats." They were glad to get inside the NAVFORV compound. The O in Cs from COS DIV 13 were already there when they arrived.

Shumadine says, "We were accorded just grand treatment. We were shown around, given hors d'oeuvers and a meal." Then they were ushered into a large room that looked, according to Bob Elder, like the CIC of an aircraft carrier. Waiting in the room were Captain Hoffmann, Charley Plumly and George Elliott. They heard, "Attention on deck!" and Admiral Zumwalt and General Creighton Abrams ("A great military man," Shumadine says) walked in. Roy Hoffmann says that it was a total surprise General Abrams attended.

The meeting lasted about 20 minutes, during the course of which Captain Hoffmann, Admiral Zumwalt and General Abrams spoke to the men. Individual memories of the meeting vary to some degree, but Terry Costello says, "How I remember it is totally different from how John Kerry remembers it."

Kerry relates in *Tour of Duty* he remembered they were called up because the Swifties were refusing to go on patrols. Costello says, "I almost fell out of my chair when Kerry said in *Tour of Duty* we were refusing to go on patrol. I can't remember anybody refusing to go on patrol. I'm sure we were a brash bunch and probably griped and complained. We always thought the only happy sailor was a bitching sailor." Bob Elder relates, "We had made enough noise about the incredible danger to ourselves and our crews, and were trying to understand what our real mission was." Elder's attitude was that he would follow the orders because he was a naval officer, but wanted a clearer understanding of their mission. Shumadine says with a laugh, "We felt unappreciated and unloved."

Costello's overview of the senior officers' speeches was, "They were having trouble with the Paris Peace Talks and they needed a foothold in IV Corps and we were it. They were sending us In Harm's Way and they appreciated what we were doing. I appreciated being called up and told that." Bob Elder also got the same theme from the conference. The Paris Peace Talks were languishing, and Elder quotes Abrams as saying:

> As you know the Paris Peace talks are going on, and Ho Chi Minh is dismissing us there. He is saying to us that we only control a part of South Vietnam. The South Vietnamese Army and the U.S. military do not control the Ca Mau peninsula and therefore you have no jurisdiction to even be here at the negotiating table.

Abrams said that the word came directly from Kissinger that the Allies *must* demonstrate a presence in the area for the talks to go anywhere. "We're not going to get any Army down there," Abrams said, "only the Navy can do it."

Abrams pledged to get media recognition for the great sacrifices the crews were making, and assured them that they would be chronicled as owning the Ca Mau peninsula. "Your mission," Abrams said, "is not to take ground and hold it, but it is to change the dynamics of the Peace Talks, get us to substantial talks so we can end this war."

"Well," Elder says, "as far as I was concerned that was the most noble thing in the world. I came out of that meeting with a great sense of renewed mission." Larry Thurlow said that Zumwalt, in his speech, paraphrased Churchill ("Never have so many owed so much to so few").

The senior officers opened the floor to questions. Costello says, "We certainly weren't chastised while we were there and I don't remember a lot of questions being asked." Bob Elder remembers John Kerry speaking up briefly at only one point, making Elder wince with Kerry's cerebral whining about the mission, "to the officers who owned the mission."[66]

At the end of the meeting Abrams and Zumwalt said they wanted to shake the hands of the men who were winning the war. They said they felt that little group of Swift boat officers and their crews could influence the policy of the United States.

As they were getting ready to leave someone said, "Let's get a group picture," and that how the picture, which became a *cause celebre* during the 2004 presidential election, came to be taken.

By the 24th all the crews were back patrolling, with PCFs 6, 31, 50 and 71, during the early morning hours, encountering evading sampans in the Cua Lon. The units captured the ten occupants and destroyed their sampans and 600 pounds of food. Then the same boats conducted cordon and search operations from the Song Ong Doc to Ca Mau, and then exited through the Song Canh Hau, a total run of 62 miles. The boats received light sniper fire throughout the day.

On January 25, in Paris, formal truce negotiations began. That day in Vietnam PCFs 6, 21, 50, 71 and 93 conducted a cordon and search mission in

---

66. As one would expect, there were few questions of the senior officers. Most of the men interviewed for this book do not remember future Senator Kerry saying anything. Admiral Hoffmann was standing behind Abrams and Zumwalt observing how his men were reacting to the speeches. He remembers Kerry sitting separated several seats to the left of the rest of the men. Hoffmann does not remember Kerry asking one question or otherwise participating in the dialogue.

The famous Swift boat officer's photo taken on January 22, 1969 in Saigon, Republic of South Vietnam. Standing, left to right: Elder, Thurlow, Crosby, Hoole, McCann, Bernique, Kerry, Hildreth, Herritage, Elliott, Bates, French, Galvin and Costello. Kneeling left to right: Imbrie, Barker, Baker, Shumadine, Dobson, Gilbert. Not present: Brant, Locke, Murphy, Patton and Lathrop. OFFICIAL U.S. NAVY PHOTO, HOFFMANN COLLECTION

the Bo De/Dam Doi/Bo Gui river complex. They were unable to complete their mission of destroying barricades due to low tide. The boats came under fire and PCF 21 received damage from rocket and small arms fire. PCFs 66 and 94 proceeded up the Song Ong Doc in support of ground forces. The boats encountered hostile fire; PCF 66 (Lieutenant William B. Hoole, Jr.'s boat) received two rocket hits. Three Navy sailors were wounded during the engagement.

The *Point Orient* and PCFs 56 and 80, operating in Quang Nam province, discovered a large group of people transiting the waterway near An Ky. They captured five sampans, three basket boats and detained approximately 175 people.

On January 26, PCFs 21, 71 and 72 conducted operations on the Bay Hap with RF/PF units from Cai Nuoc. The units destroyed materiel used to support the enemy; the Swifts drew fire four times during the operation. The next day PCFs 5, 6, 72, 93, and 95 conducted operations in the Cua Lon and Dam Doi, receiving fire twice during the operation, which left one of the sailors wounded.

On the 28th two PCFs patrolling the Ham Luong came under fire. Two B-41 rockets and automatic weapons fire hit the lead PCF. The O in C and one of the crewmen went into the water when the boat was struck. The second boat rescued the sailors and then both boats made firing runs through the kill zone before exiting the river to medevac the wounded.

Nine other boats commenced a three-phase operation at 1300 when they entered the Song Ganh Hao from the South China Sea and proceeded to the Gulf of Thailand via Ca Mau City. They transited the Song Ong Doc taking targets of opportunity under fire and suppressed heavy enemy rocket and automatic weapons fire.

Meanwhile, Pat Sheedy, whom the reader encountered in Chapter 6 on the *Adams*, arrived at An Thoi from Qui Nhon.[67] When Sheedy arrived in An Thoi he was assigned PCF 50, which had been George Bates' boat; Sheedy and Bates were Academy classmates. He moved to Qui Nhon and took over Sheedy's old boat there. Sheedy spent his first four months in country in Qui Nhon, where the CO was Lieutenant Commander Chuck Miller. Because of the heavy combat in the Delta, Miller had to transfer two crews down. He just called them in and said, "You're going"; Sheedy to An Thoi and Jeff O'Grady to Cat Lo.

Miller told Sheedy that he had talked to Captain Hoffmann after selecting the two crews. Hoffmann said, "I'll bet one of them is Sheedy."

Miller told him he was right and was informed that Captain Hoffmann thought highly of Sheedy, whom he knew from his old command on the *Adams*. Miller did not inform Hoffmann that Sheedy had not volunteered for the duty.

Hoffmann followed what the young officer was doing in An Thoi. When Sheedy was there the then single officer went through a period when he didn't write home much. His mother in Charleston became concerned and called Mary Linn, whom she had met on an *Adams* family cruise. Mary Linn assured her that as far as she knew everything was fine, and that the captain thought highly of Pat. Not long after Roy Hoffmann was in An Thoi and told Sheedy, "Write home! Your mother called Mary Linn."

MEANWHILE, A SEAL TEAM detachment was assigned to TF 115 to enable the Market Time forces to gather and act on intelligence in Captain Hoffmann's area of responsibility. One of the first things the SEALs did was

---

67. He would remain at An Thoi until August 4, 1969.

to investigate VC extortion and black market activities at the Ca Na Salt Flats, which were adjacent to Secret Base 35 in the Nha Trang area.

The Ca Na was a popular anchorage. Small boats shuttled between the mainland and coastal freighters anchored offshore. It was an ideal situation to move contraband, and the Market Time forces maintained a close surveillance of the area.

Nguyen Lam was the Ca Na Salt Flats manager—he probably had dealings with the VC. He was of Japanese extraction and had served in both the Japanese and Vietnamese armies.

The SEALs also operated on Hon Tre Island, and in Nha Trang, and Than Phu. In the middle of February one platoon of the SEAL detachment was detached to Cai Nuoc (New Nam Can in the Ca Mau). They established a local intelligence base for missions into the Cai Nuoc, Dam Doi and Nam Can districts.

One month later a mission in the north led by Robert Kerrey resulted in his receiving the Medal of Honor.

ON WEDNESDAY, JANUARY 29, 1969, Swifts from An Thoi and Cat Lo conducted a two-day raid of enemy base areas in the Ca Mau. The operation began when four Swifts raided enemy base areas along the intersecting Ganh Hao and Ong Doc rivers, taking targets of opportunity under fire.

In the second phase of the operation eight of the Swifts (including PCFs 5, 72, 93 and 94 from An Thoi) entered the Cua Lon and steamed back across the peninsula to the Bo De, there exiting into the South China Sea. Three crewmen were injured when PCFs 72 (O in C Rocky Hildreth) and 94 (O in C Tedd Peck) were probing a side canal.[68] The boats were hit by B-40 rocket grenade and automatic weapons fire, leaving one of the boats badly damaged.

All six boats then proceeded up the Cua Lon, where PCFs 72 and 94 again probed another canal. Douglas Brinkley describes the action in *Tour of Duty*. It started with a booming explosion that literally lifted PCF 94 out of the water. Peck was standing in the pilothouse doorway with an M-16. As he commenced firing two machine gun bullets hit him, one in his arm and the other in his chest. The boats came under fire from both banks, taking out their radio and radar. Although Peck was bleeding profusely he managed

---

68. The enlisted crew on Peck's boat included LPO Del Sandusky, engineman Eugene "Gene" Thorson, boatswain's mate Michael Medeiros, gunner's mate David M. Alston, and radarman Thomas M. Belodeau.

Tedd Peck's battle damaged PCF 94, after the action of January 29, 1969. Machine gun rounds tattooed the boat. Gunner's Mate David Alston was wounded in the gun tub, and Tedd Peck was seriously wounded. John Kerry would briefly replace Tedd Peck, and Fred Short replaced the wounded Alston, until he returned around March 4, 1969. Hoffmann photo

continue firing until a third bullet struck his ankle, breaking his leg. Peck realized he couldn't move. Sandusky managed to get the boat turned around and they exited the canal.

The pilothouse caught fire. David Alston was grazed in the head by a bullet and another struck his arm.[69] Belodeau rushed into the pilothouse with a fire extinguisher. "Only God saved us," he later told Brinkley. "It was a miracle. We should have all been gone."

Peck was going in and out of shock. "They were trying to give me morphine, but I waved them off. In case we were hit again, I wanted to be able to swim." The boats cleared the river and rendezvoused with a USCG cutter, where corpsmen put Peck on a stretcher and he was transferred to a nearby WHEC. Corpsmen began pumping Peck with IVs and irrigating his wounds with saline solution. The first and second bullets had gone through his upper body, but the third was lodged in his ankle. The next morning Peck was

---

69. Fred Short replaced David Alston on the crew on February 18, 1969.

medevaced to a Saigon hospital. He was going home.[70] John Kerry inherited Peck's boat and crew for the brief one and a half months he was to remain in country.

The remaining boats on the operation moved up the coastline to the My Thanh River, where they conducted a three-hour raid on enemy positions along the river.

The next day PCFs 5, 50 and 72 conducted a MEDCAP at Cai Nuoc, treating 216 Vietnamese. The boats fired on targets of opportunity on the way in and out of the river. The 5 and 50 boats then conducted a night ambush, catching two 30-foot sampans with a substantial amount of rice. In the process they killed two Viet Cong.

CHARLEY PLUMLY CAME DOWN from Cam Ranh for an operation in the Cua Lon/Bay Hap Rivers. Plumly was going in with the lead boat, and Bob Elder remembers Plumly's briefing well: "Guys," he said, "we're going in so deep we're going to take casualties and we are not going to turn back. When we take casualties we are going to soak them up and keep going."

Bob Elder thought, "Holy shit. When someone gets hit your first instinct is 'let's get out of here.'" Plumly then gave each of the boats a code name that indicated their place in line. Elder says, "I was so rattled after what he said that when I went back to my crew to tell them where we fit in line, and what the objective was, I had totally forgotten my code name, which meant I didn't know where I was in line. 'What kind of skipper am I?' I thought. When Plumly called, 'Bulldog, take your place,' I guessed and fell into third place in line, which was where I belonged."

IF, AS THIS AUTHOR DOES, one accepts Mark Twain's definition that, "Courage is resistance to fear, mastery of fear—not absence of fear," one reporter that covered the war was particularly courageous. Bob Elder tells the story. He had been on patrol and got word he was to pick up a reporter, and take that person around the horn of South Vietnam for delivery to an LST for an operation the next morning. "All of us used to get fed up," he says, "with these daisy chain things which would take you off patrol and turn you into a taxi cab."

Elder's 43 boat rendezvoused with another Swift to pick up the reporter, who turned out to be a woman, Liz Trotta. She had just spent six hours of pounding on heavy seas getting to the rendezvous, and she had four more

---

70. All descriptions of this action taken from Brinkley, *Tour of Duty*, p. 265.

The rugged transit from the Ca Mau to An Thoi, 1969. WEYMOUTH SYMMES PHOTO

to get to the LST. Meanwhile, she was a woman on a boat with no toilet, no privacy, and no amenities.

It was a dark night for the transit, the crew was in the cabin and Elder was driving the boat. Trotta came into the pilothouse and stood beside the eerie, glowing radar scope. She was understandably uncertain, afraid. "Bob," she asked, "what's this going to be like? I've got to go in tomorrow on a river raid. This will be my first Swift boat raid, I've heard these terrible stories and I'm so frightened."

Elder responded, "Liz, don't worry, a lot of it is just noise. When the noise starts, you're not going to like it, but for the most part they turn out to be mostly noise." As the morning wore on Trotta became comfortable as the calm officer talked to her about what to expect.

They got to the LST and tied up alongside. Elder says, "There is this 25 foot climb up the side of the goddamn thing, hand over hand on a net." They let Trotta go first. The boat was slamming against the LST with the heavy seas, and the Jacob's ladder was barely within reach for her. To climb the ladder she had to time the jump, pull herself up until she got her feet on the ladder. In her fatigues, Trotta managed to struggle to the top. Elder followed her up and introduced her to the CO of the LST.

Trotta asked him, "Are you expecting trouble today on this raid?"

His response was less than reassuring, "Oh, Miss Trotta, you need not fear, I have a wonderful hospital on this ship."

Elder had been on patrol for the preceding 48 hours and so another crew took his boat for the raid. He watched the four boats transit the open water and disappear into the jungle. Elder went into CIC to follow the boats as they transited the river. While in the interior they encountered a horrendous firefight. Liz Trotta survived.[71]

One other reporter wasn't so lucky. A *Time* magazine reporter once rode Bob Elder's boat on a run from the Bo De through the Cua Lon to Square Bay. The reporter told Elder what it was like being in firefights without a weapon. Because of the terrible reputation of the Bo De/Cua Lon run, the reporter asked for a weapon and Elder gave him an M-16. The reporter made it through the run. One week later there was an editorial in *Time* chronicling the reporter's death during an Army operation.

On another mission into the Bay Hap, Roy Hoffmann came down to the LST to fly overhead in a Seawolf to observe the operation. He pulled Elder aside before the mission and asked him what was the maximum elevation a mortar round would reach. Elder didn't have a clue—he knew the maximum effective range but not the maximum height. "I made up an answer," he says. "Twenty five hundred feet." Hoffmann replied, "That's what I'm going to fly at."

Elder says, "Well, he flew at 800 feet."

On February 2, 1969, PCFs 5, 38, 43 and 50 conducted operations in the Cua Lon River. The units took an evading sampan under fire at the mouth of the river, killing one of the occupants. The boats continued on and about halfway through the transit PCF 38 received a B-40 rocket hit on the fantail. O in C Terry Costello rushed to the stern and found after gunner Marvin Sedlacek lying in a pool of blood. Costello searched for the wound and found Sedlacek was losing copious amounts of blood from his upper arm. The skipper had a hard time getting the bleeding stopped.

---

71. Liz Trotta went on to spend 30 months in Vietnam, going on every conceivable Army, Marine and Navy mission, during the course of which she exhibited great courage. She was the first woman to cover a war for broadcast news. She is a graduate of the Columbia University Graduate School of Journalism. In her career she won three Emmy awards and two Overseas Press Club awards; and wrote *Fighting for Air: In the Trenches with Television News*. She is also the former New York bureau chief of *The Washington Times* and is a contributor to the FOX News Channel. Bob Elder and Liz Trotta reestablished contact during the 2004 presidential election. Because of her experiences on Swift boats she fairly covered Swift Boat Veterans and POWs for Truth.

"Latch" in an LST operations center, Vietnam, 1969.
Tom "Tommy Trees" Forrest and Joe Ponder photo

What it was like: Swifts in a narrow and overgrown canal. PCF 23 takes the lead.
Hoffmann photo

He asked the wounded man if he wanted a morphine shot as he was in a great deal of pain. Sedlacek nodded and Costello got the needle in but couldn't get the morphine out. He remembers thinking, "Here he is hurting and I'm hurting him more." The morphine packet required that you pull a wire and poke it up the needle to break the seal, after which you then squeeze the morphine out. Costello felt terrible; he had jammed the morphine needle into Sedlacek's arm without making the required hole in the foil.

The next day the 38 boat went onto skids for repair of battle damage, while the other three boats conducted a night operation in the Bay Hap. As the boats exited the river PCF 43 received small arms fire and two rockets hit close aboard, wounding one of the sailors and causing light damage to the boat.

On February 7 the boats hit the enemy hard, as PCFs 23, 31, 43 and 44 conducted operations with ground forces in the Rach Ong Quyen and Rach Ba Thanh, canals branching off the Cua Lon. During the sweep substantial amounts of enemy materiel were seized. That same day PCFs 5, 9, and 38, with MSF troops aboard, entered the Bay Hap for a mission to Cai Nuoc, after which the boats transited the Cai Nhap canal. They disembarked the troops, and after pickup they exited through the Cua Lon. While in the Cai Nhap the PCFs received heavy fire, wounding seven U.S. Navy sailors and causing heavy damage to all the boats.

A sweep on the 9th by troops inserted by PCFs 10, 23, 31 and 43 in a canal near the mouth of the Rach Duong Keo resulted in the destruction of numerous bunkers, structures, sampans, junks and a bridge. The troops also picked up 43 suspected VC and large quantities of food and medicine. The troops searched on shore for a camouflaged headquarters, which they found and destroyed. The next day the boats delivered a half ton of captured rice to Cai Nuoc villagers.

For actions on February 11-12, 1969, Captain Roy F. Hoffmann received a Silver Star Medal for "conspicuous gallantry and intrepidity in action against the enemy." He had come down from Cam Ranh as an observer for the large operation. The operating forces consisted of ten PCFs divided into two sections, the USS *Washtenaw County*, USS *White River*, USS *Pivot*, USS *Cypress*, and a Mobile Strike Force consisting of paid Cambodian and ethnic Chinese troops.

At approximately 1225 hours PCFs 28, 53, 60 and 103 entered the Rach Nuong and were immediately attacked by an enemy force entrenched in

Captain Hoffmann in a flak jacket on the stern of a Swift boat, Ca Mau peninsula, 1969. Hoffmann photo

heavily fortified bunkers. The enemy opened up with rockets and intense automatic weapons fire from both banks of the river. PCF 60 almost immediately took two B-40 rocket hits at the waterline and began to rapidly sink. The crew performed emergency damage control and kept the boat afloat. PCF 103 then took a direct rocket hit in the engine room, disabling one engine. Captain Hoffmann ordered the four Swifts to clear the area to make temporary repairs to the crippled boats. The *White River* then conducted NGFS on the area as an air strike pounded the enemy positions.

At about 1630 on the 12th, PCFs 3, 10, 31, 43, 44 and 71 entered the Rach Duong Keo. Captain Hoffmann, aboard PCF 71, coordinated the insertion of the Mobile Strike Force below the area of a firefight on the 9th. The troops swept along the banks of the Duong Keo, destroying bunkers and mines. The Swifts then extracted the troops and inserted them again for a sweep of the Rach Nang. PCF 71 received a rocket hit on the port side shortly after ground forces made contact with the enemy. Roy Hoffmann was sitting on the port door coaming with an M-16 resting on his knee when the rocket struck. "I actually saw the damn thing coming," he says. The rocket hit almost directly under him, spraying shrapnel into the forward bunk area. Stacked mattresses in the space absorbed

The stern of PCF 23 packed with RSV troops for insertion. Hoffmann photo

most of the shrapnel, although Hoffmann ended up with shrapnel in his flak jacket. PCF 10 was sprayed by small arms fire, wounding three of the sailors aboard. The ground forces got into an intense firefight with the enemy as well; during the exchange of fire two VC were killed and an American Army advisor to the troops was killed.

The commander of the task force, Captain Hoffmann, at war with an M-16 and the ever present cigar on the bow of a Swift boat. HOFFMANN PHOTO

Although jarred by the explosion, Captain Hoffmann continued to direct the Strike Force, which advanced on the enemy. Under a withering hail of fire from the boats and the troops, the enemy retreated into the jungle. The boats stayed on the scene as all units pursued the enemy force until darkness fell and contact was broken. The boats fired on both banks on the way out of the river.

PCF 71 began taking on water upon exiting the river. Captain Hoffmann helped put on a temporary patch to attempt to arrest the alarming flow of water. They exited the river onto fairly heavy seas, which threw the boat around and dislodged the temporary patch. The water again came pouring in.

The O in C at one point asked Hoffmann what he thought they should do, and Hoffmann replied, "Well, you better make sure you've got your life jackets, because I think we're going swimming." He further advised the O in C to stay in constant radio contact as long as possible and make sure to keep their position reports going in.

As it turned out one of the other Swifts came back for them, "and we stepped aboard without getting wet." Within two to three minutes the Swift sank in about ten feet of water. It was the second, but not last time, Roy Hoffmann would be aboard a sinking Navy vessel.

The next morning, despite dangerous sea conditions, the 44 boat was able to salvage most of the electronic gear and the majority of weapons from the 71 boat, including the mortar. Shortly thereafter the HCU 1 Salvage Team, working from the USS *Pivot*, successfully refloated the boat. The boat had been easy to find; at low tide the mast was sticking out of the water.

ON FEBRUARY 18, 1969, PCFs 50, 66, 72 and 94 conducted operations in the Bay Hap. The 50 and 66 boats were first in and proceeded to Cai Nuoc for a Medical Civic Action Program (MEDCAP). An underwater mine exploded in front of PCF 66 and both boats came under small arms fire. The boats cleared the kill zone and continued to Cai Nuoc for the MEDCAP. PCFs 72 and 94 (under O in Cs Rocky Hildreth and John Kerry, respectively) entered the river about four hours later. Two more mines exploded as the 72 and 94 boats proceeded up the river. Rocky Hildreth told Douglas Brinkley, "We got bracketed with five B-40 rockets. We could actually see them go by. Then they started hitting us with small arms fire."[72]

On February 20, PCFs 37, 44 (O in C Tom Wright), 72 (Rocky Hildreth), 93 and 94 (John Kerry) probed the Dam Doi River to the outpost of Dam Doi. On the return transit the units received rocket and small arms fire. PCF 94 received a rocket-propelled grenade on the port side, resulting in minor injuries to the O in C (John Kerry). The engineman, Eugene Thorson, received a Purple Heart for "shrapnel wounds in the right arm."

On the 21st PCFs 5, 31, 50 and 93 proceeded up the Song Ong Doc to conduct operations near Thoi Binh. The units were forced to turn back when they received heavy rocket fire ten minutes after entering the river, resulting in serious damage to PCF 93.

On February 24 in I Corps the *Point Gammon, Point Glover, Point Lomas* and PCFs 12, 15, 70, 79, 81, and 99 conducted a combined sweep of a restricted area 15 miles south of Da Nang. The combined forces destroyed numerous junks, sampans, hootches and basket boats. The *Point Welcome* fired on beached sampans in a restricted area 25 miles north of Qui Nhon, and destroyed them.

That same day Terry Costello's boat took a mine while on the Ha Tien patrol. Costello's 38 boat and Rich McCann's 21 boat were coming out of the river when they passed a Buddhist shrine on one side and fish stakes on

---

72. Gunner's mate Fred Short made his first patrol on PCF 94 on this date, replacing David Alston. Short was raised in North Little Rock, Arkansas. He enlisted in the Navy in September 1967, and arrived in country at the same time as this author in early 1969.

the other. Costello's boat was in the lead, and he preferred being on one bank or the other, which on this day probably saved the boat. The mine detonated right in the center of the river as they passed by.

THE SWIFT BOATS GREATLY appreciated the support given them by the ships off the coast. On February 25, 1969, the USCG *John C. Spencer* (WHEC 36) arrived in Area 9 and relieved the USCG ship *Wachusett* (WHEC 44). Area 9 covered the southern tip of South Vietnam and the western coastline up to the Cambodian border. The *Spencer* took over as the "mother ship" to the Swifties, to which they returned after their daily river patrols. The "A" Gang provided the PCFs fuel and water, while the "*Spencer* Hilton" provided the Swifties a real rack to sleep on and good chow. They provided some entertainment to the weary crews with movies, soft drinks, popcorn and pizza. They were able to repair damage the boats sustained in firefights, and the Medical Department attended to the wounded. During the three-week patrol the *Spencer* cared for the 17 Swifties who received Purple Hearts during that period.

ON FEBRUARY 25 the Market Time Delta SEAL platoon was inserted into the Thanh Phu secret zone to collect intelligence. During the patrol the SEALs received hostile fire from a group of hootches. The SEALs returned the fire, killing 21 of the VC (body count). It is little wonder the enemy feared the storied SEALs.

The next day PCFs 43 and 44 spotted five VC crossing the river in a sampan near the mouth of the Cua Lon. The VC jumped off the sampans and attempted to swim away, but the PCFs closed on them. The Swifties jumped into the water to force the VC back aboard. During the capture PCF 44 took a rocket grenade close aboard, wounding one of the sailors. With their valuable enemy intelligence sources aboard, the Swifts shot their way out of the river.

BY THIS TIME, Bob Elder and his crew had been transferred to COS DIV 14 at Cam Ranh Bay. He took his coastal patrols in Cam Ranh as seriously as he had down south. One morning in late February or early March they were underway at 0500 hours. He was standing beside his helmsman, who said, "Mr. Elder, we have a steel hull out there. We gotta go get it. Look at the size of that thing."

The steel hull was over the horizon, but the signal from the radar was unbelievable. Elder called his crew to general quarters and gave the helmsman a course to the steel hull. They put on their ID lights and went charging out to sea at 25 knots. Elder got on the radio and said, "Any ship this net, any ship this net, this is Inky Bite Delta, over."

The sun was just coming up and when they got within range they see *it is the battleship New Jersey*. The ship transmitted back, "Inky Bite Delta, this is Onrush, over." Elder then realizes he is in *the same ocean with the New Jersey*, and he is attacking it with a 50 foot Swift boat. Elder informed the ship they were a Swift boat, and Onrush, not realizing their size, came back and said, "Inky Bite Delta, would you care to come alongside and take our mail into Cam Ranh Bay?"

Elder gave an affirmative response and the huge ship, on a northerly course, slowed down and "my little Swift boat comes alongside this warehouse in the water." They sent down a Jacob's ladder and Elder climbed the 25 feet to the ship. He was taken to the bridge where he met the captain. "I'd be delighted to take your mail, sir," Elder said.

"My boy," the CO asked, "how big is that boat of yours?"

"Fifty feet, sir."

The CO said with a smile, "How much can you carry? I have about two tons of mail here." The CO was kidding the Swift skipper, but it was still too much for the little boat to carry. The CO then informed Elder that the *New Jersey* had just received a call for a fire mission, and asked if the Swift crew would like to watch the battleship fire her guns. With Elder's positive response the CO told him to stand about 300 yards off the bow to watch the barrage.

Elder got back aboard the Swift and they got amidships of the battleship, which took off to get in position, creating a bow wave about four feet high. Elder instructed his helmsman, "All ahead full, take off to your right and stand off about 300 yards." Meanwhile the bow wave had reached about six feet high, and the little boat was not only forced by the bow wave back against the battleship, but under the bow. Above him was 40 feet of looming ship, and Elder looked above and back and all he could see was iron. Ahead was a six-foot wave the boat couldn't get over. They were in danger of getting crushed by the huge ship.

Elder got on the radio to request that the ship stop, but because his antennas were totally masked by the ship he couldn't reach the ship. Elder says, "For at least the tenth time in Vietnam I think I'm near death. I'm going to my death swamped by Onrush." Elder's helmsman, QM2 Rex Young, in a great feat of seamanship, plunged them through the bow wave. The *New*

Three noted Swifties (left to right): Don Droz, killed in action on board PCF 43, April 12, 1969; Captain Roy F. Hoffmann, CTF 115; and Mike Bernique, legendary Swift boat skipper. HOFFMANN PHOTO

Jersey got into firing position, the forward turret came around and the three guns commenced firing.[73]

Elder eventually became XO of COS DIV 14 under Paul Dodson, and he turned his 43 boat over to Don Droz, whom the then 29-year-old Elder describes as "looking so young." Droz then transferred to An Thoi with his crew.[74]

Droz was a handsome, married officer who had left in the United States

---

73. The *New Jersey* was decommissioned after short service in the Vietnam War, and ended up permanently docked in Philadelphia as a museum. Years later, Bob Elder took his son aboard, they stood on the quarterdeck and Elder told his son the story.

74. Almost everyone interviewed for this book disagreed with Brinkley's portrayal of Don Droz in *Tour of Duty* as an almost cowardly, antiwar Navy officer. Larry Thurlow, who knew him well, says that Droz had turned against the war, thinking it was wrong both politically and militarily. Terry Costello says, "I don't remember anybody, even Kerry, saying the war was wrong. Maybe Don Droz felt that way, but I don't remember him saying it." Droz also had decided by this time not to make the Navy his career. But rather than look for an easy way out, Don Droz remained a professional Navy officer to the end, one who courageously followed orders and led his crew into battle again and again. He never let his fellow officers or crew down.

a wife, Judy, and a three-month-old daughter, Tracy. His nickname in Vietnam was "Dinky Dau," an Americanization of the Vietnamese *dien cau dau*, meaning to be crazy. Droz hailed from Rich Hill, Missouri. Pat Sheedy knew Droz from his first day at Annapolis in 1962. They each owned a Pontiac GTO, which was the "class car" that year. After they both graduated from the Academy they parted, only to meet again in Cam Ranh when Sheedy arrived in country. Sheedy describes Don Droz as "a great guy, always friendly, always smart." Terry Costello describes Droz as "an aggressive guy, and a nice guy—I liked him."

ON FEBRUARY 28, 1969, PCFs 23 (O in C Bill Rood), 43 (O in C Don Droz) and 94 (O in C John Kerry) returned to the Bay Hap to land Cai Nuoc RF/PF troops at ambush sites along the river. The sweep by the troops uncovered numerous spent small arms ammo and spider holes. The boats took the troops aboard and proceeded to the Dong Cung Canal, where they encountered an enemy initiated firefight.

Bill Rood was one of the outstanding O in Cs in the division.[75] George Elliott relates that Rood on March 12, 1969, "received shrapnel in the face from a shattered windshield and we all thought he was blinded in, at best, one eye. He was medevaced . . . and returned to An Thoi after about two weeks of hospitalization. I had an opening on the staff and offered it to Lieutenant j.g. Rood. Rood said, 'No thanks skipper, I want my boat back.'"

On this day John Kerry was OTC. Apparently the three officers had discussed in advance that, rather than driving past an ambush, the boats would make a 90-degree turn into the face of enemy fire. It was a tactic most of the other O in Cs questioned. Terry Costello says, "Most of the ambushes I was on, if you'd run ashore you'd have been dead. Bernique got away with it but he was a different kind of guy [than Kerry]. Bernique knew what he was doing. By that time the VC had gotten more sophisticated and to go ashore in an ambush area would be suicide. That was a real dumb thing to do [on Kerry's part]." Costello went on to state, "Kerry had a lot of balls, but he did stupid things. I just thought he was a loose cannon."

At the first ambush site the OTC directed the Swifts to the beach as the

---

75. This author, through an intermediary, requested an interview with Bill Rood. He is the only former Swift boat sailor contacted who declined a request for an interview, but he did indicate he was not granting any interviews. He wrote a letter supporting John Kerry's actions of February 28 during the 2004 election. He would have been the best source for action on this day.

One of the best-known Swift boat operations photos, taken going up a small canal of the Dam Doi, in late February or early March, 1969. Trailing boat is Bill Rood's PCF 23; note the after gunner had added an "R" to the stern, signifying River Patrol Craft Fast. He was later made to paint it over. Making the turn is John Kerry's 94 boat.
OPERATION DESCRIPTION COURTESY OF FRED SHORT, WHO WAS IN THE GUN TUB OF THE 94 BOAT ON THE OPERATION. OFFICIAL U.S. NAVY PHOTO, HOFFMANN COLLECTION

VC attempted to escape. The boats disembarked the troops, led by a U.S. Army adviser, after the fleeing VC. The tactics worked that day. They routed the enemy and killed three of the attackers. As the troops swept away from the boats they killed another half dozen VC, wounded or captured others, and captured enemy weapons and supplies.

Kerry and Rood's boats then proceeded up the river, leaving Don Droz and his 43 boat at the site of the ambush. The two Swifts then encountered another ambush, turned into it, and again the tactic worked. The troops were at the first ambush site; Bill Rood and Richard Lamberson, a member of his crew, went ashore to search the area. Out of Rood's vision, a VC carrying a B-40 rocket launcher jumped up in front of Kerry's boat. Tom Belodeau hit the fleeing VC and knocked him down. Kerry went off the boat with an M-16, chased down the injured VC and dispatched him as he hobbled away. For the action Kerry received a Silver Star and Bill Rood a Bronze Star.[76]

SINCE KERRY'S SERVICE has been shrouded in controversy, it is appropriate to look at what his fellow officers, in interviews for this book, had to say about him. Don Droz was one of the few people that John Kerry spent any time with in Vietnam. He was later killed in action and so cannot give his impressions today. Bill Rood also is silent, other than commenting favorably about Kerry in the above action.

Terry Costello's comments were fairly typical of how most of the other officers felt about Kerry during his short stay in Vietnam, "Kerry and I didn't really talk in Vietnam. I didn't have the right pedigree for him to be interested in me. I wasn't particularly interested in him, so we never had much interchange."

Larry Thurlow says Kerry thought people like him were hicks. Kerry, Thurlow says, would size you up and put you into one of two categories. "One, can this guy help me now or maybe help me later? Two, if not, the hell with him. Kerry thinks he's the center of the universe. If you don't have any value to him he doesn't have time to be bothered with you." Thurlow said most of the officers fell into category two with Kerry.

In contrast, Mike Bernique and Kerry were friends in Vietnam, although Bernique now says, "I did not know him. I knew what he let me know." Bernique and Kerry on the surface had much in common. They were born the same month and year; Bernique thought they were both born in Massachusetts, an impression Kerry gave Bernique even though it turned out Kerry was born in Denver. Both were educated in France. Kerry led Bernique to believe he was Irish, which he was not. Both men were Catholics. Bernique says it was an "amazing group of things to have in common in a small group." They gravitated toward one another and spent some time together.

---

76. In addition to those awards, Tom Belodeau and Mike Medeiros earned Bronze Star Medals; Del Sandusky, Fred Short and Gene Thorson received Navy Commendation Medals. John Kerry probably wrote the after action report for the mission. The medals were awarded by Admiral Zumwalt, who obviously was not there that day, and relied on the after action report for the awards, including Kerry's.

Kerry in his short time in Vietnam did go up some rivers with Bernique, who says, "I will tell you he exhibited courage. In fact, sometimes he had courage bordering on foolhardy." On one mission they encountered an enemy minefield and Kerry walked through it. Bernique yelled at him, "Get the fuck out of there!" Kerry just looked at him, shrugged and walked out. Bernique further says, "I think Kerry extrapolated on everyone's experiences and made them his."

Mike Bernique went on to say, "There is no one whose opinion I respect more than Larry Thurlow's. He was salt of the earth." Thurlow thinks John Kerry was a phony, a self-centered, rich snob, and a coward in Vietnam. Mike Bernique reconciles the various opinions of Kerry's courage as either Kerry was different when operating with him, or he had grown afraid after he spent a couple of months in the rivers.[77]

ON FEBRUARY 28, 1969, Captain Roy Hoffmann received his fitness report from Vice Admiral Zumwalt. In it Zumwalt said Hoffmann was, "strongly recommended for accelerated promotion to Flag rank and is particularly well suited for assignment as a cruiser-destroyer flotilla command and for a Flag billet . . . ." The possibility of advancement to admiral had not really seemed a possibility for the Crystal City, Missouri native, who thought he had probably achieved his highest rank at captain. Achievement of Flag rank is rare and intensely competitive in the Navy; roughly ten of the top 50 captains in the Navy are chosen for the honor and responsibility.

Zumwalt's report was glowing. Even allowing for the hyperbole one sometimes sees in these reports, clearly Zumwalt held his TF 115 commander in the highest esteem. Hoffmann, Zumwalt said:

> Has personally led many of these missions and thus exposed himself many times to the enemy in order to gain first hand knowledge of the problems involved in executing these missions. Task Force 115 forces have made numerous incursions into territory that has been for many years been completely controlled by the Viet Cong. Capt. Hoffmann's forces have contributed significantly to the failure of the enemy's post-TET offensive in the Delta. Capt. Hoffmann possesses all the qualities of a great combat leader.

---

77. Mike Bernique was eventually rotated out of An Thoi to the north. The pounding of the guns had severely damaged his hearing, and the posting in the north further assaulted a serious condition. He eventually spent six months in the Philadelphia Naval Hospital because of the condition. This author sat next to Mike Bernique in a meeting in 2004, and it was evident he has serious, permanent damage to his hearing.

He is bold, imaginative, fearless and in complete control at all times. He has displayed the judgment, personal courage and competence while under fire, that is the true test of a military professional. His general reputation among the general officers in this theater is that he is one of the really great naval wartime leaders produced by the in country Navy. This leads me to state without reservation that he is a brilliant tactician and combat commander.

In March Bill Shumadine got to see his wife and five-month-old child in Hawaii for his R & R. "I went near the end," he says, "so I wouldn't have so long to go before I saw them again. It was the only time I was sick that whole year—I got the Hong Kong flu."

Dr. Larry Good, the division dentist at An Thoi, had tried to give him drugs to alleviate the symptoms, but they didn't help much.[78] When Shumadine arrived at the hotel the doctor took one look at him and said, "Keep the kid away from him." Shumadine says, "I get one five day R & R and all I can do is lie in bed.[79] I was like a limp rag when they put me on the plane to fly back to Vietnam."

While he was on R & R they put his 5 boat and the 23 boat on skids, took his Decca 202 radar off the mast and installed a Raytheon 1900. The retrofit was to allow the boats to go farther up the rivers. On installation they cut the mast in half and hinged it. They used coaxial cable that could be bent and not damage the wave guides. With the retrofit they could get under fish traps, low hanging brush and bridges. It turned out to be a worthless modification because there were only two boats that had it, and they couldn't go in the dangerous rivers by themselves.

On March 3, 1969, the pier area at Cam Ranh Bay came under 140mm rocket fire. Shrapnel from a rocket hitting close aboard Skimmer 75 killed the Boat Captain. When the skimmer returned to the pier they found 38 holes had perforated the boat. On the 5th Communist forces fired seven rockets into Saigon, killing at least 22 civilians and wounding scores more. There were no secure areas in Vietnam.

---

78. Dr. Larry Good performed great service for the Swifties and Vietnamese villagers during his time in An Thoi (including taking out an impacted wisdom tooth from this author). Larry Good has practiced dentistry in Hays, Kansas, since he left the Navy. Larry Thurlow lives nearby and Dr. Good has been his friend and dentist for many years.

79. He says with a laugh, "A lot of guys lay in bed on their R & R, but they were more active."

On March 7 a Boston Whaler inserted a SEAL team up a stream in An Xuyen province. The SEAL mission was to capture a VC extortionist. After inserting the SEALs the crew on the Boston Whaler opened fire on an approaching sampan. The SEAL team took fire from an abandoned village and killed six and captured one VC. The VC guerrilla detainee identified the dead VC as the first and second lieutenant and the tax collector.

The next day PCFs 5, 9 and 38 entered the Cua Lon River with MSF troops. The Swifts proceeded to the Nhung Mien and Bien Nhan canals to look for signs of command-detonated mines. Roy Hoffmann, who liked to be addressed by his call sign "Latch," was aboard Terry Costello's 38 boat for the dangerous run. In the canal they encountered the extremely strong currents that occurred when the tide was going in or out. Costello's helmsman fought the current, and as he attempted to beach the boat to disembark troops, he beached the boat right into a large banyan tree. Then Costello heard, "Man overboard!"

It was not uncommon for the boats to lose someone overboard. The walkways were narrow, slippery and the boats pitched and rolled continually. Costello thought to himself, "Jeeze, one of the little guys [Vietnamese troops] has fallen off the boat and will get caught in the screws. Imagine my horror when I look back and there's the somewhat bald head of Latch bobbing down the canal holding an M-16 out of the water."[80]

Fighting the current, while trying to stay afloat and swim with one arm is exhausting for a young man, let alone the then 44-year-old commander of the task force. They pulled the boat off the bank and managed to get the boat up to the struggling Latch, who grabbed the troop net. With water logged flak jacket, boots and one free arm it was impossible to climb the net. The crew grabbed him by the flak jacked and "pretty much unceremoniously dumped him on the deck."

Shumadine says, "He's laying there panting and we're thinking, 'Lord, our careers are at an end.'" The helmsman, RD3 Gregory Cybulski, said, "Latch, I'm very sorry sir."

Latch growled back, "You sons of bitches, you'll never let me live this down." Costello was relieved to have the commander back aboard, and happy he hadn't

---

80. Although going off the boat wasn't that rare, it was an unpardonable sin to loose your piece in the process. Roy Hoffmann kept his M-16.

lost the M-16, "because it was one of mine." The boats then inserted the troops and they swept 1,000 yards along both canals. After picking up the troops the boats were to proceed to the Cai Nhap canal for a psychological operations broadcast. They never got that far.

As they resumed the mission they headed down the Cua Lon, and somewhere past Old Nam Can, in the evening, they came under heavy enemy fire, during the course of which all of the boats received substantial damage.[81]

Costello normally liked to be on the port side of the boat during the river runs, but for this one he was on the starboard side because Hoffmann was on the port side. When the firefight started Costello remembered looking over and seeing Latch fall backwards into the main cabin, and he thought, "Oh, Christ, he's been hit. How am I going to report this?" What happened was the concussion from the boat being hit had knocked Latch into the cabin.

As the crew and Captain Hoffmann returned fire the boat took a rocket in the bow. Costello, Ratliff, the twin .50s gunner, the peak tank gunner, two of the Nungs and Cybulski were all wounded. The peak tank gunner took a hit in the arm; Ratliff got hit in the foot with a .50 caliber slug. Costello was hit with shrapnel in various parts of his body. A .50 caliber round went through the pilothouse, hit the base of the pilot's chair and ricocheted up, hitting Cybulski in the upper thigh. He stood up in his helmsman chair and Costello asked, "What are you doing?"

"I'm hit," he responded.

Costello said, "Sit down and drive," which he did. The boats fought their way clear. When they cleared the kill zone Costello asked Cybulski if he was all right. Cybulski showed him the wound and Costello thought, "Good lord, that had to hurt." There was an entry hole and around the wound it looked like someone had beaten him with a baseball bat. Cybulski stayed at his station until they got all the way out, and then he was medevaced.[82]

The immediate problem was the large hole in the bow, and they temporarily patched it with life jackets. Costello, who was OTC, called for medevac, which he says took forever to arrive. He had the boats beach, two on the south bank and one on the north bank. There was an Army Green Beret captain with the troops and Costello had him set up a defensive perimeter in front of the boats. The

---

81. Later in the summer of 1969 the site of Old Nam Can would be the river setting of Operation Sea Float, a barge-anchored base for the SEALORDS Forces.

82. Costello did not see Cybulski again in Vietnam, and he often thought, "I bet he's pissed at me," for making him continue to drive the boat. But years later they saw each other and the helmsman wasn't upset at all.

Nungs were reluctant to leave the boats—apparently they thought they would be left. After the Green Beret yelled at them they finally went off the boats.

An Army medevac helicopter responded, and he didn't want to land in the hot area. Costello argued with him over the radio, assuring the pilot they had a defensive perimeter out and they had to get the severely wounded men off the boats. The helo finally came in about dusk and picked up the worst of the wounded.

After the medevac they were down to three crew members on the boat. Roy Hoffmann, rather than taking the helo out, decided to ride the boat back to An Thoi. "Why he decided not to go out by helicopter," Costello says, "I don't know."

The boats then exited to the Square Bay area as Costello thought, "This is not the best way to live." They passed Square Bay and started north to An Thoi, with Costello driving and his men rotating, watching the hole in the bow while Latch and the other exhausted men slept. As they transited the open seas, Costello noticed two things, "One, we weren't going very fast and two we were riding low in the water." He checked and saw water in the main cabin. "We were sinking," he says. The exhausted enlisted man watching the hole had fallen asleep and water was pouring in. Meanwhile, Latch was sound asleep on one of the two racks in the forward compartment.

Costello got on the radio and tried to raise someone to bring pumps out to him, but no one responded. The crew started hauling water out with buckets. They finally got ahead of the water, stuffed the hole again and made it back to An Thoi. "Captain Hoffmann never knew what happened and we never told him," Costello now says.

When they got back to An Thoi it took a week to patch the boat, which had numerous bullet holes, blown out windows and the large hole in the bow.

On March 12, PCFs 23 (Bill Rood), 43 (Don Droz), 51 (Larry Thurlow) and 94 (John Kerry), with MSF troops aboard, conducted a SEALORDS operation in the Cua Lon and adjoining canals. During the operation two of the Swifts were mined and two of the sailors were wounded.

On the 23 boat, the after gunner had painted an "R" in front of the PCF to indicate River Patrol Craft, Fast (he was later ordered to remove it). Fred Short was the twin .50 gunner that day.[83] He remembers the boats were ambushed and disembarked the troops to pursue the enemy. They later went

---

83. Comments taken from an e-mail to this author, October 11, 2005.

far enough upstream that the canal became so narrow they had to run the bows up on the bank to turn the boats around.

Short, who had just turned 21 on February 18, says the crews referred to the series of patrols as the "Days of Hell." "I was so glad my parents had the good sense to send me to Sunday school. I never really appreciated those classes until An Thoi. I was one scared Arkie."

LARRY THURLOW WAS SELECTED as the officer to work with the VNN, to train them to operate and maintain Swift boats. By January he had had enough of the duty and requested to go back on the boats. He was distressed by the lack of ambition exhibited by the Vietnamese and wanted to get back on the boats. He was assigned PCF 51, but often took other boats out.[84]

On March 12 he was in the rivers with John Kerry, Don Droz and Bill Rood's 23 boat when, during a firefight, Rood was temporarily blinded as his windshield exploded, spraying glass into the officer's eyes. A mine also exploded off the starboard bow of Thurlow's boat, injuring the bow gunner. As Kerry and Droz waited for the Nungs to return to the boats, Thurlow's boat towed the 23 boat back to the LST, where Rood was medevaced out. All of the men that day thought Rood had lost his eye. As related earlier in this chapter, Rood returned to his boat two weeks later.

MARCH 13, 1969: THE MINING OF PCF 3

The next day was John Kerry's last river operation, the "No Man Left Behind" incident.[85] Whatever else may be said about the day, Larry Thurlow deserved the Bronze Star he was later awarded for the action. The boats and officers on the mission were, PCFs 3 (Dick Pees, O in C), 23 (Jack Chenoweth), 43 (Don Droz), 51 (Larry Thurlow), and 94 (John Kerry).

---

84. Douglas Brinkley in *Tour of Duty*, p. 299, relates accurately, "PCF 53 was in good hands with Larry Thurlow, among the toughest and ablest Swift boat officers in Vietnam."

85. Sources for this operation were the COS DIV 11 Command History; interviews with Larry Thurlow and Robert Hornberger; Brinkley, *Tour of Duty* and "John Kerry's Final Mission in Vietnam;" and O'Neill, *Unfit for Command*. In John Kerry's version of the day, a mine went off alongside his boat, Lieutenant Rassmann was blown overboard, Kerry was terribly wounded from the underwater mine, Kerry turned back into the fire zone while bleeding heavily from his arm and side, and reached into the water and pulled Rassmann out, all while under heavy enemy fire. John Kerry spent more than $50 million in paid political advertising during 2004, promoting his version of this day.

Vietnamese forces, inserted by U.S. Navy Swift boats, move on a sweep in the Mekong Delta, 1969. Hoffmann photo

The boats were to conduct operations in the Bay Hap River and Dong Cung Canal. The day started at 0600 as Kerry's PCF 94 and Rich McCann's PCF 24 left the LST to join three other boats for the raid on the Bay Hap. It was a dark, cloudy gray and humid day. The boats loaded the Nung aboard (Chinese and Cambodian mercenaries), along with a U.S. Special Forces team of Green Berets, and got underway. As they neared the entrance to the Bay Hap, McCann's boat developed engine trouble and was forced to stop. The troops aboard McCann's boat were then transferred to Kerry's boat for the operation. The 94 boat arrived at the rendezvous point at the mouth of the Dong Cung, joining boats skippered by Skip Barker, Don Droz and Larry Thurlow, which had Ruff Puffs (SVN Popular Force troops) aboard, that they had picked up at Cai Nuoc. At the mouth of the canal Barker cut a wire connecting fish stakes to make a hole wide enough for the Swifts to enter. The canal was so narrow the leading boats roiled the water for the following boats, causing them to roll. It was a twisting, winding canal with mangroves thick on the banks on each side.

On this early morning operation, Kerry, Rassmann, and Thurlow went ashore, where they discovered a large rice cache. After making the decision to destroy the food, Kerry and Rassmann threw concussion grenades into the cache, and then ran for cover. Rassmann got away from the rice explosion, but Kerry was caught in the backside by flying rice. Kerry and Rassmann thought the foregoing was hilarious.[86]

When the boats reached the designated point they disembarked the troops and Nungs, who were paid based on the number of confirmed enemy they killed. A few moments after the Nung went ashore the men on the boats heard a load explosion. One of the Army Green Berets called on the radio, "Can you come back here and pick up a body? I've got one of my boys killed by a booby trap."

The trail the troops had followed was booby-trapped. The VC had put poles on either side of the trail and run wire across at about the 5-foot 10-inch level (probably to get the taller Americans). When the wire was tripped the line pulled the pin out of a grenade, exploding it close by. Generally the wires could be seen during the day, but night and inattention were devastating. That day the troops walked under the wires and got into a village, where

---

86. The self-inflicted "fanny wound" would become the basis for Kerry's third Purple Heart, which he claimed for action later in the day.

South Vietnamese soldiers sweep away from a burning hooch. HOFFMANN PHOTO

one of the Nungs, Bac She De, sliced open a bag of rice, which was wired with a booby-trap.

Characteristically, Larry Thurlow got off his boat with a couple of military issue ponchos to carry out Bac She De's remains. Thurlow says about coming upon the Nung, "I didn't realize you could still kind of look like a human and have that much blown up on you." The claymore explosion scooped out Bac She De's innards, and shattered the bones in his forearms and upper arms. "The muscles just sucked his hands up toward his shoulders," Thurlow says. "His teeth were gone, his eyes were gone, and there was a hole out the back of his helmet. It was a tremendous blast. A guy that might have weighed 120 pounds, there was like 90 pounds of him left when I rolled him up."

He thought to himself, "I'm not making anybody else take this guy back." He wrapped Bac She De up in a poncho, and carried him across a rice paddy instead of down the booby-trapped trail. Thurlow, who is a large man, carried Bac She De about a hundred yards to the boats. Carrying the burden, Thurlow now says, "Oh my god, I thought I was going to die." Thurlow deposited the body on the fantail of the 94 boat, on which the Nung had ridden into the canal.[87]

After Thurlow returned to the boats they got the troops back aboard and exited the Dong Cung. They then transited the Bay Hap to Cai Nuoc, where they unloaded their troops and moved out. Earlier in the day, when they had gone up river it had looked to Thurlow like Vietnamese had just started setting fish stakes in the river, and there was an empty sampan at the site. Thurlow now believes the VC were setting mines at the location and the boats had interrupted them as they went up the river. The VC had run what looked like #9 wire from pole top to pole top, leaving gaps on either bank. It looked like if you hit the wire you would trigger a mine, when in fact the wires were to funnel the boats to the side where there were command detonated mines beneath the water.

The boats moved down the river in a reverse arrowhead, with Kerry's 94 boat in the lead on the right side, followed by Don Droz' 43 boat. On the left side Dick Pees' 3 boat was in the lead, followed by Jack Chenoweth's 23 boat, with Van Odell manning the twin .50s. Larry Thurlow was following right in the middle of the river. He had the best view of the developing

---

87. When Douglas Brinkley called Thurlow to interview him for *Tour of Duty*, he asked him, "Were you there when John Kerry carried the Nung's body back to the boat?" Thurlow replied, "Kerry did not carry the body back, I did."

situation and was just getting on the radio to warn the other boats of the danger of passing through the two narrow openings in the wire, when "I could see daylight under his [Dick Pees'] keel." A mine exploded on the left side under PCF 3. There was clearly no explosion on the right side.[88] The explosion lifted the Swift about two feet out of the water, engulfing it in mud and spray, and then it settled heavily back into the water, rocking from side to side. The entire crew of the 3 boat, some of whom were thrown into the water, was injured. Jack Chenoweth's boat maneuvered over immediately to help pick the men up out of the water.

The 43 boat made a left turn toward the 3 boat. All of the boats except John Kerry's did as standard operating procedure would suggest, pulling up to cover the crippled 3 boat and its crew, and opened up, firing on the banks in case the enemy had set up an ambush. They stopped firing almost immediately, as there was no return fire from the banks.[89] GMG2 Robert Hornberger, on the twin .50s of the 43 boat says, "We opened fire that day, but when we didn't get return fire we stopped." Thurlow relates, "John Kerry hits the throttles" and his boat accelerated away from the action, down the river, leaving the other three boats to assist the 3 boat. Hornberger relates that the 43 boat guarded one bank while the other boat guarded the other, as the third boat pulled men out of the water. "The boat ahead of us [Kerry's 94 boat]," he says, "took off down the river, and I asked Mr. Droz, 'Where are they going?'" Droz replied, "I don't know."

The 94 boat was crowded with Nungs, and Army officer Jim Rassmann got dumped in the river as the boat accelerated, leaving him 100 yards from the other three boats. Rassmann was justifiably confused at water level, as the 94 boat had left him behind, and he heard the guns of the other Swifts firing at the banks. The other boats had a sinking boat and wounded to attend to, and Rassmann was in no danger given the lack of enemy return fire. Chenoweth's boat eventually moved to pick him up as Kerry finally returned to the scene of the mining and got him out of the water.

Meanwhile, one of the engines on the 3 boat was disabled and the other was locked at 500 rpm. The boat veered dangerously, hitting sandbars in the river. Thurlow maneuvered the 53 boat over to render assistance. He

---

88. Larry Thurlow believes both sides were mined, but for some reason the mine on the right side failed to explode.

89. Most credible witnesses to the action, including Chenoweth, his twin .50s gunner Van Odell, Robert Hornberger, and Larry Thurlow indicate there was no return hostile fire that day.

finally got aboard the 3 boat and got it under control as it began to sink. He checked on and stabilized the wounded, and as he was moving from the bow to the stern, holding his M-16 in his left hand and holding the railing on the cabin with his right, he missed his handhold, "and I could feel myself suspended in mid-air, thinking, 'I know I'm going in.'" Thinking the river is like the Cua Lon and 20 feet deep, he hit the water with his M-16 in his hand. "I just straightened out, and my feet hit the bottom." The river was about eight feet deep, so he just kept bobbing until his boat came over and picked him up.

Thurlow returned to the 3 boat, working to keep the damaged Swift afloat. Only one engine was running and the overboard discharge pipes were destroyed in the engine room, rapidly filling the hull with water. Two Swifts tied up alongside the 3 boat as tired and bloody sailors kept bailing for all they were worth to keep the boat afloat.

Larry Thurlow stayed on board as they towed PCF 3 in a race to get the boat out before it sank. Jack Chenoweth's boat went out to a USCG cutter offshore with the wounded and returned with a damage control team to help save PCF 3.

The spot report for the action reported that Lieutenant j.g. Richard Pees received head and back injuries and was medevaced; Ensign Kenneth Tryner received a back injury and was medevaced; Lieutenant j.g. John Kerry received a shrapnel wound [sic] to the left buttock and a contusion on the right forearm (described as minor); GMG3 Earl N. Hollister received a shrapnel wound to the groin and was medevaced; RD3 Leslie Vorphal received a back injury and was medevaced; GMG3 Wolfe received a back injury, contusions and abrasions; and EN3 Fred Arp received contusions and abrasions.[90]

March 13, 1969, was the last time Larry Thurlow saw Kerry. By the time Thurlow returned to An Thoi, Kerry was gone. Thurlow and his crew wanted a drink, and the only facility open was the Officer's Club. Thurlow took his five enlisted crew members in for a drink; a Navy lieutenant arrived and took umbrage to enlisted men being in the club. Basically, the lieutenant was invited to leave.

---

90. John Kerry's wounds, for which he received his third Purple Heart and a ticket out of Vietnam, were minor. He received the self-inflicted "fanny wound" to the buttocks earlier in the day, as we have seen. A contusion may also be defined accurately as a bruise. Had a mine actually gone off next to his boat, as he reported, one could at least give him some credibility on the point. The only mine that went off that day exploded under Dick Pees' 3 boat.

Years later, when Thurlow saw an enlisted man from his crew, the crew member said, "If you can tell me what happened at the O club in An Thoi after we towed the 3 boat out, I'll know it is you." The enlisted man said the incident was one of the highlights of his tour in Vietnam.

March 14, 1969: Robert Kerrey and the SEALs Assault an Enemy Position

U.S. Navy SEALs served in Vietnam from 1964 to the end of the war. Although their numbers never exceeded 200, their impact on the enemy was enormous. In six years the SEALs accounted for 600 confirmed VC killed, and another 300 killed, captured or detained.

Robert Kerrey and his SEAL team arrived in Vietnam in January of 1969, where they reported to the office of Captain Roy Hoffmann. Hoffmann briefed the SEALs on the successes of Market Time Forces and their assault on the interior rivers of the lower Mekong Delta. Hoffmann, according to Kerrey, said he would provide the SEALs with Swift boats for almost any operations they wanted to conduct, but informed them he had limited helicopter gun ships available, and most of those were committed to covering the operations of his crews.

On March 14, 1969, 25-year-old Lieutenant Bob Kerrey and a five-man SEAL team, under the administrative, but not tactical control of Captain Roy Hoffmann, were ferried by Swift boat to Nha Trang. There they interrogated a VC sapper who was willing to lead the SEALs to other sappers, in exchange for his freedom, thus becoming a "Hoi Chanh" (former VC who have gone over to the South Vietnamese government). With the Hoi Chanh they got back aboard the Swift and headed a mile east beyond Hon Tam Island in the Bay of Nha Trang, which was known to be a well-defended VC sanctuary, and home to several important members of the VC's political cadre. The mission was to penetrate the enemy's defenses and bring back the VC officers—alive if possible.[91]

---

[91]. Former Senator Robert Kerrey did not respond to an interview request for this book. His narrative in *When I Was a Young Man* is a pretty straightforward account of the actions on the 14th, and provides the quotes for this section. Although an earlier incident involving the former senator has become somewhat controversial, this author has no reason to question Kerrey's actions or heroism.

The SEALs left the Swift boat on a pitch-dark night on two small rubber boats and paddled to the seaward side of the island. The VC camp was almost impregnable, located on a ledge halfway down a 350-foot sheer cliff. To climb straight up to the ledge was deemed suicidal by Kerrey, so he decided to scale the cliff at another point and descend on the enemy from above.

Kerrey split his team into two three-man sections, keeping the Hoi Chanh with him. They climbed the treacherous cliff, and then descended to the ledge, staying in touch by whispered radio communications. If one of them fell, or dropped a piece of equipment they would be exposed on the cliff to an alerted enemy.

The two groups reached the ledge, where they found the first group of VC without a problem. Kerrey then continued to where the Hoi Chanh told him the next group would be. The VC saw the oncoming SEALs—Kerrey got off a short burst as the sound of an explosion ripped the air. He was thrown backwards and his rifle was torn from his hands. He smelled burning flesh and sensed immediately he had been seriously wounded. In the pitch dark he reached down to his leg to assess the damage and found his foot was detached from his calf. Meanwhile, gunfire rocked the night as the VC attacked at close range. Kerrey tied a tourniquet on his leg above the knee, then pulled himself up so he could direct his men, who circled around and got the enemy in a deadly cross fire. Kerrey then broke the styrette of morphine and injected it into his thigh, tasting it almost immediately in his mouth. The SEALs secured the prisoners, and then called in medevac helicopters. Kerrey's men brought him out in a sling to where he could be extracted. On the way up the cliff he caught a finger on his left hand on a tree limb and it snapped. Thanks to the effects of the morphine he felt no pain.

Kerrey was evacuated by helicopter and sent first to the Army hospital at Nha Trang, and then flown on to Yokosuka, Japan. Roy Hoffmann rode a Swift boat to visit him in Nha Trang before Kerrey was transferred to Yokosuka.

On March 24, 1969, Bob Kerrey wrote Roy Hoffmann a letter from Yokosuka. He indicated he wasn't completely free of drugs, but "I'll be making the final trip by bus to the U.S. Naval Hospital in Phil., Pa. after . . . flying there from Yokosuka. I couldn't feel better. The corpsmen and nurses have been outstanding right down the line. They haven't taken anything off the leg as yet . . . ."

He had been told by the head orthopedic surgeon at Yokosuka that the leg should be taken off just below the knee, "I'm optimistic about the outcome," Kerrey said, closing the letter with:

The last few years had undermined my confidence in the strength of the leadership in the U.S. Navy. I had seen weak willed people in command positions whose actions were controlled almost completely from regulations and not from their heart and mind. My short period of contact with you has shown me there are men who can still combine courage with Naval obligations. It was a pleasure working for you and an honor knowing you. Thanks for everything.

Kerrey was flown to the Navy hospital in Philadelphia. His leg was so badly mangled that amputation at the knee was required. When he awoke from the operation his mother was nearby. "Is there anything left?" he asked her.

"There's a lot," his mother Elinor Kerrey replied, pointing at his heart.[92]

ON MARCH 16 President Nixon received intelligence reports that indicated over 40,000 Communist troops had secretly amassed in a zone ten to 15 miles wide just inside the Cambodian border. Nixon decided to secretly bomb those sanctuaries, thus denying the enemy safe harbor, from which they launched attacks against Americans and their South Vietnamese allies. The bombing began the next day.

For the first time in the war, the Communists felt the sting of war in their base camps and supply areas in Cambodia. B-52s made 3,630 flights over Cambodia and dropped 110,000 tons of bombs over the 14-month period that ended in April of 1970. Soon after the bombing began there was a steady decline in the number of American casualties in Vietnam. The bombing was the right action for the Commander in Chief to take; withholding the information from the American people made the right strategy wrong.

ON MARCH 17, four days after the mission of March 13, 1969, John Kerry requested reassignment out of Vietnam. He used the three Purple Hearts he was issued as his exit ticket.[93] His request was forwarded to the Navy Bureau of Personnel at 0742 hours that day. Shortly thereafter he turned PCF 94 over

---

92. After the Admiral returned from Vietnam, the family made a trip to Missouri, visiting both sets of grandparents. On the way back home they went through Philadelphia, because Roy Hoffmann wanted to stop at the Veteran's hospital and visit Bob Kerrey. The family stayed in the car while Hoffmann made the visit. Chris Carnahan says, "He had a high regard for him [Kerrey]." Hilarie Hanson, even though she was only 11 years old during the visit, says, "I can specifically remember my father saying, 'Bob Kerrey is a hero.'"

93. As far as is known, he became the only Swiftie in the history of TF 115 to make such a request before the end of his tour. He served four months and nine days out of a one year tour of duty.

(John O'Neill would eventually get the boat), and he was transferred to Cam Ranh to await further orders. He spent five or six days in Cam Ranh, after which he was assigned to Brooklyn. His short time in Vietnam was over.

Pat Sheedy ran into him in the passageway of the APL right after a St. Patrick's Day Party. Kerry asked Sheedy, "What do you think. Should I leave or stay?" Of course, by then Kerry had already put in to leave. Sheedy told him, "If you want to leave, and have a ticket out, you should go." Kerry left, mostly unnoticed.

March 19, 1969: Three Market Time Raiders Go Missing in Action

On March 19, 1969, PCF 58, with Lieutenant Jim Winandy and crew aboard, entered the Cua Dai River complex 20 miles south of Da Nang.[94] They relieved another crew, and set up a patrol schedule with PCF 101, which had already been on station the preceding one or two days. The two boats made a run to Hoi An City, and then the two boats, with 58 in the lead, headed down river. On the transit the lead boat spotted a fishing net partially across the river and stopped to remove it. Winandy instructed the 101 boat to proceed.

One of the men on the 101 boat was Lieutenant Robert Andretta, from Coastal Group (CG) 14. The reader will recall Bob Andretta from Chapter 6 on the *Adams* (the Bull Ensign). Andretta had been assigned as senior advisor at Coastal Group (CG) 14, known as the Junk Force, which operated under Captain Hoffmann's task force. CG 14 consisted of from five to nine junks and operated under the Swift Coastal Division. They had about 135 sailors, half of which had river experience and about 50 who were more like Marines, designated as a landing force. Andretta was the direct liaison with the Vietnamese CO of the Junk Force (a counterpart lieutenant). They were stationed at a little outpost at the mouth of the Cua Dai River and worked extensively with the Swift boats. He says of the Swift crews, "Those guys were crazy; they'd go up to where they couldn't even turn around."

---

94. Accounts of the events of March 19–20, 1969, are from information provided by Bob Shirley, a knowledgeable source of Swift history; an interview with Judge Robert Andretta on August 17, 2006; an article from the *Swift Current*, "An Evening on the Cua Dai" by Sonny Barber; and an unpublished article by Bob Andretta, "A Night to Remember."

On the 19th the boats had asked Andretta to give them a river orientation, as the Swifts wanted to step up operations in the Cua Dai waterways. Prior to the run they had visited RF/PF headquarters and the Marine artillery base. For the trip each PCF carried five to six VN sailors whom they had picked up at Hoi An. The VN were instructed to stay in the cabin, unfortunately probably the most dangerous place to ride on the boats.

As the boats approached "ambush corner" at about 1730 hours, Andretta advised the O in C it was likely they would take some fire as they headed down the river. Andretta was at the port side pilothouse door and the O in C was on the starboard side. As the 101 boat slowed to wait for the 58, they passed across a sand bar. At this point, they would have turned west toward CG 14, into the main river channel. The 101 boat dragged bottom, then drifted free. The helmsman, Bill Pfeffer, poured on full throttle and spun the wheel to exit the mouth of the Cua Dai.

Suddenly, there was a flash from the bank and a 75mm recoilless rifle round struck the starboard side above the main deck and detonated in the main cabin. The blast that came through the pilothouse doorway was enormous, and smoke and flames filled the small space. EN2 Ronald L. Wood, on the M-60 in the peak tank, returned fire from the bow. Pfeffer spun the wheel to port but got no response from the steering mechanism. He also pulled back on the throttles but again got no response. Heat and flames seared the hair off Sonny Barber's eyebrows, arms and the front of his head. PCF 101 was in dire straits, heading at flank speed directly toward the south bank and the enemy.

Pfeffer and Barber, amid swirling smoke, exited the pilothouse and headed for the after steering, to get the boat under control. As they raced down the port side a second recoilless round struck the starboard side, forward below the main deck level directly below the pilothouse. The second detonation propelled both men overboard and into four to five feet of water. The blast blew Andretta a good distance from the boat and he also tumbled into the water. Meanwhile the 58 boat raced close aboard to engage the enemy.

Wood emptied his ammo can into the enemy positions, and was attempting to reload when he saw smoke boiling from both pilothouse doors. Under enemy fire, Wood made his way to the after helm and regained control of the boat about 15 feet from where it would have run aground. He managed to get the boat about a half-mile down the river and beached it before it sank completely in the channel. Wood then attended the wounded men, who were unable to move. He helped them get ashore and then went back to the boat, now engulfed in flames, as .50 caliber machine gun bullets cooked off in the white-hot flames burning in the cabin. He found a fire extinguisher and attempted to fight the raging fire. As dusk fell and they were offloading and medevacing injured crew members, they realized that three of the men from the boat were missing in action.

Meanwhile, the men who had gone off the boat stood in chest-deep water watching the action as the boats engaged the enemy. As the boats cleared the area, enemy gunners on the south bank began to focus on the three men in the water, Andretta, Barber and Pfeffer. "Small arms fire crackled and splashes appeared around [us]," Barber relates. "We were like targets in an arcade—nowhere to run or hide."

Barber had a head wound; Pfeffer had a deep cut on his finger, which was broken. Pfeffer had a Ka-bar, but none of the men had side arms. Andretta's flak jacket was smoldering and he got rid of it. Barber dove down and pulled himself along the bottom using the roots of trees and plants on the bottom. "I would come up frequently," he says, "and gasp for air, and the shots would begin again with splashes all around us." While Andretta was underwater he could hear little "zings" of bullets hitting the water and see the bubbly trails of the heavy fire. He soon was nearly beyond his ability to go on—gasping for breath, and unable to stay underwater for any length of time. He finally had to just plow on, "bullets be damned."

The men decided to head downstream to the easternmost island, bypassing Tuan Tinh and Cam Thanh islands, which were enemy held. They then started drawing fire from the north side of the channel on Cam Thanh Island. They got to the shallows, still under small arms fire. Finally they made it to the tip of the island and out of the line of fire. They had been in the water about an hour and fifteen minutes, taking fire for most of that time. It was a miracle they were alive. Barber had been wounded again; this time he had a half dollar sized hole in his left arm. "Blood was dripping down mixed with the muddy river water." As night fell they could hear the Swifts sweeping up and down the main channel laying down an almost constant barrage of fire on the enemy position.

Andretta decided to go around to the side of the channel and try and get the attention of the Swifts. The other two huddled on the riverbank, partly on the bank and partly in the water. After the Swift firing runs an AC-47 *Spooky* (a Puff the Magic Dragon gunship) pounded the enemy area, drawing enemy fire as tracers crossed in the night air. When Andretta didn't return the other two men decided to seek better shelter. They came on a deep depression in the sand, found some vegetation and covered themselves as best they could.

During the night they came under "friendly fire" from a 105 howitzer. They heard the thud of the howitzer, and then the splash of the shell 75 to 100 yards away. Then a second round followed, closer, and a third, all walking across the river toward them. The shells stopped before they reached them. "My heart was pounding so hard I thought anyone within earshot might detect it," Barber says. Also during the night two helicopters crisscrossed the area in an apparent attempt to find the men. The helos left as it got pitch dark, and were replaced by helicopters dropping flares over the area. Swifts also swept the area with their searchlights.

Andretta found a shallow hole about five feet long, two feet wide and a foot or so deep. "I realized how much like a grave was this hole as I settled into it." About 0200 hours, quiet talking and the sounds of movement in the water awakened Andretta. He saw a dozen or so VC in three sampans. He could barely see them, but he could hear their equipment rattling. They came ashore at a bunker that Andretta had earlier rejected as a shelter. They were 15 feet away from him, and he froze, hugging his "grave." He believes they had been sent out to find the sailors, but they seemed nervous with the Swifts and helicopters sweeping the area. The nervous VC settled in and didn't move around, although during the night one of them walked toward Andretta. It sounded like he might step right into the hole; Andretta froze and held his breath. The VC urinated and returned to the others.

Andretta was suffering from one of his usual bouts of dysentery that plagued all the advisors. After swallowing the foul and brackish river water the dysentery came back with a vengeance. Unable to hold it any longer, he let go "with power and with sound which I thought the VC must have heard. Would I finally be captured in this humiliating way? I thought that was the lowest point to which I had ever fallen. I would die in this mess and because of it." He began to quietly cry, and then by sheer force of will got himself back under control.

Later in the night a small pig came rooting around, got into the hole, and discovered the stinking human and went squealing off into the brush. Still, the nervous VC did not investigate. Just before dawn two more Swifts made a firing run on the ambush site—Andretta's night companions, the VC, fired at the Swifts but fortunately the Swifts didn't respond. At about 0530 the VC left in their sampans and Andretta washed up as best he could in the river.

Dawn finally arrived. The two Swifties stood up to signal a friendly outpost and were taken under fire again. They found a log and floated it out to the channel, hoping to flag down a boat. By then Andretta had persuaded a fishing boat to pick him up. They stopped and picked up the other two men as well. The men were so grateful to be picked up they gave the fisherman their watches.

They went by the group of Swifts with their bows on the beach around the 101 boat. It was lying over on one side, burnt black, with debris littering the deck and a huge hole in the side, and what looked like dozens of wooden pegs plugging bullet holes. Finally, 15 hours after they had gone off the boat, they were delivered to CG 14. Their arms and faces were swollen with mosquito bites, but they were alive.

As they arrived on the scene the Swifties greeted them joyfully, after which they were taken to Da Nang for medical treatment, a shower and clean clothes. Pfeffer had to have his wedding band cut off to treat the swollen finger. The Swifties were sent out the next day on patrol to relieve the 24 boat, which had been hit by two recoilless rifle rounds while patrolling with PCF 99.

On September 8, 1969, Engineman Second Class Ronald L. Wood was awarded the Silver Star for his heroism on March 19. Bob Andretta continued his outstanding tour of duty in Vietnam after the incident. "I was put in for a Silver Star and didn't get it, and I thought I'd done a lot more for mine than Kerry did for his." Andretta also got a third Purple Heart and turned it down so he could continue with Coastal Group 14. Typically, three weeks later the Navy transferred him to CG 13, where he didn't want to be.

During his tour in Vietnam, while on a skimmer during a firefight, Andretta was shot through his right leg and the bullet continued on to strike his left leg. His thigh swelled up horribly over the next couple of days. Doctors decided to leave the bullet in his left leg. Two years later the bullet hole became badly infected and the bullet oozed out.

ON MARCH 23 THE *Point Orient's* small boat, while boarding three sampans, came under heavy automatic weapons fire from the beach. Chief Engineman Morris S. Beeson was hit and died instantly. The Coast Guard men returned fire and suppressed the fire from the beach.

ON MARCH 25, 1969, Terry Costello turned PCF 38 over to Ensign Williams. Costello was getting short and "I had no desire to stretch my luck any further." However, Captain Hoffmann, who was down for a major operation, requested he go with him because he needed Costello's experience.

"What do you want me to do?" Costello asked.

"Just be here," Hoffmann replied.

Both Hoffmann and Costello ended up going into the Cua Lon, probing a couple of canals. Costello, an excellent naval officer, still thought, "This is no man's land and we shouldn't even be in here. We have no support, I'm short, and I don't need this."

Hoffmann was asking questions about operations. After the boats cleared the area he decided they needed to see the area from the air. They got in an Army *Loach*, a small observation helicopter, flown by, Costello says, "an Army warrant officer that looked like he was about 16. My pre-flight brief was, 'If you're sitting in the back don't worry if we go down because the blades will go through there and kill you." Costello, who had never been in a helicopter, thought, "I don't want to do this."

The helo pilot spent most of the time over the jungle at the same elevation as a Swift boat pilothouse. "I'm thinking, 'we're going to hit a fish stake and die.'" They flew up and down the rivers and canals in the enemy held area, checking out areas for future operations.

TEDD PECK, THE SKIPPER of PCF 94 eventually ended up at St. Albans Naval Hospital for treatment of the terrible wounds he suffered on January 29, 1969. Peck says he was "horrified" when he learned PCF 94 and his crew had been turned over to John Kerry. Still in pain and suffering from his wounds, he was stunned in early April to see John Kerry, back from Vietnam eight months early, jauntily pop into his hospital room in dress whites and an attaché cord.

Peck asked him what he was doing back in the States. Kerry told him that "the Navy" had decided it was time for him to come home. He was visiting the wounded as an admiral's aide. Then astoundingly, Kerry tried to recruit Peck for the radical Vietnam Veterans Against the War (VVAW), which Kerry said was a group he had helped organize.

Peck asked, "John, how can you do this? All of our guys are still over there in Vietnam." Kerry had no answer.[95]

ON APRIL 4, 1969, Commander Paul A. Yost, who would be the OTC for the bloody events to follow in the Duong Keo, relieved Commander Adrian L. Lonsdale as Commander, Gulf of Thailand Surveillance Group and Senior

---

95. O'Neill and Corsi, *Unfit for Command*, p. 95.

Naval Advisor, 4th Coastal Zone.[96] The Change of Command Ceremony was held at An Thoi, and Lonsdale's speech is worth noting:

> When I arrived, Market Time was in a static defensive position. It had long before accomplished its mission of preventing sea infiltration. The Viet Cong controlled most of the coastline. Our new Task Force Commander [Captain Roy Hoffmann] changed all that. He removed the tight restrictions on gunfire missions and river intrusions. He demanded enforcement of restricted areas denying the enemy their livelihood. The rigid enforcement coupled with increased gunfire moved the enemy inland. The Captain encouraged us to go after them. The first significant ventures into the previously forbidden rivers were by lone Aces; among them Lieutenants Bernique and Brown. They proved that the VC were not invincible. Nothing was the same after that. When I came here two months after Tet last year, the populace of the Fourth Coastal Zone was huddled within the confines of the defensive perimeters of their cities and towns. The VC freely crossed the border northeast of Ha Tien, they occupied the coastline from Ha Tien to Rach Gia, there was little traffic from Rach Gia eastward, and to the south, places like Cai Nuoc came under regular VC attacks. The Nam Cau District was 100 per cent controlled [by the enemy]. But our new Admiral [Zumwalt] changed all of that [with operation SEALORDS]. The results have been spectacular. There is now little or no infiltration northeast of Ha Tien; Cai Nuoc, which until last December was considered constantly in jeopardy of being over run, is now considered safe from enemy threat; and our boats now rove freely through the Nam Can District. And as for the officers and men of the U.S. Navy and Coast Guard who served under me, I have nothing but the highest respect and admiration. Their professionalism, courage, and endurance, in my view match that of any of our country's heroes. Their days have been long ones, their living conditions harsh, and their missions have been filled with tension and terror. Almost always their battles have been fought with an unseen enemy whose rockets and weapons fire can hit at any moment or place. But our men, in all cases have withstood the test and to them belongs the credit for our successes.

APRIL 5–6 THOUSANDS of antiwar demonstrators marched in New York City to Central Park, demanding the United States withdraw from Vietnam. The weekend of protests ended with demonstrations and parades in San Francisco, Los Angeles, Washington, D.C., and other cities. On April 9 the

---

96. Admiral Paul A. Yost, USCG (ret.), had a long and distinguished USCG career, including a stint as Commandant of the Coast Guard from 1986 to 1990. He graduated from the Coast Guard Academy in 1951, and commanded the cutters *Agassiz* (WSC 126) and *Resolute* (WMEC 620). He was in Vietnam as part of the naval command structure from 1969–1970, and commanded the Sea Float facility in the Ca Mau.

Chicago Eight, indicted on March 20 of federal charges of conspiracy to incite riot at the 1968 Democratic convention in Chicago, pled not guilty.

A Gallup poll reported that three out of every five people expressing an opinion on the Vietnam War backed President Nixon. On April 10, police forced students out of University Hall at Harvard University, where a mass strike protested Harvard's ties to the national security and military apparatus. The next day, Senators Frank Church and John Sherman Cooper proposed an amendment forbidding the funding of American Ground operations in Cambodia, Thailand or Laos.

April 12, 1969: The Rach Duong Keo and the Destruction of PCF 43

USCG Commander Paul Yost was the new commander of Task Group 115.4 and was the OTC of the Duong Keo operation. He relates in the article "Hard Day on the Bo De [sic]":

> My boss in the operation was . . . Roy Hoffmann. He was very hands on. He knew everything going on in his command, and he was a night owl. Hoffmann would call all of his four commanders . . . at about 2300, sometimes later, to get a report for the day. He was a taskmaster. He was very tough. And he wanted to know everything that was happening.

The command ship for the operation was the USS *Westchester County* (LST 1167). This was Paul Yost's first big operation. When he got aboard the LST he received a message that Hoffmann was coming to the *Westchester County* to observe the operation. Yost hoped to remain as OTC, which turned out not to be a problem since Roy Hoffmann had already been ordered to stay off the boats by Admiral Zumwalt.

Hoffmann had ridden the boats almost up to the events of April 12, but Zumwalt finally concluded they were too dangerous, and Zumwalt did not want to lose his task force commander, whom he hoped to convince to extend his tour. (Hoffmann told him he wouldn't extend—if he did he wouldn't have a family. He had back to back long deployments and been gone from home almost the better part of two years).

Hoffmann now says of switching from the boats to flying over in attack helicopters, "I would not disobey a direct order, but if I could circumvent it . . ."

The USS Westchester County (LST 1167), with Swift boats tied alongside. These workhorse ships provided support for the Swifts working the inland waterways of South Vietnam. Hoffmann photo

The operation started on April 11, in a river north of the Duong Keo. After the day operations, the boats beached for the night, half on one side of the river and half on the other. Bill Shumadine beached his 5 boat with Rich McCann's 21 boat beside him. Yost was on the other side of McCann, on Skip Barker's 31 boat. They beached on a mud flat as the tides were going out. The experienced Shumadine stepped across to Yost's boat. "What's the plan tomorrow?" he asked.

Yost replied, "We're going to get underway at dawn, we're going back out the river to the coast, and then down to the Rach Duong Keo south of here."

Shumadine asked, "You said we're going to go at dawn? Look right now at what time it is. It's 6:30 or 7:00 in the evening, we just had dinner and we're sitting on the mud. The tides are going to be high at midnight and we'll be back on the bottom at dawn."

Yost said he had tide charts, and his quartermaster had assured him they'd have enough water to get underway in the morning.

Shumadine said, "We're dealing with big forces here Commodore. It's the same the world over. I've been in these rivers, the tides come and go and you can't change that. We're going to be sitting here on the mud in the morning."

Yost told him they'd be able to get underway, that was the plan, and it was all coordinated. During the night the men got eaten alive by biting ants assaulting the boats from overhanging branches. The men couldn't sleep, and were tired in the morning.

"Early next morning," David Hemenway relates, "the tide had gone out—we're high and dry—beached." It was after 10:00 A.M. before they could get enough water under the boats to get underway. Shumadine thought, "Oh, this is a great start."

"That," he says, "was the start of that horrible day. Everything was late, everything was rushed, and everything was off track."[97] After the boats had enough water to get underway they rendezvoused at the LST.

Terry Costello was on the LST. Hoffmann had asked him to assist in CIC and help monitor the operations. Costello played gin with Don Droz ("He beat me") right before they loaded his 43 boat with UDT and explosives. Droz had said, "Well, I gotta go."

Don Droz had just come back from R & R, and had just arrived from An Thoi. Bill Shumadine says that when Droz had come back from R & R he asked him, "Don, how was it?"

Droz replied, "I just left the two most beautiful girls in the world [his wife and daughter]." Droz could hardly wait to get back to them. Shumadine says, "I'll never forget him saying that."[98] Droz had just received orders to be the NROTC instructor at Dartmouth, orders he was proud of.

Hoffmann says, "I didn't know Droz personally, but I knew who he was, because he had a good reputation. He was a fighter, respected by everyone. Everything I knew about him was positive." His twin .50s gunner, Robert Hornberger, says that Droz never complained about the war to the crew. "If he got orders, he followed them," he says.

There are many questions from the Duong Keo operation; one was whether the 43 could turn up enough rpms that day to stay with the other boats, and had fallen behind in the river as a result. Roy Hoffmann had

---

97. Shumadine now questions the decision to let Yost, who had been in country only a few days, run the mission. Yost had no idea how Swift boats operated. He thought, "This is crazy, letting him run the show. That appalled me. Yost was willing to listen, he was just inexperienced." Yost had just replaced Adrian Lonsdale, the experienced man. Bill Shumadine had far more experience. Admiral Zumwalt had just ordered another officer with excellent tactical experience and judgement, Roy Hoffmann, off the boats.

98. "Don had been a buddy," Shumadine says. "We were the only two married guys in our class at Coronado. Don married Judy, my wife's name is Judy, she was pregnant with her first child, and my wife was pregnant with our first child; we had common things."

Bringing them back aboard. Official U.S. Navy photo, Hoffmann collection

a policy that boats had to be able to turn up 2,000 rpms, so as to not be a danger to themselves and the other boats by slowing the column down. Hoffmann says he had a discussion with Droz before the operation, where he ordered him to offload his C-4 and the UDT personnel at the Special Forces base at the mouth of the river, because the 43 boat was not turning up sufficient rpms.

Virgil Erwin supports Roy Hoffmann's version of the conversation. He said the 43 boat was " . . . tired, needing repair, not scheduled for this river incursion." Erwin goes on to relate that, ". . . Don is arguing with Captain Hoffmann that his Swift boat is OK. This is a big operation and I know Don doesn't want to be left behind. 'All right . . . you can go,' I hear Captain Hoffmann tell Don. 'But you drop the Demolition Team at the first insertion point and then you get the hell out of that river. Is that understood.'"

For reasons that will probably never be known, Don Droz chose to ignore those orders and was in the process of catching up with the column as the firefight ensued. The 43 boat survivors this author interviewed did not indicate the boat had any engine problems.

Another question is whether Don Droz was ordered into the river against his will, particularly since his boat was a late arrival. Roy Hoffmann remembers Droz talking to him and telling him he wanted to go on the operation. Shumadine says of the two versions, that Droz was forced to go, or he wanted to go, the latter rings true. Shumadine believes that Droz would have wanted to be in the river because that's where his buddies were. "That sounds like Don. He would not have wanted to be held back. He's got all this stuff they need in the river, 'let me take it to them,' is how he would have felt. It was not because he loved the war. He was very much ready for it to be over so he could go home." Had the boats not been stranded the previous night when the tide went out, and had the operation started in the early morning as planned, the 43 boat might not have been on the operation at all.

The 43 boat crew consisted of Lieutenant j.g. Don Droz, BM2 Wayne D. Langhofer, RD2 Stephen A. Miller, RD3 Michael S. Modansky, EN2 Lloyd Jones, and GMG2 Robert Hornberger. It was an experienced crew.

Robert Hornberger, whom we previously encountered on Mike Bernique's crew, had volunteered to go back to An Thoi on the 43 boat.[99] Mike Modansky, who is Jewish, was born in Brooklyn, New York, and went to high school in a suburb of Long Island called Jericho. He spent two years at Bowling Green University in Ohio before enlisting in the Navy.

His father was in the Eighth Air Force, 94th Bombing Division during World War II, flying missions over Germany from Cambridge, England.

---

99. The operation on the Rach Duong Keo of April 12 is one of the most extensively documented, yet confusing operations Swift boats engaged in during their time in Vietnam. This author, who was not on the operation that day, has relied on several sources to put together an account of the two-day operation. A good starting point for the day is Robert B. Shirley's excellent Web site "Operation Silver Mace II April 12, 1969 Duong Keo River, Vietnam" (http://pcf45.com/SEALORDS/silvermace/silvermace.html). There also is a tape of the radio transmissions that day, which starts basically when the lead boats are beached after the firefight and right as the Seawolves are passing the coastline. Terry Symmes did the tape transcription for this book. Additional sources were interviews conducted with Terry Costello, October 11, 2005; David Hemenway, March 19, 2007; Roy F. Hoffmann, December 28, 2005; Robert Hornberger, February 10, 2007; Mike Modansky, March 27–28, 2007; Pat Sheedy, August 21, 2006; Bill Shumadine, January 25, 2007, and Jack Chenoweth, April 5, 2007. There was an oral history done of the incident during the 2007 Swift Boat Sailors Association reunion in San Diego. Participants included Virgil A. Erwin III, Lawrence Hortt, Michael Lohnes and William Miller. Virgil Erwin has provided to this author an article covering the events from the first drop-off point, "Death of a Swift Boat." Additionally this author consulted Cutler, *Brown Water Black Beret*, pp. 308–309; and Admiral Paul A. Yost, Jr., USCG, Ret., "Swift Boats: Hard Day on the Bo De [sic]," *Naval Institute Proceedings*, October, 2004.

He was the lead navigator in a B-17 *Flying Fortress* and flew over 50 missions, receiving five Distinguished Flying Crosses. Like his father, Modansky had intended to enlist in the Air Force, but there were no parking places in front of the Air Force recruiters, so he went a little farther up the street to the Navy, which had a place to park. He enlisted, and the recruiter assured him that with two years of college he could have his pick of rates. Modansky told him, "Anything but electronics." Of course, he ended up in radar, which had a high electronic component.

He was ordered to the aircraft carrier USS *Ticonderoga* (CVA 14), and made two Far East Cruises to Vietnam from 1966-1968. One day after the second cruise he was standing with a group of his fellow radarmen, complaining about the coffee, when Les Garrett came in and asked, "Did you guys see what's on the bulletin board outside CIC?" They looked, and it was a notice asking for volunteers for Swift boats in Vietnam. The Navy was only looking for five ratings, radar being one. Six of the radarman on the ship volunteered for Vietnam, including Modansky, this author, Les Garrett, Mike "Mugsy" Montgomery and two others. The orders to go came in almost immediately.

When he got to Coronado he was informed he was too heavy to go through the school (the result of long days at sea and eating all the starchy food on the carrier). Modansky ate cabbage for three weeks, took off 20 pounds, and started Swift training. He was sent to Qui Nhon initially, after which he was assigned to duty on PCF 43.

At about 1720 on April 12, 12 Swifts entered the Rach Duong Keo, each heavily loaded with approximately 23 Sixth Battalion Vietnamese Marines with equipment and supplies for a five-day operation. The 13th boat, PCF 43, had a ten man UDT aboard, with 1,000 pounds of explosives. Just past the pre-planned Objective 20, at coordinates WQ010500, the first five boats, PCFs 23 (O in C Ensign Steve Carroll), 67 (O in C Lieutenant j.g. Virgil Erwin), 93 (O in C Jack Chenoweth, whom we encountered in the mining of PCF 3), 94 and 103 (O in C Chuck Mohn), beached on the left bank and inserted their troops. The remaining eight boats proceeded up the river to insert their troops at a point to be determined by the OTC, Commander Yost, and the Vietnamese Company Commander and his U.S. Marine advisors.

The plan was to box the enemy in on two sides with troops, with the Swifts blocking escape from the river and the Seawolves closing the backdoor. Yost later claimed that he called the ship and asked that the helicop-

SEALORDS forces patrolling the serpentine waterways of the Mekong Delta.
Hoffmann photo

ters be launched, but Hoffmann held them back. Roy Hoffmann has no recollection of the radio transmission, and it's doubtful it occurred. The tape recording of the day starts after this point, so it's impossible to tell what actually happened. The helos were on standby on the LST to assist the boats if they got in trouble, and Hoffmann would have been concerned an early launch of the Seawolves would have left them too short of fuel to give the boats and troops support if they ran into trouble (they could only be in the air for 45 minutes with their fuel load under combat conditions).

At coordinates WQ045545, at about 1734 hours, two Viet Cong companies hit the eight Swifts from both banks with claymore mines, 75mm recoilless rifle fire, B-40 rockets, .30 and .51 caliber machine guns and automatic weapons fire. David Robert Hemenway was driving the lead 5 boat, and he relates they were hit at a point in the river where it made a right, 45 degree bend, where fish stakes came out from the shore about half way into the river. PCFs 5 and 21 were blasted with several claymore mines, and small arms fire; PCF 21 was hit on the port quarter aft just below the main deck with a B-40 rocket. Shumadine says, "All of a sudden I thought I had hit an ammunition dump because a huge explosion went off on the port side of the boat." The men on the following boat, PCF 21, later told Shumadine, "We thought you guys had been destroyed," as the 5 boat disappeared in smoke. The after gunner on the 5 boat was seriously wounded, and one VN Marine was killed instantly and four other VN Marines were seriously wounded on the boat. The object of the enemy had been to knock out the lead boat so the following boats would pile up behind, leaving them exposed in the river. Instead, all boats hit full throttle.

The next three boats through, PCFs 45, 9, and 31 were raked with gunfire; the forward gunners on both PCFs 9 and 45 were seriously wounded, but stayed at their stations until the boats were clear of the ambush. One of the Vietnamese Marines on PCF 45 was also seriously wounded. The 45 boat took a B-40 rocket in the gun tub; twin .50s gunner Lawrence Hortt passed out twice but kept firing. Yost says, "I thought the end of the world had come—B-40 rockets were exploding . . . all nine [sic] boats had their .50 calibers chattering . . . everybody who had a weapon was firing at something."

The twin .50s gunner on Yost's boat was wearing a flak jacket and flak pants, but a bullet went through the gun tub and hit him in the gut in the four-inch gap between the flak jacket and pants. He slid out of the gun tub, unconscious, with blood pouring out of his wound.

PCF 51 was rocked by automatic weapons fire and was also hit by two B-40 rockets, which blew out all of the main cabin windows. One of the rockets hit five inches above the waterline on the port side, knocking out the port engine. QM3 Thomas Holloway was killed by a single gunshot wound. The 51 boat exited the kill zone on one engine, which overheated and also became disabled.

As the 43 boat entered the kill zone it was hit with a claymore mine, a 75mm recoilless rifle round and three B-40 rockets. Lieutenant j.g. Don Droz was killed in the initial barrage, along with 35-year-old HMC Robert Worthington of UDT Team 13. He took a B-40 rocket to the stomach. Two other members of the UDT team were seriously wounded in the initial attack. The crippled boat, with steering out, didn't make the turn and instead ran at full throttle almost straight up on the muddy bank dead ahead and than canted to the right.

Robert Hornberger, the twin .50s gunner, had yelled at the men on the stern to man the after conning station after the hits, but all the steering was out. Hornberger says of the rocket strike in the pilothouse:

> I heard a bang when it went off, I saw all this smoke; you could hardly see anything. I got sprayed with shrapnel and felt my leg—I was afraid it had been blown off. I felt down and I had holes in my pants and a little bit of blood. I looked down and Don Droz was lying there with his head up, facing me. I couldn't see his eyes at all.

Hornberger believes Droz died instantly. He later went down into the pilothouse and checked on the helmsman, whose face was bloody—he was unconscious. Hornberger remembers hitting the bank. He says, "It happened so fast. If the boat had turned the opposite way we'd all be dead. We're getting all kinds of fire."

Terry Costello's old boat, PCF 38, sprayed by small arms and heavy machine gun fire, turned back to assist the 43 boat. The 38 boat then received two B-40 rockets in the pilothouse and cabin area, seriously wounding the O in C, Ensign Williams. The hits disabled the pilothouse steering and the port engine. Williams, despite serious wounds to his left leg and loss of hearing from the blast, regained control of the boat from the after steering station. The boat then fought through the kill zone and joined the other boats.

A Chief Warrant Officer with the UDT team on the 43 boat remembered, "I was on the 43 when she got hit. I remembered the 38 trying to get back to us and getting hurt so badly that she had to turn back."

Yost radioed Shumadine and told him to keep going until he found a clearing for medevacs. The remaining seven damaged boats cleared the kill zone and transited upstream another couple of miles and beached at coordinates WQ058558 on orders of the OTC. The Swifts beached on either side of the river, odd numbered boats to the right and even numbered boats to the left. PCF 38 tried to inform the OTC by radio of the 43 boat's dire circumstances, but there was confusion as to which boat it was and where it was located. Virg Erwin, monitoring the radio transmissions, heard the 43 boat trying faintly to break through. "No one is responding to this call," he says. "Christ, am I the only one that can hear this?"

The Seawolves, from Helicopter Attack (Light) Squadron Three, Detachment One, were on the deck of the LST, at the ready with the engines warmed up. Roy Hoffmann relates, "The next thing I hear is there's a firefight going on with the main group. That's when I jumped in the Seawolf 16." The two helos were Seawolf 14, piloted by Lieutenant Commander Don Hartman, and Seawolf 16, piloted by Lieutenant j.g. Bill Wallen. They would prove more than courageous, making firing run after firing run against the enemy positions.

Bill Shumadine says there was a lot of confusion as to how many boats were in the river. They initially thought there were only 12 boats, which meant that all were accounted for. As Shumadine says, "I didn't want to go back into the kill zone unless I was sure there was another boat back there in distress. We'd go back in a heart beat if someone's in there."

Yost (call sign Dipsy Doodle) began to ask for casualty assessments from the boats, not all of which were in radio contact.[100] PCF 21 responded [all quotes from the radio tape transcript in italics]: *This is 21. I say again, I've got one KIA Victor November November* [Vietnamese Navy] *type. I've got one Uniform Sierra* [U.S.] *type needs medevac. I've got five Uniform Sierra types with slight shrapnel wounds, I've got three Victor November November types with slight shrapnel wounds. Over.*

Shumadine reported that one of the Vietnamese Marines on his boat had lost both legs and the Swift crew had put tourniquets on the stumps. One of the Vietnamese had his head blown off; there was just the trunk of his body left.

Seawolf: *I'm off this time. I'm just passing the coast now. We're going up the upper edge.*

Yost: *Seawolf, I need a medevac. I'm at 058558. I have seven boats with me on the port and starboard banks. Are you in my area? Over.* Yost's radio transmission indicates the confusion of the day. There were seven boats with him; the eighth, the 43 boat, was in dire straits behind them.

Seawolf: *It's* [your area] *coming up now.*

---

100. These sometimes silly call signs were created in part to make it hard for the enemy to pronounce the words if they transmitted false messages from their own radios. "I've heard them try," Virg Erwin says. "They struggle, saying things like 'Brack Widow Spryder.' It helps to hear the enemy's voice, helps make them seem almost human."

Attending to a wounded South Vietnamese soldier on the stern of a Swift boat.
HOFFMANN PHOTO

Yost: *On the port bank, on the port bank. You take a look at it and see if that little clearing right ahead of the boat furtherist is large enough. If not, maybe we can make a pickup off the boats. Over.*

Seawolf: *I don't think I can. I'll have to expend in order to pick up anybody, over.*

Yost: *Hafta do—we want to pick up as soon as you can make it, over.*

Dipsy Doodle, Seawolf 16, how many medevacs do you have?

This is Dipsy Doodle, it looks like I'm gonna have, uh, six or seven all together here, six or seven all together.

There was a brief discussion about where to expend the rockets. A couple of times on the tape a faint transmission from the 43 boat may be heard, trying to break through. The 103 boat, back with the first group, tried to come on the line: *Dipsy Doodle, this is 103, I'd recommend those rockets be . . .* The 67 boat and 103 boat had gotten underway to assist the 43 boat. Virg Erwin says, "I'm scared, knowing we are heading into certain hell."

Meanwhile, the Seawolves, now aware of the 43, circled back down river and came on the scene of the 43 boat. They immediately came under heavy enemy small arms fire. "I looked down," Hoffmann says, " and saw the 43 boat laying over on its starboard side. I could see smoke coming out the exhaust. I thought, 'What the hell is this? How did they get up on the beach?'" The Seawolves reported back to Yost that the 43 boat was about one mile from his position.

Yost: *The 43 boat is disabled one-mile back, did you say? Over.*

Seawolf: *43 is high and dry, one-mile back. I see, uh, one of your Swift boats is firing like mad. Can I unload in that general area?*

Yost: *[Provide] air cover while we send someone back to get her. Over. Seawolf, this is Dipsy Doodle, did you get my last, over?*

Negative.

Seawolf, I have my 43 boat one mile from the bank in the river [firing and helicopter noise] *high and dry disabled. I will send somebody back to tow him to my position—require you provide air cover, over.*

I'm over him now.

Dipsy Doodle, Seawolf 16, we have 43 in sight and we're opening fire around his position this time [noise, shooting].

Seawolf 16 made the first firing run, then 14 made a firing run, laying down a barrage of M-60 machine gun fire and 2.75 inch rockets into the enemy positions, providing relief for the men of the stricken 43 boat, who had taken cover in the water and alongside the boat. The Seawolves came under attack at point blank range from .51 caliber machine guns. Captain Hoffmann, in the face of this point blank fire, calmly passed information, and instructions, when asked, to the OTC.[101]

Seawolves: *They are shooting in all directions. 14, this is 16, continue straight ahead and you'll come right to* [unintelligible, sounds of firing, helicopter] *they're firing at us at this time . . . 14, we just received fire . . . no troops, no troops in area.*

16, 14

16 go ahead.

Do you see our green smoke down there at 3:00 o'clock?

Yep.

Roger, we received fire out of there.

OK, that's green smoke; let's hose it down.

Roger.

Hose it down where the green smoke is [gunfire]. *OK, right where the smoke was, let's hose that area down.*

We're taking fire!

Circle in for the rocket strike in here?

Right about heading 240.

Meanwhile, Yost wanted the downriver Swifts to insert their troops below the ambush site. *67, this is Dipsy Doodle, over . . . and 103, go back, get your troops, bring 'em up and insert 'em just short of the ambush and let 'em sweep up* [gunfire].

This is 67, roger that.

Ordered back to pick up their troops, the 67 and 103 boats turned around in the river. As was Jack Chenoweth, Erwin was haunted by the event. "We've been ordered *not* to dive into this maelstrom of death. God help me, I am willingly accepting an order that should be ignored."

Latch: *Relay to Dipsy Doodle, pick up troops and take 'em to ambush area and insert 'em and let 'em work up* [gunfire and helicopter noise].

Seawolf: *Receiving fire! Receiving fire!*

Roger, lay it on them.

---

101. For Captain Hoffmann's actions that day he was awarded a Gold Star in lieu of a Third Bronze Star Medal with Combat "V." The descriptions of his actions are taken from the citation. The award states: "His coolness and courage in the face of enemy fire were instrumental in extracting the crew of Inshore Patrol Craft 43 from the 'kill zone.' Captain Hoffmann's outstanding professionalism, sense of responsibility and courage under fire were in keeping with the highest traditions of the United States Naval Service."

A cacophony of sound, shooting, noise, helicopters and overlapping communications followed.

Meanwhile, the crew of the 43 boat was in desperate straits. "We're getting all kinds of fire," Hornberger says. He opened up with the .50s, but because of the elevation he couldn't fire on the port side. He swung the guns around and opened up on the bank opposite the boat. When he ran out of .50-caliber ammunition he grabbed the M-16 the twin .50s gunners always kept close. "But when I did, a VC fired at me, the bullet hit the gun tub, ricocheted, hit the stock of the M-16 and it went flying out of my hands. Langhofer saw the VC and shot him."

Since Hornberger was weaponless he climbed out of the gun tub, grabbed another M-16 and jumped in the water. As he attempted to fire the gun he realized it was jammed. Langhofer threw him another M-16, which worked. Eventually there were three of them in the water, two firing and one loading clips. They fired on the opposite bank while the men behind the boat (including Modansky) returned fire on the VC moving in on the port side of the boat. The men behind the boat were exposed from the starboard side but the men in the water covered for them. Hornberger says the helos probably saved their lives.

Modansky, the M-60 gunner on the bow, remembers, "I was firing in every direction because I had no idea where the bullets were coming from." He was seriously wounded in the attack, but still managed to throw his M-60 over the side with belts of ammunition, and take a position behind the boat, returning enemy fire.

At the medevac site, Shumadine wanted to get the troops off the boats to set up a defensive perimeter, because he was concerned they could have beached at another enemy position. But the troops wouldn't move. "They were in shock," Shumadine says. "They didn't return fire the whole time we were going through the kill zone. They were hunkered down, scared." Shumadine took them by their backpacks and physically threw them off the bow. "I got their attention and they got off the boat."

Shumadine then heard the following transmission from Yost: *21, 21, this is Dipsy Doodle, over.*

This is 21, over.

21, the 43 boat [is] back about one klick. I've got the Seawolf overhead providing cover. He [the 43 boat] got through the ambush all right, but he is disabled on the bank. Take yourself and 5 and go back and bring him—tow him up to this direction, over.

This is 5 [Shumadine]. I'm taking a com guard for 21. He has negative communications of any sort. We both have too many wounded to take off. You'll have to send someone else, over. The crew of the 5 boat was plugging the many bullet holes in the boat with wooden pegs, breaking out more ammunition, and "licking their wounds."

5, Dipsy Doodle, are you being able to get the casualties together over there, over?

This is 5. We have . . . ambulatory cases that we need stretchers [for]. We have to have stretchers. I cannot take anyone off of 5 and put them on 21. 21 can do that. However, 21 has lost all com.

Seawolf: Receiving fire, receiving fire . . . way the hell out there.

We're still taking fire 14.

103, Dipsy Doodle.

This is 103, roger; we have five boats down here [noise, unintelligible] can get 43 out with beau coup protection, over.

Yost: You can get 43 out with beau coup protection? Over. You can get 43 out, is that true, over?

I don't know, but we're down here just north of 20 at this time... At this point the 103 boat requested permission to go after the 43.

Yost: I concur, but I'm not sure that I want . . . you to come through the ambush. I'm going to see if we can get him from this end, over.

103, roger, out.[102]

The lack of a relief effort for the 43 boat got to Shumadine: "I finally got frustrated, got on the radio and told Yost 'I'm going back up the river. Please advise.'"

Yost: 5, standby, I don't want you to go by yourself . . . 5, standby.

Meanwhile, the 67 and 103 boats had gone back to the insertion point, where the Vietnamese Marines were sitting in a circle, calming eating rice from a bowl with chopsticks. They ignored the O in Cs frantic appeals to get them aboard. Erwin spotted an American Marine and yelled, "Get these assholes aboard my boat! Now! There's been an ambush!"

---

102. It is very easy to criticize decisions made under the stress of heavy combat, but often not fair. Yost could be fairly criticized for not sending the five undamaged downriver boats back into the kill zone to rescue the 43 boat. Probably he was concerned about more heavy casualties in what was an intense ambush. His decision to go back himself speaks well of him personally, but it was not necessarily the best command decision. He was really only considering the resources immediately available to him. According to Jack Chenoweth, the five downstream boats wanted to go up to the 43 boat, and he remains frustrated today that they were not allowed to do so.

"They won't move," he yelled back. "Not without direct orders from their senior officer. He's up river with Yost."

As Erwin now says, "Five fully functional Swift boats sit useless. One hundred Marines sit eating lunch. All of us sit without direction while the crew of the 43 boat is fighting to stay alive."

The OTC made the decision to attempt the rescue of PCF 43's personnel with PCFs 5 and 31 (O in C Skip Barker, with Yost aboard). Yost commendably later said of his decision to go back himself, "If you can't lead them [back to the 43 boat] don't do it."

Yost asked for another twin .50 gunner from an adjacent boat and they took the wounded gunner off the 31 boat.

Shumadine's boat was on the other side of the river. Hemenway was tending to the wounded on the back of the boat when Shumadine came up to him and said, "We have to go back." Hemenway thought, "Wow, really."

Shumadine backed his boat off the bank and idled in the middle of the river, then started downstream. Yost came on and said, "Hold on, we are coming." As they transited the river they passed the 9 boat which was all shot up; the O in C was laying on the deck with his foot shot off. The 9 boat had lost steering and the crew was trying to navigate up the river on emergency tiller and one engine. Shumadine thought initially that might have been the last boat in line, but of course it wasn't.

The 5 boat then led the way back to the kill zone, ahead of the 31, which then arrived on the scene. The Seawolves were still overhead and Yost relates that the engines on the 43 boat were still running at full speed, and the screws were still chopping water. Shumadine says they came around the bend, "and there is the disgusting, ugly sight, a boat high and dry out of the water, taking fire. Most of the crew were off the boat and behind it, some in the knee-deep water. The VC in the bunkers on both banks were still firing at them."

The Chief Warrant UDT Officer on the 43 boat said, "I . . . remember the . . . boats coming back into the kill zone to get us. We were out of bullets and about to swim for it. You guys saved my ass—Thanks."

Hornberger says, "I was just trying to stay alive. I could see the bullets hitting the water. I don't know how long we were there fighting it out." By the time the 31 boat got them out of the water the fire was pretty well suppressed.

The two Swifts opened up on the VC. Yost initially told Shumadine to try and pull the 43 boat off the bank, while the 31 boat covered him. Shumadine thought, "I don't have a tug boat, I don't have the capability of a big fat, power screw, I've got a speed screw. There's no pulling power, the aluminum cleats pull out easily, there's no way I'm getting that boat off the bank."

Still under fire, Shumadine pulled his boat in close and lassoed the starboard aft quarter bit and pulled away. The nylon rope stretched to the snapping point and the boat didn't budge. Shumadine gave up the effort, and carefully backed down so the rope didn't get fouled in the screws. He put the bow up to the stern of the 43 boat and jumped over to retrieve the line. He then saw the big corpsman who had taken a B-40 round in his gut. "We need to get him off," he told his crew. Shumadine says, "He was opened and coming apart." They got him over to the boat and covered him with a blanket.

Yost's boat pulled up to the bank and got the men in the water and the two still firing from the boat. "Get aboard! Get aboard!" Yost yelled, but the men on the 43 said, "You've got to take our skipper." There were 12 seriously wounded men on the 43 boat and two KIAs aboard. The 31 boat got all but the corpsman aboard.

Shumadine then went back to the cabin of the 43 boat to retrieve classified materials. While he was in the cabin his crew shouted at him, "The other boat is leaving!" Shumadine returned to his boat and joined the 31 boat. He says now, "I was looking for Dinky Dau [Don Droz]. I asked my crew, 'Where is he?'"

His crew pointed over to Barker's boat. "Look on the bow," they said.

Shumadine said, "I don't see him." He looked and saw people hunched down, he looked at the faces and didn't see his friend Don Droz. "I don't see him," he said again.

His crew replied, "On the bow—look at the shoes."

Shumadine said, "The shoes?" and then he saw brown shoes sticking out from under a blanket. "He always wore those brown shoes," Shumadine says. He thought, "Oh my God, it's Don—they got him. It's one thing when somebody dies and you don't know them, but when it's a friend it's hard to take. It was a tough thing to handle."

The 5 and 31 boats returned to the medevac area with the wounded and dead. After they had placed them in the medevac area, Yost radioed, *PCF 5 and PCF 9, take on the troops over there. Take on all the Marines on that bank right now, over. 9 and 5 acknowledge.*

5 roger.

9 roger.

Yost: *Okay, take on all the troops and we're gonna insert the troops down just* short of the 43 boat, and have them go ashore and sweep down on the 43 and put a circle around it, over.

5, roger, out.

9, roger, out.

This is Seawolf 16, the boat is on fire right now. The boat is on fire.

Yost: Understand the boat is on fire at this time. Is that affirmative?

Seawolf: That's affirmative the boat is on fire.

Yost: Seawolf, the boat has demolition.

Dipsy Doodle, this is Latch, over.

This is Dipsy Doodle, over.

Latch: All right, the boat is now fully aflame. I think it's too late to do much about it. It may be too dangerous [to put a perimeter around it]. I think you better call it off. It's about to go up.

Yost: Latch, I concur. Uh, I'm intending now to wait until the sun goes down and I get my medevac off. I'll be towing one boat from my location and make a run through and come on out. Do you concur, over?

Latch: Negative, I do not concur. You've got those troops unprotected. You better discuss this with the ground commander on this side, over.

Dipsy Doodle, this is 103, do you desire that 67 and 103 proceed to disabled boat, over?

Negative 67 and 103, stay by your troops. Go back down by your troops. Out.

Latch, Latch, this is Dipsy Doodle. I've got all my troops right here. I'm gonna take 'em aboard. I have the rest of the troops at 20 . . . and I'm gonna run through the ambush after dark and join them. Do you concur? Over.

This is Latch, concur, over. I don't think that you need to wait until nightfall if you can get your medevac off and get through there, I think you're better off right now.

Seawolf: That gas tank looks like it's just ready to go. There it goes!

Latch: 014, in reference to your last . . . we have observed several secondary explosions, and she's just engulfed in flames at this time, over.

Yost: You say it is engulfed in flames? Over.

Latch: That's affirmative. That's affirmative. And also there have been several secondary explosions.

Yost: 6 Bravo . . . if you can give me any information as to sightings of VC, bunkers and so on, I would appreciate it, over.

Seawolf: This is 14. We have been spraying the area with door gun and we haven't seen any [recent] movement down there. No movement at all, and stand by—we'll see if we can find any bunkers in the area.

Yost then tried to get the Vietnamese Marines to sweep the area in front of the boats. He told the Marine major, "Get those Marines down the beach." The Marine disagreed, saying they needed to dig in in front of the boats. "We're liable to get overrun tonight. I'm going to need your mortars." Ultimately, it was the VN Marine colonel who refused to move the troops. The U.S. Marine informed Yost that the troops weren't going to move. "He isn't going to move," the U.S. Marine told Yost. "We're going to be here. Get used to it."

Yost got back on the radio: *Leatherneck 6, this is Dipsy Doodle; the land commander here wants to stay in my location overnight. He doesn't want to go back through the ambush. Check with Latch and see what you think about that, over.*

Seawolf: *Hey, the ammo is starting to go on the boat! I know I don't want to fly over the damn boat. I don't see any bunkers out here, but it's pretty hard to see.*

Twenty minutes after the survivors and dead were extracted from the 43 boat, the over 1,000 pounds of explosives and mortar rounds exploded in a fireball, hurling flame, smoke and twisted metal into the air. Latch had instructed the helo pilots not to fly directly over the 43 boat because he knew, "it was going to be a hell of an explosion. It shook the hell out of us when it did explode." Hartman agreed, "I'd have been a hell of a lot farther away if I knew it was going to be that big an explosion."

At the medevac site Hemenway says, "They piled up the dead on the 38 boat, next to our boat." The helos flew medevac until nightfall. After that the rest of the wounded waited until morning for medevac. Hornberger, who was given morphine for his wounds, was among the men that were medevaced out the next day. He was taken to the LST, but they couldn't get all the shrapnel out of his body. Hornberger was eventually returned to the boats at An Thoi and went on subsequent operations there.

Modansky was also medevaced out by helicopter, and eventually transferred to the Philippines for treatment. He returned to An Thoi and went back on the boats. He was later transferred to Cam Ranh where he finished out his tour on coastal patrol. When he left An Thoi he said to himself, "I'm not going to get killed—I'm going to make it home."

Yost calls the night in the river "the most miserable night I ever spent." The VN colonel claimed the little task group was up against a combined VC/NVA battalion, and Yost had no idea whether he was right or wrong. Yost thought it likely they would be attacked.

The boats conducted defensive mortar firing during the night. The next morning Yost finally got the VN Marines to sweep both banks. The large enemy force had faded into the jungle.

All that remained of the 43 boat after the devastating firefight on April 12, 1969.
OFFICIAL U.S. NAVY PHOTO, HOFFMANN COLLECTION

The final toll for the men on the boats was three U.S. Navy killed, 33 wounded, and two VN Marines killed and 13 wounded. At least 18 VC were killed in the fight. The rest, including the wounded, faded away to fight another day.

The next day the boats exited the river and returned to the LST. Pat Sheedy was on the LST because his PCF needed work and was not available for the operation. "That afternoon," he says, "the boats came out of the river and had a debriefing in the wardroom of the LST. All of the O in Cs and the helicopter guys got up and told their stories. It was a real time after action report and a very sad time."

Two Swifts tow PCF 51 out of the Duong Keo, April 13, 1969. This was the day after the devastating firefight that resulted in the loss of PCF 43.
Official U.S. Navy photo, Hoffmann collection

"It could have been us," Jack Chenoweth said to Virg Erwin. Erwin now says of the next day, "I look at the faces of men, their somber expressions, everyone avoiding eye contact. The smell of depression is as strong as diesel fumes. It's the scent of survivors' guilt."

Bob Elder was awakened in Cam Ranh the next morning and told his old boat had been destroyed and Don Droz had been killed. He again felt the same overwhelming feeling of guilt that he had felt when his friend Jim Harwood had lost part of his leg in November in the Bo De.[103]

---

103. The 43 boat was destroyed exactly one week after Larry Thurlow left Vietnam. Roy Hoffmann had the sad task of writing to Judy Droz of the tragedy. Thirty-two years after the events of April 12, Don Droz' daughter, Tracy Droz Tragos, set out on a journey to know and grieve for the father she had grown up without. The result is the documentary film "Be Good, Smile Pretty," a journey of discovery, healing and remembrance. In 2002 Bob Elder got in contact with Tragos. She was most gracious to Elder, telling him not to feel badly about her father. The conversation finally gave Elder some closure after all the intervening years. An embittered Judy Droz became active in the antiwar movement. As Terry Costello says, "I can understand why his wife was upset. She has the right to say what she wants, even though she may be wrong."

As Roy Hoffmann wound down his time as CTF 115, he provided a summary of TF 115 casualties during his tenure. There were 188 wounded, which included 168 Swifties in COS RON One; USCG, four; IUWG, four; SEALs, two; EOD, two; UDT, five; NFV Staff, one; CTF 115 Staff, one; and Skimmers, one. Killed in action totaled 29; they included 17 Swifties in COS RON One; IUWG eight; UDT, one; USCG, two; and Australian, one. There was one VNN missing in action and one U.S. Marine MIA. The Market Time forces engaged in over 289 enemy initiated firefights and 20 mining incidents. The enemy almost never came out ahead in an engagement. Forty-eight PCFs (60 per cent of the in country total) were seriously damaged, although only two were totally destroyed. The Market Time Forces continued the blockade from the sea, and it's doubtful any Communist infiltration occurred by sea. Since October the Market Time Raiders made more than 270 river raids, the result of which was in many areas pacification and trade was established or accelerated. The casualty rate overall for Roy Hoffmann's tour of duty as commander of TF 115 was just over six per cent.

For the Market Time casualties the enemy paid a terrible price. Again, from Hoffmann's Summary, the Task Force was responsible for killing 730 VC/NVA (body count), 744 KIA, (estimated), 382 Wounded In Action (body count) and 198 WIA (estimated). In addition, the Market Time Raiders destroyed or damaged thousands of enemy sampans, junks, structures and bunkers.

The psychological effect of the Market Time Raiders was even more striking. The Americans struck VC/NVA redoubts and sanctuaries and cast doubt and fear into the enemy, concerning their strength, safety and ultimate victory. The Market Time incursions also tied down VC/NVA troops that could have been otherwise deployed for offensive operations against friendly ground forces.

Roy Hoffmann sent out the following message with the report:

> We have made the enemy acutely aware of and fear TF 115. This has been possible only because of the courage, aggressiveness and professionalism of the officers and men who make up the Task Force. You have all given your best and served your country well. That made the difference. I am very proud of you and am honored to have served with you. Well done.

FOUR DAYS BEFORE Roy Hoffmann's scheduled departure from Vietnam he participated in his last action there, for which he received a Gold Star in lieu of the second award of the Bronze Star Medal with Combat "V." The boats were again assaulting known enemy strongholds along the Rach Duong Keo. For the operation Hoffmann assembled a force consisting of seven Swifts, two USCG Cutters, one LST, four helicopter gun ships, a medical evacuation helicopter, a UDT Team and a Vietnamese Mobile Strike Force.

On May 5 the units entered the Duong Keo and immediately began to receive heavy enemy rocket, automatic weapons and small arms fire. The units executed a pre-planned pincer movement despite the fact one of the Swifts had beached to prevent sinking after an enemy rocket hit. The coordinated arrival of air strikes and helicopter gun ships (with Captain Hoffmann again aboard), and the close proximity of the LST for helicopter refueling and rearming turned the tide for the Allied forces.

Ten VC were known killed in the battle, although the number was probably higher. The Americans pounded the area with heavy air strikes, helicopter rockets and mortar fire from the Swifts. The enemy fortifications were severely damaged and the troops captured significant amounts of enemy munitions, weapons, documents and equipment. It was a complete rout of the enemy, and Captain Roy Hoffmann's last mission in Vietnam.

Hoffmann would later receive the Distinguished Service Medal for his tour as Commander Coastal Surveillance Force and Commander Coastal Flotilla One, for the period May 1968 to May 1969. The award said in part:

> Ever alert for even greater utilization of his forces, Captain Hoffmann inspired and actively led his units to new heights and superb combat records while carrying out additional inshore operations, one of which was SEALORDS. . . . As a result of Captain Hoffmann's brilliant leadership, professionalism, knowledge, and exceptional organizational and planning ability, Market Time Forces were utilized to the utmost in all facets of naval warfare to aid the Republic of Vietnam in her fight for freedom from communist aggression.

In Hoffmann's final fitness report, a grateful General Creighton Abrams wrote:

> As Commander U.S. Military Assistance Command, Vietnam, I have been exceptionally impressed with Captain Hoffmann's brilliant combat leadership. Combining intelligence and foresight, Captain Hoffmann's Market Time forces have mounted a new and brilliant record against the enemy. The damage and destruction wrought on the Viet Cong and North Vietnamese Army by the Market Time units bear tribute to Captain

Hoffmann's aggressiveness, outstanding tactical ability, and willingness to take the fight to the enemy. Under Captain Hoffmann's leadership his forces... displayed a boldness and courage that has become the hallmark of the Swift Raiders. Captain Hoffmann continued his bold and daring Swift river raids throughout the secret zones of South Vietnam... dealing the enemy crushing blows in areas heretofore long standing Viet Cong sanctuaries. A great tactician, an intelligent, articulate, and forceful military officer, a man who conducts his campaigns boldly, and who led his men brilliantly, Captain Hoffmann is unreservedly recommended for immediate promotion to Flag rank and positions of even greater responsibility.

ON MAY 9, 1969, Roy Hoffmann flew back to the United States. When he arrived at the airport in Charleston, Mary Linn met him at the airport. He arrived in undress whites and she took him directly to the Mamie P. Whiteside Elementary School. Emilie Hoffmann Crow says, "I remember looking out the window and there were Mom and Dad walking in. He was in that white uniform and it was the tannest I ever remember him being." Hilarie Hoffmann Hanson remembers, "We were in school. I remember him coming to the school in his white uniform. I looked out the classroom door and he was there at the door. And I remember how really proud that moment was."

Change of Command ceremony, TF 115, Cam Ranh Bay, 1969. L–R, chaplain, Admiral Zumwalt, Captain R. F. Hoffmann, VNN CNO Chon, Commander Richard Nicholson, Commander Charley Plumly. The wind carried Hoffmann's prepared remarks into the Bay and he delivered his speech from memory.
OFFICIAL U.S. NAVY PHOTO, CAPTAIN CHARLEY PLUMLY, USN, RET., COLLECTION

8

COMMANDS AND RETIREMENT

USS *Sierra* (AD 18)

Roy Hoffmann left Cam Ranh Bay and flew to Honolulu at the request of Admiral Zumwalt, who wanted to know what happened to Zumwalt's recommendation that Bob Kerrey receive the Medal of Honor for the action of March 14, 1969. Hoffmann learned that the Fleet Commander was sending the nomination for the award on, recommending it be approved. Hoffmann then flew to Charleston via San Francisco. He was greeted on arrival in Charleston by a city that was under martial law due to violent civil rights protests.

In the meantime, Mary Linn found a home for rent in Virginia Beach that belonged to a naval aviator. The location entailed a long commute to the new command, the *Sierra*, but the house was a nice four-bedroom, four-bath home with a screened in back porch. She had initially requested Navy quarters while her husband was still in Vietnam, but was told that only he could apply. Two months later, after the Hoffmanns signed a year lease on the rental, the Navy called and informed Mary Linn their quarters were ready. Mary Linn told them, "I can only tell you you're lucky it's me answering the phone and not my husband." She told them they had ten months to go on their lease and couldn't move.

The Navy left them on the quarters list and ten months later housing became available. It was the first time they had ever lived in quarters and it was very convenient. Roy Hoffmann went from a 17-mile commute to a one-mile walk to the pier. It allowed a more normal life as Hoffmann came home about 6:00 P.M. most every evening and the family had dinner together.

ADMIRAL ZUMWALT WANTED Roy Hoffmann to go to the Pentagon from Vietnam, because he thought he needed more senior staff experience. Hoffmann responded that he appreciated the offer, but he didn't want to go to the Pentagon at that time. He wanted to go to a destroyer tender command that would allow him to spend some time with his family. The decision probably delayed a likely advancement to admiral. He put an AD on his preference card and was granted the request. Whether Zumwalt had anything to do with the assignment is unknown.

ON MAY 11–12, 1969, Saigon came under the worst wave of terror attacks the city had experienced that year. Communist forces shelled 159 cities, towns and military bases, the largest number of attacks since the 1968 Tet offensive. President Nixon, on May 14, outlined an eight-point peace offer to the Communists, which included a mutual pullout of all major forces over the next 12 months. The silence of the response from the North Vietnamese, both in Hanoi and Paris, was deafening.

Supreme Court justice Abe Fortas, appointed to the Court by President Lyndon Johnson in 1965, resigned on May 15, the first justice in history to give up his office under public pressure. He had received a $20,000 fee from convicted securities seller Louis Wolfson; Fortas resigned when it was disclosed he was receiving $20,000 a year from a Wolfson foundation.

President Nixon realized that the antiwar movement was undermining support for an honorable end to the Vietnam War. He astutely recognized that although much of the leadership for the movement came from radicals, rank and file members were often college age men subject to the draft, and their families and friends. He sent a special message to Congress on May 19 calling for an overhaul of the Selective Service System, thus changing and eventually ending the draft. He proposed that 19-year-old men get the first call, and he wanted to reduce the period of prime draft vulnerability from seven years to one year. He continued the undergraduate student deferment; the maximum vulnerability to the draft came whenever the deferment expired. As Stephen Ambrose stated, "The net effect was that twenty year olds and up were no longer threatened by the draft, and, just as Nixon hoped and expected, most of them stopped marching for peace and started getting on with their lives."

Meanwhile, Nixon's "Vietnamization" policy, the gradual replacement of American troops by South Vietnamese forces, became the defining strategy of the Vietnam War. It was, simply stated, a phased withdrawal unrelated to the situation on the ground in South Vietnam. U.S. military commanders were instructed to keep American casualties to an absolute minimum.

As a consequence, the goal of winning the war was replaced by the policy of withdrawal. Once that policy was announced all incentive for negotiation by the North Vietnamese ceased, and it became difficult for the military to maintain morale among its fighting forces. It was a slow, phased-in retreat, and was, according again to Stephen Ambrose, the worst mistake of the Nixon Presidency, particularly in light of polls of the day indicating more than 60 per cent of Americans opposed a total withdrawal.

On June 23, 1969, liberal Earl Warren retired as Chief Justice of the Supreme Court after serving nearly 16 years through the Eisenhower, Kennedy and Johnson administrations. He was nominated by President Eisenhower, who considered Warren, "the biggest damn fool mistake I ever made."

ON JUNE 27, 1969, Captain Roy F. Hoffmann assumed command of the USS *Sierra* (AD 18), relieving Captain Paul C. Boyd. The *Sierra* was a destroyer tender, essentially a mobile naval shipyard. She was designed primarily to tend destroyers and cruisers, although she could repair all types of ships, from landing craft to carriers. She had more than 30 shops and laboratories aboard, enabling her to perform any ship repair task short of a major overhaul. For example, she could change the propellers of a destroyer without the necessity of dry-docking, she could pour large steel castings, accomplish heavy machine and structural steel work, wind large electric motors, repair watches and binoculars, and calibrate the most intricate and sophisticated electronic equipment.

The *Sierra* was an old ship, commissioned on March 20, 1944. She deployed to the Pacific at the end of World War II, and then served the destroyers of the Atlantic Fleet after the War. She was 530 feet long, with a beam of 73 feet, and displaced 17,100 tons. Her normal complement was 45 officers and 979 men, although there were only 33 officers and 828 men aboard when Roy Hoffmann reported aboard. She carried enough food to feed her own crew and a division of destroyers for three months, as well as thousands of rounds of ammunition for issue to other ships. She could fuel destroyers or provide tubes for their boilers. She provided medical and dental services, and could act as the commissary for fleet personnel, providing clothing, "gedunk," and personal toiletries. Deep within her vast storerooms, she carried over 55,000 separate kinds of repair parts; what she didn't carry she might well be able to make. It was a complex command.

Roy Hoffmann took command at a time of continued political unrest in the Mediterranean and an increased Soviet naval presence worldwide. The

USS Sierra *(AD 18)* underway. Official U.S. Navy photo, Hoffmann collection

Ship's crew, USS Sierra *(AD 18).* Hoffmann photo

Change of Command ceremony, USS Sierra, *Captain Hoffmann (right) saluting.*
OFFICIAL U.S. NAVY PHOTO, HOFFMANN COLLECTION

U.S. Navy was called on to intensify its commitments overseas at a time when a reduction of manpower was taking place. The *Sierra* successfully met the challenge to insure the cruiser-destroyer force was maintained at a high state of material readiness. Doing more with less, Captain Hoffmann maintained high morale, and increased work output, quality and productivity.

IN A HARBINGER OF THINGS to come, then Senator George McGovern (South Dakota Democrat) met privately with the chief North Vietnamese and NLF negotiators in Paris on May 22. Undercutting the diplomatic efforts of the United States, he declared that fruitful peace negotiations could not begin unless the U.S. agreed to "unconditional withdrawal" from Vietnam, and discontinued its "unqualified embrace of the Thieu-Ky government." Aside from the obvious point that "unconditional withdrawal" was an enormous disincentive for the North Vietnamese to negotiate, the implications of having 535 congressmen and women negotiating on behalf of the U.S. was destructive to American foreign policy.

On July 8, 1969, 3,000 people at McChord Air Force Base, located near Tacoma, Washington, welcomed back the first American soldiers to return under the new troop reduction policy. The largely symbolic return of 94 soldiers was the first reduction in force in Vietnam since 1965.

On July 18, 1969, Senator Edward Kennedy, brother of the slain President John F. Kennedy and Attorney General Robert Kennedy, drove his car off a bridge on Chappaquiddick Island off Martha's Vineyard. He had left a rented cottage in a 1967 Oldsmobile where he had been partying with the "boiler room girls." He had with him Mary Jo Kopechne as he drove off the Dike Bridge. The Olds turned over and sank beneath the relatively shallow, dark waters, trapping Kopechne in a metal coffin, where she died. Kennedy escaped with his life and did not report the drowning to authorities until he returned to Chappaquiddick the next day and discovered the body had been found. In the week following his reporting of the drowning the best lawyers in Massachusetts were flown in to Hyannis to prepare his defense. Kennedy, a week later, pled guilty to leaving the scene of an accident. For causing the death of the young secretary, Judge James A. Boyle sentenced Kennedy to the minimum sentence of two months in prison, which sentence he suspended. Kennedy neither spent a day in jail for the crime, nor felt the disfavor of the Massachusetts voters. He returned to the Senate where he remains today, lionized by the Democratic left.

On July 20, 1969, astronaut Neil Armstrong became the first human to walk on the moon. He said, "That's one small step for man, one giant leap for mankind." Nixon, forgetting his history, announced that it was the greatest event since the creation. The return trip back to earth by Apollo 11 took 60 hours.

Nixon still harbored some hope of winning the Vietnam War. Henry Kissinger had commissioned a study within the office of the Chief of Naval Operations, code named Duck-Hook, which proposed measures for military escalation against North Vietnam. The military options included massive bombing of Hanoi, Haiphong and other key areas of North Vietnam; a ground invasion of North Vietnam; the mining of harbors and rivers; and a bombing campaign designed to sever the main railroad links to China. Twenty-nine major targets were pinpointed for destruction in a series of air attacks that were to continue until Hanoi capitulated. Had some or all of these measures been instituted at the beginning of the war rather than considered in 1969, the outcome of the war would most likely have been far different. However, by that juncture it was far too late.

On August 9, 1969 film actress Sharon Tate and four others were found brutally murdered in Tate's home overlooking Benedict Canyon in California. Tate had been stabbed 16 times. The bodies were hideously mutilated and arranged in grotesque positions. The killers, led by Charles Manson, a 35-year-old ex-con, committed two more murders two days later. He used a bizarre blend of sexual perversion, drugs and religion to hold his followers. He was ultimately arrested, convicted and remains behind bars today.

On August 15, 400,000 young hippies gathered at a 600-acre pasture for three days of drugs, sex and music.[1] During what became known as Woodstock, two tremendous cloudbursts turned the farm into a swamp. After three days of incessant rain, and inadequate sanitary facilities, even *The New York Times* was appalled:

> The dreams of marijuana and rock music that drew 300,000 to 400,000 fans and hippies to the Catskills had little more sanity than the impulses that drove the lemmings to march to their deaths in the sea. They ended in a nightmare of mud and stagnation that paralyzed Sullivan County for a whole weekend. What kind of culture is it that can produce so colossal a mess?

On September 3, 1969, 79-year-old Ho Chi Minh, President of North Vietnam and source of the misery of his fellow Vietnamese in both North and South Vietnam, died after suffering a heart attack. Most of the people around him had been with him for years and so his death did not portend a change of heart or direction for North Vietnam.[2] His body was placed in state at Hanoi's Ba Dinh Hall and millions queued by to pay homage. All wore white in the traditional Vietnamese color for mourning. Ho wanted to be cremated but instead his embalmed body lay in a Leninesque mausoleum for all to see.

On September 5, 1969, criminal charges were formally brought against Lieutenant William Calley for the "My Lai massacre," where poorly led American troops slaughtered at least 109 Vietnamese villagers. After a four-month trial Calley was found guilty and sent to prison, the only one so punished for the crime. My Lai, a sorry exception in a war where American troops in general showed great restraint with the civilian population, be-

---

1. Performers included Santana, Janis Joplin, Sly and the Family Stone, Jefferson Airplane, Grateful Dead, Jimi Hendrix, Blood Sweat and Tears, the Who, Creedence Clearwater Revival, Arlo Guthrie, Joe Cocker, John Sebastian and Sha Na Na.

2. The North Vietnamese formed a collective leadership led by Le Duan, first secretary of the Communist Party; Truong Chin, member of the Politburo and chairman of the National Assembly; General Vo Nguyen Giap, defense minister; and Premier Pham Van Dong.

came a cause célèbre for the antiwar left, and a false paradigm for what was considered by many to be typical of Vietnam veterans.

Dr. Benjamin Spock, whose conviction for aiding draft dodgers had recently been overturned, announced that he and ten other representatives of the New Mobilization Committee to End the War in Vietnam planned a 36-hour "March Against Death" in Washington, D.C. in mid-November. On September 25, Senator Charles Goodall proposed legislation that would require withdrawal of all U.S. troops from Vietnam by the end of 1970, and bar the use of congressionally appropriated funds after December 1, 1970 for maintaining U.S. military personnel in Vietnam. The next day President Nixon held a news conference during which he said he hoped to end the war by the end of 1970. He rejected moves to set a deadline for the withdrawal of all U.S. forces, and urged the American people to support him and give him the time he needed to end the war honorably. David Broder shortly thereafter wrote in the *Washington Post*: "It is becoming more obvious with every passing day that the men and movement that broke Lyndon Johnson's authority in 1968 are out to break Richard Nixon in 1969. The likelihood is great they will succeed again."

On October 14 radio Hanoi broadcast a letter to the American people from North Vietnamese Premier Pham Van Dong that in another time would have outraged U.S. citizens:

> This fall large sectors of the U.S. people, encouraged and supported by many peace- and justice-loving American personages, are launching a broad and powerful offensive throughout the United States to demand that the Nixon administration put an end to the Vietnam aggressive war and immediately bring all American troops home.... May your fall offensive succeed splendidly.[3]

On October 15 hundreds of thousands of Americans demonstrated to protest or support Nixon's Vietnam War strategies. Two hundred and fifty thousand people went to Washington, D.C. for the so-called "Vietnam Moratorium Day." The *Washington Star* said in an editorial: "What counts is whether the demonstration, regardless of intention, does in fact give encouragement to Hanoi and thereby presumably prolong the war." Viet Cong Radio said that the Communists had gained "strong encouragement from the Moratorium." By this date John Kerry was flying former Robert Kennedy speech writer Adam Walinsky around New York State and making antiwar speeches.

---

3. Imagine should such a message have been received from Adolf Hitler or Hideki Tojo during World War II, or from Kim Il-Sung, the North Korean Communist dictator who launched the Korean War.

On November 3, 1969, Nixon made his "Silent Majority" speech to the nation, in which he stated, "And so tonight, to you, the great silent majority of my fellow Americans—I ask for your support. Let us be united for peace. Let us be united against defeat. Because let us understand: *North Vietnam cannot defeat or humiliate the United States. Only Americans can do that* [emphasis added]."

The response to Nixon's speech was overwhelmingly positive: A Gallup Poll telephone survey reported 77 per cent of those interviewed backed the president, while only six per cent opposed him. More than 500,000 telegrams and 30,000 letters poured into the White House favoring the speech. This elemental truth of presidential power was demonstrated once again: The real power of the presidency comes primarily from his ability to go directly to the people with a powerful and truthful message.

On November 13–15, 800,000 people massed in Washington, D.C. for an event organized by the New Mobilization Committee to End the War in Vietnam. The protesters were mostly young, white and middle class. Senator George McGovern and Dr. Benjamin Spock spoke; entertainers such as Peter, Paul and Mary, and Arlo Guthrie warbled. In a great show of disrespect for those who had died for their country in the war, and those still serving, some 46,000 people carried a placard bearing the name of an American soldier killed in Vietnam; or alternately, to equate their sacrifice with "atrocities," they carried the name of a village allegedly destroyed by U.S. troops.

On the 14th Washington riot policemen were forced to use tear gas to rout 2,000 demonstrators who were marching on the South Vietnamese embassy. At least 20 were arrested and seven policemen were injured. The next day tear gas dispersed 10,000 gathered at the Justice Department Building, there to protest government prosecution of antiwar demonstrators. The demonstrators were led by members of the Youth International Party (Yippies). The mob threw rocks and bottles and burned U.S. flags. Some actually broke into the Justice Department, shouting "Smash the state!" There they tore down the American flag, burned it, and raised the Viet Cong flag in its place.

As 1969 came to its sorry conclusion, U.S. troop strength in Vietnam was at 474,000, down from the peak of 543,000 in June. United States combat deaths during the year totaled 9,414, down from 14,592 the preceding year. The drawdown and the antiwar activities in America began to affect the morale of the remaining troops in Vietnam.

In Vietnam the North Vietnamese were increasingly forced to replace Viet Cong troops with their own. About two-thirds of the Communist regulars in the south were NVA, deployed to replace main-force Viet Cong devastated by their losses during the Tet Offensive of 1968.

On January 3, 1970, John Kerry requested an early discharge from active duty, which was granted.[4] On May 23, 1970, Kerry married Julia Thorne. Shortly after their honeymoon he joined the radical group Vietnam Veterans Against the War.

MEANWHILE, CAPTAIN ROY HOFFMANN was compiling a stellar record as skipper of the *Sierra*. His fitness report by Rear Admiral John D. Chase, Commander Cruiser-Destroyer Flotilla Four (COMCRUDESFLOT Four), indicates how well the ship performed despite general adverse conditions in the Navy at that time. During the reporting period of 1 March to 26 June 1970, there was an upsurge in tender work at a time of reduction of tenders available to do the work. Admiral Chase commented on the smartness of the crew and cleanliness of the ship. "The honor guard," he said, "would do credit to a cruiser Marine detachment.

"*Sierra* has also continued to be an outstanding Flagship. Her support for my embarked Flag is continuous, effective and substantial. It is a pleasure to be on board." Roy Hoffmann served as the Chairman of the Destroyer Flotilla Four Gunnery Board, tasked with improving gunnery throughout the Force. He worked with Fleet personnel and the Destroyer School in Newport on gunnery curriculum.

Admiral Chase further stated:

> All of this attests to the abilities, energy and drive of Captain Hoffmann. He is meticulous and demanding but of himself first of all. He is personally acquainted with the tender jobs his ship is performing and his own hours are as long as any of those the men actually doing the work . . . I consider that Captain Hoffmann should be a Flag officer and should be selected early. As a first step, I strongly recommend him for a major command at sea now.

The major command at sea soon followed, Roy Hoffmann's last in a job he loved and excelled at. He left the *Sierra* after a Change of Command ceremony on December 17, 1970. Captain Richard A. Bihr, another graduate of the Navy's V-12 program, relieved him.

---

4. Or so it appears. As will be seen, the circumstances of his discharge are controversial and unknown since he has never released his complete military records.

Rear Admiral J. B. Hildreth, who relieved Admiral Chase, conducted Roy Hoffmann's last performance review while he was CO of the *Sierra*. Hoffmann was, Hildreth said:

> ... a truly exceptional commanding officer, destroyer man and an inspirational leader. Here is an officer with unlimited capability, totally committed with the finest sense of personal dedication to the profession. Here also is an officer whose advice and opinion is sought for the clarity, common sense, depth of consideration and professional acumen and expertise which he applies to the subject. Captain Hoffmann is a man who demonstrates complete courage in his convictions without the slightest regard for personal recrimination. He undertook major repair works normally considered the sole capability of shore based industrial facilities. Captain Hoffmann realized savings of $600,000 to the Navy as actually documented by records of costs of repairs in 18 destroyer types. ... Hoffmann's ability to motivate and instill a "can-do" spirit in his command was the key to *Sierra's* most commendable achievements. Captain Hoffmann's prowess as a seaman and ship handler are deserving of special mention and recognition. In Norfolk, Virginia and Mayport, Florida he moored to piers and got underway without the assistance of tugs and pilots. These evolutions were commented upon by numerous senior officers and witnessed by scores of others—examples of ship handling that were significantly influencing and inspirational.[5] I consider his services as a Flag Officer will be of inestimable value to the Navy and the nation and unreservedly support his selection for such service.

USS *Leahy* (DLG 16)

As Roy Hoffmann prepared to assume command of the *Leahy*, Admiral Zumwalt had advanced to Chief of Naval Operations, the highest uniformed position in the Navy. Zumwalt sent a letter to Hoffmann on January 18, 1971, which read in part:

> During your tour ... as Commander Coastal Surveillance Force (CTF 115) ... you had the unique opportunity to demonstrate your leadership and command capabilities in combat. Your magnificent performance has placed you at the forefront of your contemporaries for competitive consideration for future positions of broad responsibilities. Few individuals are afforded

---

5. Destroyer tenders are large, underpowered and an awkward ship to land and get underway. As the Admiral says, "you would ring up all back full, get a cup of coffee, and wait to see what happens."

such a challenging assignment in their captaincy and those that have been are the future leaders of our Navy. In my judgment your assignment carried more than Major Command responsibility and is at the flag level. I will watch with interest your continued rise up the Navy's ladder of success.

From January 31 to February 2, 1971, the so-called "Winter Soldier Investigation" took place in Detroit, Michigan. The Vietnam Veterans Against the War (VVAW) and actress Jane Fonda sponsored the event. Fonda was in her Mao period, wearing a red star Viet Cong flag costume. She was the key financial supporter and the honorary national coordinator of the event.

John Kerry attended the event and listened as so-called "combat veterans" told grisly horror stories about American soldiers in Vietnam. They told of decapitations, torture of prisoners, shelling villages for fun, corpsmen killing wounded prisoners, napalm torching villages, women raped, and innocents, including children, massacred for fun. Further testimony told "of using prisoners for target practice and throwing them out of helicopters, of cutting off ears of dead VC, of burning villages and gang-raping women."[6] Kerry, of course, knew better from personal experience.

As the witnesses piled on the stories, each seemed to try and outdo the previous speaker. The impression was that only sadists or psychopaths were in the U.S. military. "Reciting horrors became an unofficial badge of courage, a required ritual for acceptance into the ranks of antiwar activists."[7]

One of the organizers of the event was Al Hubbard, the VVAW's executive secretary. He claimed he was a decorated Air Force captain who had caught shrapnel flying a plane into Da Nang in 1966. In fact he was a staff sergeant (E-5) with no record of service in Vietnam. Hubbard was typical of the scruffy lot. As Scott Swett has written:

> All the Winter Soldier allegations were considered for possible investigation.... The U.S. Army CID (Criminal Investigation Division) declined to open cases for a number of the allegations ... 33 of the 76 Army witnesses

---

6. B. G. Burkett and Glenna Whitley. *Stolen Valor* (Dallas, Texas: Verity Press, Inc, 1998), p. 131. *Stolen Valor* has become a vital source in restoring the honor of the Vietnam veteran, and Burkett has done great service in exposing the false Vietnam vet. The slander of the military continues today: "Although it has been thoroughly discredited, the Winter Soldier 'investigation' is still being cited today as proof of American servicemen's barbarity." p. 134.

7. John E. O'Neill and Jerome R. Corsi. *Unfit for Command* (Washington, D.C.: Regnery Publishing, Inc., 2004), p. 111.

were discarded at the outset—because their claims were either obviously false or did not qualify as criminal violations. Of the remaining 43 witnesses, 25 "refused to provide factual data," 13 provided information that "did not support the allegations," and the remaining five could not be located. None of the investigations resulted in criminal indictments. But telling the truth was never the purpose of Winter Soldier and other war crimes tribunals. Like the North Vietnamese and Viet Cong representatives they worked with and supported, VVAW leaders relentlessly exaggerated American war crimes in Vietnam as a political tactic.[8]

These false stories of atrocities would provide the basis for John Kerry's testimony before the Senate Foreign Relations Committee three months later.

ON FEBRUARY 13, 1971, in Naples, Italy, Captain Roy Hoffmann relieved Captain Orlin N. Putman as CO of the USS *Leahy* (DLG 16). The *Leahy* was built by Bath Iron Works of Bath, Maine and commissioned on August 4, 1962.[9] She was named after Fleet Admiral (five-star) William D. Leahy. Leahy had been a close advisor to both Franklin Roosevelt and Harry Truman. After commanding nearly every kind of surface ship, Leahy was appointed CNO in 1937, during the course of which he started the buildup of the Navy that became the most powerful sea force the world has ever known. After his retirement from the Navy he was appointed Ambassador to France at Vichy during the German occupation. President Franklin Roosevelt then appointed him Chief of Staff to the Commander in Chief. In the White House he, along with Roosevelt and Harry Hopkins, was one of three men most involved with directing World War II. Hopkins concentrated more on production and on relations with Churchill and Stalin; Leahy dealt more with strategies and plans. Leahy informed President Truman, at the death of Roosevelt, on all matters pertaining to the war. Hopkins had been ill and out of touch for weeks and Leahy filled in admirably with the new president, who had been kept in the dark by Roosevelt about war plans. Leahy died in 1959.

Comparable to the old cruisers, the *Leahy* was 533 feet long and had a beam of 55 feet, with a 26-foot draft. She had four high temperature and pressure propulsion steam boilers that drove two shafts, each with 85,000

---

8. Scott Swett, "Still Slandering the Troops," FrontPageMagazine.com, August 24, 2006.
9. The *Leahy* was decommissioned on October 1, 1993, at the Naval Station San Diego, where she was home ported. When her commissioning pennant was hauled down she had served for 31 years.

SHP, to a speed of 30 knots. Her screws were 12 feet in diameter, with five manganese/bronze blades. She burned 93.3 gallons of fuel per mile, produced 24,000 gallons of fresh water daily, and served over 1,300 meals per day to her crew of 30 officers and 400 enlisted men. She was home ported in Norfolk, Virginia, although she was in Naples as part of a Mediterranean deployment when Hoffmann reported aboard.

On April 18, 1971, John Kerry arrived in Washington, D.C., there to represent the Vietnam Veterans Against the War (VVAW). The VVAW sponsored weeklong antiwar demonstrations, called Operation Dewey Canyon III. Kerry's participation almost insured that his path would cross with that of Roy Hoffmann, and over 350 Swifties and POWs during the 2004 election. "Dewey Canyon III featured Vietnam veterans marching on Washington in a very dramatic, emotional way. Longhaired, scruffy, dressed in camouflage and the remnants of military garb, and draped in medals, they presented the image of men who had obviously been tested in battle and had seen the horrors of war..."[10] It was all political theater made for television cameras, featuring many who were not Vietnam veterans, or in some cases, not veterans at all.

The electrifying event of Dewey Canyon III was the testimony of John Kerry before the Senate Foreign Relations Committee, chaired by J. William Fulbright, on April 22, 1971. Kerry was testifying on behalf of the VVAW, and his testimony was based on the mostly unsubstantiated and fraudulent Winter Soldier Investigation in Detroit. Kerry's testimony was a remarkable indictment of the men with whom he had served in Vietnam, and in fact was a stain on everyone serving in the military. It was particularly shocking in that he knew most of what he said was untrue. He said in part, in sworn testimony:

> I would like to talk, representing all those veterans, and say that several months ago in Detroit, we had an investigation at which over 150 honorably discharged and many very highly decorated veterans testified to war crimes committed in Southeast Asia, not isolated incidents but crimes committed on a day-to-day basis with the full awareness of officers at all levels of command.
>
> It is impossible to describe to you exactly what did happen in Detroit, the emotions in the room, the feelings of the men who were reliving their experiences in Vietnam, but they did. They relived the absolute horror of what this country... made them do.

---

10. Burkett and Whitley, *Stolen Valor*, p. 135.

They told the stories at times they had personally raped, cut off ears, cut off heads, taped wires from portable telephones to human genitals and turned up the power, cut off limbs, blown up bodies, randomly shot at civilians, razed villages in a fashion reminiscent of Genghis Khan, shot cattle and dogs for fun, poisoned food stocks, and generally ravaged the countryside of South Vietnam in addition to the normal ravage of war, and the normal and very particular ravaging which is done by the applied bombing power of this country.

Kerry called for an immediate pullout from Vietnam. Asked during questioning of the consequences for Vietnam and the rest of Southeast Asia if America abandoned her allies, Kerry estimated 3,000 might lose their lives if American forces pulled out. Kerry missed the number by a factor of 1,000, as three million people lost their lives in the genocide that followed in Southeast Asia after the American pullout in 1975.

Kerry further stated, "I have been to Paris. I have talked with both delegations at the peace talks, that is to say the Democratic Republic of Vietnam [the Communists of North Vietnam] and the Provisional Revolutionary Government [the Viet Cong]." He took these actions while still serving out his military obligation and while U.S. troops were still fighting in Vietnam.

Kerry concluded his testimony with, "How do you ask a man to be the last man to die for a mistake?"[11]

It is difficult to overstate the adverse impact his testimony had on those who had served, and were still serving in the military during the Vietnam era. Essentially branding them all as war criminals, the impact on American POWs still held under brutal conditions in North Vietnam was even more severe. Paul Galanti was a U.S. Navy pilot shot down in June of 1966 who spent seven years in Communist captivity. He said that during torture sessions his North Vietnamese captors cited antiwar speeches as an example of why the POWs should cross over to the Communist side.

Galanti says, "Kerry broke covenant among servicemen never to make public criticism that might jeopardize those still in battle or in the hands of the enemy.... John Kerry was a traitor to the men he served with."[12]

A few days after Kerry's testimony, in early May, POW guards in Hanoi called

---

11. For the full text of Kerry's testimony and his responses to questions, see Lieutenant Colonel Robert "Buzz" Patterson, *Reckless Disregard* (Washington, D.C.: Regnery Publishing, Inc., 2004) pp. 199–230.

12. O'Neill and Corsi, *Unfit for Command*, p. 107. For a remarkably powerful video of the impact of the antiwar movement on POWs, see the documentary *Stolen Honor Wounds that Never Heal*, produced by Carlton Sherwood.

a group of American POWs into a courtyard, where they showed the POWs a 16 mm film clips of Kerry's testimony. Colonel Bud Day, U.S. Air Force, Retired, who would later be awarded the Medal of Honor for his resistance while a POW, when informed of the Senate testimony, asked who had testified. "John Kerry," he was informed. Day shrugged. "A no-name dingbat."[13]

The day after Kerry's testimony, approximately 800 men from all branches of the service threw their medals over a barricade at the Capitol in Washington, D.C., John Kerry tossed his ribbons, not medals, although he did throw the medals of two veterans who had not shown up.[14]

"From start to finish, the public took Dewey Canyon III at face value, not understanding that they were watching brilliant political theater. Kerry, a Kennedy protégé with white-hot political aspirations, ascended center stage as both a war hero and as an antiwar hero throwing away his combat decorations."[15]

ON APRIL 23, 1971 in Palma, Mallorca, Vice Admiral Isaac C. "Ike" Kidd, Jr., commander of the 6th Fleet, presented the Meritorious Unit Citation to the *Leahy*. Kidd's Navy career spanned some 40 years by the time he retired on October 2, 1978. He served 23 years at sea, 15 of which were in command of destroyers, destroyer divisions and squadrons, a flotilla and three U.S. Fleets in the Pacific, Mediterranean and Atlantic.

He graduated from the Naval Academy on December 14, 1941 and was commissioned an ensign on December 19, 1941, just 12 days after his father, Rear Admiral Isaac C. Kidd, was killed on board his flagship, the battleship *Arizona*, during the Japanese attack on Pearl Harbor. The senior Admiral Kidd was posthumously awarded the Congressional Medal of Honor.

Ike Kidd, Jr., supposedly a descendent of the infamous pirate Captain Kidd, during World War II served as Gunnery Officer on the destroyer *Cowie*, participated in North Atlantic convoy duty, and in the invasions of North Africa, Sicily and Italy. During the Sicily invasion the *Cowie* directly engaged, at point blank range, German "Tiger" tanks on the beach. Kidd went from the *Cowie* to the destroyer *Putnam*, where he saw action in the Leyte Gulf, Saipan, and Tinian operations. He went on to participate in

---

13. Robert Coram, *American Patriot The Life and Wars of Colonel Bud Day* (New York: Little, Brown and Company, 2007), p. 243.

14. Kerry's medals turned up on the wall of his Capitol Hill office. When questioned by a reporter he acknowledged that the medals he had thrown away were not his.

15. Burkett and Whitley, *Stolen Valor*, p. 135.

operations off Iwo Jima, and Okinawa, and was involved in the rescue of the few survivors of the destroyer *Twiggs*, which was sunk by a kamikaze attack. He was also aboard when the *Putnam* assisted in the salvage of the battleship *Pennsylvania*, hit at Buckner Bay, Okinawa.

In 1971 Kidd was promoted to full admiral (four-star), and was appointed Chief of Naval Materiel, functioning as the Navy's top procurement and logistics officer, with a civilian and military workforce of over 350,000 men and women. He became Supreme Allied Commander, Atlantic, and Commander in Chief U.S. Atlantic Fleet on May 30, 1975. He was, Roy Hoffmann says, "One tough son of a bitch. Ike Kidd was going to be an admiral from the day he was born. He was a little bit difficult, to put it mildly."

Once, Kidd approached the moored *Leahy* in a small boat and came aboard unannounced, by climbing up the fantail. It was a breech of Navy etiquette for a senior officer to come aboard unannounced. The Command Duty Officer (CDO) knocked on Hoffmann's door and said, "Captain, Admiral Kidd is on board."

"What? Why didn't he tell us, for God's sake?"

The CDO replied, "I didn't know it either, but he came up over the fantail."

Kidd wandered around the ship, making his own inspection of the readiness of the *Leahy*. When he was done he knocked on Hoffmann's door and asked, "Can I come in?"

"It would be an honor, admiral," Hoffmann replied.

Kidd told him it was an informal visit, and what he had found. He said, "I just wanted to see what you are doing."

When Roy Hoffmann reported aboard the *Leahy* he encountered the problems that were rampant in the Navy at the time: Racial and discipline problems, and drug use. On his visits to the mess decks he could see the races were segregated at meals, with blacks sitting together and whites sitting separately. "You don't have to be a genius to see what that's about," Hoffmann says.

There were also considerable discipline problems on the ship, and the appearance of the ship and sailors was not as sharp as Hoffmann expected. Unfortunately, the discipline problems had much to do with the CNO, Admiral Zumwalt, whose Z-grams split the Navy. There were those in the fleets who took the loosened discipline with the attitude, "Give us an inch and we'll take a mile." Then there were the traditionalists, particularly older chiefs and senior officers, who didn't like the changes. Their attitude was, "Fuck it—it ain't like it used to be."

Somewhat insulated in the Pentagon from the problems, Zumwalt probably wasn't fully aware of what was going on. A difficult situation was exacerbated by the Zumwalt "Mod Squad" teams who sometimes came on board fleet ships, unannounced, thus undermining the authority of the senior officers aboard. The Squads interviewed ship's personnel without the captain even knowing they were aboard. The discipline and morale problems certainly existed before Zumwalt became CNO, but his loosening of discipline at that moment in the Navy's history did not help the situation.

On the *Leahy*, Hoffmann increased the use of non-judicial punishment through Captain's Masts, after consultation with the leading chief petty officers and Master at Arms. He had two capable black CPOs on board with whom he worked to alleviate the segregation problem. Personal inspections by the captain became routine; an officer ate every meal on the mess decks and provided written reports to Hoffmann; and the *Leahy* drill team was the sharpest outfit in the Fleet.

The ship began to shape up. C. K. Moore, Commander of Destroyer Squadron Ten, had this to say about the ship and her captain:

> Captain Hoffmann . . . is an expert ship handler, perhaps the best I have been associated with in the USN in years. He is the captain of his ship in the oldest tradition, fully conversant with his capabilities and limitations, and always firmly and fully in command. His officers will learn much from his example. Captain Hoffmann is clearly an officer with tremendous drive, a vast background of operational expertise, a firm understanding of the essentials of discipline in today's Navy. His standards are high and clearly understood. The response of *Leahy's* crew to this aggressive professional is a heartening demonstration that relaxation of standards does not equate with sloppiness . . . without hesitation I recommend his selection to flag rank.

The *Leahy* returned to the U.S. from the Mediterranean deployment on May Day, 1971. On her return, Commander Don Campbell relieved as Executive Officer (XO) and, he says, "I stepped into a whirlwind."

Don Campbell was from Idaho and had the nickname "Spud" aboard the *Leahy*. He graduated from the Naval Academy in 1954 and was initially assigned to the surface destroyer fleet. He went from there to duty in the Pacific on six submarines, the last of which he commanded. He wanted to return to the surface Navy, affording him an opportunity for more commands. He was sent to the *Leahy* as preparation for command of a surface ship.[16]

Don Campbell took on the role of ameliorator of what he considered the sometimes too harsh disciplinary tactics of Captain Hoffmann. It is a difficult and sometimes frustrating role to play, but Campbell was a professional Navy officer, who received voluminous and glowing fitness reports from Hoffmann.

Campbell admired Hoffmann, saying he "was one of the most professional naval officers I ever encountered or served with. If you had to go to war with someone, that's the guy I'd go with." He further states, "We turned that ship around. It was because of his [Hoffmann's] leadership, but also he needed that counterpart in someone like me. It wasn't a warm ship. Roy could be tougher than hell, unbending, never wavering and I could be the other half, the gentle fellow, the nice guy."

The captain, he says, "seldom slept. He roamed the ship night and day. His method was effective; you could eat off the decks of that ship, which was professional in every way." Hoffmann always, Campbell says, treated his opinions with respect, and backed him up in his decisions.

Campbell's comments about the captain are illuminating:

> I think he [Hoffmann] got tougher because he got even more professional. He was more senior, he'd seen combat, he knew what the consequences were for a ship to survive in today's environment. If we're going to get into a shooting war we've got to be able to do our part. It's going to be hard on everybody, but they're going to have to learn how to do it.
>
> There's not a lot of compassion outwardly, but inside it's eating him up. He would have made a hell of a Marine. It was almost like being a football player with a very tough coach. You've got it in you and he's going to get it out of you and make you the very best player you can be.

During the summer of 1971 the *Leahy* operated in the Atlantic between Newport, Rhode Island, and San Juan, Puerto Rico. There was a short dry dock period for rudder repairs; then a dependents' cruise to

---

16. All quotations from an interview conducted May 1, 2006. Campbell went from the *Leahy* to command of the *Adams* class USS *Conygham* (DDG 17). Campbell achieved the rank of captain; Roy Hoffmann always had a high regard for him and thought he should have made Flag rank. However, Campbell says, "I had a higher calling and had to leave the Navy [in 1980]." His father developed Alzheimer's disease and his parents needed help. In those days there was no place to put Alzheimer's disease patients, and Campbell said, "I had to get out of the Navy and make some money." His father lived 12 years after the diagnosis.

Yorktown, Virginia; midshipmen training in Newport; ASW and AAW exercises on the Atlantic Fleet Weapons Range in Puerto Rico; and liberty in Boston, New York, Newport and San Juan. The ship was awarded the COMCRUDESLANT Battle Efficiency "E" for her competitive class.

ON JUNE 8, 1971, William F. Buckley, founder of *National Review* magazine, gave the commencement address to the United States Military Academy at West Point. Buckley felt compelled to address the testimony of John Kerry before the future leaders of the United States Army. He said that Kerry's rhetoric was "the indictment of an ignorant young man" willing to charge military commanders and those serving under them; three presidents; and the American people with waging an immoral war in a criminally atrocious manner.[17]

Buckley went on to say Kerry was "the crystallization of an assault upon America which has been fostered over the years by an intellectual class given over to self-doubt and self-hatred, driven by a cultural disgust with the uses to which so many people put their freedom." Buckley reminded the graduating West Point cadets of the nobility of their sacrifice. He thought Kerry's and other's assaults on America must be countered.

"If America is the monster of John Kerry," Buckley said to the cadets, "burn your commissions tomorrow and take others, which will not bind you in the depraved conspiracy you have heard described. If it is otherwise, remember: The freedom John Kerry enjoys, and the freedom I enjoy, are, quite simply, the result of your dedication. Do you wonder that I salute you?"[18]

On June 30, 1971, John O'Neill, standing up for all veterans so slandered by John Kerry, debated him on the "Dick Cavett Show." The two former Swift boat skippers faced off in an ABC special broadcast, Kerry representing the Vietnam Veterans Against the War and O'Neill representing Vietnam Veterans for a Just Peace. The show was widely watched. John O'Neill was then as he is today: Articulate, forceful, with an encyclopedic knowledge of the facts. Kerry came across as supercilious, vacillating and vague. The audience, which had been solidly behind Kerry at the beginning, was booing him by the end. Even Dick Cavett, an antiwar sympathizer, seemed uneasy with Kerry's performance. O'Neill's moral outrage was evident, leading him later to comment that Kerry was "a self-promoted war hero who in reality was the greatest moral coward I had ever met, willing to sell out friends and comrades for political fame."

---

17. O'Neill and Corsi, *Unfit for Command*, pp. 175–176.
18. *Ibid.*

On June 13, 1971 the *New York Times* began publication of the "Pentagon Papers," the top-secret history of American involvement in Vietnam. Pentagon employee Daniel Ellsberg turned the papers over to *Times* reporter Neil Sheehan. It was a disturbing event, in that someone within the government "leaked" a top-secret document related to a policy with which he disagreed. The Nixon administration attempted to stop the publication of the documents, but on June 30 the Supreme Court ruled that the *Times* and the *Washington Post* could resume publication. Today, the *New York Times* believes it may publish top-secret papers regarding current operations, even though so doing might endanger troops or operatives in the field.

It is not an understatement to say that the publication of the "Pentagon Papers" led to Watergate, which brought down the Nixon presidency. Nixon ordered an investigation of Ellsberg, and a group was set up as a corollary to the White House, called the "plumbers." Their purpose was to try and stop "leaks." The plumbers expanded their activities to the Nixon "enemies list," and ultimately to the 1972 presidential campaign. Whether Nixon knew about their activities or not is not as relevant as the fact he created the environment in which they could flourish.

ON SEPTEMBER 15, 1971, Rear Admiral James B. Hildreth conducted Roy Hoffmann's Report on the Fitness of Officers. In the report he said:

> Captain Hoffmann is an outstanding naval officer and gentleman in every sense of the word. His vast professional background coupled with his no nonsense leadership are an inspiration to his crew ... Captain Hoffmann is an outstanding seaman and ship handler. He set an example in the Norfolk area for other DLG captains to follow in the large number of junior officers of his command who routinely make unassisted landings with the 8,000-ton ship. He is firm and fair in his dealings with subordinates regardless of race or creed.

Dave Wallace reported aboard the *Leahy* in September of 1971.[19] He graduated from college in 1968, "during the years when it wasn't 'what do you want to do,' but 'what kind of uniform do you want to wear when you're doing it.'" He went on to OCS, where one of his instructors was a former O in C on Swifts. Upon graduation in November of 1968 he tried to volunteer for Swifts, but was told they were only taking fleet-qualified officers. He was instead assigned to the USS *Skagit* (LKA 105), an attack cargo ship.

---

19. All quotations taken from June 5, 2007 interview.

By the time he finally did receive his orders to Swifts, the training had been moved to Vallejo, California, where the PBRs also trained. He arrived in the summer of 1969, completed training and then was assigned to Cat Lo, RVN (COS DIV 13), where he spent his entire year tour. From there he was assigned to BUPERS, where he was told he needed to go to a tin can if he wanted to make the Navy a career. He was assigned to the *Leahy*, where "shock of the world," Roy Hoffmann, "whom we'd all heard of," was CO. Wallace was two weeks away from promotion to full lieutenant.

Going from the 'gator Navy, which was very casual ("everything but put your feet up on the wardroom table"), to Swift boats, where the uniform of the day was flip-flops and cut-offs, to the east coast destroyer Navy was culture shock. "I reported aboard," Wallace says, "with all these career-chaser, academy types. Even Omar Bradley's grandson was aboard."[20] Without any experience for the position, Wallace was assigned as the ship's navigator.

HARRY TRAIN, ROY HOFFMANN's roommate on the *Hubbard*, and who was on the submarine desk at BUPERS during Hoffmann's time there, had by this time made Rear Admiral.[21] Train, who went on to retire as a four-star admiral, graduated in 1949 from the U.S. Naval Academy. His father, Harold C. Train, had served as Director of Naval Intelligence and retired from the Navy as a rear admiral. He served as CO of the *Arizona*, prior to Pearl Harbor, and became the last living CO of the *Arizona*.

In late 1971 and 1972, his son, Admiral Harry Train, was Commander Cruiser/Destroyer Flotilla Eight (COMCRUDESFLOT Eight); his flagship was the USS *Leahy*. On January 31, 1972, Train had this to say about Roy Hoffmann:

> Of the twelve commanding officers and unit commanders of the rank of Captain under my command, Captain Hoffmann is without question the standout and the most superbly qualified for selection to flag rank. He knew his ship better than anyone on board, made face to face contact with virtually every member of the crew everyday, knew himself as well as he knew his men, was . . . honest with both himself and his men, was a hard but fair taskmaster, was . . . loyal both up and down, and was worshipped by every man on board. He is the personification of the enlightened leader who views men, not as representatives of a certain race or creed, but as individuals, with individual needs and . . . capabilities that can be honed and tuned to the fine edge of professionalism that is the hallmark of the U.S. Navy . . . It is my firm conviction that Captain Hoffmann is far

---

20. Bradley must have turned over in his grave to have a grandson in the Navy.
21. All quotations taken from an interview conducted on October 10, 2004.

and away the best ship handler in the Navy today. As such, he has developed among his officers, the finest group of junior officer ship handlers in the Navy. I strongly urge Captain Hoffmann's immediate selection to flag rank and his assignment to the most demanding and unforgiving assignments the Navy has to offer.

Admiral Train, in an interview with this author, gave an example of Hoffmann's ship handling ability, and his unyielding requirements for excellence. The story came about as the result of a ship handling competition for all of the destroyers from CRUDESFLOT Eight that wished to compete. A competition board, composed of Hoffmann, Train, COMDESFLOT Two, and two others, judged the all day competition.

As part of the competition, the destroyers, mostly with junior grade officers as OODs, were to land in succession. The last junior officer in the competition had apparently been told that speed was the answer to every landing. Meanwhile, as the day wore on the tide currents were getting stronger. The officer came in to the landing at two-thirds speed; the board became alarmed as the ship sped toward the pier. Train first suggested to the CO of the destroyer that the officer might want to back off the speed. The CO made the suggestion to the young officer, who came to a stop bell. The pier loomed ever closer and collision was imminent.

At this point, Roy Hoffmann could stand it no longer—even though he was just a guest aboard. He took off his hat, threw it on the deck and said, "Oh, shit, I have the conn." His first command was "port ahead flank." Train says, "I damn near died."

Hoffmann's next command was "right full rudder." Then, "starboard back emergency." His objective was to get as high a powered twist on the ship as he could. He then ordered port back emergency and got the speed off, and Train says, "We just glanced the pier. The bow—the bows are really long over hangs—hit a tractor-trailer on the pier, running the nose all the way down the side of the tractor-trailer. The ship was absolutely stopped right there a foot from the dock.

"He [Hoffmann] reached down and picked up his cap with a scowl on his face, as only he can do, left the bridge and went down to the quarterdeck. It [the landing] was an amazing thing."

Rear Admiral J. B. Hildreth also commented on Hoffmann's ship handling excellence. "He is an outstanding ship handler who has trained his officers to maneuver *Leahy anywhere* [emphasis added by Hildreth] without outside assistance."

Hildreth also commented on one area in particular in which the Navy of that time was struggling: Retention of personnel. A Navy that cannot retain solid, capable sailors will suffer the consequences over the long run. In a Navy that was struggling with morale issues, the *Leahy*, under the command of Roy Hoffmann, raised the first term reenlistment rate percentage from 3.5 to over 45 per cent.

ON FEBRUARY 14, 1972, the *Leahy* deployed for another Sixth Fleet Mediterranean cruise. The Task Force of which *Leahy* was a part included the aircraft carrier USS *Franklin D. Roosevelt* (CVA 42). It was an eventful cruise.

Shortly after deploying from Norfolk, the Task Force rendezvoused and formed a larger Task Force consisting of British, Dutch and American ships, in an exercise called LANTREADEX 3-72. The Task Force participated in continuous war games with submarines, aircraft or both. During the first 35 days the ship made port twice. The first stop was a one-day logistics stop in Roosevelt Roads, Puerto Rico. The second stop was scheduled for the Bay of Biscay, off the west coast of France.

The *Roosevelt*, accompanied by her screening destroyers, including the *Leahy*, set sail in weather that was initially good. The closer the ships got to Europe the lower the barometer fell. By the time they arrived at the Bay of Biscay seas were 30 to 35 feet high and all hands were hanging on for dear life. The seas were so bad Admiral Engen told Roy Hoffmann that he actually had fish in his sea cabin that had come through the air intakes. The heavy seas caused the *Leahy* to roll almost to the righting arm (that means if you go any farther you don't come back). "Everyone was green [seasick]," Dave Wallace says, "and here comes Hoffmann out of his sea cabin smoking a cigar."

Early on March 6, *Leahy* was detached from her picket station in NATO exercise MAJIC SWORD V, to search for and assist the Dutch ship *Evertsen* as she wallowed helplessly in heavy weather north of Spain. With a large topside hatch torn off and heavy seas rolling over her bow, the *Evertsen* was in danger of going down. The French frigate *Sufferin* moved toward her position as the *Leahy* crashed through huge seas in the same direction. The next afternoon *Evertsen* was located and *Leahy* escorted her toward Bilbao, Spain, until relieved by the German ocean tug *Atlantic*.

The *Leahy* then resumed steaming with the *Roosevelt*, arriving at Rota, Spain to officially join the 6th Fleet on March 10. They got underway through the Straits of Gibraltar at night, the Anti-Submarine Team chasing submarines for several days, after which the ship's crew had liberty at Palma de Mallorca. In Palma there were many parallels with American life with discotheque nightclubs, restaurants, sight seeing, beaches and hundreds of curio shops. The ship berthed near the head of a long quay wall called Porta Pi. Taxis waited in line to transport the sailors into town. The men took advantage of Spanish wine and food, which included octopus, mussels, squid and crayfish.

Don Campbell relates that when they were in port, Roy Hoffmann would want a fast car with which to tour, and he wanted Campbell to ride with him. "We'd get in that damn car and go racing around Europe. He drove like a son of a bitch."

Campbell relates another "Nails" Hoffmann story, this about entering port. On one particular occasion Campbell asked Hoffmann what uniform he wanted the crew to wear.

"White hats, blues and pea coats," Hoffmann responded. (Campbell says, "This was when half the Navy was wearing baseball caps, and there were no baseball caps on *Leahy*. Hoffmann didn't give a damn what Zumwalt said.")

Campbell went to see the leading chief petty officer and told him, "Chief, we've got to be in blues and white hats and pea coats."

"What did you just say?" the chief asked.

"I said we've got to be in blues, white hats and pea coats."

"XO," the chief responded, "the crew doesn't have pea coats."

"What do you mean the crew doesn't have pea coats? What are all those lockers for I'm inspecting all the damn time?"

Chief: "They *sell* their pea coats."

"Jesus," Campbell said, "these guys have got to be in pea coats, you understand?"

The chief, who had been in the Navy a long time, replied, "If you keep the captain looking forward, I'll take care of it."

As they entered port, the captain stood on the port side forward. The sailors lined the port side rail; those sailors that had pea coats lined up forward, and those without lined up beside them toward the stern. Campbell, who is larger than Hoffmann, stood aft of him, trying to block his view. Just beyond the break of the ship, about halfway down, there were no more pea coats. Those sailors were in foul weather jackets. "Captain Hoffmann never noticed," Campbell says.

Captain Hoffmann liked to let his sailors blow off steam in port as long as they stayed out of trouble. His general quarters boatswain's mate of the watch, a squared away sailor on board, loved to go on the beach and fight

Marines. He usually won the encounters. After one fight, the Shore Patrol (SP) brought him back, under arrest. Hoffmann and the XO were afraid the SP would prefer charges again the boatswain, escalating the incident and taking it out of the hands of the ship. The captain and XO decided to hold a Captain's Mast right away, to protect the boatswain from outside charges, since that would be double jeopardy.

Hoffmann took the sailor to Mast and read him the riot act, telling him what a crap sailor he was. Then, according to Dave Wallace, the captain looked at the sailor and "gave that little tilt of his head and said with a wry smile, 'I heard you kicked their [the Marines] asses, Boats.'"

The sailor got a big smile and said, "Yes, captain, I did! Do you want to hear about it?"

Hoffmann replied, "You'll have plenty of time to tell me about it, because you're restricted to the ship for 90 days." However, the captain didn't bust the boatswain, because he didn't want to lose him as his general quarters boatswain's mate of the watch. "Roy Hoffmann was toughest on people he thought should be doing better or he had high hopes for," Wallace says. "The others he wouldn't give the time of day to."

The *Leahy* next stopped at Naples, Italy, then steamed to Cannes, France, after which the Task Force participated in exercise QUICKDRAW with the Italian Navy. The Sixth Fleet on April 10, 1972, rendezvoused with all available ships for a Fleet Review in honor of a remarkable man, Admiral Horacio "Rivets" Rivero. Rivets retired on May 1, 1972, after 46 years of service.

A Fleet Review is a rare honor paid to only a few great men. "Operation Rivets" was held with no publicity and was a private salute from the U.S. Navy to one of its own. Rivero was born in Poncie, Puerto Rico, the son of a carpenter. He entered the U.S. Naval Academy at the age of 16, speaking Spanish while taking English as his foreign language. One of the smallest men in physical stature to enter the Academy, he graduated number one in his class with ease. He went on to post graduate work at MIT, again finishing first in his class. He specialized in radar, at a time few people knew of its existence.

As a lieutenant in the early phases of World War II, he evaluated, contracted for and supervised the installation of all of the fire control radars in the ships of the U.S. Navy. He went on to distinguish himself as XO on a cruiser during combat. He played a major role in saving the ship and her crew after a hurricane tore the bow loose from the rest of the ship. He went on to plan weapons systems and operational tactics for the Navy, and played a large role in the design of modern missile ships.

USS Leahy, *Naples, Italy, 1972.* Dave Wallace photo

He made Flag rank at age 43, one of the youngest in modern history to be so honored, and served in Flag capacity for over 18 years. Advanced to full admiral (four-star) in 1964, he served as Vice Chief of Naval Operations for four years. On retirement he was Commander of Allied NATO Forces, a position he held for four years. A superb diplomat, he was credited with bringing about one of the greatest periods of NATO cooperation in the history of the alliance.

On April 10, the USS *Springfield* (CLG 4) broke Admiral Rivero's flag, and the admiral and his wife were taken to a rendezvous in the Tyrrhenian Sea. There, with precise timing, the participating Sixth Fleet ships (33 in number) steamed in two columns, one led by *Leahy*, past the admiral's Flagship as he received his Fleet Review.

The *Leahy* spent a week in Barcelona, Spain, and then transited to the Eastern Mediterranean, where they once again encountered the continuous presence of Soviet shadowing ships and frequent over flights by Soviet reconnaissance aircraft.

May 2–8, 1972, the *Leahy* made the first of two visits to Athens, Greece. Getting underway again the ship participated in the huge NATO exercise DAWN PATROL, which inclued 78 ships of six nations. As part of the exercise, two Greek gunboats tested *Leahy's* detection systems.

"Under Roy Hoffmann," Dave Wallace says, "you didn't just detect, you detected and then *killed them.*" They found the Greek gunboats cruising among the vast network of Greek islands, and the 533-foot *Leahy* chased the gunboats around the islands. Wallace and CIC tried to keep up with position reports, and the boatswain's mate of the watch called out Fathometer readings to Wallace on the bridge.

Hoffmann moved from one side of the bridge to the other yelling out instructions, "All ahead flank! Right full rudder! There they are, I can see the sons of bitches!" as his stressed Navigator thinks they are going to run straight on to an island dead ahead.

"Navigator recommends all back emergency, left full rudder!" Wallace called out in alarm as the ship entered water with a depth of 50 feet.

Wallace says the captain turned around, "and gave me a look that could have killed an elephant."

"Make it so," the captain said.

Wallace says, "If the U.S. Navy were ever down to one World War II destroyer and needed the Suez Canal opened up, the captain would have to be Roy Hoffmann. The *Leahy* was one of the few ships I observed in my last two years in the Navy that was really ready for a combat mission."

One night *Leahy*, while steaming independently, anchored within sight of the Soviet-used anchorage at Kithira Bank; eight or nine Soviet ships were anchored there. The Soviets lacked the sophisticated replenishment system U.S. ships had, and usually anchored to replenish.

The next morning, a Sunday, Captain Hoffmann said, "Why don't we have some fun?"

Navigator Dave Wallace asked, "Captain, what are your intentions here?"

Hoffmann replied, "We're going to go through the middle of the Soviet anchorage."

"Sir?" Wallace asked.

One of The Black Aces from Fighter Squadron 41 dogs a Russian "Bear" (a spy plane). OFFICIAL U.S. NAVY PHOTO, HOFFMANN COLLECTION

Hoffmann said, "Boatswain's mate of the watch, get that John Philip Sousa music on, and put some missiles on the rail."

Wallace says, "We then go blazing through at close to 30 knots in the middle of the Kithira anchorage with unarmed missiles on the rail, blaring 'The Stars and Stripes Forever,' over the 1MC [speakers], with Hoffmann standing on the port wing waving at the Russians." When they got there the Soviet ships were all at General Quarters.

"Undaunted, we did a wide circle and came back through. The crew loved it."

"The Soviets knew us," Hoffmann says, "from the time we arrived in the Med until the time we left. They probably said 'Thank God' when we left."

On May 25 the ship anchored in Soudha Bay and "Swim Call" was piped down as most of the crew took advantage of the deep, clear water. On May 31, *Leahy* anchored at the island of Rhodes for six days of well-earned liberty, after which the ship went into Athens again, for 14 days.

There is a large basin east of Sicily bordered on the north by Italy,

Captain Hoffmann, Lieutenant Ken Reid, Lieutenant Dick Fates, Lieutenant Dean Steele and Lieutenant Jim Olwin are briefed before the flight mission, June 9, 1972, by Commander Ed Hickey. Aboard the USS Franklin D. Roosevelt (CVA 42).
OFFICIAL U.S. NAVY PHOTO, HOFFMANN COLLECTION

USS Franklin D. Roosevelt (CVA 42) underway with air wing aboard.
OFFICIAL U.S. NAVY PHOTO, HOFFMANN COLLECTION

Part Three: Vietnam to Retirement 357

The Black Aces in formation. Official U.S. Navy photo, Hoffmann collection

Back aboard the Roosevelt (Official U.S. Navy photo, Hoffmann collection).

Greece, and Turkey, all NATO members, and the Aegean Sea. Along the African coast lie the Arab countries, then mostly politically aligned with Soviet Russia. To the east is the explosive Middle East. Into this confined area the two most powerful fleets in the world, the Soviet and U.S. navies, operated while training, asserting their political influence, and protecting their international rights of commerce. The close proximity of the two antagonists created a tense drama as they asserted their rights while attempting to prevent the start of war.

As Soviet shipping transited the Black Sea through the Aegean Sea and into the Med, the Sixth Fleet kept close watch on their movements. Each Soviet over flight (done by planes called "Bears," the equivalent of an American B-52) was identified, tracked on radar and escorted by U.S. fighter jets if they threatened the Fleet.

The *Roosevelt* was on her last cruise and her Air Ops and CIC were at best obsolete. The *Leahy* was a Naval Tactical Data (NTDS) ship, and so *Leahy's* CIC ended up controlling the *Roosevelt's* aircraft once they were airborne. On an intercept the ship would give the aircraft a course to come up

USS Leahy *(DLG 16), Captain Hoffmann commanding, steaming in company with the* USS Franklin D. Roosevelt *(CVA 42), and the* USS Rigel *(AF 58).*
OFFICIAL U.S. NAVY PHOTO, HOFFMANN COLLECTION

under the Soviet Bear from the stern. When the aircraft had visual contact of the Bear he would say "Tally Ho" and resume command of his own aircraft. The Americans would often get above the wing of the Bear where the pilot could look into the Soviet aircraft.

The constant exercises, training and tracking meant a life underway of hard work and long hours for the crews of the Fleet. CIC was on port and starboard watches of five hours on and five off. Still, the slogan of the Fleet was "more sweat in peace means less blood in war."

On June 9, 1972, Roy Hoffmann got the chance to see first hand what it was like to be in on an aerial intercept in a U.S. Navy jet. He left the *Leahy* in a helo and was transported to the *Roosevelt*. Once aboard he went through a briefing, strapped himself into the rear seat of an AE 104, F4J Phantom, and was catapulted off the USS *Franklin D. Roosevelt*. During his flight the plane flew supersonic at 1.5 mach, and participated in what the pilots called "daisy cutters" flying a few feet off the water. Don Campbell says Hoffmann's flight group, with the captain in the lead aircraft, came out of the sun, and passed the *Leahy* a few feet off the deck. The passing planes "blew the windows out of the bridge as they hit afterburners and went straight up." While in the air Hoffmann's plane received fuel in flight from an A-7, and then made an arrested landing aboard the *Roosevelt*.

Hoffmann arrived back at the *Leahy* in a helo, and according to Campbell, "gave me a big grin and he proceeded up to his cabin. I looked at him and he's got blood coming out of both ears. He ruptured both eardrums during the flight and couldn't hear a word I was saying. He really loved those pilots and would do anything for them."

The *Leahy* continued with antisubmarine and air defense war games, and was stationed astern of the *Roosevelt* as rescue destroyer. One night an F-4 Phantom jet approached the carrier deck when suddenly over the radio circuit came, "Wave off! Wave off!" The Squadron Commander piloted the plane; his plane was low on fuel and he broke into the landing pattern out of turn as he attempted a second landing. He caught the hook the second time but it didn't hold. He hit the throttle as the rear seat airman, who controlled the ejection, hit the ejection button, blowing the canopy off. The jet hit low and skidded off the side, now absent the two ejected pilots. Rescue crews aboard *Leahy* ran to their stations as the OOD backed the engines down hard.

"Two men in the water," the radio crackled as searchlights probed the dark sea. *Leahy* picked up the Squadron Commander by throwing him a horse collar, and the rescue helicopter found the navigator. Hoffmann says,

"That was a sad situation because the crash landing finished the Squadron Commander's career."

As American troops left South Vietnam in greater numbers, the Communists became more emboldened. On March 30, 1972, North Vietnam launched a massive offensive across the DMZ into South Vietnam. President Nixon responded on April 15 by ordering the resumption of bombing in North Vietnam. On May 1 the Communists captured the city of Quang Tri, and Nixon responded again on May 8 by announcing the mining of Haiphong harbor and stepped-up bombing raids against North Vietnam.

The vast effort to save South Vietnam as an independent, non-Communist country was lost, in essence, on June 17, 1972. On that date, five men were arrested at the Democratic National Committee offices at the Watergate Office building. The men were carrying cash and documents that showed they were employed by the Committee to Reelect the President, Nixon's campaign group for his 1972 reelection campaign. The purpose of the break-in was to plant listening devices in the phones of Democratic leaders and to obtain political documents related to campaign strategy.

Subsequent to the arrests of the five men, two former intelligence operatives, G. Gordon Liddy and E. Howard Hunt, were arrested for their involvement in the break-in. Hunt, it turned out, was one of the CIA agents responsible for planning the Bay of Pigs debacle, and some of the Cubans arrested in the initial group also took part in the invasion of Cuba. The wheels had been set in motion to bring down the presidency of Richard Nixon. Ultimately, Watergate and the aftermath would embolden the Democrats in Congress to cut off all funding for support of our allies in South Vietnam, leading directly to the fall of the country to the Communists in 1975.

Meanwhile, in July of 1972, Jane Fonda engaged in the remarkably treasonous act of visiting the capital of our enemy combatant during wartime, there to denounce the American soldiers fighting for her right to be so vacuous. Fonda, who has acting talent but little common sense, made the highly visible and publicized trip to Hanoi while the war still raged and while POWs were held under brutal conditions; and after more than 40,000 Americans had already been killed on the battlefields of Vietnam. Others of the far left wing in America, including Senator Ted Kennedy, former attorney general Ramsey Clark, Jesuit priest Daniel Berrigan, Reverend William Sloan Coffin and one-time Fonda husband Tom Hayden, had visited Hanoi, but none had the fame of "glamorous" Jane Fonda.

Fonda put on the helmet of a North Vietnamese soldier, sang antiwar songs, and sat in the gunner's seat of an AAA battery presumably used to shoot down "American imperialist air raiders." The North Vietnamese fully capitalized on her folly, using her radio broadcasts and films to help break the morale of U.S. troops and to encourage the enemy fighting them. In one broadcast from the enemy capital she said, "I am speaking particularly to U.S. servicemen . . . your weapons are illegal and . . . the men who are ordering you to use these weapons are war criminals according to international law. In the past, in Germany and Japan, men who committed these kinds of crimes were tried and executed."

She returned home wearing a necklace made from the melted parts of an American B-52 bomber shot down by the North Vietnamese. She told the media our prisoners of war were safe and well taken care of. The reality was different.

She went to Hoa Lo and met with seven POWs. One of them, Navy lieutenant commander David Hoffman, shot down while flying his F-4 over Vietnam on December 30, 1971, was tortured until he agreed to appear. Hoffman's guards got violently angry when he refused to go, and they broke again an arm broken when he was shot down. They twisted the arm as great pain shot through him. John McCain was beaten in an unsuccessful attempt to get him to meet with Fonda.

Hoffman says, "I was dragged out to see Fonda. When I . . . heard her antiwar rhetoric, I was almost sick to my stomach. She called us criminals and murderers."[22]

North Vietnamese Colonel Bui Tin has said of the American antiwar movement:

> It was essential to our strategy. Everyday our leadership would listen to world news over the radio at 9 A.M. to follow the growth of the American antiwar movement. Visits to Hanoi by people like Jane Fonda and former Attorney General Ramsey Clark and ministers gave us confidence that we should hold on in the face of battlefield reverses. We were elated when Jane Fonda, wearing a red Vietnamese dress, said at a press conference that she was ashamed of American actions in the war and that she would struggle along with us.[23]

Lewis Sorley said, "After the war Admiral Elmo Zumwalt visited Vietnam and talked with Communist leaders. 'General Giap was very clear,'

---

22. Patterson, *Reckless Disregard*, pp. 48–49.
23. Lewis Sorley, *A Better War* (New York: Harcourt Brace & Company, 1999), p. 93.

said Zumwalt. 'They always knew they had to win it here [in the United States] and the Jane Fondas of the world were of great use to them.'"[24]

Other than the disgust of veterans and their families, Jane Fonda suffered no adverse consequences from her visit, and is, in fact, today lionized by the left and adored by her movie fans.

BY THIS TIME VICE ADMIRAL ENGEN had assumed command of Carrier Division Four. Engen had entered the Navy through the aviation cadet program and was designated a naval aviator in June of 1942. In 1943–44 he flew a SB2C Helldiver and participated in the Battle of Leyte Gulf. In the Korean War he was part of the U.S. Navy's first-ever jet sortie in combat. He commanded the ammunition ship *Mount Katmai* (AE 16) and in 1966–67 commanded the aircraft carrier *America*.

As COMCARDIV Four Admiral Engen appreciated the professional support provided by the *Leahy*. In a message to Captain Hoffmann on July 23 he said, "*Leahy* has no equal in professionalism. No carrier has ever had a better partner. Anytime that I hear AAW or excellence or both I will always think of *Leahy*."

With the high accolades from his superiors, it was a disappointment, to say the least, when Captain Roy Hoffmann was not selected for Flag rank the first time he was up. The highly competitive process considers something like the top 50 captains in the Navy, and the board selects maybe ten of those for Flag rank.

The Flag Board met when Campbell was with Roy Hoffmann on the Med cruise. Campbell says, "When the Flag Board met, he didn't make it, and there was an odds-on chance he was going to. He had the right seniority; he'd punched all the holes in his career. He was really hurt when he was not selected, and I guess I would have been too."

The reasons for the non-selection are unclear, as the deliberations of the Flag Board are done in secret. As Hoffmann says, "You had to have 'water walker' fitness reports to make admiral, but that still was no guarantee."[25] Perhaps the blunt, outspoken captain had offended someone, or maybe he was number 11 on the list. In any event, it was the first setback in a career that had marched steadily along.

---

24. *Ibid.* pp. 93–94.
25. John D. Bulkeley, one of the finest naval officers this country has produced, took three trips before the Selection Board to make it—and President John F. Kennedy probably made the difference for him.

The *Leahy* finally arrived home on August 12, 1972. On the ship's return from the Med cruise Rear Admiral R. O. Welander, COMCRUDESFLOT Eight wrote:

> I am convinced that this was one of the rare instances when a ship directly and faithfully mirrored the qualities of the commanding officer.... As she was was the only NTDS ship in the task group, *Leahy* regularly fulfilled the role of Anti-Air Warfare Commander and did a superb job. Captain Hoffmann ... is one of the most professionally competent destroyer men I have ever met. His leadership is such that he transmits this same dedication and drive for excellence to his entire wardroom and crew ... There is ample evidence of deep mutual trust and respect between this uniquely effective commanding officer and his officers and men. I recommend without reservation and strongly urge that Captain Hoffmann be selected for flag rank at the earliest selection opportunity; the Navy should not delay in giving this unique officer the scope and responsibility within which he may attain his obvious potential.

On September 11, 1972, the Change of Command Ceremony occurred at the Destroyer-Submarine Piers, wherein Captain Watt W. Jordan, Jr., USN, relieved Captain Hoffmann as CO of the *Leahy*. And so it ended, the position Roy Hoffmann most enjoyed in the Navy, command of a ship at sea. The born sea captain would now have to adjust to the Navy bureaucracy. It was not smooth sailing ahead.

Captain Roy and Mary Linn Hoffmann at the Leahy *homecoming.*
OFFICIAL U.S. NAVY PHOTO, HOFFMANN COLLECTION

ADVANCEMENT AND RETIREMENT

In September 1972 the Hoffmanns left Norfolk for 672 South Harrison Street in Arlington, Virginia, and Captain Roy Hoffmann reported to the Office of CNO at the Pentagon in Washington, D.C. He assumed the position of Head, Current Plans Branch, and reported to the Deputy CNO for Operations (a three-star). It was a highly desirable job and a stepping-stone to admiral.

The bureaucracy was a world of its own, and Hoffmann says, "It takes six months to get up to the language and the system." There was a maddening set of acronyms to learn, and a pecking order to navigate. In addition, every Navy officer goes there swearing he wasn't going to forget his roots in the seagoing Navy ("Don't forget the fleet" was the mantra). The reason the Pentagon exists is to support the troops and it's very easy to forget that. For a quintessential man of action, the process of writing memos to do business and the agonizing budget process must have been a difficult adjustment.

Having just come from his own ship, Hoffmann was appalled at what he perceived as the lack of discipline in the fleet and shore Navy. He believed discipline and morale went hand in hand. One of the first things he did on arrival was to request a personal interview to address the problem with the CNO, Admiral Elmo Zumwalt. Hoffmann believed that Admiral Zumwalt did not fully appreciate that his Z-grams had the net effect of bypassing the Navy's senior officers. Hoffmann knew that Zumwalt did not want yes men on his staff, and he knew he could approach Zumwalt from a position of mutual trust and respect.

As it turned out, one did not just walk in and talk to the CNO. Zumwalt was surrounded by what was called his Z-gram or kitchen cabinet, and a member of "the team" came to Hoffmann and requested he write a memo to Zumwalt so he would know the subject of the interview. Hoffmann responded, "If I have to go through all that to see the admiral, you can forget it."

"Is that what you want us to tell the admiral?" asked the functionary. (No doubt someone else was thinking, "There goes *his* career.")

"Yes," Hoffmann responded. The functionary went back and about a day later Hoffmann was informed the CNO wanted to speak with him. When he arrived in Zumwalt's office, he looked up and said, "What's up, Roy?"

Hoffmann led off with, "You're going to have a mutiny, admiral."

"Those are pretty strong words."

"Yes, they are," Hoffmann responded, "but I mean them sincerely. I don't know if it's going to be aboard a minesweeper, submarine, destroyer, or aircraft carrier, but it's going to happen." He expanded on the problems he had seen in the fleet as the intense CNO listened carefully. He asked Hoffmann what he recommended.

"The simplest thing," he said, "is to reemphasize 'The Watch Officer's Guide.' It should be required reading for every officer on board. It's just basic discipline, that's all it is. Discipline is slipping away from us; in fact we are precariously close to losing it."

Although Roy Hoffmann now says, "I don't think Zumwalt really wanted to hear what I said about discipline," he did ask him to write a memo. Hoffmann responded with a short one; shortly thereafter there was a walk-off on an aircraft carrier in San Diego. A series of ugly incidents followed which exposed much of what was wrong with the Navy.

In late 1972, at least four ships experienced racial violence in which small groups of blacks attacked whites. There were other reports of rioting, disobedience and threats of sabotage. "FTN" (Fuck the Navy) signs began to appear on base and in the fleet. Some of the problems related to the problems of recruitment and retention of quality sailors. Woefully unprepared young men, both white and black, were recruited into an increasingly technologically oriented Navy. This was particularly true of many blacks who lacked the basic skills required for advancement, but had been promised a career opportunity in the Navy. They thought the menial tasks, lacking advancement potential, to which they had been assigned were the results of institutionalized racism.

Many in the Navy thought that Zumwalt's reforms, expressed in his Z-grams, went too far, too fast. Zumwalt vigorously defended the reforms, saying the Navy merely reflected turmoil occurring in the rest of the country. He thought the Navy had to change and adjust to the new conditions.

An increasingly aging and obsolete fleet compounded the problems on the Navy's ships, which sailed with undermanned and overworked crews.

ON NOVEMBER 7, 1972, President Richard Nixon defeated his Democratic challenger, Senator George McGovern, burying him in a landslide. Nixon got 60.8 per cent of the popular vote and 520 of 537 electoral votes. McGovern was really a fringe antiwar player on what was then the far left of the Democratic Party. Watergate had not attracted the attention of the public yet, but even if it were better known it's doubtful McGovern could have won. He carried only Washington, D.C., and Massachusetts.

In liberal Massachusetts John Kerry was defeated in his race against Republican Paul Cronin for the Fifth Congressional seat. Kerry had thought his radical antiwar activities would help him in the state, but the voters rejected him. From this election on, Kerry de-emphasized his antiwar record and began to promote his "war hero" image as the way to political office.

On January 22, 1973, a heart attack felled former president Lyndon Johnson. Ironically, the next day, Dr. Henry Kissinger and Le Duc Tho initialed an agreement "ending" the war in Vietnam and providing for the release of American prisoners of war. The agreement was formally signed January 27. On March 29 the last American troops left Vietnam and on April 1 the last known American prisoners of war arrived at Clark Air Base in the Philippines.

On February 7, 1973, the U.S. Senate established a Select Committee on Presidential Campaign Activities, chaired by North Carolina Senator Sam Ervin. The committee was formed to look into rumors of political dirty tricks, corrupt financing and other wrongdoing by the Nixon reelection committee. Begun in part as a political witch-hunt by the Democratic Congress, disturbing signs of wrongdoing showed up as they turned over the rock and found out what lay beneath. Led by a crusading judge, John Sirica, the trail soon led directly to John Mitchell, Nixon's former Attorney General, who became the chairman of the Committee to Reelect the President (later given the appropriate acronym "CREEP").

On April 20, L. Patrick Gray, acting director of the FBI, resigned after admitting he had destroyed evidence relating to Watergate. Ten days later Nixon's chief of staff, H. R. Haldeman, domestic affairs assistant John Ehrichman, and presidential counsel John Dean III, all resigned. The wheels were coming off the Nixon administration.

On June 25 John Dean went before Ervin's Senate committee and accused Nixon of involvement in the Watergate cover up, and further stated that Nixon had authorized payment of "hush money" to the seven men arrested in the break-in. The allegations were true, as it turned out.

Three weeks later, White House aide Alexander Butterfield electrified the nation when he disclosed that President Nixon had secretly recorded all Oval Office conversations. A constitutional crisis ensued, with Nixon asserting "executive privilege" to keep his conversations private, and the Senate insisting the tapes be released to that body. The release of the tapes was fatal to the Nixon presidency.

On October 10, 1973, the sorry mess in Washington became even more sordid as Vice President Spiro Agnew resigned after pleading nolo contendere (no contest) to tax evasion charges dating from his days as governor of Maryland. Two days later Nixon nominated House Minority Leader Gerald Ford to succeed Agnew under the provisions of the Twenty-fifth Amendment.[26] As it turned out, Nixon had picked the next president.

---

26. Ford, a decent and honorable man, was characterized by Lyndon Johnson as "a nice fellow, but he spent too much time playing football without a helmet."

On October 20, "The Saturday Night Massacre" occurred when Nixon ordered Attorney General Elliot Richardson to fire Watergate Special Prosecutor Archibald Cox, who had demanded the actual Oval Office tapes, rather than the synopsis Nixon offered. Richardson and his assistant, William D. Ruckelshaus, resigned rather than fire Cox. Solicitor General Robert Bork did the deed.[27]

The weakened presidency of Richard Nixon allowed the Congress, on November 7, to override his veto of the War Powers Act, which restricted the President's power to commit troops to foreign countries without congressional approval.

IN 1973 THE FLAG SELECTION BOARD met; this time Harry Train was on the board. Hoffmann now says, "I knew that was a big plus from the very beginning." The Flag Board, which generally consists of at least seven flag officers, this time selected Roy Hoffmann for advancement to Rear Admiral. It was a well-deserved promotion and appropriate recognition for an outstanding career. By this time the second oldest Hoffmann daughter, Chris, was dating Steve Carnahan, whose father, submariner Ralph Carnahan, was selected for advancement to admiral in the same group.

With the selection, Admiral Hoffmann was moved to the position of Director of Surface Warfare. In the position he had more contact with the CNO, Admiral Zumwalt, who tended to focus fully on what he was doing at the moment. One time he was walking to a meeting with the Admiral (Roy Hoffmann) and other staffers. Zumwalt was reading a briefing paper as they navigated the corridors of the Pentagon. The staffers got around a corner and realized Zumwalt had disappeared. He had walked into a broom closet while reading the paper. He came out laughing at himself, and said, "You guys booby trapped me."

ON SATURDAY MORNING, October 6, 1973, Syria and Egypt attacked Israel, catching both the U.S. CIA and armed services establishment by complete surprise.[28] The attack also caught the Israelis by surprise, in

---

27. The Democrats got their revenge on Bork in 1988, when Ronald Reagan nominated him to the Supreme Court. The eminently qualified jurist was rejected for his views on judicial restraint, not his qualifications. The Senate hearings on Supreme Court nominees have been something of a circus since.

28. Descriptions of the Yom Kippur War were taken from Stephen E. Ambrose, *Nixon Ruin and Recovery 1973–1990* (New York: Touchstone, 1991), pp. 229–259.

part because the attack began on their religious holy day of Yom Kippur. Egypt and Syria crashed into territory occupied by Israel since the 1967 war, with tanks, missiles, planes and infantry. The Syrians drove the Israelis off the Golan Heights, and the Egyptians destroyed the vaunted Bar-Lev defense line. They drove several miles into the Sinai and entrenched. The stunning victories shocked an Israel prepared for a short war, not one lasting weeks.

In a sense it was another proxy war, with the Americans backing Israel and the Soviets backing the attacking Arabs. President Nixon had to walk a delicate line between preserving his détente policy, while keeping the Soviets from further incursions into the Middle East, and preventing an Arab victory. Looming in the background was a direct superpower confrontation, with all of the nuclear risks implied.

With Watergate Nixon's most immediate crisis, Secretary of State Henry Kissinger stepped into the diplomatic breech, ignoring the President while he dealt with the crisis. Kissinger focused on starting a peace process immediately.[29]

Meanwhile, the Israelis launched devastating counterattacks that threatened the overextended Egyptian Army, which was cut off from supplies. Israel built a causeway across the Canal, allowing them to control both banks. The Soviet Union responded by moving its naval forces into the Eastern Mediterranean, and prepared to fly paratroopers into Egypt. They were determined to prevent Israel from completely crushing the Egyptians. Nixon responded by putting U.S. forces on worldwide alert, and he ordered the Sixth Fleet into the waters off Egypt as a signal to the Soviets that he would brook no interference from them.

Kissinger worked to convince a reluctant Israel to accept a cease-fire. At 12:52 A.M. on October 22 the U.N. Security Council adopted Resolution 338, jointly sponsored by the U.S. and the Soviet Union, which mandated a cease-fire in the Middle East. The Israelis ignored that Resolution, and another one, causing Anwar Sadat to publicly call on both the U.S. and the Soviet Union to make them comply. The Soviets were threatening "the gravest consequences" if the Israelis didn't comply; finally, under U.S. pressure, they did.

---

29. Watergate had crippled the Nixon presidency, and thus the Nation's ability to deal with the war. Kissinger justified his usurpation of presidential authority thusly, "It was not clear that Nixon retained enough authority to manage the manifold pressures about to descend on him."

NIXON MANAGED TO HANG ON to his shattered presidency into 1974. On August 5, 1974, in a televised address to the Nation, Nixon released transcripts of a conversation with chief of staff H. R. Haldeman, which showed that six days after the Watergate break in, Nixon ordered the FBI to stop investigating the incident. It was the "smoking gun" that Nixon's enemies had been looking for. Nixon's congressional support faded after the speech, and his removal from office became certain.

Three days later he announced his resignation, effective at noon on August 9, 1974. On August 9 he formally resigned and left for California after a maudlin speech to his staff. Vice President Gerald Ford was sworn in as President. Almost a month later, President Ford granted Nixon a "full, free and absolute pardon ... for all offenses against the United States which he ... has committed or may have committed or taken part in while President." The pardon would, two years later, usher in the unfortunate presidency of Jimmy Carter.

ON JULY 1, 1974, Roy Hoffmann was officially advanced to Rear Admiral, and in November moved to the U.S. Naval Station at Charleston, South Carolina (Mary Linn followed in February 1975), where he relieved as the Commander Mine Warfare Force. It was not the command he hoped for.

What he wanted was command of a destroyer flotilla, the position he was most suited for by experience and disposition, and which would have been the most beneficial to the Navy. Unfortunately, fate had intervened in the form of a horrific plane crash.

The Admiral, still in the Pentagon at the time, had been scheduled to go with the Commander of the Mine Warfare Force to jointly brief the Chairman of the Senate Armed Services Committee, John Stennis, on the plan to reopen the Suez Canal. The Commander, his Chief of Staff, Ops officer and four other staffers were flying from Charleston, South Carolina to Washington, D.C., via Charlotte, North Carolina, on Flight 212, a DC-9-31 carrying 78 passengers and four crew members. The plane crashed while on an instrument approach in dense fog into Douglas Municipal Airport at Charlotte. The crash, which occurred just short of the runway, killed 71 of the occupants of the plane, including most of the senior staff of the Mine Warfare Force. The aircraft was destroyed by the impact and resulting fire.

As soon as he heard of the crash the Admiral knew he would be ordered to Charleston and the Mine Warfare Force. He had the experience, and the Navy was then engaged in the planning stages of Operation "Nimbus

A C-130 refuels an RH-53D helicopter, used for mine warfare countermeasures during the clearing of the Suez Canal. Hoffmann photo

Bomb craters, Suez Canal, 1974. Hoffmann photo

Stream," the second phase of clearing the Suez Canal. He got message orders (meaning "come yesterday"). He went immediately to Charleston.

Chris Hoffmann and Steve Carnahan were to have been married in January 1975, but they moved the wedding up to November 1974 to accommodate the change. Harriet entered the Northern Virginia Training Center that November; just Emilie remained at home with the Admiral and Mary Linn.

FROM APRIL TO DECEMBER 1974, U.S. Navy Task Force 65 operated to clear and reopen the Suez Canal (Operation Nimbus Stream). To facilitate the clearing of the Suez Canal, the 18,300-ton helicopter carrier USS *Iwo Jima* anchored six miles from war-battered Port Said in Egypt. The ship was there to help our former enemies clear and reopen the Suez Canal of explosives and wreckage that had blocked it since the Six-Day War of 1967. U.S. Navy RH-53 Sea Stallion helicopters, units of the Mine Warfare Force, flying off the carrier, were involved in the first stage of the project. Working with British minesweepers, they located thousands of mines, shells, rockets and bombs that had gone into the 107-mile canal during the Six-Day War of 1967 and the Yom Kippur War. The operation was initially under the

Battle damage after the Yom Kippur War, 1973. HOFFMANN PHOTO

RH 53 Delta helicopter, Suez Canal, 1974. Hoffmann photo

Reopening the Suez Canal after the 1973 Yom Kippur War. Hoffmann photo

Returning to the ship, reopening of the Suez Canal. HOFFMANN PHOTO

command of Rear Admiral Brian McCauley, who had previously directed the minesweeping of Haiphong harbor.

During the minesweeping phase, the U.S. Navy used Sea Stallion helicopters towing minesweeping sleds for airborne mine countermeasures, and the Brits used conventional ship minesweepers. The Brits went from the Red Sea to the Med and the U.S. swept from the Med to the Red Sea, thus achieving double coverage.

The helicopters swept for magnetic, acoustic and pressure mines and mapped the bed of the Suez Canal to plot the detritus blocking shipping.[30] The second phase of the clearing, called "Nimbus Moon," used the information to find, defuse, or explode the munitions. The minesweeping took over two months, and it took a year to detonate all the explosives in the Canal and along its banks.

The final phase involved a massive salvage effort to remove the tanks, trucks, boats, and 12 large ships buried in the mud of the Canal. There were an additional 16 rusting ships still afloat in the Great Bitter Lake, trapped since the 1967 fighting.

---

30. See Chapter 3 for an explanation of the various types of mines used in mine warfare.

At Charleston the Admiral oversaw Nimbus Star, while working with the American State Department and Vice Admiral Bell-Davies, the British attaché in Washington, D.C. The Admiral's flag lieutenant was Dick Reass (who eventually retired as a Navy captain).[31] Reass wanted to go over to the Canal for the operation. The Admiral agreed, but told him he was going to be working with Egyptian Admiral Mohammed Ali Mohammed.[32] Normally, it wouldn't be an issue, but Reass was Jewish, and Nimbus Star was an important part of the reestablishment and normalization of relations with Egypt.

Reass responded, "I'm an officer of the United States Navy, sir." ("I loved that answer," the Admiral said). The Admiral picked Reass for the assignment.

Admiral Ike Kidd, the Atlantic Fleet Commander during Nimbus Star, proved to be the most difficult part of the operation for Roy Hoffmann. Kidd was a qualified deep-sea diver (he had a diving helmet on his desk), and was as usual hands on. The Navy did not have the salvage equipment available to clear the Canal of all the sunken debris and ships (two of the ships had actually been sunk perpendicular to the channel). American salvage ships, purchased from the Germans and left over from clearing operations during the Vietnam War, had to be towed from Subic Bay in the Philippines to the Red Sea, across the Indian Ocean. They first had to be towed to Singapore for overhaul. At least twice a day Ike Kidd would ask for a position report on the heavy lift craft. Kidd couldn't understand why the seagoing tugs, towing the heavy lift craft, were taking so long.

The Admiral's chief of staff at the Mine Warfare Command was Captain Charles Stratmann, a naval aviaator and fellow native of Crystal City, Missouri.[33] Hoffmann and Stratmann had grown up together and lived across the street from each other as youths. Stratmann was good friends with the Admiral's younger brother, Paul. Of his job as chief of staff, Stratmann says, "There was nothing to do—he [the Admiral] did everything. It was the most boring job I ever had."

---

31. Captain Dick Reass, USN, Ret. interview, August 3, 2007. Reass was an NROTC graduate of the University of Texas; he was commissioned on June 4, 1966 and retired in November of 1993. During his distinguished Navy career he had five ship commands and one shore command. He is married to Madelyn Reass, and they have a son, Matthew, and had a disabled daughter, Alexis, who has passed away.

32. Mohammed Ali had been standing next to Gamel Abdel Nasser, the president of Egypt, when he was assassinated in 1970.

33. Quotes taken from an interview conducted June 6, 2007. Stratmann retired as a captain in 1977. He enlisted June 3, 1946, and was later commissioned in the USNR.

The cost of the minesweeping to the U.S. was estimated at about $15 million, part of the $250 million in aid for Egypt that the Nixon administration requested from Congress. The reopening benefited Egypt, but also Europe, the Middle East and Asia. One-third of the world's tanker tonnage could cut the journey from the petroleum fields of the Persian Gulf to the ports of the Mediterranean by 16 days of sailing time. It was not, however, strategically beneficial to the Americans, as it reduced the Soviet navy's supply lines distance from its Black Sea bases to the Straits of Malacca, the doorway to the Pacific and Japan. Formerly the distance was 11,000 miles, via the Cape of Good Hope. They would now only have to transit 2,200 miles.

By the mid-1970s the Soviets were spending vast resources on their military establishment, taking advantage of the post Vietnam retrenchment by the U.S. The Soviets deployed thousands of mobile, intercontinental ballistic missiles and other nuclear weapons; built up large ground and air forces in Eastern Europe and the Far East; and supported Communist guerilla movements in Africa, Asia and Latin America.

At a time when the American Navy was struggling with quality and retention of personnel, and an aging fleet, the Soviet naval forces increased their presence around the world, challenging U.S. control of the oceans.

In 1975 the Soviet Navy conducted exercise Okean 75, which involved 220 ships. Long range Soviet bombers made mock strikes against the continental U.S. Soviet warships steamed in all the world's oceans, and probed the Gulf of Mexico. To add insult to injury, Soviet ships and planes operated from the former American base at Cam Ranh Bay in Vietnam. Admiral James L. Holloway III, who replaced Admiral Zumwalt as CNO on June 29, 1974, said the U.S. Navy had only a "slim margin of superiority" over the Soviet navy.[34]

On April 30, 1975, Duong Van Minh ("Big Minh"), the last President of South Vietnam (a position he held for two days), surrendered Saigon to Communist North Vietnamese forces. There was a panicked withdrawal as the few remaining Americans and some of their terrified South Vietnamese allies were evacuated. The North Vietnamese had swept through South Vietnam, emboldened by the termination of support by a Democratic American Congress, which cut off all funding for the war effort there. The betrayal of our ally brought misery to all of Southeast Asia.

---

34. Mid-1970s assessment drawn from the Naval Historical Foundation, *The Navy*, (New York: Barnes & Noble Books, 2000).

When the North Vietnamese took over, a mass exodus began from South Vietnam, as people fled for their lives and their freedom. Somewhere between one and one-half to two million people set out by sea on anything that would float, risking starvation or drowning. Over a quarter of a million people were lost at sea, while others were captured, tortured and murdered by pirates. The boat people dispersed to Thailand, Malaysia, Hong Kong, and the Philippines, and were scattered in refugee camps throughout Asia.

In Vietnam, the Communists established nearly 100 "reeducation camps," essentially political prisons where anyone who supported or worked with the U.S could be held indefinitely. Somewhere between a half million to a million people were so incarcerated.

The Vietnamese Communists then turned their armies against Laos, Cambodia and Thailand; and conducted a campaign of ethnic cleansing against the Montagnards, Christian mountain people who had courageously fought alongside American forces against Ho Chi Minh.

One example of the consequences of the Communist takeover was Toi Dang, a Vietnamese sailor who served on Swifts in Coastal Division 11 at An Thoi. Caught up in the terrible Communist takeover, he managed to escape to the United States, leaving behind his family, heritage and country. Nineteen of his fellow sailors were placed in reeducation camps and disappeared forever.[35]

IN JULY 1975 THE MINE WARFARE FORCE was reorganized into the Mine Warfare Command, still under Admiral Roy Hoffmann, who then reported directly to the Chief of Naval Operations and the Fleet Commanders, for all matters concerning mine warfare worldwide. He held that position until November 1976. By this time the Suez Canal was open for commerce again. Canal pilots, who had formerly guided ships through the narrow canal, came back in droves from all over the world. The Israelis had pulled back into the Sinai and both banks of the Canal were again under Egyptian control.

During the clearing operation, divers and dredgers retrieved 8,524 pieces of unexploded ordnance, 127 pontoon-bridge sections, 16 trucks, eight

---

35. O'Neill and Corsi, *Unfit for Command*, pp. 121–122. Toi Dang was particularly offended by the testimony of John Kerry before the Senate Foreign Relations Committee in 1971. "His testimony was all lies," he says. "He is a brother only to other liars—not to my Swift brothers." Toi Dang attends reunions today with his American counterpart Swift boat sailors, most recently at the Swift Boat Sailors reunion held in San Diego in 2007 (see the Epilogue).

tanks, 104 small boats and barges, ten large sunken ships and 15 airplanes. Some 686,000 mines and other explosives were removed from both banks, and the Israeli causeway, which they had used to supply their forces on the west bank during the Yom Kippur War, was dismantled.

For his command of the Mine Warfare Force and for his guidance of Operation Nimbus Stream, the Admiral received the Legion of Merit issued on behalf of the President of the United States.

ON NOVEMBER 22, 1975, the guided missile cruiser *Belknap* collided with the aircraft carrier *John F. Kennedy* during maneuvers in the Mediterranean Sea. Eight sailors died, 48 were injured and damage to the cruiser was so severe that it took four years to repair the ship. The collision triggered fires and explosions within 40 feet of nuclear weapons aboard the cruiser—a so-called "broken arrow" incident, involving the possibility of detonation of nuclear weapons.

The *Kennedy* was conducting routine night flight operations in the Ionian Sea, and the *Belknap* was plane guard. The *Belknap* was subject to standing night orders that she not approach closer than 2,000 yards of the hemisphere forward of the beam of the carrier. The *Belknap* was abreast the carrier when she received orders to take station astern as the plane guard ship. As the cruiser turned, so did the carrier, maneuvering to catch the wind for air ops. The ships turned into each other and the *Belknap* passed under the huge overhang of the angle deck on the carrier's port side. As the *Belknap's* aluminum superstructure crumpled it cut aircraft refueling lines on the carrier, spraying aviation fuel onto the *Belknap*. Fires burned on both ships for up to four hours.

Rear Admiral (later Vice Admiral) Donald Engen, whom we encountered earlier with the *Leahy*, conducted an Article 32 investigation. Admiral Roy Hoffmann was selected for the court martial court, because he had commanded the same type of ship and was a legend in the Navy for his ship handling. Engen, then vice commander of U.S. Naval Forces, Europe, recommended that the Navy court martial the captain of the *Belknap*. Clearly, he had failed to adequately exercise command authority and train his bridge team, and his OOD in particular.

In a harbinger of the problems with the military justice system that would entangle the Admiral later at the Naval Base Charleston, the captain of the *Belknap* was ultimately acquitted of wrongdoing. The defense team for the captain had given him little chance of avoiding responsibility for the collision. Initially he was summarily relieved of command under the Fleet Commander's orders. The Court of Military Appeals (see below) intervened and reversed the decision against the captain, restoring him to duty. The traditionalists in the Navy were absolutely appalled. It was the first time anything like that had ever happened. CNO Admiral James L. Holloway felt compelled to issue a 1976 reminder to the fleet about the responsibility of a captain for his ship and crew.

On January 21, 1976, in one of his first acts as president, Jimmy Carter unconditionally pardoned most of the 10,000 men who had evaded the draft during the Vietnam War. In a lesser-known directive, he provided for upgrades of military personnel who had received a less than honorable discharge during the War. The upgrades, which particularly focused on military personnel who had protested the war, were nearly forced on the military.

In June 1976 Admiral Roy Hoffmann assumed the additional duties of Commandant, Sixth Naval District. In addition to his duties as Commandant he was the Commander of the Naval Base at Charleston. It was a large responsibility. As Base Commander, he managed all Navy and Marine Corps activities in the Charleston, South Carolina area, including more than 30,000 military and civilian personnel. His responsibilities at the Naval Base included the following facilities: The Naval Shipyard, Polaris Missile Assembly Facility, Supply Center, Naval Weapons Station, Naval Regional Medical Center and a Naval Facilities Engineering Command.

He was additionally responsible for providing total administrative material, and waterfront and harbor support for 65 operating fleet ships. He was given the responsibility to reduce the shore side support budget of $12 million by $1.5 million annually, while at the same time improving mission effectiveness (doing more with less). He was responsible for the appearance of the base and for establishing good relations with the civilian community outside the base.

As Commandant of the Sixth Naval District, he was responsible for representing the Secretary of the Navy and CNO in coordinating all Naval shore activities in the seven southeastern states.

The Admiral attacked his new responsibilities with gusto. He would do what he thought was right, to make it an effective command, regardless of the consequences. And one consequence would be a charge of unlawful command influence, for insisting on tougher sentences for sailors facing disciplinary action.

The new orders entailed a move next door from the Hoffmann's previous living quarters. They went from Quarters "B" to Quarters "A," which were the Commandant's Quarters. They were fancy digs (Mary Linn describes them as "lovely"). The Quarters were built in 1905, and were built for entertaining. The rooms were huge, and the home had five fireplaces. The home and grounds had been neglected, but, says Mary Linn, "We took care of that." They cared for the home and both worked outside on the flower beds. Mary Linn found time to volunteer at the base hospital, mostly in the pharmacy.

The Admiral had a personal steward (for him, not for Mary Linn). He prepared the evening meal and did the Admiral's laundry. ("I did my own laundry," Mary Linn says. "I don't want anybody doing my laundry.") The steward took care of all the Admiral's uniforms, seeing they were clean and pressed.

The new assignment was, both the Admiral and Mary Linn realized, a "pasture job." It was an end of career assignment without much chance of further advancement. At the level the Admiral had attained, it was "Up or out" (promotion or retirement). He was not going to go quietly.

He thought he needed to address what he felt were discipline problems, drug problems, and the generally seedy and rundown appearance of the base itself. To clean up the base, he took detainees, incarcerated in detention barracks on the base, and put them to work. Previously they had been sitting around watching television. They were put to work cleaning, painting, planting trees, and landscaping. The Admiral insisted the base be policed—he cracked down on littering. The base began to shape up and become something the sailors took pride in.

The Admiral was appalled by the number of sailors and Marines who were seriously injured while riding motorcycles off base. Working with the CPOs, he instituted motorcycle training and safety programs, and required that the men under his command wear leathers and a safety helmet when they left the base. Dissatisfied with the loose motorcycle requirements in South Carolina, he said, "If the state won't control it—I will," Eventually he worked with the state to reinstate the old law which had stricter requirements.

There were ceremonial duties, one of which put him together once again with the irascible Admiral Ike Kidd. The occasion was a visit by the French Ambassador, and the very hands-on Ike Kidd wanted to serve him local food at the ceremonial banquet.

"You've got to do something that's Charleston," he told Roy Hoffmann.

"Well, you want to serve him grits?"

Kidd exploded, "This is nothing to be joking about!"

When the ambassador arrived Kidd went down to Charleston to greet him. There was a delay getting the ambassador through U.S. customs processing and Admiral Kidd went berserk. He got involved in handling the suitcases to speed up the process.

On another occasion President Jimmy Carter made an official visit to Air Force and Navy commands in Charleston,

Rear Admiral Roy F. Hoffmann.
OFFICIAL U.S. NAVY PHOTO, HOFFMANN COLLECTION

South Carolina. He didn't like protocol and confused everyone when he walked off the plane without "Hail to the Chief." "Hail to the Chief" was the signal to the honor guard to start the welcoming ceremony, including a 21-gun salute, which Carter didn't want either. No one knew what to do.

As Carter greeted the Admiral he said, "How are you, Roy?" The greeting surprised the Admiral, since the only other time they had met was during an annual drill, when the president has to go through the required by law exercise of releasing nuclear weapons. The Admiral was on the Navy team for the drill, which included all NATO and other U.S. allies. As they counted down from ten to one, Carter failed to release the weapons. The then Chairman of the Joint Chiefs of Staff, Admiral Moorer, looked at the president and said, "Mr. President, you blew it."

Carter got a sheepish grin and asked, "Admiral, I know it; can we start over?"

As it turned out, it took 24 hours to reset the program. Carter asked if he had fulfilled his duties by being there, and Moorer said, "Yes, sir, you did."

THE MORE SERIOUS PROBLEMS the Admiral felt he had to address related to discipline problems and drug use on the base. Running counter to the re-

Activation of YR 26 (Advanced ship repair base—ASRB), July 1976. L-R: Captain Ed Whelan (DESRON 28), Rear Admiral Tom Morris (REDCOM ONE), Captain John Culver (Commanding Officer ASRB 201), Rear Admiral Roy F. Hoffmann (Commander, Mine Warfare Forces, Atlantic). CAPTAIN JOHN CULVER, USN, RET., PHOTO

laxed standards of the time, he moved to aggressively track down drug users and sellers. He was upset by the widespread use of marijuana on the base, and the lax attitude taken by some of the officers and chief petty officers in reporting marijuana offenses.

He called a meeting of all chiefs (E-7 and above) into the base theater for a conference. He arranged for a few of his staff CPOs to get some confiscated marijuana and burn it while the chiefs were coming in the door. It smelled like an alfalfa field on fire.

He asked the chiefs if they noticed a particular smell when they came in. "Raise your hands," he said. Almost all raised their hands.

"How many of you can identify the substance? Raise your hands." Two dozen or so raised their hands.

"What you smell is marijuana," the Admiral said. "When was the last time any of you put someone on report for smoking pot or having possession of it? Raise your hands—no repercussions—I just want to see how many." A few hands went up.

"Therein lies the problem," he said. "Some of you may have come from environments where it was tolerated. Well let me get right to the point: It will not be tolerated on this base. We've got chief petty officers and officers who are not taking responsibility and are looking the other way. I'll tell you that you are not going to wear that chief's crow [eagle] very much longer if you don't accept your responsibility and authority *and use it*." He made the same point to the officers.

He also cracked down on the detention barracks, which were drug pools, with drugs passing back and forth continually. To alleviate the problem, he put a fence up around the barracks. When the Fleet command got wind of what he had done they said it was a violation of Navy directives. He justified what he had done by saying there was no gate; he was merely controlling and funneling through who and what came in and went out of the barracks. It was an indicator that all might not appreciate his aggressive campaign to clean up the base.

He also cleaned up the area outside the base, working with the mayor to clean up and reduce the number of strip joints and tattoo parlors. The newly disciplined sailors became less of a problem to the greater Charleston community, and the citizens reacted positively and with support.

The number of drug arrests rose by 100 per cent. Before he took command roughly 15 sailors each month were arrested for drug offenses. That number rose to 25 to 30 per month. He brought in drug sniffing dogs for random searches of autos and barracks. Plainclothes drug agents were used on base, and tighter security—including occasional car searches—was put in effect at the base gates.[36]

Sailors caught using marijuana were restricted to base and in some cases forced to do hard labor. Others received a reduction in rate and a concomitant pay cut. The Admiral made clear that those caught selling drugs on base would probably face court martial.

The Charleston County Metro Narcotics Unit estimated that an incredible 50 per cent of the sailors at the base used marijuana. (The same was probably true in the fleet, an even more dangerous situation.) Admiral Hoffmann commented at the time, "It's absolutely vital to the operational security of the Navy and vital to the security of men and equipment that the drug laws are enforced."

The commander of the Atlantic Fleet agreed in a directive: "Personnel under the influence of marijuana and other illicit drugs create an unacceptable risk of personal injury to themselves, their shipmates and of damage to vital equipment."

---

36. The military operates on a different set of standards than civilian life. With the seriousness of the mission, and the danger, the standards are higher than civilians are accustomed to. It was a violation of military law to have knowledge of someone's drug use and not report it.

IT WAS AN ADJUSTMENT for the family with the Admiral's position as commander of the base. Emilie was still at home and Hilarie came home for the summers, where she had a position of lifeguard on the base. Once one of the Admiral's aides came up to her, took her hands and rotated the palms up. He said, "Well, it doesn't look like you suffered too much."

"What are you talking about?" she asked. She was informed that there was a rumor (false) going around the base that she had been arrested by the Shore Patrol (SP) because of drugs. The Shore Patrol had gone through the yard, as someone in the brig had made the allegations about her. "Mom thought it was funny," Hilarie says, "that those guys were out there in their 'whitey-tighties' looking under bushes. My dad's exact words were, 'We live in a glass house.'

"You became more conscious of what you said and did," she says. One night she was late for curfew and had to call her father to the gate to get on base—they wouldn't let her date drive her to the house.

THE ADMIRAL'S CLASH with the military legal establishment over the application of the rules was about to break into the open. Pat Sheedy, whom we encountered on the *Adams* and on Swift boats in Vietnam, says, "It was a clash of the old Navy and the new Navy." Morale was so bad in the fleet that he had two white hats on PCFs who extended in Vietnam rather than go back aboard ship. One of Sheedy's classmates at the Academy had a father who was a retired Chief Boatswain's Mate, and his opinion of the early 1970s was that Zumwalt was dismantling the machinery of the Navy. "It was a wonder," Sheedy says, "that the whole military establishment survived all that [the 1970s]."

Another career officer, Charley Plumly, says that the post Vietnam Navy was falling apart because of discipline problems, drugs, sex, race issues, etc. "Roy was a spit and polish guy," he says. "It was a miserable time for him."

On March 9, 1978, the Charleston *News and Courier* ran an editorial called the "Parlous State of Military Justice."[37] In the editorial they approvingly quoted Rear Admiral Roy Hoffmann, who had said the judges on the U.S. Court of Military Appeals were tearing down the system they should be protecting. In an unusual move, the Admiral had challenged the

---

37. Editorial, *The News and Courier*, March 9, 1978, p. 8A. All articles from the newspaper relating to this period are cited under "Sources."

wisdom of the civilians on the Court. Although it was a courageous position, representing much of the thinking of the traditional Navy, it was a lonely position in the lead of an issue that needed to be addressed. As the editorial stated, "Straight talk about many of the most critical aspects of national defense is rare. The public . . . hears little about the . . . troublesome areas of morale and discipline and what Congress is—or more usually, is not—doing about them."

Hoffmann charged that members of the court were writing military law instead of interpreting it, and he asked them to stop. " . . . One knows," the editorial continued, "that what the admiral says is exactly true: courts everywhere are rewriting the law in defiance of Congress, the voters and democratic process. The Court of Military Appeals is no different from the rest."

Hoffmann further charged the collapse of military justice was only a step behind the collapse of military discipline. He pointed to an unsupportable high rate of desertion, six times that of World War II and triple the rate of the Korean and Vietnam wars. The deserters, he said, were getting away with it.

The Court of Military Appeals was strongly influenced by Senator Strom Thurmond, and some of the members were inept political hacks with little or no experience with the military. The three-member body was set up to handle appeals from special and general courts martial. They were civilians appointed by the president for 15-year terms.

The Court of Military Appeals (COMA) had become a force for liberal change, and as a consequence a source of consternation for the traditional military. It was steadily working, as the Warren Court did with civilians, to expand the rights of defendants in uniform. COMA was steadily eroding the authority of military commanders over the court martial process. COMA was resented by officers in the Pentagon, who regarded the COMA directed "civilianization" of military justice as damaging to an essential ingredient of military life: Discipline. Rear Admiral William O. Miller, who retired in 1978 as Judge Advocate General (JAG) of the Navy, openly charged COMA of "excesses harmful to the military society."

On May 31, 1978, Admiral Roy Hoffmann was relieved of judicial authority, following allegations that he interfered in courts martial proceedings. As the convening authority for the naval base it was Hoffmann's responsibility to convene courts martial, appoint panels of judges and trial defense counsel, and review trials. His authority was transferred to Rear Admiral Albert J. Monger, his successor at the Mine Warfare Command.

The Admiral had worked with and respected then Lieutenant Commander William L. Schachte, Jr. (from Charleston originally), who was one of the more outstanding O in Cs on Swift boats while the Admiral was CTF 115.[38] Schachte was the senior head trial counsel at the Legal Services Office in Charleston. He says beneath the Admiral's tough exterior, "he was tender deep down inside."

"Roy was so pissed off at the lawyers that he started convening his own courts like they used to in the old days." When the charges hit, the Admiral called in Bill Schachte and said, "Well, what do you think, Bill?"

"Admiral, they are going to hang you out to dry on this one," Schachte replied. The Admiral needed a four striper to defend him, and Captain Ken Bridges ended up with the job. He was a good, aggressive attorney, according to Schachte.

The News and Courier stood solidly behind the Admiral, saying, "Knowing the man [Hoffmann], we plead guilty to prejudice in his favor. People like him are the hope of our nation. They are all too few." MCPO Kenneth R. Cook, USN, Ret. wrote in defense of the Admiral, "As one who has worked directly for the admiral in years past to my knowledge he never interfered with any command that acted responsibly. Everyone knows the justice system in the armed forces is a disgrace. Lawyers have been successful in destroying military discipline . . . "

The investigations, requested by the Admiral, related to allegations that he promoted improper and illegal disciplinary procedures at the Charleston Naval Base. Rear Admiral Milton P. Alexich arrived in Charleston to conduct the investigation of over-restrictive practices at the detention barracks, and the unlawful command influence charge. The allegations arose during the court martial of a submarine fireman who was charged with unauthorized absence and possession of marijuana. Both charges were dismissed, the absent without leave charge because he had been confined "illegally" prior to his trial. On the possession charge,

---

38. All quotations from an interview conducted with Bill Schachte June 5, 2007. Rear Admiral Schachte, USN, Ret., has had a distinguished legal career both in the Navy and in civilian life. He served as Judge Advocate General of the Navy, the Navy's top uniformed lawyer. While stationed at Cam Ranh Bay he was in charge of the operation in which John Kerry received his first Purple Heart, one of the three that allowed him to exit Vietnam early. Schachte was the credible witness on scene, as he was in the skimmer with Kerry, and witnessed the self-inflicted wound that Kerry received. He also indicated there was no incoming enemy fire that night. Today, Schachte is "retired," living in Charleston with his wife of 41 years, Carmen, although he continues to practice law and consults as an expert in international law of the sea conventions. He is a most articulate, spiritual and impressive man.

Military judge Commander Jean E. Van Slate of the Naval Legal Affairs Office, found him innocent. The allegations against the Admiral came from a defense motion in the trial, alleging that Hoffmann had exercised unlawful command influence in the case. To buttress his claim he brought in a parade of witnesses. The defense lawyer said he had attempted to talk to the Admiral about the case, but had been blocked by members of the Judge Advocate General's (JAG) staff. Van Slate ruled that although Hoffmann had not unlawfully influenced the current case, he had done so in previous cases. It was clear the lawyers had set him up.

Van Slate's ruling stated that Hoffmann had prevailed on naval station commander Captain John V. Smith to try disciplinary offenders before lay officers rather than military judges. Van Slate concluded that Hoffmann and Smith were using the procedure "to gain what they perceived to be less lenient sentences." He also ruled that Hoffmann interfered with former naval station commander Captain Theodore W. Pstrak to the extent that Pstrak couldn't use his proper authority to deal with discipline cases.

The court's outrageous behavior was particularly galling as the Admiral was then in Pascagoula, Mississippi, for the dedication of a ship, when the charges hit. Mary Linn heard about the charges at a party. Hoffmann's chief of staff, Captain M. I. McCreight, III, called the situation a very deliberate effort to discredit the admiral. "I'm sure those young fellows over there have absolutely no concept of what they're doing," he said.

On May 23 the Charleston *Evening Post* ran an editorial titled "In Defense of Tough Admirals." The editorial said in part:

> The testy admiral [Hoffmann] is said to have "encouraged subordinate commanders to bring military offenders to trial before line officers rather than military lawyers . . . . We would rather have the Navy run by one ADM Hoffmann than by a whole corps of lawyers in uniform. Like many other naval officers, ADM Hoffmann is concerned by the sorry state of good order and discipline in the Navy. Unlike too many of them, he decided to do something about it. He cracked down on sloppy performance of duty at the naval base. He campaigned against drug trafficking. He cleaned up service clubs . . . He gave the base a smart, squared away appearance—the best it has had in years.
>
> He spoke out vigorously, against ill-advised attempts to civilianize the military justice system and he castigated the Court of Military Appeals for decisions he said were destroying naval discipline. Inevitably, he made powerful enemies.
>
> Well, it is high time somebody had the guts to say the things he has said

and take the action he has taken. The Navy's desertion rate is the highest in history, twice as great as it was during the Viet Nam war . . . Almost half of the Navy's new breed of volunteers fail to finish a first-term enlistment. Must everyone go over the hill; must all ships become rusting hulks unable to leave the pier, before the nation realizes what is being done to the Navy?

The former naval station commander, retired Captain Theodore W. Pstrak, made a remarkable admission when he was called to testify about the issue. He said that he adopted a tougher non-judicial punishment policy because of the influence of the Admiral. "It's not the right thing," he said, "but that's what I did." He estimated that he was called before the Admiral 20 to 30 times to explain why he had handed down various punishments. Showing a remarkable lack of spine, he said there was doubt in his own mind of the guilt of some of those charged with marijuana offenses, but because of the Admiral's influence, he sent the cases to court martial. He said if he had been left to his own discretion he wouldn't have done it. He also felt pressured by criticism from the Admiral because of the lightness of his sentences in other cases, such as AWOL cases. *Pstrak said Hoffmann never exercised his influence on any one particular case* but did it on the general subject of punishment.[39] Pstrak's successor, Captain John V. Smith, said that the Admiral hadn't exercised influence on him in judicial punishment matters.

On June 1, 1978, the board of directors of L. Mendel Rivers Branch #50 of the Fleet Reserve Association[40] overwhelmingly adopted a resolution of support for the Admiral. The resolution said in part:

> The Navy has brought upon itself . . . a military justice system that delays, and based on minor technicalities, clerical or procedural errors, sets aside or excuses required disciplinary actions . . . We firmly believe that ADM Hoffmann had the duty and responsibility to exercise "command influence" to maintain good order and discipline . . . Rules and regulations supported by discipline are the basic foundation of our Navy; traditions, pride, respect, and the acceptance of responsibility and the execution of authority, by its supporting members.

---

39. The Admiral said at the time that "the biggest mistake I ever made in my life" was not removing Pstrak from his command. He had considered removing him, but since Pstrak was nearing retirement he let him stay. Bill Schachte says that the Admiral was "a great warrior and sea dog," but shore duty wasn't necessarily his forte. Schachte says that at this juncture the Admiral needed someone who would stand up to him, talk to him about the consequences, and if he didn't follow the advice tell him to get someone else to give it. The Admiral was always willing to listen to people he respected.

40. Retired former enlisted Navy and Marine Corps military advocates.

Two weeks later, at a change of command ceremony at the Fleet Ballistics Missile Submarine Center, the Admiral fired back in a speech. Naval responsibility, authority and accountability were being eroded by recent interpretations of the code of military justice, he charged. The erosion was undermining discipline, which led to a decrease in readiness. He went on to say that "responsibility, authority and accountability" were the three key words in the operation of any command.

"Today's Navy," the Admiral said, "is one which preaches and practices equal opportunity. I suggest we give similar attention to equal accountability because everyone from the newest recruit up must be equally accountable if the system is to survive.

"But for too many years . . . the Navy tried to substitute 'improved management practices' for fair and firm military discipline and we have suffered from it. We must constantly remind ourselves that good order and discipline are absolute fundamentals to an organization that expects accountability and responsibility from its members."

He called the Uniform Code of Military Justice (UCMJ) essentially sound law, and said that the UCMJ authority, "exercised by commanding officers, brought forth acceptable accountability of those overseeing command and responsibility to those viewing it from below.

"However, over the past decade we have witnessed an accelerating condition that I will label 'erosion of authority' through judicial manipulation of the military justice system." The roots of the erosion, he said, came from a series of decisions handed down by military appellate courts and the interpretation of those decisions by the officers who form the Navy-Marine Corps Trial Judiciary. He said the system must respect every man's rights and protect the accused, but the system must place equal importance on protecting the rights of law-abiding members of society as well.

Referring to Article 37 of the code, which was designed to prevent command influence in judicial proceeding, the Admiral said the article had been interpreted by the judge advocate general to mean that no one in command could complain about the action of a military judge, no matter how illegal or ill advised the action might be.

At the root of the problem, he said, was a system that was increasingly administered by judges who were products of academic institutions with little knowledge of command experience, rather than line officers.

He closed with advice to those in command, or who aspired to it: "I say to you: Study and fully appreciate the authority that goes with command and then use it! Don't be reticent. Don't equivocate. Use it. For I submit the integrity of military command authority is as fundamental to the future of the American way of life as the word liberty itself."

ON AUGUST 26, 1978, at 9:30 A.M., the Change of Command and retirement ceremony occurred wherein Rear Admiral Albert J. Monger assumed command of the Charleston Naval Base and the Sixth Naval District from Rear Admiral Roy F. Hoffmann. The ceremony was, as an editorial in *The Evening Post* indicated, ". . . a more somber occasion than it ought to be. . . . Uncertainty about the eventual outcome of a confrontation between him and the Navy lawyers is a cloud over glittering ceremony at which he turns over command today."

As part of the ceremony, Vice Admiral William L. Read read the Admiral's second Legion of Merit citation. The Legion of Merit was "For exceptionally meritorious conduct in the performance of outstanding service as Commander, Naval Base, Charleston . . . and as Commandant, Sixth Naval District." It probably reflected how the traditional Navy felt about the Admiral; one reads it with a sense of irony at the accolades from the Navy in light of his troubles with the lawyers. It read in part:

> Rear Admiral Hoffmann's dynamic leadership, planning ability and special military knowledge were instrumental in the successful accomplishment of the missions of his Commands. His organizational skill and meticulous attention to detail resulted in major improvements in the Naval Base's appearance, good order and discipline, morale and Fleet supports. Rear Admiral Hoffmann established programs that included effective physical security, improved investigative techniques, and an aggressive attack on drug abuse violations. In addition, he established, organized, and administered a regimented program to maximize utilization of legal-hold personnel at the Naval Station . . .

In his closing remarks the Admiral returned to the values that he believed in passionately. "The military is not a democracy," he said. "Its job is defending and making democracy live. In order to do that we must give up a few civil rights." He emphasized that individual's rights should be protected, but not at the expense of weakening the Navy.

He also noted the weakened state of readiness. The Navy had declined from 1,000 active ships in 1968 to 458 a scant ten years later. There were fewer ships in 1978 than before Pearl Harbor.

The panoply of a U.S. Navy Retirement and Change of Command ceremony, Charleston Naval Base, August 31, 1978. Official U.S. Navy photo, Hoffmann collection

Rear Admiral Albert J. Monger (right) relieved Rear Admiral Roy F. Hoffmann (center) as Commandant Sixth Naval District and Commander Naval Base Charleston. Vice Admiral William L. Read (left) accompanies them.
Official U.S. Navy photo, Hoffmann collection

Part Three: Vietnam to Retirement 391

Congratulations on an outstanding career by Vice Admiral William L. Read. OFFICIAL U.S. NAVY PHOTO, HOFFMANN COLLECTION

A kiss from the Admiral's lady, Mary Linn Hoffmann, August 31, 1978. OFFICIAL U.S. NAVY PHOTO, HOFFMANN

Rear Admiral Roy F. Hoffmann admires the bo's'n's pipe, presented by the Command CPO, during his retirement ceremony. OFFICIAL U.S. NAVY PHOTO, HOFFMANN COLLECTION

The *Post* further editorialized about his retirement:

During his tour of duty in Charleston, ADM Hoffmann improved the image of the Navy in military and civilian eyes. He has cleaned up a Naval Base run down by neglect on the part of officers perhaps more popular than he. He has reminded naval personnel . . . of obligations to duty that some had let slip from their minds. In the process, however, he has made enemies as well as friends. Morally and professionally . . . ADM Hoffmann has had the best of the confrontation so far—a judgment sustained by the obvious signs of reluctance of superiors in Washington to carry the matter to a desirable conclusion. In presenting that challenge—without, we are convinced, any motive beyond a wish to do his duty—ADM Hoffmann sounded an alarm which might have awakened in sleeping Navy hearts a wish to return to the spirit which wins wars, as opposed to merely running a happy, sloppy ship.

The *Post* concluded, with remarkable prescience, "Detachment and retirement soon to come . . . do not terminate the usefulness of this distinguished and energetic officer. Out of uniform, ADM Hoffmann will serve the interests of his country."

THE INVESTIGATION INTO THE UNDUE command influence charge had an almost theater of the absurd beginning and end. After the attempt by the military judiciary to tarnish the reputation of one of the Navy's finest officers, the Admiral ended up with a non-punitive letter from Chief of Naval Operations Admiral Thomas B. Hayward. A non-punitive letter of censure is not part of a serviceman's permanent record.[41]

Admiral Hayward became CNO on July 1, 1978, relieving Admiral James L. Holloway III. He took over the Navy at a time when it had taken huge cuts under presidents Nixon and Ford. Before the Vietnam War there had been 33 carriers, and by the time President Carter took office there were 13. Carter had no plans to build any more, and in fact talked about an eight carrier Navy.

By all objective standards the Navy Hayward had inherited was a mess, unable to retain top-notch sailors and officers. Incredibly, many of the sailors manning the fleet were high school dropouts, many with criminal records. Drug and alcohol abuse was rampant throughout the fleet. Forty seven per cent of Navy personnel were smoking marijuana; another 11 per cent were snorting cocaine. Manpower shortages were so acute several ships could not

---

41. Quotations taken from an interview with Admiral Hayward September 2, 2005.

get underway and leave port. Hayward sent videotape almost immediately to the fleet in which he included a stern warning: "We're out to help you or hammer you; take your choice."

Admiral Hayward, a Naval Academy graduate, saw extensive combat in Korea and Vietnam as a carrier aviator. He was Air wing commander on the *Intrepid*, commanding officer of the aircraft carrier USS *America*, commander of the U.S. Seventh Fleet, and commander in chief of the United States Pacific Fleet, prior to becoming CNO.

It fell to Admiral Hayward to rebuild the Navy after the neglect of the Nixon/Ford/Carter years, and he understood what it would take. As such, he is an admirer of Admiral Roy F. Hoffmann. Hoffmann, he says, "Demands a lot of others and of himself. He is a man of character, integrity, courage, and boldness. He is the kind of guy you'd go to war with."

The Navy began to change, and to return to traditional values. Roy Hoffmann, attacked for his views at the end of his service, saw vindication as the Navy began to return to its roots. *The Evening Post*, in an editorial on February 21, 1981, harkened back to "a short, crusty, two-star admiral named Roy Hoffmann" as they noted approvingly:

> Reports from Norfolk say that the admiral heading the Atlantic Fleet Training Command there has banned civilian clothes for sailors in Navy apprentice schools, removed beer from the barracks, ordered regulation haircuts for all hands and demanded properly executed salutes. He even ordered parades, complete with Navy bands, each Friday at the Norfolk Naval Station.
>
> In that spirit, Rear Admiral J. F. Frick, the naval base commander in Norfolk, said, "Personal appearance, pride, performance and professionalism are the attributes of any first-class organization." Roy Hoffmann said the very same thing, and he was right.

PART FOUR

CIVILIAN AND SWIFT BOAT VETERANS AND POWS FOR TRUTH

You shall judge of a man by his foes as well as his friends.
—JOSEPH CONRAD
Lord Jim 1900

9

CIVILIAN

Port of Milwaukee

The St. Lawrence Seaway, which brought ocean-going traffic into the Great Lakes, opened in 1959. The old seaway could accommodate ships up to 250 feet, a rowboat by today's standards. The new seaway, a joint American-Canadian effort, enlarged the locks, and all the ports of the Great Lakes, Chicago, Detroit, Cleveland, Toledo, Milwaukee, and Duluth, had to readjust to international shipping.

Geography, climate and the size of the waterways were impediments to the growth of the ports of the Great Lakes. The Asian markets were difficult to obtain because of the added expense and distance of transiting the Panama Canal. Winter was another obstacle—most shipments couldn't be scheduled after October. And finally, as technology expanded oceangoing vessels to more and more colossal proportions, inland ports couldn't compete for the behemoth ships.

The ports of the Great Lakes did have an advantage over the Gulf Ports, however. Because of the curvature of the earth, the voyage across the North Atlantic to Europe is 1,000 miles shorter from the mouth of the St. Lawrence than from New Orleans. The advantage is offset by the winter, which lasts sometimes from November to May, when the Lakes are not necessarily hospitable to the world's sailors.

The winter storms were notorious. On November 11, 1940, a cold front raced across the Canadian prairies and struck Lake Michigan by early afternoon. Thirty-foot waves and winds topping 75 miles an hour caused the deaths of nearly 200 sailors by dusk, as their ships went down. In November

1976, one of the largest ships on the lakes, the *Edmund Fitzgerald*, went down on Lake Superior. The entire crew went to a watery grave.

Vessels sailing in the 45-mile-an-hour winter winds can collect freezing spray on their superstructures, sometimes piling up a couple of feet of ice from bow to stern. The extra weight drives the ship deeper into the water, interferes with buoyancy and makes ship handling difficult as the vessels roll and plunge almost unpredictably.

The Milwaukee port reached its peak in 1970–71, when it handled over a billion tons of foreign cargo for the first time in history. By 1973–74, however, the worldwide recession brought the tonnage numbers down 25 to 30 per cent. It was a slow climb back. The port was a business subsidized by the city; the deficit in 1977 was $750,000. The costs were justified by the economic benefits the port brought to the community, somewhere in the area of $22.1 million that same year. Still, it was a large subsidy which added to the intense scrutiny the politicians gave the port.

The port consisted of a Bulk Terminal and Handling Facility with 60,000 square feet of space, used for salt storage and salt packaging operations; General Cargo Terminals and Reefer Facilities; a Liquid Cargo Pier for liquid fats, oils and petroleum products; a City Heavy Lift Dock, featuring a 220-ton stiff-leg derrick; a Bulk Handling Facility; a Scrap Handling Facility; a Grain Elevator with a three and one half million bushel capacity; and a Municipal Mooring Basin with winter space for commercial lake vessels.

The Port of Milwaukee needed a new director, and the search took a year. They were looking for someone with both marketing and managerial skills. The Harbor Commission formed a Search and Screen Committee. Admiral Zumwalt was then in Milwaukee as head of a company that built hospitals as a turnkey operation. His number two man, a retired admiral, at Zumwalt's suggestion called Roy Hoffmann and asked if he knew of any candidates for the job. The Admiral eventually called back and said, "I've got a name for you."

"Who is it?"

"Roy Hoffmann—me." He saw it as an opportunity to learn the stevedoring business, although he knew it was a limited opportunity, due to the winter freeze up problem.

It was a big job. The director had full management authority and responsibility for the port, a city corporation. He reported directly, as a head of a city department, to the Mayor of Milwaukee and the Board of Harbor Commissioners. The full-service international port handled primarily capital equipment, general cargo and processed grain. He was responsible for enforcement of harbor laws and ordinances, including public operational safety in conformance to OSHA guidelines. He negotiated facility contracts, and was responsible for relations with various labor unions including the International Longshoreman's Association (ILA), American Federation of State, County & Municipal Employees, Teamsters, and the International Union of Operating Engineers. He also was responsible for planning and conducting a six-year harbor rehabilitation and improvement program including dredging, dock walls, railroads and construction of a heavy lift dock and container yard. He had responsibility for directing the port's marketing and sales efforts, and for the development, presentation and management of the port's $2 million annual staff operating budget.

Milwaukee's longshoremen were members of Local 815 of the International Longshoremen's Association. Ten years before there were 700 of them, but with the advent of containerization (freight contained in giant metal cases, easily lifted by a crane at the dock), their numbers were down to 290. They had gone from unloading every single box or crate to becoming mechanics, crane and pulley operators and dockside engineers. The work was seasonal, lasting about nine months out of the year.

According to Dan Meehan, the port's primary stevedore (see below, Port of Richmond), the Port of Milwaukee was always a highly charged, political situation.[1] The port initially had a fine director in Harry C. Brockel, who was there in one capacity or another for 35 to 40 years. He was, Meehan says, "capable and articulate, with a mind like a filing cabinet." He was there from the time the port dealt with local Lake Michigan traffic to the advent of international trade. He was always on the hot seat because he was a highly political operative.

In 1959 a strong and effective mayor by the name of Henry Meier was elected, who immediately began to clash with Brockel.[2] There was always conflict between the two, and, Meehan says, "when there's conflict at the top, everybody suffers. They would try to destroy each other."

Additionally, the port director job was a fish bowl. Once Brockel had a $50 ashtray on his desk and it made the front page of the newspapers. Brockel was not in the long run going to survive the situation. Meier finally made a change and promoted one of the superintendents to the directorship.

---

1. All quotations from an interview conducted with Dan Meehan on July 13, 2007.
2. Meier served 28 years as mayor.

He was a good man, but politically naïve. He went directly to Congress to expand the port without going through the mayor. When Meier found out his string of profanities ended with, "He's got to go."

Into the volatile political mix came Roy Hoffmann, who had just come from the highly disciplined military environment. Meehan says, "Roy had to adjust himself from this highly militarized culture to this political scene, which took the cooperation of everyone to make it work—and he did a wonderful job."

"He was always willing to listen," Meehan says, "always willing to contribute. There were times when he and I crossed swords, but I always knew he was capable and focused. We had some tough times, but we never, ever lost respect for each other."

Richard W. Weening, an influential business executive and politician, was the president of the Milwaukee Harbor Commission when the Admiral arrived. He was head of the Democratic Party in the State of Wisconsin, but also was a pragmatic politician and business owner. Roy Hoffmann reported to the very liberal board, and the capable mayor, who had been a supply officer in the Navy during World War II.

The Board members were all political appointees. One was a professor at the University of Wisconsin, "a pain in the ass," the Admiral says, "but harmless." There was one industrialist who understood business well and who was very good. The Admiral got along with the chairman well enough.[3]

One of the men on the board was an individual named Dan Steininger. Steininger was the grandson of the former socialist mayor of Milwaukee during World War II. Dan Steininger was a Yalie with a lot of money, and a lawyer. He eventually became the CEO of the Catholic Knights. Not long after the Admiral was hired Steininger confronted him about the controversy at the Charleston Navy Base, telling him that had he known of those circumstances at the time the Admiral applied for job as Port Director, he would have blocked the nomination. Thereafter they had little contact, but it set the stage for what was to come.

---

3. Bill Drew, a one-time City Hall powerhouse, said that Roy Hoffmann kept his military demeanor when dealing with the board, a group that some viewed as a bunch of self proclaimed little generals. "He always had a presentation that was backed with charts and numbers," Drew said. "He was very precise, very military. I don't think he was easy to push around. He was no cream puff." "Hoffmann once rocked the boat in Milwaukee," by Cary Spivak and Dan Bice, *Milwaukee Journal Sentinel*, August 23, 2004.

MARY LINN ENDED UP loving Milwaukee. "It was the cleanest, prettiest place I ever lived." They purchased a home in a nice friendly neighborhood, a block from Lake Michigan. The home, stone with a slate roof, was built in 1925, and the Admiral rebuilt the kitchen cabinets and they tiled the floors together.

They had no children at home; Harriet was at the Northern Virginia Training Center in Fairfax, Virginia. Mary Linn would drive to pick her up for a month in the summer and for a month at Christmas. She would generally make the 900-mile trip in two days going over, so she could pick up Harriet during the day. Sometimes she drove straight through coming back.

"I had a social life in Milwaukee," Mary Linn says, "that had nothing to do with Roy's rank. I had learned as the wife of an admiral not to suggest 'let's go here or let's go there,' because there were never any objections, so I always waited for someone else to make suggestions. It was in Milwaukee I made friends—nobody could care less about position."

Mary Linn learned to cross country ski in the winter, and she golfed in the summer. Her husband worked hard, but his Saturdays and Sundays were generally free, for the first time since they had married. "I thought we had roots," she says. "I thought it was where we would spend the rest of our days."

IN JANUARY 1980, one of the difficult passages of life occurred, when the Admiral's mother, Zettamae, died. Harriet was home with the Hoffmanns when the death occurred. The Hoffmanns took off immediately for Crystal City, over treacherous, icy winter roads. As they traveled, Mary Linn says, "they closed the interstate and we had no choice but to stop." They missed the visitation, which left the Admiral's father very upset. "Mr. Hoffmann," Mary Linn said, "we are very lucky to be here at all."

Nine months later, World War I veteran Roy Walter Hoffmann died, suddenly and unexpectedly. Brother Paul's wife called Mary Linn to let them know. The Admiral was at work at the port and Mary Linn called him there to tell him. "It was," she says, "a shock to say the least." Mary Linn's father, the master mechanic and machinist, Robert Linn Thompson, died in February 1981. Her mother, Christine Marchand Thompson, died on November 4, 1988.

On July 31, 1982, Steve Carnahan, son of Rear Admiral Ralph Carnahan, and second eldest Hoffmann daughter Chris Carnahan's husband, was out mowing the lawn at their home. He suffered a massive heart attack that day and died. He died of hypertrophic cardiomyopathy, the killer of many young athletes. It is a disorder that often has no obvious warning signs; the heart muscle (predominantly of the left ventricle) inexplicably becomes excessively thick. The condition is thought to cause one of every three cases of sudden death among athletes.

Steve's death was a shock to the entire family. Prior to his death, Hilarie Hanson says, they had not been a particularly demonstrative family, but became much more so after the death of Steve. "There were more 'I love you's' expressed," she says.

LONGEVITY IN A POLITICIZED job such as port director is short, and in a way it is remarkable the Admiral lasted the eight years he did. His nemesis, Dan Steininger, became chairman of the Harbor Commission, which he controlled. He wanted Roy Hoffmann out. In a 2004 article in the *Milwaukee Journal Sentinel*, Steininger said, "I have never said one thing publicly about the reasons I sought Roy Hoffmann's resignation. I never will."[4]

The admiral now says, "I resigned, but I resigned under duress. I would have been fired had I not resigned. I wasn't ready to retire." He walked away from his $65,000 per year job, saying he had no legal grounds to challenge his removal. The Harbor Commission quickly and unanimously accepted his resignation.

PORT OF RICHMOND AND RETIREMENT

In 1986 Roy Hoffmann left the Port of Milwaukee for what seemed certain retirement in Milwaukee, and so it would have remained had it not been for a Fourth of July circus parade. There, while observing the parade with the Carnahan granddaughters, Erin and Kalin, Roy Hoffmann ran into Dan Meehan, a remarkable entrepreneur and philanthropist.

Daniel E. Meehan was born in 1930 on Staten Island, New York. He graduated from the U.S. Merchant Marine Academy in 1951, after which he went to sea for five years, primarily sailing along the south and east coast of Africa, from Cape Town, South Africa, to Mombassa, Kenya in the north. He now says, "You find the world is not like it is back home."

He was eventually offered a job ashore in New York, a job that paid

---

4. "Hoffmann once rocked the boat in Milwaukee," by Cary Spivak and Dan Bice, *Milwaukee Journal Sentinel*, August 23, 2004.

$5,000 per year, less than half what he had earned aboard ship. He spent seven years on the docks, and then was made superintendent of the pier. There he learned, "when a ship is in port there is no clock and no calendar—everything depends on the ship's schedule. You have to do whatever it takes to sail her on schedule."

He got a call after the opening of the St. Lawrence Seaway from a man in Milwaukee by the name of Ted Hansen, who wanted someone to build a company for him. The Hansen family was in warehousing, and Ted Hansen recognized the new paradigm of international shipping would present new challenges.

Meehan went there in 1962, and bought Hansen's company in 1978, the year the Admiral arrived. Hansen's philosophy had been Milwaukee first and always, but Meehan expanded his operation to eventually include ports in Superior, Wisconsin; Duluth, Minnesota; Albany, New York; Richmond, Virginia; Moorhead City, North Carolina; and Tampa and Manatee, Florida.

Meehan's challenge in growing his company was finding quality people to run the subsidiaries, and so it was that he approached Roy Hoffmann in 1989 at the circus parade in Milwaukee. "All I said to him was, 'Roy, what are you doing since you retired?'"

"I'm still adjusting," the Admiral replied. Something in the tone of his voice must have tipped Dan Meehan off, because he said, "Can we have breakfast or lunch someday?" He says, "I knew right away I needed Roy's leadership."

When they met, Meehan said to him, "I've got an ideal port in Richmond, but they need a leader." He then asked if the Admiral had any interest in running the Port of Richmond.

The Admiral told Meehan that he was going to Charlottesville to visit Cecile, and that he would go and check out the Richmond port. The port, it turned out, was a mess ("a shit-house," he says), and they were losing money, because of labor problems. The Teamsters Union hadn't trusted the previous director, as they thought he wanted to replace them with the International Longshoreman's Association.

Initially, Roy Hoffmann wasn't interested in the opportunity, but he saw there were advantages with the port, particularly since the Philip Morris and Dupont companies were neighbors. Additionally, he had always wondered how successful he could be in private industry. The latter reason turned out to be the main attraction.

He wasn't sure Mary Linn would be willing to leave Milwaukee. As it turned out, the move to Richmond appealed to her. It was closer to Harriet (only 109 miles away); Chris was in North Carolina and Cecile was in Charlottesville, much closer than the more remote Milwaukee.

The Admiral talked to Meehan and told him, "If you give me a piece of the action, as a partner, and if we have an understanding that once you give me the mission statement, I'm going to say 'hands off.' I'm going to run the place.

"To my surprise, Dan agreed, and followed up with a written contract." The Admiral, at age 65, went to work as Executive Vice President for Meehan Overseas Terminals, Ltd., which operated the port under contract with the city. When the Hoffmanns arrived in Richmond they purchased the red brick Colonial style home where they still reside.[5]

The terminal consisted of four ship berths; a railroad terminal; trucking facilities; 284,000 square feet of warehouse space; 40 acres of container storage space with modern lift and handling equipment; and after Roy Hoffmann arrived, a well-equipped repair/maintenance facility to competitively and expeditiously move cargo in and out of the port.

The Admiral sat down with the president of the local union and assured him he wasn't looking to change unions or cut wages. However, he wasn't going to tolerate liquor or drugs on the job. He asked the union leader for his support. Fortunately, the union leader understood that to stay in business the firm had to make money, which in the long run benefited the union. Relations with the 50 longshoremen who loaded and unloaded the ships smoothed out.

In return for the support of the union, the Admiral vastly improved working conditions, particularly as related to safety and cleanliness. The port was able to emphasize low freight damage rates and the quality workforce. When the ships moored, the workers hit the decks running, until the ships sailed. The only times the cranes came down were during severe thunderstorms, when the cranes acted as lightning rods.

In addition to the work with the containerized Dupont goods, and the bulk tobacco and finished products from Philip Morris entering and leaving the port, they made money on newsprint coming down from Canada, designated for their largest customer, *The Virginia Pilot* in Norfolk. They got the job because of their superior job on damage control. The rolls of newsprint weighed about four tons, and they had to be handled like eggs. A nick on the

---

5. The home is a two-story with a walk out basement that contains the Admiral's shop and a guest bedroom. It is spacious, befitting their five children and seven grandchildren, with five bedrooms and three and a half baths.

edge could result in a tear when the presses were turning out something like 16,000 to 20,000 newspapers an hour. If the newsprint ripped, they had to stop the presses and change the roll, a process that resulted in lost time and additional labor costs. Similarly, a small pebble picked up in the warehouse could be a disaster for the presses. They continually ran a vacuum sweeper in the warehouse to keep the floor clean.

Within six months, the port was returning a profit. As with the situation in Milwaukee, Richmond was a challenge. It was a long 100-mile transit, through a winding, narrow and shallow river, for large ships to get to the port. The river was subject to shoaling and was virtually unnavigable at night. Depth restrictions limited the largest vessels from entering or leaving the Upper James under full load, even though they sailed at high tide.[6] But the success of the port, according to port authorities, was the plain speaking former admiral. "The full time, personal attention of Roy Hoffmann is really what makes this place go," Martin J. Moynihan, the port's executive director said.[7] "You've got to give him a heck of a lot of credit for what's going on around here."

IN 1995, FORMER SWIFT BOAT SAILORS gathered in Washington, D.C., most together for the first time since their service in Vietnam 25 or more years earlier. The event came about because the first two Swift boats, built by Sewart Seacraft, were found at Rodman in Panama. PCFs 1 and 2 were part of the training inventory of the U.S. Naval Small Craft and Technical School. Senator John Kerry was instrumental in requesting that the two boats be preserved for historical purposes. The Navy Museum in Washington, D.C. provided space to display one of the boats. The boats, in late November 1994, were transported aboard the flight deck of an LST to the Norfolk Naval Station.

They were retrofitted to appear mostly as they had while on patrol in Vietnam, and former Swifties brought the two boats from Norfolk to the Washington Navy Yard (called "The Last River Run"), where they were made available for former crew members and their families to take a last ride aboard before they were retired from service. Swifties came into Washington, D.C. from all over the country for the dedication ceremonies.

---

6. The Army Corps of Engineers' minimum draft requirement was 26 feet; the Port of Richmond was dredged to 28 feet. There was tidal action all the way to Richmond (from six to eight feet), enough to impact all loads going and coming.

7. "Port chief here keeps dream alive," Charles Slack, *Richmond Times-Dispatch*, September 5, 1995. Moynihan was a retired U.S. Coast Guard captain.

On June 16, 1995, former Swiftie and Congressman Jim Kolbe (R-Arizona) hosted a reception for the group in the Rayburn House Office Building.[8] On Saturday, June 17, Kolbe led a tour of the U.S. Capitol and took the Swifties and their families on a tour of the House floor. On the 17th the dedication ceremony occurred at the Navy yard.

It was an emotional time for the aging warriors and their families. The ceremony was moving, full of the pomp and circumstance of Navy ritual. Admiral Zumwalt was there, as were Admirals Boorda, Will, Moore, and Hoffmann.

During the ceremony, Admiral Zumwalt addressed the group, wearing his dress blues in the heat, because, he said, it was the only uniform he had left. He said that he had saved the uniform anticipating he would die in winter and be buried in the dress blues. He told his wife, "If I die in summer, I'll just sweat it out."

"I'm sweating it out today," he said in his speech. He praised the service and sacrifice of the Swift crews, and spoke of the successes of Operation SEALORDS. He spoke of renewed ties with Vietnam, and of the respect the country had for those who had fought in that faraway place.

---

8. Bill Garlow and Steve Hayes co-sponsored the event with the congressman.

Former Swifties and their families ride the boats once again, Washington Navy Yard, 1995. TERRY SYMMES PHOTO

Part Four: Civilian and Swift Boat Veterans and POWs for Truth   407

Admiral Elmo Zumwalt, Swift boat dedication ceremony, June 17, 1995.
TERRY SYMMES PHOTO

Senator John Kerry spoke, giving a moving speech about service on Swifts, which appeared heartfelt and left many in the audience in tears.[9] The only discordant note was an off-key antiwar song delivered from the podium by the then Deputy Assistant Secretary of the Navy for Reserve Affairs, Wade Sanders, a Clinton appointee.[10]

It was Sanders who first notified the Hoffmanns of the event. His secretary, without identifying who she worked for, had called Mary Linn at home and asked for the Admiral's work number. Mary Linn informed the secretary that her husband did not accept social calls at work. The next

---

9. The full text of the speech and a more detailed description of the event may be found in Weymouth D. Symmes, *War on the Rivers* (Missoula, Montana: Pictorial Histories Publishing Company, Inc., 2004), pp. 234–240 and 251–254.

10. Mary Linn Hoffmann says of the Wade Sanders' song, "I was appalled." Her husband was more direct. "I was absolutely appalled when Sanders got up there and sang that protest song. That was absolutely unacceptable—I was so damn mad I almost got up and walked out. It was absolutely disgusting."

Senator John Kerry, Swift boat dedication ceremony, 1995. TERRY SYMMES PHOTO

call was from a very officious Wade Sanders, who said, "Well, he *would* want to take a call from the [Deputy] Assistant Secretary of the Navy."

Mary Linn, mistakenly thinking her husband would want a call from Sanders, passed the number along. A formal invitation followed, both to the dedication and to an alfresco dinner at Teresa Heinz' home in Georgetown following the event.[11] When the Admiral heard about it he said there was no way he was going. Mary Linn now says, "I knew he didn't like Kerry, but I didn't realize how deep this more or less hatred was."

Mary Linn had been suffering for a year with temporal arteritis (sometimes called giant cell arteritis), a condition in which certain arteries in the head and elsewhere become inflamed. The pain of the disorder can make everyday living difficult; if not treated promptly, temporal arteritis can cause blindness. In Mary Linn's case, she totally lost vision in her right eye.[12] She had to take the corticosteroid, prednisone, which, she says, "caused me to gain weight, which made me even more angry." Another side effect of the disease was that she had trouble walking. She hadn't had much of a social life and was looking forward to getting out. She talked her husband into going to the event. "We went," she says, "because I wanted to go."

She could see what the dedication ceremony meant to the men attending. "My observation of the people in the audience and how these men treated each other still makes me get goose bumps," she says. "These men were seeing each other for the first time in so many years. It was an emotionally draining thing for them, and to see how they helped each other. I'd not seen men react like that before—totally unabashed, they hugged, they cried—it was very heartwarming."

Rocky Hildreth and Friar Tuck Brant were there, and Tuck brought one of his scrapbooks, which they were going through when the Admiral came up to them. "What are you guys doing?" he asked.

Tuck replied, "We're just playing a little acey duecey here and looking through my scrapbook."

"Can I look in there?" the Admiral asked.

"Sure," Tuck replied. The Admiral started going through it, and came across a picture of Brant's PCF on a sandbar.

"What the hell's this, Brant?"

---

11. The dinner was served on bone China, and the meat was lamb—not your traditional southern meal. John Kerry and Teresa Heinz had been married ten days when the event occurred.

12. Her vision eventually returned in the eye.

"Oooh, that's when I was kind of aground on a sandbar."

"Did you report this?"

"Nooo, I didn't. We just waited for the water to come back in and refloat us, then we left."

The Admiral turned away and said, "I've seen enough here."

Tuck Brant now says, "I think he really wanted to chuckle."

The night of the dedication the Hoffmanns took a cab with a former Swiftie and his wife to the Heinz home. The cab driver, who was black, was a great deal of fun. When he pulled over to pick them up, someone behind him started honking. The cab driver, Mary Linn says, "called him a very coarse name." As they pulled away, she said to the driver, "By the way, what did you call that man that honked at you?" She says, "Well, if black people can blush—he did!"

They had a great time with him on the way over, and he was very accommodating. As they were getting out of the cab another car drove up, and the driver asked, "Where does the [Deputy] Assistant Secretary of the Navy park?" The Swiftie in the cab said, "Any place you can find."

Admiral Zumwalt was at the home, as were other dignitaries, along with the men who had gone on the "Last River Run." Mary Linn met many of the Swifties for the first time. Mary Linn says Teresa Heinz was a gracious hostess, and says she thoroughly enjoyed the affair.

The Admiral was introduced and asked to make a few comments, which he did. Kerry and the Admiral were cautious toward each other, but the evening went well.

ROY HOFFMANN PUT IN FIVE productive years at the Port of Richmond, until he was nearly 70 years of age. Finally, the demands of the position became too much, which he realized after suffering a fall off a crane at the port. He wasn't hurt badly—he chipped a tooth and messed up a suit—but they took him straight to the doctor. They didn't think he had a misstep or stumbled—he most likely blacked out. "He was doing things at 70," Mary Linn says, "that he shouldn't." It was time to retire for good.

On December 31, 1995, Roy Hoffmann retired from all active business activities. His retirement ceremony was a positive celebration of his successes at the port. Dan Meehan says, "Everybody loved him for his leadership, knowledge, wisdom and judgment."

The next year, Dan Meehan called him with the news he had sold the company to Federal Commerce and Navigation of Montreal, headed by

Egyptian immigrant Laddy Pathy. Pathy owned 60 ships and chartered an additional 60.[13]

ADJUSTING TO RETIREMENT, the Admiral says, "took a long time—I missed being part of the action." Hilarie says, "He was at odds with what to do with himself, to still feel like he was producing something worthwhile. That's when he started doing a lot of his woodworking—he made some beautiful things. And, of course, he's always been the lawn man, no matter where he lived he always had the nicest grass."[14]

He and Mary Linn made a Rhine-Danube European tour. He belongs to various veterans' organizations,[15] and they attend reunions, of his high school in Crystal City; and Navy reunions including the *Cromwell, Harry E. Hubbard, Lloyd Thomas, Sierra, Leahy, Adams*; and the Swift Boat Sailors Association reunions in New Orleans in 1998 and San Diego in 2000 and 2007.

From December 30, 1999, to January 2, 2000, the Hoffmanns celebrated their 50th wedding anniversary. Held at the turn of the millennium, when the world was expected to go to pieces, it turned out to be a very special occasion.

"Dad wanted to do something special for the anniversary," Chris Hoffmann Carnahan says. He rented several rooms at the Peaks of Otter in the foothills of the Blue Ridge Mountains of Virginia. Nineteen people attended; everyone was able to make it except the oldest and youngest daughters, Harriet and Emilie. "It was such a special time," Chris says. "It was a time where we could show our appreciation for our parents, but it was also a time where they could show their appreciation for one another."

---

13. Dan Meehan did not retire from life, however. He had set up the Meehan Family Foundation initially to award scholarships. To date the Foundation has awarded 53 four-year scholarships to various educational institutions. He placed the proceeds of the sale of his business into the Foundation, which currently has an endowment of over $13 million. The Foundation operates in Mexico, Guatemala, South Africa, the Ukraine, the Republic of Georgia, Cuba and Haiti. Meehan and his wife have been honored for their initiative in providing an average of 20,000 supplemental family food packages per month since 1992. The Foundation has built five medical clinics around the world, and the Meehans have been given many awards for their philanthropy.

14. His outdoor work didn't always turn out well. Once we talked and he admitted somewhat sheepishly that he had gone for Weed and Feed for his lawn, but had come home with Weed only. After applying it to the back yard, the yard turned an ugly brown.

15. Including the American Legion, the Retired Officers Association, Veterans of Foreign Wars, Navy League, Military Order of the Purple Heart, and the Tin Can Sailors Association.

The Hoffmann women in 1999, left to right: Cecile, Hilarie, Christine, Emilie, Mary Linn and Harriet. HOFFMANN PHOTO

As they were leaving the celebration they heard of the death of Admiral Zumwalt on the radio. The great Navy man had passed away after an operation to remove a lung. He had contracted asbestosis, a chronic condition affecting the tissue of the lungs, from his lifetime of duty aboard ships.

The Admiral and Mary Linn attended the dedication of the installation of a plaque at the Navy Memorial for the *Hubbard* in 2003. After the event they went to a restaurant, where they ran into Ernest Borgnine. Borgnine had a long and produc-

Roy F. and Mary Linn Hoffmann, USS Hubbard reunion, 2003. HOFFMANN PHOTO

Former U.S. Navy men: Roy Hoffmann and Ernest Borgnine. Hoffmann photo

tive television and Hollywood career, appearing as Commander McHale in *McHale's Navy* (1962), Sergeant "Fatso" Judson in *From Here to Eternity* (1953), Major General Worden in *The Dirty Dozen* (1967), and Detective Lieutenant Mike Rogo in *The Poseidon Adventure* (1972). In 1955 he received the Best Actor Academy Award for his role in *Marty*.

Perhaps lesser known is Borgnine's U.S. Navy service. He joined the Navy in 1935 after high school. He was discharged in 1941, but he reenlisted when the United States entered World War II, and he served until the end of the war in 1945. He achieved the rate of Gunner's Mate Chief Petty Officer.[16]

When the two old sea dogs got together, Borgnine asked Roy Hoffmann, "How old are you now?"

---

16. Unlike today's movie stars, many of whom despise the military and seem to hate America, the World War II generation of actors produced many who served their country during the war. A partial listing would include Alec Guinness, who operated a British Royal Navy landing craft on D-Day; Donald Pleasance (*The Great Escape*) was an RAF pilot who was shot down, held prisoner and tortured by the Germans; David Niven was Lieutenant Colonel of the British Commandos in Normandy; James Stewart was a bomber pilot who flew more than 20 missions over Germany, and who as a reservist retired with the rank of Brigadier General in the Air Force; Clark Gable (*the* mega-star of the day), enlisted as a private in 1942 and flew operational missions over Europe in B-17s; Charles Bronson was a tail gunner in the Army Air Corps; George C. Scott was a decorated Marine; Eddie Albert was awarded a Bronze Star for heroism at the horrific battle on the island of Tarawa in 1943; Brian Keith was a Marine rear gunner in the Pacific; Lee Marvin was a Marine on Saipan during the Marianas campaign, during which he was awarded the Purple Heart; and of course, Audie Murphy (*To Hell and Back*), the 5-foot 5-inch tall Texan, was the most decorated serviceman of World War II.

"Seventy-seven," replied the Admiral.

"You're just a kid; I'm 86," Borgnine replied.

The Admiral asked him, "What's the thing you remember most about the war?"

Without hesitation, Borgnine said, "I remember coming back at the end of the war. When we sailed past Diamond Head into Pearl Harbor. I thought to myself, 'We did it.'"

IN RETIREMENT, THE HOFFMANNS took a great deal of pride and satisfaction in their children. The girls were still in their first marriages and were enjoying successful lives.[17] It appeared that the proud parents would settle in to enjoy their children and grandchildren. And then in 2003, John Kerry, at the USS *Yorktown*, announced he was running for president, and hence Commander in Chief of the armed forces.

---

17. Chris, widow of Steve Carnahan, has two children, Erin and Kalin; Cecile is married to Pete Gorham, and her children are Seth and Todd; Hilarie is married to Jack Hanson, and their children are Kelsey and Alex; Emilie is married to Rory Crow, and her child is Brooke.

10

SWIFT BOAT VETERANS AND POWS FOR TRUTH

The only unforgivable sin in war is not doing your duty.
—President Dwight D. Eisenhower

You and I have a rendezvous with destiny. We will preserve for future generations this, the last best hope of man on earth, or we will sentence them to the first step into a thousand years of darkness. If we fail, at least let those future generations say of us we justified our brief moment here. We did all that could be done.
—President Ronald Reagan

The efforts of the Swift Boat Veterans and POWs for Truth in 2004 are nearly incomprehensible without an objective and intellectually honest appraisal of a few facts. First, the vast majority of men who served on Swift boats in Vietnam felt a strong sense of betrayal by John Kerry, who used two disputed Purple Hearts, and a third which did not require a day in a hospital, to exit Vietnam barely four months into his 12-month tour. He was the only Swiftie known to take such an advantage during the long and distinguished time the Swifts served in Vietnam. It goes without saying that someone had to take his place, and assume the dangers of serving on the boats, when he left.

Second, he compounded that betrayal by coming home and slandering, in Senate testimony, not only the men he served with on Swift boats, but *all* Vietnam veterans. He dishonored his Navy commission by meeting with the enemy in Paris, throwing away his medals (or ribbons), and he outraged most veterans with his association with Jane Fonda and her ilk.[1]

Third, Swift Vets was undertaken by ordinary American citizens with nothing to personally gain and much to lose by their involvement. The group was composed of Republicans, Democrats and Independents. There was never any communication, cooperation or coordination with the Republican Party, the Bush White House, or the Bush campaign by the Swift Boat Veterans or POWs. The Federal Election Commission (FEC) confirmed the foregoing statement after the election.

Fourth, there was an astonishing mainstream media bias during the 2004 presidential election. It was a media that did not really want to report anything that would disparage John Kerry, for fear it would help George Bush. To understand the depth of the bias, one must assume that it was the Republican nominee who had chosen to make his service the centerpiece of his qualification to be president. Then assume that he had exited his wartime service under very questionable circumstances, come home and engaged in radical antiwar activities, and had almost assuredly received a less than honorable discharge when he left the service. Finally assume that in the face of all that, he refused to release his pertinent military records. In another election, and perhaps another time, the revelations about the character of John Kerry would have forced his withdrawal from the race.

ON SEPTEMBER 2, 2003, John Kerry stood in front of the aircraft carrier USS *Yorktown* at Mount Pleasant, South Carolina, and announced his candidacy

---

1. The extensively documented facts about the Purple Hearts, the Silver Star, "No Man Left Behind" and "Christmas in Cambodia"; and his radical antiwar activities may be found in *Unfit for Command* by John E. O'Neill and Jerome R. Corsi, Ph.D. Neither Kerry nor his supporters have ever refuted the facts in the book. Most defense of Kerry has centered on the "Silver Star incident," which O'Neill has referred to as "wrapping a small truth around a big lie." By Kerry's own admission, he shot a wounded, fleeing VC youth in the back that day. As with nearly everything else regarding Kerry's service in Vietnam, the documentation has either not been released or is suspicious. The Silver Star citation on Kerry's Web site is signed by former Navy Secretary John Lehman, who is on record as saying he had no idea where it came from. "It is a total mystery to me," he says. "I never saw it. I never signed it. I never approved it. And the additional language it contains was not written by me." There were two previous versions of the Silver Star, the first signed by Admiral Zumwalt and the second by Admiral John Hyland. Each successive version was more favorable to Kerry. Thomas Lipscomb, "Kerry citation a 'total mystery' to ex-Navy chief (John Lehman)." *New York Sun Times*. August 28, 2004.

for President of the United States. He was joined by some crew members of PCFs 44 and 94, with whom he had served in Vietnam. He emphasized his military service, saying, "George Bush's vision does not live up to the America I enlisted in the Navy to defend, the America I have fought for in the Senate—and the America that I hope to lead as president."[2]

He seemed an unlikely candidate for president. He was a very liberal Massachusetts senator, with a relatively undistinguished record. His political mentor was Senator Ted Kennedy, whose questionable ethics made him appealing to a narrow group of far left Americans. His radical antiwar activities were another weakness, which Kerry hoped to offset with his record as a Navy officer in Vietnam. Kerry had been on the campaign trail for months, but he had slipped into fourth place among registered Democrats since July. Senator Joe Lieberman of Connecticut was first, while former Vermont Governor Howard Dean was moving up in the polls.[3]

When Kerry announced at the *Yorktown*, John O'Neill, who had debated Kerry on June 30, 1971, on the "Dick Cavett Show," was at home in Houston. His wife, Anne, was on dialysis and very ill at the time. O'Neill was then getting ready to donate a kidney to her. When he heard Kerry had announced he thought it was a joke. He thought that no one would take Kerry seriously as a candidate.

And so it seemed, until January 19, 2004, when the Iowa caucus results came in, indicating John Kerry had taken 38 per cent of the state's delegates, and John Edwards had taken 32 per cent. Former front-runner Howard Dean got 18 per cent, and compounded his poor showing by giving the widely ridiculed "I have a scream" post caucus speech. On January 27, John Kerry won the New Hampshire primary with 38.4 per cent of the vote. On February 3, called "Mini Tuesday," Kerry won the Missouri, Arizona and Delaware primaries; and the New Mexico and North Dakota caucuses. On the 7th he won Michigan and Washington caucuses, and on the 8th won the Maine caucus. On the 10th he won Tennessee and Virginia, after which Wesley Clark endorsed him. On February 14 he won caucuses in Washington, D.C., and Nevada; and Wisconsin on the 17th. The next day Howard Dean called it quits. What had been formerly

---

2. Readers looking for a comprehensive history of the 2004 election will have to consult other sources. The Swift Vets were never concerned with George Bush, or Kerry's record other than his military service and his antiwar activities.

3. It was worse for Kerry in December, as he polled four per cent, to 23 per cent for Howard Dean, ten per cent for Wesley Clark and Joe Lieberman, Richard Gephardt at six per cent, Al Sharpton at five per cent, and John Edwards at two per cent.

unthinkable for the former Swift boat sailors of Task Force 115 was now looking more and more certain: John Kerry was the presumptive Democratic Party's presidential candidate.

As Kerry swept through the primaries, John O'Neill was then in the critical care unit of Methodist Hospital in Houston recovering from donating a kidney to his critically ill wife, Anne. "I looked up at the television," O'Neill says, "and Kerry was in his brown leather jacket and was claiming victory in a primary, and it said he was the presumptive Democratic nominee. My reaction was: I thought I was hallucinating."

Larry Thurlow was probably indicative of many of the Swifties; he was at wits end over a Kerry candidacy. He knew he was going to speak out, but didn't know what to do. Then, "out of the blue, the Admiral called."

Admiral Hoffmann was also alarmed over the prospect of a Kerry candidacy. The country, after all, was at war, in Afghanistan and Iraq. He considered John Kerry totally unqualified to be the Commander in Chief of American troops during wartime. He incredulously called Chuck Horne (COMCOSRON One during Vietnam), to ask him if thought Kerry could be a serious candidate for president. Horne asked him if he had read the just released *Tour of Duty* by Douglas Brinkley. It was the first the Admiral had heard of it. He immediately purchased a copy, read it, and phoned Horne again.

"I've never seen so many lies and gross exaggerations in my life," the Admiral told him. "Where in the hell did all this come from?" Horne gave the Admiral the strong impression that he did not want to be involved.

The Admiral next called retired Rear Admiral Bill Schachte. Schachte had not read *Tour of Duty*, but supported the Admiral's concerns about the true nature of John Kerry's character. He also warned the Admiral about how vicious a presidential campaign could be.

"You know," Schachte told him, referring to the abuse of command charge at Charleston, "you've got some warts in your career."

"Yes I do," the Admiral replied, "and I'm proud of every damn one of them."

The Admiral faxed the "skimmer incident" portion of *Tour of Duty* to Schachte, who e-mailed back: "Roy, you know damn well I wouldn't have put that rookie [Kerry] in a situation like that by himself."[4]

---

4. This is the first Purple Heart incident at Cam Ranh Bay, wherein Kerry wounded himself with an M-79 round, was turned down for a Purple Heart, and somehow managed to get it reissued later in his tour. Bill Schachte was the credible on scene witness that night, in the skimmer with Kerry.

Almost everyone interviewed for this chapter acknowledges that had there been no *Tour of Duty*, there would have been no Swift Boat Veterans and POWs for Truth (SBVFT). Many political commentators also feel that without SBVFT Kerry may well have been elected president. Kerry and Brinkley certainly hadn't intended it to be that way.

Tour of Duty was to be Kerry's campaign biography, establishing him as the Vietnam War version of John F. Kennedy. Ironically, Brinkley is a respected historian with an impressive list of books to his credit. Unfortunately, in this case he didn't understood the military ethos, and he is a biased liberal professor who had a liar as his primary source. Using the Kerry private journals from Vietnam, which Brinkley compared with the literature of World War I poet Wilfred Owen, Brinkley created a hagiography of a fatally flawed hero.

What had been intended to establish Brinkley as the court historian of a Kerry administration, as Arthur M. Schlesinger, Jr. had been for Kennedy, backfired. It exposed to all the Swifties the full extent of Kerry's character, and they were appalled.

Former O in C Andy Horne says, "When I read *Tour of Duty* it had to be with an empty stomach." George Elliott, Kerry's Division Commander at An Thoi, says, "I didn't know or much care about the little details of Kerry's two months in An Thoi. Kerry's diaries, as recorded by Brinkley, were a revelation. The book was galvanizing and, coupled with what we all knew about his Vietnam Veterans Against the War (VVAW) activities, made it imperative to oppose his campaign."

Bill Shumadine wasn't aware of the book until the Admiral called him. He went out and bought a copy of the book and read it cover to cover with growing outrage. "I hadn't talked about Vietnam in years," he says. "I don't know who John Kerry thought he was going to fool. Kerry can be a senator, but not the president."[5]

Shumadine sent this author a ten page, single spaced review of all the technical mistakes in the book, concluding, "throughout the sections of the book dealing with facts with which I am familiar, the author has carelessly inserted 'best guess' information and not made any effort to alert the reader that the narrative is based on his opinion. The numerous inaccuracies and lazy approach to checking the facts makes the book a useless tool for defining John Kerry's experience in Vietnam."

---

5. From a January 25, 2007 interview.

John O'Neill says the book is, "garbled, and it's obvious that Brinkley ran into all sorts of criticism [while researching the book] about Kerry, and problems Kerry had. He decided to write around them and not report them. That set up his book as a perfect target, because he was unwilling to take the truth and deal with it."

"Brinkley was trying to write a campaign biography," O'Neill continues, "but he didn't know enough about the military to ferret out that which would really hurt Kerry from that which would really help him. His quotes about Kerry are some of the most damaging things in the book. He makes clear in his analysis of Kerry's journal that Kerry was lying to himself."

Retired Vice Admiral Rex Rectanus told this author, "The reason I became a plank owner on Swift vets was that I became so incensed when I read *Tour of Duty*. It brought back to me things I hadn't thought about in years." Rectanus was particularly upset that the book portrayed senior officers in Vietnam as incompetent, and that they were condoning atrocities.

Brinkley also failed to realize how respected Admiral Roy Hoffmann was with his former sailors. In the book he disparages the Admiral as a promotion hungry officer who launched "ludicrous missions aimed at sacrificing the best Americans to satisfy a president's geopolitical ambitions." He compared the Admiral to the colonel in the movie *Apocalypse Now*, who loved the "sweet smell of napalm in the morning."[6]

The reader will not be surprised that the Admiral was going to act on what he thought was right, regardless of the consequences. Working with Charley Plumly, he went up to his attic and pulled out an old TF 115 roster, then started calling the former Swifties' last known state area code, followed by 555-1212. He scored on about one out of three former sailors with the 35-year-old list. Most were astounded to hear from their old Task Force Commander. Almost all were appalled at the prospect of a Kerry presidency. Almost all said 'sign me up.'[7]

The Admiral called Bob Elder at home. "Bob Elder," he led off, "Roy Hoffmann."

Elder told this author, "I'm in my den, and *I stood up*. 'Yes, sir,' I responded. I hold him in great reverence."

---

6. Mary Linn Hoffmann had heard her husband called everything from "Rotten Roy" to "Nails," and she says she just tried to consider the source. "However," she says, "you dislike having your spouse maligned."

7. This author's call came on March 9, 2004. I had just finished reading *Tour of Duty*. As with most of the other men, I was so appalled at the portrait of the Swifties I had served with, and of our entire chain of command, that I immediately said, "Sign me up."

The men of Swift Boat Veterans and POWs for Truth. "Friar Tuck" Brant holding a banner that flew on his boat in Vietnam, flanked by Van Odell and Tom Wright. "Latch" second from right next to Charley Plumly. LYNN WRIGHT PHOTO

Bob "Friar Tuck" Brant wouldn't read *Tour of Duty*. His wife Barb and daughter Jen had seen the book at Borders, and Barb came home and told him, "There's a new book out about John Kerry called *Tour of Duty*. Would you like me to buy you the book for your birthday?"

"No way," he said.

"You don't want to read it?"

"No."

Barb got the book and looked up "Brant," and then went to the section on the "Bo De Massacre." It was hardly a complimentary account of the action where her husband had served as OTC. She bought the book, read it cover to cover, flagging with yellow stickers the portions that didn't seem right. She knew some of the people involved from Swift Boat Sailors Association reunions. She worked on the book for a couple of weeks, and then asked Tuck, "I know this book upsets you, but can I ask you a couple of questions?"

"I guess."

The session ended up lasting three hours. She started with the part about Admiral Hoffmann. "That's not the man I know," she said. "Was he like that?"

"Absolutely not," Tuck said. "The book isn't right. He is a warrior and I'd go anywhere with him."

By the time they had been through the book, Tuck Brant was ready for the phone call that came from the Admiral in late February. The Admiral led off with, "Have you read *Tour of Duty?*"

Tuck replied, "No, but we know about it and are upset about it." The Admiral asked if he wanted to be part of a group opposing Kerry. Tuck told him he would have to think about it for a while. He knew of the repercussions of getting involved, particularly for his family. He spent about ten days thinking about it as he looked through his old scrapbooks, thinking about his dad.

Barb asked him, "Have you thought about it?"

"Yes."

"You've made up your mind, haven't you?"

"Yes."

"You're going to do it, aren't you?" Barb asked.

"Yes."

"What if there are repercussions?"

"I'll live with them," Tuck replied. "But I couldn't live with myself if I didn't get involved."

ON MARCH 2, 2004, President Bush called Kerry to congratulate him on his decisive wins in the Democratic primaries; Kerry was his presumptive opponent in the election. But it was apparent to the Kerry campaign they had a problem with *Tour of Duty*. Brinkley was the first to call Admiral Hoffmann, after hearing the Admiral was calling Swifties about Brinkley's book. Brinkley asked the Admiral to cooperate in correcting the manuscript. The skeptical Admiral refused.

Next, on March 15, at around 8:30 p.m., the phone rang at the Hoffmann home in Richmond. He picked it up and heard the familiar voice of John Kerry, who wanted to discuss the negative portrait of Hoffmann in *Tour of Duty*. Kerry knew that the Admiral was organizing Swifties against him. He made the Admiral an offer (consider it a bribe): If the Admiral would drop his efforts against Kerry, Kerry would insure that *Tour of Duty* would be changed to reflect favorably on the Admiral. He went on to say that the Admiral had been unfairly maligned in the book, that he respected him, and considered him a good leader in Vietnam.

"It sure as hell doesn't look like it," the Admiral responded. The blunt Roy Hoffmann told Kerry that he and the vast majority of his shipmates could never forgive him for his defamation of the Navy and other U.S. forces in his slanderous and undocumented accusations of atrocities in Vietnam. He went on to cite Kerry's leadership of the VVAW and his association with Jane Fonda and others of her ilk.

Two days later, the Admiral sent out by e-mail what he called "SITREP NUMBER ONE FROM SWIFT BOAT TOUR OF TWELVE COMMITTEE."[8] The Admiral, who neither types nor uses the Internet, prevailed on Mary Linn to prepare the message. Next-door neighbor Roseanne Walling taught her how to put the addressees into nine groups. When the message to the groups was ready Mary Linn said to the Admiral, "It's ready to send, do you really want to do this?" On receiving an affirmative answer she hit "Enter," and the message went out.[9]

In the e-mail, the opening communication of Swift Vets, the Admiral struck the themes that would dominate the Swift effort to inform the public of the character of John Kerry. It read in part:

> Our mission is: "to set the record straight" regarding Senator John F. Kerry's tour of four months, 12 days of in-country duty during the Vietnam War.
>
> Our thesis is . . . Kerry is not fit to be the Commander in Chief of the Armed Forces of the United States of America.
>
> Our response must be irrefutably factual, from witnesses who were there, with minimal opinionating and rhetoric. We now have seventy Swifties, officers and enlisted, solidly "on board." We believe two hundred or more is reasonably attainable [the final number was over 350].

The Swifties were alarmed at the prospect of a man most considered a traitor to his country, leading the United States in time of war. The prospect of Kerry becoming the Commander in Chief seemed a real possibility, in large respect because of the weaknesses associated with the presidency of George Bush.

The attacks of September 11, 2001, by Islamic terrorists crashing two planes into the Twin Towers in New York, one into the Pentagon in Washington, D.C., and one into a field in Pennsylvania, had initially united the country behind the president. His move into Afghanistan after Osama

---

8. The Tour of Twelve alluded to the fact that Swifties served twelve months unless medevaced out earlier.

9. Daughter Cecile Gorham says, "I know he was a little nervous. He knew this was not going to be popular with everybody. I admired him for doing what he had to do." Daughter Hilarie Hanson says, "The issue was character. They [the Swift Boat Veterans] put their honor on the line once again."

Bin Laden and the Taliban was widely hailed as the right response to the 9-11 attacks. But the invasion of Iraq in 2003 had aroused the antiwar forces that were personally repelled by the president anyway.

On March 22, Richard Clarke, Bush's former chief counter terrorism aide, released a book that, although critical of previous administrations for their handling of Al-Qaida prior to 9-11, caused there to be focus on whether the Bush administration had done enough to thwart the attacks. Then, on April 29, photographs broke showing Iraqi prisoners in the Abu Ghraib prison outside Baghdad being abused by U.S. soldiers. The resulting firestorm reflected the reflexive response of a media more than willing to believe the worst of U.S. troops. The disproportionate coverage of Abu Ghraib in relation to the daily heroics of troops in Afghanistan and Iraq was an indicator of how the antiwar press would hammer home the problems in Iraq.

On May 8 the body of reporter Nick Berg was found in Iraq. A few days later a video of his beheading by terrorists was distributed, sparking outrage throughout the world. In this mix were calls for the resignation of Secretary of Defense Donald Rumsfeld, over Abu Ghraib. Bush's overall job approval rate was at 42 per cent; approval for his handling of the Iraq War stood at 35 per cent. The low poll numbers coincided with the release of the sleazy Michael Moore "documentary," *Fahrenheit 911*.[10]

April 6, 2004: Organizational meeting in Dallas, Texas

On Friday, March 19, 2004, John O'Neill, after establishing contact with Bill Franke and the Admiral, sent an e-mail message to the Admiral, Mike Bernique, Jim Zumwalt, Andy Horne, Bill Lannom and Bill Franke, confirming that they would all meet at Spaeth Communications in Dallas, Texas, on April 6, 2004, to "discuss the Kerry matter."[11] O'Neill closed the e-mail with, "It is, of course, a great honor to be involved with you all. I'd ride the rivers with any of you."

---

10. John O'Neill says, "Bush was a relatively weak candidate and the Iraq War had gone poorly, which set him up very easily to be defeated. There was a real chance the country would look for an alternative without examining the alternative; there is a huge difference between the mediocre and horrendously bad."

11. Jim Zumwalt, the son of Admiral Elmo Zumwalt and the brother of Elmo Zumwalt III, was fully supportive, but could not attend. This author had been invited to the meeting but had not yet committed to attend.

Earlier in the year, while O'Neill was recovering from donating a kidney to his wife Anne, he began getting media calls about Kerry, because of their debate in 1971. He called Merrie Spaeth to seek her advice on what he should do about Kerry.

MERRIE SPAETH SAYS, "Without my husband, I wouldn't have been involved."[12] She describes her husband, Tex Lezar, as "brilliant but eccentric." She was grateful to John O'Neill for having hired Lezar and making him a partner in his law firm in 1998. It showed, she says, O'Neill's generosity of spirit. Merrie Spaeth and her three children were stunned when Tex Lazar dropped dead of a massive heart attack in their home early in 2004, an event from which Spaeth was still recovering when she hosted the Dallas meeting.

Merrie Spaeth is an accomplished woman in her own right. She graduated Cum Laude from Smith College and went to the Columbia Business School. She was the first woman to serve on the staff of the Director of the FBI. She spent two years in the Reagan White House as Director of Media Relations, an office set up during the Carter administration. As such, she was responsible for the local press and special press (anything that covers citizens' work or interests). It was an important job. "When you look at how people get their information," she says, "they get it from their local press and they get it from the specialty press. No one reads the *Washington Post*."

Spaeth had spent the previous 20 years building her business, Spaeth Communications. In the course of her normal business she worked for O'Neill's law firm in developing trial strategy and coaching witness for trials. Spaeth was astounded when O'Neill called her in the second or third week of February, ranting about John Kerry. "I was stunned. You'd think if you knew someone for 15 to 20 years you would hear him mention Kerry."

O'Neill told her about his Swift boat service and his debate with Kerry in 1971. Spaeth asked, "What do you want from me?"

"I want your advice," he said. Her advice was "don't get involved, forget about it, it can't benefit you in anyway."

He told Spaeth, "I have to get involved, and I just can't let this happen."

She advised him to at least wait until he had somewhat recovered from the kidney transplant. By mid March he was on the phone again, saying that Admiral Roy Hoffmann wanted to get together as a group. Dallas seemed a good central place for the meeting, and Spaeth agreed to host the meeting.

---

12. All quotes from Merrie Spaeth are from an interview conducted July 13, 2006.

Meanwhile, she read everything she could about Kerry. "I was mortified by my own ignorance [of Kerry and the antiwar movement]," she says. "Kerry's Senate testimony was carefully hedged as to whether he had personally committed atrocities. I was terribly embarrassed that for 30 plus years I had believed that stuff."

The meeting opened in the offices of Spaeth Communications at 10:00 a.m.[13]; attending the meeting were Spaeth, the Admiral, B. G. "Jug" Burkett (the author of *Stolen Valor*, who was invited to the meeting by John O'Neill),[14] O'Neill, Andy Horne, Bill Lannom, Charley Plumly, Bill Franke, Mike Bernique, and this author.

John O'Neill came from a Navy background. His father was a 1931 Naval Academy graduate, who went on to a long career in that service, retiring as a rear admiral. O'Neill also had two uncles who served in the Navy. One uncle was killed at the beginning of World War II; another was killed while flying off the *Oriskany* during the Korean War. His body was never recovered and he left behind five children.

O'Neill says, "I grew up in the environment that nurtured Admiral Hoffmann.[15] They believed in honor over life. They had contempt for self-promoters. They had no great attachment to money. When you measured people's worth, it was by their deeds, not the country club they belonged to, the house they lived in, or the cash they had. They thought that people who measured themselves by those standards were people to feel really sorry for. They measured people by: 'He was on the *Lexington* when it went down;' or 'He won a Navy Cross on Iwo Jima.' It's a different value scale."

John O'Neill had two brothers who preceded him at the Naval Academy. Brother Brian, a submariner, graduated in 1957; and Ed, a surface line officer, who graduated in 1959. O'Neill graduated in 1967 from the Naval Academy.

O'Neill volunteered for Swift boat duty, and arrived at Coastal Division 11 not long after Kerry left. Then Captain Hoffmann was finishing his tour of duty when O'Neill arrived, and they didn't meet there. O'Neill says, "I

---

13. The meeting came at a difficult time for Mary Linn Hoffmann. Her brother Lee died the Sunday before the Dallas meeting. The death was not a shock, as he had been ill, and the Hoffmanns had visited him the week before he died. Hilarie and Cecile went to Richmond, and then they and Mary Linn picked up Chris and drove to Atlanta for the funeral.

14. Burkett served in Vietnam with the 199th Light Infantry Brigade; his book exposed the massive distortion of history surrounding the Vietnam War and those who fought in it.

15. All quotations are from an interview conducted with John O'Neill, July 30, 2007.

had heard about him. He was famous. One of the stories that circulated was that Hoffmann was on a Swift boat under heavy fire saying, "I'll plug the holes, just keep shooting!" O'Neill also heard stories, even then, about Kerry's questionable Purple Hearts.

O'Neill experienced the losses of war while in Vietnam. A close friend, Ken Norton, was killed while serving in Da Nang. "One man," he says, "died in my arms while I was serving at Sea Float."

O'Neill says, "Admiral Zumwalt's son, Elmo, became my closest friend in Vietnam." Elmo had arrived in Vietnam four or five months after Admiral Zumwalt arrived. Zumwalt received the unsettling news that his son had volunteered for duty aboard Swifts. Admiral Zumwalt had the power to deny the request, but Elmo "politely but firmly told his Dad to keep hands off." Zumwalt told BUPERS to handle the request as they would any other.[16]

O'Neill and young Elmo tried to operate together whenever they could while serving at Sea Float. They ended up serving together for nearly six months. "He was," O'Neill says, "a wonderful and courageous guy."

They remained friends and stayed in touch after Vietnam. "My friend Elmo Zumwalt detested Kerry," O'Neill says, "to the point where anytime Kerry did something Elmo would send a note saying, 'We've really got to do something about this weasel.'"

O'Neill, after his honorable discharge from the Navy, debated Kerry in 1971. When the debate was over O'Neill called his dad to ask how he had done. His father replied, "Well, son, after you called him a coward and he didn't punch you out, it was all over."

O'Neill says, "Kerry represented a form of moral cowardice that was so unusual, it was so at war with everything my father, Roy Hoffmann and other military officers stood for."

John O'Neill went on to receive his J.D. from the University of Texas in 1973, graduating first in his class. He clerked for Justice William H. Rehnquist on the U.S. Supreme Court from 1974-75, and then entered the private practice of law in Houston, specializing in large-scale commercial litigation.

---

16. Admiral Zumwalt always had a special place in the heart of the Swift boat sailors. He decided once to go on a night ambush mission with one of the boats. Admiral Rex Rectanus says, "General Abrams was very unhappy when he learned Zumwalt spent a night on a Swift boat on a night ambush. If he had been captured or killed, it would have been a real blow to everybody. Zumwalt's night ambush worked—word spread to the troops and it was a huge moral boost. Had it not worked . . ." Admiral Rectanus interview, January 26, 2007.

Andy Horne is a Houston native who practiced law there. O'Neill and Horne knew each other, and it was Horne who had put O'Neill in contact with the Admiral. Horne graduated from the University of Texas law school in 1964 and went to work for the Harris County (Texas) District Attorney, where he worked until 1967, after which he resigned to enter the U.S. Navy. He went to OCS in Newport, Rhode Island, and was commissioned as an ensign in September 1967. He wanted Swift boat duty but was told he first needed to be fleet qualified. He was assigned to the USS *Princeton* (LPH 5), where he relieved Larry Thurlow, who was going to Swift school.

Horne reapplied for Swift boats, was accepted, and ended up going to Vietnam in September 1969. He was assigned to Coastal Division 13 in Cat Lo, where he served as the O in C of PCF 59. In March he was transferred to Cam Ranh Bay as an Operational Readiness Inspections Officer. When the Squadron offices moved to Cat Lo he transferred back.[17] While he was at Cat Lo he met Bill Lannom, with whom he stayed in contact after the war. And that is how Lannom came to be at the meeting.

Lannom was born and raised in Grinnell, a small farm and college town in east central Iowa. He graduated in 1968 from the University of Iowa, after which he entered OCS in Newport, Rhode Island. A new "In Country Vietnam" program had just opened for newly commissioned ensigns. Lannom volunteered, was selected for Swift school, which he attended with Bill Franke and this author. After graduation he was assigned to Cat Lo in Vietnam, where he was O in C of PCF 37. Upon receiving his honorable discharge from the service he returned to Grinnell where he joined his two older brothers in the family business.[18]

The Admiral had tracked down Bill Franke, whom he did not personally know. Matt D'Amico had given the Admiral Franke's name, as he had been looking for someone with the business acumen, communications network and horsepower to support the fledgling Swift operation.

Franke received an economics degree from Principia College, after which he entered the Navy. Upon completion of OCS he volunteered for Swift boat duty. He served one year in Vietnam, primarily in Coastal Division 11 at An Thoi. He was O in C of PCFs 56 and 93, and then became Tactical Commander of a task group that included 12 Swift boats, multiple aircraft and approximately 300 ground troops. While in Vietnam Franke received the

---

17. Andy Horne and his wife, Sylvia, currently live in Galveston, Texas.
18. Lannom's wife's name is Anne, and he has two sons.

Silver Star, Bronze Star, Purple Heart and Vietnamese Cross of Gallantry.

Franke is the President and Chief Executive Officer of Gannon International, a privately held corporation engaged in real estate development, computer technologies and international trade. He invited this author to attend the Dallas meeting, which offer was accepted.[19]

Admiral Hoffmann invited Charley Plumly and Mike Bernique to the meeting.[20] John Kerry had particularly offended Bernique after he returned from Vietnam. "He [Kerry] went before the Senate and lied like a son of a bitch," Bernique says.

Shortly after Kerry's testimony he called Bernique to invite him to his wedding to Julia Thorne. Bernique told him, "'John, frankly, no. Not only am I not going to the wedding, but also this is our last conversation. You lied like a son of a bitch.'

"I remember him hemming and hawing," Bernique says, "and basically I hung up." Bernique would not hear from him again until 2004.

The Swifties, Spaeth and Burkett crammed themselves into Spaeth's second floor conference room. They introduced themselves to each other, and then discussed their proposed objective (to set the record straight regarding Kerry's tour of duty in Vietnam and antiwar activities), and their proposed plan (to issue a letter to Kerry calling on him to sign a Form 180 to release his military records; and possibly hold a proposed press conference in late April or early May). The proposed guidelines for the group were that there be no coordination, support or communication with the Bush campaign, any political party or outside political organization. The effort was to be a non-partisan, information only.

The meeting in Dallas stretched to 12 hours, interrupted only by lunch and a "Texas barbeque" in the evening. There was a grand debate over strategy.[21] Should the group only go after Kerry's assertions that U.S. soldiers committed atrocities in Vietnam, or should they expand their effort to include Kerry's combat record, which as they shared information, they found was increasingly suspect. Bernique and O'Neill, in particular, thought they should focus on his antiwar activities, but Franke and the Admiral thought his record in Vietnam was so suspect that it had to be brought up.

---

19. I spent nearly a year as Franke's Leading Petty Officer, mostly in An Thoi, first on PCF 56, then on PCF 93, after the 56 boat was severely damaged by an enemy underwater mine.

20. For background on Charley Plumly see Chapter 7, Operation SEALORDS, and for Mike Bernique see Chapter 7, starting with October 14, 1968: Bernique's run up the Rach Giang Thanh. All quotes from Mike Bernique from an interview conducted June 14, 2006.

21. Bill Franke has likened getting Swifties on the same page to herding cats.

Disquieting stories were beginning to surface from those who had served with Kerry that his record there was fraudulent.

Jug Burkett made the telling point to the group, saying that if Kerry's record in Vietnam were as suspect as it seemed, they were the only group in America that could question it. They had been with him on operations, serving in the same rivers, and knew the Swift boat environment intimately. Any other group that questioned his record would simply be quoting second hand information; it would seem the typical political attack in the heat of a presidential campaign.

Merrie Spaeth sat listening at the head of the table. "The first thing I thought was, 'holy crap, the story's true.' Second, I thought 'these guys are going to be destroyed.'"

Admiral Hoffmann sat to her left listening to the long debate. Spaeth says he impressed her in several ways. "First, was his approachable manner. He was a military man in a *very* different environment. Despite two hearing aids, his ears were wide open.

"The second thing is he was a sponge, wanting to learn, and he never seemed to take umbrage by what my husband used to call 'the pushy broad.'

"Third, his demeanor through all this was enormously respectful of all of you, and he was respectful of the process. He never showed the anger that some of you showed."

John O'Neill says, "Admiral Hoffmann was the inspiration for the whole thing, and without him none of it would have come about. He was in a field, politics, which he really didn't know. But he understood honor, so his judgments were largely very good. He had a real understanding of what's in people's hearts—unusual for a guy that is so gruff."

At the Dallas meeting the men arrived at several tasks that had to be completed, but most importantly, the meeting cast the die for the involvement of the aging warriors. It is safe to say none of them really knew what was in store.

First, they chose a name for themselves. Merrie Spaeth stood at a board and asked them what they were about. "Swift boats and truth," the men responded. And so, "Swift Boat Veterans for Truth" would be what they would call themselves.

Second, they agreed to send Senator Kerry a letter, in which they said that he had "grossly and knowingly distorted the conduct of the American soldiers, sailors and airmen of that war.

"Further, we believe that you have withheld and/or distorted material facts as to your own conduct in this war.

"Your conduct is such as to raise substantive concerns as to your honesty and your ability to serve, as you currently seek, as Commander in Chief of the military services . . . . We the undersigned formally request that you authorize the Department of the Navy to independently release your military records (through your execution of Standard Form 180), *complete and unaltered*, including your military medical records."

The letter concluded, "Senator Kerry, we were there. We know the truth. We have been silent long enough. The stakes are too great, not only for America . . . But, most importantly, for those who have followed us into service in Iraq and Afghanistan."[22]

Third, the group agreed that Kerry would not release his military records, because the truth was contained within them. They felt that they would have to hold a press conference to expose Kerry's record to the media, which, they thought, would take it from there.

Fourth, they formed a Steering Committee composed of Admiral Hoffmann, Charley Plumly, Andy Horne, Bill Lannom, John O'Neill, Bill Franke and this author.[23] The group left Dallas with an awareness of and some trepidation for the significant actions they had just initiated, and convinced that once they had sent the letter and held a press conference the press would show the same concerns about Kerry's character the Steering Committee held.

The next day NewsMax.com carried an article by B. G. Burkett titled "Navy Commanders to Cast Doubt on Kerry's War Record." In the first public announcement of the group's forthcoming activities, Burkett announced to WABC Radio's Steve Malzberg that the group would allege that Kerry's Purple Hearts were awarded for "self-reported injuries that were virtually nonexistent.

"He never got a day of treatment, he never spent a day in a medical facility," Burkett continued. Burkett disclosed that he had spoken personally to the Navy men.

By then it had become obvious to the Kerry campaign that *Tour of Duty* was a problem. Kerry sycophant Wade Sanders sent an e-mail out on April

---

22. The full text of the letter may be found on page 188 of *Unfit for Command* or on Swiftvets.com. The release of the records would have been routine in any other campaign. As Bill Schachte says, "The truth is not scattered, it's in John Kerry's records. This debate is unnecessary and Senator Kerry should end it once and for all and authorize the release of his military records. He owes it to America to do just that." John Kerry has as of this writing never authorized the full release of his military records.

23. Mike Bernique did not join the Steering Committee, but he remained in close contact with Admiral Hoffmann during the 2004 campaign.

9, which said in part, "For those of you who have read Tour of Duty there is an opportunity to correct any inaccuracies, errors and/or for you to provide your suggestions/contributions to the revised edition of Tour of Duty."

On April 15 the Admiral fired back in an e-mail titled "Tour of Duty Review." Headed "Dear Swifties," the e-mail, referring to Sanders' message, said, "I suggest you ignore this 'opportunity to correct.' Kerry, Sanders and Brinkley were aware or should have been aware of the many exaggerations, distortions of fact and several outright lies at the time of original publication. Let them stew in their own brew."

On April 10 Merrie Spaeth introduced a woman to the group who would play a key role in SBVFT, Jennifer Webster.[24] "You will start hearing from Jennifer Webster," Spaeth e-mailed. "I decided you needed a dedicated staff person to work on this, and Jennifer has offered to take the assignment because of the deep respect we have for all of you."

Webster had done contract work for Spaeth for the preceding six years, and Spaeth thought SBVFT needed her expertise. Webster owned The Webster Group, which specialized in media relations and consulting, since 1999. Spaeth called her the night before the Dallas meeting and told her to purchase and read two books: *Tour of Duty* by Douglas Brinkley and *Stolen Valor* by B. G. Burkett.

After she read the books she met with John O'Neill, who "was sitting on a lot of unanswered media calls. At that point I was just called on to manage those calls and to prepare him and line him up for live interviews."

She began working with O'Neill, practicing with him on camera. "He has such a wealth of information in his head," Webster says. "We worked on condensing his knowledge." She was always cognizant of O'Neill's health, because he was having a slow recovery from his surgery. She did set up interviews with NBC, CBS, ABC and FOX; FOX was the only interview they planned to fly to New York for.

A reporter from NBC met with O'Neill in Houston for an hour interview. Webster became concerned O'Neill was tiring, so she said to the reporter, "You really need to wrap this up, he just had surgery."

The reporter replied, "Well, you have to understand, I think I'm witnessing history."

---

24. Jennifer Webster resides in Houston, Texas, and is married to Jamey Webster; they have three children, Catherine, Faith and Julia. Jennifer Wammack assisted Webster throughout much of 2004; they were known affectionately by the Swifties and POWs as "the Jennifers." All quotations are from an interview with Jennifer Webster, July 19, 2007.

"That was the first person who ever said anything like that," Webster says. "I didn't know what kind of impact this would have."

Webster and O'Neill flew to New York for the Linda Vester show on FOX. After it was over, Webster says, "these young people kept coming up to John and thanking him because their fathers or uncles had served in Vietnam. This was new to me."

The next day they had breakfast with Jerry Corsi (who was co-writing *Unfit for Command* with O'Neill). "My eyes were as big as saucers," she says, "as he got into Kerry and the Vietnam Veterans Against the War, meeting with the enemy in Paris, and participating in discussions of assassinations of Senators supporting the war. I was starting to think, 'what was I getting into?' I never heard any of that. It turned out it was all true."

MEANWHILE, BILL FRANKE was putting his considerable resources to bear to get the group organized. He searched for (and the Admiral called) the Swift boat O in Cs in the picture taken in Saigon (14 of them opposed Kerry at that point)[25]; he established and registered a Web site (Swiftvets.com); and, working with the Admiral, had completed the letter to Kerry.

With all of this going on, John Kerry was focusing his campaign on his military service. The April 13, 2004 issue of *USA Today* featured an article headlined, "John Kerry's Vietnam," with the subhead, "The Democratic presidential candidate says lessons learned as a young lieutenant in the Mekong Delta have made him the leader he is now."

The article featured pictures of Kerry and his crew of the 94 boat; a picture taken from a video of Kerry's stalking toward the camera with an M-16 gripped in his right hand; and a reunion with Jim Rassmann at a campaign rally in January in Des Moines, Iowa. "Kerry saved the Green Beret's life in Vietnam," the caption stated.

But the article pointed out that "A smaller number of veterans remember an ambitious self-promoter who left Vietnam after only four months, his ticket the three Purple Hearts he earned for minor wounds." Steve Gardner, Kerry's twin 50's gunner on PCF 44, and the enlisted man who served the longest with Kerry, "called Kerry a 'hesitant' commander who shunned danger."

Rassmann said he was alive today because of Kerry's courage during a vicious battle in March 1969.[26] The *USA Today* article stated, "His [Kerry's]

---

25. See Chapter 7, January 22, 1969: The O in Cs are called to Saigon.
26. See Chapter 7, March 13, 1969: The mining of PCF 3.

campaign is considering legal action against what officials call lies and slander spread on the Internet."[27]

THE SWIFTIES ORGANIZE AS A 527 ORGANIZATION

Claudia Standiford, John O'Neill's legal assistant, began working to establish a 527 organization for SBVFT in mid April, retaining Susan Arceneaux of Political Compliance Services, Inc. to set the 527 up, handle all reports and keep an accounting of the group's then meager funds.

The so-called 527 organizations arose out of an egregious attack on the First Amendment (free speech), the McCain-Feingold Act of 2002.[28] Cosponsored by Senators John McCain (R.-Ariz.) and Russ Feingold (D.-Wis.); and Representatives Chris Shays (R.-Conn.) and Marty Meehan (D.-Mass.), the act was to supposedly clean up financing of federal election campaigns, following various investigations of the financing of the 1996 Clinton-Gore reelection campaign. Disregarding the Constitution, and in a breakdown of all three branches of the federal government, Congress passed it; Bush signed it while questioning its constitutionality; and the Supreme Court, unable to convincingly state why it didn't violate the First Amendment, upheld its constitutionality, in the 2003 case McConnell v. Federal Election Commission.

The act prevented political parties from raising funds not allocated to specific candidates (the so-called "soft money"), and barred citizens' groups from using candidates names or photographs in broadcast advertising for 30 days before a primary and 60 days before a general election. Not only did the act restrict free speech, it had the effect of protecting the political class from challengers and from issue-oriented groups that oppose the way they vote in Congress. The effect was that only candidates and news organizations (notoriously biased), as opposed to regular citizens, were permitted to criticize a politician's record at election time.

The 527 organizations arose from a section of the IRS code that allowed non-profit organizations to engage in "issue advocacy." It was a loophole in McCain-Feingold that one could drive a truck through. Although the 527s were not to coordinate with any party or candidate, and were not to engage

---

27. Andrea Stone, "John Kerry's Vietnam," *USA Today*, April 13, 2004, p. 18A.
28. The official name was the Bipartisan Campaign Reform Act of 2002 (BCRA).

in electioneering, by the time SBVFT was forming, the Democratic 527s had already spent $60 million violating the spirit if not the letter of the law.

The regulations prevented 527 political organizations from using corporate or union funds to pay for electioneering communications within 60 days of a general election; imposed strict new reporting obligations for 527 organizations, and prohibited the 527s and their agents from coordinating their activities with a federal candidate, campaign or political party.

The reporting requirements were particularly onerous. The FEC's Form 9 had to be filed with 24 hours of the first air date of any electioneering communication. All disbursements over $200 had to be reported, including the transaction date and the person receiving the funds. Additionally, the name and address of each donor who in the aggregate had contributed more than $500 since the first day of the preceding calendar year had to be reported. The 527s were fully transparent as to what they took in and what they spent.

Ads by 527s could not expressly advocate the election or defeat of a clearly identified federal candidate or group of candidates. It was an unclear environment in which to operate; the federal government would ultimately decide which "free speech" was allowable under its rules.

AT ABOUT THE TIME Susan Arceneaux joined the group, John O'Neill asked this author if he would serve as treasurer for SBVFT. Arceneaux had been a principal of Political Compliance Services, Inc. since June 2001.[29] The firm assists political candidates, seated members of Congress, 527s and Political Action Committees (PACs) in filing FEC reports, state election law reports, and accounting.

In April of 2004 she got a call from someone she had never heard of, John O'Neill. He filled her in on the activities of SBVFT to date, and kept reiterating, "This is *not* a political group, this is an anti-Kerry group." It was evident to Arceneaux that O'Neill was not a Bush fan, and that the group was looking for a non-Bush operative.

He told her they hoped to raise $100,000 to conduct their information campaign. "Because I was so leery of the finances of the group," Arceneaux says, "I told him I had to get the first quarter payment up front." She was informed the treasurer was a retired banker and that he would call her.

---

29. Susan Arceneaux is a native of West Monroe, Louisiana. She was previously the Director of Administration for the Forbes 2000 campaign. Her husband, Mike, works on Capitol Hill, and she has three daughters, Alyssa, Carrie Arceneaux Kirby, and Emily. All quotations are from an interview conducted July 29, 2007.

ON APRIL 19, 2004, John Kerry threw down the gauntlet. An article the next day by Michael Kranish in the *Boston Globe*, stated:

> The day after John F. Kerry said he would make all of his military records available for inspection at his campaign headquarters, a spokesman said the senator would not release any new documents, leaving undisclosed many of Kerry's evaluations by his Navy commanding officers, some medical records, and possibly other material [relating to the nature of his discharge]. Kerry, in an interview Sunday on NBCs "Meet the Press," was asked whether he would follow President Bush's example and release all of his military records. "I have," Kerry said. "I've shown them—they're available for you to come and look at . . . ." But when a reporter showed up yesterday morning to review the documents, the campaign staff declined, saying all requests must go through the press spokesman, Michael Meehan. Late yesterday, Meehan said the only records available would be those already released to this newspaper . . . . By comparison, retired General Wesley K. Clark released hundred of pages of his records during the Democratic primary campaign . . . . Bush earlier this year released 300 pages of documents after media outlets raised new questions about the extent of his National Guard service.[30]

On April 27 a message went out to dozens of former Swifties from latch@swiftvets.com (Roy Hoffmann), soliciting their support for the letter to John Kerry. "We believe we need to stand up and be counted on this issue," Latch said. The letter was cosigned by 87 men, including all of the Steering Committee, Admiral Rex Rectanus, Tuck Brant, Bill Shumadine, George Bates, Bob "Rocky" Hildreth, Joe Ponder, Jack Chenoweth, Terry Costello, Bob Elder, George Elliott, Grant "Skip" Hibbard, Tedd Peck, Pat Sheedy, Dave Wallace, Steve Gardner and Jim Zumwalt, on behalf of his father and brother.

On the Swift Vets Web site positive responses to the e-mail began to pour in, with 95 per cent in favor. Meanwhile, Wade Sanders was attempting to dissuade Swifties from joining Admiral Hoffmann, and SBVFT. He e-mailed one of the Swifties and said, "I'm saddened to see you have cast your lot with one of the worst Naval Officers [Hoffmann] I ever served with. He was a bully and a butcher." Sanders referred to the Swift Vets as "bitter drunks," which deeply offended the honor-driven Swifties. He referred to Joe Ponder (whom the reader will recall from Chapter 7 was severely wounded while serving on Swifts in

---

30. Michael Kranish, "Kerry refuses to release more records." The *Boston Globe*, April 20, 2004.

Vietnam) as a "whining crybaby."[31] The attacks on the Swifties served to unify the group as they had been in Vietnam; and brought new members in.

May 4, 2004: The National Press Club Press Conference, Washington, D.C.

The Swifties had naively thought that the media would treat their letter to Kerry seriously, but it was met with deafening silence. They felt they had no choice but to go ahead with the press conference they had agreed to in Dallas. The group, which had no formal fund-raising apparatus and few funds, paid for the conference with a $25,000 advance from John O'Neill.

The Swifties thought the press conference would finally force the mainstream media to deal with the allegations against Kerry. They based that belief on the scrutiny Bush was receiving over his National Guard service, questions the Swifties also thought were legitimate.

Merrie Spaeth, who had dealt with the media for years, had concerns about the press conference. "I was concerned that to the extent that anyone paid attention to you [the Swifties], they were going to tear you apart. You were all terminally honest and terminally polite, which means when someone asks you a question you do your best to respond."

However, she says, "I also thought you were all incredibly believable."

The Swift group reserved a room at the National Press Club in Washington, D.C., and scheduled the press conference for May 4, 2004. Eighteen Navy Vietnam combat veterans, including John Kerry's entire chain of command above him in Vietnam, went on record opposing Kerry's bid to be Commander in Chief of the Armed Forces. By this time they had more than 250 Swift boat veterans who had signed the open letter to Kerry backing them.[32]

The Swifties met with Merrie Spaeth and Jennifer Webster the night before the press conference, in the basement of the motel where they all stayed. They worked on consolidating the statements the Swifties had prepared, and then on preparing them for something none of them had ever done: Go before a largely

---

31. O'Neill and Corsi, *Unfit for Command*, p. 69, and an e-mail from Sanders to Jim Thomas. Jim Thomas was the radarman on Bob Elder's 43 boat in Vietnam. After the completion of his Navy service he completed college and was commissioned in the U.S. Air Force, eventually retiring as a major. He lives today in Las Vegas, Nevada.

32. "We had some damn fine officers and men," the Admiral says. "It was an elite group. I have been amazed at how successful they have been in their lives."

hostile national media and accuse a candidate for President of the United States of lying, and betraying them. The two exhausted women got back to their hotel rooms after 2:00 in the morning. When Webster got back to her room, "That was one of the early indicators, my cell phone [and it turned out her home phone] were buried with requests for interviews. To look on caller I.D. and see CBS, NBC, ABC—it was a little daunting."

The next day John O'Neill and Admiral Roy Hoffmann stood at the front of the standing room only crowd, with the January 22, 1969 picture of the 20 Swift boat officers in Vietnam on one stand behind them, and a VVAW picture on the other. John O'Neill led off, saying, "We resent very deeply the false war crimes charges he [Kerry] made coming back from Vietnam in 1971.... We think those cast an aspersion on all those living and dead, from our unit and other units in Vietnam. We think that he knew he was lying when he made the charges, and we think they are unsupportable."

Admiral Hoffmann was next:

> I do not believe John Kerry is fit to be Commander in Chief of the armed forces of the United States. This is not a political issue. It is a matter of his judgment, truthfulness, reliability, loyalty and trust—all absolute tenants of command.... His contempt for the military and authority is evident... In an abbreviated tour of four months and 12 days, and with his specious medals secure, Lt.j.g. Kerry bugged out and began his infamous betrayal of all United States forces in the Vietnam War... Senator Kerry is not fit for command.

Charley Plumly[33] said:

> During Lt.j.g. Kerry's tour, he was under my command for two or three specific operations before his rapid exit. Trust, loyalty and judgment are the key, operative words. His turncoat performance in 1971 in his grubby shirt and his medal-tossing escapade, coupled with his slanderous lies in the recent book portraying us that served, including all POWs and MIAs, as murderous war criminals, I believe, will have a lasting effect on all military veterans and their families.

Andy Horne: "Thirty five years ago, many of us fell silent when we came back to the stain of sewage that Mr. Kerry had thrown on us, and all of our colleagues who served over there. I don't intend to be silent today or ever again. Our young men and women who are serving deserve no less."

---

33. See Chapter 7 starting with Operation Market Time.

Bob Elder:[34] "It is a fact that in the entire Vietnam War we did not lose one major battle. We lost the war at home . . . and at home, John Kerry was the Field General."

Joe Ponder:[35] "My daughters and my wife have read portions of the book *Tour of Duty*. They wanted to know if I took part in the atrocities described. I do not believe the things that are described happened."

Grant "Skip" Hibbard:[36]

> The briefing . . . the morning after revealed that they had not received any enemy fire, and yet Lt.j.g. Kerry informed me of a wound—he showed me a scratch on his arm . . . that appeared to be from one of our own M-79s . . . . I do not recall being advised of any medical treatment, and probably said, "Forget it." He later received a Purple Heart for that scratch, and I have no information as to how or whom.
>
> Lt.j.g. Kerry was allowed to return to the . . . USA after four months and a few days in country, and then he proceeded to betray his former shipmates, calling them criminals who were committing atrocities. Our rules of engagement were quite strict, and the officers and men of Swift often did not even return fire when they were under fire if there was a possibility that innocent people—fishermen in a lot of cases—might be hurt or injured.

Jim Zumwalt:[37]

> Lt. Kerry gave numerous speeches and testimony before Congress inappropriately leading his audiences to believe that what was only an anomaly in the conduct of America's fighting men was an epidemic. Furthermore, he suggested that they were being encouraged to violate the law of war by those within the chain of command.
>
> Very specific orders, on file at the Vietnam archives at Texas Tech University, were issued by my father [Admiral Elmo Zumwalt] and others in his chain of command instructing subordinates to act responsibly in preserving the life and property of Vietnamese civilians."

Dave Wallace:[38]

---

34. See Chapter 7, starting with Operation SEALORDS.
35. See Chapter 7, November 24, 1968: The Bo De "Massacre"
36. Hibbard was Kerry's COS DIV commander at Cam Ranh Bay.
37. Lieutenant Colonel James Zumwalt, USMC, Ret., signed up to oppose Kerry on behalf of his deceased father, Admiral Elmo Zumwalt; and his deceased brother, Elmo Zumwalt III. He was convinced that they would be as appalled at the idea of Kerry being Commander in Chief as he was.
38. See Chapter 8.

In a whole year that I spent patrolling, I didn't see anything like a war crime, an atrocity, anything like that. Time and again I saw American fighting men put themselves in graver danger trying to avoid . . . collateral damage.

When John Kerry returned to the country . . . he told my family—my parents, my sister, my brother, my neighbors—he told everyone I knew and everyone I'd ever know that I and my comrades had committed unspeakable atrocities.

George Elliott:[39]

I served with these guys. I went on missions with them, and these men served honorably. Up and down the chain of command there was no acquiescence to atrocities. It was not condoned, it did not happen, and it was not reported to me verbally or in writing by any of these men, including Lt.j.g. Kerry.

In 1971, '72, for almost 18 months, he stood before the television audiences and claimed that the 500,000 men and women in Vietnam, and in combat, were all villains—there were no heroes. In 2004, one hero from the Vietnam War has appeared [John Kerry], running for President of the United States and Commander in Chief. It just galls one to think about it.

Adrian Lonsdale:[40]

During the Vietnam War, I was Task Force Commander at An Thoi, and my tour of duty was 13 months, from the end of Tet to the beginning of the Vietnamization of the Navy units.

Now when I went there right after Tet, I was restricted in my movements. I couldn't go much of anyplace because the Vietcong controlled most of the area. When I left I could go anywhere I wanted, just about. Commerce was booming, the buses were running, trucks were going, the waterways were filled with sampans with goods going to market, but yet in Kerry's biography he says that our operations were a complete failure. He also mentions a formal conference with me, to try to get more air cover and so on. That conference never happened.

Bill Shumadine:[41]

I was in An Thoi from June of '68 to June of '69, covering the whole period

---

39. See Chapter 7, starting with Operation Market Time. Elliott was Kerry's COS DIV 11 commander.
40. See Chapter 7, starting with Operation Market Time. Lonsdale was the area commander when Kerry was in An Thoi.
41. See Chapter 7, starting with Operation Market Time.

that John Kerry was there. I operated in every river, in every canal, and every offshore patrol area in the IV Corps area, from Cambodia all the way around to the Bo De River. I never saw, even heard of all of these so-called atrocities and things that we were supposed to have done.

This is not true. We're not standing for it. We want to set the record straight.

Steve Gardner:

I served in 1966 and 1967 on my first tour of duty in Vietnam on Swift boats, and I did my second tour in '68 and '69, involved with John Kerry in the last 2 ½ months of my tour. The John Kerry that I know is not the John Kerry that everybody else is portraying. I served alongside him and behind him, five feet away from him in a gun tub, and watched as he made indecisive moves with our boat, put our boats in jeopardy, put our crews in jeopardy . . . . If a man like that can't handle that six man crew boat, how can you expect him to be our Commander in Chief?

Bob "Friar Tuck" Brant:[42]

My service was three months in Coastal Division 13 out of Cat Lo, and nine months with Coastal Division 11, based in An Thoi. John Kerry was in An Thoi the same time I was. I'm here today to express the anger I have harbored for over 33 years, about being accused with my fellow shipmates of war atrocities.

All I can say is when I leave here today, I'm going down to the Wall to tell my two crew members it's not true, and that they and the other 49 Swifties who are on the Wall were then and are still now the best.

Jennifer Webster says, "at the news conference the press was very hostile because the room was too small. They were literally fighting for camera space." One of the reporters came up to her and said, "You *had* to know the interest."

"No," she replied, "we really didn't know what to expect."

Even though the room had been booked in Merrie Spaeth's name, the Kerry campaign operatives were fully aware what was going on with the Swifties' press conference. The Kerry campaign had a mole inside the SBVFT organization.[43] As a result, the Kerry forces had rented a room one

---

42. See Chapter 7, starting with Operation Market Time, and November 24, 1968: The Bo De "Massacre."

43. It's common knowledge among the Swifties who the individual is.

floor above where the Swifties held their conference, and had scheduled a press conference immediately following the SBVFT press conference. They also had a thick package of questions for the press to ask with backup documentation, and a DVD promoting Kerry's war "heroics."

Bill Franke was in Singapore on business during the press conference, so he asked his wife, Ruth Franke, to attend and give him a report of what transpired. She stood at the back of the crowded room with the reporters as the Kerry people circulated in the room, handing out their packets. Mistaking her for a reporter, she was handed a packet, which she immediately took to Merrie Spaeth at the front of the room.

Merrie glanced at the document. She now says, "The Kerry people were so stupid and arrogant. They couldn't believe that citizens would step forward to do this. I think that was their downfall from the beginning. They didn't understand anything about the military."

"Kerry wants you to answer these questions," she said to O'Neill. "Why don't you?"

Webster says, "Merrie and John did a masterful job—they got the Kerry questions and read them one by one, and went through and answered them."

"I know Kerry's people are here," O'Neill said to the assembled reporters, "and I know they are giving you this packet." Jennifer Webster believed the press reaction showed their bias; rather than questioning the SBVFT issues raised at the press conference, they used the Kerry questions, related to the "ties" O'Neill and Spaeth had to the Republicans, as the basis for their questions.

After he was finished a handful of the press went to the Kerry conference, but the majority stayed to question the Swifties individually. But the tenor of the attitude of the members of the press had changed. Webster says, "When the press got the Kerry questions with the allegations of the O'Neill and Spaeth Republican connections, that seemed to mean everything to them. The attitude of the press seemed to be relieved—we really don't have to report this." They asked questions, "but," says Webster, "with a much more cynical tone. They desperately wanted a reason not to report the story."

That point really struck home when she arrived back in Houston that evening, in time for the 5:30 news. CBS was the only news organization that covered the event, and they did a hatchet job, pointing out that George Elliott had supported Kerry in a 1996 conference. The media had hours of footage with John O'Neill and of the press conference, and they used none of it.

"We all made a misjudgment on the press conference," John O'Neill says, "because we didn't realize the nature of the mainstream media. We thought we would get honest and honorable treatment, and we didn't. I was shocked. That was stunning to me. It never occurred to me the fix was on in the American media."[44]

Not long after that he and Bill Franke met with a reporter for a major wire service and explained the whole Kerry situation to him. The reporter said, "Well, I understand exactly what you are talking about, and I know you are telling me the truth."

O'Neill asked him, "Well, are you going to write a story about it?"

"No," the reporter replied.

"Why not?" O'Neill asked.

"Because it would help Bush," the reporter replied.

Jennifer Webster had a similar experience with a CNN reporter, except this time the reporter wanted to report the story and kept getting shot down by the network. Webster started calling to try and get interviews for the individual Swifties, but it was difficult because the media had successfully buried the issue, and no one had heard of the press conference. "You always had the feeling," she says, "that they thought they were going out on a limb to grant interviews."

As John O'Neill says, "The only people willing to cover the story early were Sean Hannity, the *Wall Street Journal*, *Investor's Business Daily*, several Web sources, and of course C-SPAN, which aired the original press conference."[45]

It became obvious the Swifties needed a new strategy, and they turned to a fifteenth century method of communication, writing a book; and to the twenti-

---

44. The Swifties were not totally naïve about the issue. Candidates had withdrawn before for scandals far less serious than the one the Swifties were exposing. George Romney, the former Republican Governor of Michigan, had said in an August 31, 1967, interview, "When I came back from Vietnam [in November 1965] I'd just had the greatest brainwashing that anybody could get." He withdrew as a candidate for president on February 28, 1968, largely as a result of the remark. Thomas Eagleton was briefly George McGovern's running mate in 1972. It was disclosed that Eagleton had checked himself into a hospital three times for physical and mental exhaustion between 1960 and 1966. In a lesson on the loyalty of politics, McGovern first said he would back him "1,000 per cent," then dumped him from the ticket. Gary Hart, considered the front-runner for the Democratic nomination in 1988, was plagued by rumors of marital infidelity. He withdrew from the race when a picture appeared with Donna Rice sitting on his lap on the appropriately named luxury yacht, "Monkey Business." Ms. Rice was not his wife.

45. Contributing later to the story in a significant way were the Drudge Report, Rush Limbaugh and Laura Ingraham, who went through the SBVFT allegations point by point and permitted rebuttal—there was none.

eth century technology of television. They knew they had to resort to advertising to go over the heads of the media directly to the American people.

But as George Elliott says, "It was not until the press conference that it sunk in that this was not a Quixotic fantasy; rather it was a declaration of total commitment to stopping Kerry from becoming Commander in Chief of the U.S. Armed Forces. Even then, I didn't know how really difficult the next few months would be."

MEANWHILE, AFTER THE press conference the deluge struck the Hoffmann household. "Mom was a novice computer user," daughter Chris Carnahan says, "and the next thing you know they are getting 1,000 e-mails a day. She [Mary Linn] learned the computer on the fly. I think it stressed her out terribly. Dad can be impatient; he wants things done and she is trying to learn this new piece of machinery.

"Mom would get so incensed over some of the obscene language that came in. Initially she said, 'Oh my God, the f-word,' but she really developed a tough skin. It never ruffled Dad."

"Day after day," Mary Linn said, "I was maxed out at 999 e-mails [the most her in-box could handle]. Roy would sit on my left, read them, and dictate responses." Those that required a longer or mail response Mary Linn printed. She worked from morning to late at night on the computer, with one exception: "Monday mornings, I bowled, come hell or high water! I took out my all frustrations on the bowling alley."

One morning she was on the computer at 2:00 A.M. when an instant message popped up from Chris: "GO TO BED!"

Mary Linn sent her one back: "What are YOU doing up?"

She also fielded some of the phone calls. One woman called and said, "What you doing is despicable—he gonna win!" The phone was a huge problem, as every time it rang they had to get off the Internet. They solved that by installing DSL, so they could be on the phone and Internet at the same time.

Meanwhile, the Web site Swiftvets.com was under assault by Kerry supporters. An individual logged in under the name "sparky" and posted almost 40 messages a day (over 21 per cent of the more than 1,100 total), replying to virtually every criticism of Kerry. Meanwhile, other Kerry supporters flooded the site, "totally bollixing your board," as one supporter of the Swift Vets, who logged on to the Swiftvets forum, wrote. "None appear to be Vietnam vets (or vets, for that matter)," he wrote. "The Swift Boat Vets are an honorable group comprised of very credible people," he went on, "but

I've got news for you: you are getting trashed by these—I think—professional Kerry operatives."

It was past time for professional help with the Web site, and help arrived in the form of Scott Swett and Bob Hahn.[46] Swett had originally gotten hooked up with Jerry Corsi, who had volunteered to help him with his Web site WinterSoldier.com. Swett grew interested in the topic of Kerry and his Vietnam Veterans Against the War (VVAW) activities and war crimes testimony after reading a threat by a Kerry supporter on FreeRepublic.com. It was where he learned about the book *The New Soldier* by John Kerry.

Swett found a copy of the book on e-bay and purchased it for $400. "Once I started looking into the contents of the book," he says, "which is a photo essay of various protest activities of the VVAW, I became curious about the war atrocity and war crimes allegations that were made in it. I discovered a lot of them came from the Winter Soldier investigation held in Detroit."[47] As he began to research the issue, "it struck me that these were the guys that fabricated the myth immortalized in Hollywood of the dysfunctional, drug addicted, brutal baby killer Vietnam veteran."

In early February 2004 Swett was working during the day as a mainframe software developer. He thought that the antiwar issue was going to become the central issue of the upcoming presidential campaign. "I decided I was going to find out everything I could on the antiwar movement and publicize it."

Swett had grown up in a military family on SAC bases, thus his interest in the issue stemmed in part from his father, who is a Vietnam veteran. "When he came back he made it very clear that what actually happened in Vietnam had very little relation to what the media was reporting."

Bob Hahn had written the Web site for the nonprofit FreeRepublic network, and Swett was impressed with his computer skills, especially his background in online technology. Hahn had done the technical side of WinterSoldier.com.

John O'Neill asked Swett to interview with Bill Franke to do the Swift Vets Web site. Swett and Hahn came up with a proposal on May 19, for a public Web site, to be used as an information resource for the activities of SBVFT, and where visitors could receive a newsletter and donate to the

---

46. All quotations from Scott Swett are from an interview conducted January 4, 2006. Swett holds a degree in Marketing from the University of Maryland. He has spent the last 20 years as a software developer.

47. See Chapter 8.

cause; and a private Web site, where "members" could log in. The site would retain records in the database to meet the 527 reporting requirements. Hahn would do the framework and Swett the contents. Hurricane Electric was the support company that actually hosted the Web site.

Another member of the team joined on June 8. Retired Navy Commander Tom Wyld spent his first ten years in the Navy at sea, and then spent the last ten in public affairs assignments. After his retirement he went to work for the National Rifle Association (NRA) as PR director and later chief of staff for their lobbying and political arm. Merrie Spaeth, who had become a friend of Wyld's during his NRA days, referred him to the Swift boat veterans. He would make valuable contributions while working directly with Bill Franke and the Admiral.

On June 10, this author presented a financial report to the Steering Committee, which was then meeting via a weekly phone conference call on Wednesdays. The finances of the group were precarious—the organization was rapidly running out of funds. SBVFT had taken in just over $60,000 in donations since inception, and disbursed nearly $50,000 in expenses. There were not enough funds on hand to meet anticipated expenses. John O'Neill was eventually able to get pledges of $125,000 from friends of his in Houston, which allowed the group to keep the doors open.

In June Bill Franke called Washington, D.C., lawyer Benjamin L. Ginsberg, a partner in the firm Patton Boggs, LLP, and told him, "We've got this group, we're not able to break through the media, and we know we're getting into a legally dangerous area. We hear you really know this stuff—would you mind meeting with us?"

Ben Ginsberg grew up in Cleveland and Philadelphia in what he describes as a liberal Democratic household.[48] The oldest of four children, his father was a medical school professor and his mother was a lawyer.

In both the 2000 and 2004 election cycles Ginsberg served as the national counsel to the Bush-Cheney presidential campaigns. He also played a central role in the 2000 Florida recount that decided the presidential election that year.

---

48. All quotations from an interview with Ben Ginsberg conducted August 3, 2007. He received an A.B. degree in 1974 from the University of Pennsylvania and a J.D. from the Georgetown University Law Center in 1982. Before he entered law school he spent five years as a newspaper reporter. He specializes in Political Law, Public Policy and Lobbying, and Litigation and Dispute Resolution. He is married to Joanne Ginsberg and has two children; his son works for Romney for President and his daughter works for Google.

"I met with Bill Franke." Ginsberg says, "I really liked him a lot, and I'm always sympathetic to groups that have a cause that's important to them, and who are having a problem getting their message out. I was particularly touched when Bill described all of you [the Swift Boat Veterans]."

By the time Franke met with him, the 527 concept was well established. The Democrats had already spent $60 million on 527s, through the contributions of George Soros, Steven Bing, Peter Lewis and others. Ginsberg attended a barbeque in early July at Bill Franke's home, "and I was tremendously impressed by the men. And that's what heightened my interest in making it work." He agreed to represent the Swift Boat Veterans, a decision that was to come with a high personal cost.

The Swift Boat Veterans needed a Washington, D.C., public relations firm, and through the suggestion of John O'Neill's cousin they contacted the DCI Group, which is a strategic public affairs consulting firm. The group helps clients with "direct contact" that bypasses the media and helps get the message out through regular mail and/or the Internet. The advantage of the group is it frees its clients from the filters created by news outlets. In the first week of June DCI called in one of its political consultants, Chris LaCivita, and asked him to talk to a group of veterans that was having a problem getting their message out. They had gone to LaCivita because he is a decorated former Marine.

Chris LaCivita is from Pittsburgh originally.[49] He enlisted in the U.S. Marine Corps in 1984, and is a decorated veteran of the first Iraq War. LaCivita says, "I was the first political guy they [the Swift Vets] met with." He met with John O'Neill and Bill Franke. "Bill was very passionate," LaCivita says, "John more low key." He had never met them before, "but there was an immediate connection because I completely understood what a combat environment was like. That put them at ease. It is a privilege and honor for me to work with combat veterans."

---

49. All quotations from an interview conducted with Chris LaCivita July 31, 2007. He was attached to the First Battalion, Eleventh Marines, during Operation Desert Storm. His unit moved into Kuwait on February 22, and on February 24 the unit earned their Combat Action Ribbons engaging enemy armor at 1,500 to 1,800 yards. On February 25 they moved up in advance of the main unit, where the Iraqis counterattacked and the Marines fired artillery and small arms at them at point blank range. LaCivita was wounded when " a round literally landed at my feet." He was blown about 15 feet away, taking shrapnel through the chin. Shrapnel also hammered his Kevlar vest, cracking one of his ribs. He was medevaced out and later returned to his unit. One of his buddies stepped on a mine and was medevaced out with him; he died the next day.

Franke and O'Neill expressed their frustrations with the media. As LaCivita listened to them he thought, "How could this not be an issue?" He told them the only way to combat that was through television. "You're relying on a media that is a filter for the information," LaCivita told them. "Screw the filter, let's make an ad they can't ignore."

O'Neill handed him the manuscript for the book *Unfit for Command*, which O'Neill and Jerry Corsi were getting ready for publication. LaCivita took it home and read it cover to cover that night.

"I was absolutely flabbergasted," he says, "at the extraordinary level of detail in that book." He told the two Swifties he would develop a plan and start the process of developing an ad. No one had the slightest idea how they would pay for it.

A $100,000 CHECK FROM Bob Perry arrived in the law offices of John O'Neill on July 1, 2004. It was the first significant donation to SBVFT, which sorely needed the funds. A grateful Admiral Roy Hoffmann immediately wrote Perry a letter. "Up to this time our organization has been largely self-funded," his letter said, "however, self-funding has its limitations since most of our members are of modest financial means, and we have no political affiliation. Thus, we are ever more dependent upon private donations from patriots like you."

Perry's donation was followed by a mid July donation of $100,000 from Dallas oilman Boone Pickens, and another $25,000 from a Houston businessman.[50]

On July 23, 2004, Scott Swett and Bob Hahn brought the Swiftvets.com Web site on line, after a review by Bill Franke, John O'Neill, Admiral Hoffmann and the Patton Boggs lawyers. Swett says, "We wanted to make sure we weren't saying anything actionable."

With the launch of the Web site, the world of the Swifties changed irrevocably. "One of the reasons for the success of the Web site," Swett says, "is there was a lot of pent-up interest in Swift Vets. The story hadn't been carried in the mainstream media." The Web site barely preceded the advance release of *Unfit for Command* and the launching of the first ad. "At that point traffic on the Web site increased exponentially," Swett says, "and the Web site went from two dedicated servers to four."

The convergence of the factors caused what could only be called a perfect storm in politics—the Swifties had gone from continual crises over lack of

---

50. By July 21, 2004, SBVFT had collected nearly $350,000.

funds to a crisis of too much support. "As contributions started to roll in," Swett says, "we hit the intitial limit with the bank."

Swift Vets' bank's credit card division was originally reluctant to extend much of a limit to the new and unknown 527. Susan Arceneaux was able to arrange for a $10,000 secured monthly credit card limit for donations.[51] Everyone thought that would be plenty, a stance that now seems laughable.

MEANWHILE, THINGS HAD TURNED around on talk radio for Jennifer Webster. The radio show producers were calling her, wanting Swifties for interviews. She had 20 to 30 Swifties available to do interviews, so her job (assisted by Jennifer Wammack), became finding available men to do the interviews. "It was our favorite part of the job," she says. "We got to know you guys [the Swifties] so well, we got to match the man with the interview. It made for happy radio hosts. Michael Savage needed Steve Gardner [Kerry's former crew member]; Laura Ingraham needed Bob Elder. We had such a wide array of personalities."

They also tried to find local radio connections with the Swifties, who were scattered all over the country. Early on Webster would call the Admiral to get his advice on who to use in the interviews. "He had so much pride in all of you guys," she says. "It was like he was picking among his children—he was proud of all of them."

The word was going out to millions of Americans at the time the mainstream media was still trying to ignore the Swifties. From July 24 through September 2 it seemed the Swifties were everywhere. A representative sampling follows: Bob Elder was on Laura Ingraham, the Mike Gallagher Show, and on the Michael Reagan Show. This author was on Janet Parshall's America and on Mark Furman's show (Furman is the former police detective who became famous during the O. J. Simpson trial). Van Odell was on NPR and BBC; Dr. Louis Letson, Larry Thurlow and Admiral Hoffmann were on Judicial Watch. Steve Gardner was on the Michael Savage Show, the Jerry Doyle Show and the Bill O'Reilly Show on FOX News. Andy Horne and Admiral Hoffmann were on the Tony Snow Show; and Van Odell and Jack Chenoweth were on Hannity and Colmes on FOX. John O'Neill was on Bill O'Reilly on FOX, Wolf Blitzer on CNN, and the radio shows of Michael Savage, Larry Elder, Jerry Doyle, and Alan Colmes. In

---

51. John O'Neill and this author personally guaranteed the intitial limit.

addition, Rush Limbaugh covered Swift Vets extensively on his show.[52]

During the period July 24–September 2 a quick sampling indicates the Swift speakers made more than 200 appearances on national and regional radio and television, and print media interviews, in addition to the local radio, television and print coverage they received in their home towns.

Chris LaCivita continued to work on the first ad, which he was able to develop from 13 hours of footage with the Swift Boat Veterans, and a $25,000 budget. He thought that the Swifties did have some advantages: They were well organized, had the truth on their side, and had the 527 already in place. "You [the Swifties] had an established chain of command, which to me was mind-boggling. This was where I encountered the Admiral for the first time."

The reserved Admiral and the loud, boisterous, profane and gregarious former Marine never developed a warm working relationship. Other than the daily media calls, which occurred between the P.R. people and the Swifties at 9:00 A.M. Eastern Time, Bill Franke tried to keep their contact to a minimum.

As he was working on an ad strategy, LaCivita contacted Greg Stevens (he has since passed away) of the media firm Stevens, Reed, Curcio & Potholm. Stevens suggested he contact Rick Reed of the firm, whose uncle is Adrian Lonsdale.

Rick Reed had attended the May 4 press conference at the National Press Club, but only to see his uncle. After the conference Reed was surprised that there wasn't more of a media response. "The thing that struck me," he said in a 2006 interview, "is that the Swift Boat Veterans were not political people. They probably had no idea that this would really shake up the political process."

Reed readily joined with LaCivita, and together they wrote, produced and directed the ads. "Our whole goal," LaCivita says, "was to get the Swifties on camera and let them speak from their hearts—which wasn't hard to do. We couldn't script them—it had to be their words."

The final group to work directly with the Swift Boat Veterans was Creative Response Concepts (CRC), a firm dealing in issues management and media relations. The company works for nonprofits, major corporations,

---

52. A partial listing of the Speaker's Bureau would include Jack Chenoweth, Ken Cordier (POW), Bob Elder, Steve Gardner, Mike Gann, Admiral Hoffmann, Andy Horne, Grant "Skip" Hibbard, Dr. Lou Letson, Van Odell, John O'Neill, Richard O'Mara, Joe Ponder, Charley Plumly, Weymouth Symmes, Larry Thurlow, Jim Thomas, Shelton White and Dave Wallace.

small businesses and trade associations. The firm had come to the attention of the group through John O'Neill's first cousin, Commander James Carter, USN, Ret. (USNA 1963). The firm was known for its reputation in dealing with the national media. Their first contact was with president and CEO of the privately held firm, Greg Mueller.

After listening to the Swifties he called Mike Russell into his office and told him that an organization made up of Vietnam veterans, who either knew Kerry or served with him, were neither happy with the way he characterized his military service, nor his treatment of his fellow veterans when he got back.

Russell's first question was, "Are they legitimate?"

Mueller replied, "Yes, this is the real thing." He told Russell that they were going over to Bill Franke's home, where John O'Neill would join them on the phone, for a more detailed briefing.

Mueller had gone to Russell because he knew of his father's military background. Russell's father, Paul Edward Russell, who passed away in 1999, had enlisted in the Navy at age 18. He ended up serving 30 years and retiring as a captain. His father was a Midwest farm boy. His mother, Virginia Russell, the daughter of Greek immigrants, was raised in Chicago, three blocks from the site of the St. Valentine's Day Massacre.

Mike Russell spent 15 years in radio as a news anchorman, news director and program director. He then spent four years with the Christian Coalition, working as Communications Director for Ralph Reed. He has been with CRC since 1998, as a senior vice president.

"The thing that really got me energized and dedicated to the Swift boat campaign," Russell says, "was meeting so many of these men and later their wives, and later still when the POWs joined the group. It ignited something in me that took this campaign, for me personally, way above a job.

"This was something I felt was important. It became obvious to me that I had the same serious problems with Kerry's qualification to be Commander in Chief, as did these men who were relaying the information to me.

"The thing that really hammered it home was that these were not political operatives. These were retirees that just had a belly full of John Kerry."

Russell realized immediately the Swifties needed help dealing with the media strategy, which would be, "First, they were going to ignore you [the Swifties] and then they were going to try and destroy you, and that's exactly what happened. They thought that by listening to what you had to say, but keeping their pens in their pockets, they could let this go.

"What they hadn't counted on was this grassroots outcry actually taking hold. In today's environment, the Swift Boat Veterans, probably better than any other organization that has been formed to date, demonstrated that you could absolutely bypass the liberal media with other outlets and get your message out, and do it so effectively that the press was forced to cover the organization.

"Swift Vets became this grassroots leviathan—people were contributing online, O'Neill's book was a national bestseller, the Kerry campaign was inept at best in dealing with the controversy.

"The Swift Boat Veterans turned over a number of stones regarding Kerry's service, his commendations, his activities, his statements and his discharge from the armed forces, that under any other circumstances, if it had been a Republican candidate or a sitting president, the full investigative resources of major news outlets would have been dedicated to getting to the bottom of that story. It personally astounded me the degree that some of these reporters at major news outlets could turn a blind eye to the questions the Swift Boat Veterans were raising."

CRC ended up on the front lines with the media, but they made a conscious decision not to be the public face of the organization. "The message was going to carried by the men themselves," LaCivita says. When the first ad hit, CRC had to deal with a firestorm.

LaCivita and Reed had already pulled the Kerry vice presidential running mate John Edwards clip, for the first SBVFT ad. "If you have any questions about what John Kerry is made of," Edwards said in the clip, "just spend three minutes with the men who served with him."

"John Edwards gave a huge presence," LaCivita says. "He set the whole thing up."

LaCivita screened the ad in advance for Greg Mueller and Mike Russell. As he played it, LaCivita says, "I thought Greg was going to have a heart attack."

"OH-MY-GOD," Mueller said.

"I know," LaCivita replied, "This is going to cause a shit-storm."

July 26 to 29, 2004: The Democratic National Convention, "Reporting for Duty"

The 2004 Democratic National Convention took place from July 26 to July 29, 2004, at the Fleet Center in Boston Massachusetts. Chairman of the convention was New Mexico Governor Bill Richardson. The Democrats convened to confirm the nomination of John Kerry as candidate for President, and John Edwards as candidate for Vice President, to face incumbents President George W. Bush and Vice President Dick Cheney in the 2004 presidential election. Political neophyte Barack Obama, candidate for the U.S. Senate from Illinois, gave the keynote speech.

The Kerry strategists clearly thought highlighting Kerry's combat record was his path to the presidency. They thought, by using his relations with his Swift boat crew, he could be presented as a "regular guy." They thought his "war heroism" would prove his "steely resolve" in the War on Terror. The convention hall was festooned with photos of Kerry in combat. A few Swifties stood on stage, and Jim Rassmann retold the story of how Kerry had supposedly saved his life while "under fire" in Vietnam.

Chris LaCivita says, "His campaign knew all there was to know about his antiwar activities. What they didn't know about was the medals. That came out of left field. They never expected that." LaCivita believes that Kerry never discussed with his senior campaign staff in any great detail the level of discontent and accusations that were present with the men who had served with him. "He never prepped his staff to deal with the issue," LaCivita says. "He also expected a pass from the press."

Jennifer Webster believes the SBVFT organization got a huge break when Van Odell went to the convention on behalf of the Swifties. He was the only one the group had the money to send, and there were members of the SBVFT who were opposed to him going, thinking he would get eaten alive by the media. But they misjudged their man. Using borrowed press credentials from a radio station, Odell got on the convention floor. Webster instructed him to go to "Radio Row" and say, "I served with John Kerry and I'm not supporting him."

He ended up doing 30 interviews. Webster says of Odell, "He's so good. He was the perfect person, because he didn't shy away from it at all even though it had to be very intimidating to be on the floor of the Democratic Convention."

When it came time for Kerry's speech, on Thursday, July 29, the man who had made his name opposing the Vietnam War, strode across the stage, gave a salute and said, "I'm John Kerry, and I'm reporting for duty." Apparently the line was former Senator Max Cleland's idea, and Kerry co-opted it for his speech.

His speech sickened the Swift Boat Veterans for Truth. He said he would "never hesitate to use force." He said he knew "what kids go through when they are carrying an M-16 in a dangerous place." He said the American flag, "flew from the gun turret right behind my head," and that he would wage the war in Iraq "with the same lessons I learned in war."

Chris LaCivita was watching the speech at home. "I never realized," he says, "how big this was going to be until John Kerry took the stage to accept his party's nomination for President of the United States, and he stood there like a schmuck, saluted the camera and said, 'I'm John Kerry and I'm reporting for duty.' I looked at my wife and said, 'Holy shit!'

"My phone rang—it was my mother. She had seen the speech and she said, 'Chris, change your home phone number.'

"John Kerry is such an arrogant son of a bitch," LaCivita says, "that he had the audacity to say that ["Reporting for Duty"], because he knew this [the Swift Vets] was coming. He felt himself untouchable on the topic."

Mike Russell says of Kerry at the convention, "He never realized what a huge mistake that was. Here was a guy who did everything he could to describe his comrades in the U.S. Navy as war criminals and baby killers. He tossed his medals [or ribbons] over the fence in an act of defiance not only to the armed forces but also to this country. And then for him to get up and recast himself as a war hero and friend to the armed forces was the height of hypocrisy. It was a powder keg that got lit the night he stood on that stage."

Just after the convention, voters who thought Kerry would keep America strong militarily outnumbered by 19 percentage point voters who said he would not, extraordinary numbers for a Democratic candidate. Just over a month later, that margin slid to three percentage points, and his numbers on whether he would be a strong leader went from 18 percentage points over those voters who thought he would, to one per cent. He had a similar slide in the "trust John Kerry to be Commander in Chief"—those numbers went from 16 percentage points to three points. Many analysts would later attribute the difference to the Swift Vets information campaign.

The First Ad Runs, *Unfit for Command* Becomes a National Bestseller, and the Kerry Counterattack

Mike Russell says, "I think Chris LaCivita is one of the best in the business, but you're only as good as the material you have to work with. These [SBVFT] ads were heartfelt messages from real people. It made the ads unbelievably effective. It was a perfect combination of message, talent and strategic use of resources."

There weren't many resources at that point to use. The organization funding continued hand to mouth. The Web site donations had yet to pour in, and the last large donation had come on July 19 from Boone Pickens ($100,000). The first ad was originally scheduled to run on July 28, the night before Kerry's acceptance speech at the Democratic National Convention, but it had to be delayed until after the convention, because the bank had put a hold on a donation check.

John O'Neill signs a copy of his best selling book, Unfit for Command. LYNN WRIGHT PHOTO

The Swifties finally managed to accumulate enough money to run the ad in smaller markets in three states (Ohio, Wisconsin and West Virginia). The ad started running on August 5–12 and cost just over $545,000.

First though, they had to meticulously document the content of the ad. Television stations were under no obligation to run the so-called "issue ads." The issue ads paid the same corporate rate a McDonalds or Coca Cola would pay. "The ads," LaCivita says, "if they're controversial, have to be scrubbed by the stations' legal departments. Every single line of every single ad had to be backed up with proof."

The meticulous John O'Neill, with the assistance of Claudia Standiford, put together a thick, bound document, with all the evidence backing up the statements of the men in the first ad. There were 27 sections of documentation, covering the backgrounds of the men in the ads; and documentation of the March 13, 1969: "No Man Left Behind" Incident; The Purple Hearts; Christmas in Cambodia; and War Crimes. One cannot read this document without understanding the underlying truth behind the ad. Apparently the lawyers for the television stations agreed, because 19 of them ran the ad immediately, and the 20th ran the ad the following Monday, only because their lawyers couldn't get to it sooner.

The now famous ad, "Any Questions?" called one of the most effective ever, opened with the January 22, 1969, black and white photo of Kerry and 19 other Swift boat officers, followed by inspirational music and the visage of John Edwards, looking every bit like the slick plaintiffs lawyer he was, intoning, "If you have any question about what John Kerry is made of, just spend three minutes with the men who served with him."

Edward's image is replaced by one line on the screen: "Here's what those men think about John Kerry."

Then the former Swift boat sailors are shown on screen, one by one.

Al French: "I served with John Kerry."

Bob Elder: "I served with John Kerry."

George Elliott: "John Kerry has not been honest about what happened in Vietnam."

Al French: "He is lying about his record."

Louis Letson: "I know John Kerry is lying about his first Purple Heart because I treated him for that injury."

Van Odell: "John Kerry lied to get his Bronze Star . . . I know, I was there, I saw what happened."

Jack Chenoweth: "His account of what happened and what actually happened are the difference between night and day."

Admiral Hoffmann: "John Kerry has not been honest."

Adrian Lonsdale: "And he lacks the capacity to lead."

Larry Thurlow: "When the chips were down, you could not count on John Kerry."

Bob Elder: "John Kerry is no war hero."

Grant Hibbard: "He betrayed all his shipmates . . . he lied before the Senate."

Shelton White: "John Kerry betrayed the men and women he served with in Vietnam."

Joe Ponder: "He dishonored his country . . . he most certainly did."

Bob "Rocky" Hildreth (off-camera): "I served with John Kerry . . . John Kerry cannot be trusted."

Narrator: "Swift Boat Veterans for Truth is responsible for the content of this advertisement."

And so it went, one minute of a devastating ad for a presidential candidate of any party, any time. As LaCivita says, "People already had a general opinion of Kerry, that he was a slick, slippery Senator from Boston, who changes his mind a lot. Now, these guys that served with him in Vietnam come out and start lambasting him—it fit with the perception already out there. The public was blown away by what this group of warriors from Vietnam was doing."

It is safe to say the media had never dealt with anything like it before. "The media weren't dealing with political types," LaCivita says. "They were dealing with normal people. People who had nothing to gain, but everything to lose."

Mike Russell believes that, "Swift Vets was the perfect example of how grassroots American politics should work in the country. It was a legitimate citizens group who insisted they were going to be heard."

That said, the Swifties, with the running of the first ad, and *Unfit for Command* becoming a national bestseller, found themselves at the center of a maelstrom of the type none of them had ever experienced. But Mike Russell thought they had advantages to weather the heavy seas ahead.

"I look at Bill Franke as the business genius of the organization, along with you [this author; the Admiral and Bob Elder were also on the Finance Committee] running the finances. You had a great leader in Admiral Hoffmann. To have the key people in place to make decisions and not get caught up in a lot of bureaucracy or red tape. The people running the organization were the best I've ever seen."

Further, Russell says, "O'Neill was unflappable, he had every fact down, he had every incident in his head, and he is a supreme orator. John was so effective the Kerry campaign tried to shut down debate style shows because they had no one to counter him."

Finally, "We didn't have any of the 'elders' of political parties telling us what to do. We had our own resources, our own message. We had a group of people who knew what they wanted to say, and they weren't going to be dissuaded by what the political handlers wanted to say."[53]

LaCivita knew that free airing of the ad on national news shows would increase the ad's impact exponentially, and that's exactly what happened. He also made the ad available to Internet sites like the Drudge Report and HumanEvents Online, which had a combined audience in the millions.

Journalists denounced the ad almost immediately. Mike Barnicle of MSNBC said, "This isn't an ad, it's political pornography." Douglas Brinkley said, "These are malicious fabrications in the heat of an election."

And the media went to their then go-to guy, Senator John McCain, for a comment. Defending his colleague in the Senate, the POW Vietnam war

---

53. John O'Neill says, "When we came out Dick Morris said this [SBVFT] would be a disaster for the Republicans. We didn't really know whether it would be a disaster or not, but we had to speak the truth. Bismarck said that God protects drunks, little children and the United States of America, and this was another instance of that happening."

hero, without having any of the facts, shot back immediately. "I deplore this kind of politics. I think the ad is dishonest and dishonorable." For many in the media, his remarks provided all the coverage they needed to ignore and/or attack.[54]

Bob Novak had a much fairer assessment of O'Neill's book. "I have read the book and found it neither the political propaganda nor the urban legend that its detractors claim. It is a passionate but meticulously researched account of how Kerry went to war, what he did in the war and how he conducted himself after the war. The very serious charges by former comrades deserve answers, but so far have produced only ad hominem counterattacks."

ON AUGUST 4, 2004, Human Events Online noted, "As originally reported on the Drudge Report, a new, yet to be unleashed, bombshell book from John O'Neill, a leader of the anti-Kerry group Swift Boat Veterans for Truth . . . will hit stores soon and already has shot up to as high as #2 on Amazon."

More than 60 people who were physically involved in the incidents reviewed the extensively documented book on the great Kerry deceptions. The book soon topped the bestsellers list and ultimately sold 850,000 copies.

"I was not at all surprised it was a bestseller," O'Neill says. "I thought it would break him [Kerry]. If we'd had a neutral media he would have been run out of the presidential race. Any reasonable investigation would show that he lied and lied about the centerpiece of his campaign. The only thing that saved him was the 'slime and ignore' strategy."

"WE HAD MORE THAN $80,000 in credit card donations the first 48 hours," Susan Arceneaux says of the two days after the Web site was launched. She was at that time on vacation, and she kept getting repeated calls from the credit card fraud people telling her the limits had been exceeded. They shut the credit card donations down because of sheer volume and that the group had exceeded its limit by eight times. Because of her track record with the bank, she was able to talk to a manager in Charlotte, North Carolina, and get the limits increased to $500,000.[55] By the 6th of August the group had taken in $160,000 in credit card donations and it was evident the $500,000 would not be near enough.

---

54. For the remark, McCain earned the enmity of most of the Swifties, who believed they had taken on Kerry for honorable reasons. As will be seen, the political class was deeply offended by the 527s in general.

55. She eventually got the limit increased to $1 million, and then to no limit.

When she returned from vacation there were 16 or 17 tubs of mail for Swift Vets waiting for her at the post office. She hired everyone she could find, her kids and friends included, to process the mail, but the volume was too high to handle. SBVFT soon went into a lock box arrangement with the bank to process donations and mail.

"We never envisioned the volume," she says. "It was difficult because Swift Vets wasn't my only client." She began working 15 to 18 hours per day; at the same time the caging people at the bank were doing ten to 12 deposits a day.

Most of the mail was supportive, in the vein of, "Tell the Swift boat guys to fight on!" There was, of course, hate mail, saying, "You will get yours," or "You are horrible people."

"When I realized how nasty and vulgar some of the letters were," she says, "I quit letting my daughter open the mail." One night as they were opening mail, white powder fell out of one of the envelopes. She called the police who tested it and found it was benign. They told her to be very careful.[56]

Someone from the media somehow convinced the post office to let them look at the signature card for the Swift Vets post office box. They got her name off the card and a list of her clients soon appeared in print. "I was worried how it would affect my other clients," she says. As it turned out, she only lost two clients over her work for Swift Vets. However, she says, "I felt very protected. I felt you and the Admiral were there for me. If anything, it made me feel more obligated because I didn't want to let you guys down."

As the campaign wore on she grew to have a deep respect for the Admiral. "It's not hard for me to understand why after all these years you guys [the Swift Vets] would back him up and be there for him," Arceneaux says. "I respect him greatly, but I also have a little bit of fear of him. When he called I felt like I had been called to the principal's office . . . it was 'yes, sir, yes, sir, yes, sir.'

"But he was the kindest man," she continues. "You could tell Swift Vets touched him deeply, and he felt it deeply. I would do anything for him that he ever asked, and I didn't know anything about him [before Swift Vets]."

THE KERRY CAMPAIGN apparently decided the only strategy they could employ was to attack the Swift Vets. He had approved of the vast sums of money spent on 527s initially, as they attacked Bush and left him the high

---

56. The letters got worse after the election, as an e-mail from Susan Arceneaux indicated, "Wey, as we've discussed, the hate letters are much worse now than they were during the campaign. I just thought everyone should be advised." (December 8, 2004)

ground. Now that he was under attack, he sent out lawyers to threaten any TV stations that ran the Swift Vets ad.

In a letter dated August 5, 2004, signed by both the General Counsel for Kerry/Edwards and the General Counsel for the Democratic National Committee, the lawyers attempted to intimidate station managers into canceling the ad. The letter alleged that the ads were full of lies, and implied that the stations would be held legally accountable for the objectionable content in those ads. It was the worst approach Kerry could have taken, because it created intense interest in the ad: What exactly was Kerry trying to cover up?

The attacks, John O'Neill says, "helped us tremendously. The threats against the station mangers led to extensive publicity . . . More than 1.4 million people downloaded that first ad, and it swept through the Internet."

By August 11, 2004, the Swift Vets Web site was experiencing more traffic than either Moveon.org or johnkerry.com. Swiftvets.com was ranked sixth on Internet traffic ratings. On August 10 there were nearly 100,000 visitors, and for every ten main site visitors, there was one contribution page visitor. The total Internet donations had gone to over $319,000, with an average donation of $63.80.

August 17, 2004: The Key Bridge Marriott Meeting— the POWs Join with Swift Boat Veterans for Truth

The Swift Boat Veterans had suddenly become radioactive, and they began to pay a personal price for their involvement. The attention came on them suddenly. Mike Russell was sitting in his home with his remote going through CNN, FOX and MSNBC, back and forth. "Every single news talk show was talking about the Swift boat ad and the impact it was going to have on the Kerry campaign. I'd never in my life as a P.R. professional gone across the full spectrum of cable news talk shows and seen my client up there being discussed in a 360-degree window. I realized at that moment that this is something that I'll never see again in political public relations."

"On the day Kerry specifically attacked Swift Vets," Scott Swett says, "the mainstream media switched from trying to ignore them to a full-throated attack on Swift Vets. It had the unintended effect of calling the attention to another segment of the population that didn't know about it yet. The day after Kerry attacked was the largest single donation day in the history of the Web site; $600,000 rolled in that day."

As the focus shifted sharply to the Swift Vets organization, the work and attacks increased exponentially. Swett says he went "six months on four hours sleep a night. It was a whirlwind."

Terry Symmes says:

> All hell broke loose. Our personal names, phone number and e-mail address were accessible. After a few days of vicious e-mails, and phone calls 24/7, we learned to unplug our phone at night. No matter what one might think they are ready for, you cannot prepare yourself for the hate that these people have inside. Many would express feelings that they were sorry the men of Swift Boat Veterans for Truth hadn't come home in body bags, or their names weren't on the Wall in Washington, D.C.[57] I will have to say that after the first few weeks of the threats and filth, that we did receive many supportive calls and e-mails. We actually only had about six or seven breaks during the year when we would leave the house to have dinner with friends without phones ringing constantly.

At least one private investigator was hired to try and intimidate one of the Swifties. A big white SUV with blackened windows pulled into a neighbor's driveway across the street from the Swiftie. The neighbor challenged the man, who had a large camera, asking him why he was there. He informed her that he was a private investigator.

Two of the Swifties in the first ad lost their jobs after it came out, almost certainly because of Swift Vets. Bill Franke received threats that his building in St. Louis would be burned. Charley Plumly got three death threats during 2004. John O'Neill's home was picketed during his daughter's wedding and he received many threatening letters and voicemails during the course of 2004. One was so explicit the FBI was called in. It said in part:

> I found four of your gang in California and disposed of these criminals. It was easy. They were old men and weak. And have accidents. And I have others who hate you. And help. Now I am in texas because you have made my quest much easier. You have given me many names and pictures of swift boat veterans that will make my revenge. I vow to dispose of every one of you criminals as I can. You o'neill are not safe from me. None of your family

---

57. One of the e-mails said: "THE ONLY REGRETTABLE THING IN ALL OF THIS IS THAT THE NAMES OF ALL YOU LYING SWIFTVET A-HOLES AREN'T ENGRAVED ON THE VIET NAM MEMORIAL WALL." Another e-mail was sent to the Symmes' computer 450 times during the wee hours of one night: "LYING FUCKING BASTARDS!!! I WAS THERE!!! FUCK YOU!!!" It was not one of the more reasoned and thoughtful responses that came in.

is safe from me. None of your veterans are safe from me... I watch. I follow. I will know where everyone lives... But I watch you.

Patty Thurlow, Larry's wife, was from a small Kansas town and was not used to or comfortable with the limelight; she was reluctant initially to get involved. Mary Linn and the late Trenny Elliott took her under their wings and made her feel part of the effort. Still, she was not prepared for the harassment they got because of Larry's involvement.

The phone rang constantly with harassing calls. One caller said, "If you're smart at all, you'll kill yourself so I won't have to," and then hung up. Thurlow called the sheriff. The calls were particularly heavy after opponents found his Bronze Star citation, which indicated there was enemy fire on the day of the mining of PCF 3. The harassment was galling for the other Swifties, who do consider Thurlow a hero for his actions on March 13, 1969 (the mining of PCF 3). A bemused Thurlow says, "There is not a guy that served over there on Swifts, besides John Kerry, who considers himself a hero. Besides, was I running for president, or even dog catcher?"

Admiral Rex Rectanus says about his involvement in Swift Vets, "I got some negative repercussions from contemporaries of mine, who let me know it in no uncertain terms."

Some attacks were just silly. Tina Brown of the *Washington Post* said, "The worst thing about the Swift boat movement has been the steady march of aggrieved sexagenarians across our TV screens, banging the hollow drums of their pasts. They were heroes once and young, but look what politics has wrought: Gabby, flabby John O'Neill... shifty George Elliott; Van Odell with his sorrowful Wyatt Earp mustache."[58] Odell immediately fired off an e-mail to the Swifties: "They have attacked my mustache—have they no shame!?"

And the Admiral came under the harshest attack of any of the Swift Vets. John O'Neill says watching the Admiral during 2004 was like watching Dick Butkus during a football game on a freezing day in Chicago. "Whatever insults Admiral Hoffmann got," he says, "it was like water off a duck's back. He was able to ignore the extraneous stuff almost better than anyone else I ever saw. He was motivated by something the Kerry guys never understood—the concept of honor. Because they never understood that they were never able to cope with the Swift Vets.

---

58. An e-mail came in on that vein August 20: "I sincerely hope you rodents get hung up by your tiny little balls."

"They tried to intimidate him, they tried to insult him, they had Kerry call, essentially to bribe him, but they were dealing with a person motivated in a way they did not understand, almost a person in a parallel universe."

The four Hoffmann daughters were proud of their father, but the personal attacks on him were upsetting. Chris and Hilarie in particular got into it, reading everything they could get their hands on. Chris says, "I went to visit my parents one weekend, and I went up to Dad's office and it looked like a tornado had gone through there. He had this sheepish look—he's usually very organized and neat. I was shocked—I'd never seen so much paper and books and mess."

Emilie Crow says, "I remember sitting in the break room at work one day when CNN was on and I looked up and said, 'That's my Dad.' And everyone looked at me like I was crazy. I bought the Dallas paper every day and cut out article after article."

On August 10 Gary Aldrich, the former FBI agent who had exposed some of the underside of the Clinton presidency in *Unlimited Access* came out with an article titled "Former FBI agent warns the Swift Boat Vets":

> . . . for a lot of Americans, all they will ever remember about my attempt to tell the truth is that the president's [Clinton] top advisor, George Stephanopoulos, called me a pathological liar . . . So, my warning to the Swift Boat Vets is this: When you take on the establishment, be prepared to suffer serious assaults to your reputation . . . The mainstream media will work diligently to alter the population's perception of you in ways that you could not possibly imagine. They will demonize, and then marginalize you so that your impact on this coming election will be minimal . . . If your 60-second ad were given honest exposure, the election would be all but over, and the people who have seen it know this. That's why they will destroy you, then ignore you.

It all seemed very discouraging; then Scott Swett sent out an e-mail with a picture of bombers flying through heavy flak. Under the picture it said:

> If you aren't taking flak, you're not over the target.
> Best regards, Scott.

THE ADMIRAL SENT out the invitations to the Swift Vets meeting, August 16-17 at the Key Bridge Marriott Hotel in Arlington, Virginia. The meeting was designed to get everyone together to plan strategy, meet with the media, and do more filming for future ads. Each veteran attending was requested to prepare a one-minute message on "why you are here."

Image accompanying Scott Swett's e-mail. ASAF Museum Photo

"Stick to facts and facts only," the Admiral said, "in your own words!

"We also want this to be a camaraderie event," he said, "an opportunity to greet old friends after 34–35 years and renew that mutual loyalty and trust we attained forever through combat experience. Bring your wife; she has always been a part of the team."

Mary Linn Hoffmann says, "I loved going to the Key Bridge Marriott and meeting some of the nicest people I've ever known in my life."

The meeting also brought together the lawyer who was daily advising the group, and some members of the Steering and Financial committees. William J. McGinley, a member of the Patton Boggs firm, had, at Ben Ginsberg's suggestion, been acting as the adviser to the group on 527 rules and regulations, handling contributions and disbursements, and reporting requirements. This author and Susan Arceneaux had almost daily contact with the capable and personable lawyer.

Bill McGinley specializes in Political and Tax Law, and in the law of Nonprofit Organizations. He holds a B.A. degree in History from the University of California; and M.A. degree in History from California State University, Fresno; and a J.D., with honors, from George Washington University Law School. During the Arlington meeting he met with Susan Arceneaux, this author, the Admiral, Charley Plumly and Bob Elder to insure that the now radioactive group did all that could be done to comply with the somewhat vague laws governing the 527s.[59]

---

59. Arceneaux well understood the dangers of a Kerry presidency. "As it got closer to the election and it looked like Kerry was going to win I did have many sleepless nights. I knew the Kerry campaign was going to be vengeful and if they had the power to wield, they would."

SBVFT held a Sunday group dinner for the men and their wives. The Admiral opened the meeting with a strong reminder to be direct, straightforward and honest in all activities. "Swift Vets' integrity is paramount," he told the group. John O'Neill described for the group the content of *Unfit for Command*. Bill Franke then briefed the group on activities of SBVFT, and introduced for the first time Chris LaCivita and Mike Russell. He also announced to the group there would be a POW ad forthcoming expressing the feelings of the POWs about Kerry's lies.

Monday night Bill and Ruth Franke invited everyone to their home for a reception. There the Swifties sat around a table and signed 100 copies of *Unfit for Command*, for each to take back home. That night the Swifties gathered in front of two television sets and watched John O'Neill, on FOX News, debate Kerry's veterans' coordinator. The Swifties cheered O'Neill on as though they were at a football game.

WITHOUT QUESTION the defining moment of 2004 for the Swifties was the uniting of the former POWs (Prisoners of War) of Vietnam with the Swift Boat Veterans for Truth, which partnership created Swift Boat Veterans and POWs for Truth. Bill Franke speaks for all of the Swifties when he says, "When the POWs arrived, we held them in such reverence; it was a special moment."

Mike Russell says, "It profoundly affected me. I understood how these POWs and Swift boat veterans felt, because I grew up in a military household. You could argue over Swift boat allegations, but you couldn't argue with a POW wife who said, 'every time John Kerry opened his mouth my husband was beaten.' Kerry had no way to refute that. The media tucked their pens in their pockets and looked the other way."

Former POW Paul Galanti was at home when he got a phone call from Roy Hoffmann inviting him to a meeting with former Swift boat sailors to discuss the Kerry candidacy.[60] Galanti brought to the meeting, held at a Holiday Inn, POWs Ken Cordier and Jim Warner.

---

60. All quotations from an interview conducted July 18, 2007, with Commander Paul Galanti, USN, Ret. Galanti is a 1962 U.S. Naval Academy graduate. He and his wife, Phyllis, were married in 1963; they live today in Richmond, Virginia. They are involved with the Families of the Wounded Fund (FOTWF.org), to support wounded veterans. The group helps with transportation, cash cards and provides other support. The group is mostly made up of Vietnam combat veterans, although they have a young SEAL in the group and a veteran of Iwo Jima.

Then Lieutenant Commander Paul Galanti was shot down on June 17, 1966 near Vinh, North Vietnam. His A-4 Skyhawk, flying off the USS *Hancock* (CVA 19), was hit after he attacked a railroad siding. He could see rescue destroyers offshore after his plane was hit, but the plane went out of control before he could reach them. He ejected from his plane at nearly 600 mph, was shot on the way down, and was captured and forced north to Hanoi, where he was paraded in what was "ostensibly a 'spontaneous demonstration' on the part of the North Vietnamese." He was paraded through the streets with other POWs. One of the North Vietnamese broke out of the crowd and kicked Galanti in the groin; he went down in a heap.

He ended up enduring nearly seven years (2,432 days) of harsh treatment and imprisonment in various POW camps in North Vietnam, collectively called the "Hanoi Hilton" by the POWs. He initially expected to be held six months to a year, but he hadn't counted on the lack of resolve in the United States to win the war. During that time the "Peace Talks" dragged on for five long years. During his captivity he spent more than a year in solitary confinement and lived in ten camps scattered all over North Vietnam. He credits the leadership of Colonel Robbie Risner and Commander Jim Stockdale (Stockdale received the Medal of Honor) for holding the POWs together.

"We were proud to be serving our country" Galanti says, "and openly ridiculed our North Vietnamese captors . . . We discounted trips to Hanoi by various American personalities such as Jane Fonda, Ramsey Clark, and a few antiwar no-names who were referred to as 'comrade' by the Vietnamese." Galanti's courage and endurance were rewarded when he was released, February 12, 1973.

"I think I was there [in prison] an extra four years because of the kind of crap Kerry was putting out," Galanti says. "It should have been over in 1968. North Vietnam was on its knees."[61]

Galanti had known Admiral Hoffmann before the meeting at the Holiday Inn. "Phyllis calls him Roy, and a few others do, but I don't know anyone that ever worked for him that called him Roy. Everybody called him by his first name, 'Admiral.' He commands respect."

At the Holiday Inn meeting Bill Franke brought a tape recorder and played Kerry's testimony before the Senate in 1971. Galanti says, "I heard 'Genghis Khan' and I sat up and said, 'I heard that in Hanoi.' Hanoi Hanna

---

61. Galanti says, "President Bush is fighting all the same things we were talking about in Swift Vets—the antiwar movement, the media, the sarcasm of the comedians."

was very positive it was a Navy lieutenant that was talking about war crimes being perpetrated by Americans."

Galanti says, "The meeting at the Holiday Inn was an epiphany. Pilots are cocky guys. We looked down on the [Swift] boats doing 20 knots and thought, 'they make nice targets, maybe.' It wasn't until I got to that meeting that I got riled up. We went to Bill Franke's house that night and I thought, 'God, what a great bunch of guys.'"

Another POW who joined the effort was Medal of Honor recipient Colonel George "Bud" Day, USAF, Ret. Colonel Day was shot down over North Vietnam on August 26, 1967. He was the forward Air Control Pilot in an F-105 on a strike mission over a missile site near the DMZ when he was hit. He was doing about 500 mph when he took a hit in the aft section. The front seat pilot was on his first mission, and Day, in the back seat, had to punch out first. A rescue helicopter picked up the front seat pilot, just as the VC got to Day. His left arm was broken in three places in the ejection, and he was blinded in the left eye due to a blood clot or bruise. He hit the ground unconscious, dislocating his left knee on impact.

Early in his captivity he was able to escape. He was 40 miles north of the DMZ when he started out, but after ten days on the run he began having hallucinations and talking out loud, one of the symptoms of starvation. The hallucinations drove Day right into the path of the VC. He attempted to run, but they started firing and he was hit in the leg and hand. He was recaptured and taken back to the same camp where he had originally escaped.

During his captivity he was brutally tortured; his stoic resistance made him a revered figure among the other POWs. He was finally released on March 14, 1973.[62]

Bud Day had seen pictures of Kerry with fellow VVAW people prior to the 2004 election. "I couldn't help but wonder," Day says, "what kind of guy would take up with people that looked so disreputable. They looked like street trash, wearing parts of old uniforms, boonie hats, beards—scruffy looking people. My first thoughts [while a POW in Hanoi] were right—another antiwar dingbat."

---

62. All quotations from an interview on July 30, 2007. Bud Day was born in 1925; he dropped out of high school in 1942 to join the Marine Corps, where he spent 30 months overseas in the Pacific Theater. He holds a Juris Doctor degree from the University of South Dakota. He married the former Doris Sorensen in 1949. They reside today in Florida, where he is still actively engaged in the practice of law. For the full story on this remarkable American man and hero, see the biography, *American Patriot*, by Robert Coram (2007).

Day says, "It was an anathema to me that anybody with his background would entertain the idea of leading a country he had rejected."

Day had started following the campaign in Iowa when Howard Dean was succeeding as an antiwar candidate. Kerry saw the issue was resonating with the Democratic primary voters and he began to move to the left. "He got traction," Day says. "Suddenly he becomes the leading figure—not surprisingly because he's incredibly glib. He can stand there and lie on his feet faster than a horse can trot."

"I truly felt," Day says, "he kept us in jail two to three years longer, but far worse than that were the POWs who were killed during that extra time.

"It's natural that he would boil up to the top of the McGovern, Fulbright, Hatfield left wing of the Democratic Party, that was still alive and well. When I recognized that he was going to be the candidate it just repulsed me to the point where I said, 'I've got to do something.'

"You guys [the Swift Vets] were already out there making a big wake. I instantly said, these guys are my friends. Here these guys who served with this snake charmer have his number. They certainly can speak more vividly and authentically than any other group about the real character and the real nature of this man. So I want to get in their corner. Anything I can do to help them I will do. I got real frustrated when I saw how the media was stiffing Swift Boat Veterans."

On allying with the Swifts, Day says, "I started getting concerned messages from the POWs (including Paul Galanti). It became real clear that we needed an alliance with the Swift boaters." Of the alliance, Day says, "It was like putting on an old pair of shoes. I never had an untoward comment by any POW [about joining Swift Vets]—never, ever.

 "Another thing that was so fulfilling to me was to get up there and meet you all. I've been in a lot of trials and a lot of courtrooms and I've dealt with a lot of people. You get to the point where you have an almost gut feeling for truth and integrity. As soon as I started meeting all of you I had that feeling that these guys were absolutely, totally on the level. Truthfulness just boiled over. You knew you were dealing with an issue that you didn't have to worry about exploding in your face. I felt all that much better about it. I knew we had hit a home run.

"I was just instantly struck by Admiral Hoffmann. He has that ability that good leaders have, and you instantly recognize that this is a guy that genuinely is concerned about the troops and is a truthful and honest guy. You know with Latch when he gives you his word or he tells you something, it will get done and you can believe him. I was instantly taken with him."

Soon many POWs had joined the effort, men like Ron Webb, Smitty Harris, Kevin McMannis and his wife Mary Jane. Eventually about ten POWs were involved in the ads, and somewhere between ten and 20 of the POWs were active in Swift Boat Veterans and POWs for Truth. "But," Paul Galanti says, "we got lots of atta-boys from POWs, behind the scenes."

However, pro-Kerry forces attacked Galanti. "I got hate e-mail because my name's all over the Internet. I was at a college football game and a woman came up to me and said, "How dare you do that. How dare you say such things about a distinguished combat veteran."

Galanti's standard response was, "The real heroes are in military hospitals after losing their legs and they feel guilty because they can't go back to Iraq and rejoin their unit. Kerry, the first time he gets in a boat in Vietnam, he puts himself in for a Purple Heart."

Galanti says with a laugh, "People probably thought, 'this guy's getting mad, he's probably got PTSD and he's going to blow his cork in a minute.'"

ONE OF THE MYTHS to arise from the 2004 campaign is that John Kerry did nothing to counter the Swift boat veterans. Actually he tried every tactic he could to shut it down. Merrie Spaeth says, "Mike Bernique could have made Kerry president." Kerry realized as well as anyone that there were few Swifties supporting him, and none with the kind of reputation and respect a Mike Bernique had.[63] He also realized that the entire chain of command above him in Vietnam was supporting Swift Boat Veterans for Truth. If he could just tip over a couple of the early, respected O in Cs ...

On a Sunday night in August, Tuck Brant was watching the Summer Olympics at home. He was sitting in a chair watching women's volleyball for the Olympic Gold Medal. At 7:50 P.M. the phone rang.

"Hello," Brant said.

"Bob, this is Senator Kerry, what are you doing?"

Brant, who recognized the voice, responded, "Well, I'm watching Olympic volleyball."

"Well," Kerry responded in a pompous voice, "I'd like to do that too, but I've been very busy lately. I just wanted to give you a call because there's a group of Swift people out there saying bad things about me. Have you heard of them?"

---

63. Bill Rood was another of the respected, early An Thoi Swift boat O in Cs, and apparently Kerry called to try and persuade him to get involved in his campaign. Rood did write one article of support on Kerry's Silver Star, but he didn't involve himself beyond that.

Brant thought to himself, "Doesn't he know I'm involved? I did the initial press conference." To Kerry, he replied into the phone, "Yes, I've heard there's a group out there. They're called Swift Vets for Truth—and I are one!"

There was a pause, not a long one, and Kerry said, "Well, I'm sorry to hear that, but I appreciate your honesty. As long as I have you on the phone, can I ask you why you are?"

Brant replied, "Well, for 35 years I've been stewing about what you said about our guys over there in Vietnam—that everyone who was over there was a baby killer who committed atrocities. That's a crock of crap."

Kerry, again in a pompous voice, replied, "Well, you know there were some atrocities, and there were violations of the Geneva Convention."

"In general that didn't happen—you labeled everybody. Do you know the scar tissue you caused on some of those young minds and their families who read that?"

Kerry said, "I'm sure that if you and I could get together—I—we could come to an agreement in which I convince you you are wrong."

"That will be a cold day in hell," Brant replied. "As far as I'm concerned this conversation is over."[64]

Mike Bernique had not heard from Kerry for 35 years, since their last conversation when he was invited to Kerry's first marriage. Then, Swift Vets happened, "and you guys were pounding away at him," Bernique says. "I had not joined your group. I get home to La Jolla in August of 2004, and there are a whole bunch of messages on my recorder and they're all from John Kerry, each sounding more frustrated than the last."

The phone rang again, and Bernique picked it up. It was John Kerry.

Bernique asked this author in a June 14, 2006, interview, "What's the first thing you would ask me after 35 years?"

"How have you been doing?"

Bernique said, "That's pretty good. Kerry asks me 'where have you been?'"

Bernique told Kerry, "John, sorry about that, I have been at my home in La Jolla."

"La Jolla!" Kerry says. "Boy, you really made it big on those stock options, didn't you?"

Bernique says, "That's the second thing he said. Now I'm sitting down in

---

64. The story of the phone call was eventually picked up by the Drudge Report and that night of the Drudge Report Brant had about 40 phone calls. Not many of them were to tell him what a nice man he was.

my chair and I'm *really* ready to help him out. I'm thinking, 'At least I didn't marry it John, not once, but twice.'"

Kerry then went into a long rambling speech about how Skip Barker (a Kerry supporter) had suggested he call. When he finished Bernique said, "I'm pissed at you John—you lied."

Kerry responded, "Well, I'm on record for saying I exaggerated."

Bernique declined to help him.

THERE ARE THREE THINGS Kerry could have done to address Swift Boat Veterans for Truth, aside from going on the attack as he did, or making a couple of phone calls. The first, releasing his complete military records, was problematical for him, as we have seen. In addition to the complete medical records, and fitness reports, there is what one might call not a smoking gun, but a smoking cannon, and that is the records would likely disclose the nature of his discharge from the military.

"Kerry was stripped of his medals when he left the Navy," Admiral Rex Rectanus says, "and he could have had an officer's Bad Conduct Discharge when he left the Navy. Jimmy Carter and Teddy Kennedy wrote the amnesty program that included Kerry, and that's where he got all his awards back.[65] We all know that, but a lot of the American public does not know that."

Former JAG officer and retired Navy Captain Mark Sullivan has built a compelling case that Kerry received less than an honorable discharge from the Navy in 1975. The "honorable discharge" on Kerry's Web site appears to be a Carter administration substitute for the original discharge. Kerry's discharge was issued at least three years after it should have been. He most likely received an "other than honorable" discharge certificate, or worse, no certificate at all. In either case, there would have been a total loss of all of Kerry's medals, and the suspension of all benefits of service.[66]

The second thing he could have done is sincerely apologize for leaving Vietnam well before his completed tour, and not being honest about how he had characterized his service. He could have sincerely apologized for his

---

65. "Carter issued Executive Order 11967, under which thousands received pardons and upgrades for harsh discharges or other offenses under the Selective Service Act. . . . All officials with knowledge of what specifically happened in Mr. Kerry's case are muzzled by the Privacy Act of 1974. The act makes it a crime for federal employees to knowingly disclose personal information or records." Thomas Lipscomb, "Kerry's Discharge Is Questioned by an Ex-JAG Officer." *New York Sun Times.* November 1, 2004.

66. *Ibid.*

Senate testimony in 1971, acknowledging that it wasn't truthful and that it was hurtful to all Vietnam veterans. Of course to have done so would have angered many of his supporters on the left, and may not have helped him much with veterans, who had more than 30 years of resentment built up; it may also have cost him his mainstream media protection.

Ben Ginsberg has identified the third, and perhaps only real alternative Kerry could have used. "John Kerry would have been president," Ginsberg says, "if he had said after the ad came out, 'This is awful, these are wounds of the war that have not healed and should heal. These men and I have a completely different view of this, but it's wrong for this wound to fester. I want to meet with them and hash it out, as painful as that is going to be.'" Ginsberg says, "I always thought that if he had said that, and offered to meet with you [the Swift vets] he would have been president, because all of a sudden he would have been the uniter, not the divider. He would have defused the whole rancor and looked like a leader. Instead, he got into that screechy, 'they're ignorant scumbags,' mode."

Ginsberg also makes an interesting point about the mainstream media. He says their bias in 2004 went beyond simply not wanting to help Bush. "A lot of people who opposed the Vietnam War," Ginsberg said, "saw Kerry as almost a mythical figure, because he had been so outspoken about it.

"You all [the Swift vets] told your story of what it was really like in Vietnam, and that crumbled a lot of the myths that a lot of liberal journalists had about the rectitude of the antiwar movement and their activities. There were some legitimate issues with policies about the war, but that's different from what Kerry did, demonizing troops who fought in the war.

"All of you Swift Vets touched a vein that was really interesting to see. I think people of my generation thought that Vietnam was an issue that the country had put behind it. And I think Kerry's candidacy and your reaction to him showed that wound still had some freshness to it."

ON AUGUST 18, 2004, the *Washington Times* published the first of three front-page excerpts of *Unfit for Command*. The next day CBS released a poll that showed support for Kerry among veterans had plummeted. The veteran vote had been equally split between Kerry and Bush after the Democratic convention, but three weeks later Bush was a staggering 18 points ahead of Kerry among veterans.

According to Evan Thomas in *Election 2004*, "Kerry wanted to blister the Swift Boat vets in a speech he was scheduled to give to the Veterans of Foreign Wars on August 18. 'We need to get these guys,' he said.

"But at the last minute his handlers on the road were ordered by headquarters in Washington to restrain the candidate. Cahill and Shrum were worried that Kerry would seem too bitter and angry."[67]

Apparently Edwards also wanted to hit back, but again Kerry headquarters said no. "Historian Douglas Brinkley cautioned [the Kerry campaign] that Kerry's diary included mention of a meeting with some North Vietnamese in Paris. Edwards was flabbergasted. 'Let me get this straight,' the Senator said. 'He met with terrorists? Oh, that's good.'"[68]

Thomas then goes on to make a rather extraordinary indictment of the "big" liberal newspapers. "The Kerry campaign did work closely with the major dailies, feeding documents to *The New York Times*, *The Washington Post*, and *The Boston Globe* to debunk the Swift Boat Vets. The articles were mostly (although not entirely) supportive of Kerry, but it was too late. The old media may have been more responsible [?] than the new media, but they were also irrelevant."[69]

The above was why many felt the major liberal newspapers became little more than newsletters for the Kerry campaign in 2004. Their credibility today is still severely damaged because of it.

On August 19, Kerry did, after all, fire back at the Swifties, at a firefighters union gathering in Washington. "More than 30 years ago I learned an important lesson," he said. "When you're under attack the best thing to do is turn your boat into the attack. That's what I intend to do today."

He then said of SBVFT, "Of course, this group isn't interested in the truth and they're not telling the truth. But here's what you really need to know about them . . . They're a front for the Bush campaign," he said. "And the fact that the president won't denounce what they're up to tells you everything you need to know. He wants them to do his dirty work.

"Of course," Kerry continued, "the president keeps telling people he would never question my service to our country. Instead he watches as a Republican funded attack group does just that. Well, if he wants to have a debate about our service in Vietnam, here is my answer: bring it on."[70]

---

67. Evan Thomas and the Staff of *Newsweek*, *Election 2004* (New York: Public Affairs, 2004), p. 117.

68. Ibid., p. 118.

69. Ibid., p. 120.

70. Ken Mehlman, Bush's campaign manager, later confided to Bill Sammon, "These [the Swifties and POWs] are people who are incredible. You may disagree with what they are saying. But they are heroes. These are people who suffered in prison camps for America. And to respond and say, 'these are bums who don't have a right to speak. But other veterans who agree with us do,' is responding with a hammer and not a scalpel." Bill Sammon. *Strategery* (Washington, D.C.: Regnery Publishing, Inc., 2006), p. 100.

ON AUGUST 20 the Kerry campaign called on Regnery, the publisher for *Unfit for Command*, to withdraw the book from bookshelves. A campaign spokesman said, "No publisher should want to be selling books with proven falsehoods in them, especially falsehoods that are meant to smear the military service of an American veteran." The next day the Kerry campaign filed a complaint with the Federal Election Commission (FEC), alleging the SBVFT violated "the law with inaccurate ads that are illegally coordinated with the Bush-Cheney presidential campaign and the Republican National Committee."

The Kerry campaign, in a classic case of "if I say it, it must be so," said there was "overwhelming evidence" that SBVFT was coordinating its spending on advertising and other activities with the Bush campaign. They offered not a scintilla of evidence to support the claim, and the FEC later held there had been no coordination with the Bush campaign.

On August 24–September 1, the second ad ran in Albuquerque, New Mexico; Las Vegas, Nevada; Harrisburg, Pennsylvania; and on Washington, D.C., cable. The ad alternated clips of Kerry's Senate testimony with charges from the SBVFT, particularly former POWs, that Kerry's accusations had demoralized and betrayed soldiers in Vietnam. Perhaps the most devastating line was from Paul Galanti: "John Kerry gave the enemy for free what I and many of my comrades in the North Vietnam prison camps took torture to avoid saying."

The ad cost $700,000 to run, which, due to ever increasing grassroots support, the SBVFT could pay. Main site visitors on the Web site totaled over one million by August 20, 8,734 had contributed to the SBVFT for a total of nearly $1 million. Belying the "big money" charge, the average contribution was less than $60.

On August 23, former Senator Bob Dole, whose right arm is withered from wounds received during World War II, weighed in on the Kerry controversy. "One day he's [Kerry] saying that we were shooting civilians, cutting off their ears, cutting off their heads, throwing away his medals or his ribbons," Dole said. "The next day he's standing there, 'I want to be president because I'm a Vietnam veteran.'"

One Vietnam veteran said, "Anybody who did not spit on a Vietnam veteran in 1968 can do so now by voting for John Kerry." The truth about Kerry was costing him the one constituency he most needed to have, veterans. On August 23 the number of donors on Swiftvets.com was over 15,000, for a combined total of over $1.5 million; the average donation was $63.21.

That bad news for the Kerry campaign was followed by their admission that it was indeed possible his first Purple Heart commendation was the result of an unintentional, self-inflicted wound. It was an extraordinary admission, because with it collapsed Kerry's rationale for leaving Vietnam nearly eight months early with three Purple Hearts. Admiral Hoffmann immediately issued a statement saying, "When Grant Hibbard and Doctor Letson appeared in our ad, they were attacked and vilified by the Kerry campaign, but now we see news reports saying the Kerry campaign is now sheepishly acknowledging that what we said was true. John Kerry's own journal reinforces the fact that neither Kerry nor his crew had seen hostile enemy action."

The campaign had been forced also to change their stories on the "No Man Left Behind Incident" (the mining of PCF 3) and "Christmas in Cambodia." "John Kerry's stories are falling apart," the Admiral said.

Meanwhile, Barnes and Noble, the nation's largest bookstore chain, was facing fierce complaints because they did not have the bestseller *Unfit for Command* available in its stores. They had to issue a statement they had no political agenda, and that the publisher, Regnery, had not been able to keep up with customer demand for the book.

On August 24, 2004, Ben Ginsberg resigned as attorney for the Bush campaign. It was he says, "on a personal level tremendously painful to have to leave the presidential campaign. But I've never felt as strongly about helping a client as I did you guys [the Swift Boat Veterans and POWs]."

Of course, lawyers are ethically bound to maintain attorney client confidentiality. Ethically Ginsberg could not and would not have disclosed to the Bush campaign or Swift Vets information regarding what the respective groups or both were doing. But once the old media discovered the connection, they were all over the issue. It was, as Ginsberg says, a "stunning double standard," in 527 media coverage.

The mainstream media had given almost no coverage to the $63 million spent by Democratic 527 groups on negative advertising against Bush, and had made no effort to expose the revolving door connections to the Kerry campaign.

Kerry campaign lawyer Bob Bauer and Democratic National Committee counsel Joe Sandler also represented 527s. Jim Jordan, Kerry's previous campaign manager, represented three 527s. Harold Ickes, an executive committee member of the Democratic Committee, actually headed the Media Fund, and Bill Richardson simultaneously chaired the Democrat's national convention and a 527. Zack Exley went from an executive position with Moveon.org to the Kerry campaign.

The Kerry-Edwards campaign had far more direct connections with Democratic 527 groups, but the mainstream media kept their pens in their pockets. The old media had lambasted the Swift Vets for the Republican "big money" connections, yet John Edward's top donor, Steven Bing, contributed $8 million to Democratic 527s. Susie Buell, Kerry vice chairman, gave more than $1 million to 527s, and Lewis Cullman, who raised more than $100,000 for the Democratic Party gave $1.65 million to the 527s.

When Bush-Cheney filed a detailed 70-page complaint detailing illegal coordination by Democrats, there were 14 articles about it, and there was no follow up. When Kerry-Edwards filed an unsupportable charge of coordination against Swift Vets ads, there were 74 articles, and as Ginsberg says, "the pack swarmed. The double standard in reporting on 527s suggests that some of the withering scrutiny visited on the Swift Boat Veterans should be directed inward."[71]

Ginsberg's principled stand won him the further admiration of the Swifties and POWs. Bill Franke says, "Ben Ginsberg could have finessed the issue and stayed as counsel for Bush-Cheney and resigned from representing Swift Vets. It is a tribute to him that he chose what he thought was in the best interests of the nation to get the story out. It speaks volumes on Ben Ginsberg."

THE SWIFTIES AND POWs went into a grind it out mode, putting their lives on hold and coming together in brotherhood as they had in Vietnam. The Speakers Bureau could be counted on at any time for an interview or appearance, John O'Neill was indefatigable, and the SBVFT media people and Swifties developed a sometimes-uneasy alliance.

Mike Russell had been diplomatically warned that Admiral Hoffmann was running the SBVFT show. Fortunately, he was used to the personality type, because of his father. Russell immediately realized, "this is a very strong personality, this is not someone to be trifled with, and if you butt up against him he's like an old, angry mule who'll kick your teeth out if he feels you are stonewalling him or are an obstructionist in some way."

Russell and the rest of the media people thought that the early strategy of having press conferences was no longer viable. He thought they would turn into a media circus with "a lot of shouting and finger pointing by Kerry supporters." Unfortunately, press conferences were near and dear to the Admiral's heart.

---

71. Ben Ginsberg, "Swift Boats and Double Standards," washingtonpost.com, September 1, 2004, p. A19.

Six mornings a week, at 9:00 A.M. Eastern Time, media strategy sessions were held by conference call between the Swifties and the media types. For the Swifties they were a necessary evil, to insure that the hard earned money of the SBVFT donors was employed responsibly and to the greatest effect. One may be quite certain the media people sometimes endured the meetings with the politically naïve Swifties who adamantly wanted to stay in control of their message.

Each morning the Admiral, Bill Franke, this author, Jennifer Webster, Mike Russell, Chris LaCivita, Greg Mueller, and John O'Neill when commitments allowed, would conference to hammer out the issues. A news conference was scheduled, and the debate about whether to hold it went on for several days, with the Admiral arguing for it and Mike Russell against it. The group finally agreed to cancel the press conference, at which point the Admiral grew so angry he shut down the call.

"The Admiral is a point-blank man," Russell says. "He will hit you with both barrels. His job was to get a mission accomplished."

Russell called him about the press conference after the meeting. He told the Admiral, "You are not a political operative and you are not media savvy.[72]

"Admiral," Russell went on, "we're going to cancel this press conference."

"Now just a goddamned minute," the Admiral exploded. "This is the goddamned tail waggin' the goddamned dog!"

"In that moment," Russell says, "the Admiral knew I wasn't going to be trifled with either. We disagreed over this tactic, but there was a connection that we made and a respect for each other that allowed us to work together going forward."

After the election was over, the Admiral, who was always leery of the P.R. people, told Russell, "You know, I didn't like you much when we started out, but I grew to respect you and I learned a lot from you."

Mike Russell says, "That was a big moment for me."

ON AUGUST 26 AN L.A. *Times* poll put Bush ahead of Kerry for the first time, although within the margin of error it was a statistical tie. And the Swifties kept raising money and buying ads. The 30-second ad showing Kerry throwing his medals/ribbons away opened with a shot of Marines marching.

LaCivita screened it for the Admiral, who asked, "Why do you have Marines marching in that commercial? We are a group of sailors."

---

72. Mike Russell says, "We knew that was one of our greatest strengths and at the same time our greatest weakness."

LaCivita looked at him and replied deadpan, "Because Admiral, we couldn't find any sailors that could march."

The ad, another devastating one produced by LaCivita-Reed, showed Kerry in a convoluted interview saying, "I gave back—I can't remember—six, seven, eight, nine [ribbons or medals]."

The ad concluded, "How can the man who renounced his country's symbols now be trusted?" At the same time, the Swift vets went national for the first time, with an $800,000 cable TV buy with the prior ad in which the former POWs talked about Kerry. After that *Time* magazine polls suggested that 77 per cent of registered voters had either seen the ads or heard about them. *Time* went on to assert "And while *Navy records and eyewitnesses contradict nearly all the groups claims* [emphasis added], 35% (including 25% of swing voters) suspect there's some truth to the charges."

When the Republicans held their National Convention the Swift Vets were harshly criticized by some for "creating a distraction" with the ads during the convention. John O'Neill says, "When we came out Dick Morris said this would be a disaster for the Republicans. We didn't really know whether it would be a disaster or not, but we had to speak the truth. Admiral Hoffmann had an understanding of the sense of fairness of the American people."

In early September, Carlton Sherwood, an independent producer of documentaries, released "Stolen Honor." The devastating documentary, which featured an analysis of how the behavior of John Kerry as a leader of the antiwar movement impacted American POWs, stated, "Perhaps more than any living group of combat veterans, it was American POWs who suffered most, forced to endure the immediate consequences of Kerry's traitorous falsehoods."

The interviews with the POWs, many of whom had appeared in SBVFT advertisements, were a shocking indictment of Kerry and the antiwar movement. A momentous sea change was occurring in the veterans' community and with their families. It would not manifest itself until the November 2 election, but Kerry had lost the vast majority of one of the most influential and united groups in America: the veterans.

To this author, that sea change is best exemplified in an e-mail sent to Lou Letson, which he with permission shared with the Swifties:

> Keep the faith Lou. You have some pretty big names supporting you, and you also have most of the 2.5 million Vietnam Vets behind you as well. It is these same media personalities (and outlets) that created the lies and stereotypes that have become the image of the Vietnam Veteran. Those of us who served know they are lies, but until now we had no credible voice to

speak our anger. In the 60's and early 70's there was no Internet, no FOX News, no Swift Boat Veterans for Truth. All the country had was ABC, NBC and CBS, along with the NY Times and the Washington Post, all of whom lied about us.

You and the Swifties have given us a voice and we are grateful beyond words. Lou, you know that I lost my closest brother in Quang Ngai Province in September 1966. He was a Marine Staff Sergeant who died DEFENDING a village with a squad of Marines. Yes, defending the village, not burning it or killing and raping the villagers . . . He was 25 years old and left a wife and two children. Multiply his story by 58,000 and you have 58,000 families who have been quietly seething for 30 years over the lies and negative stereotypes that were created by the likes of John Kerry, Fonda, Ramsay Clark and the (then) national media. They still don't get it. They still don't understand that even after all this time we are as angry as ever, because those lies cut very deep and the wounds never healed.

If John Kerry hasn't done anything else, his posturing and chest pounding . . . have finally brought about a forum for us . . . It is you, the Swift Boat Veterans, who are representing us in this fight for our history and our dignity. All I can say, as one who served in the jungles of III and IV Corps as an infantryman in the First Cavalry Division, and as a brother who lost a brother and more friends than I want to count, is thank you for taking on this fight for us. Thank you and I salute you all.[73]

THERE WERE TWO RATHER PATHETIC attempts by the old media to counter the Swift Vets and promote Kerry. In mid September CBS's "60 Minutes II" aired a report which claimed to have obtained "long lost" records of Bush's senior officer in the Texas Air National Guard. The documents were the "documentary evidence" that Bush had shirked his duty.

Even before the segment had finished airing, a blogger was on the Web questioning the authenticity of the documents. As it turned out, the documents were faked, and it backfired on Dan Rather, who insisted CBS had not made an error. The incident, which became known as "Rathergate," ultimately caused him to resign.

This sorry episode of "journalistic ethics" was followed another perhaps worse, on the Ted Koppel "Nightline" show. Koppel's staff traveled to Vietnam to prove that the Swift Vets' version of Kerry's Silver Star incident was false. They interviewed five or six former Viet Cong, who went along with Koppel (probably for a fee), saying there were as many as 20 Viet Cong when Kerry went

---

73. See also in the Appendix, "The Last Battle of Vietnam," a poem by Russ Vaughn, which also captures the spirit of that 2004 campaign.

ashore. Everyone on Kerry's crew said there was a single VC, and in *Tour of Duty* Kerry said of the incident, "I thought to myself, 'Thank God there was only one. If there were five or ten we would have all died.'"

Koppel chose to believe four former American enemies, rather than Kerry, Kerry's own crew, and the SBVFT, because it fit his political agenda. There was an Orwellian aura on his show as he told John O'Neill not to quote Kerry anymore. John O'Neill finished by saying, "You've been had, Ted."[74]

On September 22, Sean McCabe, on behalf of the SBVFT, announced that the group had launched a $1.3 million TV blitz in Pennsylvania, Ohio, West Virginia, Nevada and New Mexico. The subject of the ad was Kerry's secret meeting with the enemy leaders of North Vietnam in Paris in May of 1970. As with the other ads, it was true and devastating.

Douglas Brinkley then made a rather extraordinary admission, in the *New York Times*, "Every American now knows that there's something really screwy about George Bush and the National Guard, *and they know that John Kerry was not the war hero we thought he was* [emphasis added]."

Medal of Honor recipient and Senator McCain's cellmate in the Hanoi Hilton, Colonel Bud Day, issued a statement that got to the heart of the problems Kerry was increasingly having with the American people. "The issue is trust," Day wrote. "Can anyone trust John Kerry? I draw a direct comparison of General Benedict Arnold of the Revolutionary War, to Lieutenant John Kerry. Both went off to war, fought, and then turned against their country . . . John Kerry for President? Ridiculous. Unthinkable. Unbelievable. Outrageous."

As the 2004 election drew to a close, the Hoffmann home had the surface appearance of a typical retirement house. The downstairs was orderly, there were photos around of the Admiral in uniform surrounded by his five daughters, and there were formal shots of the grandchildren arranged on side tables. There was a woodworking shop in the basement; the home looked typical for a retirement couple the ages of the Hoffmanns: 78 for the Admiral and 76 for Mary Linn.

---

74. John O'Neill believes that the 2004 election exposed the bias of the media for all to see. Network ratings dropped, as did the readership of newspapers like the *Los Angeles Times* and the *Chicago Tribune*. "Whatever shreds of credibility the major media had before the election are gone. They operated so clearly as extensions of the Kerry campaign. . . . These folks simply start off with an opinion and then either gather or manufacture facts to support the opinion." It is a sad commentary on formerly venerated papers like the *New York Times*, which have become a laughing stock because of their biases.

But Mary Linn was spending most of her time in her basement office, handling hundreds of e-mails, while the Admiral was upstairs in his office, now so full of open boxes that Mary Linn couldn't get in to vacuum. The woodworking shop was silent, the yard wasn't what it once was, and they mostly saw each other only at dinner.

As the leader and driving force behind SBVFT, the organization had turned into more than a full time job for the Admiral and Mary Linn. From the first press conference to the 1st of October the organization had raised more than $14 million from tens of thousands of contributors. The Web site had over 3.5 million visitors, 71,671 contributors, and over $5 million in contributions. The simple outrage of one man over the candidacy of John Kerry had started it all.

From the Second Key Bridge Marriott Meeting to the Election

The Swifties and POWs gathered one last time before the election at the Key Bridge Marriott in Arlington. The meetings opened with a buffet dinner at 6:30 P.M. in the Marriott Ballroom, followed by a strategic/planning meeting with the Steering Committee.

The Admiral opened the meeting by welcoming everyone. Bill Franke then introduced a special guest, T. Boone Pickens, who had traveled to Arlington for the event.[75] John O'Neill gave a report on *Unfit for Command*, Jennifer Webster updated everyone on her Speakers Bureau radio appearances, and Chris LaCivita commented on the ads and the impact of the SBVFT. His report was followed by a financial report by this author, who also introduced Susan Arceneaux to the group. Bill Franke gave a report on strategies going forward; Van Odell spoke on the upcoming Speakers Bureau's schedule; the Admiral made the concluding comments and specific assignments.

At 8:00 A.M. the next morning designated Swifties and POWs headed to Atlantic Video for the filming of mini-documentaries by Harry Kloor and more footage for commercials. The remaining participants in the conference stayed for training on dealing with local media, led by the Webster Group and CRC, after which they headed for Atlantic Video for the "Big Shoot."

---

75. Pickens was so impressed by the men he met and their families, and their commitment, he committed to an additional $1 million donation to SBVFT that night.

These aging warriors stood under hot lights on hard concrete for the filming. Seventy-nine-year-old Bud Day was there in a leather flight jacket and with his Medal of Honor around his neck. The Swifties who had not yet met him, respectfully went up to shake his hand and tell him how honored they were to be with him that day. The Admiral was there, as was Joe Ponder, on crutches, 92 men in all, POWs and Swifties, filmed together for the last ad, where they jointly proclaimed, "John Kerry is unfit for command." They shared their stories with the cameras; at times their emotions showed; and at other times they laughed, breaking once into an off-key rendition of "Row, row, row your boat."[76]

That evening the men and their families embarked on the cruise ship *Odyssey* on the Potomac River. Admiral Hoffmann told the men, "As we will be perceived by the public as representatives of the Sea Services, coat and tie are recommended."

On Sunday morning the Steering Committee met again, after which all hands boarded buses for the Vietnam Memorial Wall. It was a poignant reminder of why they were all serving once again.

Meanwhile, the Kerry campaign did everything in their power to stop the showing of "Stolen Honor," scheduled to run on 62 nationwide affiliates of the Sinclair Broadcasting Group. They eventually succeeded in intimidating Sinclair into showing parts of the documentary only.

As the campaign wound down to its weary end, the Kerry forces had to resort to attacks to try and counter John O'Neill. The Kerry surrogates came nearly unhinged when they went head to head with him. Kerry forces dredged up James Carville, the attack dog from the Clinton administration, to try and shout the dignified O'Neill down. And it was difficult to watch Lawrence O'Donnell on MSNBC, on Scarborough Country, interrupt O'Neill every few seconds, calling the decorated Vietnam veteran O'Neill, "Liar, liar, liar . . . " and "creep." For his unprofessional screeches, he lost his job.

---

76. The SBVFT purchased their then largest ad buy, $3.14 million, to run the two ads that came from that filming. The first, "They Served," portrayed the men who had banded together to tell the true story of John Kerry. The second, "Why?" ends with Bud Day asking John Kerry, "How can you expect our sons and daughters to follow you, when you condemned their fathers and grandfathers?" Admiral Hoffmann had long insisted to the media people they needed to film the Swifties and POWs as a group. By all accounts, the ads were powerful and moving. All ads may be viewed on Swiftvets.com.

The Election, Orlando and the Post-election

On November 2, 2004, President George W. Bush defeated John F. Kerry for President of the United States. The Swifties and POWs were relieved, and grateful to the American people for carefully listening to what the SBVFT had to say. The Swifties and POWs, and their families, had the utmost respect for the voters. They had never tried to tell them how they should vote; rather the SBVFT trusted the collective judgment of the American people.

Admiral Hoffmann issued a statement that said in part, "We [SBVFT] were the true embodiment of grassroots citizen action, complied fully with federal election law, and had every right to participate in the public discussion of John Kerry's qualifications as Commander in Chief."

To John O'Neill, Admiral Hoffmann's founding and leadership of SBVFT brought to mind the Alfred Lord Tennyson poem, *Ulysses*, which closes thusly:

> Tho' much is taken, much abides; and tho'
> We are not now that strength which in old days
> Moved earth and heaven; that which we are, we are;
> One equal temper of heroic hearts,
> Made weak by time and fate, but strong in will
> To strive, to seek, to find and not to yield.

THE REST OF THE STORY of the SBVFT may be quickly told. The men of Swift Vets and their families met in January 2005 in Orlando for a celebration of "Mission Accomplished" and "The record is set straight." There were two business meetings to discuss the future of Swift Vets, and to let everyone know how much support the people of America had given the group. There were over 150,000 individual contributors to Swift Vets; they flooded the group with over $26 million in contributions.[77]

Swift Vets took seriously their fiduciary responsibility for the money entrusted to them. The Steering and Financial Committees believed that

---

77. Contrary to the "Republican Big Money" canard that the Kerry supporters attempted to foist on the American public, SBVFT had remarkable grass roots support. There were three donors over $1 million (Bob Perry gave $4.45 million, and Harold Simmons and T. Boone Pickens each gave $2 million). These American patriots never asked for any consideration or input into the group for their donations. Only 25 individual donors gave over $25,000; the remainder came from small donations from all over the country.

"Latch" and Mary Linn Hoffmann, Orlando, Florida, 2005. LYNN WRIGHT PHOTOS

contributors had given money with the expectation that the organization would responsibly spend it. As it turned out, an incredible 94 per cent of donations (total ad costs divided by contributions less retainage for legal costs) went directly to inform the American people about John Kerry.

At an evening banquet on the 29th of January 2005, the Swifties, POWs and their families gathered to honor the effort. Charley Plumly was in charge of the banquet, and, as we would expect, he fulfilled those duties in his no nonsense style. Paul Galanti presented John O'Neill with an appreciation for his grace and courage in 2004, and Bob Elder gave an etched crystal bowl and a moving speech honoring Admiral Hoffmann's leadership during 2004.

Elder closed his remarks with, "And so tonight, as we gather one last time to celebrate the restoration of our honor, we keep faith with the voices of the 58,000 names whom when we again reach out and touch, will forever cry out and say, "God bless you, Admiral Hoffmann, we knew you'd come."

The women who had been so instrumental in Swift Vets then went to the front to be honored, after which, in an extraordinary showing of knowing his troops and what they had done for Swift Vets, the Admiral lined up all the key players to the left and right of the podium, and one by one, singled them out by name and told what they had done in 2004. It was to be last time they would all be together.

TO THE POLITICAL LEFT, who couldn't believe Kerry couldn't beat the "incompetent" George Bush, "to swiftboat" became a pejorative verb. It was invoked by them to deflect criticism of Cindy Sheehan, John Murtha, Al Gore and others. The left attempted to define "swiftboating" as an ad hominem attack, mere name-calling or smearing of an honorable person.

Bob Elder presents an appreciation to the Admiral for his leadership of Swift Boat Veterans and POWs for Truth. LYNN WRIGHT PHOTO

Former POW Paul Galanti presents an award to John O'Neill for his courage and grace under the force of the intense media scrutiny of 2004. LYNN WRIGHT PHOTO

The leadership of Swift Vets, (left to right) John O'Neill (Co-Chairman), Bill Franke (Operations), Weymouth Symmes (Treasurer and Compliance), Rear Admiral Roy F. Hoffmann USN, Ret. (Chairman). LYNN WRIGHT PHOTO

Medal of Honor winner Col. Bud Day, Jim Zumwalt, Mission Accomplished, Orlando, Florida, January 2005.

Tribute to Admiral Roy F. Hoffmann USN (Ret.)
Delivered by Robert G. Elder
Orlando, Florida—January 29, 2005

We are here tonight to talk about gratitude and about honor. A generation ago most of us came off of ships in the navy to gather in a far away place to uphold the sacred oath that all of us are bound by. On May 4, 2004, we gathered once again, this time coming off of farms and schools, businesses and professions, some even came on crutches to once again uphold our devotion to that oath. And tonight, we gather for perhaps the last time, to acknowledge with humility the gratitude bestowed upon us, and to celebrate the restoration of our honor.

Gratitude . . . the gratitude of millions of Americans for preventing a great injustice. And honor . . . the restoration of honor and dignity to 2.7 million veterans who for thirty-five years suffered the humiliating effects of a terrible betrayal visited upon them by one of their own. Honor restored to so many brave men whose tour of duty lasted up to seven years in lonely captivity. And for 58,000 names, forever enshrined on a wall, who say to every hand that reaches out to touch them—"who will come forward to tell the truth?"

We are humbled by the poignant words of a grateful America. By the words of a woman from Youngstown, Ohio who said "God bless and keep all of you wonderful Americans." From a retired army officer in California—"Thank you Swiftvets and POWs, one more time, for providing an invaluable service to our country—a job well done—Welcome home." From a veteran in Louisiana—"I have been inspired by your courage—and that restores my esteem as a veteran myself—you are honorable soldiers—and worthy of great respect." And from a man who never served, "it would have been an honor to have served with such fine men as yourselves." And from the daughter of a deceased veteran—"God bless you wonderful heroes—you won this fight for us." And from a 1st Air Cav veteran in Michigan, "thank you for helping me to finally be proud of my humble sacrifice". From the son of a two-tour veteran—"you helped me understand my father better, and to be more proud of him than ever—I will always be in your debt." From an ex-patriot during the 70's—"today you not only redeem your own names—you redeem us all." And from the wife of a firefighter in New York—"God help me—how do you say thank you for saving our country." And from the daughter of a veteran in New York—"you spoke for the man I honor—Thank you—thank you for honoring him and allowing him to believe once again that there is a code of honor." And from a proud daughter of a veteran—"I have learned quite a bit from all of you—I have learned that my American values are still intact—God, family, country are still in existence—God bless you my dear friends—thank you for giving me the momentum to care, and to never forget—those who have not returned, those who will never return—I will never fail to thank those who serve—I will never forget—and one more time . . . just in case I have missed one of you—Welcome home."

So many touching expressions of gratitude. We are here tonight to ourselves express gratitude to our leaders. I want to do so by telling you a true story—a story told to me by a young special forces officer one night in Ha Tien as we were preparing for a mission the next morning. It is a story about honor and keeping faith. An army platoon was suddenly ambushed as they were on a search and destroy mission somewhere in III Corps. They were pinned down and subject to withering enemy fire. A rifle squad was under particularly heavy fire and the platoon sergeant saw one of his men out on the skirmish line suddenly fall badly wounded. While the battle raged a young medic came up to the sergeant and asked for permission to go out on the flank and retrieve the wounded soldier. Believing such a risk to be futile the sergeant replied "it's no use—he is probably already dead." Despite his sergeant's words, the young medic, at the risk of his life crawled out to the fallen soldier. Minutes later he returned carrying the body of the soldier and laid him at the feet of his sergeant. The sergeant looked at his medic and said "You see Corporal, I told you it was of no use, you risked your life for nothing, he is already dead." The young medic looked up at his sergeant and said "Oh no sergeant, I did not risk my life for nothing—you see when I got to this man's side he was still alive, and as I knelt down he looked into my eyes and in his dying breath he whispered "God bless you Corporal, I knew you'd come."

And so tonight, as we gather one last time to celebrate the restoration of our honor, we keep faith with the voices of 58,000 names who, when we again reach out and touch them, will forever cry out and say "God bless you Admiral Hoffmann, we knew you'd come." Ladies and gentlemen, I give you Admiral Roy F. Hoffmann.

Waiting for the Admiral to speak (left to right) Joe Ponder, Van Odell, Larry Thurlow, John O'Neill, Weymouth Symmes. LYNN WRIGHT PHOTO

Waiting for the Admiral to speak about their service during 2004 for Swift Vets (left to right): Jim Deal, Tony Snesko, Jennifer Webster, Tom Wyld, Ken McGhee, Rocky Hildreth. Jennifer Webster handled much of the radio from the beginning.
LYNN WRIGHT PHOTO

The men of Swift Vets (left to right): John O'Neill, Weymouth Symmes, Andy Horne, Bob Elder, Bill Schachte, Dick Pees, Adrian Lonsdale, Bill Franke, Pete Webster and Grant Hibbard. LYNN WRIGHT PHOTO

They also served; the wives of the Swifties. Left to Right: Rebecca Ponder, Anne O'Neill, Mary Linn Hoffmann, Sibyl Plumly, Sylvia Horne, Terry Symmes, Trenny Elliott, Ruth Franke, Patty Thurlow, Barbara Brant, Marsha Gardner.
LYNN WRIGHT PHOTO

Men of SBVFT (left to right): Rocky Hildreth, Dave Wallace, Steve Gardner, Jim Thomas, Jack Chenoweth, George Elliott, Joe Ponder, Van Odell, Larry Thurlow, John O'Neill, and Weymouth Symmes. LYNN WRIGHT PHOTO

A poignant moment: Admiral Hoffmann, flanked by Jack Chenoweth and George Elliott, thanks Joe Ponder for his service. LYNN WRIGHT PHOTO

That was the least of the worries for the leadership of Swift Vets, who had two items of concern left over from 2004: Another John Kerry presidential run, and the Kerry-Edwards complaint brought against SBVFT with the FEC.

In January of 2006 it appeared Kerry was positioned for another White House run. As the AP put it, "It's almost as if Sen. John Kerry never stopped running for president. He still jets around the country, raising millions of dollars and rallying Democrats . . . His campaign Web site boasts of an online arm of three million supporters."

Even Kerry began to use Swift Boat as a pejorative. "That's another one of their 'Swift Boat'-style tactics where they throw up the mud and stick it," he said in 2006. But then he led the ill-fated "flopibuster" against Supreme Court nominee Samuel Alito, angering Democrats who knew the capable jurist would be confirmed in the Senate.

But then, the John Kerry the SBVFT had exposed to the American public came to light in an unguarded moment, in the now famous "botched joke." Kerry, in a speech to a group of students in California, said, "You know, education, if you make the most of it, you study hard, you do your homework and you make an effort to get smart, you can do well. If you don't, you get stuck in Iraq."

The firestorm that resulted from the remark was made worse by Kerry's response to the firestorm, first by stonewalling, then by "apologizing" for what he said was a botched joke. Whether it was a Freudian slip, a botched joke, or exposed the heart of John Kerry really didn't matter. It seemed to be consistent with what he really thought, and he was reverting back to his old form of dishonoring military service.

The irony is that the old media, which had covered so ably for him in 2004, now turned on him like a pack of wild dogs, when he was no longer useful to them.

THE FEDERAL GOVERNMENT, in the form of the FEC, relentlessly pursued SBVFT after the election of 2004. The FEC charged SBVFT with two transgressions in its activities in 2004: Electioneering (that is, expressly advocating the defeat or victory of a candidate), and coordination (that is, coordinating activities directly with a campaign, party or candidate).

With the full force of the federal government behind them, the FEC did everything they could to prove the Swifties had violated the law in 2004. They subpoenaed the records of the vendors that had worked for the group, eventually gathering over a million pages of documents. They found . . . nothing.

The FEC based its action against the SBVFT on legal points that were not in effect in 2004, during which the FEC had failed to provide solid guidelines for the 527s. Ben Ginsberg feels the Republican appointees to the FEC board acted in an intellectually insupportable way. "They had a legal theory that did not stand up and has in fact been rejected by the U.S. Supreme Court [after the SBVFT conciliation] in the Wisconsin Right to Life Case."

Still, the Swift Vets paid nearly a million dollars in legal fees to chart a proper legal course in 2004, and to defend themselves after the election. Ginsberg said that the FEC allowed the process of defense to be the penalty in the case of SBVFT. "To put all of you through the subpoena of maybe a million pages of e-mail, and then they never used any of them in any of the legal process.

"The FEC didn't find evidence of anything, which is the aggravating part, and you paid a nuisance amount of money [in a fine] that was somewhere just over one per cent of the money raised, just to end the litigation."

The Swift Vets leadership opted to conciliate with the FEC, in part because a lengthy legal battle, likely to go all the way to the Supreme Court, would have required another two years of legal battles and perhaps another two million dollars in legal fees. The Steering Committee felt the money and effort could be better used to support badly injured veterans coming home from Iraq and Afghanistan.

Bradley A. Smith, the former chairman of the FEC in 2004, had this to say about the conciliation settlements of SBVFT and two other 527s with the FEC:

> These groups aren't being punished for making errors in their filing papers. They're being punished for criticizing politicians. No doubt many Americans think that the Swift boat veterans and POWs were terrible, smearing the reputation of an honorable Vietnam War veteran. Many Americans think that Moveon.org was terrible, making misleading and unfounded charges that undermined American unity in war. That is what political speech often does. Bob Perry and Boone Pickens' contributions made it possible for the Swifties to be heard. When the Swifties held their first news conference in Washington about John Kerry's war record and post-Vietnam war testimony to congress, the press ignored them. Only when it got money to run ads did the group get wide media coverage. Then tens of thousands of citizens, learning of the group, flooded it with millions in small contributions. Big money did not drown out the voices of average Americans—it allowed them to be heard. In what other country can ordinary people have such a profound political effect? If last week's fines have the desired effect, in future elections we will not hear from groups such as the Swifties.

Ben Ginsberg considers McCain-Feingold an assault on the free speech First Amendment rights of Americans. "Now that the Supreme Court has finally thrown out a portion of it" he says, "and given a roadmap on how to throw out the rest of it, it is getting its just reward." The Supreme Court suggested that many of the legal theories the FEC used to come after the 527s were improper under the law. Under the Supreme Court's reading of the law, the FEC would not have been able to do what it did to Swift Vets, and the other 527s, after the 2004 election.

EPILOGUE

THE ADMIRAL ROY F. HOFFMANN FOUNDATION

War is an ugly thing, but not the ugliest of things. The decayed and degraded state of moral and patriotic feeling which thinks that nothing is worth war is much worse. The person who has nothing for which he is willing to fight, nothing which is more important than his own personal safety, is a miserable creature and has no chance of being free unless made and kept so by the exertions of better men than himself.

—John Stuart Mill
English economist and philosopher (1806–1873)

There had never been any understanding or intent that any of the Swifties or POWs associated with the Swift Boat Veterans and POWs for Truth would profit in any way from the organization. John O'Neill as co-author of the bestselling *Unfit for Command* was entitled to receive nearly $1 million in royalties from the publisher. In an extraordinary act of generosity, he assigned all rights and control of those royalties, without reservation, to endow a foundation honoring the leader of Swift Vets, Admiral Roy F. Hoffmann.

The Admiral Roy F. Hoffmann Foundation was formed on January 2, 2005, as a nonprofit corporation regulated by the provisions of United States Code section 501 (c) (3). The corporation was managed by a Board of Directors, which consisted of Admiral Roy F. Hoffmann, Chairman of the Board; Larry Thurlow, President; and board members Van Odell, Joe Ponder and Weymouth Symmes. The board decided at the onset to scrupulously avoid publicity, partly in order to shield the dignity of recipients,

Joe Ponder presents an Admiral Roy F. Hoffmann Foundation check for the Vietnam Unit Memorial Monument in Coronado, California. JOE PONDER PHOTO

Admiral Hoffmann at the presentation of an Admiral Roy F. Hoffmann Foundation check, 2005. MARY LINN HOFFMANN PHOTO

and to allow the Foundation to operate without the usual administrative expenses associated with charitable organizations. The board was also determined, as were all the Swift boat veterans, that returning servicemen never be treated as they had been when they returned from Vietnam.

The Foundation began awarding grants on May 4, 2005; the first grant was to a Vietnam veteran in dire need of the funds. That donation was followed by a significant contribution to the Vietnam Unit Memorial Fund to honor and perpetuate the memory of fallen shipmates who are still on patrol from the Vietnam war. Then the Foundation settled into what has become its primary purpose: Direct financial support to severely wounded veterans returning from the Iraq and Afghanistan theaters of war. Working mostly with federal medical centers such as Walter Reed and the Naval Medical Center Bethesda in metro Washington, D.C., the Brooks Army Medical Center in San Antonio, Texas, and various military bases and VA hospitals, the board personally reviews and verifies all applications. Because the board consists of uncompensated volunteers, approximately 95 per cent of donated money is returned to the veterans.

John O'Neill's opening donation was later matched by T. Boone Pickens, who gave one million dollars in April of 2006 to continue the work of the Foundation. The awards to the veterans are unrestricted direct grants that average just over $9,000. As this is written the Foundation has made over 300 awards totaling nearly $2.4 million.

Each check has been hand delivered by either a Swift boat combat veteran, or in some cases, by affiliated personnel.[1] The Admiral had this to say about the Foundation:

> It is a rewarding experience for those of us to materially help these courageous men and women in serious need of financial support. It can also be heart-rending and difficult for one to maintain composure when a proud sergeant reaches out to thank you with a steel claw. Yet the spirit of the recipients to date has been amazingly and uniformly good, with no apparent bitterness or despair, but a determined willingness to move on with life. For example, I was welcomed aboard enthusiastically by a young Marine sergeant at a Combat Training Command in Quantico, Virginia, who lost both lower arms, most of the muscle and flesh from his left leg, and multiple shrapnel wounds. He clamped a pen in his right prosthesis and with deliberation, signed his name to the receipt—not beautiful, but legible.

---

1. A listing of those who have assisted in delivering the checks is included in the Appendix.

The Admiral then asked the young Marine, "This is a combat training command. What's your assignment?"

"Martial arts, sir!"

"Including bayonet?"

"Yes, sir. Would you like a demonstration?"

The Admiral assured him it wouldn't be necessary. The Marine was 6-foot 4-inches and the Admiral 5-foot 7-inches.

Swift Boat Sailors Association Reunion, San Diego 2007

Larry Thurlow's first time aboard a Swift boat in 38 years. Swift Boat Sailors Association Reunion, San Diego, 2007. Left to Right, Terry Symmes, Weymouth Symmes, Larry Thurlow, and Patty Thurlow. Bud Kittle photo

Epilogue: The Admiral Roy F. Hoffmann Foundation

IT IS PERHAPS BEST to close the circle with the Swift Boat Sailors Association (SBSA) reunion, held May 2–6, 2007, in San Diego. The SBSA is the fraternal organization for former Swift boat sailors and their families. It was the highest attended reunion in the Association's history, as the aging warriors came together once again to respect the past and look forward to the future. As it has always been, the event was free of political acrimony—it was a renewal of the bonds of war.

Admiral Harold W. Gehman, former Swiftie and in his last assignment before retirement, NATO Supreme Allied Commander, Atlantic, was the keynote speaker at the evening banquet. Honored guests included Vice Admiral Rex Rectanus, there with Jinny Martin, and of course, Rear Admiral Roy and Mary Linn Hoffmann.

The Hoffmann's spent much of their time in the hospitality room, graciously making themselves available to the many Swifties and their families who wanted to speak to them.

Mike Bernique's crew reunited for the first time in 38 years. Swift Boat Sailors Association Reunion, San Diego, 2007. Left to Right, Jimmy Sanford, Edward Kesselring, Mike Bernique, David Hemenway, and Robert Hornberger.
JIMMY SANFORD PHOTO

On Saturday there was a remembrance at the Vietnam Unit Memorial Monument, for those fallen Swift boat sailors still on patrol. The sailors in attendance stood at attention with their families, as each of the more than 50 names were read as a bell tolled. A Marine honor guard gave the traditional 21-gun salute, after which taps was sounded. The closeness of the group, and their sorrow over those who didn't return, was palpable in the air.

The ceremony closed with the Navy Hymn.

> Eternal Father, Strong to save,
> Whose arm hath bound the restless wave,
> Who bid'st the mighty Ocean deep
> Its own appointed limits keep;
> O hear us when we cry to thee,
> For those in peril on the sea.

And so it has always been, and always will be. Honor those who have served, but more importantly, honor those who are In Harm's Way today, for they are the future of America.

APPENDIX

The Last Battle of Vietnam

It never occurred to me, ever before,
That our Navy would win the Vietnam War.
When they took to their boats in this year of elections,
with the mission of making some major corrections
I shared their belief, John should not be elected,
And their view overdue, truth should be resurrected.
Yet I questioned the course they'd set themselves for,
Knowing how John was loved by the media whore.

Ignored and dismissed by the media queens
Being shrewd, savvy sailors they still found the means
To reach out to the people, to open their eyes
To a phony John Kerry and his war story lies.
With their very first ad, they torpedoed his boat,
A Cambodian Christmas would no longer float.
His heroics unraveled, his stories fell flat,
Especially that one 'bout his magical hat.

John called on his lawyers and media whores,
And threatened the Swiftees with vile legal wars.
But these warriors kept charging back into the fire,
And made the folks wonder, "Is Kerry a Liar?"
Till the question of whether he's telling the truth
Was still in their minds in the election day booth.
So the brave Swiftees gave us what we'd not had before,
They gave us our victory in the Vietnam War.

Those brave, stalwart sailors, falsely labeled as liars,
Stood firm and stood tall, kept directing their fires,
Steadfast, unrelenting, they served once again,
And defeated John Kerry, these honorable men.
All Vets can take pride, yes all, not just some,
That we won the last battle of Vietnam.
It took far too long to bring an end to our war
But we did, November Second, Two Thousand Four.

To our Brothers, forever, on that long black Wall,
You've been vindicated now, one and all.

Russ Vaughn
2D Bn, 327th Parachute Infantry Regiment
101st Airborne Division
Vietnam 65-66

By virtue of the authority vested in me as President of the United States and as Commander-in-Chief of the Armed Forces of the United States, I have today awarded

THE PRESIDENTIAL UNIT CITATION (NAVY)

FOR EXTRAORDINARY HEROISM TO

COMMANDER TASK GROUP 194.0
(Units Participating in Operation SEA LORDS)

For extraordinary heroism and outstanding performance of duty from 18 October to 5 December 1968 while engaged in armed conflict against enemy forces in the Republic of Vietnam. Commander Task Group 194.0 initiated and prosecuted the first of several interdiction campaigns to sever enemy lines of communication and resupply and to establish the legal government in areas previously held by the enemy. The naval units engaged in Operation SEA LORDS consistently displayed the striking power and professionalism which were to mark this and following campaigns. Tasked with routing a myriad of enemy forces from their previous sanctuaries, personnel of Commander Task Group 194.0 ventured courageously into little-known canals and back-water areas, fighting valiantly through countless intense enemy rocket and automatic weapons attacks. The naval units, through their persistent and aggressive strikes against enemy strongholds, were eminently successful in their campaign to interdict enemy resupply routes and base areas throughout the lower Mekong Delta region. The courage, professionalism, and dedication displayed by the officers and men of Commander Task Group 194.0 reflected credit upon themselves and were in keeping with the highest traditions of the United States Naval Service.

Richard Nixon

The following Swift boat veterans (and related veterans) directly delivered financial assistance checks to the courageous and dedicated military men and women in the Iraq and Afghanistan wars. All of the recipients have suffered grievous wounds and lifelong disabilities as a result of direct combat, or in a few cases, non-combatant military support:

Edward J. Bergin	Clearwater, Florida
Kenneth "Ken" Briggs	Philadelphia, Pennsylvania
Jack Chenoweth	Spring Branch, Texas
Captain Terry W. Costello	Stockton, Missouri
John Hart Davis	Yolo, California
SCPO Grady E. DeLoach, Jr.	Dallas, Texas
Virgil Erwin	San Diego, California
William E. Franke	McLean, Virginia
Lester D. Garrett	Highland Ranch, Colorado
MCPO Charles Green	Cadiz, Kentucky
Curtis D. Hatler	Coon Rapids, Minnesota
Thomas M. Heritage	Novi, Michigan
Robert W. "Rocky" Hildreth	Cedar Grove, New Jersey
Rear Admiral Roy F. Hoffmann	Richmond, Virginia
Ernest J. "Bud" Kittle	Rockport, Texas
William Lannom	Grinnell, Iowa
Captain Adrian Lonsdale	Mattapoisett, Massachusetts
David P. Marion	College Station, Texas
Donald W. Matras	Lemont, Illinois
Captain Kenneth B. McGhee	San Diego, California
Van H. Odell	Katy, Texas
John O'Neill	Houston, Texas
Richard W. Pees	Ada, Ohio
Captain Charley Plumly	Ellijay, Georgia
Joseph L. Ponder	Keystone Heights, Florida
Charles R. "Chuck" Rabel	Vista, California
Sandy Reid	Florissant, Missouri
William R. Rogers	Gig Harbor, Washington
Captain David R. Stefferad	Madisonville, Louisiana
CPO James W. Steffes	Sun City, California
Weymouth D. Symmes	Missoula, Montana
W. P. "Sonny" Taylor	Oakland, Tennessee
Larry Thurlow	Bogue, Kansas
David B. Wallace	Atlanta, Georgia
Bernard Wolff	Marietta, Georgia

Glossary

ACTOV—Accelerated turnover to Vietnam.

ADM—Admiral; four stars. Equivalent—General.

AK-47—Standard infantry piece of Communist forces; 7.62 mm gas operated single shot or fully automatic rifle. The most successful assault rifle ever made.

AM—Steel hulled fleet minesweeper—the workhorse of the mine fleet.

AMS—Auxiliary Mine Sweeper; wooden hulled.

APL—Non self-propelled barracks ship.

ARVN—Army of the Republic of Vietnam—a South Vietnamese soldier.

ASW—Antisubmarine warfare.

Beaucoup—Many. Passed down to the Americans from the Vietnamese, who got it from the French.

B-40—A shoulder fired, rocket propelled grenade launcher, similar to the American 3.5 inch rocket launcher, carried by Viet Cong and North Vietnamese soldiers, used for antitank and antipersonnel targets.

B-41—RPG 7, effective range about 500 yards. Capable of penetrating one foot of armor. The weapon was more feared than the B-40

Bridge—The area in the superstructure of a ship from which the ship is operated.

Broach—To get crosswise to the direction of wave travel.

BUPERS—Bureau of Naval Personnel

CAPT—Captain; eagle. Equivalent—Colonel.

CDR—Commander; silver oak leaf. Equivalent—Lieutenant Colonel.

Charlie—U.S. troops nickname for the Viet Cong, based on Victor Charlie from the military phonetic alphabet.

CINCPAC—Commander in Chief, Pacific.

Chieu hoi—Vietnamese for "open arms." A program whereby enemy soldiers could surrender without penalty. Also, an enemy soldier who has surrendered.

CNO—Chief of Naval Operations. The senior uniformed officer in the Navy, equivalent to the Chief of Staff of the Army.

CO—Commanding officer.

COMNAVFORV—Commander Naval Forces, Vietnam.

COMUSMACV—Commander, U.S. Military Assistance Command, Vietnam.

CONN—Station, usually on the bridge, from which the ship is controlled; the act of so controlling.

COS DIV—Coastal Division.

CPO—Chief Petty Officer.

C-RATS—C-rations, the standard meals eaten in the bush from World War II through Vietnam. The meals came in cartons containing 12 different meals, instant coffee and four very stale cigarettes.

Glossary and Selected Sources 505

CTF—Commander task force
CTG—Commander task group
CTZ—Corps Tactical Zone. One of four military subdivisions of the Republic of South Vietnam.
DD—Destroyer.
DE—Destroyer Escort.
DEROS—Date Eligible for Return from Overseas.
DESRON—Destroyer Squadron.
Di Di Mau—Vietnamese for "Drive, drive faster," or "Run, run quickly," depending on context. The term was frequently used to direct fishermen to clear an area.
Dinky Dau—An American bastardization of *Dien cai dau*, to be crazy in Vietnamese.
DIV COM—Division Commander.
Dixie Station—Operations in the Gulf of Tonkin conducted south of 15 degrees North.
DLG—Guided Missile Frigate.
DMS—Destroyer Minesweeper, used for open water clearance where deep draft and less maneuverability were more acceptable.
DMZ—Demilitarized zone. In Vietnam, the Seventeenth Parallel, established by the 1954 Geneva accords.
Dung Lai—Vietnamese for "Stop!"
ENS—Ensign; gold bar. Equivalent—Second Lieutenant.
EOD—Explosive ordinance disposal.
Free fire zone—In Vietnam, an area in which one had on scene discretion to fire upon sighting the enemy, without first checking with headquarters. The authority required restraint, and was not a war crime.
GDA—Ground damage assessment.
GQ—General quarters. The condition of full readiness for battle.
H & I—Harassment and interdiction.
HE—High explosive, usually referring to artillery and mortar shells.
Hoi Chanh—Former Viet Cong soldier who has switched to the South Vietnamese side.
Hook—Anchor.
Hooch—Any dwelling, as in a Vietnamese villager's home.
IUWG—Inshore Undersea Warfare Group
KIA—Killed in action.
Lai Dai!—Vietnamese for "Come here!"
LCM—Landing Craft, Mechanized
LCPL—Landing Craft, Personal, Large.
LSM—Landing Ship, Medium.
LST—Landing Ship, Tank.
LT—Lieutenant; two silver bars. Equivalent—Captain.
LCDR—Lieutenant Commander; gold oak leaf. Equivalent—Major.
LTJG—Lieutenant, junior grade; silver bar. Equivalent—First Lieutenant.
MACV—Military Assistance Command, Vietnam.

MEDCAP—Medical Civic Action Program.
MEDEVAC—To medically evacuate a wounded or ill soldier.
MIA—Missing in action.
MRF—Mobile Riverine Force.
MSB—Minesweeping Boat.
MSC—Minesweeper, Coastal.
MSL—Minesweeper, Light.
MSM—Minesweeper, Medium.
MSO—Minesweeper, Ocean.
MSF—Mobile Strike Force. Mercenaries.
M-79—.40 mm grenade launcher, that shot spin-armed small grenades.
M-16—Standard rifle carried by American soldiers. 5.56 mm, gas operated single shot or fully automatic gas operated weapon. The clips held 17 bullets, but soldiers rarely loaded it that full because of endemic problems with jamming. The rifle was accurate to about 400 yards.
M-60—Light machine gun that uses belted 7.62 mm ammunition. The weapon had a firing rate of 550 rounds per minute, but the maximum sustained firing rate was 100 rounds per minute.
NGFS—Naval gunfire support.
NILO—Naval Intelligence Liaison Officer.
NVA—North Vietnamese Army. A North Vietnamese soldier.
OCS—Officer candidate school.
O in C—Officer in Charge.
OOD—Officer of the Deck. Officer on the bridge entrusted with operations at sea.
PBR—Patrol Boat, River
PCF—Patrol Craft Fast (Swift boat).
POW—Prisoner of war.
Rach—Canal in Vietnamese.
RADM—Rear Admiral (Lower Half); one star. Equivalent—Brigadier General.
RADM—Rear Admiral (Upper Half); two stars. Equivalent—Major General.
RF/PF—Regional Forces/Popular Forces, South Vietnamese militia. The "Ruff Puffs."
RAG—River Assault Group.
R & R—Rest and recreation leave.
RPG—Rocket propelled grenade.
SBVFT—Swift Boat Veterans and POWs for Truth
SEAL—Sea Air Land Team—Navy commando.
SEALORDS—Southeast Asia Lake, Ocean, River and Delta Strategy.
Sea Wolves—Navy UH-1B Iroquois ("Huey") helicopters.
SERE—Survival, evasion, resistance, escape.
Song—River in Vietnamese.
Squadron—Two or more divisions of ships or aircraft.
Stable Door—Harbor surveillance and patrol operations in Vietnam under control of CTG 115.9.

Swift boat—PCF
Task Force 115—Coastal Surveillance Force (Operation Market Time)
TF—Task Force. A major subdivision of a naval fleet or unified command.
TG—Task Group. Component of a naval task force.
TU—Subdivision of a task group.
UNREPS—Underway replenishments.
USA—United States Army
USAF—United States Air Force
USCG—United States Coast Guard
USMC—United States Marine Corps.
USN—United States Navy.
USS—United States Ship
VADM—Vice Admiral; three star. Equivalent—Lieutenant General.
VC—Viet Cong
VNN—Vietnamese Navy.
VVAW—Vietnam Veterans Against the War.
WHEC—USCG High Endurance Cutter.
WIA—Wounded in action.
Willie Peter—A white phosphorous artillery or mortar round.
WPB—Patrol craft; an 82-foot U.S. Coast Guard cutter.
XO—Executive Officer.

Selected Sources

Interviews

The more than 60 interviews this author conducted for *This is Latch* constitute a rich primary source about the Admiral and Mary Linn Hoffmann, Navy life in general, and the history of the times from the mid Twentieth Century through 2004. All of those interviewed were extraordinarily forthcoming in relating the parts they played in the foregoing narrative. It is my opinion the following individuals represent the best of America, and I once again extend my appreciation for the time and candor.

Judge Robert A. Andretta (*Adams*, TF 115)
Susan Arceneaux (SBVFT, Hoffmann Foundation)
Mike Bernique (TF 115, SBVFT)
Commander Robert "Friar Tuck" Brant, USN, Ret. (TF 115, SBVFT)
Captain Don Campbell, USN, Ret. (*Leahy*)
Christine Linn Hoffmann Carnahan
Jack Chenoweth (TF 115, SBVFT)
Captain Louis Colbus, USN, Ret. (*Cromwell*, *Leahy*)

Captain Terry Costello, USN, Ret. (TF 115, SBVFT)
Emilie Hoffmann Crow
Captain John A. Culver, USNR, Ret. (*Hubbard, Cromwell*, Commander Mine Warfare Force)
Matt D'Amico (*Adams*, TF 115)
Colonel Bud Day, USAF, Ret.—former POW, Vietnam (SBVFT)
Bill Dudley (*Cromwell*)
Bob Elder (TF 115, SBVFT)
Captain George Elliott, USN, Ret. (TF 115, SBVFT)
Virgil A. Erwin III (TF 115)
Bill Franke (TF 115, SBVFT)
Ruth Franke (SBVFT)
Commander Paul Galanti, USN, Ret.—former POW, Vietnam (SBVFT)
Benjamin L. Ginsberg (SBVFT)
Cecile Hoffmann Gorham
F.L. "Skip" Gunther (TF 115)
Hilarie Hoffmann Hanson
Admiral Thomas Hayward, USN, Ret.—former CNO (Commandant Sixth Naval District/Commander Charleston Naval Base)
David Hemenway (TF 115)
Kent Hewitt (*Cromwell*)
Mary Linn Hoffmann
Rear Admiral Roy F. Hoffmann, USN, Ret.
Robert Hornberger (TF 115)
Lawrence Hortt (TF 115)
Edward E. Kesselring (TF 115)
Chris LaCivita (SBVFT)
Dr. Louis Letson (TF 115, SBVFT)
Mike Lohnes (TF 115)
Captain Adrian Lonsdale, USCG, Ret. (TF 115, SBVFT)
Jinny Martin (SBVFT)
Dan Meehan (Ports of Milwaukee and Richmond, VA.)
Mike Modansky (TF 115)
Greg Nolan (*Cromwell*)
Van Odell (TF 115, SBVFT, Hoffmann Foundation)
John E. O'Neill (TF 115, SBVFT, Hoffmann Foundation)
Captain Charley Plumly, USN, Ret. (TF 115, SBVFT)
Joseph L. Ponder (TF 115, SBVFT, Hoffmann Foundation)
Vice Admiral William L. Read, USN, Ret. (*Cromwell*, Commander Mine Warfare Force, Commandant Sixth Naval District/Commander Charleston Naval Base)
Captain Dick Reass, USN, Ret. (Commander Mine Warfare Command)
Vice Admiral Earl "Rex" Rectanus, USN, Ret. (TF 115, SBVFT)
Joe Roxe (*Cromwell*)
Mike Russell (SBVFT)

Jimmy Sanford (TF 115)
Rear Admiral William Schachte, USN, Ret. (TF 115, Commandant Sixth Naval District/Commander Charleston Naval Base, SBVFT)
Jack Shamley (TF 115, SBVFT)
Commander Pat Sheedy, USN, Ret. (*Adams*, TF 115, SBVFT)
Robert B. Shirley (TF 115)
Fred Short (TF 115)
Commander William Shumadine, USN, Ret. (TF 115, SBVFT)
Merrie Spaeth (SBVFT)
David Stevenson (TF 115)
Captain Charles Stratmann, USN, Ret. (Commander Mine Warfare Force)
Scott Swett (SBVFT)
Major James P. Thomas, USAF, Ret. (TF 115, SBVFT)
Larry Thurlow (TF 115, SBVFT, Hoffmann Foundation)
Admiral Harry Train, USN, Ret.—former CINCLANTFLEET (*Hubbard*, BUPERS, *Leahy*)
Dave Wallace (*Leahy*, SBVFT)
Commander Larry Wasikowski, USNR, Ret. (TF 115)
Jennifer Webster (SBVFT)

Books

Allen, Frederick Lewis. *The Big Change 1900–1950*. New York: Bantam Books, 1952.
_____. *Only Yesterday*. New York: Harper & Brothers Publishers, 1931.
_____. *Since Yesterday*. New York: Harper & Row, 1968.
Ambrose, Stephen E. *Nixon—The Triumph of a Politician 1962–1972*. New York: Simon and Schuster, 1989.
_____. *Nixon—Ruin and Recovery 1973–1990*. New York: Touchstone, 1991.
Brinkley, Douglas. *Tour of Duty*. New York: William Morrow, 2004.
Burkett, B.G. and Whitley, Glenna. *Stolen Valor*. Dallas, Texas: Verity Press, Inc., 1998.
Carey, John. *Eyewitness to History*. New York: Avon Books, 1987.
Carruth, Gorton. *What Happened When*. New York: Signet, 1989.
Coram, Robert. *American Patriot*. New York: Little, Brown and Company, 2007.
Croizat, Victor, LTCOL, USMC. *Vietnam River Warfare 1945–1975*. New York: Blandford Press, 1986.

Cruise Books
_____. *Hubbard's Far Eastern Forays 1951*. USS *Hubbard* (DD 748)
_____. Operation Unitas II 1961 USS *Norfolk, Courtney, Hammerberg, Cromwell*, SS *Clamagore*, Patrol Squadron II, Commander Destroyer Flotilla Two.
_____. Mediterranean Cruise 15 February–10 July 1966 USS *Charles F. Adams* (DDG 2)
_____. Mediterranean Cruise 15 August, 1967–29 January, 1968 USS *Charles F. Adams* (DDG 2)

_____. Mediterranean Cruise 1970–71 USS *Leahy* (DLG 18)
Cutler, Thomas J., LTCDR, USN. *Brown Water Black Beret*. Annapolis, Maryland: Naval Institute Press, 1988.
Davis, Kenneth C. *Don't Know Much About History*. New York: Avon Books, 1990.
Forbes, John, and Robert Williams. *The Illustrated History of Riverine Force The Vietnam War*. Toronto: Bantam Books, 1987.
Garfinkle, Adam. *Telltale Hearts*. New York: St. Martin's Press, 1995.
Goulden, Joseph C. *Korea The Untold Story of the War*. New York: McGraw-Hill Book Company, 1982.
Halberstam, David. *The Fifties*. New York: Villard Books, 1993.
Hicks, John D., George E. Mowry, and Robert E. Burke. *A History of the American Democracy*. 4th ed. Boston: Houghton Mifflin Co., 1970.
Johnson, Ellis A., and David A. Katcher. *Mines Against Japan*. Naval Ordnance Laboratory, White Oak, Silver Springs, Maryland, 1973.
Johnson, Paul. *A History of the American People*. New York: HarperCollins, 1997.
_____. *Modern Times The World from the Twenties to the Nineties*. New York: HarperPerennial, 1991.
Kane, Joseph Nathan. *Facts About the Presidents*. New York: Ace Books, 1976.
Karnow, Stanley. *Vietnam A History*. New York: The Viking Press, 1983.
Kearns, Doris. *Lyndon Johnson and the American Dream*. New York: Harper & Row, Publishers, 1976.
Kerrey, Bob. *When I Was a Young Man*. Orlando: Harcourt, Inc., 2002.
Kleinfelder, Rita Lang. *When We Were Young*. New York: Prentice Hall, 1993.
Larson, David L., ed. *The "Cuban Crisis" of 1962*. Boston: Houghton Mifflin Company, 1963.
Larzelere, Alex. *The Coast Guard at War Vietnam 1965–1975*. Naval Institute Press, 1997.
Leckie, Robert. *The Wars of America*. Edison, NJ: Castle Books, 1998.
Lewis, Jon E. *The 20th Century*. New York: Carroll & Graf Publishers, Inc., 1994.
Manchester, William. *American Caesar*. Boston: Little, Brown and Company, 1978.
_____. *The Glory and the Dream*. New York: Bantam Books, 1974.
McCain, John. *Faith of My Fathers*. New York: Random House, 1999.
McMaster, H.R. *Dereliction of Duty*. New York: HarperCollins, 1997.
Morison, Samuel Eliot. *The Oxford History of the American People Vol. 3: 1869 to the Death of John F. Kennedy 1963*. New York: New American Library, 1972.
Naval Historical Foundation. *The Navy*. New York: Barnes & Noble Books, 2000.
Neft, David S. and Richard M. Cohen. *The Sports Encyclopedia: Baseball*. 8th ed. New York: St. Martin's Press, 1988.
O'Neill, John E., and Jerome R. Corsi. *Unfit for Command*. Washington, D.C.: Regnery Publishing, Inc., 2004.
Palmer, David. *Summons of the Trumpet*. Novato, California: Presidio Press, 1978.
Patterson, LT COL Robert "Buzz," USAF, Ret. *Reckless Disregard*. Washington, D.C.: Regnery Publishing, Inc., 2004.

Ritter, Lawrence, and Donald Honig. *The Image of their Greatness.* New York: Crown Trade Paperbacks, 1992.
Sammon, Bill. *Strategery.* Washington, D.C.: Regnery Publishing, Inc., 2006.
Schreadley, R. L. Cdr. USN, Ret. *From the Rivers to the Sea.* Annapolis, Maryland: Naval Institute Press, 1992.
Sorley, Lewis. *A Better War.* New York: Harcourt Brace & Company, 1999.
Steffes, James. *Swift Boat Down.* X Libras, 2006.
Symmes, Weymouth D. *War on the Rivers.* Missoula, Montana: Pictorial Histories Publishing Company, Inc., 2004.
Taranto, James, and Leonard Leo, eds. *Presidential Leadership.* New York: Free Press, 2004.
Thomas, Evan and The Staff of *Newsweek. Election 2004.* New York: Public Affairs, 2004.
Toland, John. *In Mortal Combat Korea 1950-1953.* New York: William Morrow and Company, 1991.
United States Naval Institute. *The Bluejackets Manual.* Annapolis, Maryland: United States Naval Institute, 1978.
Ward, Geoffrey C., and Ken Burns. *Baseball An Illustrated History.* New York: Alfred A. Knopf, 1994.
Westmoreland, General William C. *A Soldier Reports.* Garden City, N.Y.: Doubleday, 1976.
Whitburn, Joel. *The Billboard Book of Top 40 Hits.* New York: Billboard Publications, Inc., 1985.
Young, Peter, ed. *The World Almanac of World War II.* New York: Bison Books, 1981.
Zumwalt, Elmo R., Jr. *On Watch.* New York: Quadrangle, 1976.
Zumwalt, Elmo, Jr., Admiral, and Lieutenant Elmo Zumwalt III. *My Father My Son.* New York: MacMillan Publishing Company, 1986.

PERIODICALS, NEWSPAPERS, INTERNET AND UNPUBLISHED ARTICLES

"Admiral's Punishment Policy Cited." *The Evening Post.* Charleston, South Carolina. May 29, 1978.
"Admiral Upset at Criticism." *The Evening Post.* Charleston, South Carolina. May 22, 1978.
Andretta, Robert. "Amateur Heroics." Unpublished article. February 14, 2001.
_____. "A Night to Remember." Unpublished article. November 14, 1999.
Barber, Sonny, "A[n] Evening on the Cua Dai." *Swift Current.* Third Quarter, 2005, p. 7.
"Baseball's 20 Greatest Teams of All Time." *Sports Illustrated*, 1991.
Brinkley, Douglas. "John Kerry's Final Mission in Vietnam." *American History.* April 2004.

Burkett, B. G. "Navy Commanders to Cast Doubt on Kerry's War Record." NewsMax.com, April 7, 2004.

Cagle, Malcolm W., and Frank A. Manson. "Wonsan: The Battle of the Mines." *U.S. Naval Institute Proceedings*. Vol. LXXXIII No. 6, June 1957, pp.598–611.

"Change of Command." *The Evening Post*. Charleston, South Carolina. August 26, 1978.

Clayton, Vincent J. "Welcome to Engineering." *Vietnam*. February 2006, pp 28–33.

"Clean Sweep of the Canal." *Time*. May 6, 1974.

Cullen, Dr. Leslie J. "Creating a Main Line of Resistance Tet and the Genesis of Operation Sea Lords." *Naval Historical Center* (Internet). September 23, 2003.

Editorial. *The News and Courier*. Charleston, South Carolina. March 9, 1978, and August 31, 1978.

Edwards, Lieutenant Colonel Harry W. "A Naval Lesson of the Korean Conflict." *U.S. Naval Institute Proceedings*. Vol. LXXX No. 12, December 1954, pp. 1,337–1,340.

Erwin, Virg. "Death of a Swift Boat." Unpublished article. May 26, 2007.

Galanti, Paul. "An Ex-POW reflects, a quarter century out." *Richmond-Times Dispatch*. Richmond, Virginia, February 15, 1998.

Galanti, Paul. "35 Years After Shoot-Down: Ex-POW Reflects on Life After Hanoi." *Times-Dispatch*. Richmond, Virginia, June 17, 2001.

Ginsberg, Ben. "Swift Boats and Double Standards." Washingtonpost.com. September 1, 2004, p. A19.

"Hoffmann Acts Ruled Illegal." *The News and Courier*. Charleston, South Carolina. May 20, 1978.

Hoffmann, Rear Admiral Roy F. "Offensive Mine Warfare: A Forgotten Strategy?" *U.S. Naval Institute Proceedings*, Volume 103, Number 891, 1977.

Hoffmann, Rear Admiral Roy F. "Recollections of Mine Warfare Experience in the Early Months of Korean War—1950." Unpublished article, October 31, 2000.

"Hoffmann Requests Investigation." *The Evening Post*. Charleston, South Carolina. June 3, 1978.

"In Defense of Tough Admirals." *The Evening Post*. Charleston, South Carolina. May 23, 1978.

"Investigators to Visit Base." *The Evening Post*. June 2, 1978.

Kranish, Michael. "Kerry refuses to release more records." *Boston Globe*. April 20, 2004.

Letters. *The Evening Post*. Charleston, South Carolina. May 30, 1978.

Lipscomb, Thomas. "Kerry citation a 'total mystery' to ex-Navy chief (John Lehman)." *New York Sun Times*. August 28, 2004.

Lipscomb, Thomas. "Kerry's Discharge is Questioned by an Ex-JAG Officer." *New York Sun Times*. November 1, 2004.

"Mideast Erupts, The." *Newsweek*. October 15, 1973. pp 38–41.

"Most Amazing 60 Years in History, The." *Time*. 1983.

"Navy Discipline Eroding." *The Evening Post.* Charleston, South Carolina. June 14, 1978.

"Navy—Shape Up or Ship Out, The." *The Evening Post.* Charleston, South Carolina. February 21, 1981.

O'Neill, John E. August 2, 2004, letter and supporting evidence provided to station managers in support of the television advertisement, "Any Questions?" by the Swift Boat Veterans for Truth (Unpublished document).

O'Neill, John E. "We're Not GOP Shills." *The Wall Street Journal Online (WSJ.com).* August 27, 2004.

"Rejuvenated COMA Has Military Bristling." *The Evening Post.* Charleston, South Carolina. December 3, 1978.

Rosin, Hanna. "Unfriendly Fire." Washingtonpost.com. October 3, 2004.

Sherwood, Carlton. *Stolen Honor Wounds That Never Heal* [DVD]. Red, White and Blue Productions, Inc., 2004.

Shumadine, William. *"Tour of Duty* Review." Unpublished article. 2004.

Slack, Charles. "Port chief here keeps dreams alive." *Richmond Times-Dispatch.* September 5, 1995.

Spivak, Cary, and Dan Bice. "Hoffmann once rocked the boat in Milwaukee." *Milwaukee Journal Sentinal.* August 23, 2004.

Stone, Andrea. "John Kerry's Vietnam." *USA Today.* April 13, 2004.

"Suez: The Seas Rejoined." *Time.* June 9, 1975.

Sweetman, Jack. "Great Sea Battles of World War II." *Naval History Magazine U.S. Naval Institute Proceedings.*

Swett, Scott. "Still Slandering the Troops." FrontPageMagazine.com. August 24, 2006.

Swiftvets.com

Symmes, Terry. "Swift Boat Veterans for Truth—Perspective from a Wife." Unpublished article. 2006.

Woods, Spec. 5 Randy. "VC Gunners Pounce on Cruising Swift Boats." *Stars and Stripes.* November 28, 1968.

Wright, Tom. "Meeting Report, Key Bridge, Marriott, Washington, D.C." Unpublished article, August 18, 2004.

Yost, Jr., Admiral Paul A., USCG, Ret. "Swift Boats: Hard Day on the Bo De." *Naval Institute Proceedings.* October 2004.

Public Documents

Federal Election Commission. *Conciliation Agreement (MURs 5511 and 5525).* December 13, 2006.

RECORDINGS:
    Bo De Run Firefight, Vietnam. November 24, 1968
    Rach Duong Keo Firefight, Vietnam. April 12, 1969.

Report on the Fitness of Officers: Capt. Roy F. Hoffmann
    1. 1 Oct 68 to 28 Feb 1969 by Vice ADM Elmo Zumwalt, Jr. USN
    2. 1 Mar 1969 to 9 May 1969 by Gen. Creighton W. Abrams USA
    3. 1 March 1970 to 26 June 1970 by RADM John D. Chase USN
    4. 27 June 1970 to 17 December 1970 by RADM J. B. Hildreth USN
    5. 13 Feb 1971 to 25 April 1971 by Capt. C. K. Moore USN
    6. 14 Feb 1971 to 25 April 1971 by RADM George C. Talby, Jr. USN
    7. 26 Apr 1971 to 15 Sept 1971 by RADM James B. Hildreth USN
    8. 15 Sept 1971 to 31 Jan 1972 by RADM Harry D. Train USN
    9. 15 Sept 1971 to 31 Jan 1972 by RADM J. B. Hildreth USN
    10. 25 May 1972 to 11 Sept 1972 by RADM W. O. Welander USN

U.S. Navy. *USS Pirate War Diary for the period of 14 August 1950 to 12 October 1950.* Naval Historical Center, Washington, D.C.

U.S. Navy. *Report of Loss of USS Pirate (AM-275).* Naval Historical Center, Washington, D.C.

U.S. Navy. *Report of Sinking of U.S.S. Pledge (Am 277) on 12 October, 1950.* Naval Historical Center, Washington, D.C.

U.S. Navy. *Log Book of the USS Harry Hubbard (DD-748).* 1 June 1951 to 30 June 1950.

U.S. Navy. *Log Book of the USS Walke (DD-723).* 1 June 1951 to 30 June 1951.

U.S. Navy. *Action Report Commander Destroyer Squadron 7 USS Walke War Damage.* 12 June 1951.

US. Navy *Report of Circumstances surrounding mining of USS Walke while operating with Task Force 77 in the Japan Sea.* 17 June 1951.

U.S. Navy. *Action Report Commander Carrier Division Five (Commander Task Force 77 Underwater contact.* 12–13 June 1951.

U.S. Navy. *Narrative Report of Circumstances Incident to mining of USS Walke morning of 12 June 1951 to 26 June 1951.*

U.S. Navy. *Coastal Division Eleven Command History.* 1 January 1968 to 31 December 1968 and 1 January 1969 to 31 December 1969.

U.S. Navy. *The U.S. Navy in Vietnam.* 1968.

U.S. Navy. *An Evaluation of the Coastal Surveillance Force (CTF 115) For the Third Quarter 1968.*

U.S. Navy. COMCOSURVFOR *Quarterly Evaluation Report.* 29 December 1968.

U.S. Navy *Commander Coastal Surveillance Force Operation Order.* 28 February 1969.

U.S. Navy. *Commander Coastal Surveillance Force (COMCOSURVFOR) Quarterly Evaluation Report.* 29 March 1969.

INDEX

Abrams, General Creighton 181, 182, 197, 198, 202, 203, 226, 261, 262, 325, 426, 514
Adams, Charles Francis 139
Adams, John and Mary Ellen 231
Agnew, Spiro 221, 366
Albert, Eddie 412
Aldrich, Gary 462
Alexich, Rear Admiral Milton P. 385
Alito, Samuel 491
Alston, David M. 265, 266, 275
Ambrose, Stephen 257, 328, 329, 367, 509
America's Cup 125, 126
American Expeditionary Force 4
American Patriot, by Robert Coram 342, 466, 509
Anderegg, John R. 180, 181
Anderson, EN2 Danny Lee 208
Andrea Doria 104
Andretta, Judge Robert A. 137, 139, 140, 143, 145, 147, 150, 153, 296–300, 507, 511
An Nhon 254
An Thoi 166, 175, 177, 178, 185, 187, 190, 191, 195, 204, 206, 207, 209, 210, 215, 220, 222, 224, 226, 232–234, 238, 242, 244–246, 248, 249, 251, 255–257, 260, 264, 265, 268, 278, 279, 282, 283, 286, 287, 292, 293, 302, 305, 307, 321, 376, 418, 427, 428, 439, 440, 468
antiwar movement ix, 14, 19, 20, 134, 139, 172, 179, 180, 188, 257, 278, 302, 323, 328, 334, 335, 338, 340–342, 346, 361, 365, 407, 415, 416, 423, 425, 428, 444, 452, 465, 466, 467, 471, 477
An Xugen Province 192, 195
Arceneaux, Alyssa 434
Arceneaux, Emily 434
Arceneaux, Mike 434
Arceneaux, Susan 433, 434, 448, 457, 458, 463, 480, 507
Armstrong, BM2 Daniel 234
Armstrong, Doug 206, 332
Armstrong, GMC2 Billy S. 180
Arp, EN3 Fred 292

Badoglio, Prime Minister Pietro 30
Baker, Rich 215, 234, 237
Barber, Sonny 296, 297, 298, 299, 511
Barker, Skip 263, 288, 304, 318, 319, 470
Barnicle, Mike 456
Barrow, Mr. 28
Bassac River 200, 210, 222, 224
Bataan Death March 23
Bates, George 207, 215, 220, 228, 229, 263, 264, 435
Bath Iron Works 104, 139, 339
Battle of Midway, 24
Battle of the Bulge 30, 83
Battle of the Coral Sea 24
Battleship Row 20
Bauer, Bob 474
Bay Hap River 215, 227, 228, 248, 251, 256, 263, 267, 269, 271, 275, 279, 288, 290
Bay of Nha Trang 293
Bay of Pigs 127, 360
BBC 448
Beeson, Morris S. 300
Bell-Davies, Vice Admiral 374
Belodeau, Radarman Thomas M. 181, 265, 266, 281
Ben Hai Raiders 174
Ben Hai River 174, 180, 219
Bergin, Edward J. 503
Bernique, Mike 191, 204, 208, 209, 210, 211, 212, 213, 214, 215, 220, 222, 224, 225, 226, 245, 246, 248, 249, 263, 278, 279, 281, 282, 302, 307, 423, 425, 428, 430, 468, 469, 470, 499, 507
Bernique's Creek 214, 215, 222, 245, 246, 249
Bernique's Run 208
Berrigan, Daniel 360
Bethany, Jack 129
Bien Hoa 97
Bien Nhan 284
Bihr, Captain Richard A. 336
Bill O'Reilly Show 448
Bing, Steven 446, 475
Binh Thuan 221

515

Black Aces 355, 357
Blasko, BM3 Peter P., Jr. 222
Blinn, Gary 153
Blitzer, Wolf 448
bloopy bags 86, 88
Bo De "Massacre" 231–242, 420
Bo De River 184, 216, 231, 232, 236, 257, 440
Bo De run 233, 243, 245
Bo Gui 263
Bonne Terre, Missouri 13, 36, 38, 42, 63
Boorda, Admiral 406
Borgnine, Ernest 84, 411–413
Bork, Robert 367
Boston Globe 435, 472, 512
Boston Navy Shipyard 121
Bowman, Frank 180, 181
Boyd, Captain Paul C. 329
Boyle, Judge James A. 332
Branch, Lieutenant Commander Alvin D. 132, 133, 363, 387, 503
Brant, Barbara 420, 421, 489
Brant, Commander Robert "Friar Tuck" 182–184, 192–195, 220, 222–225, 232, 233, 237, 238, 242, 243, 245–249, 254, 260, 263, 408, 409, 420, 421, 435, 440, 468, 469, 489, 507
Braun, Eva 31
Bredenko, BM3 Steve 253
Bridges, Captain Ken 385
Brinkley, Douglas ix, 161, 165, 181, 188, 195, 232, 242, 244, 253, 260, 265, 266, 267, 275, 278, 287, 290, 417, 418, 419, 421, 431, 456, 472, 479, 509, 511
Brockel, Harry C. 399
Broder, David 334
Bronson, Charles 412
Brooks, Commander Clarence "Breezy" 92–94
Brooks Army Medical Center 497
Brown, Lieutenant David C. 185
Brown, Lieutenant Mike 203, 204, 213, 214
Brown, RD2 Anthony B. 253
Brown's Run 204, 216
Bryan, Rear Admiral Louis A. 108
Buckley, William F. 346
Buell, Susie 475
Buie, GMG3 Roger 196
Buis, Major Dale 97
Bulkeley, Vice Admiral John D. 72–76, 362
BUPERS (Bureau of Naval Personnel) 35, 85, 98–103, 152, 348, 426, 504, 509

Burkett, B. G. "Jug" 338, 340, 342, 425, 428–431, 509, 512
Burns, Lieutenant Commander Harry A. 10, 61, 62, 82, 83, 511
Bush, President George W. 415, 416, 421–423, 428, 433–436, 442, 445, 452, 458, 465, 471–476, 478, 479, 482, 483
Butterfield, Alexander 366
Byer, Commander Bob 94

C-SPAN 442
Cai Lon River 222
Cai Nhap 271, 285
Cai Nuoc 227, 229, 230, 248, 263, 265, 267, 271, 275, 279, 288, 290, 302
Calley, Lieutenant William 333
Ca Mau 175, 187, 191, 192, 202, 216, 217, 222, 232, 249, 251, 261, 262, 264, 265, 268, 272, 302
Cambodia 198, 202, 210, 212, 222, 225, 254, 295, 303, 376, 415, 440, 454, 474
Campbell, Captain Don 344, 345, 351, 359, 362, 507
Cam Ranh Bay 160, 163–166, 168, 176, 183, 188, 190, 201, 206, 226, 244, 249, 257, 267, 271, 276, 277, 279, 283, 296, 321, 323, 326, 327, 375, 385, 417, 427, 438
Cam Thanh Island 298
Ca Na Salt Flats 265
Cape Batangan 175, 249
Carnahan, Christine Linn Hoffmann 70, 157, 295, 371, 401, 410, 443, 507
Carnahan, Erin 402, 413
Carnahan, Kalin 402, 413
Carnahan, Ralph 367, 401
Carnahan, Steve 367, 371, 401, 413
Carroll, Steve 308, 510
Carson, Johnny 29
Carter, Commander James 450
Carter, President Jimmy 96, 108, 369, 378, 380, 470
Carville, James 481
Castro, Fidel 76, 96, 127, 129, 130
Cat Lo 184, 192, 193, 194, 202, 206, 215, 222, 244, 258, 260, 264, 265, 348, 427, 440
Cavett, Dick viii, 346, 416
CBS 431, 437, 441, 471, 478
Chandler, BM2 Anthony G. 180
Charleston Naval Shipyard 33, 142, 385, 389, 390
Chase, Rear Admiral John D. 336, 337, 514
Chau Doc 210

Chenoweth, Jack 287, 290–292, 307, 308, 315, 317, 323, 435, 448, 449, 455, 490, 503, 507
Chiang Kai-shek 41, 208
Chicago Tribune 479
Chin, Truong 333
Chu Lai 172, 173, 175, 181, 196, 221, 243
Church, Frank 303
Churchill, Winston 14–16, 30, 262, 339
CINCPAC (Commander in Chief Pacific) 161, 504
Clark, Commodore 94
Clark, Wesley 416
Clark Air Base 366
Clayton, QM2 David 118, 204, 512
Clinton administration 407, 433, 462, 481
CNN 442, 448, 459, 462
Coastal Group 14 300
Coastal Group 16 175
Coastal Surveillance Force 166, 325, 337, 507, 514
Co Chien River 202, 251, 252, 254
Coffin, Reverend William Sloan 180, 360
Colbus, Captain Louis 105, 209, 507
Colmes, Alan 448
COMA (Court of Military Appeals) 378, 383, 384, 386, 513
COMCARDIV 362
COMCOSRON One 249, 417
COMCRUDESFLOT Eight 348, 363
COMCRUDESFLOT Four 336
COMCRUDESLANT Battle Efficiency "E" 346
Commander Robert R. Monroe 137
COMNAVFORV (Commander of Naval Forces Vietnam) 165, 182, 200, 219, 253, 504
COMUSMACV 181, 182, 504
Cone, J. I. 91
Cook, MCPO Kenneth R. 385
Cooke, Cardinal Terrence 137
Coolidge, Bill 12
Cooper, John Sherman 36, 38, 80, 303
Cordier, Ken viii, 449, 464
Coronado, California vii, 7, 153, 161, 163, 173, 178, 183, 187, 188, 190, 206, 209, 210, 234, 305, 308, 496
Corsi, Jerome R. "Jerry" 301, 338, 341, 346, 376, 415, 432, 436, 444, 447, 510
COS DIV 11 (Coastal Division 11) 175, 181, 185, 198, 214–216, 232, 234, 254, 255, 287, 376, 425, 427, 439, 440
COS DIV 13 (Coastal Division 13) 215, 251, 254, 261, 348, 427, 440

COS DIV 15 (Coastal Division 15) 222
Coset, Lieutenant Albert W. 77
COSRON ONE (Coastal Squadron One) 166
Costello, Captain Terrance W., USN, Ret. 37, 187, 188, 191, 203, 204, 207, 208, 214, 224–226, 232–237, 243, 251, 256, 257, 261–263, 269, 271, 275, 276, 278, 279, 281, 284–286, 300, 301, 305, 307, 311, 323, 435, 503, 508
Cox, Archibald 73, 367
CRC (Creative Response Concepts) 449, 450, 451, 480
Cromwell, Captain John Philip 104
Crosby, Bob 215, 263
Crow, Brooke 413
Crow, Emilie Hoffmann 92, 157–159, 326, 371, 383, 410, 411, 413, 462, 508
Crow, Rory 413
Cruz, EN2 Edward C. 180
Crystal City, Missouri 5, 6, 25, 282, 374, 401, 410
Crystal City Works Nine 5
Cua Dai River 296, 297, 511
Cua Lon River 179, 192, 203, 204, 215, 216, 222, 232, 251, 255, 262, 263, 265, 267, 269, 271, 276, 284–286, 292, 301
Cuba 4, 96, 127–131, 360, 410
Cuban Missile Crisis 84, 127, 128, 210
Cullen, Leslie J. 197, 200, 203, 512
Cullman, Lewis 475
Culver, Captain John A., USNR, Ret. 75, 76, 126, 381, 508
Cummings, Lieutenant Commander E. J., Jr. 104
Current, D. C. 184, 253, 296, 363, 511
Cybulski, Radarman Gregory 187, 237, 284, 285

D-Day 30, 73, 74, 412
D'Amico, Matt 137, 143, 145, 148, 149, 151, 153, 427, 508
Dam Doi 232, 263, 265, 275, 280
Dam Dong Cung (VC Lake) 214
Da Nang 166, 172, 173, 175, 183, 186, 221, 243, 275, 296, 300, 338, 426
Dang, Toi 92, 175, 376
Davis, Boatswain's Mate 187
Davis, John Hart 503
Davis, Lieutenant j.g. John 180, 181
DAWN PATROL 354
Day, Colonel George "Bud" viii, 342, 466, 479, 481, 485, 508

DCI Group 446
Deal, Jim 488
Dean, Howard 416, 467
Dean, John III 366
DeLoach, SCPO Grady E., Jr. 503
Democratic National Convention 451, 454
Democratic Party, Democrats 71, 72, 91, 172, 188, 360, 365, 367, 400, 415–417, 446, 451, 467, 475, 491
DESFLOT TWO 85–88, 104
Deutermann, Rear Admiral Harold E. "Dutch" 86, 90
Dauntless 24
Devastator 24
Dewey Canyon III 340, 342
Dewey Rifle 221
Diachenko 51
Dick Cavett Show viii, 346, 416
DiMaggio, Joe 19, 82
Dobrynin, Anatoly 127
Dobson, Ralph 245, 246, 247, 263
Dodson, Paul 278
Dole, Senator Bob 473
Donahue, Dr. Lieutenant j.g. 67
Dong, Premier Pham Van 333, 334
Dong Cung Canal 214, 253, 279, 288, 290
Dong Ha 177
Donitz, Admiral 108
Doolittle, Lieutenant Colonel James H. 23, 24
Doolittle's Raiders 23
Doyle, Jerry 448
Drake, Lieutenant j.g. Robert 110, 111, 183
Drew, Bill 244, 400
Droz, Don 278–281, 286–288, 290, 291, 305–307, 311, 319, 323
Droz, Judy 323
Drudge Report 442, 456, 457, 469
Duan, Le 333
Duclap 186
Dudley, Bill 105, 111, 116, 123, 131, 508

Eagleton, Thomas 442
Edwards, John 416, 451, 452, 455
Ehrichman, John 366
Eisenhower, General Dwight D., President 29, 30, 31, 71–73, 79, 85, 91, 97, 329, 414
Elder, Larry 448
Elder, Lieutenant j.g. Robert G. "Bob" viii, 204–208, 220, 228, 232, 234, 238, 249, 250, 254, 261–263, 267–269, 276–278, 323, 419, 435, 436, 438, 448, 449, 455, 456, 463, 483, 484, 486, 489, 508

Elliott, Captain George M., USN, Ret. 185, 187, 207, 211, 212, 220, 222, 224, 225, 232, 233, 238, 260, 261, 263, 279, 418, 435, 439, 441, 443, 455, 490, 508
Elliott, Trenny 185, 461, 489
Engen, Vice Admiral Donald 350, 362, 377
Enola Gay 32
Erwin, Virgil A. III 25, 206, 306–308, 312, 314, 315, 317, 318, 323, 503, 508, 512
Exley, Zack 474

Falkland Islands 117
Farragut, Admiral 47
Fates, Lieutenant Dick 356
FEC (Federal Election Commission) 415, 434, 473, 491, 492, 493
Feingold, Russ 433, 493
Feller, Bob 82, 83
Fighter Squadron 41 355
Flat River, Missouri 32
Fonda, Jane 188, 338, 360–362, 415, 422, 465, 478
Fontaine, E. P. 107
Foote, Lieutenant Commander 34
Ford, Captain John 72
Ford, President Gerald (Vice President) 36, 366, 369
Foreman, EN2 Don 196
Fortas, Supreme Court Justice Abe 328
FOX 269, 431, 432, 448, 459, 464, 478
Franke, Ruth 441, 464, 489, 508
Franke, William E. "Bill" 243, 423, 425, 427, 428, 430, 432, 441, 442, 444–447, 449, 450, 456, 460, 464, 465, 466, 475, 476, 480, 485, 489, 503, 508
French, Al 455
Frick, Rear Admiral J. F. 36, 393
Frondizi, Arturo 116
Fulbright, J. William 340, 467
Fultz, EN2 David E. 245
Furman, Mark 448

Gable, Clark 36, 38, 412
Galanti, Commander Paul, USN, Ret. viii, 185, 341, 464–468, 473, 483, 484, 508, 512
Gallagher, Mike 448
Game Warden 165
Ganh Hao 264, 265
Gann, Mike 449
Gardner, Marsha 489

Index   519

Gardner, Stephen M. "Steve" 244, 432, 435, 440, 448, 449, 489, 490
Garlow, Bill 406
Garrett, Lester D. "Les" 308, 503
Gehman, Admiral Harold W. 173, 499
Gephardt, Richard 416
Giap, General Vo Nguyen 333, 361
Gilbert, Frank 256, 263
Gilbertson, GMG3 Larry Wayne 208, 250
Ginsberg, Benjamin L. "Ben" 445, 446, 463, 471, 474, 475, 492, 493, 508, 512
Ginsberg, Joanne 445
Go Cong River 251
Goff, GM2 259, 260
Golburg, QM2 196
Golden, Ken 245
Goodall, Senator Charles 334
Gorham, Cecile Hoffmann 81, 144, 157–160, 403, 404, 411, 413, 422, 425, 508
Gorham, Pete 413
Gorham, Seth 413
Gorham, Todd 413
Gravely, Vice Admiral Samuel L. Jr. 29
Gray, L. Patrick 366
Great Crash 7
Great Depression 7, 8, 10, 11, 12, 37, 73
Green, Arthur 28
Green, MCPO Charles 503
Guantanamo, Gitmo 76, 129, 143, 144, 145
Guinness, Alec 412
Gulf of Thailand 175, 210, 217, 264, 301
Gulf of Thailand Surveillance Group 175, 301
Gunther, Francis L. "Skip" 173, 175, 181, 195, 196, 508

Hahn, Bob 444, 445, 447
Haiphong 332, 360, 373
Haldeman, H. R. 366, 369
Halsey, Vice Admiral William F. "Bull" 23, 24, 32
Ham Luong River 202, 251, 264
Hannity, Sean 442, 448
Hannity and Colmes 448
Hanoi 176, 328, 332–334, 341, 360, 361, 465, 466, 479, 512
Hanoi Hanna 465
Hanson, Alex 413, 510
Hanson, Hilarie Hoffmann 86, 157–159, 230, 295, 326, 383, 402, 410, 411, 413, 422, 425, 462, 508
Hanson, Jack 413
Hanson, Kelsey 413

Harrison, George (AFL/CIO) 144
Hart, Gary 442
Hart, Gene 237
Hartkemeyer, EN2 J. R. 253
Hartman, Lieutenant Commander Don 312, 321
Harwood, Lieutenant j.g. James "Jim" 204, 206, 207, 234, 237, 238, 239, 241, 243, 323
Hatch, BM Steve 244
Ha Tien 177, 207, 210, 211, 215, 222, 224, 246, 249, 256, 275, 302, 487
Ha Tien/Rach Gia canal 215
Hatler, Curtis D. 503
Hayden, Tom 188, 360
Hayes, Steve 406
Hayward, Admiral Thomas, USN, Ret. 392, 393, 508
Heinz, Teresa 408, 409
Hemenway, David Robert 191, 209, 210, 211, 212, 214, 220, 305, 307, 310, 318, 321, 499, 508
Henderson, Rear Admiral G. R. 65
Hensley, BMSN Howard 208, 250
Heritage, Thomas M. II 503
Hewitt, J. Kent 105, 106, 111, 115, 125, 130, 131, 508
Hibbard, Grant "Skip" 257, 435, 438, 449, 455, 474, 489
Hickam Field 20
Hickey, Commander Ed 356
Hildreth, Rear Admiral James B. 347, 514
Hildreth, Robert W. "Rocky" 191, 263, 265, 275, 337, 349, 350, 408, 435, 455, 488, 490, 503
Hitler, Adolf 8, 12–15, 17, 19, 31, 334
Hoa Lo 361
Ho Chi Minh 169, 188, 200, 208, 233, 257, 261, 333, 376
Ho Chi Minh Trail 169
Hodge, Alan J. 249
Hoffa, Jimmy 142
Hoffman, David 361
Hoffmann, Frederick Herman 3
Hoffmann, Hannah Mary 3, 4
Hoffmann, Harriet Ann 42, 63, 64, 68, 70, 71, 81, 98, 105, 133, 136, 157, 158, 231, 371, 401, 404, 410, 411
Hoffmann, Juanita 6
Hoffmann, Mary Linn Thompson 6, 8, 12, 13, 18, 23, 28, 32, 33, 37, 38, 42, 43, 56, 57, 61, 63, 64, 68, 70, 71, 81, 86, 93, 98, 104, 105, 128, 131, 137, 138, 144,

148, 157–161, 230, 231, 264, 326, 327, 363, 369, 371, 379, 386, 391, 401, 403, 407–411, 419, 422, 425, 443, 461, 463, 479, 480, 483, 489, 496, 499
Hoffmann, Paul Ivan 6
Hoffmann, Rear Admiral Roy F., USN, Ret.
  Early Life 6–25
  World War II 25–33
  USS *Quick* (DD 490) 33–35
  Civilian to Korean War 35–42
  USS *Pirate* (AM 275) 43–57
  USS *Harry E. Hubbard* (DD 748) 58–68
  NROTC, Illinois Tech. 80–84
  DESFLOT TWO 85–90
  USS *Lloyd Thomas* (DD 764) 91–98
  BUPERS 98–103
  USS *Cromwell* (DE 1014) 104–133
  Naval War College 133–137
  USS *Charles F. Adams* (DDG 2) 137–153
  CTF 115 157–326
  USS *Sierra* (AD 18) 327–337
  USS *Leahy* (DLG 16) 337–363
  Head, Current Plans Branch 363–367
  Director Surface Warfare 367–368
  Commander Mine Warfare 369–377
  Commandant Sixth Naval Dist./
    Commander Charleston
    Naval Base 378–393
  Port of Milwaukee 397–402
  Port of Richmond 402–410
  SBVFT 414–493
  Hoffmann Foundation 494–497
Hoffmann, Roy Walter 3, 4, 5, 8, 25, 401
Hoffmann, Zettamae Pruneau 4, 5, 6, 28, 401
Hoffmann Foundation v, 242, 495, 496, 507–509
Hofheinz, Judge Roy 147
Hoi An 296, 297
Hollister, GMG3 Earl N. 292
Holloway, Admiral James L. III 375, 378, 392
Holloway, QM3 Thomas 310
Hon Tam Island 293
Hon Tre Island 265
Hoole, Lieutenant William B. 263
Hornberger, Robert 209, 210, 212, 214, 287, 291, 305, 307, 311, 316, 318, 321, 499, 508
Horne, Andy 418, 423, 425, 427, 430, 437, 448, 449, 489
Horne, Commander Charles F. "Chuck" 249, 417
Horne, Sylvia 427, 489

Horrell, BM3 Gerald R. 256
Hortt, Lawrence 307, 310, 508
Hubbard, Al 338
Hubbard, Commander Harry E. 62
Hue 175, 186
Hughes, Engineman Richard 187
Human Events Online 457
Humphrey, Vice President Hubert 36, 38, 179, 188, 219, 221
Hunt, E. Howard 360
Hurricane Electric 445
Hyatt, Lieutenant Commander Bruce 44, 49, 51, 52, 57

Ickes, Harold 474
Inchon Harbor 46
Ingraham, Laura 442, 448
Inland Straits 111
Investor's Business Daily 442
IUWG ONE (Inshore Undersea Warfare Group One) 168
Iwo Jima 31, 343, 425, 464

Janet Parshall's America 448
Jerry Doyle Show 448
Joe Pratte 37
Johnson, President Lyndon B. 134, 188, 203, 217, 221
Jones, EN2 Lloyd 307
Jordan, Captain Watt W., Jr. 363
Jordan, Jim 474
Judicial Watch 448

kamikaze 30, 62, 343
Keith, Brian 412
Keith, Rear Admiral Robert Taylor Scott 86
Kennedy, President John F. 1, 76, 84, 102, 127, 128, 134, 182, 332, 362, 418, 510
Kennedy, Robert F. 29, 127
Kennedy, Senator Edward 332, 360, 416, 470
Kerrey, Robert "Bob" 265, 293, 294, 295, 327, 510
Kerry, Senator John vii–x, 161, 188, 226, 244, 248, 251, 254, 257, 259, 261, 262, 266, 267, 275, 279–282, 286, 287, 290–292, 295, 301, 334, 336, 338–342, 346, 365, 376, 385, 405, 407, 408, 413–418, 420–422, 424, 428–430, 432, 433, 435–440, 444, 450–453, 455, 461, 464, 468, 469, 471, 473, 474, 477–483, 491, 492, 511, 513
Kerry/Edwards campaign 459

Kesselring, Edward E. 209, 214, 499, 508
Key Bridge Marriott Meeting 459
Khrushchev, Nikita 84, 91, 97, 127, 129
Kidd, Rear Admiral Isaac C. 342
Kidd, Vice Admiral Isaac C. "Ike", Jr. 342, 343, 374, 379, 380
Kim Il Sung 41
Kimmel, Admiral Husband E. 22
King, Martin Luther, Jr. 85, 142, 160, 179
King Neptune, the Imperial Ruler of the Raging Main 110
Kirby, Carrie Arceneaux 434
Kissinger, Henry 262, 332, 365, 368
Kittle, Ernest J. "Bud" 498, 503
Kloor, Harry 480
Knutson, EN3 Wade 209, 214
Kobe 24, 57
Kolbe, Jim 406
Kopechne, Mary Jo 332
Koppel, Ted 478, 479
Korean War 7, 41, 42, 44, 47, 50, 57, 63, 64, 65, 68, 70, 71, 79, 83, 165, 334, 362, 425, 512
Kranish, Michael 435, 512

LaCivita, Chris 446, 447, 449, 451, 452, 453–456, 464, 476, 477, 480, 508
LaCivita-Reed 477
Lam, Nguyen 265
Lamberson, Richard 280
Lambert Field 28, 43
Landon, Alf 13
Langhofer, BM2 Wayne D. 307, 316
Lannom, Anne 427
Lannom, William "Bill" 423, 425, 427, 430, 503
LANTREADEX 350
Laos 254, 303, 376
Last Battle of Vietnam, The 478
Last River Run, The 405, 409
Leahy, Fleet Admiral William D. 339
LeMay, General Curtis 34
Lemmon, Jack 29, 97
Letson, Dr. Louis "Lou" 257, 448, 449, 455, 474, 477, 508
Lewis, Peter 446
Leyte Island 30
Lezar, Tex 424
Liddy, G. Gordon 360
Lieberman, Joe 416
Limbaugh, Rush 442, 449
Little Creek Amphibious Base 152
Lodge, Ambassador Henry Cabot 134

Lohnes, Michael "Mike" 307, 508
Long Tau River 165
Lonsdale, Captain Adrian, USCG, Ret. 168, 175, 177, 178, 186, 207, 217, 301, 302, 305, 439, 449, 455, 489, 503, 508
Los Angeles Times 22, 479
Louis Sicka 37
Lucovich, Gunner's mate 187
Lukasiewicz, Gunner's mate Paul 237
Luke, Steve 195, 224, 245, 247, 248, 249

Mabery, Pat 13
Mabery, Terry 13
MacArthur, General Douglas 23, 30, 32, 35, 41, 46, 58, 59, 65, 73
Madam Nhu "Dragon Lady" 134
Mahan, Captain Alfred 133
Mariano, Frank 233, 234
Marion, David P. 252, 254, 255, 503
Marshall, Missouri 29, 31
Martin, Jinny 499, 508
Matras, Donald W. 503
McAuliffe, General Anthony 30
McCabe, Sean 479
McCain, Admiral John S., Jr. 161, 163
McCain, Senator John 161, 163, 361, 433, 456, 457, 479, 493, 510
McCain-Feingold Act of 2002; 527 Organizations 433, 434, 446, 457, 458, 463, 474, 475, 492, 493
McCann, Rich 263, 275, 288, 304
McCarthy, Senator Eugene 172, 179
McCauley, Rear Admiral Brian 373
McChord Air Force Base 332
McCreight, Captain M. I. III 386
McDermott, BM2 John P. 195
McElwain, Commander Harry W. 49
McGhee, Captain Kenneth B. 488, 503
McGinley, William J. "Bill" 463
McGovern, Senator George 331, 335, 365, 442, 467
McGowan, QM3 Robert "Mac" 234, 235, 236, 239, 241, 243
McKenney, ET2 Norman L. 253
McMullen, Lieutenant Cornelius E. 43, 44, 50, 52, 56, 57
McNamara, Defense Secretary Robert 142
Meany, George 144
Medeiros, QM2 Michael 245, 265, 281
Meehan, Daniel E. 399, 402, 403, 409, 410, 508
Meehan, Marty 433
Meenan, RM2 Thomas J. 253

Mehlman, Ken 472
Meier, Henry 399, 400
Mekong Delta 165, 200, 202, 223, 234, 242, 288, 293, 309, 432
Merrill, David 221
Michael Savage Show 448
Midway 24, 25, 64, 69, 91, 210
Miller, Commander Chuck 264
Miller, Rear Admiral William O. 384
Miller, Stephen A., RD2 307
Miller, William 307
Mine Warfare Force 44, 47, 50, 369, 371, 374, 376, 377, 381, 384, 508, 509, 512
Minh, Duong Van 375
Mitchell, John 366
Mobile Riverine Force 165, 506
Modansky, RD3 Michael S. 307, 308, 316, 321, 508
Mohammed, Admiral Mohammed Ali 374
Mohn, Chuck 308
Monger, Rear Admiral Albert J. 384, 389, 390
Monroe, Commander Robert R. 137
Montagnards 376
Montgomery, Mike "Mugsy" 308
Montgomery, Robert 72
Moore, Admiral 406
Moore, Captain C. K. 344, 514
Moorer, Admiral Thomas H. 155, 200, 380
Morris, Dick 456, 477
Morris, Lieutenant j.g. William T. 253
Morris, Rear Admiral Tom 381
Moveon.org 459, 474, 492
Moynihan, Daniel Patrick 29, 405
Moynihan, Martin J. 405
MSNBC 456, 459, 481
Mueller, Greg 450, 451, 476
Murphy, Audie 412
Murphy, B. Franklin 37
Mussolini, Benito 15, 29
My Lai 333
My Tho 254

Nagasaki 32
Nagoya 24
Nagumo, Admiral 19, 20, 24
Nam Can 216, 265, 285, 302
National Press Club 436, 449
Naval Medical Center 497
Naval War College 131, 133, 176
NAVFORV 190, 203, 224, 261
NBC 431, 437, 478

New Deal 13
Newport, Rhode Island 107, 121, 125, 133, 209, 345, 427
Newport News, Virginia 5
New Soldier, The, by John Kerry 444
New York Times 333, 347, 472, 479
Ngo Dinh Diem 134
Ngo Dinh Nhu 134
Nha Trang 166, 168, 265, 293, 294
Nhung Mien 284
Nicholson, Commander Richard 326
Nickerson, Lieutenant Commander R. B. 33
Nightline 478
Nimitz, Admiral Chester 20, 33
Ninh Thuan 221
Nitze, Paul 200
Niven, David 412
Nixon, President Richard M. 60, 71, 91, 97, 134, 179, 182, 219, 221, 226, 257, 295, 303, 328, 329, 332, 334, 335, 347, 360, 365–369, 375, 392, 393, 509
Nolan, Greg 105, 106, 109, 112–115, 119, 508
Norton, Ken 426
Novak, Bob 457
NPR 448
NROTC 31, 33, 80, 187, 305, 374
Nutt, Captain Tom 161

O'Connor, Father John Joseph 136, 137
O'Donnell, Lawrence 481
O'Mara, Richard 449
O'Neill, Anne viii, 416, 417, 489
O'Neill, Brian 425
O'Neill, Diane viii
O'Neill, Ed 425
O'Neill, John E. v, viii, 287, 296, 301, 338, 341, 346, 376, 415–417, 419, 423–434, 436, 437, 441, 442, 444, 445–451, 454–457, 459–461, 464, 475–477, 479–485, 488–490, 495, 497, 503, 508, 510, 513
O'Reilly, Bill 448
Obama, Barack 452
Odell, Van H. 290, 291, 420, 448, 449, 452, 455, 461, 480, 488, 490, 495, 503, 508
Olwin, Lieutenant Jim 356
Operation Bold Dragon 251
Operation Foul Deck 222
Operation Giant Slingshot 202
Operation Market Time 161, 162, 164–171, 173, 174, 178, 182, 184, 188, 201,

Index 523

242, 256, 258, 264, 265, 276, 293, 296, 302, 324, 325, 437, 439, 440, 507
Operation Stable Door 168
Operation Swift Kick 181
Operation Unitos II 107, 108
Osaka 24
Oswald, Lee Harvey 134
Ovnard, Master Sergeant Chester 97

PACs (Political Action Committees) 434
Pagano, Sylvester "Syl" 12
Panama Canal 105, 108, 109, 110, 397
Paris Peace Talks 172, 179, 217, 261
Parks, Rosa 85
Parshall, Janet 448
Parsons, Charles 37
Pathy, Laddy 410
Patton, George S. 25, 149, 220, 263
Patton Boggs, LLP 445, 447, 463
PCF 3 181, 192, 209, 210, 212, 215, 222, 224, 272, 287, 290–293, 308, 432, 461, 474
PCF 5 181, 191, 192, 228–230, 249, 263, 265, 267, 268, 271, 275, 283, 284, 304, 310, 317–319
PCF 6 256, 262, 263
PCF 9 204, 215, 271, 284, 310, 318, 319
PCF 10 181, 271–273
PCF 11 214
PCF 12 181, 275
PCF 13 249
PCF 15 275
PCF 19 180, 181
PCF 21 173, 174, 196, 256, 262, 263, 275, 304, 310, 312
PCF 23 270, 271, 273, 279, 280, 283, 286, 287, 290, 308
PCF 24; 288, 300
PCF 27 181
PCF 28 215, 271
PCF 31 222. 234–236, 238, 239, 240, 243, 262, 271, 272, 275, 304, 310, 318, 319
PCF 32 215
PCF 36 184, 195, 215, 220, 222, 224, 245, 246, 247, 249, 250
PCF 37 275, 427
PCF 38 181, 187, 203, 204, 214, 224, 233, 237, 243, 251, 269, 271, 275, 284, 300, 311, 321
PCF 43 204, 205, 207, 220, 228, 249, 250, 267, 269, 271, 272, 276, 278–280, 286, 287, 290, 291, 303, 305–308, 310–312, 314, 316, 317–323, 436

PCF 44 170, 244, 271, 272, 275, 276, 432
PCF 45 310
PCF 50 207, 214–216, 220, 222, 228, 256, 262, 264, 267, 269, 275
PCF 51 286, 287, 310
PCF 53 271, 287, 291
PCF 56 263
PCF 58 296, 297
PCF 60 271, 272
PCF 66 253, 263, 275
PCF 67 308, 314
PCF 70 221, 275
PCF 71 253, 256, 262, 263, 267, 272, 274, 275
PCF 72 187, 222, 234, 237, 239, 243, 263, 265, 267, 275
PCF 75 249
PCF 79 249, 275
PCF 80 249, 263
PCF 81 275
PCF 82 228, 230, 234, 237, 238, 243
PCF 86 253
PCF 88 245, 247
PCF 89 222
PCF 93 181, 187, 214, 215, 232, 233, 243, 256, 262, 263, 265, 275, 308, 428
PCF 94 viii, 174, 214–216, 256, 262, 263, 265, 266, 275, 279, 280, 286–288, 290, 291, 295, 301, 308, 432
PCF 95 263
PCF 98 195, 260
PCF 99 275, 300
PCF 101 296, 297, 300
PCF 103 215, 271, 272, 308
Pearl Harbor 18–24, 34, 42, 63, 69, 82, 161, 187, 256, 342, 348, 389, 413
Peck, Edward "Tedd" 181, 244, 245, 265, 266, 267, 301, 435
Pees, Richard W. "Dick" viii, 287, 290, 291, 292, 489, 503
Pennington, B. D. 50
Peron, Gerealissimo Juan Domingo 116
Peron, Maria Eva Duarte de 116
Perry, Bob 447, 482, 492
Pershing, "Black Jack" 4
Pfeffer, Bill 297, 298, 300
Pfeiffer, Gerald (Jerry) 12
Pfeiffer, James 12
Phu Quoc Island 175, 176, 254
Pickens, T. Boone 447, 454, 480, 482, 492, 497
Pittsburgh Plate Glass Company 5
Plain of Reeds 256
Pleasance, Donald 412

Plumly, Captain Charley, USN, Ret. 183, 188–190, 261, 267, 326, 383, 419, 420, 425, 428, 430, 437, 449, 460, 463, 483, 489, 503, 508
Plumly, Sibyl Ann Middleton 188, 190, 489
Pochel, Gerald "Pooch" 193, 194
Political Compliance Services, Inc. 433, 434
Poncho 108
Ponder, Joseph L. "Joe" viii, 232, 234–236, 239, 240–243, 270, 435, 438, 449, 455, 481, 488, 489, 490, 495, 496, 503, 508
Ponder, Rebecca 489
Port of Milwaukee 397, 398, 399, 402
Port of Richmond 399, 402, 403, 405, 409
Pratte, Joe 37
Price, Rear Admiral Walter 86–89, 165, 202
Pruett, BM2 224
Pruneau, Leo 4, 5, 9
Prysock, Fred S. 184, 224, 243, 245, 247
Pstrak, Captain Theodore W. 386, 387
PT boat 72, 73, 74, 76, 102, 196
Pusan, South Korea 42, 45, 46
Putnam, Captain Orlin N. 342, 343

Quang Nam 263
Quang Tri 180, 186, 360
QUICKDRAW 352
Qui Nhon 166, 168, 185, 264, 275, 308

Rabel, Charles R. "Chuck" 503
Rach Ba Thanh 271
Rach Cai Bai 254
Rach Duong Keo 204, 271, 272, 301, 303, 304, 305, 307, 308, 323, 325, 513
Rach Gia 215, 222, 224, 302
Rach Giang Thanh 204, 208, 209, 210, 214, 238, 244, 249, 428
Rach Nang 272
Rach Nuong 271
Rach Ong Quyen 271
Rach Soi (canal) 224
Rach Soi (town of) 224
Rainbow Division (U.S. Army) 3
Ramsey Clark 360, 361, 465
Rassmann, Lieutenant Jim 287, 289, 291, 432, 452
Ratcliff, GMGSN Vern E. 245
Rather, Dan 478
Rathergate 478
Ray, James Earl 179

Ray, QM2 R. H. 196
Read, Vice Admiral William L., USN, Ret. 389, 390, 391, 508
Reagan, Michael 448
Reagan, President Ronald 36, 80, 117, 367, 414, 424
Reass, Captain Dick, USN, Ret. 374, 508
Rectanus, Vice Admiral Earl "Rex" 29, 196, 197, 200–203, 243, 419, 426, 435, 461, 470, 499, 508
Reed, Lieutenant Commander Charles 137, 145
Reed, Ralph 450
Reed, Rick 449
Rehnquist, Justice William H. viii, 426
Reid, Lieutenant Ken 356
Reid, Sandy 503
Republican Party; Republicans; 13, 72, 182, 415, 441, 456, 473, 477
Rhee, President Syngman 46
Rice, Donna 442
Richardson, Bill 451, 474
Richardson, Elliot 367
Richardson, GMG3 David L. 245
Ridgway, Lieutenant General Matthew 65
Risner, Robbie 465
River Assault Force 165
Rivero, Admiral Horacio "Rivets" 352, 353
Rogers, William R. 503
Rokowski, Ernie 125
Rommel, Field Marshal Erwin 25
Romney, George 442, 445
Rood, Bill 279–281, 286, 287, 468
Roosevelt, President Franklin D. 13, 16–20, 23, 25, 30, 31, 50, 60, 110, 339, 350, 356–359
Rosenberg, Julius and Ethel 79
Rowdy 77
Roxe, Joe 105, 107, 113, 114, 115, 116, 117, 131, 508
Rumsfeld, Donald 423
Rung Sat Special Zone 165
Russell, Mike 450, 451, 453, 456, 459, 464, 475, 476, 508
Russell, Paul Edward 450
Rutherford, Lucy 31

Sadat, Anwar 368
Saigon 172, 176, 183, 184, 186, 187, 188, 190, 196, 197, 198, 202, 206, 210, 212, 214, 215, 219, 222, 224, 225, 226, 233, 242, 256, 257, 260, 261, 263, 267, 283, 328, 375, 432

Salzer, Robert S. 165
Sammon, Bill 472, 511
Sanders, Wade 260, 407, 408, 430, 431, 435, 436
Sandler, Joe 474
Sandusky, QM1 Del 245, 265, 266, 281
Sanford, Jimmy 209, 212, 214, 499, 509
Sasebo, Japan 44, 45, 49, 64, 68
Savage, Michael 448
SBSA (Swift Boat Sailors Association) 237, 242, 307, 410, 420, 498, 499
SBVFT (Swift Boat Veterans for Truth, Swift Boat Veterans and POWs for Truth) v, 208, 269, 414–416, 418, 420, 422, 429, 431, 433–435, 440–449, 451–453, 455–462, 464, 465, 467–485, 488–493, 495, 506–509, 513
Schachte, Rear Admiral William, USN, Ret. 385, 387, 417, 430, 489, 509
Schermerhorn, Captain 165
Scott, George C. 412
SEALORDS (Southeast Asia Lake, Ocean, River and Delta Strategy) 161, 197, 198, 200, 202, 203, 210, 215, 216, 221, 223, 226, 231, 236, 243, 244, 253, 255, 256, 260, 285, 286, 302, 307, 309, 325, 438, 506
SEALs 165, 168, 169, 178, 217, 464, 506
Sea of Japan 46, 47
Seawolves (Navy UH-1B Iroquois "Huey" helicopters) 169, 203, 222, 232, 233, 247, 307–309, 312, 314–318, 320, 321, 506
Sedlacek, Marvin 269, 271
Semmes, Rear Admiral B. J. 98
Seven Mountains 224
Shamley, Jack 210, 232, 233, 234, 235, 236, 240, 509
Sharpton, Al 416
Shays, Chris 433
Sheedy, Commander Pat, USN, Ret. 137, 143, 144, 146, 149, 152, 153, 191, 264, 279, 296, 307, 322, 383, 435, 509
Sherwood, Carlton 341, 477, 513
Shirley, Robert B. 296, 307, 509
Short, Fred 266, 275, 280, 281, 286, 509
Short, Lieutenant General Walter C. 22
Shumadine, Commander William, USN, Ret. 190–192, 228–230, 243, 248–250, 261, 263, 283, 284, 304, 305, 307, 310–312, 316–319, 418, 435, 439, 509, 513
Sicka, Louis 37
Sihanouk, Prince 212

Simmons, Harold 482
Simon, BM3 Richard 220
Sirhan, Bishara Sirhan 179
Sirica, Judge John 366
Smedberg, Vice Admiral William II 98
Smith, Bradley A. 492
Smith, Captain R. S. 65
Smith, Layton Dale 105
Smokey Bear 184, 193, 194, 195
Snesko, Tony 488
Snodgrass, Lieutenant j.g. John C. and Mary 70
Snow, Tony 448
Song Ganh Hao 264
Song Ong Doc 187, 214, 217, 220, 256, 262–265, 275
Soros, George 446
South China Sea 210, 222, 235, 258, 264, 265
Southern Attack Group 33
Spaeth, Merrie 423–425, 428, 429, 431, 436, 440, 441, 445, 468, 509
Spahn, Lieutenant Warren 83
Sparkman, Senator John J. 71
Speakers Bureau (SBVFT) 475, 480
Spofford, Captain Richard T. 49, 50, 51
Square Bay 203, 269, 286
SS *Clamagore* 108, 110, 509
SS *Nautilus* 86
SS *Sample* 187
SS *Sculpin* (SS 191) 104
SS *Seawolf* 86
St. Joseph Lead Company 6, 12, 33, 36
Standard Form 180 428, 430
Standiford, Claudia 433, 454
Steele, Lieutenant Dean 356
Steering Committee (SBVFT) 430, 435, 445, 480, 481, 492
Stefferad, Captain David R. 503
Steffes, CPO James W. 180, 503, 511
Steininger, Dan 400, 402
Stennis, John 369
Stevens, Greg 449
Stevens, Reed, Curcio & Potholm 449
Stevenson, David 509
Stevenson, Governor Adlai E. 71, 129
Stewart, General James "Jimmy" 80, 84, 97, 163, 412
Stockdale, Jim 465
Stolen Honor Wounds That Never Heal 341, 477, 481, 513
Stolen Valor 338, 340, 342, 425, 431, 509
Stoneberg, Lawrence "Larry" 234–237, 243

Straits of Magellan 111, 113
Strategic Interdiction Campaign 202
Stratmann, Captain Charles, USN, Ret. 374, 509
Struble, Vice Admiral Arthur D. 45, 48
Subic Bay, Philippines 41, 177, 374
Suez Canal 354, 369–373, 376
Sullivan, Captain Mark 333, 470
Swett, Scott 338, 339, 444, 445, 447, 448, 459, 460, 462, 463, 509, 513
Swift Boat Sailors Association; see SBSA
Swift Boat Down 180, 511
Swift Boat Veterans for Truth; see SBVFT
Swift Boat Veterans and POWs for Truth; see SBVFT
Swifties ix, x, 191, 195, 203, 211, 215, 216, 222, 229, 230, 237, 247, 253, 254, 260, 261, 276, 278, 283, 300, 324, 340, 405, 406, 409, 417–419, 421, 422, 428, 431, 433, 435, 436, 440–442, 447–450, 452, 454–457, 460, 461, 464, 468, 472, 475–478, 480–483, 489, 491, 492, 495, 499
Swiftvets.com 430, 432, 443, 447, 459, 473, 481, 486, 513
Sylvester "Syl" Pagano 12
Symmes, Terry 132, 307, 406, 407, 460, 489, 498
Symmes, Weymouth D. iii, iv, xi, 10, 47, 71, 90, 123, 127, 139, 165, 237, 243, 267, 275, 283, 286, 293, 306–308, 349, 407, 418, 419, 425, 427, 428, 430, 434, 445, 448, 456, 463, 469, 476, 477, 480, 503, 507
Tan Son Nhut 224, 257
Task Force 115 v, vii, x, 152, 164, 166, 173, 185, 189, 190, 227, 259, 264, 282, 295, 324, 326, 417, 419, 507, 508, 509
Task Force 116 165, 202, 203, 211
Task Force 117 165
Task Force 135 127
Task Force 136 127
Task Force 65 371
Task Force 77 51, 65, 514
Taylor, Radarman 187
Taylor, W. P. "Sonny" 503
Tay Ninh City 256
Tet Offensive 160, 175, 179, 197, 200, 203, 302, 328, 336, 439, 512
Thang, Commander Dang Cao 175, 176
Than Phu 265
Thant, UN Secretary-General U 225
Thatcher, Prime Minister Margaret 117

Thiele, QM2 Kurt, Jr. 245
Tho, Le Duc 365
Thoi Binh 275
Thomas, Lieutenant j.g. Lloyd 91
Thomas, Major James P., USAF, Ret. "Jim" 208, 436, 449, 490, 509
Thompson, Captain 66
Thompson, Christine Marchand 6, 401
Thompson, Elizabeth 6, 7
Thompson, Robert Lee 6, 7
Thompson, Robert Linn 6, 401
Thorne, Julia 336, 428
Thorson, EN2 Eugene "Gene" 245, 265, 275, 281
Thurlow, Lieutenant j.g. Larry viii, 177–179, 187, 191, 204, 208, 243, 257, 262, 263, 278, 281–283, 286–293, 323, 417, 427, 448, 449, 455, 461, 488–490, 495, 498, 503, 509
Thurlow, Patty 461, 489, 498
Time magazine 269, 477
Tin, Colonel Bui 361
Tojo, General 18, 334
Tonkin Gulf Resolution 134
Tony Snow Show 448
Tour of Duty ix, 161, 165, 181, 188, 195, 232, 244, 253, 260, 261, 265, 267, 278, 287, 290, 417–421, 430, 431, 438, 479, 509, 513
Tragos, Tracy Droz 323
Train, Admiral Harold C., USN, Ret. 63, 77, 103, 348, 349, 367, 509, 514
Trotta, Liz 267, 268, 269
Truman, President Harry 31, 32, 41, 42, 46, 58, 60, 65, 339
Tryner, Ensign Kenneth 292
Tuan Tinh 298
Turner, Marine Lance Corporal Frederick R. 221

UCMJ (Uniform Code of Military Justice) 388
Unfit for Command viii, 287, 301, 338, 341, 346, 376, 415, 430, 432, 436, 447, 453, 454, 456, 464, 471, 473, 474, 480, 495, 510
University of Nebraska 36
Unlimited Access 462
USCG *Bibb* 229
USCG *Ingham* 222
USCG *John C. Spencer* (WHEC 36) 276
USCG *Owasco* 221
USCG *Point Banks* 258, 259, 260
USCG *Point Cypress* 214, 244
USCG *Point Dune* 180

Index 527

USCG *Point Gammon* 275
USCG *Point Glover* 275
USCG *Point Lomas* 275
USCG *Point Orient* 263, 300
USCG *Point Welcome* 275
USCG *Wachusett* 215, 216, 276
USCG *Winona* 168
USS *Acme* 181
USS *America* 126, 416
USS *Arizona* (BB 39) 20, 21, 348
USS *Atlanta* 83
USS *Barney* 204
USS *Barry* (APD 29) 62
USS *Barton* (DD 723) 78
USS *Belknap* 377
USS *Bon Homme Richard* 65, 66
USS *Boyle* (DD 755) 332
USS *Bradford* (DD 545) 62, 67
USS *Brown* (DD 546) 62, 210
USS *Brush* 48, 56
USS *Charles F. Adams* (DDG 2) 137, 138, 139, 140, 142, 143, 144, 145, 147, 141, 142, 147, 148, 149, 150, 151, 152, 153, 264, 296, 345, 383, 509
USS *Chatterer* 49
USS *Conygham* (DDG 17) 345
USS *Courtney* 108, 116, 147, 509
USS *Cowie* 342
USS *Cromwell* (DE 1014) 103, 104, 105, 106, 107, 109, 110, 111, 112, 113, 114, 115, 118, 120, 122, 119, 108, 122, 120, 121, 123, 124, 125, 126, 127, 128, 129, 130, 131, 133, 410, 507, 508, 509
USS *Cypress* 214, 244, 271
USS *Douglas Fox* 183
USS *Doyle* (DMS 34) 51
USS *Endicott* (DMS 35) 44, 51, 55, 57, 74
USS *Enhance* 187
USS *Enterprise* 24, 32, 92, 127
USS *Esteem* (MSO 438) 167
USS *Evans* (DD 552) 62
USS *Franklin D. Roosevelt* (CVA 42) 350, 356, 357, 358, 359
USS *Hadley* (DD 774) 62
USS *Hammerberg* (DE 1021) 105, 108, 110, 120, 128, 509
USS *Harry E. Hubbard* (DD 748) v, 58–78, 103, 108, 338, 348, 410, 411, 508, 509, 514
USS *Helena* (CA 75) 67, 69
USS *Hornet* 23, 24
USS *Incredible* (AM 249) 44, 45, 49, 50, 51, 52, 54

USS *Indianapolis* 73
USS *Intrepid* 393
USS *Iwo Jima* 371
USS *John F. Kennedy* 377
USS *John R. Perry* (DE) 187
USS *John R. Pierce* (DD 753) 129, 210
USS *John Willis* (DE 1027) 188
USS *Joseph P. Kennedy* (DD 850) 129
USS *Kermit Roosevelt* 50
USS *Kite* (AMS 22) 44, 50, 51
USS *Leahy* (DLG 16) 337, 339, 342, 343, 344, 345, 347, 348, 350, 352, 353, 354, 358, 359, 362, 363, 377, 510
USS *Lexington* 24, 425
USS *Lloyd Thomas* (DDE 764) 89, 90, 91, 92, 98, 92, 93, 94, 98, 410
USS *Magpie* 48, 56
USS *Mansfield* 56
USS *McCoy* (DE 1038) 209
USS *Meridith* 62
USS *Missouri* 26, 29, 32, 416
USS *Mockingbird* 49
USS *Mount Katmai* (AE 16) 362
USS *New Jersey* (BB 62) 67, 68, 277, 278
USS *Nipmuc* (ATF 157) 185
USS *Norfolk* (DL 1) 108, 110, 347, 393, 405, 509
USS *O'Brien* (DD 725) 62, 65, 67
USS *Oklahoma* (BB 37) 21
USS *Osprey* (AMS 28) 44, 45, 49
USS *Partridge* 49
USS *Pennsylvania* 343
USS *Philippine Sea* (CV47) 64
USS *Pirate* (AM-275) v, x, 43–45, 49–57, 61, 514
USS *Pivot* 271, 275
USS *Pledge* (AM 277) 44, 49, 50–52, 54–57, 514
USS *Princeton* 35, 66, 177, 178, 427
USS *Putnam* 342, 343
USS *Quick* (DD 490) 33, 35
USS *Redhead* (AMS 34) 44, 50, 51, 54
USS *Rich* 74
USS *Rigel* (AF 58) 358
USS *Rochester* (CA 124) 41, 44, 45, 48, 61
USS *Sacramento* (PG 19) 73
USS *Samuel Gompers* 185
USS *Shenandoah* (AD 26) 111, 188
USS *Sierra* (AD 18) 102, 327, 329, 330, 331, 336, 337, 410
USS *Soley* (DD 707) 205
USS *Springfield* (CLG 4) 353
USS *Tennessee* 21

USS *Terrill County* (LST) 257
USS *Ticonderoga* (CVA 14) 308
USS *Tide* 74
USS *Valley Forge* (CV 45) 41, 64
USS *W. S. Sims* 188
USS *Walke* (DD 723) 65, 66, 67, 68, 514
USS *Washoe County* (LST 1165) 215, 232, 239, 240, 241
USS *Washtenaw County* 271
USS *Weiss* 251
USS *Westchester County* (LST 1167) 303, 304
USS *West Virginia* 21
USS *White River* 271, 272
USS *Worchester* 49, 50
USS *Yorktown* 24, 177, 346, 413, 415, 416

Van Slate, Commander Jean E. 386
Vaughn, Russ 478
Veth, Rear Admiral 165, 166, 172, 182, 196, 197, 198, 200
Victoria, Missouri 3
Vietnam Unit Memorial Monument 496, 500
Vietnam Veterans for a Just Peace 346
Vietnam War 157–366
Villarreal, EN2 Larry D. 258, 259, 260
Vinh Te 210, 249, 250
Volz, BM3 Stephen T. 222
Vorphal, RD3 Leslie 292
Vung Ro Bay 253
Vung Tau 166, 168, 206, 232, 233
VVAW (Vietnam Veterans Against the War) 301, 336, 338–340, 346, 418, 422, 432, 437, 444, 466, 507

Wake Island 23, 26
Walinsky, Adam 334
Wallace, David B. "Dave" 347, 348, 350, 352–355, 435, 438, 449, 490, 503, 509
Wallace, George 221
Wallace, Lieutenant j.g. Richard C. 222
Wallen, Lieutenant j.g. Bill 312
Wall Street Journal 442, 513
Walter Reed 497
Wammack, Jennifer 431, 448
Warner, Jim viii, 180, 464
War on the Rivers, by Weymouth D. Symmes 407, 511
Warren, Earl 329
Washington Post 334, 347, 424, 461, 472, 478
Washington Times 269, 471

Wasikowski, Commander Larry, USNR, Ret. 509
Wasser, RD2 James R. 244
Watkins, Lieutenant Commander William D. 148
Webster, Catherine 431
Webster, Faith 431
Webster, Jamey 431
Webster, Jennifer 431, 436, 440, 441, 442, 448, 452, 476, 480, 488, 509
Webster, Pete 489
Webster Group 431, 480
Weening, Richard W. 400
Welander, Rear Admiral R. O. 363, 514
Wentzville, Missouri 28
Westmoreland, General William C. 169, 172, 181, 182, 198, 511
Whelan, Captain Ed 381
White, Shelton 449, 455
Whitlow, BM3 Drew 244
Will, Admiral 406
Williams, Ensign 300, 311
Williams, SN Billy A. 245
Williams, Ted 81, 82, 83
Willkie, Wendell 17
Winandy, Lieutenant Jim 296
WinterSoldier.com 444
Winter Soldier investigation 338, 339
Wolff, Bernard 503
Wonsan Harbor 45, 46, 47, 48, 49, 50, 51, 56, 57, 69, 118
Wood, Commander Burris D., Jr. 62, 69
Wood, EN2 Ronald L. 297, 300
Woods, Randy 232, 234, 235, 513
World War I x, 3–7, 13, 15, 20, 37, 57, 71, 401, 418
World War II v, viii, x, 7–14, 20, 26, 29, 31, 34–37, 41–45, 48, 62–65, 72, 73, 83, 89, 91, 104, 107–109, 148, 178, 187, 196, 204, 205, 208–210, 229, 230, 307, 329, 334, 339, 342, 352, 354, 384, 400, 412, 425, 473, 504, 511, 513
Worthington, HMC Robert 311
Wright, Lynn 420, 454, 483–485, 488, 489, 490
Wright, Tom 275, 420
Wright; BM2 Barry E. 245
Wyld, Tom 445, 488

Yamamoto, Admiral Isoroku 19
Yellow Sea 45, 47
YMS 504 48
YMS 509 48

Yom Kippur War 367, 371, 372, 377
Yost, Commander Paul A 301–305, 307, 308, 310–312, 314–321, 513
Young, Lieutenant Richard O. 55
Young, QM2 Rex J. 208, 250, 277

Zaladonis, EN3 William 244
Zondorak, Bill 153
Zumwalt, Admiral Elmo, Jr. vii, 148, 166, 186, 189, 197, 198, 200, 201, 212–214, 225, 227, 242, 243, 247, 254, 260, 261, 281, 282, 303, 305, 326–328, 337, 343, 361, 364, 367, 375, 398, 406, 407, 409, 411, 415, 423, 426, 438
Zumwalt, Elmo III 243, 423, 438, 511
Zumwalt, Jim 423, 435, 438, 485